A

Treasury of

Evangelical

Writings

Greatheart: "But here was great odds, three against one." " 'Tis true," replied *Valiant-for-Truth,* "but little or more are nothing to him that has the truth on his side. . . ."

Pilgrim's Progress

A
Treasury of
Evangelical
Writings

Valiant for the Truth

Compiled and Edited by

David Otis Fuller, D.D.

Introductions by Henry W. Coray

KREGEL PUBLICATIONS
Grand Rapids, Michigan 49501

Library of Congress Catalog Card Number 61-9768
ISBN 0-8254-2613-8

First Kregel Publications Edition 1974
Second Printing 1978

Printed in the United States of America

To

the memory of
Mabel Elizabeth Fuller
1944–1956
who was ever valiant for the truth

Acknowledgments

The following men kindly served as consultants on this book:

W. A. Criswell, D.D., Pastor, First Baptist Church, Dallas
William Culbertson, D.D., President, Moody Bible Institute
V. Raymond Edman, D.D., President, Wheaton College
John P. Walvoord, D.D., President, Dallas Theological Seminary

Also, Dr. David Hedegard, theologian and writer of Mjolby, Sweden, whose suggestions and comments have been most helpful.

A hearty thank-you is due those of the staff in the office of the Wealthy Street Baptist Church, Grand Rapids, Michigan, together with members of the church and our Baptist Bible Institute who assisted in the typing of the manuscript.

I am indebted to my friend, Henry W. Coray, pastor of the Sunnyvale Orthodox Presbyterian Church of Sunnyvale, California, for the splendid biographical sketches of the men included in this book.

My very special thanks go to my sister, Muriel Fuller, who served as editor on the manuscript.

David Otis Fuller

Contents

Preface

Chattering sparrows travel in flocks. The eagle soars alone above the clouds and craggy peaks, to brave the storm and scream defiance at the jagged lightning.

The servant of the Lord is often lonely. Like Elijah, he would fain wish God would take his life, "for I am not better than my fathers," but Horeb holds the key to ultimate triumph through Him who never leaves nor forsakes.

Forty days on a single meal the old prophet traveled across the barren desert. Then came the wind, the earthquake, the fire, and finally the still small voice—"What doest thou here, Elijah?"

"I have been very jealous for the Lord God of hosts . . . and I, even I only, am left; and they seek my life, to take it away."

How often the one who would be "valiant for the truth" is beset by such despondency. But in reality he should behold himself in the mirror of his reflected faith, "compassed about with so great a cloud of witnesses." In every age their serried ranks remain unbroken, although often reduced to seven thousand among the millions of earth.

Pythagoras, the Greek philosopher and mathematician who lived six centuries before Christ, prized truth so highly that he exclaimed: "Truth is so great a perfection that if God would render Himself visible to men, He would choose light for His body and truth for His soul!" Pythagoras knew not how truly he spoke, for one came who said, "I am the light of the world . . . I am the way, the truth, and the life: no man cometh unto the Father, but by me."

The following pages present men of all ages who had much in common. Courage was theirs in abundance, God-given convictions so firmly rooted in their hearts by God's grace that neither persecution, banishment, torture, nor death could dislodge or destroy them. Love for God and for His Son, Jesus Christ; a reckless abandonment of their lives in passionate service for the Son of God, characterized all of these men. These were indeed giant intellects who bowed their wills and their hearts in childlike submission to a sovereign God.

Each man possessed the same fierce conviction—that all truth is absolute, never relative. For these men, truth was never a nose of wax to be twisted to suit their system of dialectics or deceptive casuistry. Two times two made four. In mathematics, their supreme authority was the multiplication table; in theology, their absolute authority was the Bible. They held verbal inspiration essential. To them it was as much a test of Christian fellowship as any other fundamental of their faith: the virgin birth, the sinless life of Christ; His substitutionary death; His bodily resurrection. These truths, absolute in their nature, formed a golden chain forged by the Holy Spirit. If one link was missing, the whole would be in jeopardy.

The Tinker of Bedford, in *Pilgrim's Progress*, depicts a scene between Greatheart and Valiant-for-Truth. This dialogue could well apply to any man included in this book.

GREATHEART: "But here was great odds, three against one." "'Tis true," replied Valiant-for-Truth, "but little or more are nothing to him that has the truth on his side. . . ."

Then said Greatheart to Mr. Valiant-for-Truth, "Thou hast worthily behaved thyself; let me see thy sword." So he showed it to him.

When he had taken it in his hand and looked thereon awhile, he said, "Ha, it is a right Jerusalem blade."

VALIANT: "It is so. Let a man have one of these blades, with a hand to wield it, and skill to use it, and he may venture upon an angel with it. He need not fear its holding, if he can but tell how to lay on. Its edge will never blunt. It will cut flesh and bones, and soul, and spirit, and all." [Hebrews 4:12]

GREATHEART: "But you fought a great while; I wonder you was not weary."

VALIANT: "I fought till my sword did cleave to my hand; and then they were joined together as if a sword grew out of my arm; and when the blood ran through my fingers, then I fought with more courage."

GREATHEART: "Thou hast done well; thou hast resisted unto blood, striving against sin. Thou shalt abide by us, and go out with us; for we are thy companions."

Then they took him and washed his wounds, and gave him of what they had, to refresh him; and so they went away together.

It is in such a day that men like this are needed. For the prophet Jeremiah not only spoke of his own age but our own when he wrote:

And they bend their tongues like their bow for lies: but they are not valiant for the truth upon the earth; for they proceed from evil to evil, and they know not me, saith the Lord. [Jeremiah 9:3]

One of these "valiant for the truth" was Anselm of Canterbury (c.1034–1109). He was one of the purest theologians of the church. He reached the height of his powers and influence around 1100 A.D. In his monumental work, *Cur Deus Homo* (Why God Became Man), selections from which are found in these pages, he wrote:

In the first place, I shall ask how God took manhood without sin from the sinful mass, that is, from the human race which was totally infected by sin, as if He were to take something unleavened from a lump of fermented dough. For even though the conception of this man is pure and free from the sin of carnal delight, nevertheless the Virgin herself, from whom He was taken, was "conceived in iniquities" and her mother conceived her "in sin." And she was born with original sin, since she also sinned in Adam, "in whom all have sinned."

Such a profound and truly scriptural statement is most significant in the light of the date of its pronouncement and its source.

To the one who holds Scripture in this light, as did these giant intellects, valiants for the truth as they were, it is thrilling to learn that in every age God has had His man, chosen, predestined and fitted for warfare against the powers of darkness.

Augustine battled Pelagius; Athanasius exposed the Arian heresy; Chrysostom feared not the wrath of the pagan queen, Eudoxia; Luther hurled his defiance at papal Rome; Calvin put to flight the Libertines and all who opposed the Scriptures; Machen stood firm for the truth in the midst of growing apostasy. Not once in the long centuries has the light of God's truth been extinguished. It has always burned, dimly at times, but it has never gone out. Calvin discovered that he was one with Augustine in his stand for the truth, although more than a millenium stretched between them.

May "the God of all grace" use this volume to re-establish and stabilize the faith of many, thus providing a source of inspiration and encouragement to all whose hearts would faint as we face the final conflict.

DAVID OTIS FULLER

Grand Rapids, Michigan

PAUL, THE APOSTLE ? — c. 64

A caravan of horsemen clattered along the highway leading from Galilee to the city of Damascus. The hour was noon. A desert sun fairly exploded on the equestrians. Without warning, a rival light more dazzling than the sun cascaded down from the heavens, and with the power of physical force whipped the men from their horses and sent them sprawling to the road. All but one arose, presently. The single form remained prostrate.

"Saul, Saul," a voice called out in the Hebrew language, "why persecutest thou me?"

"Who art thou, Lord?" the prostrate one answered.

"I am Jesus whom thou persecutest," the voice said. "Arise, and go into the city, and it shall be told thee what thou must do."

The great apostle of the Christian faith never forgot that initial meeting with the Lord of Glory. *"God who commanded light to shine out of darkness hath shined in our hearts to bring the light of the knowledge of God in the face of Jesus Christ,"* he was later to write. The face of Jesus Christ! *The vision was impressed as a seal upon Paul's heart, as a seal on his arm, and the flashes thereof were as the very flashes of Jehovah. His enemies would deny his apostolic authority. His refutation? He had seen the risen Saviour. "Last of all he appeared to me, as one born out of due time." The words were his credentials. He took them, forged them into a keen Damascus blade, and with it smote his accusers hip and thigh. There was no rebuttal!*

The person predestinated to change the current of history was born in Tarsus, an influential center of culture in Cilicia. He was proud of the fact. *"A citizen of no mean city,"* he boasted once while under fire. He sprang from the Jewish tribe of Benjamin, but was *"free born"*: he came into the world a free Roman citizen. How his parents obtained that civic privilege he never explains.

He studied in Jerusalem under the learned Gamaliel, a grandson of one of the most illustrious of the rabbis, Hillel. His first known contact with Christianity, although he must have been aware of the movement, was when he witnessed the martyrdom of Stephen, whose execution, he says, he consented to. Fully persuaded that Christian people were completely wrong in their views, the zealous young Pharisee dedicated himself to their extermination. This, as a matter of fact, was his mission the day Jesus intercepted him outside of Damascus and changed the course of his career so radically. *"Lord, what wilt thou have me to do?" would be his watchword from then to the time of his martyrdom at Rome.*

There never was a more dramatic or tempestuous life. At every move death lurked just around the corner. "In labors more abundant, in stripes above measure, in prisons more frequent, in deaths oft," he reminds the Corinthians. "Of the Jews five times received I forty stripes save one. Thrice was I beaten with rods, once was I stoned, thrice I suffered shipwreck, a night and a day I have been in the deep; in journeyings often, in perils of waters, in perils of robbers, in perils by mine own countrymen, in perils by the heathen, in perils in the city, in perils in the wilderness, in perils in the sea, in perils among false brethren; in weariness and painfulness, in watchings, in hunger and thirst, in fast often, in cold and nakedness. . . ." None of these hazards moved him from the divine assignment that must be reckoned as one above and beyond the call of duty.

A burning heart, brimming with love for Christ and for the souls of men, sent him posting over land and ocean without rest. He lived the life of a whirling dervish, accomplished the work of a dozen ordinary men. The New Testament presents him as a vivid complex of apostle, theologian, preacher, missionary, writer, controversialist, logician, tentmaker, humanitarian, voyager, prisoner, friend. What Alexander Whyte wrote of David is equally true of Paul: "He never did anything by halves. Energy, decision, resolution, devotion, scorn of idleness, scorn of ease, love of labor, love of danger—you will always find virtues like these in him."

What was the secret of his unbelievable energy? He lets you in on it in the forthcoming passage, tracing the stream back to the fountainhead. "I labored more abundantly than they all: yet not I, but the grace of God which was with me."

The Resurrection

PAUL, THE APOSTLE
From his First Epistle to the Corinthians, Chapter 15

MOREOVER, brethren, I declare unto you the gospel which I preached unto you, which also ye have received, and wherein ye stand; by which also ye are saved, if ye keep in memory what I preached unto you, unless ye have believed in vain.

For I delivered unto you first of all that which I also received, how that Christ died for our sins according to the scriptures; and that He was buried, and that he rose again the third day according to the scriptures: And that He was seen of Cephas, then of the twelve: after that, he was seen of about five hundred brethren at once; of whom the greater part remain unto this present, but some are fallen asleep.

After that, He was seen of James; then of all the apostles.

And last of all He was seen of me also, as of one born out of due time.

For I am the least of the apostles, that am not meet to be called an apostle, because I persecuted the church of God.

But by the grace of God I am what I am: and His grace which was bestowed upon me was not in vain; but I laboured more abundantly than they all: yet not I, but the grace of God which was with me.

Therefore whether it were I or they, so we preach, and so ye believed.

Now if Christ be preached that He rose from the dead, how say some among you that there is no resurrection of the dead?

But if there be no resurrection of the dead, then is Christ not risen: and if Christ be not risen, then is our preaching vain, and your faith is also vain.

Yea, and we are found false witnesses of God; because we have testified of God that He raised up Christ: whom He raised not up, if so be that the dead rise not.

For if the dead rise not, then is not Christ raised: and if Christ be not raised, your faith is vain; ye are yet in your sins.

Then they also which are fallen asleep in Christ are perished.

If in this life only we have hope in Christ, we are of all men most miserable.

But now is Christ risen from the dead, and become the firstfruits of them that slept.

For since by man came death, by man came also the resurrection of the dead.

For as in Adam all die, even so in Christ shall all be made alive.

But every man in his own order: Christ the firstfruits; afterward they that are Christ's at His coming.

Then cometh the end, when He shall have delivered up the kingdom to God, even the Father; when He shall have put down all rule and all authority and power.

For He must reign, till He hath put all enemies under His feet.

The last enemy that shall be destroyed is death.

For He hath put all things under His feet. But when He saith all things are put under Him, it is manifest that He is excepted, which did put all things under Him.

And when all things shall be subdued unto Him, then shall the Son also Himself be subject unto Him that put all things under him, that God may be all in all.

Else what shall they do which are baptized for the dead, if the dead rise not at all? Why are they then baptized for the dead?

And why stand we in jeopardy every hour?

I protest by your rejoicing which I have in Christ Jesus our Lord, I die daily.

If after the manner of men I have fought with beasts at Ephesus, what advantageth it me, if the dead rise not? Let us eat and drink; for tomorrow we may die.

Be not deceived: evil communications corrupt good manners.

Awake to righteousness, and sin not; for some have not the knowledge of God: I speak this to your shame.

But some man will say, How are the dead raised up? And with what body do they come?

Thou fool, that which thou sowest is not quickened, except it die: and that which thou sowest, thou sowest not that body that shall be, but bare grain, it may chance of wheat, or of some other grain: but God giveth it a body as it hath pleased Him, and to every seed his own body.

All flesh is not the same flesh: but there is one kind of flesh of men, another flesh of beasts, another of fishes, and another of birds.

There are also celestial bodies, and bodies terrestrial: but the glory of the celestial is one, and the glory of the terrestrial is another.

There is one glory of the sun, and another glory of the moon, and another glory of the stars: for one star differeth from another star in glory.

So also is the resurrection of the dead. It is sown in corruption; it is raised in incorruption: it is sown in dishonour; it is raised in glory: it is sown in weakness; it is raised in power: it is sown a natural body; it is raised a spiritual body. There is a natural body, and there is a spiritual body.

And so it is written, The first man Adam was made a living soul; the last Adam was made a quickening spirit.

Howbeit that was not first which is spiritual, but that which is natural; and afterward that which is spiritual.

The first man is of the earth, earthy: the second man is the Lord from heaven.

As is the earthy, such are they also that are earthy: and as is the heavenly, such are they also that are heavenly.

And as we have borne the image of the earthy, we shall also bear the image of the heavenly.

Now this I say, brethren, that flesh and blood cannot inherit the kingdom of God; neither doth corruption inherit incorruption.

Behold, I show you a mystery; we shall not all sleep, but we shall all be changed, in a moment, in the twinkling of an eye, at the last trump: for the trumpet shall sound, and the dead shall be raised incorruptible, and we shall be changed.

For this corruptible must put on incorruption, and this mortal must put on immortality.

So when this corruptible shall have put on incorruption, and this mortal shall have put on immortality, then shall be brought to pass the saying that is written, Death is swallowed up in victory.

O death, where is thy sting? O grave, where is thy victory?

The sting of death is sin; and the strength of sin is the law.

But thanks be to God, which giveth us the victory through our Lord Jesus Christ.

Therefore, my beloved brethren, be ye stedfast, unmovable, always abounding in the work of the Lord, forasmuch as ye know that your labour is not in vain in the Lord.

THE EPISTLE TO DIOGNETUS

It has been said that after the close of the Apostolic Age theology fell over a cliff until restored by the great formulated creeds of the church. If so, the Epistle to Diognetus makes it plain that the fall was broken by at least one ledge unshrouded by the mists of hazy apologetics. The letter is essentially an apology for Christianity in terms of the special place of the Church in society as contrasted with the defects and corrupting influence of paganism. It glows with profound understanding of the great Biblical themes of both Testaments: the creation, the theology of history, the incarnation, the atonement, justification, the final judgment.

The document, penned by an unknown writer in classical Greek, probably first appeared in the second century. It was a type of literary Melchizedec, without father, without mother, without descent, having neither beginning of days, nor end of life; that is, enveloped in mystery, externally bearing no historical clues whatever. Not one of the church fathers quotes from it.

In 1592 Henry Stephens, third in a succession of famous French printers, issued it in Greek and Latin. He failed to give any account of its sources. Two hundred years later the manuscript Stephens used (medieval) came into the possession of the humanist Reuchlin; next it turned up in the library in Strassburg, where it was destroyed by fire. By this time, however, it had been preserved for posterity.

Who was the recipient, Diognetus? Little more is known of him than of the author. That he was an inquirer into the nature of Christianity is certain. Seemingly he was a man of culture and of high social standing. Some have guessed that he was Emperor Hadrian, which is unlikely, though there was a "lost" apology by Quadratus to him. In the second century there lived a Stoic philosopher named Diognetus, who taught Marcus Aurelius painting and composition. He may have been the recipient of the communication, as certain historians believe, but this cannot be proven, either.

The Epistle reveals a thorough acquaintance with the Bible, even though no direct quotation is present. Paul's influence is especially pronounced, and there are echoes of I Peter and the Johnnine writings. The purpose of the writer is to vindicate from experience the Christian position. Certainly, it comes to the world as a masterful apology, a sparkling defense of the faith. "It excels in fresh enthusiasm of faith," says Schaff, "richness of thought, and elegance of style, and is alto-

gether one of the most beautiful memorials of Christian antiquity, un-surpassed and hardly equalled by any genuine work of the Apostolic Fathers." Ewald ranks it first among the early Christian letters not found in the New Testament canon. Bunsen has said of it: "Indisput-ably, after Scripture, the finest monument of sound Christian feeling, noble courage, and manly eloquence." While not in the theological sense inspired writing, it merits the right to a place in the library of inspiring pieces of excellence, penned by a man asked to give a reason for the hope that is in him, and so is worthy of all acceptation.

The Epistle to Diognetus

YOUR EXCELLENCY:

I SEE, DIOGNETUS, that you are very much in earnest about in-vestigating the religion of the Christians and make very exact and careful inquiries concerning them. Who is the God in whom they trust —you wonder—and what kind of cult is theirs, because one and all, they disdain the world and despise death? They neither recognize the gods believed in by the Greeks nor practise the superstition of the Jews! And what is the secret of the affection they have for one another? And why, you wonder, has this new blood and spirit come into the world we live in now, and not before? I certainly welcome this eager-ness of yours and beg two gifts of God, who bestows upon us speech as well as hearing: may I so speak that you will derive the greatest possible benefit from hearing, and may you so hear that the speaker will have no regrets!

Well, then, purge yourself of all the prejudices clinging to you and put away your old, habitual fallacies. Make as it were a fresh start and become *a new man*, since you may yet become a hearer also of what by your own admission is a new message. Use not only your eyes, but also your judgment, to see of what stuff and nature those beings are whom you call and consider to be gods. This is stone, like the pavement under the feet; that one, metal, no better than the utensils forged for our use; this one, wood, and perhaps rotten wood by now; that one, silver, which needs a watchman to keep it from being stolen; another, iron, subject to corrosion by rust; still another, earthenware, no better to look at than anything fashioned for the most ignoble ser-vice. Is it not so? Are they not all of perishable material? Have they not been forged by iron and fire? On this one, a stonecutter has plied his craft, on that, a coppersmith, on a third, a silversmith, and on a fourth, a potter.

Is it not so? And before they were shaped by the skill of these men to represent those several objects, did not every craftsman see in every one of them—and, in fact, does see in them even now—an object of different shape? And might not utensils of the same material be made to resemble objects like these, if they happened to be handled by the same craftsmen? And conversely, might not these objects, now worshipped by you, be made by human hands into utensils resembling other utensils? Are they not all deaf and blind and lifeless and senseless and motionless? Are they not all rotting away, not all doomed to perish?

These things you call gods; these you serve; these you worship; and in the end you become like them! And here is the reason why you hate the Christians—they do not believe these objects to be gods. You, of course, are firmly convinced you are glorifying them; yet do you not show all the more contempt for them? Do you not much rather make perfect laughingstocks of them if you leave unguarded the gods you worship, when they are made of stone or clay, while you lock up for the night those made of silver or gold, and post guards beside them in the day, to prevent their being stolen? And as for the honors you imagine you pay them—well, if they are aware of them, you are actually punishing them; and if they lack sensation, you are showing them up by worshipping them with blood and victims' fat! Just let one of you submit to such treatment; let one of you permit such things to happen to him! No, there is no human being that would voluntarily submit to such a punishment; for a human being feels and reasons. A stone, of course, submits; for it has no feeling. Therefore, you really disprove its sensibility, do you not? And so I might go on and on showing that Christians are not enslaved to gods like these. But if anyone should think even the little I have said to be inadequate, I consider it superfluous to say more.

Next I suppose you most desire to hear about the difference between their worship and that of the Jews. Well, the Jews hold aloof from the worship just described, and in so far as they are right in claiming to honor one God and Lord of the universe; but in so far as they offer Him this worship in a manner resembling the one just explained, they are altogether mistaken. The Greeks, it is plain, make offerings to things insensible and deaf, and, by doing so, give proof of want of intelligence; the Jews, if they but realized that they are making offerings to God exactly as if He needed them, might rightly consider this an act of folly rather than religion.

Surely, He *who made heaven and earth and all that is in them* and supplies us with all we need, cannot Himself need any of the things

He Himself provides to those who fancy they are giving them. At any rate, people who believe they are performing sacrifices to Him by means of blood and victims' fat and whole burnt offerings, and honoring Him by such tokens of respect, do not seem to me to differ in the least from people who display the same reverence toward insensible objects. Both fancy they are making real offerings, the latter to objects unable to appreciate the honor, the former to Him who stands in need of nothing!

Furthermore, there is that fussiness of theirs in the matter of foods, their superstition about the Sabbath, their bragging about their circumcision, and the show they make of the fast days and new moons. These things are ridiculous and undeserving of consideration, and I do not suppose you wish me to instruct you about them. In fact, is it not obviously wrong to accept some of the things created by God for the use of men as created for a useful purpose, and reject others as useless and superfluous? And is it not impious to misrepresent God as forbidding an act of kindness on the Sabbath? And is it not ridiculous to vaunt the mutilation of the flesh as a mark of election, as though men were in a singular manner beloved by God on its account?

Again, they closely watch the stars and the moon to regulate the scrupulous observance of months and days, and by a distinction between the seasons which is due to God's arrangement, set aside some for festivals, others for times of sorrow—merely to suit their own inclinations! Who can consider this a proof of religion, and no, rather, of lack of understanding? Now, then, I think you have learned enough to realize that the Christians are right in holding aloof from the thoughtless aberrations common to both groups, and, in particular, from the boastful officiousness of the Jews. But as regards the mystery of their own religion, do not expect to be able to learn it from human lips.

Christians are not distinguished from the rest of mankind by either country, speech, or customs; the fact is, they nowhere settle in cities of their own; they use no peculiar language; they cultivate no eccentric mode of life. Certainly, this creed of theirs is no discovery due to some fancy or speculation of inquisitive men; nor do they, as some do, champion a doctrine of human origin. Yet while they dwell in both Greek and non-Greek cities, as each one's lot was cast, and conform to the customs of the country in dress, food, and mode of life in general, the whole tenor of their way of living stamps it as worthy of admiration and admittedly extraordinary. They reside in their respective countries, but only as aliens. They take part in everything as citizens and put up with everything as foreigners. Every foreign land is their home, and every home a foreign land.

They marry like all others and beget children; but they do not expose their offspring. Their board they spread for all, but not their bed. They find themselves *in the flesh,* but do not live *according to the flesh.* They spend their days on earth, but hold citizenship in heaven. They obey the established laws, but in their private lives they rise above the laws. They love all men, but are persecuted by all. They are unknown, yet are condemned; they are put to death, but it is life that they receive. *They are poor, and enrich many;* destitute of everything, they abound in everything. They are dishonored, and in their dishonor find their glory. They are calumniated, and are vindicated. *They are reviled, and they bless;* they are insulted and render honor. Doing good, they are penalized as evildoers; when penalized, they rejoice because they are quickened into life. The Jews make war on them as foreigners; the Greeks persecute them; and those who hate them are at a loss to explain their hatred.

In a word: what the soul is in the body, that the Christians are in the world. The soul is spread through all the members of the body, and the Christians throughout the cities of the world. The soul dwells in the body, but is not part and parcel of the body; so Christians dwell in the world, but are not part and parcel of the world. Itself invisible, the soul is kept shut up in the visible body; so Christians are known as such in the world, but their religion remains invisible. The flesh, though suffering no wrong from the soul, yet hates and makes war on it, because it is hindered from indulging its passions; so, too, the world, though suffering no wrong from Christians, hates them because they oppose its pleasures.

The soul loves the flesh that hates it, and its members; so, too, Christians love those that hate them. The soul is locked up in the body, yet is the very thing that holds the body together; so, too, Christians are shut up in the world as in a prison, yet it is precisely they that hold the world together. Immortal, the soul is lodged in a mortal tenement; so, too, Christians, though residing as strangers among corruptible things, look forward to the incorruptibility that awaits them in heaven. The soul, when stinting itself in food and drink, fares the better for it; so, too, Christians, when penalized, show a daily increase in numbers on that account. Such is the important post to which God has assigned them, and they are not at liberty to desert it.

And no wonder. It was not an earthly invention, as I have said, that was committed to their keeping; it was not a product of a mortal brain that they consider worth safeguarding so anxiously; nor have they been entrusted with the dispensing of merely human mysteries. Quite the contrary! It was really the Lord of all, the Creator of all, the invisible God Himself, who, of His own free will, from heaven, lodged among men the truth and the holy incomprehensible Word, and firmly established it in their hearts. Nor did He do this, as one might conjecture, by sending to men some subordinate, whether angel, or principality, or one of those in charge of earthly things, or one entrusted with the administration of heavenly things.

No, He sent the Designer and Architect of the universe in person—Him by whom He created the heavens, by whom He enclosed the sea within its proper bounds, whose inscrutable counsels all the elements of nature faithfully carry out, from whom [the sun] has received the schedule of the daily courses it is to keep, whom the moon obeys as He bids her give light at night, whom the stars obey in following the course of the moon, from whom all things have received their order, their bounds, and their due place in the universe—the heavens and the things in the heavens, the earth and the things in the earth, the sea and the things in the sea, the fire, the air, the underworld, the things in the heights above, the things in the deep below, the things in the intermediate space. Such was He whom He sent to them!

And did He do so, as a human brain might conceive, to tyrannize, to frighten, and to terrorize? Certainly not! On the contrary, His mission was an act of gracious clemency, as when a king sends his son who is himself a king! He sent Him as God. He sent Him [as Man] to men. The wish to save, to persuade, and not to coerce, inspired His mission. Coercion is incompatible with God. His mission was an invitation, not a vindictive measure; an act of love, not an act of injustice. Some day, of course, He will send Him as a Judge and—who will then endure His coming! . . . [Do you not see] how they are thrown before the wild beasts to make them disown the Lord, and they refuse to be overcome? Do you not see that the more of them are penalized, the more their numbers grow? Such things do not point to a human agency. Here is the power of God, here the proofs of His abiding presence!

In fact, before He came, what man at all understood what God is? Or do you accept the nonsense trumped up by those pretentious philosophers, some of whom maintained that God was fire—the very thing for which they are headed they call God!—while others said He was water, still others some other of the elements created by God? And yet, if any one of these doctrines is acceptable, then every one of the rest of the creatures might just as well be proved to be God! No, this is nothing but jugglery and imposture dished up by quacks. No man has either seen or made known God; but He has revealed Himself.

And He did reveal Himself by faith, through which alone it has been vouchsafed us to see God. For God, the Lord and Creator of the universe, who made all things and assigned to each its proper place, not only proved Himself man's friend, but long-suffering as well. But He always was and is and will be such—kind and good and unimpassioned and true; in fact, He alone is good. And after conceiving a great and unutterable purpose, He communicated it to His Son alone. Now, as long as He kept His own wise counsel to Himself and guarded it as a secret, He was seemingly wholly unconcerned about us; but once He revealed it through His beloved Son and made known what had been prepared from the beginning, He granted us all things at once. He made us partake of His benefits, and see and comprehend things which none of us could ever have expected.

After, then, He had already planned everything in His own counsels in union with the Son, He yet permitted us, all through the intervening time, to be carried away, just as we chose, by unruly passions—victims of *unbridled desires!* Not that He took at all delight in our transgressions; no, He merely exercised patience. Nor did He approve of that former era of wickedness, but, on the contrary, was all the time shaping the present era of holiness. It was His intention that we, after our own conduct in the past had proved us unworthy of life, should now be rendered worthy by the goodness of God, and that after we had demonstrated our inability, as far as in us lay, *to enter the kingdom of God*, should be enabled to do so by the power of God.

And when the cup of our iniquities was filled, and it had become perfectly clear that their wages—the punishment of death—had to be expected, then the season arrived during which God had determined to reveal henceforth His goodness and power. O the surpassing kindness and love of God for man! No, He did not hate us, or discard us, or remember our wrongs; He exercised forbearance and long-suffering! In mercy, of His own accord, He lifted the burden of our sins! Of His own accord *He gave up His own Son* as a ransom for us—the Saint for sinners, the Guiltless for the guilty, *the Innocent for the wicked*, the Incorruptible for the corruptible, the Immortal for the mortal! Indeed, what else could have covered our sins but His holiness? In whom could we, the lawless and impious, be sanctified but in the son of God alone?

O sweetest exchange! O unfathomable accomplishment! O unexpected blessings—the sinfulness of many is buried in One who is holy, the holiness of One sanctifies the many who are sinners! In the previous time He had demonstrated our nature's inability to win life, and now He revealed the Saviour who is powerful to save even what is powerless; and on both grounds He wished us to have faith in His loving-kindness, to consider Him Nurse, Father, Teacher, Counsellor, Physician, Mind, Light, Honor, Glory, Strength, Life, and—not to be solicitous about clothing and food!

If this is the faith which you, too, desire, then you should, first of all, acquire a thorough knowledge of the Father. The fact is, God loved men, and it was for their sake that He made the world; at their service He placed everything on earth; to them He gave reason and intelligence; them alone He endowed with the ability to look up to Him;

them He formed after His own image; to them *He sent His only-begotten Son;* to them He promised the kingdom in heaven, and this He will give to those that love Him. And when you have acquired this knowledge, with what joy do you think you will be filled! Or how intensely will you love Him who first loved you so! And once you love Him, you will be an imitator of His kindness. And you must not be surprised that man can become an imitator of God. He can, since He so wills.

Certainly, to be happy does not mean to tyrannize over one's neighbors, or to wish to have an advantage over the weaker ones, or to be rich and therefore able to use force against one's inferiors. It is not in such matters that one can imitate God; no, such matters are foreign to His majesty. On the other hand, he who takes his neighbor's burden upon himself, who is willing to benefit his inferior in a matter in which he is his superior, who provides the needy with what he himself has received from God and thus becomes the god of the recipients—he, I say, is an imitator of God! Then you will realize, while your lot is on earth, that God lives in heaven; then you will in good earnest discourse on the mysteries of God; then you will love and admire those who submit to punishment for their refusal to deny God; then you will condemn the deceitfulness of the world and its error once you understand the real life in heaven, once you despise the apparent death here below, once you fear the real death reserved for those who are condemned to the eternal fire, which will forever torment those delivered up to it. Then you will admire and pronounce happy those who, for conscience' sake, endure the fire that lasts but for a while—once you grasp the nature of that other fire.

There is nothing strange in my discourse, nor is my argument contrary to reason. No, after becoming a disciple of Apostles, I am now becoming a teacher of the Gentiles. What has been handed down I deliver exactly to such as become disciples of the Truth. Really, can anyone that has been correctly taught and has fallen in love with the Logos, fail to strive to learn exactly what has been plainly shown by the Logos to disciples to whom the Logos appeared in person and made revelations in plain language? He was not understood by unbelievers, but gave a detailed explanation to disciples, and these, reckoned by Him as trustworthy, came to know the mysteries of the Father.

For this reason He sent the Logos to appear in the world, who, discredited by His people, was preached by Apostles, and believed by Gentile nations. He was in the beginning, appeared new and was found to be old, and is ever born anew in the hearts of the saints. He is the Eternal One, [who] today is accounted a Son; by Him the Church is enriched, and grace, ever unfolding in the saints, is multiplied—the grace which grants understanding, reveals mysteries, announces season, glories in believers, gives freely to seekers—such as do not break their plighted troth or transgress the bounds fixed by the fathers. And then fear of the Lord becomes a theme of song, prophetic inspiration is recognized, the trustworthiness of the Gospels is firmly established, Apostolic tradition is observed, and the grace of the Church is exultant. And if you do not grieve this grace, you will appreciate what the Logos communicates through whomsoever He chooses and whenever He pleases. After all, urged by love for the revelations made to us, we but share with you whatever, in obedience to the command of the Logos, we felt prompted to speak out with difficulty.

If you read this and listen attentively, you will find out what blessings God bestows on those who love Him as they should. Since they become *a paradise of delight*, they rear in themselves a fruitful tree in fullest bloom, and are adorned with a variety of fruit; for in this garden *a tree of knowledge and a tree of life have been planted*. But mark, it is not the tree of knowledge that is fatal; no, it is disobedience that is fatal. In fact, there is deep significance in the Scripture text which states that in the beginning God planted [*a tree of knowledge and*] *tree of life in the midst of paradise*, indicating that knowledge is the avenue to life. Because the first men did not make use of it with singleness of heart, they found themselves stripped by the deceit of the serpent. Neither is there life without knowledge, nor is knowledge safe without true life. For this reason we find the two trees planted close to each other. The Apostle saw the significance of this, and so he blames knowledge when applied to life without regard to the real force of the commandment, and says: *Knowledge makes conceited; it is love that builds up*. Certain it is that he who thinks he knows anything without a knowledge that is true and attested by life as genuine, has not yet learnt to know. He is deceived by the serpent, simply because he does not love life. But he who, guided by fear, has attained to full knowledge and goes in quest of life, can plant in hope and look for a harvest.

ATHANASIUS 293-373

The Council of Nicea, meeting in the summer of 325, brought together the most colorful group of personalities ever to assemble in ancient times. Renowned scholars were there, men like Eusebius of Caesarea, the Church historian; Eusebius of Nicomedia, a churchman of royal blood; Hosius of Cordoba, the court bishop; Alexander of Alexandria, eloquent pulpiteer. Veterans of the arena were there, warriors of the Cross who bore branded in their flesh the marks of the Saviour. Ascetics were there, hermits who for years had haunted mountain dens and caves, subsisting on roots and berries. Emperor Constantine, convener of the council, was there, seated on a golden throne and arrayed in a purple robe studded with gems and gold sequins.

Why this exciting convocation? To formulate a definition of the person of Jesus Christ.

With fine acumen representatives of three segments of the Church disputed. The discussion narrowed down to one principal point: was Christ homoi-usios, of like substance with God the Father, or homo-usios, of the same substance? A single Greek letter was the pivot of the problem, with momentous issues involved in the outcome. Arius the Presbyter argued that Jesus was like God, but not truly God. Young Athanasius, an archdeacon from Alexandria, spearheaded the minority group. He maintained that Jesus was "very God of very God, begotten, not created." A mediating party, the inevitable middle-of-the-roaders, largest of the three numerically, assumed a compromising position. The two wing parties accused it of being misty, ambiguous, and unsatisfactory.

The council lasted forty-two days. At the fever point of the controversy, when the current appeared to be running strongly against the orthodox school, a certain delegate went to Athanasius and said, "You are fighting a losing battle. Does Athanasius not know that the whole world is against him?" The fiery African threw back his shoulders and his dark eyes flashed. He said quietly, "Is the world against Athanasius? Then Athanasius is against the world." He resumed the fight, wielded the sword of the Spirit with crushing effectiveness, and won the mediating party over to his side. Nicea resulted in a clear statement of the full deity of the Son of God and a condemnation of Arius' views. It was, Athanasius said, "a true monument and token of victory against every heresy."

The sturdy deacon was sprung into the floodlight of fame. Three

15

years later, the Church elevated him to the highest office in the East, Archbishop of the See of Alexandria, which included all of Egypt and Libya.

For that honor Athanasius was to pay a frightfully dear price. Stung by their defeat at Nicea, the Arians counterattacked with venom. They launched a vitriolic whispering crusade against his character. Athanasius, they said, was guilty of treason, of immorality, of sorcery, of sacrilege; Athanasius was a murderer.

Not content with slander, they resorted to every art in the ledger of political maneuvering to destroy him. They had him exiled five times. They hounded him from the Egyptian deserts to Rome. Once a band of ruffians equipped with swords and cudgels stormed into a cathedral where he was preaching. Calmly he pronounced the benediction, slipped through a rear door and rode away on a camel. On another occasion, as he was traveling on a river boat up the Nile, a pair of hired assassins hid on board intending to kill him. He learned of the plot, disguised himself, and made his escape. In his old age he was forced to flee to a cemetery and take refuge for nearly half a year in a sepulcher. In all, he spent in exile twenty of his forty-seven years as head of the Alexandrian episcopacy.

During the periods when he was allowed to serve the Church without molestation he proved to be a wise and able administrator. He passed the last seven years of his otherwise tempestuous career in Alexandria in relative peace, writing, preaching, exhorting, confirming, and defending the faith he loved with a passionate, almost fanatical love.

Edward Gibbon, certainly no sympathizer with Athanasius' convictions, wrote of him: "We have seldom an opportunity of observing, either in active or speculative life, what effect may be produced, or what obstacles may be surmounted by the force of a single mind, when it is inflexibly applied to the pursuit of a single object."

Incarnation of the Word (Selections)

ATHANASIUS

YOU ARE wondering, perhaps, for what possible reason, having proposed to speak of the Incarnation of the Word, we are at present treating of the origin of mankind. But this, too, properly belongs to the aim of our treatise. For in speaking of the appearance of

the Saviour amongst us, we must needs speak also of the origin of
men, that you may know that the reason of His coming down was
because of us, and that our transgression called forth the loving-kindness
of the Word, that the Lord should both make haste to help us and
appear among men. For of His becoming Incarnate we were the object,
and for our salvation He dealt so lovingly as to appear and be born even
in a human body.

Thus, then, God has made man, and willed that he should abide in
incorruption; but men, having despised and rejected the contemplation of God, and devised and contrived evil for themselves (as was
said in the former treatise), received the condemnation of death with
which they had been threatened; and from thenceforth no longer remained as they were made, but were being corrupted according to their
devices; and death had the mastery over them as king.

For this purpose, then, the incorporeal and incorruptible and immaterial Word of God comes to our realm, howbeit he was not far
from us before. For no part of Creation is left void of Him: He has
filled all things everywhere, remaining present with His own Father.
But He comes in condescension to show loving-kindness upon us, and
to visit us. And seeing the race of rational creatures in the way to
perish, and death reigning over them by corruption; seeing, too, that
the threat against transgression gave a firm hold to the corruption
which was upon us, and that it was monstrous that before the law
was fulfilled it should fall through: seeing, once more, the unseemliness
of what was come to pass: that the things whereof He Himself was
Artificer were passing away: seeing, further, the exceeding wickedness
of men, and how by little and little they had increased it to an intolerable pitch against themselves: and seeing, lastly, how all men were
under penalty of death: He took pity on our race, and had mercy on
our infirmity, and condescended to our corruption, and, unable to
bear that death should have the mastery—lest the creature should
perish, and His Father's handiwork in men be spent for nought—
He takes unto Himself a body, and that of no different sort from
ours.

For He did not simply will to become embodied, or will merely to
appear. For if He willed merely to appear, He was able to affect His
divine appearance by some other and higher means as well. But He
takes a body of our kind, and not merely so, but from a spotless and
stainless virgin, knowing not a man, a body clean and in very truth
pure from intercourse of men. For being Himself mighty, and Artificer
of everything, He prepares the body in the Virgin as a temple unto
Himself, and makes it His very own as an instrument, in it manifested,
and in it dwelling.

And thus taking from our bodies one of like nature, because all

were under penalty of the corruption of death He gave it over to
death in the stead of all, and offered it to the Father—doing this, moreover, of His loving-kindness, to the end that, firstly, all being held
to have died in Him, the law involving the ruin of men might be undone (inasmuch as its power was fully spent in the Lord's body, and
had no longer holding-ground against men, his peers), and that, secondly, whereas men had turned toward corruption, He might turn
them again toward incorruption, and quicken them from death by the
appropriation of His body and by the grace of the Resurrection,
banishing death from them like straw from the fire.

For the Word, perceiving that not otherwise could the corruption
of men be undone save by death as a necessary condition, while it was
impossible for the Word to suffer death, being immortal, and Son of
the Father; to this end He takes to Himself a body capable of death,
that it, by partaking of the Word Who is above all, might be worthy
to die in the stead of all, and might, because of the Word which was
come to dwell in it, remain incorruptible, and that thenceforth corruption might be stayed from all by the Grace of the Resurrection.

Whence, by offering unto death the body He Himself had taken, as
an offering and sacrifice free from any stain, straightway He put away
death from all His peers by the offering of an equivalent. For being
over all, the Word of God naturally by offering His own temple and
corporeal instrument for the life of all satisfied the debt by His death.
And thus He, the incorruptible Son of God, being conjoined with all
by a like nature, naturally clothed all with incorruption, by the promise
of the resurrection. For the actual corruption in death has no longer
holding-ground against men, by reason of the Word, which by His
one body has come to dwell among them.

And like as when a great king has entered into some large city and
taken up his abode in one of the houses there, such city is at all events
held worthy of high honour, nor does any enemy or bandit any longer
descend upon it and subject it; but, on the contrary, it is thought entitled to all care, because of the King's having taken up his residence
in a single house there: so, too, has it been with the Monarch of all.
For now that He has come to our realm, and taken up His abode in
one body among His peers, henceforth the whole conspiracy of the
enemy against mankind is checked, and the corruption of death which
before was prevailing against them is done away. For the race of men
had gone to ruin, had not the Lord and Saviour of all, the Son of God,
come among us to meet the end of death.

Why, now that the common Saviour of all has died on our behalf,
we, the faithful in Christ, no longer die the death as before, agreeably
to the warning of the law; but, corruption ceasing and being put away
by the grace of the Resurrection, henceforth we are only dissolved,

agreeably to our bodies' mortal nature, at the time God has fixed for each, that we may be able to gain a better resurrection.

For like the seeds which are cast into the earth, we do not perish by dissolution, but sown in the earth, shall rise again, death having been brought to nought by the grace of the Saviour. Hence it is that blessed Paul, who was made a surety of the Resurrection to all, says: "This corruptible must put on incorruption, and this mortal must put on immortality; but when this corruptible shall have put on incorruption, and this mortal shall have put on immortality, then shall be brought to pass the saying that is written, Death is swallowed up in victory. O death, where is thy sting? O grave, where is thy victory?" (I Cor. 15:53-55)

Why, then, one might say, if it were necessary for Him to yield up His body to death in the stead of all, did He not lay it aside as man privately, instead of going as far as even to be crucified? For it were more fitting for Him to have laid His body aside honourably, than ignominiously to endure a death like this. Now, see to it, I reply, whether such an objection be not merely human, whereas what the Saviour did is truly divine and for many reasons worthy of His Godhead. Firstly, because the death which befalls men comes to them agreeably to the weakness of their nature; for, unable to continue in one stay, they are dissolved with time. Hence, too, diseases befall them, and they fall sick and die.

But the Lord is not weak, but is the Power of God and Word of God and Very Life. If, then, He had laid aside His body somewhere in private, and upon a bed, after the manner of men, it would have been thought that He also did this agreeably to the weakness of His nature, and because there was nothing in him more than in other men. But since He was, firstly, the Life and the Word of God, and it was necessary, secondly, for the death on behalf of all to be accomplished, for this cause, on the one hand, because He was life and power, the body gained strength in Him; while on the other, as death must needs come to pass, He did not Himself take, but received at others' hands, the occasion of perfecting His sacrifice.

Since it was not fit, either, that the Lord should fall sick, who healed the diseases of others; nor again was it right for that body to lose its strength, in which He gives strength to the weaknesses of others also. Why, then, did He not prevent death, as He did sickness? Because it was for this that He had the body, and it was unfitting to prevent it, lest the Resurrection also should be hindered, while yet it was equally unfitting for sickness to precede His death, lest it should be thought weakness on the part of Him that was in the body. Did He not then hunger? Yes; He hungered, agreeably to the properties of His body. But He did not perish of hunger, because of the Lord that wore it. Hence, even if He died to ransom all, yet He saw not corruption. For [His body] rose again in perfect soundness, since the body belonged to none other, but to the very Life.

For that death is destroyed, and that the Cross is become the victory over it, and that it has no more power but is verily dead, this is no small proof, or rather an evident warrant, that it is despised by all Christ's disciples, and that they all take the aggressive against it and no longer fear it; but by the sign of the Cross and by faith in Christ tread it down as dead.

For of old, before the divine sojourn of the Saviour took place, even to the saints death was terrible, and all wept for the dead as though they perished. But now that the Saviour has raised His body, death is no longer terrible; for all who believe in Christ tread him under as nought, and choose rather to die than to deny their faith in Christ. For they verily know that when they die they are not destroyed, but actually [begin to] live, and become incorruptible through the Resurrection. And that devil that once maliciously exulted in death, now that its pains were loosed, remained the only one truly dead.

And a proof of this is, that before men believe Christ, they see in death an object of terror, and play the coward before him. But when they are gone over to Christ's faith and teaching, their contempt for death is so great that they even eagerly rush upon it, and become witnesses for the Resurrection the Saviour has accomplished against it. For while still tender in years they make haste to die, and not men only, but women also, exercise themselves by bodily discipline against it. So weak has he become, that even women who were formerly deceived by him now mock at him as dead and paralyzed.

For as when a tyrant has been defeated by a real king, and bound hand and foot, then all that pass by laugh him to scorn, buffeting and reviling him, no longer fearing his fury and barbarity, because of the king who has conquered him; so also, death having been conquered and exposed by the Saviour on the Cross, and bound hand and foot, all they who are in Christ, as they pass by, trample on him, and witnessing to Christ scoff at death, jesting at him, and saying what has been written against him of old: "O death, where is thy sting? O grave, where is thy victory." (I Cor. 15:55)

Now if by the sign of the Cross, and by faith in Christ, death is trampled down, it must be evident before the tribunal of truth that it is none other than Christ Himself that has displayed trophies and triumphs over death, and made him lose all his strength. And if, while previously death was strong, and for that reason terrible, now after the sojourn of the Saviour and the death and Resurrection of His body it is despised, it must be evident that death has been brought to nought and conquered by the very Christ that ascended the Cross.

For as, if after night-time the sun rises, and the whole region of earth is illumined by him, it is at any rate not open to doubt that it is the sun who has revealed his light everywhere, that has also driven away the dark and given light to all things; so, now that death has come into contempt, and been trodden under foot, from the time when the Saviour's saving manifestation in the flesh and His death on the Cross took place, it must be quite plain that it is the very Saviour that also appeared in the body, Who has brought death to nought, and Who displays the signs of victory over him day by day in His own disciples.

For when one sees men, weak by nature, leaping forward to death, and not fearing its corruption nor frightened of the descent into Hades, but with eager soul challenging it; and not flinching from torture, but on the contrary, for Christ's sake electing to rush upon death in preference to life upon earth, or even if one be an eye-witness of men and females and young children rushing and leaping upon death for the sake of Christ's religion; who is so silly, or who is so incredulous, or who so maimed in his mind, as not to see and infer that Christ, to Whom the people witness, Himself supplies and gives to each the victory over death, depriving him of all his power in each one of them that hold His faith and bear the sign of the Cross.

For he that sees the serpent trodden under foot, especially knowing his former fierceness, no longer doubts that he is dead and has quite lost his strength, unless he is perverted in mind and has not even his bodily senses sound. For who that sees a lion, either, made sport of by children, fails to see that he is either dead or has lost all his power? Just as, then, it is possible to see with the eyes the truth of all this, so, now that death is made sport of and despised by believers in Christ, let none any longer doubt, nor any prove incredulous, of death having been brought to nought by Christ, and the corruption of death destroyed and stayed.

When did men begin to desert the worshipping of idols, save since God, the true Word of God, has come among men? Or when have the oracles among the Greeks, and everywhere, ceased and become empty, save when the Saviour has manifested Himself upon earth? Or when did those who are called gods and heroes in the poets begin to be convicted of being merely mortal men, save since the Lord effected His conquest of death, and preserved incorruptible the body He had taken, raising it from the dead? Or when did the deceitfulness and madness of demons fall into contempt, save when the power of God, the Word, the Master of all these as well, condescending because of man's weakness, appeared on earth? Or when did the art and the schools of magic begin to be trodden down, save when the divine manifestation of the Word took place among men?

And, in the world, at what time has the wisdom of the Greeks become foolish, save when the true Wisdom of God manifested itself
on earth? For formerly the whole world and every place was led astray
by the worshipping of idols, and men regarded nothing else but the
idols as gods. But now, all the world over, men are deserting the superstition of the idols, and taking refuge with Christ; and, worshipping
Him as God, are by His means coming to know that Father also Whom
they knew not.

And, marvellous fact, whereas the objects of worship were various
and of vast number, and each place had its own idol, and he who was
accounted a God among them had no power to pass over to the neighbouring place, so as to persuade those of neighbouring peoples to
worship him, but was barely served even among his own people; for
no one else worshipped his neighbour's god—on the contrary, each
man kept to his own idol, thinking it to be lord of all;—Christ alone
is worshipped as one and the same among all peoples; and what the
weakness of the idols could not do—to persuade, namely, even those
dwelling close at hand,—this Christ has done, persuading not only
those close at hand, but simply the entire world, to worship one and
the same Lord, and through Him God, even His Father.

Let this, then, Christ-loving man, be our offering to you, just for a
rudimentary sketch and outline, in a short compass, of the faith of
Christ and of His Divine appearing to usward. But you, taking occasion
by this, if you light upon the text of the Scriptures, by genuinely
applying your mind to them, will learn from them more completely
and clearly the exact detail of what we have said. For they were spoken
and written by God, through men who spoke of God. But we impart
of what we have learned from inspired teachers who have been con-
versant with them, who have also become martyrs for the deity of
Christ, to your zeal for learning, in turn.

And you will also learn about His second glorious and truly divine
appearing to us, when no longer in lowliness, but in His own glory,—
no longer in humble guise, but in His own magnificence,—He is to
come, no more to suffer, but thenceforth to render to all the fruit of
His own Cross, that is, the resurrection and incorruption; and no
longer to be judged, but to judge all, by what each has done in the
body, whether good or evil; where there is laid up for the good the
kingdom of heaven, but for them that have done evil everlasting fire
and outer darkness. For thus the Lord Himself also says: "Henceforth
ye shall see the Son of Man sitting at the right hand of power, and
coming on the clouds of heaven in the glory of the Father." (Matt.
26:64) And for this very reason there is also a word of the Saviour
to prepare us for that day, in these words: "Be ye ready and watch, for

He cometh at an hour ye know not." (Matt. 24:42) For, according to the blessed Paul: "We must all stand before the judgment-seat of Christ, that each one may receive according as he hath done in the body, whether it be good or bad." (II Cor. 5:10)

AMBROSE 340-397

Milan, the second capital of Italy, was in a ferment. Its archbishop, Auxentius, had passed away. Who would succeed him? Neither the orthodox Catholics nor the Arians could put forth a churchman of quality to take his place. The position carried with it considerable authority: the archbishop had power to judge important civil cases, appoint officers in the church, and supervise huge sums of money.

The bishops of Milan gathered in the cathedral to elect Auxentius' successor. Crowds of citizens swarmed in to follow the election. At once a storm broke loose as orthodox and unorthodox tangled in violent argumentation over the various candidates. Tempers churned, loud cries rang out, fists struck, and not a few sustained injuries as the church seethed with excited partisans.

The Roman-trained administrator, Ambrose, consular prefect of Liquria and Emilia, with headquarters in Milan, happened to be in the city at the time. Learning of the uproar, he rushed to the cathedral, swiftly restored order, and addressed the assembly. Then a child's voice piped up, "Let Ambrose be bishop! Let Ambrose be bishop!"

Vainly Ambrose protested. They overruled his protest and forced ordination upon him. The striking fact is that he, a layman, had never entertained the idea of entering the priesthood. Actually, he had never even been baptized. But the city could not have made a wiser choice. For the next twenty-three years Ambrose was to officiate with equity and dignity and courage.

He initiated his labors by giving his estate to the poor, after providing for an income for his sister. Then he applied himself diligently to the study of the Scriptures. He preached every Sunday, lectured, catechized, wrote commentaries, hymns, and books on doctrine and morals. He often spent whole nights in prayer. He seemed always to have time for personal counseling and consultation. It was under his preaching that his great spiritual successor, Augustine, came to understand the Gospel of grace.

In the defense of the faith he rose to levels of greatness. The young emperor's mother, Faustina, a stout Arian, planned to engineer a public debate between Ambrose and one of her Arian bishops. The debate, she said, would take place in the palace, and she would sit as judge. Ambrose refused to debate on her terms. In the first place, he said, a theological disputation should be held in the church, not in the palace. In the second place, no civil ruler had the right to judge spiritual matters.

Faustina retaliated by sending a troop of soldiers to arrest Ambrose. He withdrew to the cathedral, and with him a large section of his congregation. The soldiers looked upon the interior of the cathedral as sacred territory and therefore off bounds. They stayed outside, while inside the people prayed, listened to Ambrose preach, and sang hymns he had composed.

For Faustina it meant the failure of a mission. She changed her tactics from brute force to diplomacy, from frontal attack to sly compromise. Would Ambrose not agree to turn over to the Arians one church building for worship? If so, the holy war would end and a state of peaceful coexistence would ensue.

Ambrose returned a stentorian No!

Enraged, Faustina ordered the soldiers to march straight into the cathedral and seize the obtuse ecclesiastic. But courage has a provoking way of making itself contagious. The archbishop's bold spirit filtered out of the church and into the minds of the soldiers. They disregarded Faustina's orders, continuing their casual vigil in the shadow of the cathedral, like pickets on strike.

Faustina gave up the struggle.

For the first time since the days of Peter and John, a church leader had crossed swords with a representative of the state and come off the victor. Remarkable is the fact that only twenty-seven years before, Emperor Constantine (and by curious coincidence in the city of Milano) had published an edict freeing the despised Christians from persecution. In the short period between Constantine and Faustina, the church had moved a long way forward and upward. That one man should defy a power hostile to historic Christianity and live represented a startling moral triumph for orthodoxy. Dramatically, Ambrose demonstrated to a watching world that to be valiant for truth might invite danger, but in the end it would pay rich dividends. He walked out of the conflict in the company of those heroes who "through faith subdued kingdoms, wrought righteousness, obtained promises, stopped the mouths of lions, quenched the violence of fire, out of weakness were made strong, waxed valiant in fight, turned to flight the armies of aliens."

Rules for Christian Living (Selections)

AMBROSE

Kindness

NOW we can go on to speak of kindness, which breaks up into two parts, good will and liberality. Kindness to exist in perfection must consist of these two qualities. It is not enough just to wish well; we must also do well. Nor, again, is it enough to do well, unless this springs from a good source, even from a good will. "For God loveth a cheerful giver." (II Cor. 9:7) If we act unwillingly, what is our reward? Wherefore the Apostle, speaking generally, says: "If I do this thing willingly, I have a reward, but if unwillingly, a dispensation is given unto me." (I Cor. 9:17) In the Gospel, also, we have received many rules of just liberality.

It is thus a glorious thing to wish well, and to give freely, with the one desire to do good and not to do harm. For if we were to think it our duty to give the means to an extravagant man to live extravagantly, or to an adulterer to pay for his adultery, it would not be an act of kindness, for there would be no good will in it. We should be doing harm, not good, to another if we gave him money to aid him in plotting against his country, or in attempting to get together at our expense some abandoned men to attack the Church. Nor, again, does it look like liberality to help one who presses very hardly on widows and orphans, or attempts to seize on their property with any show of violence.

It is no sign of a liberal spirit (Cicero, *De Officiis*, 1. 14. 43.) to extort from one what we give to another, or to gain money unjustly, and then to think it can be well spent, unless we act as Zacchaeus (Luke 19:8) did, and restore fourfold what we have taken from him whom we have robbed, and make up for such heathenish crimes by the zeal of our faith and by true Christian labour. Our liberality must have some sure foundation.

The first thing necessary is to do kindness in good faith, and not to act falsely when the offering is made. Never let us say we are doing more, when we are really doing less. What need is there to speak at all? In a promise a cheat lies hid. It is in our power to give what we like. Cheating shatters the foundation, and so destroys the work. Did Peter grow angry only so far as to desire that Ananias and his wife should be slain? (Acts 5:11) Certainly not. He wished that others, through knowing their example, should not perish.

Nor is it a real act of liberality if thou givest for the sake of boasting about it, rather than for mercy's sake. Thy inner feelings give the name to thy acts. As it comes forth from thee, so will others regard it. See what a true judge thou hast! He consults with thee how to take up thy work, and first of all he questions thy mind. "Let not," he says, "thy left hand know what thy right hand doeth." (Matt. 6:3) This does not refer to our actual bodies, but means: Let not him who is of one mind with thee, not even thy brother, know what thou doest, lest thou shouldst lose the fruit of thy reward hereafter by seeking here thy price in boastfulness. But that liberality is real where a man hides what he does in silence, and secretly assists the needs of individuals, whom the mouth of the poor, and not his own lips, praises.

Perfect liberality is proved by its good faith, the case it helps, the time and place when and where it is shown. But first we must always see that we help those of the household of faith. (Gal. 6:10) It is a serious fault if a believer is in want, and thou knowest it, or if thou knowest that he is without means, that he is hungry, that he suffer distress, especially if he is ashamed of his need. It is a great fault if he is overwhelmed by the imprisonment or false accusation of his family, and thou dost not come to his help. If he is in prison, and—upright though he is—has to suffer pain and punishment for some debt [for though we ought to show mercy to all, yet we ought to show it especially to an upright man]; if in the time of his trouble he obtains nothing from thee; if in the time of danger, when he is carried off to die, thy money seems more to thee than the life of a dying man; what a sin is that to thee! Wherefore Job says beautifully: "Let The blessing of Him that was ready to perish come upon me." (Job 29:13)

God, indeed, is not a respecter of persons, for He knows all things. And we, indeed, ought to show mercy to all. But as many try to get help on false pretences, and make out that they are miserably off; therefore where the case is plain and the person well known, and no time is to be lost, mercy ought to be shown more readily. For the Lord is not exacting to demand the utmost. Blessed, indeed, is he who forsakes all and follows Him, but blessed also is he who does what he can to the best of his powers with what he has.

The Lord preferred the two mites of the widow to all the gifts of the rich, for she gave all that she had, but they only gave a small part out of all their abundance. (Luke 21:3,4) It is the intention, therefore, that makes the gift valuable or poor, and gives to things their value. The Lord does not want us to give away all our goods at once, but to impart them little by little; unless, indeed, our case is like that of Elisha, who killed his oxen, and fed the people on what he had, so that no household cares might hold him back, and that he might give up all things, and devote himself to the prophetic teaching. (I Kings 19:21)

So far we have given our advice, now let us look for our authority. First, then, no one ought to be ashamed of becoming poor after being rich, if this happens because he gives freely to the poor; for Christ became poor when He was rich, that through His poverty He might enrich all. (II Cor. 8:9) He has given us a rule to follow, so that we may give a good account of our reduced inheritance; whoever has stayed the hunger of the poor has lightened his distress. "Herein I give my advice," says the Apostle, "for this is expedient for you, that ye should be followers of Christ." (II Cor. 8:10) Advice is given to the good, but warnings restrain the wrong-doers. Again he says, as though to the good: "For ye have begun not only to do, but also to be willing, a year ago." (II Cor. 8:10)

Both of these, and not only one, is the mark of perfection.

Thus he teaches that liberality without good will, and good will without liberality, are neither of them perfect. Wherefore he also urges us on to perfection, saying (II Cor. 8:11-15): "Now therefore perform the doing of it; that as the will to do it was ready enough in you, so also there may be the will to accomplish it out of that which ye have. For if the will be ready, it is accepted according to that a man hath, and not according to that he hath not. But not so that others should have plenty, and ye should be in want: but let there be equality,—your abundance must now serve for their want; that their abundance may serve for your want; that there may be equality, as it is written: 'He that gathered much had nothing over, and he that gathered little had no lack.' " (Exod. 16:18)

In giving we must also take into consideration age and weakness; sometimes, also, that natural feeling of shame, which indicates good birth. One ought to give more to the old who can no longer supply themselves with food by labour. So, too, weakness of body must be assisted, and that readily. Again, if any one after being rich has fallen into want, we must assist, especially if he has lost what he had from no sin of his own, but owing to robbery or banishment or false accusation.

Perchance some one may say: A blind man sits here in one place, and people pass him by, whilst a strong young man often has something given him. That is true; for he comes over people by his importunity. That is not because in their judgment he deserves it, but because they are wearied by his begging. For the Lord speaks in the Gospel of him who had already closed his door; how that when one knocks at his door very violently, he rises and gives what is wanted, because of his importunity. (S. Luke 11:8)

Familiarity with Good Men

It is a very good thing to unite one's self to a good man. It is also very useful for the young (Cicero, *De Officiis*, II. 13. 46.) to follow the guidance of great and wise men. For he who lives in company with wise men is wise himself; but he who clings to the foolish is looked on as a fool too. This friendship with the wise is a great help in teaching us, and also as giving a sure proof of our uprightness. Young men show very soon that they imitate those to whom they attach themselves. And this idea gains ground from the fact that in all their daily life they grow to be like those with whom they have enjoyed intercourse to the full.

Joshua the son of Nun became so great, because his union with Moses was the means not only of instructing him in a knowledge of the law, but also of sanctifying him to receive grace. When in His tabernacle the majesty of the Lord was seen to shine forth in its divine presence, Joshua alone was in the tabernacle. When Moses spoke with God, Joshua too was covered by the sacred cloud. (Exod. 24:12 ff.) The priests and people stood below, and Joshua and Moses went up the mount to receive the law. All the people were within the camp; Joshua was without the camp in the tabernacle of witness. When the pillar of a cloud came down, and God spoke with Moses, he stood as a trusty servant beside him; and he, a young man, did not go out of the tabernacle though the old man who stood afar off trembled at these divine wonders.

Everywhere, therefore, he alone kept close to holy Moses amid all these wondrous works and dread secrets. Wherefore it happens that he who had been his companion in this intercourse with God succeeded to his power. (Deut. 34:9) Worthy surely was he to stand forth as a man who might stay the course of the river (Josh. 3:15 ff.), and who might say: "Sun, stand . . . still," and delay the night and lengthen the day as though to witness his victory. (Josh. 10:12,13) Why?—a blessing denied to Moses—he alone was chosen to lead the people into the promised land. A man he was, great in the wonders he wrought by faith, great in his triumphs. The works of Moses were of a higher type, his brought greater success. Either of these then aided by divine grace rose above all human standing. The one ruled the sea, the other heaven. (Exod. 14:21. Cf. also Josh. 10:12)

Beautiful, therefore, is the union between old and young. The one to give witness, the other to give comfort; the one to give guidance, the other to give pleasure. I pass by Lot, who when young clung to Abraham, as he was setting out. (Gen. 12:5) For some perhaps might say this arose rather owing to their relationship than from any voluntary action on his part. And what are we to say of Elijah and Elisha? (I

Kings 19:21) Though Scripture has not in so many words stated
that Elisha was a young man, yet we gather from it that he was
younger. In the Acts of the Apostles, Barnabus took Mark with him,
and Paul took Silas (Acts 15:39,40) and Timothy (Acts 16:3) and
Titus (Titus 1:5)

We see also that duties were divded amongst them according to
their superiority in anything. The elders took the lead in giving counsel, the younger in showing activity. Often, too, those who were
alike in virtue but unlike in years were greatly rejoiced in their union,
as Peter and John were. We read in the Gospel that John was a young
man, even in his own words, though he was behind none of the elders
in merits and wisdom. For in him there was a venerable ripeness of
character and the prudence of the hoarhead. An unspotted life is the
due of a good old age.

Faith

"Not every one that saith unto me, Lord, Lord, shall enter into the
kingdom of heaven" (Matt. 7:21), saith the Scripture. Faith, therefore,
august Sovereign, must not be a mere matter of performance, for it is
written, "The zeal of thine house hath devoured me." (Ps. 69:9) Let us
then with faithful spirit and devout mind call upon Jesus our Lord, let
us believe that he is God, to the end that whatever we ask of the
Father, we may obtain in His name. (John 15:16; Luke 11:9,10) For
the Father's will is, that He be entreated through the Son, the Son's
that the Father be entreated. (John 16:23,24; 14:13; Matt. 7:7,8;
Mark 11:24)

The grace of His submission makes for agreement (with our teaching), and the acts of His power are not at variance therewith. For
whatsoever things the Father doeth, the same also doeth the Son, in
like manner. (John 5:19,30) The Son both doeth the same things,
and doeth them in like manner, but it is the Father's will that He be entreated in the matter of what He Himself proposeth to do, that you
may understand, not that He cannot do it otherwise, but that there
is one power displayed. Truly, then, is the Son of God to be adored
and worshipped, Who by the power of His Godhead hath laid the
foundations of the world, and by His submission informed our affections. (John 1:3; Heb. 5:7-10)

Therefore we ought to believe that God is good, eternal, perfect,
almighty, and true, such as we find Him in the Law and the Prophets,
and the rest of the holy Scriptures (Vide, e.g., Ps. 25:8; Jer. 10:10;
James 1:17,18; Dan. 9:9,10; Luke 1:37), for otherwise there is no
God. For He Who is God cannot but be good, seeing that fulness of
goodness is of the nature of God (Dan. 9:7; Exod. 34:6); nor can God,
Who made time, be in time; nor, again, can God be imperfect, for a

lesser being is plainly imperfect, seeing that it lacks somewhat whereby it could be made equal to a greater. This, then, is the teaching of our faith—that God is not evil, that with God nothing is impossible, that God exists not in time, that God is beneath no being. If I am in error, let my adversaries prove it. (See James 1:13; Luke 18:27; Ps. 90:2-4; 89:6)

Seeing, then, that Christ is God, He is, by consequence, good and almighty and eternal and perfect and true; for these attributes belong to the essential nature of the Godhead. Let our adversaries, therefore, deny the Divine Nature in Christ,—otherwise they cannot refuse to God what is proper to the Divine Nature.

Further, that none may fall into error, let a man attend to those signs vouchsafed us by Holy Scripture, whereby we may know the Son. He is called the Word, the Son, the Power of God, the Wisdom of God. (John 1:1,14; 20:31; Rom. 1:4; Matt. 28:18; I Cor. 1:24; Col. 2:2,3) The Word, because He is without blemish; the Power, because He is perfect; the Son, because he is begotten of the Father; the Wisdom, because He is one with the Father, one in eternty, one in Divinity. Not that the Father is one Person with the Son; between Father and Son is the plain distinction that comes of generation; (Begetter and begotten *must* be personally distinct); so that Christ is God of God, Everlasting of Everlasting, Fulness of Fulness. (Col. 1:19; 2:9)

Now these are not mere names, but signs of power manifesting itself in works, for while there is fulness of Godhead in the Father, there is also fulness of Godhead in the Son, not diverse, but one. The Godhead is nothing confused, for it is an unity; nothing manifold, for in it there is no difference.

Moreover, if in all them that believed there was, as it is written, one soul and one heart (Acts 4:32): if every one that cleaveth to the Lord is one spirit (I Cor. 6:17), as the Apostle hath said: if a man and his wife are one flesh (Gen. 2:24; Matt. 19:5): if all we mortal men are, so far as regards our general nature, of one substance: if this is what the Scripture saith of created men, that, being many, they are one (Acts 17:26; Gal. 3:28), who can in no way be compared to Divine Persons, how much more are the Father and the Son one in Divinity, with Whom there is no difference either of substance or of will!

For how else shall we say that God is One? Divinity maketh plurality, but unity of power debarreth quantity of number, seeing that unity is not number, but itself is the principle of all numbers.

JOHN CHRYSOSTOM 345-407

The city of Antioch was in an uproar. A cordon of unruly citizens had without provocation mobbed and slain several of Emperor Theodosius' officials. Furiously Theodosius prepared to dispatch an army to avenge the killings. Fear and remorse gripped the city. Retribution seemed inescapable. What could be done, people asked, to placate the wrath of the emperor?

Chrysostom, Bishop of Antioch, went into action. He called the residents of the city together in the Great Cathedral. Mounting the rostrum, he addressed the tense, terror-racked assembly. He spoke sternly, at first. Antioch, already known as the Sodom of the East, had added guilt to guilt, he said. There was no justification whatever for the crime of multiple murder. Antioch merited punishment. Antioch deserved no clemency.

Then gradually, subtly, the speaker mellowed. He pleaded with his hearers as a father with his erring children. One course lay open, and one only. Public wrong demanded public contrition. The citizens of Antioch must repent. The citizens of Antioch must bring forth fruit evidencing repentance. The citizens of Antioch must acknowledge that they had violated the majesty of the law, and must apologize to their emperor. The citizens of Antioch must promise never to repeat the dreadful thing they had done.

The preacher's words moved and melted men to tears. They acted out his every stipulation. In consequence, Theodosius was conciliated and suspended punishment. Such was the power of Chrysostom.

His name was John, really. Not until the seventh century did the appellation Chrysostom (literally, "The Golden-mouthed") replace his given name. The judgment of history has vindicated the change. Rightly has the Church ranked him in the top echelon of Christian preachers. The Apollos of the church fathers, he was "an eloquent man, and mighty in the Scriptures." His influence extended from the pauper in the street to the ruler in the palace.

Job once declared, "How forcible are right words!" So forcible, indeed, were Chrysostom's that his attendants would often clap hands and stamp their feet while he was preaching. He determined to put a stop to the habit. He delivered a stirring sermon condemning it as irreverent, disgraceful, dishonoring to God. The response was something less than encouraging. His congregation, Schaff records, applauded him roundly!

His popularity rose. Theodosius appointed him Patriarch of Constantinople. Archbishop Theophilus of Alexandria, in an impressive service, consecrated him to the office. Once installed, he turned upon his benefactors and exposed their evils. He accused Theophilus (and accurately) of simony, of misappropriating funds, of practicing brutality against Origen's followers. He raged against the degenerate quality of court life. He singled out for his special target Eudocia, the beautiful and treacherous empress. She was, he charged, a second Jezebel.

Ecclesiastical envy combined with imperial malice to have him unfrocked and deported. The scheme backfired. The population of Constantinople rose up and clamored for his recall. Theodosius yielded. Chrysostom's return to the city was reminiscent of his Lord's triumphal entry into Jerusalem on the first Palm Sunday: wild shouts of welcome and the spreading of garments underfoot punctuated the event.

Back in the pulpit, necessity was laid upon him, he felt, to continue to unmask the sins of Eudocia. She threatened him with deposition unless he stopped. Chrysostom would not be muzzled. "Again Herodias raves!" he thundered. "Again she dances! Again she demands the head of John in a basin!"

Great men are not always wise in the ways of the world. Chrysostom's admirers think that he went too far in his open denunciations; that having taken a stand once on court misdemeanors, he should then have given his attention to the teaching of the Gospel. But Chrysostom could not, or would not, divorce his message from the context of contemporary ills. He preached himself right out of the pulpit and back into exile.

This time public pressure was powerless to restore him. He died near Pontus, worn out, broken in health, but to the end cheerful, full of faith and love and hope, radiant in the confidence that God's will was being carried out.

The Golden-mouthed, being dead, yet speaketh. His sermons, over six hundred of which are in print, breathe a knowledge of Scripture, devotion, learning, taste, craftsmanship, a passion for beauty, an acquaintance with the Greek classics. He preached to the heart and conscience as well as to the intellect. He delighted to exalt the Christ of God, and to bring to bear on the lives of his beloved people the moral principles of the Bible. Probably he did more to make the pulpit a medium of influence for righteousness than any clergyman in the first Christian millennium.

"He regarded himsef as the bearer of momentous truth," wrote John Lord, "and soared above human praise, and forgot himself in his cause, and that cause the salvation of souls."

The Omnipotent Christ, Healer of Souls
As Well As Bodies

JOHN CHRYSOSTOM

HAVING lately come across the incident of the paralytic who lay upon his bed beside the pool, we discovered a rich and large treasure, not by delving in the ground, but diving into his heart: we found a treasure not containing silver and gold and precious stones, but endurance, and philosophy, and patience and much hope towards God, which is more valuable than any kind of jewel or source of wealth. For material riches are liable to the designs of robbers, and the tales of false accusers, and the violenceof housebreakers, and the villainy of servants, and when they have escaped all these things, they often bring the greatest ruin upon those who possess them by exciting the eyes of the envious, and consequently breeding countless storms of trouble.

But the spiritual riches escape all these occasions of mischief and are superior to all abuse of this kind, laughing to scorn both robbers, and housebreakers, and slanderers, and false accusers and death itself. For they are not parted from the possessor by death, but on the contrary the possession becomes then more especially secured to the owners, and they accompany them on their journey to the other world, and are transplanted with them to the future life, and become marvellous advocates of those with whom they depart hence, and render the judge propitious to them.

This wealth we found in great abundance stored in the soul of the paralytic. And you are witnesses who with great zeal drew up draughts of this treasure yet without exhausting it. For such is the nature of spiritual wealth; it resembles fountains of water, or rather exceeds their plenteousness, being most abundant when it has many to draw upon it. For when it enters into any man's soul it is not divided, not diminished, but coming in its entireness to each remains continually unconsumed, being incapable of ever failing: which was just what took place at that time. For although so many have applied to the treasure, and all are drawing upon it as much as they can—but why do I speak of you, seeing that it has made countless persons rich from that time to the present day, and yet abides in its original perfection?

Let us not then grow weary in having recourse to this source of spiritual wealth: but as far as possible let us now also draw forth draughts from it, and let us gaze upon our merciful Lord, gaze upon His patient servant. He had been thirty and eight years struggling with an incurable infirmity and was perpetually plagued by it, yet he did not utter a blasphemous word, he did not accuse his Maker, but endured his calamity bravely and with much meekness. And whence is this manifest? Scripture has not told us anything clearly concerning his former life, but only that he had been thirty-eight years in his infirmity; it has not added a word to prove that he did not show discontent, or anger or petulence. And yet it has made this plain also, if any one will pay careful attention to it, not looking at it curiously and carelessly. For when you hear that on the approach of Christ who was a stranger to him, and regarded merely as a man, he spoke to him with such great meekness, you may be able to perceive his former wisdom. For when Jesus said to him "Wilt thou be made whole?" he did not make the natural reply "thou seest me who have been this long time lying sick of the palsy, and dost thou ask me if I wish to be made whole? hast thou come to insult my distress, to reproach me and laugh me to scorn and make a mock of my calamity?" He did not say or conceive anything of this kind but meekly replied "Yea Lord."

Now if after thirty-eight years he was thus meek and gentle, when all the vigour and strength of his reasoning faculties was broken down, consider what he is likely to have been at the outset of his trouble. For be assured that invalids are not so hard to please at the beginning of their disorder, as they are after a long lapse of time: they become most intractable, most intolerable to all, when the malady is prolonged. But as he, after so many years, was so wise, and replied with so much forbearance, it is quite clear that during the previous time also he had been bearing that calamity with much thankfulness.

Considering these things then let us imitate the patience of our fellow-servant: for his paralysis is sufficient to brace up our souls: for no one can be so supine and indolent after having observed the magnitude of that calamity as not to endure bravely all evils which may befall him, even if they are more intolerable than all that were ever known. For not only his soundness but also his sickness has become a cause of the greatest benefit to us: for his cure has stimulated the souls of the hearers to speak the praise of the Lord, and his sickness and infirmity has encouraged you to patience, and urged you to match his zeal; or rather it has exhibited to you the lovingkindness of God. For the actual deliverance of the man to such a malady, and the protracted duration of his infirmity is a sign of the greatest care for his welfare. For as a gold refiner having cast a piece of gold into the furnace suffers it to be proved by the fire until such time as he sees it has become purer: even so God permits the souls of men to be tested by troubles until they become pure and transparent and have reaped much profit from this process of sifting: wherefore this is the greatest species of benefit.

Let us not then be disturbed, neither dismayed, when trials befall us. For if the gold refiner sees how long he ought to leave the piece of gold in the furnace, and when he ought to draw it out, and does not allow it to remain in the fire until it is destroyed and burnt up: much more does God understand this, and when He sees that we have become more pure, He releases us from our trials so that we may not be overthrown and cast down by the multiplication of our evils. Let us then not be repining, or faint-hearted, when some unexpected thing befalls us; but let us suffer Him who knows these things accurately, to prove our hearts by fire as long as He pleases: for He does this for a useful purpose and with a view to the profit of those who are tried.

On this account a certain wise man admonishes us saying "My Son, if thou come to serve the Lord prepare thy soul for temptation, set thy heart aright and constantly endure and make not haste in time of trouble"; "yield to Him" he says, "in all things," for He knoweth exactly when it is right to pluck us out of the furnace of evil. We ought therefore everywhere to yield to Him and always to give thanks, and to bear all things contentedly, whether He bestows benefits or chastisement upon us, for this also is a species of benefit. For the physician, not only when he bathes and nourishes the patient and conducts him into pleasant gardens, but also when he uses cautery and the knife, is a physician all the same: and a father not only when he caresses his son, but also when he expels him from his house, and when he chides and scourges him, is a father all the same, no less than when he praises him.

Knowing therefore that God is more tenderly loving than all physicians, do not enquire too curiously concerning His treatment nor demand an account of it from Him, but whether He is pleased to let us go free or whether He punishes, let us offer ourselves for either alike; for He seeks by means of each to lead us back to health, and to communion with Himself, and He knows our several needs, and what is expedient for each one, and how and in what manner we ought to be saved, and along that path He leads us. Let us then follow whithersoever He bids us, and let us not too carefully consider whether He commands us to go by a smooth and easy path, or by a difficult and rugged one: as in the case of this paralytic.

It was one species of benefit indeed that his soul should be purged by the long duration of his suffering, being delivered to the fiery trial of affliction as to a kind of furnace; but it was another benefit no less than this that God was present with him in the midst of the trials, and afforded him great consolation. He it was who strengthened him, and upheld him, and stretched forth a hand to him, and suffered him not to fall. But when you hear that it was God Himself do not deprive the paralytic of his meed of praise, neither him nor any other man who is tried and yet steadfastly endures. For even if we be infinitely wise, even if we are mightier and stronger than all men, yet in the absence of His grace we shall not be able to withstand even the most ordinary temptation.

And why do I speak of such insignificant and abject beings as we are? For even if one were a Paul, or a Peter, or a James, or a John, yet if he should be deprived of the divine help he would easily be put to shame, overthrown, and laid prostrate. And on behalf of these I will read you the words of Christ Himself: for He saith to Peter "Behold, Satan hath asked to have you that he may sift you as wheat: but I have prayed for thee that thy faith fail not." (Luke 22:31,32) What is the meaning of "sift"? to turn and twist, and shake and stir and shatter, and worry, which is what takes place in the case of things which are winnowed: but I, he says, have restrained him, knowing that you are not able to endure the trial, for the expression "that thy faith fail not" is the utterance of one who signifies that if he had permitted it his faith would have failed.

Now if Peter who was such a fervent lover of Christ and exposed his life for Him countless times and sprang into the foremost rank in the Apostolic band, and was pronounced blessed by his Master, and called Peter on this account because he kept a firm and inflexible hold of the faith, would have been carried away and fallen from profession if Christ had permitted the devil to try him as much as he desired, what other man will be able to stand, apart from His help? Therefore also Paul saith "But God is faithful, who will not suffer you to be tempted above that ye are able; but will with the temptaton also make the way of escape that ye may be able to bear it." (I Cor. 10:13) For not only does He say that He does not suffer a trial to be inflicted beyond our strength, but even in that which is proportioned to our strength He is present carrying us through it, and bracing us up, if only we ourselves first of all contribute the means which are at our disposal, such as zeal, hope in Him, thanksgiving, endurance, patience.

For not only in the dangers which are beyond our strength, but in those which are proportioned to it, we need the divine assistance, if we are to make a brave stand; for elsewhere also it is said "even as the sufferings of Christ abound to us, even so our comfort also aboundeth through Christ, that we may be able to comfort those who are in any trouble, by the comfort wherewith we ourselves are comforted of God." (II Cor. 1:4,5) So then he who comforted this man is the same who permitted the trial to be inflicted upon him. And now observe after the cure what tenderness He displays. For He did not leave him and depart, but having found him in the temple he saith "Behold, thou art made whole: sin no more lest some worse thing happen unto thee."

(John 5:14) For had He permitted the punishment because He hated him He would not have released him, He would not have provided for his future safety: but the expression "lest some worse thing happen unto thee" is the utterance of one who would check coming evils beforehand.

He put an end to the disease, but did not put an end to the struggle: He expelled the infirmity but did not expel the dread of it, so that the benefit which had been wrought might remain unmoved. This is the part of a tender-hearted physician, not only to put an end to present pains, but to provide for future security, which also Christ did, bracing up his soul by the recollection of past events. For seeing that when the things which distress us have departed, the recollection of them often-times departs with them, He wishing to abide continually, saith "sin no more lest some worse thing happen unto thee."

Moreover it is possible to discern His forethought and consideration not only from this, but also from that which seems to be a rebuke. For He did not make a public exposure of his sins, but yet He told him that he suffered what he did suffer on account of his sins, but what those sins were He did not disclose; nor did He say "thou hast sinned" or "thou hast transgressed," but He indicated the fact by one simple utter-ance "sin no more"; and having said so much as just to remind him of it He put him more on the alert against future events, and at the same time He made manifest to us all his patience and courage and wisdom, having reduced him to the necessity of publicly lamenting his calamity, and having displayed his own earnestness on the man's behalf, "for while I am coming," he says, "another steppeth down before me" (John 5:7), yet he did not publicly expose his sins.

For just as we ourselves desire to draw a veil over our sins even so does God much more than we: on this account He wrought the cure in the presence of all, but He gives the exhortation or the advice pri-vately. For He never makes a public display of our sins, except at any time He sees men insensible to them. For when He says "ye saw me hungry, and fed me not: and thirsty and gave me no drink" (Matt. 25:42), He speaks thus at the present time in order that we may not hear these words in time to come. He threatens, He exposes us in this world, that He may not have to expose us in the other: even as He threatened to overthrow the city of the Ninevites for the very reason that He might not overthrow it. For if He wished to publish our sins He would not announce beforehand that He would publish them: but as it is He does make this announcement in order that being sobered by the fear of exposure, if not also by the fear of punishment we may purge ourselves from them all.

And now since we have derived so much profit from the account of the former paralytic let us turn to the other who is presented to us in St. Matthew's Gospel. For in the case of mines where any one happens to find a piece of gold he makes a further excavation again in the same place: and I know that many of those who read without care imagine that one and the same paralytic is presented by the four evangelists: but it is not so. Therefore you must be on the alert, and pay careful attention to the matter. For the question is not concerned with ordinary matters, and this discourse when it has received its proper solution will be serviceable against both Greeks and Jews and many of the heretics. For thus all find fault with the evangelists as being at strife and variance: yet this is not the fact, Heaven forbid! but although the outward appearance is different, the grace of the Spirit which works upon the soul of each is one, and where the grace of the Spirit is, there is love, joy, and peace; and there war and disputation, strife and contention are not.

Let us then give our attention and observe Him as He performs the cure. For if in the case of physicians when they use the knife or cautery or operate in any other way upon a maimed and crippled patient, and cut off a limb, many persons crowd round the invalid and the physician who is doing these things, much more ought we to act thus in this case, in proportion as the physician is greater and the malady more severe, being one which cannot be corrected by human art, but only by divine grace. And in the former case we have to see the skin being cut, and matter discharging, and gore set in motion, and to endure much discomfort produced by the spectacle, and great pain and sorrow not merely from the sight of the wounds, but also from the suffering undergone by those who are subjected to this burning or cutting: for no one is so stony-hearted as to stand by those who are suffering these things, and hear them shrieking, without being himself overcome and agitated, and experiencing much depression of spirit; but yet we undergo all this owing to our desire to witness the operation.

But in this case nothing of that kind has to be seen, no application of fire, no plunging in of an instrument, no flowing of blood, no pain or shrieking of the patient; and the reason of this is, the wisdom of the healer, which needs none of these external aids, but is absolutely self-sufficient. For it is enough that He merely utters a command and all distress ceases. And the wonder is not only that He effects the cure with so much ease, but also without pain, causing no trouble to those who are being healed.

Seeing then that the marvel is greater and the cure more important, and the pleasure afforded to the spectators unalloyed by any kind of sorrow, let us now carefully contemplate Christ in the act of healing. "And He entered into a boat, and crossed over, and came into His own city; and, behold, they brought to him a man sick of the palsy, lying on a bed: and Jesus seeing their faith said unto the sick of the palsy; "Son! be of good cheer: thy sins are forgiven." (Matt. 9:1,2) Now they were inferior to the centurion in respect of their faith, but superior to the important man by the pool. For the former neither invited the physician nor brought the sick man to the physician; but approached Him as God and said "Speak the word only and my servant shall be healed." (Luke 7:7)

Now these men did not invite the physician to the house, and so far they are on an equality with the centurion: but they brought the sick man to the physician and so far they are inferior, because they did not say "speak the word only." Yet they are far better than the man lying by the pool. For he said "Lord I have no man, when the water is troubled, to put me into the pool": but these men knew that Christ had no need either of water, or pool, or anything else of that kind: nevertheless Christ not only released the servant of the centurion but the other two men also from their maladies, and did not say: "because thou hast proffered a smaller degree of faith the cure which thou receivest shall be in proportion"; but He dismissed the man who displayed the greater faith with eulogy and honour, saying "I have not found so great faith, no, not in Israel." (Luke 7:9)

On the man who exhibited less faith than this one he bestowed no praise yet He did not deprive him of a cure, no! not even him who displayed no faith at all. But just as physicians when curing the same disorder receive from some person a hundred gold pieces, from others half, from others less and from some nothing at all: even so Christ received from the centurion a large and unspeakable degree of faith, but from this man less and from the other not even an ordinary amount, and yet He healed them all. For what reason then did He deem the man who made no deposit of faith worthy of the benefit? Because his failure to exhibit faith was not owing to indolence, or to insensibility of soul, but to ignorance of Christ and having never heard any miracle in which He was concerned either small or great. On this account therefore the man obtained indulgence: which in fact the evangelist obscurely intimates when he says, "for he wist not who it was" (John 5:13), but he only recognized Him by sight when he lighted upon Him the second time.

There are indeed some who say that this man was healed merely because they who brought him believed; but this is not the fact. For "when He saw their faith" refers not merely to those who brought the man but also to the man who was brought. Why so? "Is not one man healed," you say, "because another has believed?" For my part I do not think so unless owing to immaturity of age or excessive infirmity he is in some way incapable of believing. How then was it you say that in the case of the woman of Canaan the mother believed but the daughter was cured? and how was it that the servant of the centurion who believed rose from the bed of sickness and was preserved? Because the sick persons themselves were not able to believe.

Hear then what the woman of Canaan says: "My daughter is grievously vexed with a devil (Matt. 15:22) and sometimes she falleth into the water and sometimes into the fire": now how could she believe whose mind was darkened and possessed by a devil, and was never able to control herself, not in her sound senses? As then in the case of the woman of Canaan so also in the case of the centurion; his servant lay ill in the house, not knowing Christ, himself, nor who He was. How then was he to believe in one who was unknown to him, and of whom he had never yet obtained any experience? But in the case before us we cannot say this: for the paralytic believed. Whence is this manifest? From the very manner of his approach to Christ. For do not attend simply to the statement that they let the man down through the roof: but consider how great a matter it is for a sick man to have the fortitude to undergo this. For you are surely aware that invalids are so faint-hearted and difficult to please as often to decline the treatment administered to them on their sick bed, and to prefer bearing the pain which arises from their maladies to undergoing the annoyance caused by the remedies. But this man had the fortitude to go outside the house, and to be carried into the midst of the market place, and to exhibit himself in the presence of a crowd.

And it is the habit of sick folk to die under their disorder rather than disclose their personal calamities. This sick man however did not act thus, but when he saw that the place of assembly was filled, the approaches blocked, the haven of refuge obstructed, he submitted to be let down through the roof. So ready in contrivance is desire, so rich in resource is love. "For he also that seeketh findeth, and to him that knocketh it shall be opened." (Luke 11:10) The man did not say to his friends "What is the meaning of this? why make this ado? why push on? Let us wait until the house is cleared and the assembly is dissolved: the crowds will withdraw, we shall then be able to approach him privately and confer about these matters. Why should you expose my misfortunes in the midst of all the spectators, and let me down from the roof-top, and behave in an unseemly manner?" That man said none of these things either to himself or to his bearers, but regarded it as an honour to have so many persons made witnesses of his cure.

And not from this circumstance only was it possible to discern his faith but also from the actual words of Christ. For after he had been let down and presented, Christ said to him, "Son! be of good cheer, thy sins are forgiven thee." And when he heard these words he was not indignant, he did not complain, he did not say to the physician "What mean you by this? I came to be healed of one thing and you heal another. This is an excuse and a pretence and a screen of incompetence. Do you forgive sins which are invisible?"

He neither spoke nor thought any of these things, but waited, allowing the physician to adopt the method of healing which He desired. For this reason also Christ did not go to him, but waited for him to come that He might exhibit his faith to all. For could He not have made the entrance easy? But He did none of these things; in order that He might exhibit the man's zeal and fervent faith to all. For as He went to the man who had been suffering thirty and eight years because he had no one to aid him, so did He wait for this man to come to him because he had many friends that He might make his faith manifest by the man being brought to Him, and inform us of the other man's loneliness by going to him, and disclose the earnestness of the one and the patience of the other to all and especially to those who were present.

Some envious and misanthropical Jews were accustomed to grudge the benefits done to their neighbours and to find fault with His miracles, sometimes on account of the special season, saying that He healed on the sabbath day; sometimes on account of the life of those to whom the benefit was done, saying "if this man were a prophet He would have known who the woman was who touched Him" (Luke 7:39), not knowing that it is the special mark of a physician to associate with the infirm and to be constantly seen by the side of the sick, not to avoid them, or hurry from their presence—which in fact was what He expressly said to those murmurers; "They that are whole have no need of a physician but they that are sick." (Matt. 9:12)

Therefore in order to prevent their making the same accusations again He proves first of all that they who come to Him are deserving of a cure on account of the faith which they exhibit. For this reason He exhibited the loneliness of one man, and the fervent faith and zeal of the other: for this reason He healed the one on the Sabbath, the other not on the Sabbath: in order that when you see them accusing and rebuking Christ on another day you may understand that they accused him on the former occasion also not because of their respect for the law, but because they could not contain their own malice. But why did He not first address Himself to the *cure* of the paralytic, but said, "Son, be of good cheer; thy *sins* are forgiven thee"? He did this very wisely. For it is a habit with physicians to destroy the originating cause of the malady before they remove the malady itself.

Often for example when the eyes are distressed by some evil humour and corrupt discharge, the physician, abandoning any treatment of the disordered vision, turns his attention to the head, where the root and origin of the infirmity is: even so did Christ act: He represses first of all the source of the evil. For the source and root and mother of all evil is the nature of sin. This it is which enervates our bodies: this it is which brings on disease: therefore also on this occasion He said, "Son, be of good cheer; thy sins are forgiven thee." And on the other

He said, "Behold! thou art made whole; sin no more lest some worse thing happen unto thee," intimating to both that these maladies were the offspring of sin.

And in the beginning and outset of the world disease as the consequence of sin attacked the body of Cain. For after the murder of his brother, after that act of wickedness, his body was subject to palsy. For trembling is the same thing as palsy. For when the strength which regulates a living creature becomes weakened, being no longer able to support all the limbs, it deprives them of their natural power of direction, and then having become unstrung they tremble and turn giddy.

Paul also demonstrated this: for when he was reproaching the Corinthians with a certain sin he said, "For this cause many are weak and sickly among you." Therefore also Christ first removes the cause of the evil, and having said "Son! be of good cheer; thy sins are forgiven thee," He uplifts the spirit and rouses the downcast soul: for the speech became an efficient cause and having entered into the conscience it laid hold of the soul itself and cast out of it all distress. For nothing creates pleasure and affords confidence so much as freedom from self-reproach. For where remission of sins is there is sonship.

Even so at least we are not able to call God Father until we have washed away our sins in the pool of the sacred water. It is when we have come up from thence, having put off that evil load, that we say "Our Father which art in Heaven." But in the case of the man who was infirm thirty and eight years why did He not act thus, but cured his body first of all? Because by that long period of time his sins had been exhausted: for the magnitude of a trial can lighten the load of sins: as indeed we read was the case with Lazarus, that he received his evil things in full, and thereupon was comforted: and again in another place we read, "Comfort ye my people, say ye to the heart of Jerusalem, that she hath received of the Lord's hand double for all her sins." (Isa. 40:1,2) And again the prophet says "O Lord give us peace, for Thou hast requited all things to us" (Isa. 26:12), indicating that penalties and punishments work forgiveness of sins; and this we might prove from many passages.

It seems to me then that the reason why He said nothing to that man about remission of sins, but only secured him against the future, was because the penalty for his sins had been already worked out by the long duration of his sickness: or if this was not the reason, it was because he had not yet attained any high degree of belief concerning Christ that the Lord first addressed Himself to the lesser need, and one which was manifest and obvious, the health of the body. But in the case of the other man He did not act thus, but inasmuch as this man had more faith, and a loftier soul, He spoke to him first of all concerning the more dangerous disease: with the additional object of exhibiting his equality of rank with the Father. For just as in the former case He healed on the Sabbath day because He wished to lead men away from the Jewish mode of observing it, and to take occasion from their reproaches to prove Himself equal with the Father: even so in this instance also, knowing beforehand what they were going to say, He uttered these words that He might use them as a starting-point and a pretext for proving His equality of rank with the Father.

For it is one thing when no one brings an accusation or charge to enter spontaneously upon a discourse about these things, and quite another when other persons give occasion for it, to set about the same work in the order and shape of a defence. For the nature of the former demonstration was a stumbling block to the hearers: but the other was less offensive, and more acceptable, and everywhere we see Him doing this, and manifesting His equality not so much by words as by deeds. This at any rate is what the Evangelist implied when he said that the Jews persecuted Jesus not only because He broke the Sabbath but also because He said that God was His Father, making Himself equal with God, which is a far greater thing, for He effected this by the demonstration of His deeds.

How then do the envious and wicked act, and those who repine at the good things of other people, and seek to find a handle in every direction? "Why does this man blaspheme?" they say for "no man can forgive sins save God alone." (Mark 2:7) As they persecuted Him there because He broke the Sabbath, and took occasion from their reproaches to declare His equality with the Father in the form of a defence, saying "my Father worketh hitherto and I work" (John 5:17), so here also starting from the accusations which they make He proves from these His exact likeness to the Father. For what was it they said? "No man can forgive sins save God alone."

Inasmuch then as they themselves laid down this definition, they themselves introduced the rule, they themselves declared the law, He proceeds to entangle them by means of their own words. "You have confessed," He says, "that forgiveness of sins is an attribute of God alone: My equality therefore is unquestionable." And it is not these men only who declare this but also the prophet thus saying: "who is God as thou?" and then, indicating His special attribute he adds "taking away iniquity, and passing over unrighteousness." (Mic. 7:18) If then any one else appears thus doing the same thing He also is God, God even as that one is God.

But let us observe how Christ argues with them, how meekly and gently, and with all tenderness. "And behold some of the scribes said within themselves: this man blasphemeth." They did not utter the word, they did not proclaim it through the tongue, but reasoned in the secret recesses of their heart. How then did Christ act? He made public their secret thoughts before the demonstration which was concerned with the cure of the paralytic's body, wishing to prove to them the power of His Godhead. For that it is an attribute of God alone, a sign of His deity to shew the secrets of His mind, the Scripture saith "Thou alone knowest men's hearts."

Seest thou that this word "alone," is not used with a view of contrasting the Son with the Father. For if the Father alone knows the heart, how does the Son know the secrets of the mind? "For He Himself," it is said, "knew what was in man" (John 2:25); and Paul when proving that the knowledge of secret things is a special attribute of God says, "and He that searchest the heart" (Rom. 8:27), shewing that this expression is equivalent to the appellation "God." For just as when I say "He who causeth rain said," I signify none other than God by mentioning the deed, since it is one which belongs to Him alone: and when I say "He who maketh the sun to rise," without adding the word God, I yet signify Him by mentioning the deed: even so when Paul said "He who searcheth the hearts," he proved that to search the heart is an attribute of God alone. For if this expression had not been of equal force with the Name "God" for pointing out Him who was signified, he would not have used it absolutely and by itself. For if the power were shared by Him in common with some created being, we should not have known who was signified, the community of power causing confusion in the mind of the hearers. Inasmuch then as this appears to be a special attribute of the Father, and yet is manifested of the Son whose equality becomes thence unquestionable, therefore we read "why think ye evil in your hearts? for whether is easier: to say: Thy sins are forgiven thee or to say, Arise and walk?"

See moreover He makes a second proof of His power of forgiving sins. For to forgive sins is a very much greater act than to heal the body, greater in proportion as the soul is greater than the body. For as paralysis is a disease of the body, even so sin is a disease of the soul: but although this is the greater it is not palpable: whereas the other although it be less is manifest. Since then He is about to use the less for a demonstration of the greater proving that He acted thus on account of their weakness, and by way of condescension to their feeble condition He says "whether is easier? to say thy sins are forgiven thee or to say arise and walk?"

For what reason then should He address Himself to the lesser act on their account? Because that which is manifest presents the proof in a more distinct form. Therefore He did not enable the man to rise until He had said to them "But that ye may know that the Son of man hath power on earth to forgive sins, (then saith He to the sick of the palsy) arise and walk," as if He had said: forgiveness of sins is indeed a greater sign: but for your sakes I add the less also since this seems to you to be a proof of the other.

For as in another case when He praised the centurion for saying

"Speak the word only and my servant shall be healed: for I also say to this man go and he goeth and to the other come and he cometh," He confirmed his opinion by the eulogy which He pronounced: and again when He reproved the Jews for finding fault with Him on the Sabbath day saying that He transgressed the law, He proved that He had authority to alter laws: even so in this instance also when some said "He maketh Himself equal with God by promising that which belongs only to the Father," He having upbraided and accused them and proved by His deeds that He did not blaspheme supplied us with indisputable evidence that He could do the same things as the Father who begat Him.

Observe at least the manner in which He pleases to establish the fact that what belongs to the Father only, belongs also to Himself: for He did not simply enable the paralytic to get up, but also said "but that ye may know that the Son of man hath power on earth to forgive sins": thus it was his endeavour and earnest desire to prove above all things that He had the same authority as the Father.

Let us then carefully hold fast all these things, both those which were spoken yesterday and the day before that, and let us beseech God that they may abide immoveably in our heart, and let us contribute zeal on our side, and constantly meet in this place. For in this way we shall preserve the truths which have been formerly spoken, and we shall add others to our store; and if any of them slip from our memory through the lapse of time we shall easily be able to recover them by the aid of continual teaching. And not only will the doctrines abide sound and uncorrupt but our course of life will have the benefit of much diligent care and we shall be able to pass through this present state of existence with pleasure and cheerfulness.

For whatever kind of suffering is oppressing our soul when we come here will easily be got rid of: seeing that now also Christ is present, and he who approaches Him with faith will readily receive healing from Him. Suppose some one is struggling with perpetual poverty, and at a loss for necessary food, and often goes to bed hungry, if he has come in here, and heard Paul saying that he passed his time in hunger and thirst and nakedness, and that he experienced this not on one or two or three days, but constantly (this at least is what he indicates when he says "up to the present hour we both hunger, and thirst, and are naked") (I Cor. 4:11), he will receive ample consolation, learning by means of these words that God has not permitted him to be in poverty because He hated him or abandoned him: for if this were the effect of hatred, He would not have permitted it in the case of Paul who was of all men especially dear to Him: but He permitted it out of His tender love and providential care, and by way of conducting him to a higher degree of spiritual wisdom.

Has some other man a body which is beset with disease and countless sufferings? The condition of these paralytics may be an ample source of consolation and besides these the blessed and brave disciple of Paul who was continually suffering from disorders, and never had any respite from prolonged infirmity, even as Paul also said "Use a little wine for thy stomach's sake and thine often infirmities" (I Tim. 5:23), where he does not speak merely of infirmities as such. Or another having been subjected to false accusation has acquired a bad reputation with the public, and this is continually vexing and gnawing his soul: he enters this place and hears "Blessed are ye when men shall reproach you and say all manner of evil against you falsely: rejoice ye and be exceeding glad for great is your reward in Heaven" (Matt. 5:11,12): then he will lay aside all despondency and receive every kind of pleasure: for it is written "leap for joy, and be exceeding glad when men cast out your name as evil." (Luke 6:22,23)

In this manner then God comforts those that are evil spoken of, and them that speak evil He puts in fear after another manner saying "every evil word which men shall speak they shall give an account thereof whether it be good or evil." (Matt. 12:36)

Another perhaps has lost a little daughter or a son, or one of his kinsfolk, and he also having come here listens to Paul groaning over this present life and longing to see that which is to come, and oppressed by his sojourn in this world, and he will go away with a sufficient remedy for his grief when he has heard him say "Now concerning them that are asleep I would not have you ignorant brethren that ye sorrow not even as others who have no hope." (I Thess. 4:13) He did not say concerning the dying, but "concerning them that are asleep" proving that death is a sleep. As then if we see any one sleeping we are not disturbed or distressed, expecting that he will certainly get up: even so when we see any one dead, let us not be disturbed or dejected for this also is a sleep, a longer one indeed, but still a sleep. By giving it the name of slumber He comforted the mourners and overthrew the accusation of the unbelievers.

If you mourn immoderately over him who has departed you will be like that unbeliever who has no hope of a resurrection. He indeed does well to mourn, inasmuch as he cannot exercise any spiritual wisdom concerning things to come: but thou who hast received such strong proofs concerning the future life, why dost thou sink into the same weakness with him? Therefore it is written "now concerning them that are asleep we would not have you ignorant that ye sorrow not even as others who have no hope." (I Thess. 4:13)

And not only from the New Testament but from the Old also, it is possible to receive abundant consolation. For when you hear of Job after the loss of his property, after the destruction of his herds, after the loss not of one, or two, or three, but of a whole troop of sons in the very flower of their age, after the great excellence of soul which he displayed, even if thou art the weakest of men, thou wilt easily be able to repent and regain thy courage. For thou, O man, hast constantly attended thy sick son, and hast seen him laid upon the bed, and hast heard him uttering his last words, and stood beside him whilst he was drawing his last breath and hast closed his eyes, and shut his mouth: but Job was not present at the death struggle of his sons, he did not see them breathing their last gasp, but the house became the common grave of them all, and on the same table brains and blood were poured forth, and pieces of wood and tiles, and dust, and fragments of flesh, and all these things were mingled together in like manner. Nevertheless after such great calamities of this kind he was not petulant, but what does he say—"The Lord gave, the Lord hath taken away; as it seemed good unto the Lord even so has it come to pass, blessed be the Name of the Lord for ever." (Job 1:21)

Let this speech be our utterance also over each event which befalls us; whether it be loss of property, or infirmity of body, or insult, or false accusation or any other form of evil incident to mankind, let us say these words "The Lord gave, the Lord hath taken away; as it seemed good unto the Lord even so has it come to pass; blessed be the Name of the Lord for ever." If we practise this spiritual wisdom, we shall never experience any evil, even if we undergo countless sufferings, but the gain will be greater than the loss, the good will exceed the evil: by these words thou wilt cause God to be merciful unto thee, and wilt defend thyself against the tyranny of Satan. For as soon as thy tongue has uttered these words forthwith the Devil hastens from thee: and when he has hastened away, the cloud of dejection also is dispelled and the thoughts which afflict us take to flight, hurrying off in company with him, and in addition to all this thou wilt win all manner of blessings both here and in Heaven. And you have a convincing example in the case of Job, and of the Apostle, who having for God's sake despised the troubles of this world, obtained the everlasting blessings.

Let us then be trustful and in all things which befall us let us rejoice and give thanks to the merciful God, that we may pass through this present life with serenity, and obtain the blessings to come, by the grace and lovingkindness of our Lord Jesus Christ to whom be glory, honour and might always, now and ever, world without end. *Amen.*

AURELIUS AUGUSTINE 354-430

The Spanish artist Murillo painted a remarkable portrait of Augustine. Against a backdrop of total blackness he has sketched in dazzling white an upturned face, a hand holding a quill poised over an open book, while off to the side the other hand is extended as though to receive an invisible gift. The face is singularly animated, eager, expectant.

The portrait is of course drawn from imagination. Historians record no detail of Augustine's appearance. The artist's concept, however, is true. Augustine's whole life, after his awakening, was oriented toward God. His pen became the pen of a ready writer. His hand was always open, reaching for fresh knowledge.

He was born and reared in Tagaste in North Africa. From Monica, a devout mother, and Patricius, a pagan father, the boy inherited on the one hand a strain of deep, even saintly spirituality, and on the other an unbridled sensuality. He attended school at Carthage. He studied rhetoric, involved himself in the Manichaean cult (a mixture of Zoroastrianism and Christian gnosticism), annexed a mistress, acquired a son, and made lifelong friends. His continuing studies, mixed with a developing sense of the need of salvation, led to a period of bitter disillusionment, occupied by teaching rhetoric in Tagaste, after which he moved to Rome. There he taught school for perhaps a year, then moved on to Milan.

As his success mounted, his frustrations deepened. The world and the flesh contended in his mind with divine purity. He descended, says Louis Bertrand, from the true religion to a false religion, to no religion. Skepticism ushered him to the edge of despair.

In his distress he turned for help to eloquent Ambrose, Bishop of Milan, and to the silent Scriptures. He broke with his mistress when he became engaged to marry—and promptly took on another mistress. "Oh God, make me clean," he would cry, seemingly with the reservation, "but not yet."

One day in the summer of 386, while he was in an orchard, resistless grace struck him down, cracked the power of reigning evil, renewed him from center to circumference, and opened up a new empire for a mind that ranks in fertility with the greatest in history. Ambrose baptized him. Two years later, after recasting his thoughts and purifying his life, he retired to Tagaste and founded a small religious community. About three years later, by popular clamor, he was persuaded to enter

49

the priesthood. From the priesthood it was a natural step to the next highest office, co-adjutor to the bishop, and on to become Bishop of Hippo, on Africa's Mediterranean Coast. The remainder of his life was filled with ecclesiastical duties, writings, and controversies, so universal in his time.

A list of his treatises makes Augustine sound like an arch-reactionary: Against the Pagans, Against the Astrologers, Against the Jews, Against the Manichees, Against the Priscillianists, Against the Donatists, Against the Pelagians, Against the Arians, Against the Apollinarians.

He was against so much, was he in favor of anything? Read his Confessions, his sermons, his letters, of which 224 are extant. You will come to know a personality overflowing with warmth, tenderness, and moving compassion for poor bewildered humanity.

And what a prolific writer! It has been said that so enormous was his literary output that probably no one in the world has read all that he published. "He knew every possible thing to say about every possible subject, and how to say it," Henri Marrou declares.

Augustine had as many facets as a diamond. He was preacher, author, theologian, philosopher, benefactor, world traveler, counselor at law, educator, art critic, music critic. His reference to the "vast palaces of the mind" was no mere abstraction. Probably he memorized the Bible. An ambitious statistician counted in his writings 13,276 quotations from the Old Testament, 29,540 from the New Testament, but never finished his task!

Listen to the music tumbling from Augustine's aroused soul:

"O God, most high, most excellent; most potent, most omnipotent; most piteous and most just; most hidden and most near; most beauteous and most strong; stable, yet contained of none; unchangeable, yet changing all things; never new, never old. . . . Yet, O my God, my life, my holy joy, what is it that I have said? And what saith any man when he speaks of Thee? Yet woe to them that keep silence, seeing that even they who say most are as the dumb."

Selections from His *Controversy with Pelagius on Law, Grace, and Free Will*

AURELIUS AUGUSTINE, BISHOP OF HIPPO

MAN'S NATURE, indeed, was created at first faultless and without any sin; but that nature of man in which every one is born from Adam, now wants the Physician, because it is not sound. All good qualities, no doubt, which it still possessed in its make—life, senses, intellect—it has of the Most High God, its Creator and Maker. But the flaw, which darkens and weakens all those natural goods, so that it has need of illumination and healing, it has not contracted from its blameless Creator—but from that original sin, which it committed by free will. Accordingly, criminal nature has its part in most righteous punishment. For, if we are now newly created in Christ, we were for all that, children of wrath, even as others, "but God, who is rich in mercy, for His great love wherewith He loved us, even when we were dead in sins, hath quickened us together with Christ, by whose grace we were saved."

It Was a Matter of Justice That All Should Be Condemned

The entire mass, therefore, incurs penalty; and if the deserved punishment of condemnation were rendered to all, it would without doubt be righteously rendered. They, therefore, who are delivered therefrom by grace are called, not vessels of their own merits, but "vessels of mercy." But of whose mercy, if not His who sent Christ Jesus into the world to save sinners, whom He foreknew, and foreordained, and called, and justified, and glorified? Now, who could be so madly insane as to fail to give ineffable thanks to the Mercy which liberates whom it would? The man who correctly appreciates the whole subject could not possibly blame the justice of God in wholly condemning all men whatsoever.

But why need we tarry longer on general statements? Let us go into the core of the question, which we have to discuss with our opponent solely, or almost entirely, on one particular point. For inasmuch as he says that "as far as the present question is concerned, it is not pertinent to inquire whether there have been or now are any men in this life without sin, but whether they had or have the ability to be such persons"; so, were I even to allow that there have been or are any such, I should not by any means therefore affirm that they had or have the ability, unless justified by the grace of God through our Lord "Jesus Christ and Him crucified." For the same faith which healed the saints of old now heals us,—that is to say, faith "in the one Mediator between God and men, the man Christ Jesus,"—faith in His blood, faith in His cross, faith in His death and resurrection. As we therefore have the same spirit of faith, we also believe, and on that account also speak.

Now, whereas it is most correctly asked in those words put to him, "Why do you affirm that man without the help of God's grace is able to avoid sin?" yet the inquiry did not concern that grace by which man was created, but only that whereby he is saved through Jesus Christ our Lord. Faithful men say in their prayer, "Lead us not into temptation, but deliver us from evil." But if they already have capacity, why do they pray? Or, what is the evil which they pray to be delivered from, but, above all else, "the body of this death"? And from this nothing but God's grace alone delivers them, through our Lord Jesus Christ. Not of course from the substance of the body, which is good; but from its carnal offences, from which a man is not liberated except by the grace of the Saviour,—not even when he quits the body by the death of the body. If it was this that the apostle meant to declare, why had he previously said, "I see another law in my members, warring against the law of my mind, and bringing me into captivity to the law of sin which is in my members"?

Behold what damage the disobedience of the will has inflicted on man's nature! Let him be permitted to pray that he may be healed! Why need he presume so much on the capacity of his nature? It is wounded, hurt, damaged, destroyed. It is a true confession of its weakness, not a false defence of its capacity, that it stands in need of. It requires the grace of God, not that it may be made, but that it may be *re*-made. And this is the only grace which by our author is proclaimed to be unnecessary; because of this he is silent! If, indeed, he had said nothing at all about God's grace, and had not proposed to himself that question for solution, for the purpose of removing from himself the odium of this matter, it might have been thought that his view of the subject was consistent with the truth, only that he had refrained from mentioning it, on the ground that not on all occasions need we say all we think. He proposed the question of grace, and answered it in the way that he had in his heart; the question has been defined,—not in the way we wished, but according to the doubt we entertained as to what was his meaning.

Why Heretical Writings Must Be Answered

The new heretics, enemies of the grace of God which is given by Jesus Christ our Lord to small and great, although they are already shown more openly to need to be avoided by a manifest disapproba-tion, still do not cease by their writings to try the hearts of the less cautious and less learned. And these must certainly be answered, lest they should confirm themselves or their friends in that wicked error; even if we were not afraid that they might deceive some one of the Catholics by their plausible discourse. But since they do not cease to growl at the entrances to the Lord's fold, and from every side to tear open approaches with a view to tear in pieces the sheep redeemed at such a price; and since the pastoral watch-tower is common to all of us who discharge the office of the episcopate (although you are prominent therein on a loftier height), I do what I can in respect of my small portion of the charge, as the Lord condescends by the aid of your prayers to grant me power, to oppose to their pestilent and crafty writings, healing and defensive writings, so that the madness with which they are raging may either itself be cured, or may be prevented from hurting others.

Man Does No Good Thing Which God Does Not Cause Him to Do

Wherefore God does many good things in man which man does not do; but man does none which God does not cause man to do. Accord-ingly, there would be no desire of good in man from the Lord if it were not a good; but if it *is* a good, we have it not save from Him who is supremely and incommunicably good. For what is the desire for good but love, of which John the apostle speaks without any ambiguity, and says "Love is of God"? Nor is its beginning of ourselves, and its perfection of God; but if love is of God, we have the whole of it from God.

May God by all means turn away this folly of making ourselves first in His gifts, Himself last,—because "His mercy shall prevent me." And it is He to whom is faithfully and truthfully sung, "For Thou hast prevented him with the blessings of sweetness." And what is here more fitly understood than that very desire of good of which we are speaking? For good begins then to be longed for when it has begun to grow sweet. But when good is done by the fear of penalty, not by the love of righteousness, good is not yet well done. Nor is that done in the heart which seems to be done in the act, when a man would rather not do it if he could evade it with impunity.

Therefore the "blessing of sweetness" is God's grace, by which is caused in us that what He prescribes to us delights us, and we desire it,—that is, we love it; in which if God does not precede us, not only is it not perfected, but it is not even begun, from us. For, if without Him we are able to do nothing actually, we are able neither to begin nor to perfect,—because to begin, it is said, "His mercy shall prevent me"; to finish, it is said, "His mercy shall follow me."

Nothing Is Commanded to Man Which Is Not Given by God

Since these things are so, I see that nothing is commanded to man by the Lord in the Holy Scriptures, for the sake of trying his free will, which is not found either to begin by His goodness, or to be asked in order to demonstrate the aid of grace; nor does man at all begin to be changed by the beginning of faith from evil to good, unless the unbought and gratuitous mercy of God effects this in him. Of which one recalling his thought, as we read in the Psalms, says, "Shall God forget to be gracious? or will He restrain His mercies in His anger? And I said, Now have I begun; this change is of the right hand of the Most High." When, therefore, he had said, "Now have I begun," he does not say, "This change is of my will," but "of the right hand of the Most High."

So, therefore, let God's grace be thought of, that from the beginning of his good changing, even to the end of his completion, he who glorieth may glory in the Lord; because, as no one can perfect good without the Lord, so no one can begin it without the Lord. But let this be the end of this book, that the attention of the reader may be refreshed and strengthened for what follows.

Why God Makes of Some Sheep, Others Not

But wherefore does God make these men sheep, and those not, since with Him there is no acceptance of persons? This is the very question which the blessed apostle thus answers to those who propose it with more curiosity than propriety, "O man, who art thou that repliest against God? Does the thing formed say to him that formed it, Wherefore hast thou made me thus?" This is the very question which belongs to that depth desiring to look into which the same apostle was in a certain measure terrified, and exclaimed, "Oh the depth of the riches both of the wisdom and the knowledge of God; how unsearchable are His judgments, and His ways past finding out! For who has known the mind of the Lord? or who has been His counsellor? Or who has first given to Him, that it should be recompensed to Him again? Because of Him, and through Him, and in Him, are all things: to Him be glory for ages and ages."

Let them not, then, dare to pry into that unsearchable question who defend merit before grace, and therefore even *against* grace, and wish first to give unto God, that it may be given to them again,—first, of course, to give something of free will, that grace may be given them again as a reward; and let them wisely understand or faithfully believe that even what they think that they have first given, they have received from Him, from whom are all things, by whom are all things, in whom are all things.

But why this man should receive, and that should not receive, when neither of them deserves to receive, and whichever of them receives, receives undeservingly,—let them measure their own strength, and not search into things too strong for them. Let it suffice them to know that there is no unrighteousness with God. For when the apostle could find no merits for which Jacob should take precedence of his twin-brother with God, he said, "What, then, shall we say? Is there unrighteousness with God? Away with the thought! For He says to Moses, I will have mercy on whom I will have mercy, and I will show compassion on whom I will show compassion. Therefore it is not of him that willeth, nor of him that runneth, but of God that showeth mercy."

Let, therefore, His free compassion be grateful to us, even although this profound question be still unsolved; which, nevertheless, is so far solved as the same apostle solves it, saying, "But if God, willing to show His wrath, and to demonstrate His power, endured in much patience the vessels of wrath which are fitted to destruction; and that He might make known the riches of His glory on the vessels of mercy, which He has prepared for glory . . ." Certainly wrath is not repaid unless it is due, lest there be unrighteousness with God; but mercy, even when it is bestowed, and not due, is not unrighteousness with God. And hence, let the vessels of mercy understand how freely mercy is afforded to them, because to the vessels of wrath with whom they have common cause and measure of perdition, is repaid wrath, righteous and due. This is now enough in opposition to those who, by freedom of will, desire to destroy the liberality of grace.

And if these things be so, let the Pelagians cease by their most insidious praises of these five things—that is, the praise of the creature, the praise of marriage, the praise of the law, the praise of free will, the praise of the saints—from feigning that they desire to pluck men, as it were, from the little snares of the Manicheans, in order that they may entangle them in their own nets—that is, that they may deny original sin; may begrudge to infants the aid of Christ the physician; may say that the grace of God is given according to our merits, and thus that grace is no more grace; and may say that the saints in this life had not sin, and thus make the prayer of none effect which He gave to the saints who had no sin, and by which all sin is pardoned to the saints that pray unto Him. To these three evil doctrines, they by their deceitful praise of these five good things seduce careless and unlearned men. Concerning all which things, I think I have sufficiently censured their most cruel and wicked and proud vanity.

ANSELM 1033–1109

Anselm, Bishop of Canterbury, was traveling on horseback from Windsor to Hayes. Suddenly a pack of hounds, paced by hunters, burst out of the thicket fringing the highway. Anselm saw that they were chasing a hare. He reined in his horse. The frightened hare darted under the horse and stopped, as though to take refuge there. Excited hounds surrounded the creature and, unaccountably, began to lick its fur. The hunters crowded around Anselm, laughing boisterously.

Anselm wept.

Recovering, he proceeded to turn the incident into a text for an allegorized lecture. The hare, he told the hunters, stood for the soul of man; the hounds, evil spirits; the hunt, the cruel course of life. Then he glared down at the hounds and shouted, "Go away!"

They obeyed. The poor hare skipped off into the thicket, the hunters rode away, not waiting to hear the rest of the allegory, and Anselm went on his journey rejoicing.

The story lights up two of his qualities: his tenderheartedness and his intellectual resourcefulness.

Anselm served his spiritual apprenticeship across the English Channel at Bec, Normandy. In his day the Monastery of Bec, under the leadership of the noble abbot Lanfranc, operated as the hub of classical learning. When Lanfranc was promoted to Canterbury's archbishopric, Anselm succeeded him as abbot. An unquenchable intellectual hunger assailed him. He explored the frontiers of the theological universe so long neglected by the men of the Dark Ages. He reached back to Augustine and Plato for help. He subpoenaed philosophy to confirm propositions in theology.

One day he made the startling announcement that he had discovered a method of proving the existence of God! It is all very simple, he said in effect, provided one takes his starting point with the lever of faith. Without faith there can be no real knowledge. (Shades of Augustine) The presence of certain intellectual and moral virtues lodging in man cannot possibly be explained unless we presuppose that the same qualities exist in a Supreme Being, who is completely self-contained and self-sufficient. (Shades of Plato) The conclusion is, therefore, there simply has to be a God.

To the modern mind this syllogistic reasoning may appear naïve. To the eleventh-century mind it was stupendous. Later Descartes would play on it lovingly, like a harper strumming a golden harp—until

Immanuel Kant would come along and smash the harp into a thousand pieces. Nonetheless, the effort does illustrate the boldness and vigor of an individual not content to breathe the stuffy air of traditionalism, and it was greeted with acclaim.

During his term of office as abbot, Anselm's duties took him to England. There the public received him with the enthusiasm today tendered an Eisenhower on a global junket. His gentleness, courtesy, modesty, and love of men captured the hearts of the English. When Lanfranc died, it was as natural for the islanders to clamor for Anselm to serve as Archbishop of Canterbury as it is for them today to love the Changing of the Guard.

William Rufus was the ruling monarch of England. He inherited not a single good characteristic from William the Conqueror, his father. He governed both State and Church ruthlessly and selfishly. For over four years he allowed the office of archbishop to remain vacant, meanwhile appropriating funds from the Church's coffers. He held off the appointment of Anselm as long as he could. Finally, under pressure, the king drafted him. The Abbot of Bec was so violently opposed to the move that churchmen had to force him physically to receive the ordination.

There followed a complicated triangular tug of war involving two kings, two popes and the Archbishop of Canterbury, known as the Investiture Struggle. The issues stemming from it were to have far-reaching consequences. Would the throne exercise supreme authority, or the papacy? A sturdy Catholic, Anselm threw his full support behind the popes and defied the secular powers. For his stand he was caught between the upper and nether millstones. The crown persecuted him. Rome frequently let him down. Intrigue, compromise, political maneuvering, ecclesiastical double-dealing locked him in situations well-calculated to keep him in suspense. Security was an unknown experience.

Anselm stuck to his principles. When at last the smog cleared, he emerged with an exhausted body and a clean conscience. The outcome moreover represented a triumph for the papacy that would enhance its authority and strengthen its claims for centuries to come.

Few heroes of the faith are crowned with halos by their own age. The children of light are not only less wise but also less acknowledged in their generation than children of darkness. It was four hundred years before Anselm received his formal accolade of canonization by Pope Alexander VI.

Letter of Anselm to Pope Urban II on the Incarnation of the Word

Faith and Understanding

FIRST, then, the heart is to be purified by faith—for God is spoken of as "purifying their hearts by faith"—and first the eyes are to be enlightened through keeping the Lord's commandments, because "the commandment of the Lord is lightsome, enlightening the eyes," and first we should become little children by humble obedience to the testimonies of God, in order to learn the wisdom given by the "testimony of the Lord," which "is faithful, giving wisdom to little ones." (Thus the Lord says, "I confess to thee, O Father, Lord of heaven and earth, because Thou hast hid these things from the wise and prudent, and has revealed them to little ones.")

First, I say, let us disregard the things that belong to the flesh, and let us live according to the Spirit, instead of destroying the deep things of faith by our judgment. . . . For, indeed, it is vain for a man to undertake to say, "I have understood more than all my teachers," when he does not dare to add, "Because thy testimonies are my meditation." And he is a liar when he recites, "I have had understanding above ancients," if he is not familiar with what follows, "Because I have sought thy commandments." Certainly this is just what I say: He who will not believe will not understand. For he who will not believe will not gain experience, and he who has not had experience will not know. For experience surpasses hearing about a thing, as greatly as knowledge by experience excels acquaintance by hearing.

And not only is the mind forbidden to rise to the understanding of the higher matters without faith and obedience to God's commandments, but sometimes even the understanding that has been given is withdrawn, and faith itself is overthrown by disregard for a good conscience. For the apostle says of some: "When they knew God, they have not glorified him as God, or given thanks; but became vain in their thoughts, and their foolish heart was darkened." And when he commanded Timothy to war "a good warfare," he said, "Having faith and a good conscience, which some rejecting have made shipwreck concerning faith." Let no one, then, heedlessly plunge into the obscure questions that concern divine things without first seeking earnestly, in soundness of faith, for gravity of conduct and of wisdom. Otherwise, running about with heedless frivolity through a multitude of sophistical distractions, he may be trapped by some stubborn falsehood. . . .

I have said these things so that no one will presume, before he is able, to discuss the loftiest questions of faith, and so that, if he does presume to do so, no difficulty or impossibility of understanding will be able to shake him from the truth to which he has adhered by faith. . . .

Selections from *Cur Deus Homo* (*Why God Became Man*)

The Question on Which the Whole Work Depends

THE QUESTION at issue is habitually presented as an objection by unbelievers, who scoff at Christian simplicity as absurd, while it is pondered in their hearts by many of the faithful. The question is this: For what reason or necessity did God become Man and as we believe and confess, by His death restore life to the world, when He could have done this through another person (angelic or human), or even by a sheer act of will? Many of the unlearned, as well as the learned, ask this question and want an answer. . . . Since investigations that are carried on by means of question and answer are clearer to many (especially to slower) minds, and so are more acceptable, I shall take one of those who discuss this subject—the one who among the rest presses me more urgently—to debate with me, so that in this way Boso [first a monk and then, 1124–1136, Abbot of Bec; he spent several years with Anselm at Canterbury] may ask and Anselm answer.

Boso. While the right order requires that we should *believe* the deep things of the Christian faith before we undertake to discuss them by reason, it seems careless for us, once we are established in the faith, not to aim at understanding what we believe. Therefore, since I think that by God's prevenient grace I hold the faith of our redemption so firmly that nothing can shake my constant allegiance, even if I can find no reason to help me grasp what I believe, I beg you to show me what many, as you know, seek with me. Tell me what necessity and reason led God, although He is Almighty, to take upon Him the lowliness and weakness of human nature in order to renew it.

Anselm. What you ask from me is above me, and I am afraid to handle "the things that are too high for me." If someone thinks, or even sees, that I have not given him adequate proof, he may decide that there is no truth in what I have been saying, and not realize that in fact my understanding has been incapable of grasping it.

B. You should not fear this so much, but you should rather remember what often happens when we talk over some question. You know how God often makes clear what was concealed before. You should hope from the grace of God that, if you willingly share what you have freely received, you may be worthy to receive the higher things to which you have yet to attain.

A. There is another reason for thinking that we can hardly (if at all) deal fully with this problem now. We should need to know about power and necessity and will and several other things which are so closely connected that no one of them can be fully considered without the others. . . .

B. Then you had better speak briefly about these questions, each in its proper place, so that we shall know enough to carry out the present task. . . .

A. I also hesitate to respond to your request for the serious reason that the subject matter is not only of great importance, but is fair with a reason above human understanding, just as it has to do with Him who is "beautiful above the sons of men." I am always indignant with poor artists when I see our Lord Himself painted with an ugly form, and I am afraid that I may find myself in the same position if I dare to set out such a beautiful theme in rude and contemptible language.

B. Even this should not hold you back. . . . To stop all your excuses, I am not asking you to do anything for the learned. You will be doing it for me, and for those who make the same request with me.

The Objections of Unbelievers and Replies of the Faithful

B. The unbelievers, who laugh at our simplicity, charge that we do God injury and insult when we assert that He descended into the womb of a woman, that He was born of a woman, that He grew, nourished by milk and human foods, and—not to speak of many other things that seem inappropriate for God—that He bore weariness, hunger, thirst, blows, and a cross and death between the thieves.

A. We do no injury or insult to God, but with heartfelt thanks we praise and proclaim the ineffable height of His Mercy. It is precisely insofar as He has restored us, marvelously and beyond expectation, from the great and merited evils under which we lay to the great and unmerited goods that we had lost, that He has shown greater love and mercy toward us. And if they would earnestly consider how fittingly the restoration of mankind was secured in this way, instead of laughing at our simplicity they would join us in praising the wise lovingkindness of God. For when death had entered into the human race through man's disobedience, it was fitting that life should be restored through the obedience of man. When the sin which was the cause of our condemnation had its beginning from a woman, it was fitting for the Author of our justice and salvation to be born of a woman. Since the devil, when he tempted man, conquered him by the tasting of a tree, it was fitting for him to be conquered by man's bearing of suffering on a tree. And a good many other things, when we consider them carefully, show the inexpressible beauty of our redemption thus accomplished.

How, Although the Lowly Things We Ascribe to Christ Do Not Belong to His Divinity, Unbelievers Find It Unseemly for Them to Be Attributed Even to His Manhood, and Why They Do Not Think That This Man Died Willingly

A. The will of God should be a good enough reason for us when He does anything, even though we cannot see why He wills it. For the will of God is never irrational.

B. That is true, when it is certain that God does will what is being discussed. But many will never admit that God wills something that seems contrary to reason.

A. What seems to you to be contrary to reason in our statement that God willed the things we believe concerning His incarnation?

B. To put it briefly—for the Most High to stoop to such lowly things; for the Almighty to do anything with such great labor.

A. Those who speak this way do not understand what we believe. For we affirm without any doubt that the Divine nature is impassible, and that it can in no sense be brought down from its loftiness or toil in what it wills to do. But we say that the Lord Jesus Christ is true God and true Man, one Person in two natures and two natures in one Person. Thus, when we say that God bears humiliation or weakness, we do not apply this to the sublimity of the impassible nature, but to the weakness of the human substance which He bore, and so we know no reason that opposes our faith. For we do not ascribe any debasement to the divine substance, but we show that there is one person, God and man. Therefore, in the incarnation of God we do not suppose that He undergoes any debasement, but we believe that the nature of man is exalted.

B. All right then; let nothing that is said about Christ with reference to human weakness be attributed to the divine nature. But still, can it ever be proved just or reasonable that God treated (or allowed to be treated) in this way that Man whom the Father called His "beloved Son," in whom He was "well pleased," and whom the Son made Himself to be? For what justice is there in giving up the most just man of all to death on behalf of the sinner? What man would not be judged worthy of condemnation if he condemned the innocent in order to free the guilty? The whole thing seems to go back to the same incongruity that I mentioned before. For if He would not save sinners except by condemning the just, where is His omnipotence? But if He could, but would not, how are we to defend His wisdom and justice?

A. God the Father did not treat that Man as you seem to think, or give up the innocent to death for the guilty. For He did not force Him to die or allow Him to be slain against His will; on the contrary, He Himself readily endured death in order to save men. . . .

It Is Necessary for the Same Person to Be Perfect God and Perfect Man

A. Now we must inquire how there can be a God-Man. For the divine and human natures cannot be changed into each other, so that the divine becomes human or the human divine. Nor can they be so mingled that a third nature, neither fully divine nor fully human, is produced from the two. In short, if one could really be changed into the other, the person would be God only and not man, or man alone and not God. Or if they were mingled in such a way that a third nature was made out of two corrupted natures—just as from two individual animals, a male and a female, of different species, a third is born, which does not preserve the entire nature either of father or of mother, but possesses a third composed of both—the result would be neither man nor God. Therefore, the Man-God we are seeking cannot be produced from divine and human nature, either by the conversion of one into the other or by the destructive commingling of both into a third, because these things cannot be done, and if they could they would be of no avail for the end we seek.

Moreover, even if these two complete natures are said to be united in some way, but still man is one person and God another, so that the same person is not both God and man, the two natures cannot do what needs to be done. For God will not do it, because He does not owe it, and man will not do it, because he cannot. Therefore, for the God-Man to do this, the person who is to make this satisfaction must be both perfect God and perfect man, because none but true God can make it, and none but true man owes it. Thus, while it is necessary to find a God-Man in whom the integrity of both natures is preserved, it is no less necessary for these two complete natures to meet in one person— just as body and rational soul meet in one man—for otherwise the same person could not be perfect God and perfect man.

God Ought to Take Manhood of Adam's Race, and from a Virgin

A. Now it remains for us to ask from what source God will take human nature, and how. For He will either take it from Adam or create a new man, just as He created Adam from no other man. But if He creates a new man, who is not of the race of Adam, He will not belong to the human race which was born of Adam. In that case

He will not be obliged to make satisfaction for it, because He will not come from it. For just as it is right for man to make satisfaction for man's fault, it is necessary that the sinner himself, or one of the same race, should be the person who makes satisfaction. . . . Therefore, since they themselves cannot, he who is to make it must be born from them.

Further, Adam and his whole race would have stood by themselves, without support from any other creature, if they had not sinned, and the same race must rise and be lifted up through itself, if it rises again after the fall. For if anyone restores it to its own state, so that it recovers that state through him, it will certainly stand through him. Moreover, when God first created human nature in Adam alone, and did not choose to create the woman—so that mankind might be multiplied from the two sexes—except from him, he showed clearly that He wished to create what He was going to create from human nature, from Adam alone. Therefore, if the race of Adam is raised up through some man who is not of the same race, it will not be restored to the dignity it was to have had if Adam had not sinned. But in that case it will not be entirely restored, and God's purpose will seem to fail, and these two things are unfitting. It is necessary, therefore, for the man through whom Adam's race is to be restored to be taken from Adam.

B. If we follow reason, as we planned, this is inevitable.

A. Let us now inquire whether God is to take human nature from a father and mother, as in the case with other man, or from a man without a woman, or from a woman without a man. For if it is taken in any of these three ways, it will be taken from Adam and Eve, since every human being of either sex comes from them. Moreover, no one of these three ways of taking human nature is easier for God than the others, so as to be preferable to them. . . .

God can make a man in four ways: from man and woman, as constant experience shows; neither from man nor from woman, as He created Adam; from a man without a woman, as He made Eve; or from a woman without a man, which he has yet to do. Therefore, in order to prove that this way is also within His power, and was deferred for this very purpose, nothing is more fitting than for Him to take that man whom we are seeking from a woman without a man. Moreover, we need not discuss whether this is more worthily done from a virgin or from one who is not a virgin, but we must affirm without the slightest doubt that the God-Man ought to be born of a virgin.

B. Nothing could be more substantial.

A. Then paint on the solid truth, not on empty fancies, and say that it is most fitting for the medicine for sin and the cause of our salvation to be born of a woman, just as the sin of man and the cause of our condemnation took its beginning from a woman. Also, lest woman despair of sharing in the lot of the blessed, since such great evil came from a woman, it is right that such great good should come from a woman, to renew their hope. And paint this too: if the cause of all evil for the human race was a virgin, it is still more fitting for the cause of all good to be a virgin. And paint this as well: if the woman whom God made from a man without a woman was made from a virgin, it is also very appropriate for the man who is made from a woman without a man to be made from a virgin. But for the present let these be enough of the pictures that can be painted on the truth that the God-Man ought to be born of a virgin woman.

B. These pictures are very beautiful and reasonable.

How His Death Outweighs All Sins, Great As They Are in Number and Magnitude

B. Now I pray you to teach me how His death outweighs the number and greatness of all sins, since you show how one trifling sin (as we reckon it) is so infinite that if an infinite number of worlds is spread before us, as full of creatures as our own, and they cannot be kept from returning to nothingness unless someone takes a single glance against God's will, that glance should not be taken.

A. If that Man were present, and you know who He was, and someone said to you, "Unless you kill this Man, the whole world and everything that is not God will perish," would you do this for the sake of preserving every other creature?

B. I would not do it, even if an infinite number of worlds were spread before me.

A. What if someone said to you again, "Either kill Him or all the sins of the world will come upon you"?

B. I would answer that I should prefer to bear all other sins—not only those that have been and will be in this world, but whatever else can be imagined beyond these—rather than that one alone. I think that I ought to give the same answer with respect not only to His death, but also to the slightest injury that might touch Him.

A. You are right in thinking this. But tell me why your heart judges that one sin that injures this Man is more dreadful than all the others that can be imagined, when every sin that is committed is committed against Him.

B. Because a sin committed against His person is incommensurate with every conceivable sin that does not touch his person.

A. We see, then, that no greatness or multitude of sins apart from God's person can be compared to an injury done to the bodily life of this Man.

B. That is quite evident.

A. Consider also, that sins are as hateful as they are evil, and that

that life is as lovable as it is good. It follows that this life is more lovable
than sins are hateful.

B. I cannot help seeing this.

A. Do you think that so great and lovable a good is enough to pay
what is owing for the sins of the whole world?

B. It is infinitely more than enough.

A. You see, then, how this life overcomes all sins, if it is given for
them.

B. Clearly.

A. Therefore, if to give one's life is to accept death, the acceptance
of death, like the giving of this life, outweighs all the sins of men.

B. That is certainly true for all sins that do not touch God's person.

How God Took Manhood Out of the Sinful Mass, Yet Without Sin; the Salvation of Adam and Eve

B. So, then since you have made clear the reason for what has already
been stated, I beg you to show me how God took manhood without
sin from the sinful mass, that is, from the human race which was totally
infected by sin, as if He were to take something unleavened from a lump
of fermented dough. For even though the conception of this Man is
pure and free from the sin of carnal delight, nevertheless the Virgin herself, from whom He was taken, was "conceived in iniquities" and her
mother conceived her "in sins," and she was born with original sin,
since she also sinned in Adam, "in whom all have sinned."

A. Once it is established that this Man is God and the reconciler of
sinners, there can be no doubt that He is completely free from sin. But
this cannot be the case, unless He was taken from the sinful mass without sin. If we cannot grasp the way in which the wisdom of God did
this, we must not be astonished, but must with reverence accept the
fact that in such a great matter there is something hidden of which we
are ignorant. In fact, God has restored human nature even more wonderfully than He created it. . . . Yet his restoration by God was more
wonderful than his creation, since the former was done to a sinner
against his desert, but the latter neither to a sinner nor against his desert.
Again, what a great thing it is for God and man to meet in one Person,
so that, while the integrity of both natures is preserved, the same Person
is man and God! Who, then, will dare even to imagine that human
understanding is able to discern how wisely, how wonderfully, such
an unsearchable deed was done?

B. I agree that in this life no man can fully explain so great a secret,
and I do not ask you to do what no man can do, but only to do as much
as you can.

A. I see that I cannot escape from your persistence. But if I can even
begin to prove what you ask, let us thank God. However, if I cannot,

let what has been proved before suffice. For when it is admitted that
God ought to be made man, it is unquestionable that His wisdom and
power will not fail to accomplish this without sin.

B. I willingly admit this.

A. It was certainly necessary for the redemption that Christ effected
to benefit not only those who were alive at that time, but others as well.
For suppose that there is a king, and that the whole population of one of
his cities—with the sole exception of one man, who nonetheless belongs
to their race—has sinned against him, so that none of them can manage
to escape condemnation to death. But suppose too that the one innocent
man is in such favor with the king that he is able—and so kindly disposed toward the guilty that he is willing—to reconcile all who believe
in his plan by some service, sure to please the king greatly, which he
will perform on a day set by the king's decision. And since all who
need to be reconciled cannot meet on that day, the king grants absolution from every past fault, because of the greatness of this service,
to everyone who either before or after that day confesses his readiness
to seek pardon through the deed done that day, and to ratify the agreement then made. And if they happen to sin again after this pardon, he
is ready to grant them pardon again because of the efficacy of this
agreement, if they are willing to make due satisfaction and then amend
their conduct. No one, however, is to enter his palace until the deed
through which faults are remitted is done.

As this illustration suggests, since all the men who were to be saved
could not be present when Christ effected their redemption, His death
had such power that its effect reaches even to those who lived in another place or at another time. . . .

How the Life of Christ Is Paid to God for the Sins of Men, and How Christ Should and Should Not Have Suffered

A. But now tell me what you think remains to be answered of the
question you put at the beginning, which forced so many other questions on us.

B. The heart of the question was this: Why did God become man, to
save man by His death, when it seems that He could have done this
in some other way? You have answered this by showing, by many
necessary reasons, how it would not have been right for the restoration
of human nature to be left undone, and how it could not have been done
unless man paid what was owing to God for sin. But the debt was so
great that, while man alone owed it, only God alone could pay it, so
that the same person must be both man and God. Thus it was necessary
for God to take manhood into the unity of His Person, so that he who
in his own nature ought to pay and could not should be in a person who
could. Then you showed that the Man who also was God was to be

taken from a virgin, and by the Person of the Son of God, and how He could be taken from the sinful mass without sin. Moreover, you have proved most straightforwardly that the life of this Man was so sublime, so precious, that it can suffice to pay what is owing for the sins of the whole world, and infinitely more. It now remains, therefore, to be shown how it is paid to God for the sins of men.

A. Do you not understand that by enduring with gentle patience the injuries and insults and death on the cross with thieves—all brought on Him, as we said above, by His obedience in maintaining justice—He gave an example to men, to teach them not to turn away from the justice they owe to God on account of any trials which they can experience? But He would not have given this kind of example at all if, by using His own power, He had turned away from the death brought on Him for such a cause.

B. It seems to me that there was no need for Him to give this example, since many before His coming, and John the Baptist after His coming but before His death, admittedly set an adequate example by bravely enduring death for the truth's sake.

A. No man besides Him ever gave to God, by dying, what he was not necessarily going to lose at some time, or paid what he did not owe. But this Man freely offered to the Father what he would never have lost by any necessity, and paid for sinners what He did not owe for Himself. Therefore He gave us a more striking example, to the effect that each man should not hesitate to surrender to God for himself, when reason demands it, what he is going to lose very soon. For although he did not need to do it for himself, and was not compelled to do it for others, since He owed them nothing but punishment, He gave up such a precious life—yes, nothing less than Himself—surrendering so great a person with such willingness. . . .

The Great Reason Why Human Salvation Follows from His Death

A. Now let us consider, as fully as we can, the great reason why man's salvation follows from His death.

B. My heart is struggling toward this. For although I seem to myself to understand it, I want to have the whole structure of the agrument outlined by you.

A. There is no need to explain what a great gift the Son gave freely. . . . You will not suppose that He who freely gives God so great a gift ought to be left unrewarded.

B. On the contrary, I see how necessary it is for the Father to reward the Son. Otherwise, He would seem unjust if He were unwilling, and powerless if He were unable to reward Him; but both these things are foreign to God.

A. He who rewards someone either gives what the latter does not have or foregoes what can be required from him. But before the Son did this great work, all that belonged to the Father belonged to Him, and He never owed anything that could be remitted to Him. What, then, will be given Him as a reward, when He is in need of nothing and there is nothing that can be given or forgiven Him?

B. I see on the one hand that a reward is necessary, and on the other that it is impossible. For it is necessary for God to repay what He owes, and there is no way of making repayment.

A. If such a great and merited reward is paid neither to Him nor to anyone else, it will seem that the Son performed such a great work in vain.

B. It is impious to think this.

A. Then it must be paid to someone else, since it cannot be paid to Him.

B. That inevitably follows.

A. If the Son willed to give to another what is owing to Himself, could the Father rightly forbid Him, or deny it to the other?

B. On the contrary, I think that it is both just and necessary for the Father to pay it to anyone to whom the Son wills to give it. . . .

A. To whom would it be more fitting for Him to assign the fruit and recompense of His death than to those for whose salvation . . . He made Himself man, and to whom . . . by dying He gave an example of dying for the sake of justice? For they will be His imitators in vain if they do not share in His merit. Or whom will He more justly make heirs of the debt which He does not need, and of the abundance of His own fullness, than His kinsmen and brethren, whom He sees bound by so many great debts, languishing in poverty and deepest misery—so that what they owe for their sins may be forgiven them, and what they need, on account of their sins, may be given them?

B. The world can hear nothing more reasonable, nothing more delightful, nothing more desirable. Indeed, I gain such great confidence from this, that already I cannot say how great the joy is that makes my heart leap. For it seems to me that God can repel no man who draws near to Him in this Name.

A. That is true, if he draws near as he ought to. But Holy Scripture everywhere teaches us the way to attain to a share in such great grace, and how we are to live under it—Holy Scripture, founded upon immovable truth . . . as upon a firm foundation.

B. Certainly whatever is built on this foundation is founded on a solid rock. . . .

How Great and How Just God's Mercy Is

A. When we were considering God's justice and man's sin, God's mercy seemed to you to vanish. But we have found how great it really is, and how it is in such harmony with His justice that it cannot be conceived to be greater or more just. For, indeed, what greater mercy could be imagined, than for God the Father to say to the sinner, condemned to eternal torments, and without any power of redeeming himself from them, "Receive my only-begotten Son, and give Him for yourself," and for the Son Himself to say, "Take Me, and redeem yourself"? For they as much as say this when they call us and draw us to the Christian faith. And what could be more just, than for Him to whom the price more valuable than every debt is paid to forgive every debt (if the price is given with the right disposition)?

It Is Impossible for the Devil to Be Reconciled

A. But you will understand that the devil's reconciliation, about which you asked, is impossible, if you carefully consider man's reconciliation. For man could be reconciled only by a Man-God who could die, by whose justice what God had lost through man's sin might be restored to him. Similarly, the condemned angels can be saved only by an Angel-God who can die, and by his justice can restore to God what the sins of the others took away. . . . Then their [the angels'] restoration is also ruled out by the fact that they ought to rise again without anyone's help, just as they fell without being made to fall by any injury inflicted by another. But this is impossible for them. . . . Therefore, if anyone supposes that redemption through our Saviour ought at length to be extended even to them, reason convicts him of being unreasonably deceived. I say this, not as if the price of His death might not, by its greatness, avail for all the sins of men and angels, but simply because an unchangeable reason is opposed to the raising up of the lost angels.

The Truth of the Old and New Testaments Has Been Proved in What Has Been Said

B. Everything you say seems reasonable to me, and I cannot gainsay it. Also, I think that whatever is contained in the New and Old Testaments has been proved by the solution of the one question we put forward. For you prove that God was necessarily made man, in such a way that even if the few things you have cited from our books . . . were taken away, you would satisfy not only Jews, but even pagans, by reason alone. And the God-Man Himself establishes the New Testament and proves the truth of the Old. Therefore, just as we must confess His own truthfulness, so no one can refuse to confess the truth of everything that is contained in them both.

A. If we have said anything that should be corrected, I do not refuse correction, if it is done with good reason. But if what we think we have discovered by reason is confirmed by the testimony of the truth, we should ascribe this, not to ourselves, but to God, who is blessed forever. *Amen.*

JOHN WYCLIFFE 1324–1384

"They love him most for the enemies he has made," an American politician once said in a nominating speech. If this is a criterion, John Wycliffe should have been, like Daniel, a man greatly beloved. Upon his death a fourteenth-century Catholic historian penned this diatribe: "That instrument of the devil, that enemy of the church, that author of confusion to the common people, that image of hypocrites, that idol of heretics, that author of schism, that sower of hatred, that coiner of lies, being struck with the horrible judgment of God, was smitten with palsy and continued to live till St. Sylvester's Day, on which he breathed out his malicious spirit into the abodes of darkness."

What excited so angry a blast? Wycliffe, Professor of Divinity at Oxford, had dared to assail the mendicant friars, a sizeable army of strolling monks infesting England, hawking indulgences, foisting superstitious fetishes on the public, padding their purses with coins extracted by fraud. They further disgraced the Church with a manner of life marked by laziness, ignorance, prodigality, and indifference to human suffering.

Again, Wycliffe was vocal in his objection to the pope's draining England of thousands of pounds annually from the sale of investitures, rings, crosiers, and other benefices. He appeared before one of the Parliaments of Edward III, offered a theoretical basis for denying the papal authority and stiffened its inclination to check the flow of revenue to Rome. Pope Gregory XI branded him a heretic, and demanded that he be arraigned in Saint Paul's Cathedral to answer the charge of heresy. Wycliffe obeyed, and might have received official condemnation but for the fact that the powerful Duke of Lancaster rushed to protect him, as the Elector of Saxony more than a century later would raise an umbrella of protection over Luther.

Emboldened, Wycliffe initiated a series of broadsides against the papacy that drew gasps from all who heard him. He challenged Gregory's presumptuous civil control. He labeled the pope "the anti-Christ, the proud, worldly priest of Rome, and the most cursed of clippers and cut-purses . . . who has no more power in binding the loosing than any priest." He went on to question the doctrine of the Mass, calling transubstantiation idolatry and a fable. The Communion bread represented the body of Christ, he said; but it was not His true physical body. And the Bible, not Church law, should be the rule of faith. Heresy would be contradiction of God's Word. He declared that he would follow its teaching, if necessary, to martyrdom. And to prove that he was not only interested in defending evangelical doctrines but also in spreading them, he organized a band of evangelists known as Lollards and sent them ranging over the island to preach Christ.

Long and bitter was his war with Rome. In 1382 a council known as the Earthquake Synod (for the shocks that took place during its sessions) condemned most of Wycliffe's pronouncements. Subsequently, upon the accession of unfriendly Archbishop Courtenay, he was dismissed from the Oxford faculty and forbidden to preach. In virtual retirement from active affairs he bent his efforts to teaching his followers and to writing.

Before he laid down his pen he made what proved to be his greatest contribution to Christendom: the first translation of the English Bible in the vernacular. Even though not translated from the original Hebrew and Greek but from Jerome's Vulgate, for the people of England it proved to be a benison of incalculable proportions. Besides giving breadth and beauty to the English language, it made God's revelation available to the laity. The hierarchy lifted a raucous hue and cry against what it considered a frightful breach of faith. Wycliffe replied, "The Clergy cry aloud that it is heresy to speak of the Holy Scriptures in English, and so they would condemn the Holy Ghost, who gave tongues to the Apostles of Christ to speak the Word of God in all languages under heaven."

Protestant historians call him the Morning Star of the Reformation. Certainly he, with Huss in Bohemia, Savonarola in Italy, and Wessel in North Germany, formed a constellation of silver lights destined to dispel the darkness that covered the earth until nations should come to the light of God and kings to the brightness of His rising. Surely Wycliffe was a luminary of the first magnitude.

He expired after sustaining a paralytic stroke. Twenty-nine years later the Council of Constance declared him a notorious heretic, excommunicated him, condemned his memory, and directed that his skeleton be exhumed and thrown away.

"They burnt his bones to ashes and cast them into Swift, a neighboring brook running hard by," Fuller wrote. "Thus this brook hath conveyed his ashes into Avon, Avon into Severn, Severn into the narrow seas, they into the main ocean. And thus the ashes of Wycliffe are the emblem of his doctrine, which now is dispersed the world over."

On the Apostles' Creed

JOHN WYCLIFFE, D.D.

THE GROUND of all goodness is stedfast faith, or belief. This, through grace and mercy, is obtained of God. Faith was the principal ground that enabled the woman of Canaan to obtain health of soul and of body, of Christ, for her daughter, who was evil treated of a devil, as the Gospel witnesseth. And the centurion was much praised of Christ for the stedfast belief that he had in the power of his Godhead. Faith is likened to the loadstar, for it showeth the haven of grace to men rowing in the sea of this world. Faith is the eastern star that leads spiritual kings to worship Jesus Christ, through withstanding of sin, as the east star led three kings when Christ was born.

Faith or belief is as a stone lying in the foundation of a strong building, that beareth up all the work. For as the building standeth stiffly that is well grounded upon a stone, so each virtuous deed is strong when it is grounded upon the solidity of belief. For upon this stone, that is, solid faith, Christ said that He would build His church, that is, man's soul. A man that hath lost his right eye is unable to defend himself in battle, for his shield hides his left eye, and so he has no sight to defend himself from his enemy; even so he that has lost the right eye of true faith, is unable to withstand or fight against his spiritual enemy, the devil. Saints, as St. Paul saith, through stedfastness and true faith, overcame kingdoms. (Heb. 11). They overcame the kingdom of their flesh through holiness of soul and body; and the kingdom of the world by setting at nought riches; and the kingdom of the fiend through patience and meekness.

The want of stedfast faith is the chief cause why men fall into deadly sin. For if a man truly believed that soon after he committed a sin, he should lose one of his limbs, he would, through that belief, keep himself, and flee from that sin. How much more if he believed that God would punish him in body and soul for evermore, if he died in that sin? If man's belief and trust were firmly set in God, all fear of man, fantasies, and fear of this world, would grieve him but little, or not at all. Christ said to His disciples, that if their faith were as great as the seed of mustard, and they should say to this hill, Pass hence, it should pass; and nothing should be impossible to them. St. Jerome saith that faith is likened to the corn of seed. If the corn of seed be not broken, the virtue thereof is not known; but the more it is pounded, even the stronger it smelleth; even so a man who is firmly grounded in the faith, the more he is pounded by persecution, the greater and the more fervent is his belief. Thus if man's faith were as great as the mustard seed, he should remove from himself the hill of pride, and all other false deceits of the fiend.

This faith maketh our souls so able to receive heavenly gifts, that we may get whatever we desire of the faithful Lord. Oh, blessed is the soul that believeth right and liveth well, and in well living keepeth true faith. While Peter had true faith, he went upon the sea as upon dry land; but when the firmness of his faith failed, he began to sink, and therefore Christ reproved him as of little faith. Thus it fares with us, who are staggering and unstedfast with the wind of each temptation or fear. Therefore, brethren, let us set all our belief and full trust on Him, Who is Almighty, and not in any vain thing that may fail in any time. Trust we stedfastly that nothing may grieve us farther than He will suffer it, and all things which He sendeth come for the best. And let no wealth of this failing world, neither tribulation, draw our hearts from firm belief in God. Let us not put our belief or trust in charms, or in dreams, or any other fantasies; but only in Almighty God. For it is full perilous, as holy doctors say, to scatter man's belief about any such. And let each man and woman take heed to themselves, for good living makes man to have firm belief, and trust in God, and evil works draw him into despair, as John Chrysostom saith.

After the ascension of Christ, the Holy Ghost taught His apostles all truth needful to the soul; and by His teaching they twelve settled together twelve articles, which all that will be saved must believe. [This account of the twelve apostles having united to compose the creed which goes by their name, is given by Ambrose, also by Ruffinus, and other ancient ecclesiastical historians. The ascribing of each article to a particular apostle is mentioned in a sermon attributed to Augustine. The tradition has been justly questioned, and although this symbol of Christian doctrine was of high antiquity in the primitive church, it received additions and alterations at different periods. See Lord King's history of the Apostles' Creed, and bishop Pearson on the Creed. This legend, however, does not involve any erroneous doctrine.]

The first article of belief St. Peter put into the creed, saying, *I believe in God, Father almighty, Maker of heaven and earth*. To believe *to* God, is one thing; to believe *in* God is another. The first both evil men and good men have; but the second none but good men have. The fiends believe to God, that is, that He is true, and that His words are truth; and yet some men and women fail of this point! For if they truly believed that the words of God are true, which He speaketh in Holy Writ, against their sinful living, they would amend their defaults, either for dread or for love. To believe in God, as St. Augustine saith, is, in belief, to cleave to God through love, and to seek busily to fulfil His will; for no man truly believeth in God, but he that loveth God, and by his good living believeth to have bliss of God, as a great doctor saith. And no man sinneth against God but he fails in belief, which is the ground of all good works. As the same doctor saith, In that He is Father, He will mildly do mercy to men forsaking sin; and in that He is Almighty, He is ready and of power to punish all those who will not leave their sin. We should believe that God the Father, being Almighty, without beginning and ending, made heaven, earth and all creatures, of nought, through His Word.

St. Andrew said, *I believe in Jesus Christ, His only Son, our Lord.* This article pertains to the Godhead of the Son, the Second Person in the Holy Trinity. We should believe that Jesus Christ, the Son, is equal with the Father, without beginning and ending, equal in might, and all one in might, equal in goodness, and all one in goodness; and that the Son doeth nothing without the Father; and these two Persons are One Almighty God, without beginning and ending. Jesus Christ, God's Son, and in like manner mighty with God the Father, is said plainly to be our Lord by double right; for He bought us with His precious blood, and because He shall be our Judge, and pronounce our sentence.

St. James, the son of Zebedee, said, *I believe that He is conceived of the Holy Ghost, and born of the virgin Mary.* This is the first article belonging to the manhood of Christ. We should believe that Christ, the Son of God, the Second Person of the Holy Trinity, took flesh and blood truly of the virgin by the Holy Ghost, and came into this world, very God and man together.

St. John, the evangelist, said, *I believe that He suffered pain under Pontius Pilate, upon the cross, died and was buried.* Here we should believe that the same Jesus Christ, very God and man, in the same flesh that He took of the virgin Mary, endured hard pain and sufferings, and even bodily death, by the doom of Pilate, judge of that province, without impairing of His Godhead. Christ bodily suffered hard pain, for we should have sufferance or patience in our adversities and tribulations. He suffered meekly and never trespassed, for we should suffer willingly, who have much trespassed. Christ was crucified, for we should chastise our flesh by penance [Penance is often used to express repentance. It is evident the reformer here means true repentance, and not the bodily penances of the church of Rome, as he refers to mental operations], withstanding sins and unlawful lusts; Christ died on the cross bodily, that we should endure the cross of penance, withstanding sin to our lives' end.

The cross of penance hath four parts. The first is sorrow for losing the love of God; the second is sorrow for losing the joy of heaven; the third is sorrow for deserving the pain of hell; and the fourth is sorrow for serving to the fiend and sin. Christ was buried; let this remind us that we hide our good deeds from the favour and estimation of the world, and remember that the earth is naturally the inheritor of our mortal flesh, that our thoughts may be closed from the lusts of this world, stedfastly having in mind the dreadful pains and death of Christ.

St. Thomas of India said, *I believe that He went down to hell, and the third day He rose from death to life.* Here we should believe that Christ's body lay dead in the sepulchre, without the soul, till the third day; that He rose from death to life; but the Godhead departed not from the body, neither from the soul, and after that the soul was departed from the body, it went down to hell; and delivered the holy souls that were there, through virtue of the Godhead. Christ went down into hell, giving us an example that we go thither by inward thought while we live; having mind upon the bitter pains which are there, that we come not thither after this life. Also He rose the third day, in body and soul together, very God and very Man, everlasting. He would not rise before the third day, to show the time that He was verily dead in body. For if He had risen quickly, it had not been believed that He was verily dead. And as each word of true witnessing is confirmed by the mouth of two or three, so that Christ was verily dead in the body, may be known by His lying in the tomb till the third day. On the third day He rose from death, in token that the light of His death had destroyed our double death, both of Adam and of ourselves; and that we should rise from spiritual death by three manner of medicines; by contrition or sorrow of heart, by confession and satisfaction.

St. James, the son of Alpheus, said, *I believe that He ascended to heaven, and there sitteth on the right hand of God, the Father Almighty.* Here we should believe that Jesus Christ, very God and very Man, everlasting, appeared to His disciples after His rising from the dead, teaching them of the kingdom of heaven, and eating with them to show that He was very Man as before His death, ascending into heaven raised mankind above all orders of angels. He ascended to open the gate of heaven, He ascended to show the way to men, and to lead man with Him, He ascended to pray the Father for mankind.

St. Philip said, *I believe that He is to come, to doom the quick and dead.* Here we should believe that the same Jesus Christ, very God and very Man, shall come to the judgment in the same manner, and with the same wounds that He suffered and bore with Him to heaven, and shall doom all mankind, both good and evil, according to their deeds.

That shall be a dreadful doom, and a fearful doomsman. For Christ, who shall be Judge there, is now meek as a lamb, and ready to bow to mercy; but there He will be stern as a lion to all that are damnable, and doom according to righteousness. Before the stern Doomsman, beholding all saints, angels and fiends, as John Chrysostom saith, all men and women shall yield reckoning of all their living in earth; of all the deeds that they have done; for what intent and to whose worship they wrought them; and not only of great trespasses, but also of those that seem but small. For of each idle word man shall account there, as Christ saith Himself. For as Isidore saith, "Each word that edifies not the hearer turns into peril to the speaker." That is an idle word, as Jerome saith, which profits not the speaker, neither the hearer. And since reckoning shall be holden of such, much more and without comparison, harder reckoning shall be of sinful speech, as of backbiting, slandering, scorning, false accusing, lying, swearing, cursing, and licentious speech.

Also man shall yield reckoning of all the thoughts of his heart that inclined to any sin, as God saith by His prophet. And not only we shall account for deeds done, which we should not have done, but also of deeds left undone, which we should have done. As those that have not done works of mercy to poor needy folk, nor given to them, nor lent to them, nor helped them in their suffering, as Christ shall rehearse at the doom, as He Himself saith.

Also of all the time that man hath in earth, he shall yield reckoning, how he has spent it, as it is written in the book of mourning. (Lamentations) And therefore saith Bernard, "All the time given to man, God shall seek how he hath spent it." And of misspending time, Anselm speaks, saying to man, "O thou unprofitable and dry tree, worthy everlasting fire, what shalt thou answer in that day when all the time given to thee shall be asked how thou hast spent it?" Also man shall account there of all his worldly goods, how he has gotten them, kept, spent and lent them. As Christ meaneth by the spiritual understanding of the ten pieces of money, and the five talents. Also of all powers of body, as strength, comeliness, swiftness, skill of body—in whose service these have been spent.

Also each man shall yield reckoning of the keeping of his own soul. For if a king had a daughter like to himself, to whom he thought to give great dignity and worship, and took her to any of his realm to keep; the more negligent that man were about her keeping, the stricter reckoning the king would ask of him for her. What then shall the king of heaven do to him to whom He hath committed a daughter most like to Himself, that is to say, man's soul; the much-loved daughter of this King, and ordained to great honour in the bliss of heaven, if this man keep her recklessly? Therefore God commandeth in the book of His law, that each man carefully keep his own soul. The father and mother also shall account for their children whom they chastise not; as is expressed in Holy Writ, how Eli was punished for his sons, because he chastised them not, as he should have done. Also the prelate or the curate shall account for his subjects, how he taught them by living and by word; as God saith by His prophet, a great dread shall be at His doom.

Of the multitude of accusers, man's own conscience, which is defiled with sin and not amended, shall accuse him, not privily, but openly. Also a man's own sins, which he would not leave, shall accuse him. As a stolen thing tied to a thief's neck, accuses him, so shall sins not amended in this life accuse sinful wretches. Also Holy Writ shall accuse them that knew it, and heard it, and lived not thereafter. Such shall bear with them the sentence of condemnation, as Uriah bare with him the sentence of his own death. And in example hereof, Christ said, that Moses' law shall accuse the Jews. Also God's creatures, which a man has used out of measure and in sin, shall accuse him there, and be as ready to take vengeance upon him as they were before to serve him. The fiends also shall be ready there, accusing sinful men and women, for they, as traitors, enticed to the sin, and when the sin is done they will accuse man thereof. And therefore in the book of Revelation the fiend is called accuser of Christian men. And as Augustine saith, then shall the adversary say, "Thou righteous Judge, doom these to be mine for sin which they have wrought, who would not be Thine by grace. Thine they were by nature, for Thou madest them of nought, but mine they are now, through sin and wretchedness, which they have wrought. Thine they were, for by Thy passion Thou hast bought them; mine they are now, for they did the sin that I put into their thought. To Thee they were disobedient, to me they were obedient, and to my enticing. Of Thee they took the garment of holiness, of me have they taken this coat of sin and filth. Thy garment they have lost, and with mine they have come hither. Righteous Judge, doom these to be mine, and to be damned with me." Alas! where shall that wretch abide who is so hard beset?

Also the benefits which men have received of God, who did not worship Him with due service for them, shall accuse them, and be alleged against them. And it is shown in Holy Writ where the angel came to the place of weeping (by which place is understood the doom, for there shall be weeping and wailing, as John saith in the book of Revelation). And there he rehearsed the benefits which God hath done to the people, and reproved the people, for they had not them in mind, and worshipped Him not for them. And the torment which Christ suffered in time of His passion, both wounds, cross, nails, and spear, shall accuse sinful men, as Bernard saith.

Therefore all Christian people have stedfast minds upon this sentence, and flee the unlawful lusts of your flesh, and covetings, and deceits of this deceivable world; and believe ye and have ye stedfastly in mind, that Christ shall appear in the judgment, stern as a lion to wicked men's sight, and doom both quick and dead. Of the great dread of that day God speaks by the prophet Joel. The day of the Lord shall be a great day of deliverance, a day of wrath, and of vengeance, of misery, of bitterness; the day of complaining and of accusing, the day of dread and of trembling, the day of crying and of sorrow, the day of darkness and of mourning, the day of calamity and of bitterness; a dreadful day of parting from God for ever, as Anselm rehearses.

St. Bartholomew said, *I believe in the Holy Ghost.* Here we should believe that the Holy Ghost, the third Person in the Holy Trinity, is very God, without beginning and ending, and equal in wisdom, might, and goodness, with the Father and the Son, and that these three Persons of the Holy Trinity are One Almighty God; and each one mighty, and all one might; and endless good, and all one goodness; and endless truth, and endless wisdom, and endless love, and endless righteous, and endless merciful; all are one truth, one wisdom, one beauty, one love, one righteousness, and one mercy.

St. Matthew said, *I believe in the holy church, and communing of saints.* We should believe the communion of saints, that is, that each of the three parts of holy church takes part of the other's goodness, and helps the other. The part that is in heaven helps the other two parts, praying for them, as Bernard saith; and the other two parts are said to help them that are in heaven, when their bliss and joy is increased by the fellowship of the others. For the more there are, the more is their bliss, and thus each of these three parties communes with the other.

St. Simon said, *I believe in forgiveness of sins.* Here we should believe that they who amend their life, doing true penance (repentance) with leaving off sin and keeping God's commandments, and ending in love, shall have forgiveness of all their sins. And Christ, through His passion and death, got for us of His Father forgiveness of our sins.

St. Jude said, *I believe in the rising of the body.* Here we should believe that all mankind shall rise at the day of doom, from death to life, in body and soul together, each in his own kind, and in his own body, incorruptible and immortal. And though the body were burned with fire, and the powder thereof thrown into the four seas that go about the world, yet the soul and it shall come together again, and rise from death to life, at the dreadful doom, and from that day forward never after depart. And they that have evil lived, and ended in deadly sin, shall go in body and soul to pain for evermore, and they that have lived well and kept the commands of God, and fulfilled the deeds of mercy after their power, and ended in charity to God and man, shall go, body and soul together, to bliss for evermore.

Of which bliss and life, St. Mathhias spake in the last article, where he saith, *And I believe in everlasting life.* In that everlasting life of joy and bliss, good men and women that ended well, shall dwell in body and soul, world without end.

THAT LIFE MAY HE TO US GRANT WHO BOUGHT US WITH HIS LIFE BLOOD. *Amen.*

JOHN HUSS 1369-1415

In the library at Prague there is displayed a triad of medallions dated *1572*. The first contains the figure of Wycliffe striking sparks from a stone, the second Huss kindling a fire from the sparks, the third Luther holding high a flaming torch. The medallions tell in symbolic form the story of the Reformation as it began, continued, and crystallized under the touch of an Englishman, a Bohemian, a German.

Like Luther, John Huss was born into a peasant family. His surname means Goose. John often employed it, and gradually his friends took it up. He enrolled at the University of Prague, where in 1393 he was given the degree of Bachelor of Arts, the next year Bachelor of Divinity, two years later Master of Arts.

The Church ordained him a priest. He taught at the university and preached on Sundays. Eventually, he became rector of the Bethlehem Chapel. Embracing Wycliffe's tenets, he proceeded to propound them with all boldness both orally and in the form of written articles. The university authorities, fearful of the consequences, forbade him to teach evangelical doctrines and placed his articles under ban.

The archbishop of the see of Prague, one Sbinko, at first showed a friendly regard for Huss. In 1405, Pope Innocent VII sent word to Sbinko to stop the propagation of the Huss teachings. The prelate's attitude underwent a sharp change. He turned against Huss, and renewed the public condemnation of his writings.

A crisis developed in the university. Two thousand Bavarian, Saxon, and Polish professors and students left, reducing the student body to five hundred. Immediately the authorities, recognizing the unusual ability of Huss, promoted him to the office of university rector.

He was now a controversial figure. Swarms of people filled the Bethlehem chapel whenever he preached. He grew more and more vocal in his attacks on clerical abuses, and openly questioned the Catholic doctrine of the Mass.

Sbinko ordered his writings burned. Two hundred of his manuscripts on non-theological subjects, such as philosophy and logic, were seized and thrown into the fire. The archbishop placed the city of Prague under interdict.

Events began to move rapidly. Sbinko died, and an Englishman, John Stokes, succeeded him. A sworn foe of all that Wycliffe and Huss stood for, he determined to quench the flames Huss was fanning throughout Bohemia.

Then the papacy opened a sale of indulgences in Prague. Huss, supported by his friend Jerome, inveighed against the practices with blazing indignation. Three of his sympathizers were killed for protesting. The pope accused Huss of heresy, and commanded his arrest. Even though popular sentiment favored Huss, he had to flee from Prague and live in the country, a virtual exile.

In exile, he published his most notable work, De ecclesia, (Concerning the Church). In it he challenged the authority of the pope and cardinals. They were not the Church, he said. The Church had once existed without them. The foundation of the Church was Christ, not Peter. Significantly, he took the same position on this that Augustine had in his Retractions.

A general council was called to convene at Constance, Switzerland. The pope summoned Huss to appear. Emperor Sigismund promised him safe conduct to and from the council. Accepting his word, Huss attended, arriving in Constance in November of 1414.

Within a month he was arrested and cast into a dungeon in the Dominican convent. The Church authorities changed his prison twice prior to his trial the next summer. First violent illness, then starvation, almost rendered the trial unnecessary.

The preliminary hearing turned out to be a dreadful fiasco. Whenever Huss would attempt to answer the charges of heresy or explain his position, wild shouts would go up, "Down with your sophistries. Say, Yes or No!" At the trial proper he was confronted with his written pronouncements questioning the authority of popes and cardinals, with demands that he repudiate them. He replied that he would do so only if the statements could be proven to be false to Scripture. "You are an obstinate heretic," his judges told him. A fine touch of historical irony lodges in the fact that for a short time his fellow prisoner was the deposed antipope John XXIII, who had consented to his arrest.

On July 6, he was conducted to the city cathedral. After they had celebrated the Mass, the ecclesiastical leaders had him led into the church and seated on a high stool. The sentence was read: "The holy council, having God only before its eye, condemns John Huss to have been and to be a true, real and open heretic, the disciple not of Christ, but of John Wycliffe." Without one dissenting vote, he was remanded to the civil authorities for execution. Six bishops stripped him of his vestments, crushed on his head a cap covered with pictures of the devil, and committed his soul to the devil.

They bound him to the stake by a chain. A last offer was made to free him if he would recant. "No," he said, "I shall die with joy today in the faith of the Gospel which I have preached." As the flame swirled around him he was heard to sing, "Christ, Thou Son of the living God, have mercy on me."

The council announced that it had done nothing more pleasing to

God than to punish the Bohemian heretic. It never dreamed that the fire it lighted under Huss in Constance that day would burst into a mighty conflagration that was to sweep inexorably over the whole world.

The Church—Not Men, but Christ

JOHN HUSS

THIS CHURCH the Saviour calls His church in the Gospel quoted, When He said: "On this rock I will build my church." And that He means this church is plain from the words which follow: "And the gates of hell shall not prevail against it." For seeing that Christ is the rock of that church and also the foundation on whom she is builded in respect to predestination, she cannot finally be overthrown by gates of hell, that is, by the power and the assaults of tyrants who persecute her or the assaults of wicked spirits. For mightier is Christ the king of heaven, the bridegroom of the church, than the prince of this world.

Therefore, in order to show His power and foreknowledge and the predestination wherewith He builds, protects, foreknows, and predestinates His church, and to give persevering hope to His church, He added: "And the gates of hell shall not prevail against it." Here Lyra says: "From this it appears that the church is not composed of men by virtue of any power of ecclesiastical and secular dignity, because there are many princes and high priests and others of lower degree who have been found apostates from the faith."

This comment has its proof, in part, in the case of Judas Iscariot, both apostle and bishop, who was present when Christ said: "On this rock I will build my church, and the gates of hell shall not prevail against it." But He Himself was not built upon the rock in respect of predestination, and therefore the gates of hell prevailed against Him."

From the aforesaid words of Christ it is evident that the church is taken to mean all, in a special sense, who after His resurrection were to be built upon Him and in Him by faith and perfecting grace. For Christ commended Peter, who bore [represented] the person of the universal church and confessed his faith in the words: "Thou art the Christ, the Son of the living God." And Christ said to him, "Blessed art thou, Simon Bar-Jonah." This commendation befits Peter and the whole church, which from the beginning was blessed in the way, by confessing humbly, obediently, heartily, and constantly that Christ is the Son of the living God.

This faith in regard to that most hidden article, the flesh—that is, the wisdom of the world—does not reveal; nor does blood reveal it, that is, pure philosophical science—but alone God, the Father. And because the confession was so clear and positive, the Rock *(Petra)* said to Peter (the rock): "And I say unto thee that thou art Peter," that is, the confessor of the true Rock *(Petra)*, who is Christ; and "on this Rock," which thou hast confessed—that is, upon me—"I will build" by strong faith and perfecting grace "my church"—that is, the company of the predestinate who, the probation being over, are appointed to glory. Wherefore, "the gates of hell shall not prevail against it."

Up to this point it has been deduced from the Saviour's words that there is (1) one church—namely, from the very word "church"; (2) that it is Christ's church—from the word "my"; (3) that it is holy— from the words, "the gates of hell shall not prevail against it." The conclusion, therefore, is that there is one holy church of Christ, which in Greek is *katholike* and in Latin *universalis*. She is also called apostolic, *apostolike*, because she was established by the words and deeds of the apostles and founded upon the Rock, Christ, as Jerome says in the Prologue to his *Commentary on the Apocalypse.*

The Church Founded on Christ, the Rock

The third foundation, included in the proposition (Matt. 16:18) is touched upon in the words: "On this rock I will build my church." And in view of the fact that in their utterances the popes most of all use this saying of Christ, wishing to draw from it that they themselves are the rock or the foundation upon which the church stands, namely upon Peter, to whom it was said, "Thou art Peter,"—in view of this fact, in order to understand the Lord's word it must be noted that the foundation of the church by whom it is founded is touched upon in the words, "I will build," and the foundation in which it is laid is referred to in the words, "on this Rock," and the foundation wherewith the church is founded is referred to in the words, "Thou art the Christ, the Son of the living God."

Christ is therefore the foundation by whom primarily and in whom primarily the holy catholic church is founded, and faith is the foundation with which it is founded—that faith which works through love, which Peter set forth when he said: "Thou are the Christ, the Son of the living God." The foundation, therefore, of the church is Christ, and He said: "Apart from me ye can do nothing" (John 15:5); that is, apart from me as the prime and principal foundation.

But Christ grounds and builds His church on Himself, the Rock, when He so influences her that she hears and does His words, for then the gates of hell do not prevail against her. Hence Christ says: "Every one that cometh unto me and heareth my words and doeth them,' I will show you to whom he is like: he is like a man building a house, who built a house deep and laid the foundation on a rock: and when the flood arose, the stream brake against that house and could not shake it: for it was founded on the rock." (Luke 6:48) And what this foundation is, the apostle Paul shows in I Cor. 3:11: "Other foundation can no man lay than that which is laid, which is Christ Jesus"; and I Cor. 10:4: "But the rock was Christ." Therefore, it is in this foundation and on this rock and from this rock up that holy church is built, for He says: "Upon this Rock I will build my church."

And on this foundation the apostles built the church of Christ. For not to themselves did they call the people, but to Christ, who is the first, the essential and most effectual foundation. For this reason the apostle said: "Other foundation can no man lay." Therefore this apostle, seeing how the Corinthians might err concerning the foundation, condemned them, saying: "Each one of you saith I am indeed of Paul, and I of Apollos, and I of Cephas, and I of Christ. Is therefore Christ divided, or was Paul crucified for you, or were ye baptized in the name of Paul?" (I Cor. 1:12,13) It is as if he said, No!

Therefore, neither Peter nor Paul nor any other besides Christ is the chief foundation or head of the church, so that later the holy apostle said: "What then is Apollos and what is Paul? His ministers whom ye believed and each one as the Lord gave to him" to minister to the church. (I Cor. 3:5) He said: "I planted," that is by preaching; "Apollos watered," that is by baptizing; "but God gave the increase," that is through the founding by faith, hope, and love. Therefore, "neither he that planteth," as Paul, "is anything, nor he that watereth," like Apollos, "is anything," that is anything upon which the church may be founded, but only God who giveth the increase; He is the church's foundation. And the words follow: "Let every one take heed how he buildeth thereon, for other foundation can no man lay than that is laid, which is Christ Jesus."

Now, this foundation is the rock of righteousness of which Christ spoke in the Gospel to St. Peter: "Thou art Peter, and upon this Rock I will build my church." On these words St. Augustine says, in his *Sermons on the Words of the Lord*, 13 *(Nicene Fathers, 6:340)*: "Our Lord Jesus Christ thus spake to Peter, Thou art Peter and upon this rock I will build my church—on this Rock, which thou hast confessed, on this Rock which thou hast recognized, when thou saidest, 'Thou art Christ, the Son of the Living God'—'I will build my church': I will build thee upon myself, not myself upon thee. For wishing that men should be built upon men, they were saying, 'I am of Paul, I of Apollos, and I of

Cephas,' that is, Peter. And others who did not wish to be built upon Peter *(Petrum)* but upon the Rock *(Petram)* said, 'I am of Christ.' "

Again, in his last Homily on John *(Nicene Fathers,* 7:450), Augustine says: "Peter the apostle, because of the primacy of his apostleship, had a symbolic and representative personality, for what belonged to him as an individual was that by nature he was one man, by grace one Christian, and by a more abundant grace he was one and the same chief apostle. But when it was said to him: 'I will give unto thee the keys of the kingdom of heaven, and whatever thou shalt bind on earth shall be bound in heaven, and whatsoever thou shalt loose on earth shall be loosed in heaven,' he represented the universal church which in this world is shaken by divers temptations, even as by torrents of rain, by rivers, and tempests, and yet doth not fall, because it is founded upon the Rock, the word from which Peter got his name. For Rock *(Petra)* does not come from Peter—*(Petrus)* but Peter from Rock, just as the word Christ is not derived from Christian, but Christian from Christ.

"Hence the Lord said: 'On this Rock I will build my church,' because Peter had said before, 'Thou art the Christ, the Son of the living God.' Upon this Rock which thou hast confessed, he said, 'I will build my church.' For Christ was the Rock. Therefore, the church, which is founded on Christ, received from Him the keys of the kingdom of heaven in the person of Peter, that is, the power of binding and loosing sins. For what the church is essentially in Christ, that Peter is symbolically in the Rock *(Petra)* by which symbolism Christ is understood to be the Rock and Peter the church. Therefore, this church which Peter represented, so long as she prospers among evil men, is by loving and by following Christ freed from evil, but much more does she follow in the case of those who fight for the truth even unto death."

These things Augustine teaches throughout, in agreement with the apostle, that Christ alone is the foundation and Rock upon which the church is built. To this the apostle Peter speaks, when he says: "Unto whom coming, a living stone, rejected indeed of men, but of God elect and precious, ye also, as living stones, are built upon into spiritual houses to be a holy priesthood to offer up spiritual sacrifices unto God through Jesus Christ." (I Pet. 2:4,5)

For this reason the Scripture continues: "Behold I lay in Zion a chief cornerstone, elect, precious, and he that believeth on Him shall not be put to shame. For you, therefore, that believe is the honor, but for such as disbelieve, the stone which the builders rejected, the same was made the head of the corner and a stone of stumbling and a Rock of offense. For they stumble at the word and do not believe that whereunto they were appointed." Paul also said: "Israel following after a law of righteousness did not arrive at the law of righteousness. Wherefore? Because they sought it not by faith but by works. They stumbled at the stone of stumbling and a rock of offense, and he that believeth on Him shall not be put to shame." (Rom. 9:31-33)

Behold how these two Roman apostles and bishops, Peter and Paul, prove from Scripture that the Lord Jesus Christ is Himself, the stone and the Rock of foundation, for the Lord says: "Behold I will lay for a foundation in Zion a cornerstone tried and precious, a stone of sure foundation." (Isa. 28:16) And also in the Psalms 118:22: "The stone which the builders rejected has been made the head of the corner." Therefore, Christ Himself is the foundation of the apostles and the whole church, and in Him it is fitly framed together.

From these things it is plain that Christ alone is the chief foundation of the church, and in this sense the apostle thought of that foundation, because he did not dare to speak of anything except what was built upon that foundation. Hence he says: "I will not dare to speak of any thing save those which Christ wrought through me by the obedience of God in word, and in deeds, and in the power of signs and wonders, in the power of the Holy Spirit. And so I have preached this Gospel not where Christ was already known, that I might not build upon another man's foundation." (Rom. 15:18-20) Was not this that apostle, a vessel of election, who said he did not dare to preach anything save those things which Christ spoke through him; for otherwise he would not be building on Christ, the most effectual foundation, if perchance he should say and teach or do anything which did not have its foundation in Jesus Christ. And from this it is plain, that not Peter but the Rock, Christ, was intended in Christ's Gospel, when Christ said: "On this Rock I will build my church."

Therefore, it is not a matter of much doubt to the simple Christian —faithful—that Peter did not dare to claim to be the head of the holy catholic church, for the reason that he did not rule over the whole church and did not excel above the whole church in dignity, nor was he the bridegroom of the catholic church. John the Baptist, than whom, according to the testimony of the truth in Matthew 11:11, "There hath not risen a greater among these born of women," did not dare to call himself the bridegroom, but in humility confessed himself the bridegroom's friend.

And when his disciples in their zeal for him said, "Rabbi, he that was with thee beyond Jordan to whom thou hast borne witness, behold the same baptizeth and all men come to him," John answered them and said; "A man can receive nothing except it have been given from heaven. Ye yourselves bear me witness I have said I am not the Christ, but that I am sent before Him. He that hath the bride is the bridegroom: but it is sufficient for me that I am the bridegroom's friend that standeth and heareth with joy the bridegroom's voice." (John 3:27-29) And the bridegroom said: "Ye are my friends if ye do what-

soever I command you." (John 15:14) Thus it is evident that it would
be the highest arrogance and folly for any man, Christ excepted, to
call himself the head and the bridegroom of the holy catholic church.

The Abuse of Scripture in the Interest of Clerical Power

Because many priests abandon the imitation of Christ, the high priest,
and boast of the power committed to the church, without doing works
that correspond, therefore up to this time we have been speaking of
the power of this kind. For they extract out of Matthew 18:18, "Whatsoever thou shalt bind on earth shall be bound in heaven," that whatsoever they do, every man ought altogether to approve. And from
the words of Matthew 23:2,3) "The scribes and Pharisees sit on
Moses' seat, therefore all things whatsoever they bid you, these do,"
they extract that every inferior is to obey them in all things. And so
these priests clamorously apply to themselves at their own pleasure
whatsoever appeals to them out of Christ's Gospel, and without any
ministry of love on their part to correspond. But what plainly calls
for toil and worldly self-abnegation and the imitation of Christ, that
they spurn away as something inapplicable to themselves, or make
believe they hold it when they do not.

Hence, because Jesus said to Peter, "I will give unto thee the keys
of the kingdom of heaven and whatsoever thou shalt bind on earth,"
etc., this they lay hold of with great complacency for the exaltation
of their own power. But what the Lord said to Peter (John 21:17),
"Follow me and feed my sheep," this they flee from as poison. Likewise, what He said to His disciples (Matt. 18:18), "Whatsoever thou
shalt bind on earth shall be bound in heaven," they gratefully seize
upon and glory in. But what He says, (Matt. 10:9), "Get you no
gold nor silver," they shun as hurtful. In the same way what He said to
His disciples (John 20:22,23), "Receive ye the Holy Ghost. Whosoever sins ye remit they are remitted unto them; and whosesoever sins
ye retain they are retained," very placidly they accept. But what He
says in Matthew 11:29, "Learn of me for I am meek and lowly of
heart," even the gentleness and meekness, which prepare a place for
the Holy Spirit, they do not admit to their hearts.

Also what the Lord said to His disciples (Luke 10:16), "He
that heareth you heareth me," they seize upon as meaning obedience
to themselves, but what the Lord says in Matthew 20:25-28, "Ye know
that the rulers of the Gentiles do lord it over them and their great
ones exercise authority over them. Not so shall it be among you, but,
whosoever would become great among you, shall be your minister,
and whosoever would be first among you shall be your servant: even
as the Son of Man came not to be ministered unto but to minister,"—
this most weighty saying they repudiate in word and deed—in word,

saying they ought to rule, and in deed because they do not wish to minister to the church after the custom of Jesus Christ the Lord.

And that I may gather up briefly all that the Scripture says, and especially the Gospel: what seems to indicate to them that they ought to be rich, live delicately, be famous in the world, and suffer no reproach for Christ, these sayings they ruminate over, proclaim aloud and make known all too extensively. But whatever calls for the imitation of Christ, as poverty, gentleness, humility, endurance, chastity, toil or patience—these passages they suppress or gloss over at their pleasure or expressly set aside as not pertaining to salvation. And the devil, who is the worst of sophists, leads them astray by their ignorance of the logical consequences, arguing in this way: "Christ gave such authority to Peter and the rest of the apostles, therefore also to you."

And from this they draw the inference that it is lawful for them to do whatsoever they please, and so, by reasoning of the same kind, they are most blessed fathers together with Christ in pronouncing judgment in the church and because they are to be crowned later with an everlasting crown. But blessed be Christ, the omniscient, who said these things to His apostles, knowing that the authority which was given to them they would use according to His good pleasure in ministering to His bride.

Therefore, the true worshippers of Christ, wishing to obtain that power, ought to resist every assumed power which seeks to remove them from the imitation of Christ by force or craft, for, in thus resisting such power we do not resist the ordinance of God but the abuse of power. And such abuse, in respect to the power of the keys, the simoniacs exercise who allege that they can either damn the deserving or loose those who are bound, and they do this because the obedience they falsely demand is refused them or for the sake of the gain they derive. Of such priests the Lord said: "They polluted me among my people for a handful of barley and a piece of bread that they might slay souls, which do not die, and make alive souls, which do not live, lying to my people which believe lies." (Ezek. 13:19)

Christ the True Roman Pontiff upon Whom Salvation Depends

To the honor of our Lord Jesus Christ, which honor and also Christ the aforesaid doctors nowhere mention in their writing, this conclusion is proved, namely, "to be subject to the Roman pontiff is necessary for salvation for every human being." From this it is clear, that no one can be saved unless he is meritoriously subject to Jesus Christ. But Christ is the Roman pontiff, just as He is the head of the universal church and every particular church. Therefore the conclusion is a true one. The consequence is clear from the things said above and from what is said in I Peter 2:25, "For ye were sometime going astray like sheep but are now returned unto the shepherd and bishop of your souls," and also from Hebrews 7:22-27: "By so much also hath Jesus become the surety of a better covenant and they indeed have been made free, many in number, according to the law because that by death they are hindered from continuing. But this man, because he continueth forever, hath his priesthood unchangeable, wherefore also he is able to save to the uttermost, drawing near through himself to the Lord and always living to intercede for us. For such a high priest became us holy, guileless, undefiled, separated from sinners and made higher than the heavens, who needeth not daily like those priests, to offer up sacrifices first for his own sins and then for the sins of the people, for this He did once for all when He offered Himself."

Truly this is the most holy and chief Roman pontiff, sitting at God's right hand and dwelling with us, for He said: "And lo, I am with you all the days, even unto the consummation of the age." (Matt. 28:20) For that person, Christ, is everywhere present, since He is very God whose right it is to be everywhere without limitation. He is the bishop, who baptizes and takes away the sins of the world. (John 1:29) He is the one who joins in marriage so that no man may put asunder: "What God hath joined together, let not man put asunder." (Matt. 19:6)

He is the one who makes us priests: "He made us a kingdom and priests." (Rev. 1:6) He performs the sacrament of the eucharist, saying: "This is my body." (Luke 22:19) This is He who confirms His faithful ones: "I will give you a mouth of wisdom which all your adversaries will not be able to withstand or gainsay." (Luke 21:15) He it is who feeds His sheep by His word and example and by the food of His body. All these things, however, He does on His part indefectibly, because He is a holy priest, guileless, undefiled, separated from sinners and made higher than the heavens. He is the bishop holding supreme guardianship over His flock, because He sleeps not nor is He, that watches over Israel, weary.

He is the pontiff who in advance makes the way easy for us to the heavenly country. He is the pope *(papa)* because He is the wonderful Prince of Peace, the Father of the future age. For, indeed, such a pontiff became us who, since He was in the form of God, did not think it robbery to be equal with God but emptied Himself, taking upon Him the form of a servant, because he humbled Himself by being made obedient unto death, even the death of the cross. Wherefore God hath highly exalted Him and given Him a name which is above every name, that at the name of Jesus every knee should bow, of things in heaven, of things on the earth, and things in hell. (Phil. 2:6-10)

To this the conclusion follows, namely: "To be subject to the Roman pontiff is necessary for salvation for every human being." But there is no other such pontiff except the Lord Jesus Christ Himself, our pontiff. This is so because the humanity of Christ is not subject to any other pontiff as of necessity to salvation, inasmuch as God hath exalted Him and given Him a name which is to be the most worthy above every other name, that at the name of Jesus every knee should bow and every power bend in obedience to Him "of things in heaven," that is, the angels; "things on the earth," that is, all men; and "of things in hell," that is, the devils.

And it is also so because Christ's mother was a human being; John the Baptist, also, Peter the apostle, and other saints now in heaven, and for none of these was it necessary for salvation to be subject to any other Roman pontiff besides Christ, seeing that they are already saved, persons whom no Roman pontiff can loose or bind.

Therefore, Pope Clement extended his authority too far when in his bull The Angels of Paradise, he commanded the angels to lead into the everlasting joys the soul of one who had died on a journey to Rome to secure indulgence, and who had been absolved from purgatory. For this pope wished that at his command the heavenly angels should bow their knees. And he added, "We wish that the pain of hell be not inflicted upon that soul in any degree," and so he commanded that the power or the knees of the spirits of hell should also bow at his command.

Not so did the apostles presume, for John wished not to command but to worship at the feet of angels, as he said (Rev. 22:8,9); "I, John, fell down to worship before the feet of the angel, and he said to me, see thou do it not, for I am a fellow servant with thee and with thy brethren the prophets and with them that keep the words of the prophecy of this book. Worship God." See how great is this apostle and prophet, beloved of God, who without doubt excelled modern popes and notably Clement, who gave command to the angels. He did not wish to give any command to an angel but, falling down, wished to worship before his feet, and the holy angel forbade him, showing him that he ought to worship God.

Hence holy men, when they have been praised by men, have humbled themselves and have burdened their minds with fear, lest praise should cast them down from a merit still more worthy. Therefore, Peter, Christ's apostle, when he was called by messengers went humbly to the Gentile, Cornelius, and when he was on the way, Cornelius went to meet him, instructed by an angel of Peter's holiness, and worshipped at Peter's feet. And Peter, taught of God about Cornelius and assured through revelation of his blessedness, did not permit Cornelius to lie at his feet as do modern pontiffs in whom not a scintilla of holiness is seen. Nay, often they are conscious of their sin in allowing themselves to be reverenced and, on that account, make the more ostentation, and if the ostentatious title *(titulus pompositatis)* be omitted, they at once shake with anger.

Suspension and the Interdict

Now of suspension this is to be said that, in the statement, to suspend is an administrative act or to prohibit any good thing on account of a criminal offence. Hence, what the old decretals call suspension the new law and decretals call the interdict, and then they speak of ecclesiastical suspension from an office or from a church benefice or of an ecclesiastical interdict from executing an office of the church.

This definition of suspension, therefore, being laid down, it is to be noted that, just as it is proper in itself in the first instance for God to excommunicate a man, so also it is proper for Him in the first instance to suspend him. Hence it is impossible for a pope or bishop to suspend any one justly, except as he has been before suspended of God, just as it is impossible for the pope to think anything righteously unless the thought be before suggested of God. Hence the apostle rightly says: "Not that we are sufficient of ourselves to think anything as of ourselves, but our sufficiency is of God." (II Cor. 3:5) And the supreme Bishop Himself said: "Apart from me ye can do nothing." (John 15:5)

From this it is clear that a suspension pronounced by a prelate is only worth as much as God almighty makes it to be worth. Hence, God's efficient suspension extends itself to priests, kings and every one in authority whom He removes from office or whom He takes from life by a decree of retribution. Hence, He suspends any one from the sacerdotal dignity, as it is written: "Because thou hast rejected knowledge, I will also reject thee. Thou shalt be no priest to me" (Hos. 4:6); "Bring no more vain oblations" (Isa. 1:13); and "I have no pleasure in you, neither will I accept an offering at thy hand." (Mal. 1:10)

And Christ's apostle suspended all who were guilty of criminal offence from the ministry of Christ's body and blood and the Lord, as he said: "Wherefore whoso shall eat the bread and drink the cup of the Lord in an unworthy manner shall be guilty of the body and blood of the Lord." (I Cor. 11:27) Likewise, we read of the severe suspension of Eli and his family, in that he did not duly correct his sons, as the Lord said to Eli: "Wherefore kick ye at my sacrifices and my offerings which I have commanded that they should be offered in my temple and honorest thy sons above me, to make yourselves fat with all the chiefest of the offerings of Israel my people? Therefore the Lord saith to Israel, I said indeed that thy house and the house of thy father should minister for ever before me, but now the Lord saith, Be it far from me, for he who honoreth me, him will I honor, and they that despise me shall be lightly esteemed. Behold the days come that I will cut off thy arm and the arm of thy father's house ... and this shall be the sign unto thee that shall come upon thy two sons, on Hophni and Phinephas; in one day they shall die, both of them. And I will raise me up a faithful priest, who shall do according to my heart and my mouth." (I Sam. 2:29-35) Likewise of the suspension of the king, Saul, who, in the face of God's commandments had spared God's enemies, we read: "Because thou hast rejected the word of the Lord, the Lord also hath rejected thee from being king." (I Sam. 15:23)

Who, I say, is a more foolish man than the cleric who grounds himself in the refuse of this world and holds Christ's life and teachings in derision? To such a low pitch is the clergy come that they hate those who preach often and call Jesus Christ Lord. And, when any one claims Christ for himself, immediately with carping mouth and angry face they say: Art thou the Christ? and after the manner of the Pharisees denounce and excommunicate those who confess Christ. Hence, because I have preached Christ and His Gospel and have uncovered antichrist, desiring that the clergy may live in accord with Christ's law, the prelates first arranged with Lord Zbynek, the archbishop of Prague, to secure a bull from Pope Alexander that in the chapels the Word of God should not be preached to the people. And from this bull I have appealed and never have I been able to secure a hearing. Therefore, being cited, I have on reasonable grounds not appeared because this excommunication was secured through Michael de Causis, after we had made an agreement, and now at last they have procured the interdict with which they vex Christ's common people who are without guilt.

Since, therefore, according to this method of the curia, every rational creature—angel and man—is subject to the commands of the Roman pontiff, and since the method in the processes of the same curia states that "whatsoever place, privileged or unprivileged, to which John Huss shall go, and as long as he may be there, we do subject them to the ecclesiastical interdict"—it follows that if, by the highest possibility, John Huss, according to God's absolute power, reached by death the heavenly Jerusalem, that city would be subject to the ecclesiastical interdict.

But blessed be God Almighty, who has ordered that the angels and all the saints in that heavenly Jerusalem are not subject to an interdict of this sort! Blessed also be Christ, the chief Roman pontiff, who has given grace to his faithful ones that, when there is no Roman pontiff for a given time, they may, under Christ as their leader, arrive in the heavenly country! For who would say that while the woman

Agnes, to all appearances, was for two years and five months the only pope, no one then could be saved? Or again, who would say that after a pope's death and in the interval between the pope's death and the election of his successor, no man dying in that period could be saved?

Blessed also be God Almighty, who ordains that His militant church shall have such life that, when a pope is dead, she is not on that account without a head or dead! Because not upon the pope but upon the head, Christ, does her life depend. And blessed be God that when a pope is insane or become a heretic, the church militant remains the faithful spouse of the Lord Jesus Christ! Blessed also be the Lord, the one living head of the church, who preserves her so effectually in unity that, even now, while there are three so-called papal heads, she remains the one spouse of the Lord Jesus Christ!

THOMAS à KEMPIS 1380–1471

In her novel, The Mill on the Floss, *George Eliot profiles thirteen-year-old Maggie Tolliver, the precocious, wilful, desperately lonely daughter of a home where religion was a ritual with little application. Maggie is seeking comfort at the family bookcase. She comes across an old clumsy book with its corners turned down in many places, and with certain of its passages underlined by ink marks long since browned by time. She pauses at one of the marked passages and reads:*

"Both above and below, which way soever thou dost turn thee, everywhere thou shalt find the Cross: everywhere of necessity thou must have patience, if thou wilt have inward peace. . . . It is but little thou sufferest in comparison of them that have suffered so much, were so strongly tempted, so grievously afflicted, so many ways tried and exercised. . . ."

George Eliot writes that a strange thrill of awe passed through Maggie while she read, as if she had been wakened in the night by a strain of solemn music, telling of beings whose souls had been astir while hers was in stupor. She read on and on, completely absorbed in what Thomas à Kempis had to say about the secret that would enable Maggie to renounce all other secrets: that all the miseries of her young life had come from fixing her heart on her own pleasure, as if that were the central necessity of the universe. For the first time she saw the possibility of shifting the position from which she looked at gratification of her own desires—of taking her stand out of herself, and looking at her own life as an insignificant part of a divinely guided whole.

Further on, Miss Eliot observes that Mrs. Tolliver noted the change that had taken place in her daughter—observed it with a puzzled wonder, and tried to find out what it was that caused Maggie to be "growing up so good."

History delights in the principle of striking contrasts. While in Bohemia John Huss was preparing for martyrdom because of his evangelical convictions, and while in Rome the antipope John XXIII (the first pope to bear that designation; that "jovial monster," the most profligate of mankind, guilty of every crime against God and society, if we may believe Gibbon) reveled drunkenly upon his pontifical throne, in a secluded monastery in the Netherlands an unknown monk labored to put down in a book a series of meditations due to become one of the world's classics.

At twenty, Thomas Hamerken—the name à Kempis derives from his birthplace, Kempen—had entered the Augustinian monastery on Mount St. Agnes, near Zwolle. With the exception of one brief interlude, he would pass the next seventy years of his life in cloistered obscurity. He never wrote a work on doctrine. He engaged in no controversy. He advocated no ecclesiastical reforms. He preached few sermons, though he did take the priest's orders. The world recognizes him for one achievement: he wrote The Imitation of Christ.

Even this, of course, has been denied. As Shakespeare's plays have been credited to Bacon, so The Imitation *has been attributed to a French scholar by the name of Gerson. Renan so argued, and others. The case was manufactered of old cloth, and Montmorency has ripped it to shreds. Internal as well as external evidence for the monk's authorship is too strong to be denied.*

The work has come in for its share of abuse, too. Literary pundits have made the third and fourth books the special targets for their arrows. "Loose," they charge. "Prosy and rambling," they claim. Perhaps. But they never assail books one and two. For these add up to sheer literary perfection, devotions that sparkle like rare and precious gems polished after the similitude of diamonds. To pore over them is to take an exquisite journey to the mountain of myrrh and the hill of frankincense.

Dean Milman and Thackeray criticize Imitation *for being the last effort of Latin Christianity, selfish in its aim, monastic in its structure. They overlook the fact that for all its weaknesses and limitations monasticism, in its pure form, provided the ingredients of revolt against ecclesiastical deadness, and the breath of an awakening unto newness of spiritual life.* The Imitation of Christ *represents Christian mysticism in all its warmth and grandeur.*

"The small old-fashioned book . . . works miracles to this day, turning bitter waters into sweetness," says George Eliot. "It was written down by a hand that waited for the heart's prompting; it is the chronicle of a solitary, hidden anguish, struggle, trust, and triumph. . . . It remains to all times a lasting record of human needs and human consolations."

Without a way, there is no going, without a truth, there is no knowing; without a life, there is no living.

—Thomas à Kempis

Of Consideration of Man's Misery and Death

THOMAS À KEMPIS

WRETCHED thou art wherever thou be and whithersoever thou turn thee unless thou turn thee to God.

Why art thou troubled, that all things come not to thee as thou willest or desirest? Who is he that hath all things at his own will? neither I nor you, nor no man in earth; there is no man in this world without some manner of tribulation or anguish, though he be king or pope.

Then who is in the best case? forsooth he that he may suffer anything for God's sake.

Lord, now there are many weak folk that say "O how good a life that man hath; how great, how rich, how mighty, how high he is." But behold heavenly goods and thou shalt see that all these temporal goods be as none but that they be full uncertain, and more grieving than easing; for they are never had without business and dread.

It is man's felicity to have temporal goods in abundance but mediocrity sufficeth him; verily it is a misery to live upon earth: the more spiritual that a man will be the more this present life appeareth bitter: for he feeleth better and seeth more clearly the faults of man's corruption.

For to eat, to drink, to wake, to sleep, to rest, to labour, and to be subject to the necessities of nature is very misery and an affliction to a devout man that would fain be loose and free from sin.

The inward man is full sore grieved with bodily necessities in this world.

Wherefore the prophet prayeth devoutly that he may be free from them saying "Lord, deliver me from my necessities."

But woe to them that know not their misery: but more woe to them that love this misery and this corruptible life; for there be some that so heartily clasp this wretched life that though they may scarce have their necessities with labour, yea and with begging, yet if they might live here forever, they would take no heed of the realm of Heaven.

O the mad men and out of true belief that live so deeply in earthly things that they savour no heavenly things: but these wretches yet in the end shall grievously feel how nought it was and how vile that which they have loved.

But the saints of God and all devout men and friends of Christ have not taken heed to that which pleaseth the flesh nor to them that have flourished in this world: but all their hope and all their intention hath been to things everlasting.

All their desire was borne up to things invisible and abiding lest by love of things visible they might be drawn to their lowest things.

Brother, lose not thy confidence in profiting by spiritual things: yet hast thou time and the hour; why wilt thou tarry thy purpose till to-morrow? Arise and begin anon and say "Now is the time of doing, now is the time of purging, now is the time of amending."

When thou art ill at ease then say "Now is the time of merit." Thou must go through fire and water ere thou come to refreshing.

Unless thou do force to thyself, thou shalt never overcome vice.

All the while that we bear this frail body we cannot be without sin, nor live without heaviness and sorrow.

We would gladly have quiet from all misery; but for as much as by sin we lost innocence, we lost also true blissfulness: therefore we must keep patience and abide the mercy of God till this wickedness go away and this mortality be swallowed up by life.

O how great is man's frailty that is prone and ready to vices; this day thou art shriven of thy sins and to-morrow thou dost like sins again. Now thou purposest to beware and within two hours thou dost as though thou hadst never taken such purpose; wherefore we have great cause to humble ourselves and never to feel any great things of ourselves; for we be so frail and so unstable.

Also may soon be lost by negligence what is scarce gotten in great time by grace.

What shall happen to us in the end that are sluggish so early?

Woe be to us who thus wish to decline and rest as though there were peace and safety, since there appeareth yet no step of true holiness in our conversation.

It were need that we should now be informed as young novices are in good manners, if peradventure there might be any hope of amendment to come or of more spiritual profiting.

This day a man is and to-morrow he appeareth not: full soon shall this be fulfilled in thee: look whether thou canst do otherwise.

And when man is out of sight soon he passeth out of mind.

O the dulness and the hardness of man's heart that only thinketh on things present and provided not more for things to come. Thou shouldst have thyself so in every deed and in every thought as though thou shouldst die anon.

If thou hadst a good conscience thou wouldst not much dread death.

It is better to eschew sins than to flee death: if thou be not ready to-day, how shalt thou be ready to-morrow? The morrow is a day uncertain and how knowest thou that thou shalt live to-morrow?

What availeth it to live long when there is little amendment? A long life amendeth us not always but sometimes increaseth sin. Would God we had lived well in this world one day.

Many men count the years of their conversion but ofttimes little is the fruit of amendment. If it be dreadful to die peradventure it is more perilous to live long: blissful is he that hath the hour of his death ever before his eyes and that every day disposeth himself to die.

If thou have seen any man die think that thou thyself shalt go the same way.

When it is morning think thou shalt not come to the even; and when even cometh be not bold to promise thyself the morning.

Wherefore be ever ready and live so that death find thee never unready.

Many men die sudden and unadvised: for what hour we think not the Son of Man shall come.

When that last hour cometh thou shalt begin to feel all otherwise of thy life that is past and thou shalt greatly sorrow that thou hast been so remiss and so negligent.

O how blessed is he that laboureth to be such in his life as he desireth to be found in his death.

These things shall give thee great trust in death—perfect contempt of the world, fervent desire to profit in virtues, love of discipline, labour in penance, promptitude in obedience, denying of oneself, bearing all manner of adversity for the love of Christ.

While thou art whole thou mayst do much good: but when thou art sick I wot not what thou mayst do: few there be that are amended by sickness even as they that go much on prilgrimage are but seldom the holier.

Delay not the health of thy soul through trust in friends or in neighbours; for men will forget sooner than thou thinkest: it is better now to make provision betimes and send before thee some good than to trust in other men's help.

If thou be not busy for thyself now, who shall be busy for thee in time to come?

Time now is right precious: but alas that thou spendest it no more profitably wherein thou canst deserve that whereby thou mayst live everlastingly.

Time shall come when thou shalt desire one day or one hour for thine amendment and thou wottest not whether thou shalt get it.

O my dear friend, from how great peril mayst thou make thyself free and from how great dread deliver thyself if thou be now always fearful and suspicious of death.

Study to live so now that thou may in the hour of death rather rejoice than dread: learn now to die to the world that thou mayst begin to live with Christ: learn now to despise all things that thou mayst then go freely to Christ. Chastise thy body by penance that thou mayst then have certain confidence.

And, thou fool, why thinkest thou shalt live long since thou are sure of no day?

How many are deceived and against all expectation drawn out of the body. How often hast thou heard men say "That man was slain with a sword, he drowned, he falling from high brake his neck, he in eating suddenly waxed stiff, he in playing met his end, another with fire, another with iron, another with pestilence, another slain among thieves."

And so the end of all is death and man's life passeth away suddenly as a shadow.

Who shall have mind on thee after death and who shall pray for thee?

Do, my dear brother, now what thou canst do for thou wottest not when thou shalt die and thou wottest not what shall come to thee after thy death.

While thou hast time gather riches immortal; think on nothing but thy soul's health; charge [care for] only those things that belong to thy soul.

Make thyself friends now worshipping holy saints and following their works that when thou failest in this life they may receive thee into everlasting tabernacles.

Keep thyself as a pilgrim and a guest upon the earth to whom belongeth nothing of worldly business.

Keep thy heart and rear it up to thy God for thou hast here none abiding city: thither direct prayers and daily mournings with tears that thy spirit after thy death may deserve blissfully to come to our Lord.

SAVONAROLA 1452–1498

In April, 1492, Lorenzo the Magnificent, ruler of Italy, lay dying in his palatial villa near Florence. His thoughts turned to God and to God's servant Savonarola, prior of the Dominican monastery. Ironical it was that the one churchman Lorenzo had never been able to bribe or intimidate should be the priest he would summon to administer final absolution.

Savonarola hurried to the bedside of the dissolute Medici. Would he grant Lorenzo his blessing? Only on three conditions. First, the king must exercise faith in Jesus Christ as the sole ground of his forgiveness. Lorenzo consented. Second, would he restore all the estates he had taken over from the citizens of Florence by dishonest means? He would. Third, would he agree to restore to the city the freedom it had enjoyed prior to the despotic rule of the Medici family? Lorenzo hesitated, then silently turned his face to the wall and died.

Under the Medici rule, Florence had reached the ultimate in licentiousness of court life, pagan thinking, and ruthless exploitation of the masses. Following the death of Lorenzo, Savonarola set about to reform the government. That he should succeed in accomplishing his aim is a commentary on his enormous influence. While Columbus was exploring the high seas in search of a passage to India, Savonarola was establishing a kind of Christocracy in Florence. Both represented startling experiments, shot through with grave dangers. Both achieved astonishing and unexpected success. Columbus opened up a new world in the Americas; Savonarola a new city with Jesus as the acknowledged head. And both received a bitter recompense of reward. Columbus after several trips was returned home in chains; Savonarola ended his career on the gallows.

His critics, particularly the envious Franciscan monks, charged him with rendering to God the things which were Caesar's. How dare a mere priest presume to write a constitution dictating civil laws and ordinances? Savonarola defended his stand by appealing to the case of Moses.

For some time Florence was a changed community. With a strong hand and a mighty voice Savonarola legislated and preached vice out of the city. On the surface at least, decency and freedom prevailed.

In Rome, Pope Alexander VI, the thoroughly corrupt Rodrigo Borgia, began to cast an anxious eye at Savonarola's mounting authority. To woo him over to Rome and away from Florence, Alexander of-

fered him a cardinal's hat. Savonarola turned the offer down. The pope then invited him to move to Rome. Again Savonarola returned a polite No.

Having reformed the government, the prior next shifted his attention to the cleansing of the temple. The Church, with Alexander at its head, was overrun with empty-headed leaders, and generally filled with dry rot. Savonarola imprudently sent word to the kings of England, France, Spain, and Hungary fulminating against Alexander and calling for secular help in his reform movement. Alexander intercepted one of the letters. He proceeded to denounce the reformer, suspend him from the priesthood, and excommunicate him from the Church.

Savonarola preached his farewell sermon in the Cathedral of St. Mark, where for years he had thrilled his parishioners with his powerful and eloquent messages. At the end of the service he presented his body to God, saying that he was ready to face death for the cause of truth. Soldiers seized and led him away to be tried.

His followers deserted him. Zechariah's poignant phrase, "wounded in the house of my friends," found fulfillment in the treatment accorded him. As the procession left the church, men who had once fawned on him in adulation hurled rocks at his head, brutally kicked him, and all but pulled an arm from its socket.

The city fathers concentrated on forcing him to take back his charges against the pope, and to admit that he was a false prophet. Savonarola remained adamant. With Alexander's official consent a campaign of sadistic torture was begun. They stretched him on the rack. They tied him with ropes and raised him high above the stone floor of the prison, then released the ropes and watched him fall to the floor. One day they repeated this gentle process thirteen times.

Beside himself with pain, he did recant in a moment of weakness, but quickly recovered and retracted his statement.

For a month he endured the torture. The magistrates decided he was no longer fit to live. A mock trial was held. Savonarola and two of his faithful friends were condemned to die.

The execution took place at the city square. A multitude of civilians, soldiers, and papal commissioners watched while the guard prepared fires under the gallows. An acquaintance approached Savonarola and asked if he expected to die in peace.

"My Saviour, though innocent, died for my sins," he said, "and should I not give up this poor body out of love to Him?"

Alexander's representative stood before him and pronounced the solemn words, "I exclude thee from the militant and triumphant church."

"From the church militant thou mayst," said Savonarola. "But from the church triumphant thou canst not."

They lighted the fagots under his gallows and sprang the trap. His last gesture, seen through billows of smoke spiraling about his mutilated body, was a hand lifted to bless the sea of people before him.

Introduction to *The Triumph of the Cross*

SAVONAROLA

I UNDERTAKE to defend the glorious triumph of the Cross against the impious volubility of the sophists and wise men of the world. The enterprise is bold and beyond my strength, but I hope God will aid me in a work, in these days, so useful to His glory; for although it may seem superfluous to reproduce the proofs of the faith so happily founded and established by the innumerable miracles of our Lord, by the literary monuments of the Fathers and Doctors of the Church, yet many men are so deeply plunged in the mire of vice that they do not see the light of truth, that they regard heavenly things as ridiculous, and despise Divine marvels as absurd dreams. We, inflamed by zeal for the house of God, will exert ourselves to rouse these souls slumbering in the shadow of death, and recall to their memory the authentic deeds of the past.

Although it may not be possible to demonstrate the faith by the causes and principles of nature, however, its manifested effects will furnish us with proofs so solid that every sensible man will be compelled to admit them.

But the faith does not depend upon proofs; for, says the Apostle, faith is a gift which God bestows on man through grace alone, lest any one should boast. We will, therefore, only bring forward these proofs to confirm those who hesitate, and to dispose them to receive the supernatural gift of faith, and at the same time to arm the faithful against the assaults of impiety, and to prevent the impious from undertaking anything against souls so simple whom it would be wicked to deceive. And as to what is said that faith has no merit when it is demonstrated by human reason, it does not follow that we here derogate from the mystery of grace, for this adage only refers to men who to believe will be vanquished by the arms of reason alone; but those are to be praised who by virtue of the Divine gift, having already embraced the faith of Jesus Christ, still seek for solid reasons to assure themselves in it, and to comfirm their brethren.

The prince of apostles exhorts to do this when he says, "Sanctify the Lord God in your hearts, and be ready always to give an answer to every man that asketh you a reason of the hope which is in you."

Therefore, we wish in this book to proceed only by reasonings, we shall invoke no authority, but act as if it were only necessary to believe our own reason and experience; for all men are compelled, under pain of folly, to consent to natural reason.

As we address ourselves to the learned of the times, who generally disdain familiar language destitute of ornament, we shall on their account abandon for a little our usual simplicity.

Concerning the Triumph of the Cross—Whence the Proofs of the Faith Are Drawn

As the power, the wisdom, and the goodness of God are infinite, the contemplation of a single creature can only give us an imperfect idea of Him. So the philosophers arrived at a knowledge of God through contemplating the order of the universe; but this order results not from one thing, but from innumerable things, which they could easily embrace at one view, since all beings in creation are dependent upon one another, and are united together by a natural tie. In the same manner, an isolated view of one of the works of Jesus Christ cannot give us instantly the intelligence of His virtue and wisdom, but if we offer to view all His works at once, and the effects they have produced, to draw not one proof but many, every intellect will be compelled to recognise that the Christ crucified is the true God; for if a single proof will not suffice, all the proofs united will have the power to convince every man who is not foolishly obstinate.

And just as the philosophers establish, after God, the heavens as the principal generating cause of all, we will place, after God, the Cross and the suffering of Christ as principal cause of the grace bestowed on the Church and of our salvation. After the heavens come the elements [of nature], and that is why after the Cross and suffering come the sacraments of the Church. And in the same manner as the elements draw all their virtue from heaven, *so the sacraments draw all their virtue from the suffering of Christ.* After the elementary principles in the constitution of the universe, come all the seeds, all the germs, and all the particular agents of the propagation; and so, in the same manner, in our Triumph of the Cross, we place as seed the evangelical teaching and the example of the holy. As to particular agents, they are apostles, patriarchs, martyrs, and doctors, who during their lives have, in Christ, regenerated the whole universe, and by whose merits and example the Church becomes daily fecund in renowned and fruitful works. Then in this material world come the effects which in our work are represented by that immense multitude of men, of every condition, converted to Christ by the example and exhortation of holy men whose lives have been pious and pure.

Universally Admitted Principles

When the physicist pre-supposes a moving principle, he could not enter into discussion with anyone who, like Zeno, would deny all movement. Let it then at once be granted that Jesus Christ was crucified by the Jews, and that He is recognised and adored as a God by the greater portion of all nations. That is a fact admitted not only by Christians but even by infidels. It is a fact confessed from generation to generation by heretics, Jews, Mohammedans—proclaimed in all the languages of the Gentiles and barbarians and confirmed by all the books which are published in great numbers upon Christ and His Church.

There is scarcely any region in the world where one will not meet some monument of Christian Churches, and one will scarcely find any place in the universe where Jesus Christ is not already or has not been formerly adored; or, at least, where they do not know that He is adored by the Christians as a true God, just as even the infidels call Him *the God of the Christians.*

It would then be a folly to deny this fact, which the constant tradition of word, writings, and monuments attests.

It is recognised also that the apostles have preached the Cross and that before them the prophets and patriarchs of the Hebrew people, as afterwards the martyrs and holy doctors of the Church, and an infinite multitude of monks, confessors, clerks, religious and secular men, have invariably confessed Jesus Christ.

Equally notorious is it that tyrants, philosophers, orators, and the wicked in great number, have waged against the Church and the Faith a cruel and bloody warfare; it is not the less certain that since the preaching of the Cross, idols have been overturned and the errors of the world vanquished and dissipated; that the Roman Emperors bowed their heads to the authority of the Galilean fishermen; and that an innumerable army of heretics, with their books and other impious dogmas, have been reduced to non-entity.

Method of Procedure

As, therefore, the invisible things of God are known by the visible, we must understand that there are certain invisible things of God which can be apprehended by His visible works, through the means of the natural virtue and force of the human understanding. To this consciousness even the philosophers attained, who admitted that there was a God, that there was only one God, and that He existed independent of all conditions, and other similar truths.

But it is also necessary to know that there are certain invisible things of God which cannot be brought out nor found out by any process of human reason; and certainly no one will doubt that there are in God infinite secrets and knowledge, which surpass human reason, especially when we perceive amongst men, who by nature are equal [the great philosophers], that they comprehend certain subtle truths, to the knowledge of which the intellect of the ignorant cannot attain.

Now God being infinitely superior to men, there are necessarily in Him secrets which no created reason can penetrate or sound; and as in things of sense, in which we are daily experimenting, our ignorance of a great number of their properties convinces us of the imperfection of our science, how much more palpable then should our imperfection be to us when the question is about God, since visible effects which lead up to Him are not only in equal accordance with the first cause, but infinitely removed from it.

Therefore we call those truths superhuman which we know only by faith, such as the Triune God, that God became Man, and other similar truths, incognisable by natural effects or mere reason.

Also, we may make ourselves more certain of these things by the supernatural effects of faith, for in the same manner as the observation of natural effects leads us to certain knowledge of God, and enables us to apprehend the truth of such propositions as that God exists, that He is One and Infinite, without enabling us to know Him as He is, nor to demonstrate to us His substance, so by observation of supernatural effects, we shall become more certain of such propositions that God is Triune, the Son of God is Man, without being able at the same time to comprehend what in itself is the Trinity or the Incarnation.

Now, inasmuch as grace always presupposes nature, we shall treat of the invisible things of God which can be investigated and known by means of natural effects, and we shall treat of those which are in a manner perceived by the means of supernatural effects. And we shall treat of the first summarily, because the philosophers and learned Christian doctors have written so profusely upon the subject, that there can be no room for doubt.

That There Is a God

It is then first necessary to prove that there is a God. But as it is also necessary to conform to the common usage in the name we apply to things, and as here we have to name the subject of which we are about to treat, the first question is to ascertain what men understand by the word "God."

Now it is certain that all understand by that appellation something sovereignly excellent, which some call the Prime Mover, others the First Cause, and the First Principle, and others the Supreme Good and the First Truth. Granted, then, that we understand by the word "God" the Prime Mover, the First Cause, First Principle, Supreme Good, or First Truth, or any other term, it is manifest that, even by the demonstrations of the Philosophers, we are compelled to confess the existence of God. We shall present in an abridged form, according to the order we have established in this treatise, some of these demonstrations.

I. We perceive, by means of the senses, that in this world there are certain things in motion. Now everything that moves is necessarily moved by another, nothing being at the same time under the same relation in actuality and potentiality; but it is impossible to mount from the finite to the infinite, from the being which is in motion to him who moves it, because if so there would be no intermediate movers receiving their motion from the first; necessarily, then, we arrive at a First Mover, and this First Mover we call God.

II. The argument is the same for the Efficient First Cause. We find, in fact, in the things which come within the range of our senses, an order of efficient causes. Now amongst them there is no one, nor could there be, which is to itself its own efficient cause, for in that case it must have pre-existed, which is absurd. As, therefore, it is here impossible to mount to the infinite, because subsidiary causes only act by virtue of the first, it is necessary to admit an Efficient First Cause, which by common consent is called God.

III. Besides, amongst beings there are some more or less good and this diversity can only ensue in proportion as they approach more or less to the Supreme Good, or Supreme Truth, or the Absolute Being. It is necessary, then, that there should be a Being supremely good, true, and great, and Him also we call God.

IV. In addition we observe that even beings deprived of knowledge advance towards a certain end. For they always, or at least most ordinarily, advance in the same manner, by suitable means, and arrive at their end. Manifestly, therefore, this cannot be by hazard, but by an intelligent provision which directs them, and this Intelligence we call God.

V. And, also, there is no natural propensity which can be deprived of its object—a fact perceivable to anyone who studies nature animate or inanimate. Now all men have a natural propensity to believe that there exists a Being who rules the universe, and whom they call God. The proof of the fact is that no one has ever yet succeeded in firmly establishing the conviction that there is *no God*. No nation, however barbarous, has yet appeared who has not recognised the existence of a God. In all times and places humanity has preserved that belief, and what is in all times and places the universal belief, is the result of a natural and therefore infallible propensity.

Besides, is it not from the unreflecting movements of the soul that nature draws her propensities? Well, then, the proof that the consciousness of a God is natural, is that in perils and misfortunes, when all human succour fails us, we instinctively turn to the heavens, *as the effect turns toward its cause.* The belief in a First Principle of things, in a Sovereign Moderator of the world, is natural to us. There is then a God.

That God Is One

It is certain, according to the same principles, that God is one. That which is singularly itself is not communicable. Now God is supremely Himself; He is His own nature, an independent existence; therefore He is by nature what He is—that is to say, by His own nature—God. His nature then is incommunicable; there cannot be many Gods.

Besides, God contains, as we have shown, all perfection. If there had been many Gods they would have been different, and the perfection of one would make the imperfection of the other; the rivalry and dissension of all the Gods. Complete absolute perfection is attributable to One only. There cannot then be many Gods.

All the beings we see are well ordered—the one to the other, and lend each other a mutual succour. Now, things being distinct amongst them, how could they have been able to form themselves into a harmonious whole, if they had not been co-ordained by a unique principle? (For one sole disposer is preferable to many). There is then a first and unique principle of universal order, and that principle is God.

The proof of this is latent in nature itself. For example, the bees by an admirable government are ruled by one of their number alone. Amongst men, art imitating nature, government always resumes itself into the action of one individual; and no government can last if it do not so resume itself in one form or another into the supreme arbitration of one sole power. There can be then only one God.

There Are Two Sorts of Worship of God

God may be honoured by men in two ways—by the soul and by the body. This is why we must establish the fact there are two modes of worship, the one interior and the other exterior. The interior worship is that which we render to God by the operation of the spirit and the will. The exterior worship consists of signs of religion given by the body—ceremonies and sacrifices. Now, as matter is perfected by form, it is indubitable that the exterior worship refers to the interior, and is subordinate to it.

The true interior worship is the rectitude and perfection of the life of the interior man, by which God is honoured above all. Every cause, in fact, is honoured by the effect it produces; now there is no effect more noble than man, whose perfection will honour God in the proportion of its greatness, so that this perfection itself being in the proportion of the sanctity of life, it follows that the principal honour rendered to God is the good and perfect life of a man. Consequently, the true integral worship of God consists in the life and acts of the perfect man, and in the offering up to God of that life and its acts.

It is not for himself alone that man renders to God homage and adoration, it is also that he may obtain the goodness and all the blessings that are made for him. Therefore the two modes of worship are a means and a disposition to obtain those blessings, for every agent implies the disposition of its subject. Therefore, as man is evidently better disposed by a holy life than by sacrifices to obtain happiness from God, and all blessings, *it follows that the true worship consists in holiness of life.*

The Christian Faith Is True, Because It Is the Cause of a Perfect Life

After having demonstrated the truth of the Christian religion, by the excellence of the life Christians lead, we approach the causes of that life, to draw from them a new proof.

Now, the first cause of this life is faith in Jesus Christ crucified, formed by charity; that is to say, acting by love according to the word of Scripture, "the justification of God is by faith in Jesus Christ to all those who believe on Him, and without faith it is impossible to please God."

We call a formed faith that by which, in loving Jesus Christ above all things, we believe that He is true God and true Man; that He is the Son of God, a sole God with the Father and Holy Ghost, and personally distinct from these two persons. Faith in Christ, joined to love, is, then, the cause of that Christian life of which we speak. This is proved by the experience of every day, and can be denied by no one. In fact, a Christian advances in virtue in proportion as he progresses in faith, and he recoils from the way of virtue in proportion as he recoils from faith. His progress and delay in virtue indicate equally his progress and delay in faith; these two things respond to each other necessarily. To love virtue is to love faith animated by charity, and to love such a faith is to love virtue. Such an effect, which produces itself in the Christian life, and which, since the time of our Lord, has lasted to these days, should excite our admiration, and cause us to reflect; just as the natural effects held the philosophers in admiration, and impelled them to deliver themselves up to the study of causes.

In the first place, then, the effect cannot be more perfect than its cause. If, therefore, the rectitude of the Christian life, which is better than all, depend upon the faith of Christ, it is impossible that this same faith cannot be true. And if it be true, Christ is God, as the Christians confess, and His religion is true.

In the second place, good cannot come from evil, nor falsehood from truth; for evil in that it is evil, and falsehood in that it is falsehood, are nothing positive. If, then, the faith of Christ were false, and if the love of Christ were evil, certainly the Christian life, which is good, could not depend upon it.

Thirdly, if the faith be false, it would be a still greater error; for to say that a crucified man is God, is madness in the extreme, if that be not true. The Christian life being very perfect, how then could it depend upon such a falsehood? Does not moral good come from truth, and every error in the action and the will, has it not as a principle a vice of the intelligence?

Fourthly, the more a nature is disposed, the more it is capable of receiving a perfect form. Now, the form and perfection of our intelligence is truth, and the disposition of the intelligence to receive the truth is purity of heart; whence it follows, that the more a man is disengaged from terrestrial passions, the more apt he is to receive the truth and reject error. But we have proved that this disposition is in no degree equal to that of the Christians; if, then, their faith be a lie, they would discover it as easily as others. However, they say nothing of the sort; on the contrary, in proportion as they advance in holiness, they confess their faith with greater energy, and their progress in the faith is always followed by a corresponding progress in the way of virtue. Therefore, their faith cannot be false.

Besides, God is the First Mover and Prime Cause in spiritual things, as He is in things corporeal. It is, then, He who moves human intelligence towards the truth.

That the Christian Doctrine, the Object of Our Faith, Comes from God

The reading and meditation of Holy Scripture are the causes of the Christian life, and the foundations of our religion. The truth contained in the Scripture is the object of our faith. After the reasons we have established relative to the faith of Christ, we ought now to place those which come from the Scriptures.

We know, in the first place, that it is impossible to foretell future contingencies, whether by way of experience or by way of doctrine. Hence, even the most illustrious of the philosophers attributed that knowledge to God alone.

For God, being eternal, embraces all things in His eternity, and everything is displayed naked before His eyes. On the contrary, man can only know future contingencies by a Divine revelation.

Now the Holy Scripture in all its pages, and principally in the Old Testament, has predicted not only in general, but also in particular, a crowd of contingent events depending upon the free will of man— events which should take place, not after one or ten years, but a hundred, a thousand years, and even three or four thousand years—

events which have happened among the Hebrews, deeds accomplished by Christ and His Church, the issue of which interested nearly every nation: the Assyrians, Chaldeans, Persians, Medes, Greeks, Romans, and other peoples. Now these predictions being made a long time before the events have been literally accomplished, the Holy Scripture, which contains them, is not then the work of human genius and industry, but the work of God. The predictions which have not yet been accomplished draw their truth from the accomplishment of others, whence we may conclude that God, with a sovereign goodness, extends His providence over all men and things in this world.

It belongs only to God, as we have observed, to foresee future events. It is not, therefore, in the power of man, however foreseeing and sagacious he may be, to disclose or ordain in advance the different actions, wars, and deeds of different great men and peoples, in such a manner that his prediction may be the sign of the event.

God alone has the power to signify with certainty the future by the present. Now we see in the sacred literature that the whole of the New Testament has been prefigured in the Old. It is not possible to say that it is an interpretation invented by the Christians, and arranged according to pleasure; for it would have been impossible, without the aid of an intelligent prevision, to establish in the two Testaments such an agreement of words, deeds, authors, and of different times. This agreement is no work of hazard, for we remark in it nothing clashing or strange; on the contrary, everything is admirably bound together. What is obscure in one place is cleared by another, so that the Holy Scripture in its whole serves as a commentary on each of its parts. Perhaps this may not be apparent to the eyes of those less familiar with the Scriptures; but learned and pious men, who study them diligently, have found in them a pure source of truth, and sweet effusions of grace. Let all those who desire to know the truth, read the Holy Scriptures with piety, with humility, and purity of heart, and they will certainly join with us in this opinion.

Before the diffusion of the light of Holy Scripture, humanity was plunged into a night of obscurity; but after the preaching of the apostles, after the thunder and lightning of their words, intelligencies were illuminated with the serene splendours of truth and virtue.

But, as one may be tempted to deny the past, let us pass on to the, so to speak, domestic proofs. This kind of proof has always given us more light, joy, and unction.

So from the moment when the preachers of our time, abandoning these means, had recourse to philosophy and the art of rhetoric, they had not so many auditors, nor were they so faithful as in olden times, when, using the Holy Scriptures with a simple and familiar language, the preachers marvellously spread light and love among the people.

The faithful were so happy that, in adversity as well as in prosperity they expressed their contentment by the singing of hymns and canticles.

God is my witness, that whenever I have felt inclined to employ in my sermons the subtleties of philosophy and the fine discourses of human wisdom, in order to convey to the pretended sages and fine spirits of this age some knowledge of the profundity of the Divine Word, I have observed in my audience signs of impatience and weariness, not only amongst the ignorant but even amongst educated men, who only lent a distracted attention to my words. But on every occasion when, on the contrary, I had recourse to the majesty of the Holy Scriptures, either interpreting their sense or reciting the deeds they contain, they all listened with a marvellous attention, and remained before me motionless as statues.

Now I have gained this experience, that, by putting aside tiresome questions and explaining in their stead the Holy Scriptures, the faithful have at all times been enlightened and charmed; and that, after having recognised the truth and felt compunction in their hearts, they have reformed their manners and become better. And now they can no longer support any other kind of reading or discourse, and renouncing the vanities of the age, they become almost divine. This is what also happened in the early periods, when Christianity flourished everywhere, and this is what we still see amongst us, in the effects of which we are witnesses.

Such is the doctrine which is said to be "sharper than a two-edged sword"; which has illuminated the whole world with virtue; which has overturned the worship of demons and the sacrilegious oracles of idols; and which, putting to flight innumerable errors, has worked marvels. But we shall hereafter return to this important point.

Let us add now, that our intelligence is so much the more capable of seizing the truth, in proportion as it is the more pure. Hence it comes that the best and purest spirits among men have not only exalted this doctrine in their writings, but have borne witness in its favour by their preaching, their life, and their manners, and frequently have not feared to defend it at the peril of their lives. Certainly they would not have acted in this way if they had not been so struck with its evidence, as if, as we say, they had touched it with their finger.

In the same manner, truth is always in accord with truth; but in the false, all is discord. But every other doctrine, far from opposing ours, only lends it help. The most instructed and experienced scientific men have constantly shown that there is no other philosophy which repudiates it, but that, on the contrary, all philosophy agrees with it with an admirable justice.

This is why it is praiseworthy to Christians to study the sciences, which would not be so if they were likely to injure the faith. We only object to those studies corrupted by superstition; such, for example, as the art of divination, and other arts, useless or injurious, which have always been denounced by the philosophers, and should not be reckoned amongst the sciences.

If any point of philosophy appear to contradict us, our theologians resolve such difficulties so easily, that it becomes evident that philosophy is the servant of theology; for the easy solution of difficulties is also an evidence in favour of truth.

Another peculiarity of truth is to shine the more brilliantly the more fiercely it is attacked, provided always that it be well defended. Intelligence has, in fact, truth for its object, towards which it inclines as towards its proper perfection. The more the truth shines, the more it will be loved; and it is shown in all its brilliancy when it is bravely contested, for in the fight it always comes uppermost in victory.

The Christian doctrine, after having been powerfully combated by philosophers and tyrants, has remained invincible; the innumerable works of Christians have produced faith, and, consequently, it comes from God. If not, would it have been able to survive unconquered the assaults of its numerous and powerful enemies?

The Truth of the Faith Demonstrated by the Intrinsic Effects of the Christian Life

We have, as far as our feeble intellect permits, proved the truth of the Christian faith, by reasons drawn from causes interior and exterior of the Christian life. It is now time to pass on to the reasons based upon the effects of that life.

One of the principal effects of the Christian life is peace, joy of spirit, and liberty of heart. For, besides the examples of our fathers, which we read or hear recounted, we have in our days, under our eyes, true Christians, whom the tempests and revolutions of this world do not move; who, on the contrary, glory in tribulation, and remain firm and stable in the confession of the faith of Christ. It is necessary, then, for us to seek out the source of these effects, to explain how it happens that the more one is attached to Jesus Christ by holiness, the more the soul progresses in liberty and serenity. After the Christians themselves, what is the cause of these effects? They say it is this:— "That the blessedness of man consisting entirely in the knowledge and contemplation of God, it is impossible that the desire of man can repose, as in a final end, in anything beneath God." Consequently the peace and tranquility of mind which they enjoy can only arise from their having founded their life on God, who is their true end. Ask the Christians what is their end, and they will reply, "God."

This is the reason why, counting for nothing the things of this world in comparison with God, and hoping after this life to enjoy God, they despise everything in the world and estimate it at no value. They are no longer sad at the loss of temporal things, for not valuing their present life they long for death to possess God, the only and supreme good. And because God is present everywhere by essence, presence and power, He is also in them by their love and contemplation, of which He is the Object, just as what is loved is in that which loves.

Now, when the object loved is present, the soul of him who loves delights and rejoices. This is what makes Christians experience an extreme joy at being united to God, of whose presence in them they are conscious; and because God is infinitely powerful from the moment when they feel that He is propitious to them, they count all the rest as nothing. Thus protected by a great liberty and a great confidence, neither caresses nor menaces can turn them from their end. But as man, by reason of temporal things—his great obstacle—and by reason of the feebleness of his intelligence, cannot by the mere force of nature arrive at such a degree of peace and liberty, it is necessary, they say, to attribute the cause to a celestial gift gratuitously conferred upon us, by virtue of which, God and the blessedness He has promised us are ever present.

The Truth of the Faith Proved by the Exterior Effects of the Christian Life

Another effect of the Christian life is that which manifests itself in the exterior of the Christian man in his manners, in his character, which exhale something divine; whence it happens that many are forced to respect Christians, and in some sort to render them worship.

Often their aspect, venerable by its divinity, has caused the most haughty anger to cease. This is what we read of Attila, the powerful and cruel King of the Huns. This man, whom neither the carnage he had made, nor the battalions of the enemy could restrain, was decided by the single prayer of Pope Leo to quit Italy. Attila, contrary to his custom, and to the great surprise of his own people, appeared by this retreat to obey more the order of a superior than a sentiment of veneration. The same is told of Totila, King of the Goths. This cruel conqueror, after devastating the world, could not endure the aspect of a poor monk. Scarcely had he seen St. Benedict than he prostrated his face to the earth, and only got up when bid and assisted. The Emperor Theodosius, returning to Milan from the massacre of Thessalonica, was arrested at the entrance of the temple by the authority of St. Ambrose, who reproached him with his crimes, and made him expiate them by a salutary penitence.

But the day would finish before I could recite all the illustrious examples of history.

But what is the use of proving what we see every day. It happens, commonly, that the most proud and criminal men all at once change their manner and language in the presence of the saints, and through compunction of heart completely reform their life. For it is the Spirit of God which gives to young men the grace which seduces, and to old the majesty which touches.

The cause of this effect is the supernatural beauty of the soul; it is the grace of God decorating the intelligence, the will, and the other faculties of the soul. The soul acting powerfully on the senses by the imagination, transforms the eyes and visage: now it enflames them, now it abates them: the visage is thus the mirror of the soul—sadness and joy are reflected upon it alternately. Our soul makes use of the body as an instrument: we see upon it the imprint of its passions, especially on the face and in the eyes. The proud have an arrogant look, cruel men a false one. Lightness of character is manifested in the mobility of the lips and the body; sensuality betrays itself in its languishing eyes.

It is said that certain sorcerers fascinate and entrap infants by a single look. In fact, the habitudes of the soul, good or bad, especially when they are inveterate, betray themselves forcibly on the countenance. This is the reason why, as every agent produces its like, and every effect is the expression of its cause, the exterior dignity of Christians, their honest and venerable aspect, can only have as a cause an interior beauty of soul and integrity of life. Such is the power of that exterior, that it serves more than any other to the conversion of sinners, as experience proves. The examples of pious Christians, simple and poor servants of the Lord, have more efficacy over men than the discourses of philosophers and orators, or even than miracles.

We have often seen learned and spiritual men command the most favourable attention by their fine discourses; but the life of those men did not correspond with their words; they have been without profit to the Church, and have had no other result than the praises accorded to their eloquence and wisdom. How many miracles in ancient and modern times are there which have served but little in the correction of manners! Men have run to see them, but have not returned better; on the contrary, we know and have seen that many men, as well ignorant and simple as wise and learned, have been converted by the sole example of the life of Christians. Many drawn to God by the perfume of holiness and a good fame, despising the attractions and pleasures of the world, have taken refuge from them in the purity of a new life.

After this, it is manifest that Christians have in them a certain virtue which produces all these admirable effects; for the body acts not by itself on the spirit. The proof of this is that certain bodies, especially formal, like celestial bodies, undergo no corporeal action. This is the reason why the heavens do not suffer by the action of fire which is in its vicinity. For a greater reason, consequently, the spirit by itself is not accessible to the action of the body. As, then, the exterior effects of the Christian life are corporeal, they cannot by themselves act upon the soul to carry it towards the good, without a certain virtue of which they are the instruments.

Now in a Christian of approved virtue, that virtue whence issues a perfect life, an exterior beauty and holy example is the immaculate faith and love of Jesus Christ crucified. In proportion as that love augments, the exterior beauty augments also, and becomes more efficacious in the conversion of souls. Therefore this faith which acts by love cannot be deceptive, for falsehood has no virtue capable of penetrating hearts.

Further: truth is more powerful than error. Now no remedy has yet been found more efficacious than the Christian life; as even the philosophers and other men concede those whose doctrines and examples have never won but a few disciples to good living, whilst the Christian life is every day the source of innumerable conversions and the more pure virtues. How, then, could such a perfection flourish on the dead trunk of error? Otherwise, men would be led to the correction of their manners by the doctrine and example of philosophers, rather than by the lives of Christians, which really does not happen.

And once more, God being the First Mover, without whom nothing can be moved, and His virtue conducting everything with wisdom, He manifests in the most noble effects the most noble causes. Now, after the interior exhortations and inspirations, God, to excite men to the practice of a Christian life, makes an especial use of the illustrious examples of the faithful to produce men like Him, in the same way as the heat of the sun and man are the generative principle of man. Then we must necessarily confess that a perfect Christian becomes the most noble cause, and the better instrument to produce the effect of which we speak. Therefore the virtue which co-operates with God is not a falsehood, but a supreme truth. Now this virtue is faith animated by charity. Faith, then, is true.

Truth of the Faith Proved by the Admirable Works of Christ, and First by His Power

In the contemplation of the triumph of Christ crucified, we will show that Christ has been and is much more, than any comparison can express, superior to all the gods of other religions, more powerful and more productive of good works than all those divinities, and that His wisdom and goodness are infinitely above everything, whence it will be manifest that Christ is the great God, the Lord and King, great above all gods.

Let us commence by His power, and recall to the mind, as we have to the sight, the triumph of the Cross.

Now see how we shall argue: either the crucified Jesus of Nazareth, whom the Christians adore, is the true God and First Universal Cause, or he is not the true God. If we agree to the first hypothesis, all discussion is finished, because then the Christian doctrine and faith are true; if, on the contrary, we hold to the second hypothesis, it follows that Jesus of Nazareth was a man the most proud, the most criminal, since being a man and mortal He wished to pass for a God, and to be so adored by all; so consequently He was a liar, or else it would follow He must have been a fool to undertake such and so great a work. For what could be more mad, more contrary to reason, more ridiculous, than the attempt of a man, who pretends to raise himself against the Divine Majesty, with no other help than abjection and misery—no other weapon than an uncultivated speech—no other hope than an infamous death?

What an idea! To wish to deprive God of His adorers, and to establish a new form of belief amongst men, the powerful, the wise, as well as the simple and ignorant. To wish to reverse all other religions, to give a new career to the world, to change everything, and to cause himself to be worshipped as a God by a subjugated humanity. To wish this not only during His lifetime, but to wish it to continue after his death—after an ignominious death! To promise to himself adoration and love, to exact from man, as a testimony, the most invincible attachment, a love even to death, and, if necessary, death in the most terrible torments! What an idea, we say, if such a one were no God!

Whoever you may be, I put you this question. If a mortal promised to do everything—if he had conceived such an idea, and began with you first, what would you say? Would you not suspect such a person to be foolish? Would you not simply laugh at such follies? If, then, Jesus of Nazareth is not God, how is it that, without any help, this sacrilegious seducer has prevailed against the laws of his country, against princes, against wise men, against the whole universe in opposition to him, against the powers of heaven and hell, in fine, against God Himself, even so far as to make himself equal to God, to receive honours due only to the Divinity, and to fulfil with an infinite success, in spite of difficulties and contradictions generated by long centuries, all the prophecies.

Why then, O Jews, why did your God, who governs and rules the world, permit such a great and impious crime? And you, Gentiles, I summon you as a testimony. Why did your God not extinguish this rival? How was it that this despised man, who was nailed to an infamous cross, died and was buried, has left after Him a force, a virtue, capable of generating so many and so great prodigies? Whoever, I will not say among men, but among those who have passed for gods, can be compared with Him? The angers, the sacrileges, the incestuous loves of the gods of paganism—are not they crimes even in the eyes of their worshippers?

We maintain that the Incarnation, possible to the power of God, was especially useful, and even necessary to the illumination and conduct of men, to show them the true road to felicity, and to fully satisfy the justice of God the Father for the sins of men. Then, with right, the Son of God wished to be born of a virgin, to die on the cross, in order to pay our debts, and to prove, by His example, that it is not necessary to fear death when the justice of God and the salvation of souls are concerned. In fine, Jesus Christ rose also to confirm us in the hope of the resurrection, and has been constituted the Judge of the living and the dead, because He had been condemned unjustly to death by wicked judges. Therefore, the Christian faith contains nothing repugnant to reason.

As to that which is called morality and discipline, Christianity is not less safe nor less reasonable, since the life it proposes and ordains is the most perfect of all, and there is nothing unreasonable nor absurd in the ceremonies of the Church. Certainly, the holy life which comes from the devout observation of these ceremonials, sufficiently proves it. What religion, then, in the world, can be established on such solid foundations?

The philosophers did not sufficiently comprehend the true end of life; the astrologers lost themselves in the midst of a thousand superstitions; the idolators had no truth nor modesty; the Jews are confounded by their own prophets and by the captivity to which they are now reduced; the heretics bear in their many divisions the proof of their errors; Mohammedanism falls before the attack of a simple philosophy; Christianity alone remains, confirmed and ratified by the double power and double light of nature and grace—by the holy life of Christians—by wisdom, works, and miracles, which nourish the mind: therefore, it is Divine. What man will not embrace that religion? Who will attack it without folly? Approved by God, preserved through so many centuries, maintained in spite of persecutions, sealed by the blood of martyrs; yes, that faith is Divine! If, then, we have not lost all our understanding, we must believe that the faith of Jesus Christ is the true faith; that there is another life where we shall appear in person before the tribunal of that formidable Judge, who will place the wicked on His left hand, in torments, like impure goats, and the good on His right hand, in felicity, like sacred sheep, and will give them the privilege of seeing God face to face—God Triune and One, immense, ineffable—in whom the saints will eternally possess all blessedness, by the grace of the invincible and triumphant Lord and Saviour Jesus Christ, to whom be honour, power, empire, and glory, through ages of ages. *Amen.*

MARTIN LUTHER 1483-1546

The character of any clergyman, whether priest or minister, is more readily known over the dining table than over the Communion table. Martin Luther was no exception.

In his book Table Talk, *one will find this improbable confession: "I never work better than when I am inspired of anger; when I am angry, I can write, pray, and preach well, for then my whole temperament is quickened, my understanding sharpened, and my mundane vexations and temptations depart." So wrote the Last Angry Man of the Middle Ages.*

Who can describe this mountain of a man, this human kaleidoscope, this composite of a hundred contrasting colors? At once rough and tender, poet and pugilist, boisterous and devout, deadly serious and yet possessor of a Falstaffian wit, unrelenting enemy and steadfast friend, exquisitely sensitive in hymnody and volcanic in invective, bold before men, humble before God—this begins to describe the Reformer of Saxony.

Martin Luther was born in a peasant family and never forgot it. "I am a peasant's son; my father, grandfather, all my ancestors were genuine peasants." The rough surroundings and Spartan discipline equipped him for the rapport he was to have with Germany's lower and middle classes. Educated at the University of Erfurt, he planned to practice law. The sudden and premature death of a friend, however, altered the course of his life, influenced him to enter the priesthood. He became an Augustinian monk. All acts of penance, all self-punishment, all his desperate prayers failed to bring peace to his soul. At last, through the study of Paul's epistles and the help of a godly professor, he was led to see that justification came by faith in Christ only, with no attending merit on man's part. A profound peace swept over him.

Luther continued his studies at Wittenberg, received the degree of Doctor of Divinity, joined the faculty at Wittenberg, and dedicated himself, as a zealous Catholic, to teach and preach the Gospel of grace.

The momentous developments that followed add up to material expansive enough to fill a library. The focal point of Luther's conflict with the papacy—whether it was his condemnation of the sale of indulgences or other evils, the publication of his Ninety-five Theses and the explosion it created, his debate with Eck at Leipzig, his im-

mortal defense at the Diet of Worms, his subsequent excommunication from the fold—revolved around one problem: what was to be the supreme and final authority in spiritual matters, the Church or the Word of God? Personality difficulties, Luther's marriage to a nun, the abusive language both parties resorted to, the petty misunderstandings, the tragic strictures in family units, the countless brush fires set off by the conflagration, these without exception must be accounted side issues. The battle was joined where it is still joined. Shall canon law exercise sovereign control over men's souls and consciences, or shall the Bible. Here stands the great divide, the mighty watershed which separated, and continues to separate, historic Catholicism from historic Protestantism.

Luther, aided by his friend and associate Philip Melanchthon, translated the Bible into the language of the people. It was a magnificent achievement. His fondest wish found realization. "Let the Scriptures be put into the hands of everybody; let everyone interpret them for himself, according to the light he has; let there be private judgment; let spiritual liberty be revived, as in Apostolic days. Then only will the people be emancipated from the Middle Ages, and arise in their power and majesty, and obey the voice of enlightened conscience, and be true to their convictions, and practice the virtues which Christianity commands, and obey God rather than men."

Luther's private life was as exciting as his public. He passed twenty-one joyous years with his wife, Catherine, whom he referred to playfully as "Katie, my rib," "Lady Luther," "Lady Doctor," "Lady of the Pigmarket," "my empress." They brought six children into the stirring world of their day. His home was a sort of caravansary: a constant procession of guests came and went—theological students, professors, fellow clergymen, civil authorities, noblemen, laymen burdened with problems, even beggars. After meals he would discourse on an infinite variety of subjects—his Table Talk makes for delightful reading—or play the lute, recite poetry, and sing. "The heart is satisfied, refreshed, and strengthened by music."

The tumultuous events in his life cast him upon God. He spent long hours in prayer. "How great a spirit, how great a faith, was in his very words!" records one of his biographers. "With such reverence did he ask, as if he felt he was speaking with God; with such hope and faith, as with a Father and a Friend."

In his closing years he suffered great bodily infirmity. Periods of deep melancholy assaulted him, often left him weak and on the fringes of despair. These were his battle scars. No human being could have waged the warfare he did and come out unscathed.

The world over, where free men and women gather to worship, they reach back across the centuries to take from Luther the moving words

*of his Battle Hymn of the Reformation, and with hearts aflame fling
it heavenward:*

> *A mighty Fortress is our God,*
> *A Bulwark never failing. . . .*

Luther's Prayer the Morning Before the Diet of Worms

"O ALMIGHTY and Everlasting God, how terrible is this world! Behold it openeth its mouth to swallow me up, and I have so little trust in Thee. . . . How weak is the flesh, and Satan how strong! If it is only in the strength of this world that I must put my trust, all is over. . . . My last hour is come, my condemnation has been pronounced . . . O God, O God! . . . O God do Thou help me against all the wisdom of the world. Do this; Thou shouldest do this . . . Thou alone . . . for this is not my work, but Thine. I have nothing to do here, nothing to contend for with these great ones of the world. I should desire to see my days flow on peaceful and happy. But the cause is Thine . . . and it is a Righteous and Eternal Cause. O Lord, help me! Faithful and unchangeable God, in no man do I place my trust. It would be vain. All that is of man is uncertain; all that cometh of man fails . . . O God, my God, hearest Thou me not? . . . My God, art Thou dead? . . . No, Thou canst not die. Thou only hidest Thyself. Thou hast chosen me for this work. I know it well. . . . Act then O God . . . stand at my side, for the sake of Thy Well-Beloved Jesus Christ, Who is my Defence, my Shield, and my strong Tower."

After a moment of silent struggle, he thus continues:

"Lord, where stayest Thou? . . . O my God, where art Thou? . . . Come, come; I am ready . . . I am ready to lay down my life for Thy Truth . . . patient as a lamb. For it is the cause of justice—it is Thine . . . I will never separate myself from Thee, neither now nor through Eternity. . . . And though the world should be filled with devils— though my body, which is still the work of Thy hands, should be slain, be stretched upon the pavement, be cut in pieces . . . reduced to ashes . . . my soul is Thine. . . . Yes; Thy Word is my assurance of it. My soul belongs to Thee. It shall abide forever with Thee . . . *Amen.* O God help me! *Amen.*"

[This prayer explains Luther and the Reformation.]

Defense and Explanation of All the Articles of Dr. Martin Luther Which Were Unjustly Condemned by the Roman Bull

I DR. MARTIN LUTHER by name, have with a joyful heart undertaken to demonstrate from Scripture the truth of all the articles (condemned by the pope's bull), for your further instruction and to expose the pretense of this false church, so that everyone may be able to defend himself against the blind feints these swindlers like to use. Someday, perhaps, even they will sober up and consent to exchange their hypocrisy for truth, their trickery for sincerity, and their pretensions for proofs. First, however, I must defend myself against some of the charges they bring against me.

First of all, I shall ignore the charge that I am caustic and impatient. I shall not apologize very much for that, for I have not been caustic or impatient in those books that have treated of Christian doctrine, but only in controversies, silly arguments about the papacy, indulgences, and similar foolishness. I was forced into these arguments and they were not worth all this discussion, let alone kindly and peaceful words.

They accuse me of claiming that I alone am everybody's teacher. My answer is that I have not done this, since I am always inclined to crawl into a corner. But my enemies have dragged me into the open through cunning and force to win glory and honor at my expense. Now that the game is going against them, they consider me guilty of vainglory. And even if it were true that I had set myself up all alone, that would be no excuse for their conduct. Who knows? God may have called me and raised me up [to be everybody's teacher]. They ought to be afraid lest they despise God in me.

Do we not read in the Old Testament that God generally raised up only one prophet at a time? Moses was alone during the exodus from Egypt. Elijah was alone in King Ahab's day. After him, Elisha stood alone. Isaiah was alone in Jerusalem, Hosea alone in Israel, Jeremiah alone in Judea, Ezekiel alone in Babylon, and so it went. Even though they had many disciples called "children of the prophets," God never allowed more than one man alone to preach and rebuke the people.

I do not claim to be a prophet, but I do say that the more they scorn me and the higher they regard themselves, the more reason they have to fear that I may be a prophet. God is marvelous in his works and judgments. He pays attention neither to numbers, greatness, cunning, or power. As Psalm 138(:6) says: "The haughtly he knows from afar." And even if I am not a prophet, as far as I am concerned I am sure that the Word of God is with me and not with them, for I have the Scriptures on my side and they have only their own doctrine. This gives me courage, so that the more they despise and persecute me, the less I fear them. There were many asses in the world in the days of Balaam, but God spoke only through Balaam's ass. (Num. 22:28) He says in Psalm 14 (:6) to these same prominent men: "You have confounded the sound doctrine of the poor preacher because he trusted in God," as if to say that because he is not great and high and mighty, his doctrine must be false in your eyes.

Holy Scripture must necessarily be clearer, simpler, and more reliable than any other writings. Especially since all teachers verify their own statements through the Scriptures as clearer and more reliable writings, and desire their own writings to be confirmed and explained by them. But nobody can ever substantiate an obscure saying by one that is more obscure; therefore, necessity forces us to run to the Bible with the writings of all teachers, and to obtain there a verdict and judgment upon them. Scripture *alone* is the true lord and master of all writings and doctrine on earth. If that is not granted, what is Scripture good for? The more we reject it, the more we become satisfied with men's books and human teachers.

That many of the bigwigs hate and persecute me for this reason does not frighten me at all. It rather comforts and strengthens me since it is clearly revealed in the Scriptures that the persecutors and haters have usually been wrong and the persecuted have usually been right. The lie has always had the greater following, the truth the smaller. Inded, I know if only a few insignificant men were attacking me, then what I have taught and written were not yet from God. St. Paul caused a great uproar with his teaching, as we read in Acts (17:5, 18; 18:12; 19:23-41), but that did not prove his teaching false. Truth has always caused disturbance and false teachers have always said, "Peace, peace!" as Isaiah [Ezekiel] and Jeremiah tell us. (Ezek. 13:10, 16; Jer. 6:14; 8:11)

Therefore, without regard to the pope and his great following, I will gladly come to the rescue and defense of the articles condemned in the bull, as God gives me grace. I trust, by God's grace, to protect them against the wrong that has been done them. In the face of force, nothing more is here than one poor body; that I commend to God and his holy truth which the pope has condemned. *Amen.*

It Is Heresy to Hold That the Sacraments Give Grace to All Who Do Not Put an Obstacle in the Way

In order to understand this article, it should be noted that my opponents have taught that the holy sacraments give grace to anyone, even if he does not repent his sin and has no intention to do good. They claim it is enough that he not "put an obstacle in the way," that is, that he be without wanton intention to sin. My article is stated in view of this teaching and I continue to hold and insist that this doctrine is un-Christian, misleading, and heretical. Besides the removal of the obstacle, that is, the evil intention, the reception of the sacrament requires not only genuine repentance for sin, but the worthy reception of the sacraments also requires that there be a firm faith within the heart.

Christ proved this in Matthew 9 (:2) when, in healing the paralytic, he first said to him, "Believe, my son, and thy sins are forgiven." If faith had not been necessary for the forgiveness of his sins, why should Christ have demanded it? Again, we read that Christ did no signs nor ever helped anyone unless he found faith that the person could and would do it. Thus St. John writes, "In his own country, he could do no signs because of their unbelief."

Why, does this heretical, blasphemous bull presume to teach against all of Scripture and against the faith and practice of Christians everywhere that one need not believe or repent, or intend to do good? This is so grossly un-Christian that if it were not for the bull, no one would believe that anybody even held such an absurd doctrine. I hope they will be sincerely ashamed of this bull. They would not like to have the laity read it in German.

Moreover, St. Paul says (Rom. 10:10) that, "A man believes with his heart and so is justified." He does not say that it is necessary that he receive the sacraments, for one can become righteous by faith without the bodily reception of the sacraments (so long as one does not despise them). But without faith, no sacrament is of any use, indeed, it is altogether deadly and pernicious. For this reason, he writes in Romans 4 (:3) that, "Abraham believed, or trusted, God, and it was reckoned to him as righteousness" or godliness. This Moses had previously written in Genesis 15 (:6) and it was set down in order that we might know that nothing makes us good and righteous except faith. Without faith, no one can have any dealings with God, nor receive his grace.

Do Not Try to Confess All Your Venial Sins, nor Even All Your Mortal Sins, for No One Can Know All His Mortal Sins, and in Ancient Times, Only Public, Mortal Sins of Which One Was Aware Were Confessed

They themselves teach that it is not necessary to confess venial sins, but now, because I say it, it must be heresy. I think, if I said that there is a God and then confessed all the articles of the faith, all of it would immediately be heresy, merely because I said it. This is the goodness and sincerity which the pope and his followers show toward me.

But it is the clear teaching of Scripture that not all mortal sins can be either confessed or known. In Psalm 19:12 we read, "Lord, who can discern all his sins? Cleanse thou me from secret sins." Here, the prophet teaches us that we cannot confess our secret sins, for God alone knows them, and we are to obtain remission by prayer. Furthermore, Psalm 143:2 testifies that these sins are mortal sins, "Lord enter not into judgment with thy servant; for no man living is righteous before thee." If the dear saints, God's servants (whom we regard as sinless), have such sins that they cannot be justified in God's sight, how dare you, wretched pope, justify before God those who have neither faith nor true contrition and who bring to penance only their accursed "gallows contrition"? Sins which make it impossible for the saints to be justified in God's sight must surely be mortal. Indeed, anything that prevents justification is mortal sin and vice versa.

As far as the statement is concerned which says that in ancient times only public sins were confessed, I leave the proof to the history books and to the epistles of St. Paul. I have spoken only of mortal sins known to the person himself, though they may be unknown to everybody else. Beside these sins, I say, there are still others which only God knows. We ought, therefore, leave people in peace and not force them to search out all their sins, since this is impossible anyway. We should let them confess those sins that occur to them at the time and of which they are aware. Then they can concentrate more on their faith in God's grace than on the thoroughness of their confession.

No One Ought to Say to the Priest That He Is Contrite, nor Ought the Priest Demand That He Do So

This, too, is an error in your eyes, holy father pope, but now you will have to admit it to be true, for I can prove it as follows. Whether our contrition is genuine or not is a question which cannot be left to our own discretion, but must be left to the judgment of God. Therefore, no one can say without presumption that he is truly contrite. St. Paul says in I Corinthians 10 (II Cor. 10:18), "Not the man who commends himself is accepted, but the man whom the Lord commends," and David says in Psalm 19:12, "Lord, who knows all his sins?"

If a man were required to say that he was truly contrite, he would be driven to presumption and to the impossible task of knowing all sin and evil in his heart. And since all the saints still have sin and evil

within them, it is impossble for anyone to have such contrition as will
be adequate in God's judgment, but they all say with David, "Lord,
enter not into judgment with thy servant; for no man living is righteous
before thee." (Ps. 143:2) If no one will be found justified, how will
anyone be found contrite, since contrition is the beginning of justification? Why, then, O pope, do you teach pride and presumption to
Christians so that they run head-on into God's judgment?

Christians ought to be so instructed that every penitent would know
that before God no contrition is worthy and sufficient. He ought therefore to say, "Behold, dear Lord, I know that I will not be found
truly contrite before thy judgment, and that there is still much evil
lust in me which hinders true contrition, yet, because thou hast
promised grace, I flee from thy judgment, and because my contrition is
nothing in thy sight, I put my trust and my hope upon thy promise in
this sacrament." And if the priest begins to inquire about his contrition, he ought to say, "Sir, in my own eyes I am contrite, but in the
presence of God it is but a poor contrition, with which I am not
able to stand before Him; yet I trust in His grace, which you are now,
at His command, to promise me." Thus the people should always be
urged to have faith, for at death contrition will be far too great and
faith far too small. God's promise in the sacrament is sure; our
contrition is never sure. For this reason God would have us build not
on our uncertain contrition, but on his certain promise, so that we may
be able to persevere in every time of trouble.

The Treasures of the Church, Out of Which the Pope Grants In-
dulgences, Are Not the Merits of Christ and of the Saints

The pope and his hypocrites, in order to praise the indulgences and to
make them appear valuable in the eyes of the poor people and to usurp
the treasures of the world, have invented this doctrine, and teach, to
the great dishonor of Christ, that Christ's merits are the treasure from
which the indulgences come. But if asked what evidence for this view
they have in Scripture they puff themselves up and boast of their power,
and reply, "Is it not enough that we say so?" Against this attitude I
propose this article and can base it on Scripture.

In John 6 (:51) Christ himself says that he is the living bread from
heaven, and that he who eats of this bread will live for ever. Isaiah
53 (:4) says that Christ has borne our sins. No Christian is so naive
as not to know that Christ's merits and suffering take away our sins
and save us. All believe that he died for our sins. From this it is clear
that Christ's suffering and merit are a living treasure and give everlasting life to all who share in it. But even my opponents must admit
that the indulgences do not give life, but are dead, through them no one
is made better, let alone given life. They do not take away sin, but

the penalty for sin. Now, no one but the pope and his sycophants is so foolish as to hold that discarding or remitting a penalty makes anyone better, though imposing a penalty may indeed make a man better, as we learn from reason, experience, Scripture, and truth.

This is the reason why the indulgences and the merits of Christ dovetail like life and death, day and night, Christ and Belial (II Cor. 6:15), the pope and a Christian. And they do have the right name for it, for indulgence means "to relax" or "to remit," and now everything good ceases and every kind of disaster is admitted. The pope leaves sin unpunished, indeed he takes away the penalty of sin which God has imposed and demands. So far as possible he lets sin go free and does not check it. Indeed, he protects and fosters sin, for he remits the penalty and asks and accepts money in its place. This is why St. Paul, writing to the Thessalonians (II Thess. 2:3), calls the pope a "man of sin" and "the son of perdition," for he permits and encourages sin, and thereby leads all the world with him to the devil, using his lying and deceitful indulgences.

The Roman Bishop, the Successor of St. Peter, Is Not by Christ's Appointment Vicar of Christ over All the Churches of The World

This is another of the key teachings which abolish the holy gospel and replace Christ with an idol in Christendom. Against it I have proposed this article. I stand by it and can prove it as follows:

First, since everything that is done in the church is proclaimed in clear and plain passages of Scripture, it is surely amazing that nothing is openly said in the whole Bible about the papacy. This is especially strange since my opponents consider the papacy the most important, most necessary, and most unique feature in the church. It is a suspicious situation and makes a bad impression that so many matters of lesser importance are based upon a multitude of reliable and clear passages of Scripture, while for this one doctrine no one has been able to produce a single clear reason. It is clearly stated in the gospel that St. Peter is a fisherman and an apostle, which they consider a matter of small importance compared with the papacy; yet there is not one single letter which states that St. Peter is above all the churches in the world.

At this point I would like to have it understood that I do not propose this article because I wish to repudiate the pope. Let him have as much power as he will, it makes no difference to me, and he is welcome to it. But there are two things I can neither tolerate nor keep silent about. First, he and his supporters torture, violate, and blaspheme the holy Word of God in order to establish their power. Second, they revile, slander, and anathematize the Greeks, and all others who do not submit to the pope, as though these were not Christians. They act as if being a Christian meant being bound to the pope and to Rome, while St. Paul and Christ have bound it only to faith and to God's Word, of which no one knows less or has less than the pope and his followers. And yet, though without faith and God's Word, he wants to be not only a Christian, but the god of all Christians and condemn all those who do not worship him, no matter how sound their faith and their gospel.

And it cannot be said that these people are no longer Christians because they do not obey the pope and are not built on him, since the pope himself and all his followers wish to be considered Christians, though they do not obey God in a single letter, and live, for the most part, without faith. So far they have been successful with their lies in maintaining that those who do not agree with them on this point are heretics and they themselves good Christians, though they do not take their stand with God and Christ on any point. Thus they make monkeys and fools of all the world, and define the terms "Christian" and "heretic" to suit themselves.

But let us leave their false interpretation and take up the true meaning of these words. To say that the gates of hell cannot prevail against this building must mean that the devil has no power over it; and this happens when the building is based on firm faith and stands without sin. Where faith is lacking or sin is present, there the devil rules and prevails against the building. Thus St. Peter teaches us (I Pet. 5:9) that we are to fight the devil with a strong faith, for the devil centers his attack on faith. From this it follows that this rock is Christ himself, for this is what St. Paul calls him in I Corinthians 10 (:4). The building is the believing church, in which there is no sin, and to build is nothing but to become a believer and free from sin, as St. Peter also teaches in I Peter 2 (:5) that we are to be built into a spiritual house on Christ the rock.

Now, since the pope and his authority and those who obey him walk in sin and horrible perversions and are the devil's henchmen, as everyone can see, it must be a lying invention that the rock and the building, which Christ puts beyond the reach of the gates of hell, mean the papal power and rule. If this power of the pope were the "rock" in Christ's words it could not do any evil, for Christ does not lie. But before our very eyes papal power has become the devil's power, a power for evil now as in the past.

Come on, you papists, crack this nut! This Scripture passage won't do any more, the citadel has been conquered, the pope has fallen, and he has nothing to stand on. For this saying of Christ has been the only basis on which the papacy has relied and built its claims all these many years. Now its lies and falsehoods have been revealed. If we have gained nothing else from the pope in this controversy we have at least liberated this passage of Scripture. In fact, this wins the war and decapitates the papacy, for this passage speaks stronger against the pope than for him. He who tells a single lie is assuredly not of God and everything else he says is suspect. But since the pope has lied about this fundamental doctrine and this key passage of Scripture on which it is based, and since he has perverted God's word and deceived the world with his false rule, what St. Paul says of him is certainly true, that the coming of the Antichrist shall be through the activity of the evil spirit, who enters only through lies and false interpretations of Scripture. (II Thess. 2:9)

Now you lie prostrate, dear pope! If you can honestly talk your way out of this predicament and turn your lies into truth I will admit that you have been made pope by God. But all this is not Luther's work. The credit belongs to John Huss. As it is written, "The righteous man who is dead shall condemn the ungodly who are living." (Wisd. of Sol. 4:16)

It won't do to quote some of the holy fathers who called St. Peter the rock and foundation of the church. First of all, because Christ's words take precedence over the words of all the saints. They have erred often; Christ never erred. Secondly, because no saint has ever said that the pope is this rock. They have called St. Peter the rock, not because of his power, but because of his faith, and if the pope will follow him in faith, we are ready to call him a rock too, provided only that the "rock" continues to be "faith" and does not turn into "power." But if he has no faith he shall not be called a rock.

Scripture shows clearly that St. Peter never made or sent apostles, or gave orders to them. Even with the aid of all the other apostles he could not make St. Mathias into an apostle. (Acts 1:15-26) They obtained him from heaven. Here Christ shows incontestably that all the apostles were created by him alone and are equal. This ought also to make all bishops equal and unite them, not under one authority and sovereign power as the pope's partisans deceitfully suggest to us, but in the unity of faith, baptism, love, and the Spirit, so that they would be one people, as St. Paul teaches in Ephesians 4 (:4-16). What a tempest they would raise if they could find that St. Peter sent out a single apostle, as we find that he was himself sent out! Nevertheless, they say our argument is not valid and their fable is the true version. But I think that I have produced sufficient evidence to show not only that the papacy hangs in the air, without any foundation in Scripture, but also that it raves against Scripture.

The Words of Christ to Peter, "Whatever You Loose on Earth Shall Be Loosed in Heaven," Are to Be Understood Only of Those Things That Were Bound by Peter Himself

How much the pope would like to be a god and be able to turn Christ's words around and decree, "Whatever I bind and loose in heaven, you shall loose and bind on earth." Thus he would be able to bind what God looses and loose what God binds. Then our God would be banished and could do nothing but the will of the pope. This is what happened in the days of John Huss. In those days the pope commanded the angels in heaven to lead to heaven the souls of those pilgrims who died on the way to Rome. John Huss objected to this horrible blasphemy and more than diabolic presumption. This protest cost him his life, but he at least caused the pope to change his tune and, embarrassed by this sacrilege, to refrain from such proclamation. But the rogue's face still shows. Since the pope could not keep his hold on heaven and hell, having over-extended himself, he nevertheless wants to take purgatory captive. Though he must admit that he cannot cast anyone into purgatory or bind him there, he wishes to free those that are bound there and bring them out. If you ask on what grounds he can do this, he says, "I am pope."

But enough of this! The words of Christ expressly state that his authority is on earth, not above it or beneath it. Binding and loosing apply in the same situation. The words are, "Whatever you bind on earth," and, "Whatever you loose on earth." The binding is as effective as the loosing, and the latter goes no farther than the former. We, therefore, abide by Christ's words and disdain papal sacrilege.

Moreover, all priests use the words of Christ when they absolve, and no absolution is granted except by virtue of this same word and promise of Christ. If, then, these are the very same words, why does the pope try to do more with them than the humblest priest? If the words have the same meaning, they have the same power, and if that power allows the pope to reach into purgatory, it gives every priest the same right. See how the pope fools and deceives the whole world. He selects from the divine Word whatever he wants, even though it belongs equally to everybody, and pretends to drink the best wine out of the very cask from which others can scarcely get water. God's plain and simple Word with its uniform power is gold for him, but he will not let others pass it as copper. Stop it, pope, the game has gone far enough!

Certain Articles of John Huss, Condemned at Constance, Are Most Christian, Most True, and Altogether Evangelical, and These all Christendom Together Could Not Condemn

As a matter of fact, on this point I have greatly erred, and I have already retracted and condemned this article because I said, "Certain articles of John Huss, etc." Now I say, not only certain articles, but *all* the articles of John Huss, condemned at Constance, are altogether

Christian; and I admit that the pope and his followers acted in this matter like the true Antichrist. He condemned the holy gospel along with John Huss, and replaced it with the teaching of the dragon from hell (cf. Rev. 13:1-18). I am prepared to defend this thesis, if need be, and by the help of God I will vindicate and uphold it.

In fact, St. John did not go far enough and only began to present the gospel. I have done five times as much, yet I fear that I am doing too little. John Huss did not deny that the pope is sovereign in all the world. He claimed merely that an evil pope is not a member of the body of Christendom, though he is to be endured as a tyrant. For all the members of the body of Christendom must either be holy or be on the road to holiness. But I claim that if St. Peter himself were sitting in Rome today I would still deny that he is pope and supposed to rule over all other bishops by divine right. The papacy is a human invention of which God knows nothing. All churches are equal, and their unity does not depend on the sovereignty of this one man; but as St. Paul says in Ephesians 4 (:5), their unity depends on one faith, one baptism, one Lord Jesus Christ, and these are all the common and equal possession of all the parishes in the world.

A Righteous Man Sins in All His Good Works

This article annoys the great saints of work-righteousness, who place their trust not in God's mercy, but in their own righteousness, that is, on sand. What happened to the house built on sand in Matthew 7 (:26) will also happen to them. But a godly Christian ought to learn and know that all his good works are inadequate and insufficient in the sight of God. In the company of all the dear saints he ought to despair of his own works and rely solely on the mercy of God, putting all confidence and trust in him. Therefore we want to establish this article very firmly and see what the dear saints have to say about it.

Isaiah 64 (:6) says, "We are all of us unclean, and all our righteousness is as a filthy stinking rag." You notice that the prophet makes no exceptions. He says, "We are *all* of us unclean," yet he himself was a holy prophet. Again, if our *righteousness* is unclean and stinking before God, what will our *un*righteousness be? Moreover, he says "all righteousness," making no exception. Now, if there is such a thing as a good work without sin, this prophet lies, which God forbid! Is not this passage from Isaiah sufficiently clear? Why then do they condemn my article, which says nothing but what Isaiah says? But we are glad to be condemned along with this holy prophet.

Augustine says in his *Confessions IX*, "Woe unto every human life, even the most praiseworthy, were it to be judged without mercy." Look how this great heretic, St. Augustine, speaks brazenly and sacrilegiously against this holy bull. Not only does he attribute sin to a good life, but he condemns even the very best life, which doubtlessly abounds in good works, as though it were nothing but mortal sin, if judged without mercy. O, St. Augustine, are you not afraid of the most holy father pope?

St. Gregory, too, speaks of that holy man Job and says, quoting Job 9 (:3), "Job, that holy man, saw that all our good works are nothing but sin, if God should judge them. Therefore he said, 'If one wished to contend with God, one could not answer him once in a thousand times.' " Gregory, how can you say this? How dare you say that all our good works are nothing but sin? Now you are under the pope's ban, and a heretic far worse than Luther. For he only says that there is sin in all good works; you make them out to be nothing but sin. I can see plainly that you do not want to be canonized by the most holy father pope, for you contradict him and make him into a heretic and Antichrist with this holy bull.

The same St. Gregory says later, referring to the same chapter, "We have now said many times that all human righteousness will be found unrighteousness, if strictly judged. For this reason Job (9:15) says, "Though I had done something righteous, I will not answer God and contend with him, but make supplication to my judge." God's judgment is not false or unjust, but true and just. If it finds unrighteousness in our righteousness, that unrighteousness cannot be fictitious, but must really be present. It cannot be merely a "defect" or a "weakness," but must be a damnable sin, which prevents salvation, unless mercy intervenes, and accepts and rewards our works out of sheer grace.

If these passages do not help to substantiate my article, then may God help it! I would much rather be condemned with Isaiah, David, Solomon, Paul, Augustine, and Gregory, than praised with the pope and all the bishops and papists, even though all the world were made up of pope, bishops, and papists. Blessed is he who should die for this cause! *Amen.*

The Burning of Heretics Is Contrary to the Will of the Holy Spirit

This I can demonstrate, first of all, by reference to history. From the beginning until now the church has never yet burned a heretic, and never will, though in ancient times there were many heretics of various types. Secondly, I can show the soundness of this article from their own words. For if a pope or bishop is a heretic they only depose him and do not burn him. In fact their own law, which they claim has come from the Holy Spirit, teaches that. In the third place, they have no word of Scripture which would prove that the burning of heretics is the will of the Holy Spirit. But if they say that John Huss and Jerome of Prague were burned at Constance, I reply that I was speaking of heretics. John Huss and Jerome of Prague were good Christians who were burned by heretics and apostates and antichristians, namely, the papists, for the sake of the holy gospel, as I said above. Following this example the pope and his heresy-hunters have burned other good Christians in other places, fulfilling the prophecy concerning the Antichrist that he will cast Christians into the oven. It was for this reason that Pope Alexander VI (1492–1503) ordered the burning of that godly man of Florence, the Dominican Girolamo Savonarola and his brethren. That is the way in which the holy church of the papists serves God. To do better they would consider a disgrace.

Furthermore, according to the canon law, the clergy are strictly forbidden to bear arms. Yet no one spills more Christian blood than the most holy father, the pope. Nowadays he tends the sheep of Christ with sword, gun, and fire, and is worse than the Turk. He embroils kings and princes, and lands and cities in war, yet this does not make him a heretic or Turk, a murderer or a tyrant, but he is the vicar of Christ and grants indulgences, sends out legates and cardinals in order to promote the war against the Turk. His papists make excuses for their false god and say that it isn't the pope who goes to war or burns anybody. He sits in his holy chair at Rome and prays—probably his bed-time prayers—and only commands the temporal power to fight and burn. That is exactly what the Jews did. They turned Christ over to Pilate and the Gentiles to have him crucified, but they themselves, like great saints, would not even enter Pilate's house; yet St. Stephen, in Acts (7:52) called them the murderers of Christ, and died for it. And now, because I have called the pope, who murders both body and soul, the greatest murderer the world has ever seen since its beginning, I am in the pope's eyes a heretic. God be praised, that I am a heretic in the eyes of his holiness and his papists!

This, our present Babylon, is like the first, and what the mother lacked the daughter has supplied. Genesis 11 (:1-9) shows that the first Babel defended its faith with fire only and burned Christ's ancestors. This Babylon in Rome burns Christ's children. The evil spirit knows full well that if the pope were to defend himself in books, he could not last for an instant and he would be exposed as the very dregs of all heresy and the Antichrist. To protect himself against what others write he has resorted to fire and outrageous tyranny, and now the one Babylon is as godly as the other.

They taunt me, asking why I am so timid and do not come to Rome. Did Christ run of his own accord to Annas, Caiaphas, Pilate, and Herod and ask them to kill him? I thought it was enough to stand my ground and not to flee and to wait for them where I am till they came for me, as they came for Christ. Then they could lead me wherever they want. But they say that I ought to run after them and urge them to kill me. They put everything so cleverly. Why don't they have the courage to refute my writings or to come to me and conquer me with their superior wisdom? Ah well, let the blind lead the blind!

Since the Fall of Adam, or After Actual Sin, Free Will Exists Only in Name, and When It Does What It Can It Commits Sin

This article should be sufficiently clear from what has been said above. St. Paul says in Romans 14 (:23), "Whatever does not proceed from faith is sin." Where, then, is this freedom, if of its own power it cannot do anything but sin? Again, St. Augustine says in his work, *On the Spirit and the Letter*, chapter IV, "The free will, without God's grace, can do nothing but sin." What do you say now, pope? Is it freedom to be without power to do anything but evil? You might as well say that a lame man walks straight, though he can only limp and never walk straight. It is just as if I were to call the pope "most holy," though St. Paul calls him a "man of sin and son of perdition" (II Thess. 2:3), and Christ calls him "the desolating sacrilege" (Matt. 24:15), the head of all sin and destruction. The papists have so distorted the meaning of words that they have created a new language and confused everything, just like the builders of the tower of Babel. Now "white" is called "black," and "black," "white," to the unspeakable damage of Christendom.

Paul says in II Timothy 2 (:24-26), "Teach those who oppose the truth: God may perhaps grant that they will repent and come to know the truth, and they may escape from the snare of the devil, after being captured by him to do his will." Where is the free will here? It is the prisoner of the devil, not, indeed, unable to act, but able to act only in conformity with the devil's will. Is that freedom, to be a prisoner at the mercy of the devil? There is no help unless God grants repentance and improvement. This is what Christ said in John 8 (:33-36) when the Jews claimed that they were free. He said, "Truly, I say to you, everyone who commits sin is a slave of—or owned by—sin . . . if the Son makes you free you will be free indeed." And St. Augustine changes the term, "free will," in his work *Against Julian, II*, and calls it "a will in bondage."

Furthermore, in Genesis 6 (:5) and 8 (:21) Moses says, "Everything that the heart of man craves and desires is evil at all times." Listen here, my dear papists, Moses bears witness against you, what have you to say in your defense? If there is a good thought or will in man, at any time, we must call Moses a liar, for he calls all thoughts and all desires of the human heart evil at all times. What kind of freedom is it that is always inclined to evil?

To bring the matter to an end, in the preceding pages it has been said repeatedly that godly and holy men who live out of the resources of God's powerful grace, struggle against their own flesh with great pains and peril, and the flesh fights against grace with all its strength. It is a profound and blind error to teach that the will is by nature free and can, without grace, turn to the spirit, seek grace, and desire it. Actually, the will tries to escape from grace and rages against it when it is present. Whose reason is not shocked to think that although spirit and flesh are the two greatest enemies, yet the flesh is supposed to desire and seek its enemy, the spirit? Surely, every man knows from his own experience how all his powers fight against grace in order to expel and destroy it. My opponents' position suggests that when nobody can control a wild and ravenous beast with chains you let it go free and it will chain itself and go into captivity of its own accord.

These teachings have been invented in order to insult and detract from the grace of God. They strengthen sin and increase the kingdom of the devil. Scripture says of man, in Genesis 6 (:3), that he is altogether flesh, and the flesh is most directly opposed to the spirit according to Galatians 5 (:17). And yet they confuse everything and say that the free will, which is utter flesh, seeks after the spirit. In other matters the frivolity and blindness of the pope could be tolerated, but when it comes to this chief article of the faith it is a pity that they are so senseless. Here they completely ruin everything that God has given us through Christ. St. Peter prophesied accurately when he said in II Peter 2 (:1), "There will be false teachers among you who shall deny the Master who bought them." Who is this Master but Christ, who has bought us with his own precious blood? Who denies him more than those who ascribe too little to his grace and too much to free will? For while they will not allow that to be sin and evil which is indeed sin and evil, neither will they allow that to be grace which is indeed grace and which should drive out sin. Just as a man who refuses to admit that he is sick will not allow medicine to be medicine for him.

The Speech of Dr. Martin Luther Before the Emperor Charles and Princes at Worms on the Fifth Day After Misericordias Domini (April 18) in the Name of Jesus

"Most serene emperor, most illustrous princes, most clement lords, obedient to the time set for me yesterday evening, I appear before you, beseeching you, by the mercy of God, that your most serene majesty and your most illustrious lordships may deign to listen graciously to this my cause—which is, as I hope, a cause of justice and of truth. If through my inexperience I have either not given the proper titles to some, or have offended in some manner against court customs and etiquette, I beseech you to kindly pardon me, as a man accustomed not to courts but to the cells of monks. I can bear no other witness about myself but that I have taught and written up to this time with simplicity of heart, as I had in view only the glory of God and the sound instruction of Christ's faithful.

"Most serene emperor, most illustrious princes, concerning those questions proposed to me yesterday on behalf of your serene majesty, whether I acknowledged as mine the books enumerated and published in my name and whether I wished to persevere in their defense or to retract them, I have given to the first question my full and complete answer, in which I still persist and shall persist forever. These books are mine and they have been published in my name by me, unless in the meantime, either through the craft or the mistaken wisdom of my emulators, something in them has been changed or wrongly cut out. For plainly I cannot acknowledge anything except what is mine alone and what has been written by me alone, to the exclusion of all interpretations of anyone at all.

"In replying to the second question, I ask that your most serene majesty and your lordships may deign to note that my books are not all of the same kind.

"For there are some in which I have discussed religious faith and morals simply and evangelically, so that even my enemies themselves are compelled to admit that these are useful, harmless, and clearly worthy to be read by Christians. Even the bull, although harsh and cruel, admits that some of my books are inoffensive, and yet allows these also to be condemned with a judgment which is utterly monstrous. Thus, if I should begin to disavow them, I ask you, what would I be doing? Would not I, alone of all men, be condemning the very truth upon which friends and enemies equally agree, striving alone against the harmonious confession of all?

"Another group of my books attacks the papacy and the affairs of the papists as those who both by their doctrines and very wicked examples have laid waste the Christian world with evil that affects the spirit and the body. For no one can deny or conceal this fact, when the experience of all and the complaints of everyone witness that through the decrees of the pope and the doctrines of men the consciences of the faithful have been most miserably entangled, tortured, and torn to pieces. Also, property and possessions, especially in this illustrious nation of Germany, have been devoured by an unbelievable tyranny and are being devoured to this time without letup and by unworthy means. [Yet the papists] by their own decrees [as in dist. 9 and 25; ques. 1 and 2] warn that the papal laws and doctrines which are contrary to the gospel or the opinions of the fathers are to be regarded as erroneous and reprehensible.

"If, therefore, I should have retracted these writings, I should have done nothing other than to have added strength to this [papal] tyranny and I should have opened not only windows but doors to such great godlessness. It would rage farther and more freely than ever it has dared up to this time. Yes, from the proof of such a revocation on my part, their wholly lawless and unrestrained kingdom of wickedness would become still more intolerable for the already wretched people; and their rule would be further strengthened and established, especially if it should be reported that this evil deed had been done by me by virtue of the authority of your most serene majesty and of the whole Roman Empire. Good God! What a cover for wickedness and tyranny I should have then become.

"I have written a third sort of book against some private and (as they say) distinguished individuals—those, namely, who strive to preserve the Roman tyranny and to destroy the godliness taught by me. Against these I confess I have been more violent than my religion or profession demands. But then, I do not set myself up as a saint; neither am I disputing about my life, but about the teaching of Christ. It is not proper for me to retract these works, because by this retraction it would again happen that tyranny and godlessness would, with my patronage, rule and rage among the people of God more violently than ever before.

"However, because I am a man and not God, I am not able to shield my books with any other protection than that which my Lord Jesus Christ Himself offered for His teaching. When questioned before Annas about His teaching and struck by a servant, He said: 'If I have spoken wrongly, bear witness to the wrong.' (John 18:19-23) If the Lord Himself, who knew that He could not err, did not refuse to hear testimony against His teaching, even from the lowliest servant, how much more ought I, who am the lowest scum and able to do nothing except err, desire and expect that somebody should want to offer testimony against my teaching! Therefore, I ask by the mercy of God, may your most serene majesty, most illustrious lordships, or anyone at all who is able, either high or low, bear witness, expose my errors, overthrowing them by the writings of the prophets and the evangelists. Once I have been taught I shall be quite ready to renounce every error, and I shall be the first to cast my books into the fire.

"From these remarks I think it is clear that I have sufficiently considered and weighed the hazards and dangers, as well as the excitement and dissensions aroused in the world as a result of my teachings, things about which I was gravely and forcefully warned yesterday. To see excitement and dissension arise because of the Word of God is to me clearly the most joyful aspect of all in these matters. For this is the way, the opportunity, and the result of the Word of God, just as He [Christ] said, 'I have not come to bring peace, but a sword. For I have come to set a man against his father, etc.' (Matt. 10:34-35) Therefore, we ought to think how marvelous and terrible is our God in His counsels, lest by chance what is attempted for settling strife grows rather into an intolerable deluge of evils, if we begin by condemning the Word of God. And concern must be shown lest the reign of this most noble youth, Prince Charles (in whom after God is our great hope), become unhappy and inauspicious. I could illustrate this with abundant examples from Scripture—like Pharaoh, the king of Babylon, and the kings of Israel who, when they endeavored to pacify and strengthen their kingdoms by the wisest counsels, most surely destroyed themselves. For it is He who takes the wise in their own craftiness (Job 5:13) and overturns mountains before they know it. (Job 9:5) Therefore we must fear God. I do not say these things because there is a need of either my teachings or my warnings for such leaders as you, but because I must not withhold the allegiance which I owe my Germany. With these words I commend myself to your most serene majesty and to your lordships, humbly asking that I not be allowed through the agitation of my enemies, without cause, to be made hateful to you. I have finished."

When I had finished, the speaker for the emperor said, as if in reproach, that I had not answered the question, that I ought not call into question those things which had been condemned and defined in councils; therefore what was sought from me was not a horned response, but a simple one, whether or not I wished to retract.

Here I answered:

"Since then your serene majesty and your lordships seek a simple answer, I will give it in this manner, neither horned nor toothed: Unless I am convinced by the testimony of the Scriptures or by clear reason (for I do not trust either in the pope or in councils alone, since it is well known that they have often erred and contradicted themselves), I am bound by the Scriptures I have quoted and my conscience is captive to the Word of God. I cannot and I will not retract anything, since it is neither safe nor right to go against conscience.

"I cannot do otherwise, here I stand, may God help me, *Amen.*"

ULRICH ZWINGLI 1484–1531

Protestant leaders came together in the capacity of a council for the first time at Marburg, Germany, in 1529. The purpose? To find a basis for union. The problem? How, in view of the differences of opinion concerning the meaning of the Lord's Supper, the difficulty might be resolved and a union effected. Present among others were: "the penetrating Luther, the gentle Oecolampadius, the magnanimous Zwingli, the eloquent Melanchthon, the pious Schnapf, the brave Bucer, the true-hearted Hedio."

Zwingli rose to lead the council in prayer. "Fill us, O Lord and Father of us all, we beseech Thee, with Thy gentle Spirit, and dispel on both sides all the clouds of misunderstanding and passion. Make an end to the strife of blind fury. Arise, O Christ, Thou Son of righteousness, and shine upon us. Alas! while we contend, we too often forget to strive after holiness which Thou requirest of us all. Guard us against abusing our powers, and enable us to employ them with all earnestness for the promotion of holiness."

Luther championed the view, held by the German theologians, that Jesus' statement, "This is my body," must be taken in nothing but a literal sense. Zwingli stood forth as the spokesman for the Swiss delegation, arguing that the Lord had meant that He would be present in the Communion bread spiritually, or mystically, not corporeally. The disputation waxed hot and sharp. Both parties exchanged harsh words. Luther, worn out from his exhausting encounters with Rome, was not in a good mood. When the conference broke up with not much settled, Zwingli went to the fearless German Reformer with tears in his eyes and extended his hand. Luther turned away. "We are not of the same spirit," he said.

Marburg thus became a kind of spiritual amoeba that split the Protestant Church into a pair of distinct bodies, a fountain that sent two of the multiple denominational streams coursing into the world. Rejecting the Catholic doctrine of the Mass, Lutherans have historically maintained that while Jesus' physical body is not changed into the sacred elements, nevertheless by the power of the Word of God it does upon consumption become in, sub, cum—in, under, and with—the elements. Adherents of the Reformed Faith, on the other hand, have in general followed the view of Zwingli, accepting the symbolical meaning of the Supper. Calvin differed from Zwingli chiefly in that he emphasized the spiritual presence of Christ in the elements, whereas Zwingli dwelt so strongly on the absence of Christ's body that he neglected this aspect of the service.

Ulrich Zwingli was the most clear-headed and rationalizing of the Reformers, the historian Schaff believes. "He had no mystic vein, but sound, sober, practical common sense." Born at Wildhaus, Switzerland, he studied in Austria and Germany, became a priest at twenty-two, a preacher in the minster of Zurich at thirty-four. He expounded Scripture plainly and forcefully, proclaiming evangelical doctrine over against Roman Catholic doctrine. This brought him into conflict with the Catholic leaders at Constance. His influence spread. When he did away with the Mass and images, the contours of the Swiss Reformation assumed definite shape. Zwingli in a very real sense prepared the way for Calvin.

Allowing for ordinary human weaknesses, Zwingli stands out as an emblem of Christian charity. "Let us confess our union in all things in which we agree," he used to say. "And, as for the rest, let us remember that we are brethren." Which explains why Cordus calls him "the magnanimous Zwingli."

The Certainty or Power of the Word of God

ULRICH ZWINGLI

THE WORD OF GOD is so sure and strong that if God wills all things are done the moment that he speaks his Word. For it is so living and powerful that even the things which are irrational immediately conform themselves to it, or to be more accurate, things both rational and irrational are fashioned and despatched and constrained in conformity with its purpose. The proof may be found in Genesis 1: "And God said, Let there be light; and there was light." Note how alive and strong the Word is, not merely ruling all things but creating out of nothing that which it wills. You may discover for yourselves many other proofs which for the sake of brevity we will here pass over. The earth is commanded to bud and the waters to bring forth and bear fish, and it is done that very day.

Such is the might of that eternally empowering Word. Again in Genesis 3, God said to the woman Eve: "I will greatly multiply thy sorrow and thy conception; in sorrow thou shalt bring forth children; and thy desire shall be to thy husband, and he shall rule over thee." And it all came to pass that very day, and will continue as long as life in the body. At the same time he said to Adam: "Cursed be the ground when thou tillest it; in labour shalt thou eat of it all the days of thy life; thorns also and thistles shall it bring forth to thee; in the sweat of thy face shalt thou eat bread, till thou return unto the ground out of which thou wast taken." Note here how toil and death were laid inescapably upon man by the all-powerful Word of God.

Again, when the human race corrupted itself more and more, God shortened the span of life to 120 years. (Gen. 6) And so it is to the world's end. Again, he told Adam and Eve that in the day that they ate the forbidden fruit they would die. (Gen. 2) And this assuredly came to pass as God had said. (Gen. 3) Again, God told Noah to make an ark, because it would rain forty days and forty nights and all living creatures would be destroyed. (Gen. 7) And assuredly it came to pass, for even the heathen have written about the flood, although they give Noah the name of Deucalion. Again, by his angels God declared that he would destroy Sodom and Gomorrah and the other cities, and it did not fail to happen as he said. (Gen. 19) Again, Lot and his family were commanded not to look behind, and Lot's wife was disobedient, therefore she was turned into a pillar of salt. (Gen. 19) Again, God told Abraham: "I will certainly return unto thee according to the time of life; and Sarah thy wife shall have a son, etc." (Gen. 18) Sarah herself did not believe, for she was some eighty years old, but it came to pass as God had said. (Gen. 21)

The Scriptures of the Old Testament are full of illustrations of the certainty of God's Word, for all the passages mentioned are taken from the one book Genesis, and indeed from only one part of that book. If I were to begin to tell of the great miracles which God promised Moses that he would work in Egypt and amongst the children of Israel, all of which he most certainly performed, or of what he accomplished through Joshua, Gideon and Jephthah, or through Samuel, Saul, David, and Solomon, I should never come to an end. Read these things for yourselves or take note and ponder them when you hear them preached.

We will now turn to the New Testament and consider the strength and certainty and power of God's Word as we find it there.

The divine declaration to Zechariah by the angel Gabriel seemed at first sight completely incredible, for his wife Elisabeth had always been barren and both of them were now advanced in years. And because he did not believe, Zechariah was deprived of the power of speech. But that which he regarded as impossible assuredly came to pass—such is the strength and certainty and life of the Word of God —and John the Baptist, the righteous forerunner of the Messiah, was born. The pure Virgin Mary was taken aback when the angel announced and declared the birth of Jesus Christ, for she knew not a man; but the Word of God was so alive and sure that without any detraction from her purity that holy thing was conceived and grew in her and was eventually born of her for the salvation of the world. Thus we see that the whole course of nature must be altered rather than that the Word of God should not remain and be fulfilled.

In Luke 1 again the angel said to her: "And he shall be great," meaning Christ. And when has the world seen anyone greater than he? Alexander and Julius Caesar were great, yet their dominion hardly extended over half the world, but believers in Christ have come from the rising of the sun to the going down of the same, and indeed the whole world has believed in him and recognized and magnified in him the son of the Most High, and of his kingdom there is no end. For where shall we find a ruler with dominion and authority as ancient as that of the faith of Christ, a faith which will never be destroyed, even though it be preserved only amongst the few? Indeed, this divine prophecy is visibly fulfilled before us every day.

And when Christ grew and began to teach and to work miracles, all things were subservient to him and fashioned themselves in accordance with his will. The leper said to him: "If thou wilt, thou canst make me clean." And he replied: "I will, be thou clean." And from that hour his leprosy was cleansed, for God willed it, and the words "Be thou clean," had power to accomplish it. (Matt. 8) To the centurion he said: "Go thy way, and as thou hast believed, so be it done unto thee." And his servant was healed in the self-same hour. Note that in this case the certainty of healing was made dependent upon the faith of the centurion, to teach us a sure trust in God and the work of God (Matt. 8) To the ruler he said: "Thy son liveth," and it was so (John 4), though he was not even present, to teach us that nothing is too hard or distant for the Word of God to accomplish. To the man who was blind and deaf and had an impediment he said: "Ephphatha, that is, be opened" (Mark 7), and all his bands were loosed. To the blind he said: "Receive thy sight: thy faith hath saved thee," and immediately he received his sight. (Luke 18)

To Matthew he said: "Follow me," and he followed him without delay. (Matt. 9) To the man lying on the bed he said: "Thy sins be forgiven thee." And so that the outward sign might give the assurance of inward cleansing he said: "Arise, take up thy bed and go into thine house." And he arose and departed to his house. (Matt. 9) To the woman bowed together he said: "Woman, thou art loosed from thine infirmity"—by the laying on of hands he gave her a sure sign, or perhaps testified to his good will—and immediately she was made straight. (Luke 13) Over the loaves and fishes he pronounced a blessing and they were increased, so that many thousands ate of them and there still remained far more than there had been at the first, as we may see in all the Gospels. He rebuked the unclean spirit, and immediately it left the boy possessed by it. (Matt. 17) He commanded the disciples to cast their nets on the right side and they would find, and immediately they caught 153 great fishes. (John 21) He commanded Peter to come to him on the water, and immediately he bore him up. (Matt. 14) From heaven he told Ananias that Paul was a chosen vessel to him to bear his name before kings and princes of the earth and the children of Israel (Acts 9), and so it came to pass. When Paul was journeying towards Rome, and the shipwreck intervened, he told him that no one would be lost but only the ship, and that is how it turned out. (Acts 27)

These passages from the New Testament will be quite enough to show that the Word of God is so alive and strong and powerful that all things have necessarily to obey it, and that as often and at the time that God himself appoints. And let us beware lest we murmur against God like the ungodly in the days of Ezekiel (12), who said that the Word spoken by the prophets was prolonged: for the forbearance of God is not negligence, but a respect for the most convenient time. Not that this respect is at all necessary to God, but beneficial to us, for with God there can be no time, seeing he is not subject to anything, and that which is duration to us is to him eternally present. With God, in fact, there is no such thing as past or future, but all things are naked and open to his eyes. He does not learn with time or forget with time, but with unerring knowledge and perception he sees all things present in eternity. It is in time that we who are temporal find the meaning and measure of longness or shortness. Yet what seems long to us is not long to God, but eternally present.

If you think that God often fails to punish a wicked individual or nation, suffering their arrogance far too long, you are completely mistaken. For note that they can never escape him. The whole world is before him, where then can they hide from his presence? Most certainly he will find them (Ps. 138) (A.V. 139). And if you think that he does not punish or save according to his Word you are quite wrong. His Word can never be undone or destroyed or resisted. For if it could, if God could not always fulfil it, if some other were stronger than he and could resist it, it would not be almighty. But it must always be fulfilled. If it is not fulfilled at the time when you desire, that is not due to any deficiency of power but to the freedom of his will. For if he had to act according to your will, you would be stronger than he and he would have to consult you. But what could be more nonsensical? God will never leave his Word powerless, as he says in Ezekiel 12: "O you that are rebellious, I will say the word and will perform it." And just after: "The word which I have spoken shall be done." The whole teaching of the Gospel is a sure demonstration that what God has promised will certainly be performed. For the Gospel is now an accomplished fact: the One who was promised to the patriarchs, and to the whole race, has now been given to us, and in him we have the assurance of all our hope, as Simeon said in Luke 2. "For what can he withold when he delivered up his own Son for us, and how shall he not with him freely give us all things?" (Rom. 8)

So much then concerning the power or certainty of the Word of God. And now,

The Clarity of the Word of God

Before we begin to speak of the clarity of the Word we will first forestall the objections of those who might resist it, saying: Where is this clarity? If God wants his Word to be understood, why does he speak in parables and riddles? Answer: first note that I do not undertake to give you this reply because I think that we are under no obligation to answer your insolent questions, or that the counsels of God stand in need of vindication by us, or that any man may know the grounds of all God's actions. But so far as the clear testimony of Scripture permits, I will stop your mouths, that you may learn not to blaspheme. (I Tim. 1) The fact that in times past God taught by parables but in these last days has revealed himself fully by the Lord Jesus Christ indicates to us that God wished to give his message to man in a gentle and attractive way; for it is of the nature of that which is presented in parables and proverbs and riddles that it appeals to the understanding of men and brings them to knowledge and indeed increases that knowledge.

We see the shamelessness of sin, we see everywhere covetousness and self-will, and even our righteousness is hypocrisy and men pleasing. But when it is proposed to rebuke and expose and amend our evil deeds by that evangelical doctrine which is the Word of God, we refuse to listen, we stop our ears, and that which God has sent for our good we reject so long and so often that at the last judgment falls. In II Chronicles 36 you will find that time and time again God warned the children of Israel, and when they did not amend at last he let them be taken away captive out of their own land: "And the Lord God of their fathers sent to them by his messengers, rising up betimes, and sending; because he had compassion on his people, and on his dwelling-place: but they mocked the messengers of God, and despised his words, and misused his prophets, until the wrath of the Lord arose against his people, till there was no remedy. Therefore he brought upon them the king of the Chaldees, who slew their young men with the sword in the house of their sanctuary, and had no compassion upon young man or maiden, old man or him that stooped for age: he gave them all into the hand of the Chaldean king. And all the vessels of the house of God, and all the treasures he brought to Babylon. And they burnt the house of God, and brake down the wall of Jerusalem, and burnt all the palaces thereof with fire, and destroyed all the goodly vessels thereof."

Note what calamities ensue when the Word of God is despised and condemned. And note too that failure to believe the Word of God is a sure sign that the wrath of God will soon overtake us. The Word of God and the messenger of the Word are a sweet smell or savour (II Cor. 2); but a savour of life to some, and of death to others.

When the Word of God shines on the human understanding, it enlightens it in such a way that it understands and confesses the Word and knows the certainty of it. This was the inner experience of David, and he spoke of it in Psalm 118 (A.V. 119): "The entrance of thy words, O Lord, giveth light; it giveth understanding unto the simple," meaning, those who in themselves are nothing, resembling the child whom Jesus set in the midst of his disciples to teach them humility (Matt. 18), saying: "Except ye be converted, and become as little children, ye shall not enter into the kingdom of heaven." This concurrent or prevenient clarity of the Word found outward representation at the birth of Christ when the glory of the Lord shone round about the shepherds, and then the angel began to speak with them (Luke 2), and the shepherds believed the words of the angel and found all things as he had said.

I. First then we will demonstrate the clarity of the Word with some illustrations from the Old Testament, then from the New.

1. When Noah was commanded to build the ark he believed God, that he would indeed destroy the whole earth with the flood. That he did so was not due to any human enlightenment, otherwise the many who paid no heed but built houses and married and lived according to their desires would easily have sowed doubt in his mind saying: Ah, but that which was told you is simply a delusion presented to your mind no doubt by an apparition. It may be seen, then, that the Word of God brought with it its own enlightenment, by which Noah knew that it was from God and not from any other. (Gen. 6)

2. When Abraham was commanded to offer up his son Isaac he believed that the voice was the voice of God. That he did so was not by any human enlightenment or perception, for Abraham had been promised salvation in the seed of Isaac. (Gen. 21) But now God commanded him to sacrifice his son Isaac whom he loved. (Gen. 22) Looking at it from a human standpoint Abraham must inevitably have thought: The voice is wrong. It is not of God. For God gave you this son Isaac, by your beloved wife Sarah, as a special token of his friendship. And in so doing he promised that of his seed the Saviour

of all men should be born. But if you slay him, the promise is nullified, and the gift is contradicted; for why did he wish to give him if now that you are beginning to take pleasure in him he wishes to take him away again? No, the voice cannot be of God. It is rather of the devil, to tempt you, and to destroy your best-loved son.

But Abraham did not allow himself to be deflected by such acute questioning and extremity, nor did he follow his own counsel. And that was all of God, who so enlightened him with the Word that he knew it to be the Word of God, even though he was commanded to do something quite contrary to God's former promise. The nerves and bones and muscles of faith all braced themselves. His reason could not accept the command, but faith withstood reason (Rom. 4), saying: The one who promised and gave thy son at the first can raise up again from the dead, or he can use some other means to give to the world the Saviour promised through him. He has the power and the resources to perform all that he has said. And faith gained the victory; note well that it did so by the light which the Word of God had itself brought with it.

3. When Moses had brought the children of Israel into sore straits, that is, as Josephus says, between the mountain, the sea and the enemy, he did not despair. And when the people began to murmur angrily against him (Exod. 14): "Because there were no graves in Egypt, hast thou taken us away to die in the wilderness? Is not this the word that we did tell thee in Egypt?"—he gave them assurance and comfort: "Fear ye not, the Lord shall fight for you and ye shall hold your peace." And he cried secretly in his heart to God. And God answered him: "Lift up thy rod, and stretch out thine hand over the sea, and divide it, and the children of Israel shall go dryshod through the midst of the sea." And the fact that he did not give way to despair, thinking that if the voice of God was only a delusion then all was lost, but recognized with utter certainty the voice of God; that was due, not to the understanding of Moses himself, even though he was learned in all the skill and wisdom of the Egyptians (Acts 7), but to the light of the Word of God, which comes with such clarity and assurance that it is surely known and believed.

4. Jacob knew the voice of the One who stood at the top of the ladder and said: "I am the Lord God of thy father Abraham and Isaac, etc." And the fact that he did so, and did not dismiss the voice as an empty dream, was not due to his own understanding: for where had he seen God, or heard his voice so as to be able to recognize it? But the Word of God gave him such clear understanding that he had no doubt that it was the voice of God, and when he awoke he said: "Truly the Lord is in this place, and I knew it not." Tell me, you that are wise, on the authority of what council or arbiter did he accept God's

Word as true or believe that it was really God's? You see, cavillers, that God's Word brought with it its own clarity and enlightenment, so that he perceived clearly that it was God's and believed steadfastly, and in all the promises which it contained. (Gen. 28)

5. Micaiah recognized as the Word of God the vision which God gave him and the message which accompanied it. And the fact that he did not dismiss it as a phantasy was not of man but of God (I Kings 22). For when 400 prophets stood up against him and contradicted Micaiah, especially Zedekiah who smote him on the cheek and said: "Which way went the Spirit of the Lord from me to speak unto thee?" the opposition of so many prophets of repute and the power of the two kings Ahab and Jehoshaphat ought naturally to have made him think: You cannot possibly be right, you either did not see or understand rightly. And if he had had no other light but that of the understanding there can be little doubt that that is what would have happened.

But the Word of God revealed itself to him and brought with it its own clarity, holding and assuring the understanding in such a way that he held fast by that which he had heard and seen. Tell me, you who are wise—in your own understanding—what would have become of the truth of God if the divine vision and word had been surrendered to the multitude of prophets? And where was the man who pronounced Micaiah to be right, as indeed he was? For the other prophets all promised the two kings victory. And it came to pass according to the saying of the man who was taught of God without any intervention by man, and all the rest spoke falsely.

6. Jeremiah when he was commanded to do so proclaimed the Word of God without fear, even though the people dared to lay hands on him and destroy him because of it. And the fact that he did so was because he had a firm trust in the Word of God and had been taught by God to understand it. (Jer. 26)

7. Through the Word of God in I Kings 18: "Go, shew thyself unto Ahab; and I will send rain upon the earth," Elijah perceived and accomplished the whole matter with the priests of Baal. And the fact that he did so was not of his own understanding, but by divine enlightenment, which taught him how to carry through the whole affair apart altogether from the judgment of man—for Elijah believed that he was completely alone (I Kings 19; Rom. 11)

These seven passages from the Old Testament will be enough to show conclusively that God's Word can be understood by a man without any human direction: not that this is due to man's own understanding, but to the light and Spirit of God, illuminating and inspiring the words in such a way that the light of the divine content is seen in his own light, as it says in Psalm 35 (A.V. 36): "For with thee, Lord, is the well of light, and in thy light shall we see light." And similarly in John 1.

II. We will now turn to the New Testament passages.

In John 1 it says that the Word, or Son, of God was the true light which lighteth every man that cometh into the world. But if the light lighteth every man, undoubtedly it is clarity itself; for however bright and clear a thing may be, it cannot light every man unless it is clarity itself; and if it is to continue lighting every man, it must necessarily be eternal. For all things that are clear are necessarily clear by virtue of clarity. Note, you cavillers, who have no trust in the Scriptures, that it is the Word of God, which is God himself, that lighteth every man. Away then with that light of your own which you would give to the Word of God with your interpreters. In John 3, John the Baptist says: "A man can receive nothing except it be given him from above." If we are to receive and understand anything it must come from above. But if that is so, then no other man can attain it for us. The comprehension and understanding of divine doctrine comes then from above and not from interpreters, who are just as liable to be led into temptation as Balaam was. See II Peter 2.

The Samaritan woman was clever enough to say to Christ (John 4): "I know that Messias cometh, which is called Christ: when he cometh, he will tell us all things." And our theologians have not yet learned that lesson. Ask them if they understand the words: Christ is *caput ecclesiae*, that is, Christ is head of the congregation or church which is his body. They will answer: Yes, they understand them very well, but they may not do so apart from the official pronouncements of men. What poor creatures! Rather than allow themselves to be vanquished by the truth, they deny that they are men, as if they had no ordinary intelligence and did not know the meaning of *caput*. And all that in order to subject the truth to the Caiaphas's and Annas's, its official interpreters. It is not of the slightest account to them that Christ himself said (John 6): "They shall all be taught of God," in the words of Isaiah 54.

But if all Christians are taught of God, why can you not leave them the certainty and freedom of that teaching according to the understanding which God himself has imparted? And that God himself is the teacher of the hearts of believers we learn from Christ in the words immediately following, when he says (John 6): "Every man that hath heard, and hath learned of the Father, cometh unto me." None can come to the Lord Jesus Christ except he has learned to know him of the Father. And note who the teacher is: not *doctores*, not *patres*, not pope, not *cathedra*, nor *concilia*, but the Father of Jesus Christ. And you cannot say, we are taught of men as well. No, for just before he says: "No man can come to me, except my heavenly Father draw him." Even if you hear the gospel of Jesus Christ from an apostle, you cannot act upon it unless the heavenly Father teach and draw you by the Spirit. The words are clear; enlightenment, instruction and assurance are by divine teaching without any intervention on the part of that which is human. And if they are taught of God, they are well taught, with clarity and conviction: if they had first to be taught and assured by men, we should have to describe them as taught of men rather than of God.

But Christ says (John 6): "Therefore I said, that no man can come to me, except it be given him of my Father." But if the Father give it, as the text says, then what need is there of any other teacher, or guide or interpreter? For just after, when Christ asked: "Will ye also go away?" Peter spoke on behalf of all the disciples and his answer was this: "Lord, to whom shall we go? Thou hast the words of eternal life. And we believe and are sure that thou art the Christ, the Son of the living God." Note that the disciples did not know of any other teacher who could minister comfort to them and teach them the words of life. And yet you try to convince me that I am not able to understand his words but must first learn them from some other man.

Again, in John 6, he says: "I am the bread of life. He that cometh to me shall never hunger; and he that believeth on me shall never thirst." In this verse it is quite certain that Christ is speaking of the nourishment of teaching. And this is to be found in himself. He does not say: Go to those who are robed in hoods and purple. For there is no certainty there. It is when God gives a man certainty that he is nourished and refreshed and will never hunger or thirst again. But if he has already been nourished by God, why tell him to turn away from this bread to the Fathers?

Tell me, you fools, when the rabble of carnal divines that you call fathers and bishops pronounce upon a doctrine about which there is doubt, are you enlightened, and do you know with absolute certainty that it is as they say? You answer: Yes. Oh, like the foolish Galatians, who hath bewitched you, that you believe deceitful men and do not believe those words of God which are the truth itself? How are you ever to overcome your obtusness, that you do not believe the Spirit of God who offers you the truth, but put your trust in fallible men, who can do nothing without the grace and spirit of God, subscribing and defending the abuses of which they are guilty? You believe that men can give you certainty, which is no certainty, and you do not believe that God can give it to you. Do you not know that the mind and understanding of every man must be brought into captivity to the obedience and service of God, and not of men? But I see your error, and in God's name I will show it you. You do not know that it is God himself who teaches a man, nor do you know that when God has taught him that man has an inward certainty and assurance. For you do not know what the Gospel really is. He that hath ears to hear, let him hear.

Christ stands before you with open arms, inviting you and saying (Matt. 11): "Come unto me, all ye that labour and are heavy laden, and I will give you rest." O glad news, which brings with it its own light, so that we know and believe that it is true, as we have fully shown above. For the one who says it is a light of the world. He is the way, the truth and the light. In his Word we can never go astray. We can never be deluded or confounded or destroyed in his Word. If you think there can be no assurance or certainty for the soul, listen to the certainty of the Word of God. The soul can be instructed and enlightened—note the clarity—so that it perceives that its whole salvation and righteousness, or justification, is enclosed in Jesus Christ, and it has therefore the sure comfort that when he himself invites and calls you so graciously he will never cast you out. And if you try to turn your soul away from him, saying: Here is Christ, or there, with the soul of the lover in the Song of Songs it will reply: "I held him, and would not let him go." With Magdalene, it has chosen that good part, which is the Lord himself, whose Word alone can give it encouragement and comfort. The [churchmen who are in] orders may rest in their foolish and arrogant boasting; it is we who are the true sons of Mary Magdalene and who lead the contemplative life. They may say what they like, but that is the view of Christ himself.

It was the habit of Christ always to move from earthly things to the necessary doctrine of the Spirit. Illustration: When one said to him: "Thy mother and brethren are without, desiring to speak with thee" (Matt. 12), he drew their attention away from the physical relationship to the relationship with God, and he stretched forth his hand toward his disciples, and said: "Behold, my mother and my brethren. For whosoever shall do the will of my Father which is in heaven, the same is my brother, and sister, and mother." Similarly, when the woman who had been healed cried out: "Blessed is the womb that bare thee, and the paps which thou hast sucked," he gave them instruction about a spiritual and divine birth: "Blessed are they that hear the Word of God, and keep it." It was not that he disowned his mother, but he showed the significance of what she had done. She had received the Word of God, and in the same way those who hear his Word are received and born of the Spirit of God. She bore him as a pure virgin, and in the same way those who receive the Word of God and exercise and nourish themselves in it bring forth wonderful fruit.

And so too when he was with the two sisters they both acted rightly, but he took Mary Magdalene as the starting-point for his lesson, that to choose the good part which shall never be taken away is to receive him and to seek him: for none will ever allow himself to be taken away from him. And for that reason he says to Martha: "Thou art careful and troubled about many things," and then proceeds to the discernment of the one good thing: But one thing is necessary to salvation, and Magdalene has found it; hold it fast. And do you see what that one thing is which is necessary to salvation? Or rather, who that one thing is? Your answer, Christ. You have judged rightly. Hold fast to him and never forsake him. But do you imagine that only you who are cloistered and cowled can find Christ and hear his Word? On the contrary, you are the very last to hear his teaching. For you have laid hold of other things, and you hold fast to those things and find comfort in them.

It says of Magdalene: She heard his Word: that was the good part which she had chosen. And so it is with every soul. Once it is enlightened by God, it can find no assurance or consolation or encouragement in the word of man, but only in the Word of God; and like the disciples in John 6:68 it says: "Lord, to whom shall I go? Thou hast the word of life," that is, Thy Word quickens and restores and gives life, so that the soul is comforted and bound to thee, and cannot trust in any other word but thine.

But when you are called of God you say: How am I to prepare myself, so that I may be certain to attain his grace? I reply: Put all your trust in the Lord Jesus Christ, that is, rest assured that as he suffered for us there is atonement before God for us to all eternity (Romans 5:8-11) The moment you believe, know that you are drawn by God, and that which you regard as your own work is that of the Spirit of God secretly at work within you. For in John 6 Christ says: "No man can come to me, except my Father which is in heaven draw him." Note that if you seek him and find him and cleave fast to him you are drawn by the Father, otherwise you could never have come to him.

The reason why I have spent so long over this proof is this: Those who defend the doctrines of men say: It is quite true that above all other doctrines we ought to esteem the evangelical doctrine, that is, the doctrine which is declared and taught by God—so much they will allow, praise be to God—but we understand the Gospel in a different way. And if there is a conflict between your understanding and ours, someone will have to decide between us and have authority to silence the one who is in error. And this they say in order to subject the interpretation of God's Word to men, thus making it possible to rebuke and suppress the evangelical preachers by Caiaphas and Annas.

In direct contradiction to the teaching of Paul, that all interpretation and thought and experience should be made captive to the will and service of God, they try to subject the doctrine of God to the judgment of men. Now take note of the answer: In the first place, by the Gospel we do not mean only the writings of Matthew, Mark, Luke and

John, but, as we have said, all that God has revealed to man in order
that he may instruct him and give him a sure knowledge of his will.
But God is One, and he is a Spirit of unity, not of discord. Hence we
may see that his words have always a true and natural sense; may God
grant it, no matter how we may wrest them this way or that. And here
I beg you in the name of God not to take it amiss if I draw your attention to a common error. It is that of the majority of those who in these
days oppose the Gospel—for although they dare not admit to doing
this in public, in secret they do everything within their power to that
end.

Listen to what they say. Not everything, they say, is told us in the
Gospels. There are many good things which are never even thought
of in the Gospel. Oh you rascals—you are not instructed or versed in
the Gospel, and you pick out verses from it without regard to their context, and wrest them according to your own desire. It is like breaking
off a flower from its roots and trying to plant it in a garden. But that
is not the way: you must plant it with the roots and the soil in which
it is embedded. And similarly we must leave the Word of God its own
proper nature if its sense is to be the same to all of us. And those who
err in this way we can easily vanquish by leading them back to the
source, though they never come willingly. But some of them are such
confirmed dunces that even when the natural sense is expounded in
such a way that they cannot deny it, they still allege that they cannot
presume to understand it thus unless the Fathers allow that it may so
be understood: on the ground that many expositors will always have
a better understanding than one or two.

Answer: If that is the case, then Christ himself was in error, which
God forbid, for most of the priests of the time held quite a different
view and he had to stand alone. And the apostles were also mistaken,
for they were opposed by whole nations and cities. And even today
the number of unbelievers far outweighs the number of believers: are
we to conclude then that their view is right and ours wrong simply
because they are more numerous than we? No. Consider for yourselves;
truth is not necessarily with the majority. What then of the argument?
It has no force in the present controversy. Indeed, I see that even popes
and councils have sometimes fallen into serious error, especially Ana-
stasius, and Liberius in the Arian heresy. Will you concede that? Yes.
Then your case is lost, for you must allow that if they erred once
there is always the fear that they will err again, and therefore we cannot trust in them with any certainty. Once we have discovered that—
for: *omnis homo mendax*, all men are liars, deceiving and being deceived—we see that ultimately only God himself can teach us the truth
with such certainty that all doubts are removed.

But you say: Where can I find him? Answer: Seek him in your

chamber (Matt. 6), and ask him in secret: he will see you and give you the understanding of divine truth. For as our earlier illustrations show, the doctrine of God can never be learned with greater certainty than when it is taught by God himself, for it comes from God, and he alone is truthful, indeed, he is the truth itself. This is proved by the words of I John 2 to which we have already referred: "Ye need not that any man should teach you." You hear that? We do not need human interpreters, but his anointing, which is the Spirit, teaches us of all things—all things, notice—and therefore it is truth and is no lie.

But at this point they say: I have prayed to him and I am still of the same mind as before. You will not take it amiss if I say: You lie. I allow, of course, that you prayed, but not as you ought. How then should I approach him and pray to him? In this way: First, put away that view of your own which you want to read into Scripture, for it is quite valueless, as I shall clearly show. I know that you will reply that you have worked through the Scriptures and discovered texts which support your opinion. Alas! here we come upon the canker at the heart of all human systems. And it is this: we want to find support in Scripture for our own view, and so we take that view to Scripture, and if we find a text which, however artificially, we can relate to it, we do so, and in that way we wrest Scripture in order to make it say what we want it to say.

Illustration: most of us have our doctrines and interpretations all ready, like someone asking a favour found axe in hand, as though to say: Grant it, or the axe will speak for me. And that is how we come to Scripture. The popes and foolish emperors and kings—suffer me, lords, to speak the truth—have made the majority of our German bishops into temporal princes (beggar-princes as the common man would call them). And in that way they have acquired power. They have a sword in their hands. And with that sword they go to Scripture. And they quote I Peter 2: *regale sacerdotium*: a royal priesthood. And with the sword they now force Peter: what he meant was that the clergy can be temporal princes and wield secular authority. That is what the axe can do. But Peter's real meaning was that the Lord Jesus Christ has called all Christians to kingly honour and to the priesthood, so that they are all priests, offering spiritual gifts, that is, dedicating themselves wholly to God.

Note, then, that we must not approach Scripture like that. But how are we to come? In this way: If you want to speak on any matter, or to learn of it, you must first think like this: Before I say anything or listen to the teaching of man, I will first consult the mind of the Spirit of God (Ps. 84) (A.V. 85): "I will hear what God the Lord will speak." Then you should reverently ask God for his grace, that he may give you his mind and Spirit, so that you will not lay hold of your own opinion but of his. And have a firm trust that he will teach you a right understanding, for all wisdom is of God the Lord. And then go to the written word of the Gospel. But at this point there are many who turn up their noses, not believing that if they have called upon God he will give them a different understanding, his own understanding, for they set so much store by their own human understanding that they are sure there cannot possibly be any other.

But note how falsely you speak. You must be *theodidacti*, that is, taught of God, not of men: that is what the Truth itself said (John 6), and it cannot lie. If you do not believe, and believe firmly, leaving the wisdom of men and resting only in the divine instruction, you have no true faith. And this is not merely my own view, but St. Hilary was of the same opinion, though we do not heed his help: Christ and Peter and Paul and John were all of this opinion. Thus the whole philosophical system called *theologia scholastica* falls to the ground, for it is merely a system evolved by man; and if it occupies the mind of a man, he thinks that the divine teaching is to be judged and perverted in accordance with the infallible teaching received of men.

That this is the case may be seen from the tag: "Where the philosopher leaves off, the theologian begins," which clearly means that when a man is thoroughly instructed in the human doctrine he is better able to interpret the divine, as though our light could illuminate and enlighten the divine light, and in spite of the fact that Christ says (John 5): "I receive not light from men, but I know you, that ye have not the love of God in you." For if they had had his love in them, they would not have believed any word but his: for he is the light that lighteth every man that cometh into the world, and philosophy is not such a light. Proof: who was the philosopher who taught the disciples? They were weak and foolish things when God chose them to proclaim his doctrine and, as St. Paul says (I Cor. 1), to overthrow and confound the wise of this world. Similarly today worldly or human wisdom is confounded and overthrown by those who have attained to the divine doctrine by inward longing and faith.

We see, then, that the simplicity of the disciples was instructed only by God, which is an example to us, that we might seek the form of divine doctrine from God alone. The doctrine of God is never formed more clearly than when it is done by God himself and in the words of God. Indeed, I make bold to say that those who make themselves, that is men, the arbiters of Scripture, make a mockery of trust in the Spirit of God by their design and pretension, seeking to wrest and force the Scriptures according to their own folly. For whenever anyone offers to arbitrate or testify he lays himself open to suspicion. Much more so in this particular case, in which there is one who bids us come to himself, and it is from him that the Word comes, and we resist, not because of the weakness of the Word, but because of the bondage of sinful lusts deceiving us and wresting the Word according to their own caprice.

Again, I know for certain that God teaches me, because I have experienced the fact of it: and to prevent misunderstanding this is what I mean when I say that I know for certain that God teaches me. When I was younger, I gave myself overmuch to human teaching, like others of my day; when about seven or eight years ago I undertook to devote myself entirely to the Scriptures I was always prevented by philosophy and theology. But eventually I came to the point where led by the Word and Spirit of God I saw the need to set aside all these things and to learn the doctrine of God direct from his own Word. Then I began to ask God for light and the Scriptures became far clearer to me—even though I read nothing else—than if I had studied many commentators and expositors. Note that that is always a sure sign of God's leading, for I could never have reached that point by my own feeble understanding. You may see then that my interpretation does not derive from the over-estimation of myself, but the subjection.

You were going to speak, but I will forestall you. What you wanted to say was this: It is a great error to think that you understand a matter perfectly and not to accept advice. Answer: it is indeed if we rest in our own understanding. And that is what you do, for you will not leave your human understanding, but would rather shape the divine understanding to it, if you will forgive me saying so. Hear the words of Paul (I Cor. 2): "But the natural man receiveth not the things of the Spirit of God: for they are foolishness unto him: neither can he know them, because, they are spiritually discerned. But he that is spiritual judgeth all things, yet he himself is judged of none. For who hath known the mind of the Lord, that he may instruct him." These words of Paul are more precious than all the gold upon earth. The natural man is he who brings his own mind: the spiritual man he who does not trust any mind but that which is given by God: he is pure and simple, and quite free from worldly ambition or covetousness or carnal lust.

The spiritual man judges all things, that is, he sees at once whether the doctrine is of God or not. But he is judged of none, that is, even if he is judged, which for this reason he cannot be, he will not let himself be torn or turned aside. No matter how great the human wisdom opposed to him, he replies: Who has told you the mind of God, that you declare things which God himself has not said, that is, you say that you have received them from God, but you lie, otherwise God contradicts himself, for elsewhere he says something quite different. But you would teach God and force him according to your own desires, etc.

Illustration: in Matthew 18 God instituted excommunication: sinners who commit flagrant sin and offend their neighbours are to be cut off from their fellows, just as a dead branch is cut off from a tree or a corrupt member from the body. But when the bishops undertake to collect the debts of usurers by condemning poor Christian people, I do not believe that those people are really bound or excommunicated before God. And why? Because God said: "When thy brother sins," not: "When thy brother is in debt, thou shalt cut him off." And I am certain that that is the teaching of God, and you will not change my view even if you bring against me all the lies and inventions of the canonists or the hypocrisy of the monks or the wrath of bloated prelates or the poison of Rome or the fire of Etna or indeed of hell itself. And even if God did take away his grace and for fear of death I said otherwise with my lips, yet I should still know that this abuse is not pleasing to God and that it has no authority by the divine institution.

But hear the fine way in which they cloak their actions. They say: It is not for debt that we excommunicate them, but for disobedience, as if it were possible to discharge a debt at the very moment the excommunicator demands. And yet that is not our real answer, but this: On what grounds does a Christian owe any obedience to you in a matter of this kind? Did God command you bishops to be the world's debt-collectors? You reply: "*Obedite prepositis vestris*," "be obedient to them that guide you." But does that mean: "Excommunicate men for debt?" In this and in other matters we shall not go astray if we seek only the mind of the Spirit. But if we do not, if we apply our energies to find scriptural support for our own opinions, though they are nothing but leaves and grass, we shall constantly be in error. The will of God is this, that he alone should be the teacher. And I intend to be taught by him and not by men, that is, in respect of doctrine: for in respect of sin and disobedience I will be subject to all. For it is not for us to sit in judgment on Scripture and divine truth, but to let God do his work in and through it, for it is something which we can learn only of God.

Of course, we have to give an account of our understanding of Scripture, but not in such a way that it is forced or wrested according to our own will, but rather so that we are taught by Scripture: and that is my own intention. Paul says (I Cor. 4): "For with me it is a very small thing that I should be judged of you, or of man's judgment. Yea, I judge not mine own self. For I know nothing of myself; yet am I not hereby justified: but he that judgeth me is the Lord." The Lord, who addressed and instructed Paul and all the apostles and all who proclaim his truth, he is to be their judge. We speak of Scripture, and this came from God and not from men. (II Pet. I) How then can man be its judge? Paul describes it as *theopneuston*, that is, inspired or uttered by God. (II Tim. 3) He admits that even the lowliest can speak on Scripture when the leading prophets—that is, teachers—have missed the truth, so long as he is inspired thereto by God. (I Cor. 14) At this point you might ask: Who is to tell me whether he is divinely enlightened or not? The God who enlightens him will enable you to perceive that what he says is of God. You may say: That is not my experience, but if so, take heed lest you be of those who have ears and hear not, as Christ shows from Isaiah. (Matt. 13) Even if God does leave you unenlightened in your own hostile opinion, he will still use you for good. How? In this way. Paul says (I Cor. 11): "For there must be also heresies among you, that they which are approved may be made manifest among you." Your contentiousness is the means of revealing that which otherwise would neither be sought nor asked of God.

And now finally, to make an end of answering objections, our view of the matter is this: that we should hold the Word of God in the highest possible esteem—meaning by the Word of God only that which comes from the Spirit of God—and we should give to it a trust which we cannot give to any other word. For the Word of God is certain and can never fail. It is clear, and will never leave us in darkness. It teaches its own truth. It arises and irradiates the soul of man with full salvation and grace. It gives the soul sure comfort in God. It humbles it, so that it loses and indeed condemns itself and lays hold of God. And in God the soul lives, searching diligently after him and despairing of all creaturely consolation. For God is its only confidence and comfort. Without him it has no rest: it rests in him alone (A.V. Ps. 77): "My soul refused to be comforted; I remembered God, and was refreshed." Blessedness begins indeed in this present time, not essentially, but in the certainty of consoling hope. May God increase it in us more and more, and never suffer us to fall from it. *Amen.*

THOMAS CRANMER 1489–1556

He stepped toward the stake joyfully, almost eagerly. He removed his outer garments and stood before his executioners with head erect. They bound him to the pole and applied the fire to the wood piled around him. The flames licked at him greedily. He thrust his right hand into their amber tongues, crying out, "This hand hath offended!" The member that had signed a statement of recantation, later retracted, was the first to burn in the destroying fire. "This hand hath offended!" It was a confession, a requiem, and a victory note combined. And so died Thomas Cranmer, Archbishop of Canterbury.

Cranmer came into power during the reign of Henry VIII. He had neither the passionate enthusiasm of Luther, the intellectual acumen of Calvin, nor the boldness of Knox, yet he did rise up as one of the chief architects of the English Reformation. Unassuming, flexible, cautious, Cranmer had to work with one of the most egoistic, brutal and sensuous rulers ever to sit upon a throne.

Henry wanted to cast off his Spanish queen, Catherine of Aragon, who had failed to provide him with a male heir, to marry his mistress, Anne Boleyn. He had in fact applied to the pope for an annulment. At the time, 1530, Cranmer was teaching theology at Cambridge. Henry sought his counsel on the problem. Cranmer advised him to submit it to the university divines, reasoning that they were better qualified to decide the legality of the matter than the papacy. Pleased, Henry requested Cranmer to draw up his case and present it to the authorities at Cambridge. The professor accepted the assignment. Later the king made him one of his chaplains, sent him to Rome to plead for the annulment before the pope. Cranmer failed to get the dispensation. The schools, however, decided for the king.

The whole sorry development led to the undoing of a good woman, a widened breach between England and Rome, and Cranmer's promotion to honor. In 1533, Henry appointed him Archbishop of Canterbury, successor to the pro-Catholic Wolsey.

Henry VIII was instrumental in stripping the Church of the secular powers which it had enjoyed for centuries. The reforms were long overdue. Church leaders were immersed in international politics, in the pursuit of preference and benefits, and the extortion of the ecclesiastical courts. Monks bled the people in innumerable ways. The clergy preferred to keep the common people in superstitious darkness, opposing the revival of learning then surging through the land, having *leapt across the Channel from the Continent under the exciting teaching of Colet and Erasmus. Pope and bishops fought the circulation of the Scriptures. John Lord states that two-thirds of the monks lived in concubinage. The Church owned over a third of all the property in England. Henry corrected much of this medieval holdover and immorality, not for religious reasons but for reasons of state. Anticlerical, but not a Protestant, he never broke with Rome on points of doctrine, but continued to hold to the Mass and the dogmas of Catholicism that did not affect his kingship or his reformation of the awakening nation.*

It is difficult to see how the stoutest defenders of Cranmer can clear him of the charge of compromise. He pronounced Henry's marriage to Catherine invalid, his secret marriage to Anne legal and right. In the same vein, he consistently approved the king's subsequent series of divorces and matrimonial unions. As a matter of record, he himself married while in Europe, but kept his wife in seclusion until late in life.

On the opposite side of the coin, it must be said that Cranmer, working quietly and diplomatically, succeeded in reforming the religious instincts of the people. He renounced the authority of the pope, had his name erased from the prayer book, and himself drew up forms of prayer in English which later became the basis of the Book of Common Prayer. He helped draw up the Forty-two Articles of Faith (later abbreviated to the Thirty-nine Articles), introduced the Miles Coverdale Version of the Bible in English into all the churches, and encouraged its circulation. Aware of the value of forming associations with Continental Protestants, he invited some of the very distinguished German refugees to come to England.

In one of Henry's sudden switches of policy, Thomas Cromwell was beheaded, and Cranmer's friend, Hugh Latimer, was sent into retirement. Cranmer managed to stay on. Henry VIII died in 1547. Cranmer, functioning as regent for young Edward VI in Church matters, continued to press his reforms, including a measure legalizing the marriage of the clergy and the publication of the Book of Common Prayer.

Edward passed away suddenly, not yet sixteen, in 1553, and Mary came to the throne. Daughter of the spurned Catherine, a rabid Catholic, she purged all official posts of Protestants. She introduced a minor Inquisition, burned alive over three hundred of her subjects, some of them small children. She restored deposed papist clerics to their posts and monks to their monasteries.

The new queen singled out Thomas Cranmer for her special object of wrath. He had been against the choice of Mary as Edward's successor, having favored the Protestant Lady Jane Grey, a distant relative of the royal line. Mary knew this. She promptly arrested him and had him tried for heresy.

Cranmer's courage deserted him. Under pressure, he signed seven documents declaring that he accepted the doctrines of Catholicism, that he repudiated his own writings as being contrary to the Word of God and therefore heretical. For this he was rewarded with the stake.

His noble confession in death is history now, and Cranmer must be left to the judgment of history—and a merciful God. Like Rembrandt's great paintings, he is a blend of lights and shadows. But who will exclude him from the divine beatitude: "Blessed are the dead which die in the Lord, from henceforth: Yea, saith the Spirit, that they may rest from their labours; and their works do follow them."

Thomas Cranmer (1489–1556)

PERHAPS in all English history there is nowhere else so striking an example of the sublimity of which human nature is capable in its utmost and most shameful weakness as that given by Cranmer in his speech at the stake. As a statesman he had vacillated and hesitated, sacrificing principle repeatedly for the sake of public policy or his own safety and immediate advantage. But it is hard to imagine a nobler death than his. In the full consciousness of his weakness, having put away completely his regard for public opinion, as well as what is generally considered self-respect, he used his last moments to exhort Englishmen who would survive him not to hate and hurt each other, and to entreat those who had "great substance and riches of this world," to have mercy on the weak. Then when no longer allowed to speak, and when the fire had been lighted, he gave the memorable exhibition of self-mastery, which redeemed him from surviving in history as a mere weakling, and made him one of the great heroic figures of the English race. The scene after he was silenced is thus described by his biographer, John Strype, writing in 1693 on the authority of eye-witnesses:—

"And here, being admonished of his recantation and dissembling, he said, 'Alas, my Lord, I have been a man that all my life loved plainness, and never dissembled till now against the truth; which I am most sorry for.' He added thereunto, that, for the sacrament, he believed as he had taught in his book against the Bishop of Winchester. And here he was suffered to speak no more.

"So that his speech contained chiefly three points; love to God, love to the King, love to the neighbor. In the which talk he held men in very suspense, which all depended upon the conclusion; where he so far deceived all men's expectation, that, at the hearing thereof, they were much amazed; and let him go on awhile, till my Lord Williams bade him play the Christen man, and remember himself. To whom he answered that he so did; for now he spake truth.

"Then he was carried away; and a great number, that did run to see him go so wickedly to his death, ran after him, exhorting him while time was to remember himself. And one Friar John, a godly and well-learned man, all the way traveled with him to reduce him. But it would not be. What they said in particular I cannot tell, but the effect appeared in the end; for at the stake he professed that he died in all such opinions as he had taught, and oft repented him of his recantation.

"Coming to the stake with a cheerful countenance and willing mind, he put off his garments with haste, and stood upright in his shirt; and a bachelor of divinity, named Elye, of Brazen-nose College, labored to convert him to his former recantation, he repented it right sore, because he knew it was against the truth; with other words more. Whereupon the Lord Williams cried, 'Make short, make short.' Then the Bishop took certain of his friends by the hand. But the bachelor of divinity refused to take him by the hand, and blamed all others that so did, and said he was sorry that ever he came in his company. And yet again he required him to agree to his former recantation. And the Bishop answered (shewing his hand), 'This is the hand that wrote it, and therefore shall it suffer first punishment.'

"Fire being now put to him, he stretched out his right hand, and thrust it into the flame, and held it there a good space, before the fire came to any other part of his body; where his hand was seen of every man sensibly burning, crying with a loud voice, 'This hand hath offended.' As soon as the fire got up, he was very soon dead, never stirring or crying all the while."—(From 'Memorials of Thomas Cranmer,' by John Strype, M.A. 1693.)

Three centuries after the best and greatest man of any period has done his work, the world can look back upon it and see that it is not given to any man to be "eternally right" in anything whatever except in such renunciation and self-sacrifice as Cranmer, the martyr, showed at the last in his condemnation of Cranmer, the statesman, Cranmer the prelate, and Cranmer the politician.

He was born in Nottinghamshire, July 2d, 1489, and died at Oxford, March 21st, 1556. Educated at Cambridge, he became one of the most learned men of his day, and when, in 1529, he used his learning to enable Henry VIII to divorce Catharine of Aragon, he was sent to the tower for treason, and, subsequently, to the stake, on a charge of heresy; though, of course, as generally happened in such cases during that period, the motive back of the charge of spiritual error was purely one of politics. Cranmer had pledged himself to respect the will of Henry VIII, by which the succession devolved upon Mary, and his breach of faith in violating this pledge has been called perjury, as his frequent shifting of position from the beginning of his political career up to the time when he collected all his faculties in his supreme effort at the stake has been called cowardice and lack of moral character. Macaulay denies, as others have done, his right to be called a martyr, but even if his life had been that of a coward in the last stages of moral infirmity up to the time when "with his hand seen by every one to be sensibly burning, he cried with a loud voice, 'This hand hath offended,' " and so died, his death would remain nevertheless one of the most admirable in history, so remarkable by reason of its very contrast with his life, that we can hardly imagine such strength possible for humanity, except as an antithesis to the extreme weakness, in repenting which Cranmer glorified himself and that common humanity of which his weaknesses were characteristic.

His Speech at the Stake
(As Reported in 'The Memorials,' by John Strype, 1693)

Good people, I had intended indeed to desire you to pray for me; which because Mr. Doctor hath desired, and you have done already, I thank you most heartily for it. And now will I pray for myself, as I could best devise for mine own comfort and say the prayer, word for word, as I have here written it.

(And he read it standing; and afterwards kneeled down and said the Lord's Prayer, and all the people on their knees devoutedly praying with him. His prayer was thus:)—

Father of heaven; O Son of God, redeemer of the world; O Holy Ghost, proceeding from them both, three persons and one God, have mercy upon me, most wretched caitiff and miserable sinner. I, who have offended both heaven and earth, and more grievously than any tongue can express, whither then may I go, or whither should I fly for succor? To heaven I may be ashamed to lift up mine eyes; and in earth I find no refuge. What shall I then do? shall I despair? God forbid. O good God, thou art merciful, and refusest none that come unto thee for succor. To thee, therefore, do I run. To thee do I humble myself saying, O Lord God, my sins be great; but yet have mercy upon me for thy great mercy. O God the Son, thou wast not made man, this great mystery was not wrought, for few or small offenses. Nor thou didst not give thy Son unto death, O God the Father, for our little and small sins only, but for all the greatest sins of the world, so that the sinner return unto thee with a penitent heart, as I do here at this present. Wherefore have mercy upon me, O Lord, whose property is always to have mercy. For although my sins be great, yet thy mercy is greater. I crave nothing, O Lord, for mine own merits, but for thy Name's sake, that it may be glorified thereby, and for thy dear Son, Jesus Christ's sake.

[Then rising, he said:] All men desire, good people, at the time of their deaths, to give some good exhortation that others may remember after their deaths, and be the better thereby. So I beseech God grant me grace that I may speak something, at this my departing, whereby God may be glorified and you edified.

First, it is an heavy case to see that many folks be so much doted upon the love of this false world, and so careful for it, that for the love of God, or the love of the world to come, they seem to care very little or nothing therefor. This shall be my first exhortation. That you set not overmuch by this false glozing world, but upon God and the world to come; and learn to know what this lesson meaneth, which St. John teacheth, that the love of this world is hatred against God.

The second exhortation is that next unto God you obey your King and Queen willingly and gladly, without murmur and grudging, and not for fear of them only, but much more for the fear of God, knowing that they be God's ministers, appointed by God to rule and govern you. And therefore whoso resisteth them, resisteth God's ordinance.

The third exhortation is, That you love altogether like brethern and sisters. For, alas! pity it is to see what contention and hatred one Christian man hath toward another; not taking each other as sisters and brothers, but rather as strangers and mortal enemies. But I pray you learn and bear well away this one lesson, To do good to all men as much as in you lieth, and to hurt no man, no more than you would hurt your own natural and loving brother or sister. For this you may be sure of, that whosoever hateth any person, and goeth about maliciously to hinder or hurt him, surely, and without all doubt, God is not with that man, although he think himself never so much in God's favor.

The fourth exhortation shall be to them that have great substance and riches of this world, that they will well consider and weigh those sayings of the Scripture. One is of our Saviour Christ himself, who sayeth, It is hard for a rich man to enter into heaven; a sore saying, and yet spoken by him that knew the truth. The second is of St. John, whose saying is this, He that hath the substance of this world and seeth his brother in necessity, and shutteth up his mercy from him, how can he say he loveth God? Much more might I speak of every part; but time sufficeth not. I do but put you in remembrance of these things. Let all them that be rich ponder well those sentences; for if ever they had any occasion to show their charity they have now at this present, the poor people being so many, and victuals so dear. For though I have been long in prison, yet I have heard of the great penury of the poor. Consider that which is given to the poor is given to God; whom we have not otherwise present corporally with us, but in the poor.

And now, for so much as I am come to the last end of my life, whereupon hangeth all my life passed and my life to come, either to live with my Saviour Christ in heaven in joy, or else to be in pain ever with wicked devils in hell; and I see before mine eyes presently either heaven ready to receive me, or hell ready to swallow me up; I shall therefore declare unto you my very faith, how I believe, without color or dissimulation; for now is no time to dissemble, whatsoever I have written in times past.

First, I believe in God the Father Almighty, maker of heaven and earth, and every article of the catholic faith, every word and sentence taught by our Saviour Christ, his Apostles and Prophets, in the Old and New Testaments.

And now I come to the great thing that troubleth my conscience, more than any other thing that ever I said or did in my life; and that is, the setting abroad of writings contrary to the truth. Which here now I renounce and refuse, as things written with my hand, contrary to the truth which I thought in my heart, and writ for fear of death, and to save my life, if it might be; and that is, all such bills, which I have written or signed with mine own hand since by degradation, wherein I have written many things untrue. And forasmuch as my hand offended in writing contrary to my heart, therefore my hand shall be punished; for if I may come to the fire it shall be first burned. And as for the Pope, I refuse him as Christ's enemy and Anti-christ, with all his false doctrine.

JOHN KNOX 1505-1572

On February 29, 1518, a thirteen-year-old boy watched Patrick Hamilton, a young Scot of high birth and scholarly attainments, meet his death at the stake. The horrible spectacle engraved a question in the boy's mind, written there with the point of a diamond: "Wherefore was Master Patrick Hamilton burned?" He asked the question again and again until he learned the answer: Patrick Hamilton had forfeited his life because he championed certain Protestant doctrines espoused on the Continent by Martin Luther.

John Knox read Luther and Augustine, and absorbed their views with all the intensity of his vigorous soul. He studied at St. Andrews, eventually entered the priesthood, and for some time preached evangelical tenets at Haddington.

A band of Protestants, goaded to a pitch of madness because of the inquisitorial tortures initiated by Cardinal Beaton, rose up and killed the prelate. John Knox was among the assailants. They took refuge in the Castle of St. Andrews where for two years they were besieged by French soldiers, Scotland then being a partner with France in an anti-English coalition. When the refugees at last surrendered, Knox and his friends were taken to France and sentenced to service on a galley ship.

Even under harsh conditions he remained eager to redeem the time. He revised a tract on justification by faith written by a French Protestant. Always he maintained a cheerful attitude toward life, encouraging his fellow sufferers by his buoyant spirits. His health failed, and he was swept close to the vestibule of death, but he revived and predicted that some day he would preach in St. Andrews.

After his release, Knox went to England where Protestantism under Edward VI had been given genuine stimulation. He preached in two parishes. In 1551 he received an appointment to the office of chaplaincy to the king. By his honesty and blunt eloquence he made a powerful impression on English royalty. Then Edward died and Mary, eldest daughter of Henry VIII, later to earn the name "Bloody Mary," came to the throne. For safety's sake Knox crossed the English Channel and settled on the Continent. In Geneva he met and held lengthy discussions with Calvin, thereby enlarging his fund of knowledge of Reformed doctrine and objectives.

Returning to Scotland, he married his niece, preached at St. Andrews (fulfilling his prophecy) and at Perth and Edinburgh. He was successful in winning these and other communities over to the Protestant cause. The Scottish Reformation forged ahead.

It was inevitable that Knox should become entangled with the Catholic Mary, Queen of Scots. There developed a complex of cross currents involving political maneuvering, intrigue, quarrels, a cold war, a shooting war, a division of ecclesiastical property, and a crushing defeat for Catholicism. At the Treaty of Leith (1560) three important decisions were made: (1) The authority of the papacy was abolished. (2) All acts contrary to the Confession of Faith were abrogated. (3) Only two sacraments were recognized, and Communion must be served in conformity with Protestant ritual, otherwise severe punishment would be inflicted.

Wide disagreement exists when it comes to appraising the man John Knox. He has been called a bigot, an opportunist, a self-seeking politician in priest's clothing, a rabble-rouser. On the other hand, his admirers have looked upon him as Scotland's deliverer, a heroic leader, the maker of the Scottish Reformation. There is, however, perfect agreement on one point: the important place he merits in the history of Scotland. No serious historian will deny that John Knox left an indelible stamp on that country, or that he radically altered its destiny.

His power found expression in the spoken word and in the written word. In the pulpit he was a son of thunder. It is said that his sermons had the importance of public manifestoes. "The voice of one man is able, in one hour, to put more life in us than six hundred trumpets continually blasting in our ears," Randolph declared.

His pen was no less potent than his tongue. He helped produce both The Confession of Faith and the Book of Discipline. His History of the Reformation in Scotland, a quaint and intimate account of the triumph of Protestantism, is his most massive work. He published controversial pamphlets such as Appellation to the Nobility and Estates of Scotland, and First Blast of the Trumpet against the Monstrous Regiment of Women. (He married twice.)

At his funeral, the Earl of Morton, Regent of Scotland, paid him his finest tribute: "Here lies one who never flattered nor feared any flesh."

The First Temptation of Christ

JOHN KNOX

Then Jesus was led by the Spirit into the desert that He should be tempted of the devil. (Matt. 4:1)

THE CAUSE moving me to treat of this place of Scripture is, that such as by the inscrutable providence of God fall into divers temptations, judge not themselves by reason thereof to be less acceptable in God's presence. But, on the contrary, having the way prepared to victory by Christ Jesus, they shall not fear above measure the crafty assaults of that subtle serpent Satan. But with joy and bold courage, having such a guide as here is pointed forth, such a champion, and such weapons as here are to be found, (if with obedience we will hear, and unfeigned faith believe), we may assure ourselves of God's present favour, and of final victory, by the means of Him, Who, for our safeguard and deliverance, entered in the battle, and triumphed over His adversary, and all his raging fury. And that this being heard and understood, may the better be kept in memory; this order, by God's grace, we purpose to observe, in treating the matter. *First,* What this word temptation meaneth, and how it is used within the Scripture. *Secondly,* Who is here tempted, and at what time this temptation happened. *Thirdly,* How and by what means He was tempted. *Fourthly,* Why He should suffer these temptations, and what fruit ensues to us from the same.

First, Temptation, or to tempt, in the Scriptures of God, is called to try, to prove, or to assault the valour, the power, the will, the pleasure, or the wisdom—whether it be of God, or of creatures. And it is taken sometimes in good part, as when it is said that God tempted Abraham; God tempted the people of Israel; that is, God did try and examine them, not for His own knowledge, to Whom nothing is hid, but to certify others how obedient Abraham was to God's commandment, and how weak and inferior the Israelites were in their journey towards the promised land.

And this temptation is always good, because it proceeds immediately from God, to open and make manifest the secret motions of men's hearts, the puissance and power of God's Word, and the great lenity and gentleness of God towards the iniquities (yea, horrible sins and rebellions) of those whom He hath received into His regimen and care.

For who could have believed that the bare word of God could so have moved the heart and affections of Abraham, that to obey God's commandment he determined to kill, with his own hand, his best beloved son Isaac? Who could have trusted that, so many torments as Job suffered, he should not speak in all his great temptations one foolish word against God? Or who could have thought that God so mercifully should have pardoned so many, and so manifest transgressions committed by His people in the desert, and yet that His mercy never utterly left them, but still continued with them, till at length He performed His promise made to Abraham?

Who, I say, would have been persuaded of these things, unless by trials and temptations taken of His creatures by God, they had come by revelation made in His holy Scriptures to our knowledge. And so this kind of temptation is profitable, good, and necessary, as a thing proceeding from God, who is the Fountain of all goodness, to the manifestation of His glory, and to the profit of the sufferer, however the flesh may judge in the hour of temptation. Otherwise temptation, or to tempt, is taken in evil part; that is, he that assaults or assails intends destruction and confusion to him that is assaulted. As when Satan tempted the woman in the garden, Job by divers tribulations, and David by adultery. The scribes and Pharisees tempted Christ by divers means, questions, and subtleties. And of this matter, saith St. James, "God tempteth no man"; that is, by temptation proceeding immediately from Him, He intends no man's destruction.

And here you shall note, that although Satan appears sometimes to prevail against God's elect, yet he is ever frustrated of his final purpose. By temptation he led Eve and David from the obedience of God, but he could not retain them for ever under his thraldom. Power was granted to him to spoil Job of his substance and children, and to strike his body with a plague and sickness most vile and fearful, but he could not compel his mouth to blaspheme God's majesty; and, therefore, although we are laid open sometimes, as it were, to tribulation for a time, it is that when he has poured forth the venom of his malice against God's elect, it may return to his own confusion, and that the deliverance of God's children may be more to His glory, and the comfort of the afflicted: knowing that His hand is so powerful, His mercy and good-will so prompt, that He delivers His little ones from their cruel enemy, even as David did his sheep and lambs from the mouth of the lion. For a benefit received in extreme danger more moves us than the preservation from ten thousand perils, so that we fall not into them. And yet to preserve from dangers and perils so that we fall not into them, whether they are of body or spirit, is no less the work of God, than to deliver from them; but the weakness of our faith does not perceive it; this I leave at the present.

Also; to tempt means simply to prove, or try without any determinate purpose of profit or damage to ensue; as when the mind doubteth of anything, and therein desires to be satisfied, without great love or extreme hatred of the thing that is tempted or tried. As the queen of Sheba came to tempt Solomon in subtle questions. David tempted, that is, tried himself if he could go in harness. (I Sam. 17) And Gideon said, "Let not thine anger kindle against me, if I tempt thee this once again." This famous queen, not fully trusting the report and fame that was spread of Solomon, by subtle questions desired to prove his wisdom; at the first, neither extremely hating nor fervently loving the person of the king. And David, as a man not accustomed to harness, would try how he was able to go, and behave and fashion himself therein, before he would hazard battle with Goliath so armed. And Gideon, not satisfied in his conscience by the first sign that he received, desired, without contempt or hatred of God, a second time to be certified of his vocation. In this sense must the apostle be expounded when he commands us to tempt, that is, to try and examine ourselves, if we stand in the faith. Thus much for the term.

Now to the Person tempted, and to the time and place of His temptation. The Person tempted is the only well-beloved Son of God; the time was immediately after His baptism; and the place was the desert or wilderness. But that we derive advantage from what is related, we must consider the same more profoundly. That the Son of God was thus tempted gives instruction to us, that temptations, although they be ever so grievous and fearful, do not separate us from God's favour and mercy, but rather declare the great graces of God to appertain to us, which makes Satan to rage as a roaring lion; for against none does he so fiercely fight, as against those of whose hearts Christ has taken possession.

The time of Christ's temptation is here most diligently to be noted. And that was, as Mark and Luke witness, immediately after the voice of God the Father had commended His Son to the world, and had visibly pointed to Him by the sign of the Holy Spirit; He was led or moved by the Spirit to go to a wilderness, where forty days He remained fasting among the wild beasts. This Spirit which led Christ into the wilderness was not the devil, but the Holy Spirit of God the Father, by whom Christ, as touching His human and manly nature, was conducted and led; likewise by the same Spirit He was strengthened and made strong, and, finally, raised up from the dead.

The Spirit of God, I say, led Christ to the place of His battle, where He endured the combat for the whole forty days and nights. As Luke saith, "He was tempted," but in the end most vehemently, after His continual fasting, and that He began to be hungry. Upon this forty days and this fasting of Christ do our papists found and build their

Lent; for, say they, all the actions of Christ are our instructions; what He did we ought to follow. But He fasted forty days, therefore we ought to do the like. I answer, that if we ought to follow all Christ's actions, then ought we neither to eat or drink for the space of forty days, for so fasted Christ: we ought to go upon the waters with our feet; to cast out devils by our word; to heal and cure all sorts of maladies; to call again the dead to life; for so did Christ.

This I write only that men may see the vanity of those who, boasting themselves of wisdom, are become mad fools. Did Christ fast thus forty days to teach us superstitious fasting? Can the papists assure me, or any other man, which were the forty days that Christ fasted? plain it is He fasted the forty days and nights that immediately followed His baptism, but which they were, or in what month was the day of His baptism, Scripture does not express and although the day were expressed, am I or any Christian bound to counterfeit Christ's actions as the ape counterfeits the act or work of man? He Himself requires no such obedience of His true followers, but saith to the apostles, "Go and preach the gospel to all nations, baptizing them in the name of the Father, the Son, and the Holy Ghost; commanding them to observe and keep all that I have commanded you." Here Christ Jesus requires the observance of His precepts and commandments not of His actions, except in so far He had also commanded them; and so must the apostle be understood when He saith, "Be followers of Christ, for Christ hath suffered for us, that we should follow His footstep," which cannot be understood of every action of Christ, either in the mystery of our redemption, or in His actions and marvellous works, but only of those which He hath commanded us to observe.

But where the papists are so diligent in establishing their dreams and fantasies, they lose the profit that here is to be gathered,—that is, why Christ fasted those forty days; which were a doctrine more necessary for Christians, than to corrupt the simple hearts with superstition, as though the wisdom of God, Christ Jesus, had taught us no other mystery by His fasting than the abstinence from flesh, or once on the day to eat flesh for the space of forty days. God hath taken a just vengeance upon the pride of such men, while He thus confounds the wisdom of those that do most glory in wisdom, and strikes with blindness such as will be guides and lanterns to the feet of others, and yet refuse themselves to hear or follow the light of God's word. From such deliver thy poor flock, O Lord!

The causes of Christ's fasting these forty days I find chiefly to be two: The first, to witness to the world the dignity and excellence of His vocation, which Christ, after His baptism, was to take upon Him openly: The other, to declare that He entered into battle willingly for our cause, and does, as it were, provoke His adversary to assault Him, although Christ Jesus, in the eternal counsel of His Father, was appointed to be the Prince of peace, the angel (that is, the messenger) of His testament, and He alone that could fight our battles for us, yet He did not enter in execution of it, in the sight of men, till He was commended to mankind by the voice of His heavenly Father; and as He was placed and anointed by the Holy Ghost by a visible sign given to the eyes of men. After which time He was led to the desert, and fasted, as before is said; and this He did to teach us with what fear, carefulness, and reverence the messengers of the word ought to enter on their vocation which is not only most excellent (for who is worthy to be God's ambassador?) but also subject to most extreme troubles and dangers. For he that is appointed pastor, watchman, or preacher, if he feed not with his whole power, if he warn and admonish not when he sees the snare come, and if, in doctrine, he divide not the word righteously, the blood and souls of those that perish for lack of food, admonition, and doctrine, shall be required of his hand.

But to our purpose; that Christ exceeded not the space of forty days in His fasting, He did it to the imitation of Moses and Elias; of whom, the one before the receiving of the law, and the other before the communication and reasoning which He had with God in mount Horeb, in which he was commanded to anoint Hazael king over Syria, and Jehu king over Israel, and Elisha to be prophet, fasted the same number of days. The events that ensued and followed this supernatural fasting of these two servants of God, Moses and Elias, impaired and diminished the tyranny and kingdom of Satan.

For by the law came the knowledge of sin, the damnation of such impieties, specially of idolatry, and such as the devil had invented; and finally, by the law came such a revelation of God's will that no man could justly afterward excuse his sin by ignorance, by which the devil before had blinded many. So that the law, although it might not renew and purge the heart, for that the Spirit of Christ Jesus worketh by faith only, yet it was a bridle that did hinder and stay the rage of external wickedness in many, and was a schoolmaster that led unto Christ. For when man can find no power in himself to do that which is commanded, and perfectly understands, and when he believes that the curse of God is pronounced against all those that abide not in every thing that is commanded in God's law to do them—the man, I say, that understands, and knows his own corrupt nature and God's severe judgment, most gladly will receive the free redemption offered by Christ Jesus, which is the only victory that overthrows Satan and his power.

And so by the giving of the law God greatly weakened, impaired, and made frail the tyranny and kingdom of the devil. In the days of Elias, the devil had so prevailed that kings and rulers made open war against God, killing His prophets, destroying His ordinances, and building up idolatry; which did so prevail, that the prophet complained that of all the true fearers and worshippers of God he was left alone, and wicked Jezebel sought his life also. After this, his fasting and complaint, he was sent by God to anoint the persons aforenamed, who took such vengeance upon the wicked and obstinate idolaters, that he who escaped the sword of Hazael fell into the hands of Jehu, and those whom Jehu left, escaped not God's vengeance under Elisha. The remembrance of this was fearful to Satan, for, at the coming of Christ Jesus, impiety was in the highest degree amongst those that pretended most knowledge of God's will; and Satan was at such rest in his kingdom, that the priests, scribes, and Pharisees had taken away the key of knowledge; that is, they had so obscured and darkened God's holy Scriptures, by false glosses and vain traditions, that neither would they enter themselves into the kingdom of God, nor suffer and permit others to enter; but with violence restrained, and with tyranny struck back from the right way, that is, from Christ Jesus Himself, such as would have entered into the possession of life everlasting by Him.

Satan, I say, having such dominion over the chief rulers of the visible church, and espying in Christ such graces as before he had not seen in man, and considering Him to follow in fasting the footsteps of Moses and Elias, no doubt greatly feared that the quietness and rest of his most obedient servants, the priest and their adherents, would be troubled by Christ. And, therefore, by all engines and craft he assaults Him to see what advantage he could have of Him. And Christ did not repel him, as by the power of His Godhead He might have done, that he should not tempt Him, but permitted him to spend all his artillery, and received the strokes and assaults of Satan's temptations in His own body, to the end He might weaken and enfeeble the strength and tyrannous power of our adversary by His long suffering.

For thus, methinks, our Master and Champion, Christ Jesus, provoked our enemy to battle; "Satan, thou gloriest of thy power and victories over mankind, that there is none able to withstand thy assaults, nor escape thy darts, but at one time or other thou givest him a wound: lo, I am a Man like to my brethren, having flesh and blood, and all properties of man's nature (sin, which is thy venom, excepted:) tempt, try, and assault Me; I offer you here a place most convenient— the wilderness. There shall be no mortal to comfort Me against thy assaults; thou shalt have time sufficient; do what thou canst, I shall not fly the place of battle. If thou become victor, thou shalt still continue in possession of thy kingdom in this wretched world: but if thou canst not prevail against Me, then must thy prey and unjust spoil be taken from thee: thou must grant thyself vanquished and confounded, and must be compelled to leave off from all accusation of the members of My body; for to them appertains the fruit of My battle, My victory is theirs, as I am appointed to take the punishment of their sins in My body."

O dear sisters, what comfort ought the remembrance of these signs to be to our hearts! Christ Jesus hath fought our battle; He Himself hath taken us into His care and protection; however the devil may rage by temptations, be they spiritual or corporeal, he is not able to bereave us out of the hand of the Almighty Son of God. To Him be all glory for His mercies most abundantly poured upon us.

There remains yet to be spoken of, the *time* when our Lord was tempted, which began immediately after His baptism. Whereupon we have to note and mark, that although the malice of Satan never ceases, but always seeks for means to trouble the godly, yet sometimes he rages more fiercely than others, and that is commonly when God begins to manifest His love and favour to any of His children, and at the end of their battle, when they are nearest to obtain final victory. The devil, no doubt, did at all times envy the humble spirit that was in Abel, but he did not stir up the cruel heart of Cain against him till God declared His favour towards him, by accepting his sacrifice. The same we find in Jacob, Joseph, David, and most evidently in Christ Jesus. How Satan raged at the tidings of Christ's nativity! what blood he caused to be shed on purpose to have murdered Christ in His infancy! The evangelist St. Matthew witnesses that in all the coasts and borders of Bethlehem the children of two years old and or less age were murdered without mercy. A fearful spectacle and horrid example of insolent and unaccustomed tyranny!

And what is the cause moving Satan thus to rage against innocents, considering that, by reason of their imperfections, they could not hurt his kingdom at that instant? Oh! the crafty eye of Satan looked further than to the present time; he heard reports by the three wise men, that they had learned, by the appearance of a star, that the King of the Jews was born; and he was not ignorant that the time prophesied of Christ's coming was then instant; for a stranger was clad with the crown and sceptre in the kingdom of Judah. The angel had declared the glad tidings to the shepherds, that a Saviour, which was Christ the Lord, was born in the city of David. All these tidings inflamed the wrath and malice of Satan, for he perfectly understood that the coming of the promised Seed was appointed to his confusion, and to the breaking down of his head and tyranny; and therefore he raged most cruelly, even at the first hearing of Christ's birth, thinking that although he could not hinder nor withstand His coming, yet he could shorten His days upon earth, lest by long life and peaceable quietness in it, the number of good men, by Christ's doctrine and virtuous life, should be multiplied; and so he strove to cut Him away among the other children before He could open His mouth on His Father's message.

Oh cruel serpent! in vain dost thou spend thy venom, for the days of God's elect thou canst not shorten! And when the wheat is fallen on the ground, then doth it most multiply. But from these things mark, dear sisters, what hath been the practice of the devil from the beginning—most cruelly to rage against God's children, when God begins to show them His mercy. And, therefore, marvel not, dearly beloved, although the like come unto you. If Satan fume or roar against you, whether it be against your bodies by persecution, or inwardly in your conscience by a spiritual battle, be not discouraged, as though you were less acceptable in God's presence, or as if Satan might at any time prevail against you. No: your temptations and storms that arise so suddenly, argue and witness that the seed which is sown, is fallen in good ground, begins to take root, and shall, by God's grace, bring forth fruit abundantly in due season and convenient time. That is it which Satan fears, and therefore thus he rages, and shall rage against you, thinking that if he can repulse you now suddenly in the beginning, that then you shall be at all times an easy prey, never able to resist his assaults.

But as my hope is good, so shall my prayer be, that so you may be strengthened, that the world and Satan himself may perceive or understand that God fights your battle. For you remember, sisters, that being present with you and treating of the same place, I admonished you that Satan could not long sleep when his kingdom was threatened. And therefore I willed you, if you were in mind to continue with Christ, to prepare yourselves for the day of temptation. The person of the speaker is wretched, miserable, and nothing to be regarded, but the things that were spoken, are the infallible and eternal truth of God; without observation of which, life neither can nor shall come to mankind. God grant you continuance to the end.

This much have I briefly spoken of the temptation of Christ Jesus, who was tempted; and of the time and place of His temptation. Now remains to be spoken how He was tempted, and by what means. The most part of expositors think that all this temptation was in spirit and imagination only, the corporeal senses being nothing moved. I will contend with no man in such cases, but patiently will I suffer every man to abound in his own knowledge; and without prejudice of any man's estimations, I offer my judgment to be weighed and considered by Christian charity. It appears to me by the plain text, that Christ suffered this temptation in body and spirit. Likewise, as the hunger which Christ suffered, and desert in which He remained, were not things offered to the imagination, but that the body did verily remain in the wilderness among beasts, and after forty days did hunger and

faint for lack of food; so the external ear did hear the tempting words
of Satan, which entered into the knowledge of the soul, and which
repelling the venom of such temptations, caused the tongue to speak
and confute Satan, to our unspeakable comfort and consolation.

It appears also that the body of Christ Jesus was carried by Satan
from the wilderness unto the temple of Jerusalem, and that it was placed
upon the pinnacle of the same temple, from whence it was carried to a
high mountain and there tempted. If any man can show the contrary
hereof by the plain Scriptures of God, with all submission and thanksgiving, I will prefer His judgment to my own; but if the matter stand
only in probability and opinion of men, then it is lawful for me to
believe as the Scripture here speaks. That is, that Satan spake and Christ
answered, and Satan took Him and carried Him from one place to
another. Besides the evidence of the text affirming that Satan was permitted to carry the body of Christ from place to place, and yet was
not permitted to execute any further tyranny against it, is most singular
comfort to such as are afflicted or troubled in body or spirit. The weak
and feeble conscience of man under such temptations, commonly gathers
and collects a false consequence. For man reasons thus: The body
or the spirit is vexed by assaults and temptations of Satan, and he
troubles or molests it, therefore God is angry with it, and takes no
care of it. I answer, Tribulations or grievous vexations of body or of
mind are never signs of God's displeasure against the sufferer, neither
yet does it follow that God has cast away the care of His creatures,
because He permits them to be molested and vexed for a time. For if
any sort of tribulation were the infallible sign of God's displeasure,
then should we condemn the best beloved children of God. But of this
we may speak hereafter.

Now to the temptation. Verse 2nd. "And when he had fasted forty
days and forty nights, he was afterwards hungry." Verse 3rd. "Then
came to Him the tempter, and said, "If you be the Son of God, command that these stones be made bread," etc. Why Christ fasted forty
days and would not exceed the same, without sense and feeling of
hunger, is before touched upon, that is, He would provoke the devil
to battle by the wilderness and long abstinence, but He would not
usurp or arrogate any more to Himself in that case than God had
wrought with others, His servants and messengers before. But Christ
Jesus (as St. Augustine more amply declares) without feeling of hunger,
might have endured the whole year, or to time without end, as well as
He did endure the space of forty days. For the nature of mankind was
sustained those forty days by the invisible power of God, which is at
all times of equal power. But Christ, willing to offer further occasion
to Satan to proceed in tempting of Him, permitted the human nature
to crave earnestly that which it lacked, that is to say, refreshing of

meat; which Satan perceiving took occasion, as before, to tempt and assault.

Some judge that Satan tempted Christ to gluttony but this appears little to agree with the purpose of the Holy Ghost; who shows us this history to let us understand that Satan never ceases to oppugn [impugn] the children of God, but continually, by one mean or other, drives or provokes them to some wicked opinions of their God; and to have them desire stones to be converted into bread, or to desire hunger to be satisfied, has never been sin, nor yet a wicked opinion of God. And therefore I doubt not but the temptation was more spiritual, more subtle and more dangerous. Satan had respect to the voice of God, Who had pronounced Christ to be His well-beloved Son, etc. Against this voice he fights, as his nature is ever to do against the assured and immutable Word of God: for such is his malice against God, and against His chosen children, that where and to whom God pronounces love and mercy, to these he threatens displeasure and damnation; and where God threatens death there is he bold to pronounce life; and for this cause is Satan called a liar from the beginning.

And so the purpose of Satan was to drive Christ into desperation, that He should not believe the former voice of God His Father; which appears to be the meaning of this temptation: Thou hast heard," would Satan say, "a voice proclaimed in the air, that Thou wast the beloved Son of God, in whom His soul was well pleased; but mayst Thou not be judged more than mad, and weaker than the brainless fool if Thou believest any such promise? Where are the signs of His love? Art Thou not cast out from comfort of all creatures? Thou art in worst case than the brute beasts, for every day they hunt for their prey, and the earth produces grass and herbs for their sustenance, so that none of them are pined and consumed away by hunger; but Thou hast fasted forty days and nights, ever waiting for some relief and comfort from above, but Thy best provision is hard stones! If Thou dost glory in Thy God, and dost verily believe the promise that is made, command that these stones be bread. But evident it is, that so Thou canst not do; for if Thou couldest, or if Thy God would have showed Thee any such pleasure, Thou mightest long ago have removed Thy hunger, and needest not have endured this languishing for lack of food.

But seeing Thou hast long continued thus, and no provision is made for Thee, it is vanity longer to believe any such promise, and therefore despair of any help from God's hand, and provide for Thyself by some other means! Many words have I used here, dearly beloved, but I cannot express the thousandth part of the malicious despite which lurked in this one temptation of Satan. It was a mocking of Christ and of His obedience. It was a plain denial of God's promise. It was the triumphing voice of him that appeared to have gotten victory. Oh how bitter this temptation was, no creature can understand, but such as feel the grief of such darts as Satan casts at the tender conscience of those that gladly would rest and repose in God, and in the promises of His mercy.

But here is to be noted the ground and foundation. The conclusion of Satan is this,—Thou art none of God's elect, much less His well-beloved Son. His reason is this—Thou art in trouble and findest no relief. There the foundation of the temptation was Christ's poverty, and the lack of food without hope of remedy to be sent from God. And it is the same temptation which the devil objected to Him by the princes of the priests in His grievous torments upon the cross; for thus they cried, "If He be the Son of God, let Him come down from the Cross, and we will believe in Him; He trusted in God, let Him deliver Him if He have pleasure in Him." As though they would say, God is the deliverer of His servants from troubles; God never permits those that fear Him to come to confusion; this man we see in extreme trouble; if He be the Son of God, or even a true worshipper of His Name, He will deliver Him from this calamity. If He deliver Him not, but suffer Him to perish in these anguishes, then it is an assured sign that God has rejected Him as a hypocrite, that shall have no portion of His glory.

Thus, I say, Satan takes occasion to tempt, and moves also others, to judge and condemn God's elect and chosen children, by reason that troubles are multiplied upon them. But with what weapons we ought to fight against such enemies and assaults, we shall learn in the answer of Christ Jesus, which follows: But He, answering, said, "It is written, Man lives not by bread only, but by every word which proceeds out of the mouth of God." This answer of Christ proves the sentence which we have brought of the aforesaid temptation, to be the very meaning of the Holy Ghost; for unless the purpose of Satan had been to have removed Christ from all hope of God's merciful providence towards Him in that His necessity, Christ had not answered directly to his words, saying, "Command that these stones be made bread." But Christ Jesus, perceiving his art and malicious subtilty, answered directly to his meaning, his words nothing regarded; by which Satan was so confounded, that he was ashamed to reply any further.

But that you may the better understand the meaning of Christ's answer, we will express and repeat it over in more words. "Thou labourest, Satan," would Christ say, "to bring into My heart a doubt and suspicion of My Father's promise, which was openly proclaimed in My baptism, by reason of My hunger and that I lack all carnal provision. Thou art bold to affirm that God takes no care of Me, but thou art a deceitful and false corrupt sophister, and thy argument too is vain, and full of blasphemies; for thou bindest God's love, mercy, and providence, to the having or wanting of bodily provision, which no part of God's Scripture teach us, but rather the express contrary. As it is written, 'Man liveth not by bread alone, but by every word that proceedeth from the mouth of God.' That is, the very life and felicity of man consists not in the abundance of bodily things, or, the possession and having of them makes no man blessed or happy; neither shall the lack of them be the cause of his final misery; but the very life of man consists in *God* and in His promises pronounced by His own mouth, unto which whoso cleaves unfeignedly, shall live the life everlasting. And although all creatures in earth forsake Him, yet shall not His bodily life perish till the time appointed by God approach.

"For God has means to feed, preserve, and maintain, unknown to man's reason, and contrary to the common course of nature. He fed His people Israel in the desert forty years without the provision of man. He preserved Jonah in the whale's belly; and maintained and kept the bodies of the three children in the furnace of fire. Reason and the natural man could have seen nothing in these cases but destruction and death, and could have judged nothing but that God had cast away the care of these His creatures, and yet His providence was most vigilant towards them in the extremity of their dangers, from which He did so deliver them, and in the midst of them did so assist them that His glory, which is His mercy and goodness, did more appear and shine after their troubles, than it could have done if they had fallen in them. And therefore I measure not the truth and favour of God, by having or by lacking of bodily necessities, but by the promise which He has made to Me. As He Himself is immutable so is His word and promise constant, which I believe, and to which I will adhere, and so cleave, whatever can come to the body outwardly." In this answer of Christ we may perceive what weapons are to be used against our adversary the devil, and how we may confute his arguments, which craftily, and of malice, he makes against God's elect. Christ might have repulsed Satan with a word, or by commanding him to silence, as He to whom all power was given in heaven and earth, but it pleased His mercy to teach us how to use the sword of the Holy Ghost, which is the Word of God, in battle against our spiritual enemy. The Scripture that Christ brings is written in the eighth chapter of Deuteronomy. It was spoken by Moses a little before his death, to establish the people in God's merciful providence. For in the same chapter, and in certain others that go before, he reckons the great travail and divers dangers with the extreme necessities that they had sustained in the desert, the space of forty years, and yet, notwithstanding how constant God had been in keeping and performing His promise, for throughout all perils He had conducted them to the sight and borders of the promised land.

And so this Scripture more directly answers to the temptation of

Satan; for thus does Satan reason, as before is said, "Thou art in poverty and hast no provision to sustain Thy life. Therefore God takes no regard nor care of Thee, as He doth over His chosen children." Christ Jesus answered, "Thy argument is false and vain; for poverty or necessity precludes not the providence or care of God; which is easy to be proved by the people of God, Israel, who, in the desert, oftentimes lacked things necessary to the sustenance of life, and for lack of the same they grudged and murmured; yet the Lord never cast away the providence and care of them, but according to the word that He had once pronounced, to wit, that they were His peculiar people; and according to the promise made to Abraham and to them before their departure from Egypt, He still remained their Conductor and Guide, till He placed them in peaceable possession of the land of Canaan, their great infirmities and manifold transgressions notwithstanding." Thus we are taught, I say, by Christ Jesus, to repulse Satan and his assaults by the Word of God, and to apply the examples of His mercies, which He has shown to others before us, to our own souls in the hour of temptation, and in the time of our trouble. For what God doth to one at any time, the same appertains to all that depend upon God and His promises. And, therefore, however we are assaulted by Satan, our adversary, within the Word of God is armour and weapons sufficient. The chief craft of Satan is to trouble those that begin to decline from his obedience, and to declare themselves enemies to iniquity, with divers assaults, the design whereof is always the same, that is, to put variance betwixt them and God, into their conscience, that they should not repose and rest themselves in His assured promises.

And to persuade this, he uses and invents divers arguments. Sometimes he calls the sins of their youth, and which they have committed in the time of blindness, to their remembrance; very often he objects their unthankfulness towards God and present imperfections. By sickness, poverty, tribulations in their household, or by persecution, he can allege that God is angry and regards them not. Or, by the spiritual Cross, which few feel and fewer understand the utility and profit of, he would drive God's children to desperation, and by infinite means more, he goeth about seeking, like a roaring lion, to undermine and destroy our faith.

But it is impossible for him to prevail against us, unless we obstinately refuse to use the defence and weapons that God has offered. Yes, I say, that God's elect cannot refuse it, but seek for their Defender when the battle is most strong; for the sobs, groans, and lamentations of such as fight, yea, the fear they have lest they be vanquished, the calling and prayer for continuance, are the undoubted and right seeking of Christ our champion. We refuse not the weapon, although sometimes, by infirmity, we cannot use it as we would. It suffices that your hearts unfeignedly sob for greater strength, for continuance, and for final deliverance by Christ Jesus; that which is wanting in us, His sufficiency doth supply; for it is He that fighteth and overcometh for us. But for bringing of the examples of the Scriptures, if God permit, in the end we shall speak more largely when it shall be treated why Christ permitted Himself thus to be tempted.

Sundry impediments now call me from writing in this matter, but, by God's grace, at convenient leisure I purpose to finish, and to send it to you. I grant the matter that proceeds from me is not worthy of your pain and labour to read it; yet, seeing it is a testimony of my good mind towards you, I doubt not but you will accept it in good part. God, the Father of our Lord Jesus Christ, grant unto you to find favour and mercy of the Judge, Whose eyes and knowledge pierce through the secret cogitations of the heart, in the day of temptation, which shall come upon all flesh, according to that mercy which you (illuminated and directed by His Holy Spirit) have showed to the afflicted. Now the God of all comfort and consolation confirm and strengthen you in His power unto the end. *Amen.*

JOHN CALVIN 1509–1564

John Calvin's seal depicts a heart resting on the palm of an open hand. Underneath are the words, "My heart I offer Thee, Lord, promptly and sincerely." Curious that it should serve as the symbol of the "cold theologian," of the man who "had no passions, who was all intellect"!

The thought behind the inscribed prayer was conceived in the moment of an agonizing decision. Forced by his Reformation principles to flee from France to Switzerland, in Geneva drafted to head up the government, from Geneva banished for the same principles that drew him there, Calvin settled in Strasbourg. Humiliating as the experience had been he accepted the spoiling of his office joyfully. In peaceful Germany he was able to give himself to preaching, teaching, and writing without jangling discord or maddening interference.

Suddenly a delegation from Geneva appeared and urged him to return to the city. Would he not go back and continue to direct the policies of State and Church? Nobody could possibly take his place, the delegation assured him.

He hated the idea with perfect hatred. Later he told a friend he would rather endure a thousand deaths than be tormented "in that chamber of torture." Infection center of all kinds of social and religious sores, it towered nevertheless as the political hub of Switzerland and Northern Italy. The finger of duty pointed plainly to Geneva.

It was under this tension that Calvin stroked off the memorable words, "When I remember that in this matter I am not my own master, I present my heart as a sacrifice and offer it up to the Lord." Thus was born the seal and badge of historic Calvinism.

The city of Geneva, like the Gaul of Caesar's day, was divided into three parts. The Catholics, the Evangelicals, and the Libertines, a layer of aristocrats dedicated to the pursuit of pleasure, were all contending for control. Calvin assumed the reins of the government and set about transforming Geneva into a bibliocracy, as Savonarola had made Florence a Christocracy. His program aimed at co-ordinating Church and State by bringing both in line, as he believed, with the directives of the Word of God. The Church would regulate worship. The State would preserve Christian doctrine, defend the constitution of the Church, and punish blasphemy and sacrilege. (This helps explain the later execution of Servetus.)

Calvin ran into violent hostility. The Catholics scandalized him. The Libertines threatened to end his life because be barred them from the

Communion table. On the street, children derided him by calling their dogs by his name.

In spite of all opposition, he succeeded in performing titanic feats. He carved out a civil state that virtually eliminated crime. He organized a church which turned out to be a model of efficiency. He fathered the famed Academy of Geneva. It quickly burgeoned into a college with an enrollment of fifteen hundred students. He edited the Institutes of the Christian Religion *he had begun at the age of twenty-six. This literary monolith became the textbook of Protestant theology for the next three hundred years. While no Calvinist claims inspiration for the effort, it stands as a masterful piece of systematizing of Scripture. He wrote commentaries, preached an average of six sermons a week, and corresponded with politicians, educators, and religious leaders all over the world.*

Alas, we have this treasure in earthen vessels. Who will claim exemption for the Reformer of Geneva? To a degree, Will Cuppy's sly comment on the New England Puritans applies to Calvin and his friends: "They believed in liberty—for all who agreed with them." The burning of blasphemous Servetus simply cannot be justified, the raw character of Calvin's days notwithstanding. The laws of Geneva were as rigid as iron. For the sin of gambling the police pilloried the culprit and hung a deck of cards from his neck. No bride could wear ornaments in her bonnet, nor was any woman allowed to don men's clothing. They scourged one chanteuse *for singing a popular song to a sacred tune. A mason was clapped into prison because, upon falling from a piece of scaffolding, he was overheard to say, "This is the work of the Devil."*

Unknown to most people, however, is Calvin's human side. He enjoyed throwing quoits. While he frowned on lewd plays, he never condemned drama per se. *On a certain Sunday evening, he postponed delivering his sermon in order to permit a comedy by Terence to conclude. He married an attractive widow and loved her devotedly. "From her I never experienced the slightest hindrance." Although he disdained money, he did accept a salary amounting to $125 a year, plus twelve measures of wheat and two barrels of wine. "If a man knows that he has a weak head and that he cannot carry three glasses of wine without being overcome and then drinks indiscretely, is he not a hog?" Those who accuse Calvin of being a pensioner of gloom are unaware that he wrote, "We are nowhere forbidden to laugh. . . ."*

Exhausting work, sleepless nights, extended periods of fasting, together with incredibly weighty burdens and pressures, ruined his health. Ten diseases racked his frail body and speeded his death.

He closed his earthly life apologizing to members of the council for his bursts of temper. It was appropriate that the king of Biblical scholars should with his parting breath quote from the Book of books: "The sufferings of this present time are not worthy to be compared with the glory that shall be revealed in us." "Then," says Colladon, "as the sun went down that day, the greatest light in this world was taken up to heaven."

On the Eternal Predestination of God

Extracts from the Answer of John Calvin to Albertus Pighius

THERE is not a more effectual means of building up faith than the giving our open ears to the election of God, which the Holy Spirit seals upon our heart while we hear, showing us that it stands in the eternal and immutable goodwill of God towards us; and that, therefore, it cannot be moved or altered by any storms of the world, by any assaults of Satan, by any changes, or by any fluctuations or weaknesses of the flesh.

For our salvation is then sure to us, when we find the *cause* of it in the breast of God. Thus, when we lay hold of life in Christ, made manifest to our faith, the same faith being still our leader and guide, our sight is permitted to penetrate much farther, and to see from what *source* that life proceeded. Our confidence of salvation is rooted in Christ, and rests on the promises of the Gospel. But it is no weak prop to our confidence, when we are brought to believe in Christ, to hear that all was originally *given* to us of God, and that we were as much ordained to faith in Christ before the foundation of the world, as we were chosen to the inheritance of life in Christ.

Hence, therefore, arises the impregnable and insubvertible security of the saints. The Father, Who gave us to the Son as His peculiar treasure, is stronger than all who oppose us; and He will not suffer us to be plucked out of His hand. What a cause for humility then in the saints of God when they see such a difference of condition made in those who are, by nature, all alike! Wherever the sons of God turn their eyes, they behold such wonderful instances of blindness, ignorance and insensibility, as fill them with horror; while they, in the midst of such darkness, have received Divine illumination, and know it, and feel it, to be so.

How (say they) is it that some, under the clear light, continue in darkness and blindness? Who makes this difference? One thing they know by their own experience, that whereas *their* eyes were also once closed, they are now opened. Another thing is also certain, that those who willingly remain ignorant of any difference between them and others, have never yet learned to render unto God the glory due to Him for making that difference. . . . Now, if we are not really ashamed of the Gospel, we must of necessity acknowledge what is therein openly declared; that God by His eternal goodwill (for which there was no other cause than His own purpose) appointed those whom He pleased unto salvation, rejecting all the rest; and that those whom He blessed with this free adoption to be His sons He illumines by His Holy Spirit, that they may receive the life which is offered to them in Christ; while others, continuing of their own will in unbelief, are left destitute of the light of faith, in total darkness.

"Who art thou, O man, that repliest against God?" (Rom. 9:20) Paul in this appeal adopts an axiom, or universal acknowledgement, which not only ought to be held fast by all godly minds, but deeply engraven in the breast of common sense; that the inscrutable judgment of God is deeper than can be penetrated by man. And what man, I pray you, would not be ashamed to compress all the causes of the works of God within the confined measure of his individual intellect? Yet, on this hinge turns the whole question; Is there no justice of God, but that which is conceived of by us?

Now if we should throw this into the form of one question—whether it be lawful to measure the power of God by our natural sense—there is not a man who would not immediately reply that all the senses of all men combined in one individual must faint under an attempt to comprehend the immeasurable power of God; and YET, as soon as a *reason* cannot immediately be seen for certain works of God, men somehow or other are immediately prepared to appoint a day for entering into judgment with Him. What therefore can be more opportune or appropriate than the apostle's appeal; that those who would thus raise themselves above the heavens in their reasonings utterly forget who and what they are?

And suppose God, ceding His own right, should offer Himself as ready to render a reason for His works? When the matter came to those secret counsels of His, which angels adore with trembling, who would not be utterly bereft of his senses before such glorious splendor? Marvellous, indeed, is the madness of man! who would more audaciously set himself above God than stand on equal ground with any Pagan judge! It is intolerable to you, and hateful, that the power and works of God should exceed the capacity of your own mind; and yet you will grant to an *equal* the enjoyment of his own mind and judgment. Now, will you, with such madness as this, dare to make mention of the adorable God? What do you really think of God's glorious Name? And will you want that the apostle is devoid of all reason because he does not drag God from His throne and set Him before you, to be questioned and examined?

But Pighius and his fellows are not hereby satisfied. For, pretending a great concern for the honor of God, they bark at us, as imputing to Him a cruelty utterly foreign to His nature. Pighius denies that he has any contest with God. What cause, or whose cause is it, then, that Paul maintains? After he had adopted the above axiom—that God hardens whom He will and has mercy on whom He will—he subjoins the supposed taunt of a wicked reasoner; "Why doth He yet find fault? For who hath resisted His will?" (Rom. 9:19) He meets such blasphemy as this by simply setting against it the power of God. If those clothe God with the garment of a tyrant, who refer the hardening of men even to His eternal counsel, we most certainly are not the originators of this doctrine.

If they do God an injury who set His will above all other causes, Paul taught this doctrine long before us. Let these enemies of God, then, dispute the matter with the apostle. For I maintain nothing, in the present discussion, but what I declare is taught by him. About these barking dogs, however, I would not be very anxious. I am the rather moved with an anxiety about some otherwise good men, who, while they fear lest they should ascribe to God anything unworthy of His goodness, really seem to be horror-struck at that which He declares, by His apostle, concerning Himself.

Augustine is so wholly with me, that if I wished to write a confession of my faith, I could do so with all fulness and satisfaction to myself out of his writings. But that I may not, on the present occasion, be too prolix, I will be content with three or four instances of his testimony, from which it will be manifest that he does not differ from me one pin's point. And it would be more manifest still, could the whole line of his confession be adduced, how fully and solidly he agrees with me in every particular.

In his book, *Concerning the Predestination of the Saints*, he has these words; "Lest any one should say, My faith, my righteousness (or anything of the kind) distinguishes me from others; meeting all such thoughts, the great teacher of the Gentiles asks, 'What hast thou that thou hast not received?' As if the apostle had said, From whom indeed couldst thou receive it, but from Him Who separates thee from every other, to whom He has not given what He has given to thee?" Augustine then adds, "Faith, therefore, from its beginning to its perfection is the gift of God. And that this gift is bestowed on some and not on others, who will deny but he who would fight against the most manifest testimonies of the Scripture?

"But why faith is not given to all ought not to concern the believer, who knows that all men by the sin of one came into most just condemnation. But why God delivers one from this condemnation and not another belongs to His inscrutable judgments, and 'His ways are past finding out.' And if it be investigated and inquired how it is that each receiver of faith is deemed of God worthy to receive such a gift, there are not wanting those who will say, It is by their human will. But we say that it is by grace, or Divine predestination!"

Now, that no one might attribute it to faith that one is preferred above another, Augustine testifies that men are not chosen *because* they believe, but, on the contrary, are chosen *that they might* believe. In like manner, when writing to Sextus, he says, "As to the great deep—*why* one man believes and another does not, *why* God delivers one man and not another—let him who can, search into that profound abyss; but let him beware of the awful precipice!" Again, in another place he says: "Who created the reprobate but God? And why? Because He willed it. *Why* did He will it? 'Who are thou O man, that repliest against God?' " And again, elsewhere, after he had proved that God is moved by no merits of men to make them obedient to His commands, but that He renders unto them good for evil, and that for His own sake and not for theirs, he adds, "If anyone should ask why God makes some men His sheep and not others, the Apostle, dreading this question exclaims, 'O the depth of the riches both of the wisdom and knowledge of God! How unsearchable are His judgments, and His ways past finding out!' "

Nothing therefore, is done but that which the Omnipotent *willed* to be done, either by permitting it to be done or by doing it Himself. Nor is a doubt to be entertained that God does righteously in permitting all those things to be done which are done evilly. For He permits not this, but by righteous judgment. Although, therefore, those things which are evil, in so far as they are evil, are not good, yet it is *good* that there should not only be good things, but evil things also. For, unless there were this good, that evil things also existed, those evil things would not be permitted by the Great and *Good* Omnipotent to exist at all. For He, without doubt, can as easily refuse to permit to be done what He does not will to be done, as He can do that which He wills to be done. Unless we fully believe this, the very beginning of our faith is perilled, by which we profess to believe in God Almighty!"

Augustine then adds this short sentence: "These are the mighty works of the Lord, shining with perfection in every instance of His will; and so perfect in wisdom, that when the angelic and human nature had sinned—that is, had done not what God willed, but what each nature itself willed—it came to pass that by this same will of the creature, God, though in one sense unwilling, yet accomplished what *He* willed, righteously and with the height of all wisdom, overruling the evils done, to the damnation of those whom He had justly predestinated to punishment and to the salvation of those whom He had mercifully predestinated to grace.

"Wherefore as far as these natures themselves were concerned, *they* did what they did contrary to the will of God; but, as far as the Omnipotence of God is concerned, they acted according to His will; nor could they have acted contrary to it. Hence, by their very acting contrary to the will of God, the will of God concerning them was done. So mighty, therefore, are the works of God, so gloriously and exquisitely perfect in every instance of His will, that by a marvellous and ineffable plan of operation peculiar to Himself, as the 'All-wise God,' *that* cannot be done, *without* His will, which is even *contrary* to His will; because it could not be done without His permitting it to be done, which permission is evidently not *contrary* to His will but *according* to His will." I have gladly extracted these few things out of many like them in the writings of Augustine, that my readers may clearly see with what a very modest face it is that Pighius represents him as differing from me! and makes use of him (Augustine) to support his own errors.

Paul declares in Ephesians 1:8,9: "Wherein He hath abounded toward us in all wisdom and prudence; Having made known unto us the mystery of His will, according to His good pleasure which He hath purposed in Himself." Thou hearest in these words, reader, the grace of illumination, flowing like a river from the fountain of that eternal counsel which had been before hidden. Far, very far, is this removed from the idea that God had any respect to our faith in choosing us, which faith could not possibly have existed except that God had then appointed it for us by the free grace of His adoption of us. And Paul farther on confirms all this by declaring that God was moved by no external cause—by no cause out of Himself—in the choice of us; but that He Himself, in Himself, was the Cause and the Author of choosing His people, not yet created or born, as those on whom He would afterwards confer faith; ". . . according to the purpose of Him Who worketh all things after the counsel of His own will." (Eph. 1:11)

Who does not therefore see that the Eternal purpose of God is here set in diametrical opposition to our own purpose and will? This passage also was deeply weighed by Augustine, who, in his interpretation of it, observes, "that God so works out all things, that He works also in us the very willingness by which we believe." It is thus, I think, clearly brought out and proved who they are whom God calls by the Gospel to the hope of salvation, whom He engrafts into the body of Christ, and whom He makes heirs of eternal life; that they are those whom He had adopted unto Himself by His eternal and secret counsel to be His sons; and that He was so far from being moved by any faith

in them to come thus to adopt them, that this His election is the cause
and the beginning of all faith in them; and that, therefore, election is,
in order, before faith.

On the Creation of Man

W̲E MUST NOW speak of the creation of man, not merely because
he, among all the works of God, is the most notable example of
the Creator's justice, wisdom, and goodness, but because, as we have
already said, we can have no clear and real knowledge of God without
some corresponding knowledge of ourselves.

Of this there are two branches, namely, the knowledge of man as he
was originally created, and the knowledge of man's condition since the
fall of Adam: for the present we shall confine our attention to the
former. For before we treat of the miserable state to which man has
fallen, it is worth while to remember what he was at first, lest we
should seem to attribute man's wickedness to the Author of nature.

Man thinks that he has a sufficient excuse for his wickedness if he
can allege that the faults of his nature proceed in some way from God;
and even those who affect to speak with a measure of reverence concerning the Deity gladly catch at an excuse for their depravity by
ascribing it to nature, not reflecting that this is an indirect insult to God,
who would be dishonoured by the presence of evil in the work of His
hands.

Since therefore we see that the flesh is on the watch for all sorts of
excuses by which to lay the blame of its iniquity at some other door
than its own, we must diligently seek to prevent this, by speaking in
such a way of the ruin of mankind as to cut off all excuse from the
sinner, and to vindicate the justice of God from all reproach.

It cannot justly be disputed that man consists of body and soul; and
by soul I mean an immortal, though created, essence which is the nobler
part of him. Sometimes it is called spirit. For though these two words
soul and spirit have each its own special significance when they are
used together, yet when the word spirit is used alone it has the same
meaning as soul; as, for instance, where Solomon says that the spirit
returns unto God Who gave it. (Eccles. 12:7) Christ commended His
spirit to His Father, and Stephen commended his spirit to Christ,
meaning that when the soul is released from the prison-house of the
body God is its constant guardian.

Those who imagine that the soul is called spirit because it is a mere breath, or a force infused by God into the body with no existence or essence of its own, are guilty of gross folly: this is evident from the nature of the case, and from the universal testimony of Scripture. It is true that men who are sunk in materialism are so obtuse, nay, so blinded by darkness (being alienated from the Father of lights), as to forget that they will have an existence beyond death; and yet, in the midst of their darkness, the light is not so utterly extinguished but that they are touched with some sense of their own immortality.

Conscience, which responds to the judgment of God and so discerns between good and evil, is a sure indication of immortality. How could mere motive-power, without personality, penetrate to the tribunal of God and feel terror at the approach of judgment? For the dread of spiritual punishment does not afflict the body, but falls upon the soul alone; whence it follows that the soul is endued with essence, or personal existence.

Even the knowledge which men have of God is proof enough that their souls are immortal: for a breath, or an evanescent influence, would not rise to the fountain of life. Finally, the many splendid faculties which the human mind possesses, crying out that it bears the stamp of divinity, are so many proofs of its immortal and personal existence. For the sense possessed by the brutes goes no further than the body, or at the most extends to objects with which they meet; but the activity of the human mind traverses heaven and earth, penetrates the secrets of nature, comprehends and remembers the course of ages, and infers things future from things that are past, clearly proving that something separate from the body lies hidden within man.

Our understanding conceives thoughts of the invisible God and of the angels, a power of conception which certainly belongs not to the body. We know what is right, what is just, what is honourable; and the seat of such understanding must be the spirit. Sleep itself is no uncertain proof of immortality, since it suggests thoughts of things which have never happened, and even suggests foresight of the future.

If the soul were not a something that has an existence of its own, apart from the body, the Scripture would not teach us that we "dwell in houses of clay," that at death we depart from the tabernacle of the flesh, that we "put off this corruptible," and that at the last day we shall "receive a reward for the things done in the body." For these passages and many others like them, not only distinguish the soul from the body, but speak of it as if it were the man, and thus indicate that it is the principal part of him. I will give a few additional quotations.

Paul exhorts believers to cleanse themselves from all defilement of the flesh and of the spirit, (II Cor. 7:1) showing that the filth of sin defiles these two parts of man. Peter calls Christ the Shepherd and

Bishop of souls, which would be an absurd statement if there were no souls for Christ to take care of. Moreover, if the soul has no essence or existence of its own, what sense would there be in Peter's words about the eternal salvation of souls, in his exhortation to purify our souls, in his warning that fleshly lusts war against the soul? How could the writer of the Epistle to the Hebrews say that pastors watch for souls as those that must give account?

A similar inference may be drawn from the words of Paul, "I call God for a record upon my soul," which would be meaningless unless the soul were liable to punishment. Christ expresses this in plainer words, when He bids us fear Him who after He hath killed the body hath power to cast the soul into hell. Again, in the Epistle to the Hebrews the fathers of our flesh are distinguished from God, the Father of spirits, whereby the existence of the soul is most clearly asserted. And if the soul did not survive when released from the prison-house of the body, how could Christ have spoken of the soul of Lazarus as resting in Abraham's bosom, and of the soul of the rich man as consigned to dreadful torments? The same truth is affirmed by Paul when he says that we are absent from the Lord so long as we are present in the body, but enjoy His presence when we leave it. In proof of so evident a truth I need only add that Luke tells us (Acts 23:8) that among the errors of the Sadducees was the denial of the existence of angels and spirits.

A solid proof of the existence of the soul is supplied by the statement that man was made in the image of God; for though the glory of the Creator shines in the external form of man, it is certain that the seat of the divine image is in the soul. It is true that our outward appearance, distinguishing us from the brutes, shows that we are nearer to God than they. Nor do I object to the opinion that the words "in the image of God" refer in part to the dignity of the human form. Even a heathen poet has said (Ovid, *Metamorphoses*, I 84-86):

> Brutes eye the ground: to man alone 'tis given
> To lift his head and scan the vault of heaven.

Yet it must not be forgotten that the image of God which is indicated by these outward marks is a spiritual character. It consists in the integrity with which Adam was endowed when he possessed a right understanding, affections subject to sound reason, and senses under perfect and orderly control.

The excellent faculties which man originally possessed, and which reflected the glory of God, may be best known by considering the renewal of the image of God in man by Christ, who is called the Second Adam because He has restored us to true perfection. For though Paul contrasts the quickening spirit which is given to believers by

Christ with the living soul wherewith Adam was created, and so commands the more abundant grace which is bestowed upon us in regeneration, he does not thereby contradict the truth that the object of regeneration is to form us anew unto the image of God. Accordingly he teaches us in another place that the new man is renewed in knowledge after the image of Him who created him.

What then are the special features of this renewal? First, knowledge (Col. 3:10), secondly, righteousness and true holiness (Eph. 4:24); whence we conclude that before the fall the image of God consisted in the light that filled man's mind, in the uprightness of his heart, and in the soundness of all his faculties. The same conclusion may be drawn from the words, "We all, beholding as in a mirror the glory of the Lord, are changed into the same image." Christ is the most perfect image of God; and we, being formed thereunto, are so renewed that we bear the image of God in true holiness, righteousness, purity, and understanding, an image which will reach its full splendour when we arrive in heaven.

It would not be wise to seek from the philosophers a definition of the soul of man, seeing that not one of them, except Plato, was fully persuaded of its immortality. The others so confine its powers and faculties to the present life that they practically leave us nothing but our body. We have shown from the Scriptures that the soul is an immaterial essence, an incorporeal something which has its dwelling in the body. We may add that it animates all parts of the body, fits its members for action, and holds a kind of primacy in the government of man's life. It not merely governs man's ordinary actions, but stirs him up to worship God. Though this is not clearly apparent in our present corrupt state, yet remnants of it may be seen even in our failings. For how is it men are so anxious to win fame? Because they have some sense of honour, some regard for what is seemly. The principle from which this proceeds is the knowledge that they were born to practice righteousness.

More subtle discussions of the faculties of the soul I will leave to the philosophers: a simple definition will suffice for godly edification. Some of the conclusions of philosophy are true, interesting, and useful, and I would not debar from such studies any who are eager to acquire learning; but I must point out that philosophers have always imagined that man possesses a power of reason by which he can govern himself aright. They knew not that man's nature had been corrupted by the fall, and therefore they confused two things which are entirely different, the state of man as created and the state of man as fallen.

For our present purpose it is sufficient to say that the human soul has two parts, the understanding and the will; and that it is the province of the understanding to discern between good and evil, of the will to make its choice between the two. In man's original uprightness the will was free, and by the freedom of his will he might have attained eternal life. I speak here without reference to God's predestination, because we are not now treating of that subject, but of the original nature of man.

It is clear that Adam had the power to stand if he had willed to do so: for it was by his own will that he fell. He was free to choose good or evil; and not only so, but his mind and will were perfect, and all his members were in due subjection to his mind and will, until he ruined himself and so corrupted all his faculties. On this point the philosophers were entirely in the dark: they sought the building amid its ruins; they sought close connections in the midst of dispersion. They held fast to the principle that man would not be a reasonable being unless he were free to choose between good and evil: they saw that if he did not direct his own life by his own purposes there would be no distinction between virtues and vices.

So far they were right, but only right if there had been no change in human nature: as they knew nothing of the fall, it is not to be wondered at that their reasonings were full of confusion. But those who profess to be disciples of Christ, and yet look for a free will in lost and ruined man, thus dividing their allegiance between the dogmas of philosophers and the doctrine of heaven,—what can we say of them but this: they are foolish enough to aim at heaven and earth, and they miss them both.

God, Who created the universe, sustains it by His power, and governs every part of it by His providence.

It would be but a cold and empty notion to think that God created the world at a certain epoch and then forsook the work of His hands. Indeed this is one of the principal points of difference between us and the ungodly, that we recognize the hand of God in the continuous course of nature as much as we do in its first origin. For while the mere aspect of heaven and earth compels even the ungodly to acknowledge the existence of a Creator, yet it is the peculiar province of faith to attribute to God in reality all the glory of creation. Hence it is written: "Through faith we understand that the worlds were framed by the Word of God." (Heb. 11:3)

Unless we go on to believe in God's providence, we do not truly understand that He is the Creator, however much we may seem to comprehend it with our mind and to confess it with our tongue. The carnal mind, when once it has acknowledged the power of God in creation stops there; or at the most acknowledges some general action of the Deity in preserving and governing the works of His hands. It considers that the energy originally imparted to the various creatures is sufficient to sustain them all.

Faith must go deeper: having learned that God is the Creator of all

things, it must conclude that He is their constant Governor and Preserver, and that His special providence sustains, cherishes, and cares for
every one of His creatures, even to the smallest sparrow. Thus David,
in Psalm 33, first states that the heavens and all their host were made by
the word of the Lord, and then asserts that "He looketh from heaven,
He beholdeth all the sons of men: from the place of His habitation He
looketh upon all the inhabitants of the earth: He fashioneth their hearts
alike: He considereth all their works." In fact no man seriously believes
that God created all things, unless he believes also that God cares
continually for all things that He has created.

To apprehend more clearly the distinction between the reasonings
of philosophy and conclusions of faith, we must remember that the
providence of God, as it is taught in the Scriptures, is entirely opposed
to the notion of fortune or chance. In past ages and in our own times
it has been and is the general opinion of mankind that all things
happen by chance: and it is certain that this false notion darkens,
nay, buries, all right thoughts of divine providence.

If a man falls a prey to robbers or wild beasts, if he is shipwrecked
at sea by a sudden squall of wind; or if on the other hand having lost
his way in the desert he finds a supply of his needs; if another comes
safely into port after a storm or has some hair-breadth escape from
death; all these events, whether prosperous or adverse, are ascribed by
carnal reason to fortune. But he who has learned from Christ the
hairs of his head are all numbered, will look deeper for the cause, and
will conclude that events of every kind are governed by the secret
counsel of God. Even inanimate things, whatever natural properties
they may possess, are merely instruments, the efficacy of which is maintained by God and used by Him to fulfill the purpose of His own will.

Indeed God claims for Himself, and expects us to attribute to Him,
omnipotence: not such an omnipotence as the sophists imagine, one that
is empty, idle, fast asleep; but watchful, efficacious, operative, continually engaged in action. We account Him to be omnipotent, not
because He can do all things and yet remains inactive, or merely
prolongs in a general way the course of nature; but because He governs
heaven and earth by His providence, and so rules all things that nothing
happens but according to His counsel. For when the Psalmist saith
(Ps. 115:3) that God "hath done whatsoever He hath pleased," he
refers to a fixed and deliberate purpose.

It would be senseless to interpret such words, after the manner of
philosophers, to mean merely that God is the first cause of things because He is the origin of all motion; it would rob the faithful in their
adversity of the comforting thought that they suffer nothing but by
the appointment and decrees of Him under whose hand they are. But
if the government of God thus extends to all His works, it would be

childish to limit it to the ordinary course of nature. Those who thus limit the providence of God rob themselves of a most useful doctrine, and dishonour the goodness of God towards each of His creatures.

Those who assign just honour to the omnipotence of God are thereby drawn to render to Him obedience, and to rest secure under His protection; and this is the only way of deliverance from superstitious fears. The prophet Jeremiah (10:2) forbids the children of God to be dismayed at the signs of heaven, as the heathen are. Not that he condemns all fear; but because, when unbelievers transfer the government of the world from God to the stars, they imagine that their misery or happiness depends not upon God, but upon the influences and omens of planets and comets. If we wish to escape this unbelieving superstition, we must ever remember that creatures have no random power or motion, but are so governed by the secret counsel of God that nothing happens but what is decreed by Him according to His own knowledge and will.

Let our readers therefore remember that when we speak of providence, we do not mean the providence of a God who sits idly in heaven and observes the things that are done on earth, but that of a God who controls and governs all events. His providence pertains to His hand as much as to His eye. For when Abraham said to his son, "The Lord will provide," he meant not merely to say that God had foreknowledge of the future, but that he himself was casting his care on one who delivers from perplexity and confusion.

It follows that God's providence consists in action. It is ignorant trifling to talk about mere foreknowledge. It is also erroneous to assign to God a general government which does not specially rule the actions of every creature. Those who do so, admit what they call a universal providence, but teach that this does not hinder creatures from moving hither and thither by accident, nor man from the unlimited exercise of his own free will. And thus they divide the matter between God and man, as if the former supplied the power of motion, and the latter managed his actions by his own voluntary purpose. In this manner they obscure the truth of a special providence, which is so certainly and clearly asserted in the Scriptures that it is a wonder that anyone could ever doubt it.

If we allow that the principle of motion belongs to God, but that all things drift by chance whithersoever the course of nature may carry them, it will follow that the succession of day and night, summer and winter, is the work of God so long as it runs an orderly and equable course; but that it is a mere matter of chance, or of some sidereal influence, when excessive heat burns up the fruits, or unseasonable rain spoils the crops, or hailstorms and tempests cause some sudden calamity. But this leaves no room for the exercise of God's fatherly bounty or righteous judgments. If it be said that God is bountiful enough to mankind in giving to heaven and earth their ordinary fertilizing and productive powers, we reply that this is a meagre and ungodly theory, implying that the fruitfulness of any particular year is not a special blessing from God, and that scarcity and famine are not sent by Him as a curse and a punishment. Whereas the Scripture often testifies that when the earth is refreshed with dew and rain, God thereby shows His favour; that at His bidding the heavens become as iron, and the crops are consumed by blasting and mildew; and that whenever the fields are smitten by hail and tempest it is a sure sign of His special displeasure. Finally it is, as I have said, a childish error to limit the exercise of God's providence to certain particular cases, since Christ proclaims it as a universal truth that not a sparrow falls to the ground without the will of our Father in heaven.

We know that God created the world for man: we must expect therefore to find that God governs it with a special regard to the interests of mankind. The prophet Jeremiah exclaims, "O Lord, I know that the way of man is not in himself: it is not in man that walketh to direct his steps." (Jer. 10:23) And Solomon saith, "Man's goings are of the Lord; and how shall man arrange his own way?" (Prov. 20:24) If it be objected that God gives man the natural power to move, but that man directs his movements according to his own good pleasure, I reply that in that case man's ways would be at his own disposal, whereas Jeremiah and Solomon assign to God not merely power, but choice and purpose in respect of all the ways of men.

In another place Solomon administers an elegant reproof to the rashness of men who pursue their own objects without regard to God, as if they were not led by His hand: "The disposition of the heart," saith he, "is of man; and the preparation of the tongue is of the Lord"; implying that it is ridiculous folly that men should plan their actions independently of God, inasmuch as they cannot even utter a word but in subjection to His will. But to show more clearly that nothing in the whole world is done otherwise than in accordance with God's purpose, the Scripture points out that even things which appear to be more especially matters of chance are subject to Him. If one man is accidentally slain by another, the Lord declares that He Himself has delivered the victim into the hand of the slayer. (Exod. 21:13)

In like manner the casting of lots, which most men would consider to be an appeal to blind fortune, is said to be subject to the disposal of the Lord. (Prov. 16:33) We learn the same truth from the saying, "The poor and the usurer meet together: the Lord lighteneth both their eyes." (Prov. 29:13) It reminds us that though poor and rich are mingled together in the world, each man's condition is assigned to him by God's providence; and that those who are not contented with their lot are guilty of seeking to cast off the burden which God has laid upon them.

Particular events are proofs of the universal providence of God. For instance, the Lord sent forth a wind to bring quails from the sea for the people. (Num. 11:31) When He would have Jonah cast into the sea, He sent out a wind to stir up a storm. Those who do not think that God continually rules the world, will say that this was an unusual circumstance; but I infer from it that no wind ever begins or increases but at the special bidding of God. Nor would it be true that He maketh the winds His messengers, and His ministers a flame of fire; that He maketh the clouds His chariot, and rideth upon the wings of the wind (Ps. 104:3,4), unless He directed clouds and winds at His will and showed in them the presence of His own power.

Thus also we are taught (Ps. 107:25,29), that whensoever the sea is lashed into fury by the winds, their violence is a proof of the special presence of God: "He commandeth, and raiseth the stormy wind, which lifteth up the waves thereof: He maketh the storm a calm, so that the waves thereof are still." Thus also, though it is natural that we should have children, yet God would have us acknowledge it as a favour from Himself, if He gives us children while others are left childless; for it is written that "the fruit of the womb is His reward."

One more example may suffice. Nothing is more ordinary and natural than that we should live on bread: and yet the Spirit tells us, not merely that the produce of the earth is the special gift of God, but that man doth not live by bread alone; because it is not food that keeps us alive, but the secret blessing of God: hence we are taught to pray for our daily bread to Him Who "giveth food to all flesh." Finally, when we read that the eyes of the Lord are upon the righteous, and His ears are open unto their cry, and that the eye of the Lord is upon the wicked, to cut off their memory from the earth, let us know that all creatures are so subject to the Creator, that He employs them as He thinks fit.

Those who wish to render this doctrine odious, calumniate it as being the Stoical dogma of fate; and this charge was brought against Augustine in his day. Now we have no wish to contend about words; but we reject the term fate, partly because it is one of those profane innovations which Paul bids us avoid, and partly because it is used by some, as we have said, to calumniate the truth of God.

It is a malicious falsehood to charge us with holding the heathen dogma of fate. The Stoics imagined a Necessity, arising from a perpetual chain of successive causes contained in nature; but we have no such belief. We teach that God is the Arbiter and Controller of all things, who has in His wisdom decreed from everlasting what He would do, and now accomplishes by His own power that which He has decreed. Hence we assert that not only heaven and earth and inanimate creatures, but also the counsels and purposes of men, are so governed by His providence as to be directed thereby to an appointed end.

You will say, "What! Does nothing happen by chance? Is there no such thing as contingency?" I reply that it was truly said by the great Basil that fortune and chance are words of the heathen, implying ideas which should have no place in the minds of the godly. If all success is God's blessing, and all real adversity His curse, then no room is left in human affairs for fortune or chance. A saying of Augustine deserves consideration: "I regret that in writing against the Academic school of teachers I so frequently used the word 'Fortune,' though I did not use it as the name of a goddess, but simply of the fortuitous happening of things prosperous and things adverse. It is true that I also said, 'That which is commonly called fortune is perhaps subject to some hidden method, and chance is merely that of which the reason and cause is secret.' Yet I regret that I made so much use of the word fortune; for I see that men have the mischievous habit of saying 'So fortune would have it,' where they ought to say, 'So God would have it.' "

Since, however, our minds are far too dull to rise to the heights of divine providence, we must make use of the following distinction to assist them: though all things are ordered by the sure dispensation of God's counsel, yet to us they appear to happen by chance. Not that we think that fortune rules the world and turns all things upside down at random: far from the heart of a Christian be such a foolish thought as that. But things which undoubtedly proceed from the will of God seem to us to be fortuitous, because their order, reason, end and necessity are hidden in God's counsels and are not grasped by the mind of man.

Let us take for example the case of a travelling merchant who enters a forest in company with trusty friends, strays from them unawares, falls among robbers, and is murdered. Such a death is not merely foreseen by God, but fixed by His decree: for Scripture tells us that God has not merely foreseen the length of a man's life, but has appointed his bounds that he cannot pass. (Job 14:5) And yet in such a case everything appears to us to be accidental.

We have in the history of David a remarkable instance of the way in which God directs events of all kinds by the curb of His providence. At the very moment when David was surrounded by the forces of Saul in the wilderness of Maon, the Philistines invaded the land, and Saul was compelled to depart. If God in order to save His servant threw this hindrance in the way of Saul, then, however suddenly or unexpectedly the Philistines made their attack, we cannot say that it happened by chance: faith will acknowledge that what looks to us like chance was in fact the effect of God's secret power.

The Use of the Doctrine of Divine Providence

In controlling all things by His providence God sometimes works by second causes, sometimes without them, sometimes even against them. He shows by it that He cares for all mankind, but is especially attentive to the government of His church. We must remember also that, although His goodness and severity shine forth in the whole course of providence, yet the causes of events are sometimes so hidden that we are ready to think the affairs of the world are subject to the blind power of chance. And yet, however the causes of various events may escape our view, we must firmly believe that they are hidden in His counsels, so that we may cry with David: "Many, O Lord my God, are Thy wonderful works which Thou hast done, and Thy thoughts which are to us-ward: they cannot be reckoned up in order unto Thee: if I would declare and speak of them, they are more than can be numbered."

Indeed though it becomes us, when affliction overtakes us, to seek the cause of it in our own sins, in order that chastisement may move us to repentance, yet we see that Christ vindicates His Father's right to accomplish by affliction more than the mere punishment of men according to their deserts. He saith concerning the man who was blind from his birth: "Neither hath this man sinned nor his parents: but that the glory of God should be made manifest in him." (John 9:3) Here sense raises an outcry, as if God were unmerciful in thus afflicting the innocent; whereas Christ testifies that the glory of His Father is to be seen in this thing as in a mirror, if we have eyes to see it. Let us remember that we must not presumptuously call God to account, but reverence His secret counsels and look upon His will as the righteous cause of all things.

No man can rightly and profitably consider the providence of God unless he remembers that in this matter he has to do with his own Maker, the Creator of the world, and therefore handles the subject with reverence and due humility. For lack of this many evil men assail and revile this doctrine, being unwilling to allow to God more power than their own reason approves. Us also they attack, because we not merely admit that the will of God is revealed in His word, but maintain that the world is governed by His secret counsels.

They have just enough modesty to shrink from direct blasphemy, and therefore excuse their madness by alleging that they are merely opposing our views. But if they deny that all events are governed by God's incomprehensible purposes, let them explain to us why the Scripture says that His judgments are a great deep; and why Paul saith: "O the depths of the riches both of the wisdom and knowledge of God! How unsearchable are His judgments, and His ways past finding out!"

It is true that there are mysteries both in the law and in the Gospel which are far above our powers of perception; but, since God enlightens the understanding of His people to comprehend the mysteries which He has revealed in His word, they cannot rightly be called a deep, but rather a road in which we may safely walk, a lamp to guide our feet; whereas His admirable mode of governing the world is rightly called a deep or an abyss. Hence Moses beautifully and briefly says: "The secret things belong unto the Lord our God: but those things which are revealed belong unto us and to our children." (Deut. 29:29)

A mind thus tempered to reverence and humility will not murmur against God because of the calamities which have come upon mankind in past times; neither will it blame God for crimes which man has committed, saying with Agamemnon in the *Iliad*:

> 'Tis not my fault;
> 'Tis Heaven and Destiny that are to blame.

The man who is lowly in heart will rather seek to learn the will of God, and to fulfill it by the help of His Spirit.

As to events that are yet future, we learn from Solomon that the purposes of man work in harmony with the providence of God: "A man's heart deviseth his way: but the Lord directeth his steps." (Prov. 16:9) These words teach that God's eternal decrees by no means hinder us from exercising forethought for ourselves and arranging all our affairs in subjection to His will. Nor is this unreasonable. For He who has set bounds to our life has also commissioned us to take care of it, has furnished us with ways and means for preserving it, has given us power to foresee dangers, and has taught us to apply precautions and remedies.

Our duty therefore is clear. If God has committed to us the care of our own life, we must care for it; if He supplies means, we must use them; if He forewarns us of dangers, we must not rashly run into them; if He provides remedies, we must not neglect them.

There are men who draw false and rash conclusions from a consideration of the naked doctrine of God's providential purposes. They argue, "Why should a thief be punished, if he has plundered a man whom God designed to afflict with poverty? Why should a murderer be punished, if he has slain a man whose life had reached the limit appointed by the Lord? If all such agents are subject to the will of God, why should they be punished?" But I deny that criminals are "subject to the will of God." They are subject to their own evil lusts.

A Christian heart, being thoroughly convinced that all things are subject to the dispensation of God and that nothing happens by chance, will always look up in the first place to Him; but it will give to second causes their right place. As regards men, either good men or bad men, the Christian will acknowledge that their plans, wishes, attempts and powers are under the Lord's control, and that He is able to turn them whithersoever He will, and to frustrate them as often as He pleases.

There are many promises which testify most clearly that the providence of God is always vigilantly careful for the safety of believers: it may suffice to quote the following. "Cast thy burden upon the Lord, and He shall sustain thee: He shall never suffer the righteous to be moved." (Ps. 55:22) "He careth for you." (I Pet. 5:7) "He that dwelleth in the secret place of the most High shall abide under the shadow of the Almighty." (Ps. 91:1) "He that toucheth you toucheth the apple of Mine eye." (Zech. 2:8) "Can a woman forget her sucking child, that she should not have compassion on the son of her womb? Yes, they may forget, yet will I not forget thee." (Isa. 49:15) And thus Christ, after asserting that even a miserable little sparrow falleth not to the ground without our Father, tells us that we are of more value than many sparrows, and that God therefore bestows more abundant care on us, and that we may rest assured that the hairs of our head are all numbered.

Moreover the Scripture testifies that all men are under the power of God, and that He can either render them well-disposed towards His church or prevent their malice from taking effect. He gave Israel favour in the eyes of the Egyptians. He defeated the counsel of Ahithophel when it threatened to bring about the destruction of David. The devil could do nothing against Job without divine permission.

The knowledge of such truths as these makes us thankful in prosperity, patient in adversity, and marvellously confident of our future safety. When prosperity comes, we attribute it to God's goodness whether it reaches us through the agency of men or through other channels. When men show us kindness we consider that God has inclined their hearts to help us; and when we have abundant crops, we perceive that God has heard the heavens, the heavens have heard the earth, and the earth has heard its produce. (Hos. 2:21,22)

When adversity befalls us, we lift our thoughts to God, and the knowledge that His hand has done it is most efficacious in producing patience, submission, and quietness of mind. If Joseph had allowed his thoughts to dwell on the treachery of his brethren, he could never have recovered his brotherly affection for them; but when he considered the providence of God he forgot the injury which they had done to him and said: "Ye thought evil against me, but God meant it for good, to bring to pass, as it is this day, to save much people alive. Now therefore fear ye not; I will nourish you and your little ones." (Gen. 45:8,11, 19-21)

But though the will of God is the first great cause, as it is written: "I form the light, and create darkness; I make peace, and create evil; I the Lord do all these things" (Isa. 45:7), no godly man will close his eyes to second causes. He will indeed regard a man who does him a kindness as an agent employed by God's goodness; but he will heartily feel that he is indebted to the agent, and will endeavour to show his gratitude in a suitable way and to the best of his ability. If he suffer loss through his own negligence or carelessness, he will blame himself, while he acknowledges the hand of God. If one committed to his care dies of disease through his negligence, he will consider himself guilty though he knows that the duration of life is fixed by God's appointment. He will not abuse the doctrine of God's providence to make excuses for sin of any kind.

And especially in regard to things that are yet future will a godly man take heed to second causes. He will reckon that it is the Lord's kindness that supplies him with the ordinary means of providing for his own safety, and will not be slow to seek good advice, or assistance from those who can render assistance; he will make use of various means as the legitimate instruments of divine providence, and amidst all use of means will rely upon God's providence alone. Such principles as these preserve us from presumptuous confidence, urge us to continue in prayer, and furnish us with a hope that lifts us above the dangers whereby we are surrounded.

Herein appears the inestimable happiness of those who fear God. The life of man is threatened by innumerable dangers. Not to go outside of ourselves, the body contains the seeds of a thousand diseases. If we are chilled there is danger, and there is danger if we are overheated. Go where you will, death is at hand. On board ship, the thickness of a plank or a beam is all that stands between you and death. On horseback, your life depends on the horse's foot. Walk along the street, you are surrounded by as many dangers as there are tiles on the houses. An instrument of iron held in your own or a friend's hand may bring you to your end; and there are other dangers without number which I cannot stay to mention.

You say, such things seldom happen, and happen not to all men. I admit it: but since we see that they happen to some, and thus are reminded that they may happen to us, have we not cause to fear that they will? And what can be worse than to be continually subject to fear? I wish to point out that the misery of man would be great indeed if he were subject to the government of blind chance.

But when the light of divine providence has once shone upon a godly man, not merely is he freed from the excessive fear which previously oppressed him, but he is delivered from all anxious care. He rightly dreads chance, but he calmly leaves himself in the hands of God. He is comforted by knowing that his heavenly Father so controls all things by His power, so rules them by His sovereign will, so governs them by

His wisdom, that nothing can happen but according to His appointment. Thus the Psalmist sings: "Surely He shall deliver thee from the snare of the fowler, from the noxious pestilence. He shall cover thee with feathers, and under His wings shalt thou trust: His truth shall be thy shield and buckler. Thou shalt not be afraid for the terror by night; for the arrow that flieth by day; for the pestilence that walketh in darkness; for the destruction that wasteth at noonday."

Hence it is that the saints make their boast in divine protection: "The Lord is my helper: I will not fear what flesh can do unto me. The Lord is my protector, why should I fear?" They remember that the devil and all the hosts of the wicked are so bridled by the hand of God that they can neither form malicious designs against us nor move a finger to carry them out, save in so far as God permits, or rather commands. To be brief, you may easily see, if you consider the matter, that ignorance of divine providence is the worst of miseries, and that the knowledge of it brings supreme happiness.

I have said enough for the edification and comfort of believers: I have no desire to gratify the vain curiosity of the foolish. But it is necessary to notice a few passages of Scripture which seem to imply that God's purpose is changeable. Sometimes repentance is ascribed to Him: "It repented God that He had created man." (Gen. 6:6) "It repented the Lord that He had made Saul king." (I Sam. 15:11) "If that nation, against whom I have pronounced, turn from their evil, I will repent of the evil that I thought to do unto them." (Jer. 18:8)

Sometimes we are told that His decrees are cancelled. For instance, He had proclaimed by Jonah that Nineveh would be destroyed within forty days, and yet He was moved by their repentance to spare the city. He had told Hezekiah that he should die and not live; but was moved by his tears and prayers to add to his life fifteen years. Hence many conclude that God has not fixed the affairs of men by an eternal decree, but forms His decrees year by year, day by day, and hour by hour, according to each man's deserts and the requirements of equity.

But we must remember that repentance, in the strict sense of the term, implies ignorance, or error, or lack of power. We cannot attribute repentance to God without charging Him with ignorance of the future, or inability to avoid error, or haste and inconsiderateness in His purpose. But so far is this from being the mind of the Holy Spirit, that in the very place where He speaks of divine repentance He says, "The Strength of Israel will not lie nor repent: for He is not a man, that He should repent." (I Sam. 15:11, 29)

What then are we to understand by the term repentance when it is applied to God? We must understand it as we do other forms of speech which describe God to us after the manner of men. Since His lofty attributes are above the grasp of our feeble mind, He is described in a manner adapted to our capacity. He represents Himself to us, not as He is in Himself, but as He seems to us to be. Though He is above all movements of passion, He tells us that He is angry with sinners.

As therefore, when we hear that God is angry, we ought not to imagine that any movement of passion takes place in Him, but to remember that this form of speech is adapted to our capacity; so when God is said to repent we must understand it to mean that He visibly changes His course of action. Neither His purpose, nor His will, nor His mind is changed; but, while to the eyes of men a sudden alteration appears to take place, He accomplishes in one unchanging course the things which He has foreseen, approved, and decreed, from all eternity.

Let us further ask ourselves why God sent Jonah to the Ninevites to predict the ruin of their city: and why He sent Isaiah to tell Hezekiah that he must die. For He might have overthrown Nineveh and brought Hezekiah to the grave, without any previous announcement of His design. The fact is that He willed not the destruction of the city or the king, but their reformation, that they might escape. The object of Jonah's prophecy was to defer the overthrow of the guilty city; the object of Isaiah's message was the prolongation of the king's life. Who can fail to see that by such threatenings it was the Lord's good pleasure to awaken men to repentance, that they might escape the judgment which their sins had deserved? And thus Isaiah's challenge (Isa. 14:27) remains always unanswerable: "The Lord of hosts hath purposed, and who shall disannul it? and His hand is stretched out, and who shall turn it back?"

God's Righteous Use of Wicked Agents

A *greater* difficulty is presented to us by those passages of Scripture where it is said that Satan himself and all the wicked are controlled and directed by the will of God. For the natural mind scarcely comprehends how God can work by their instrumentality, and yet remain free from all blame and pass a just sentence of condemnation on His own agents. To meet this difficulty some have invented a distinction between what God does and what He permits. But this, though well meant, is an attempt to vindicate God's honour by a false theory; for He Himself repudiates such a defence by saying plainly that He does the things referred to.

Innumerable passages of Scripture prove clearly that men accomplish nothing but according to God's secret decree. When the psalmist saith, "But our God is in the heavens: He hath done whatsoever He hath pleased" (Ps. 115:3), it is evident that this includes all the actions of men; and this truth is more clearly seen in special instances.

We know from the book of Job that Satan presents himself before God to receive orders, no less than holy angels who obey willingly.

Hence, when Satan and the Sabaeans have afflicted and robbed Job, he acknowledges that the hand of God has done it, and says: "The Lord gave, and the Lord hath taken away." In like manner when God wills that Ahab should be deceived, "there came forth a spirit and stood before the Lord, and said, I will persuade him." And the Lord saith, "Thou shalt persuade him and prevail also: go forth and do so." If the blindness and folly of Ahab came upon him as a judgment from God, the theory of a mere permission is vain; for it would be absurd for a judge merely to permit the execution of his sentence, and not to decree that it should be carried out.

Again it was the purpose of the Jews to destroy Christ: Pilate and the soldiers complied with their furious wishes: but the disciples confessed in the solemn language of prayer that all the wicked only did what God's hand and God's counsel determined before to be done. (Acts 4:27,28) I might adduce many other instances from other parts of Scripture.

What Solomon says concerning the heart of a king, that it is the hand of the Lord, who turneth it whithersoever He will, is equally true of the hearts of all men. Even the conceptions of our minds are directed by God's secret power to the accomplishment of His purposes. Nothing can more clearly prove this than the fact that God so often tells us that He blinds the minds of men, afflicts them with delirium, pours out upon them the spirit of slumber, smites them with madness, hardens their hearts. (Rom. 11:8) Many, as we have said, refer all these statements to "the permissive will of God"; but this solution appears to me unwise, since the Holy Spirit expressly states that blindness and madness are inflicted on the wicked by the righteous judgment of God.

Thus far I have merely set forth what is openly and plainly taught in Scripture; let those who brand the holy oracles with reproach consider what kind of censorship it is that they take upon themselves. If they say, "Such matters are beyond our knowledge, and we claim credit for modesty in letting them alone"; I reply: "What can be more haughty than to speak a single syllable against the authority of God, and to say, 'I think differently,' or, 'It is best not to touch such doctrines'?" Such arrogance is nothing new; for in all ages there have been impious and ungodly men who have assailed this truth like angry dogs. Such men will find that David's words are true, that God will "overcome when He is judged." (Ps. 51:4)

It has been objected that if nothing happens but according to the will of God, He must have two contrary wills, because He secretly decrees what He in His law openly forbids. This fallacy is easily exposed; but before I try to do so, let me remind my readers, that it is a cavil against the Holy Spirit, not against me; for the Holy Spirit certainly taught Job to say, "The Lord hath taken away," when robbers had despoiled him of his goods. It is also written that Eli's sons obeyed not their father because the Lord would slay them. (I Sam. 2:25) So in later times the church says that Herod and Pilate conspired together to do whatsoever God's hand and God's counsel determined before to be done. (Acts. 4:27,28) Indeed if Christ had not been crucified by God's appointment, how could we have had redemption?

The fact is that God is not at variance with Himself, neither does His will change, nor does He pretend that He wills not the things which He wills. His will is one and undivided, but appears to us, on account of the feebleness of our understanding, to be at variance with itself. On this subject Augustine has a saying with which all godly people will agree: "Some men have good wishes which are not according to God's will, and others have bad wishes which are according to God's will. For instance, a good son may rightly wish that his father should live, while it is God's will that he should die; and a bad son may wickedly wish that his father should die, when it is also God's will that the father should die. And yet the godly son pleaseth God by wishing what God willeth not; while the wicked son displeaseth God by wishing what God willeth."

God sometimes fulfills His own righteous purposes by means of the evil purposes of the wicked. The same writer (Augustine) says that the apostate angels and all the wicked did, so far as they were concerned, what was contrary to the will of God; but, so far as His omnipotence is concerned, it was impossible for them to do anything against His will; for while they act in opposition to His will, His will is done by them. He adds that a good God would not allow evil to be done, unless an omnipotent God were able to bring good out of it.

A similar answer may be made to another objection which has been made against the truth that we are now considering. The objection is this: If God not only uses the instrumentality of the wicked, but also governs their plans and passions, is He not the author of all their crimes; and are not men who are subject to His will unjustly condemned for carrying out His decrees? This false reasoning confounds God's will with his commandment, though it is evident from many examples that there is a very wide difference between them.

God willed that David's adultery should be avenged by Absalom's incest; but it does not follow that God commanded Absalom to commit incest; unless haply we may say so in respect of David, in the same way as David speaks of Shimei's cursing. When the king said, "Let him alone, and let him curse; for the Lord hath bidden him" (2 Sam. 16:11), he by no means commended Shimei for obedience to God; but recognizing that the wicked man's tongue was the scourge of God, he patiently submitted to be chastised by it. We must hold fast to the principle that the wicked, by whose agency God accomplishes His righteous judgments and decrees, are not to be held guiltless as though they obeyed His commandment, a commandment which they wantonly and deliberately break.

It is our wisdom to embrace with meekness and docility everything that is taught in Holy Scripture. Those who have the insolence to revile its doctrines let loose their tongues against God, and are not worthy of further refutation.

RICHARD BAXTER 1615–1691

Lord Macaulay once quipped that the Puritans hated bear-baiting, not because it gave pain to the bear but because it gave pleasure to the spectators. Nothing could be further from the truth. The Puritans' attitude toward the world is expressed by Sibbes in his Saint's Cordials: *"Worldly things are good in themselves, and given to sweeten our passage to Heaven. . . . This world and the things thereof are all good, and were all made of God, for the benefit of His creature." And J. B. Marsden reminds our generation that among the Puritans were found not only the greatest divines but also many of England's ablest statesmen, most renowned soldiers, and not a few gifted orators and poets. Contrary to public opinion, Puritanism acted as a grand spiritual and cultural catharsis on England under Elizabeth. It was the Puritan spirit that brought about the freedom of the press, a high view of the sanctity of the marriage vow, the invocation of divorce on the ground of infidelity, a dignified view of labor, and an active and positive program of life.*

Richard Baxter was in the vanguard of the Puritan movement. His convictions brought him into collision with powerful forces. While serving as chaplain in Cromwell's army he opposed what he believed to be the wrong actions of the general, and so incurred his displeasure. When the army turned savagely against Charles I and clamored for his life, Baxter interposed, but unsuccessfully. Again, as Cromwell obtained more and more influence until he became a virtual dictator, it was Baxter who withstood him. In 1661 Parliament passed the Act of Uniformity. This called for a revision of The Book of Common Prayer, making it mandatory for all clergymen to assent to it and use it in public worship. The revision also unfrocked ministers not episcopally ordained. Mr. Baxter, with a large bloc of pastors of Presbyterian persuasion, left the Anglican Church.

He toiled in the parish at Kidderminster for nineteen years. Through his preaching and the power of his holy life the whole community was transformed from a habitation of cruelty and immorality to a garden of true piety. Moreover the impact of his example on church leaders bound them, whether Episcopalian, Presbyterian, or Independent, into a wholesome fellowship never before known in that vicinity. The Civil War interrupted his efforts in Kidderminster, and he retired to Gloucester and later to Coventry to continue his pastoral duties.

For his nonconformity in ecclesiastical matters he was sentenced to prison for eighteen months. It stands as moral distortion that the purest of seventeenth century Protestant theologians, the man who longed for, fought for, prayed for, and would cheerfully have sacrificed his life for the unification of the church should have been imprisoned by a Protestant judge and a Protestant jury.

Probably Baxter preached more sermons, engaged in more controversies, and wrote more books than any Nonconformist of his era. In the pulpit he spoke, like Isaiah, as a messenger of God whose lips had been touched with a live coal from the divine altar; in his own phrase, "as a dying man to dying men." His books are as compelling as his sermons. His Reformed Pastor, Saints' Everlasting Rest, *and* Call to the Unconverted *probe and plumb the corners of the heart. Coleridge says of his* Autobiography, *"I could almost as soon doubt the Gospel veracity as his veracity . . . He feels and reasons more like an angel than a man."*

Baxter was an indefatigable worker. Listen to an account of his pastoral activities: two sermons each Lord's day, one in mid-week, besides occasional sermons; a Thursday evening discussion meeting; a three-hour prayer meeting with young people once a week; calls on and catechism with seven families every week. Beyond this he was a practicing physician of sorts: "Because I never took a penny of anyone, I was crowded with patients, so that almost twenty would be at my door at once."

And how does he treat this whirlwind existence? "All my labors, (except my private conferences with the families) even preaching and preparing for it were but my recreations and, as it were, the work of my spare hours."

Lord Morley has called Richard Baxter "the profoundest theologian of them all," and another, "the most learned and moderate of the Dissenters." He has bequeathed to the reading world a priceless library of books, pamphlets (some two hundred), and a few poetic fragments. And he has left the Christian world the example of a godly life, a dedicated mind, an intrepid spirit, a character unimpeachable.

How to Lead a Heavenly Life upon Earth

REVEREND RICHARD BAXTER

AS THOU DOST value the comforts of a heavenly conversation, I must here charge thee, from God, to avoid carefully some dangerous hindrances; and then faithfully and diligently to practice such duties as will especially assist thee in attaining to a heavenly life.

FIRST:—Let us consider those hindrances which are to be avoided with all possible care.

I. LIVING IN ANY KNOWN SIN, is a grand impediment to a heavenly conversation. What havoc this will make in thy soul! O, the joys that this hath destroyed! The ruin it hath made among men's graces! The soul-strengthening duties it hath hindered! Christian reader, art thou one that hast used violence with thy conscience? Art thou a wilful neglecter of known duties, either public, private, or secret? Art thou a slave to thine appetite, or to any other commanding sense? Art thou a proud seeker of thine own esteem? Art thou a peevish and passionate person, ready to take fire at every word, or look, or supposed slight? Art thou a deceiver of others in thy dealings, or one that will be rich, right or wrong? If this be thy case, I dare say, heaven and thy soul are very great strangers.

These beams in thine eyes will not suffer thee to look to heaven; they will be a "cloud between thee and thy God." When thou dost but attempt to study eternity, and gather comforts from the life to come, thy sin will presently look thee in the face, and say, "These things belong not to thee. How shouldst thou take comfort from heaven, who takest so much pleasure in the lusts of the flesh?" How will this damp thy joys, and make the thoughts of that day and state become thy trouble, and not thy delight? Every wilful sin will be to thy comforts as water to the fire; when thou thinkest to quicken them, this will quench them. It will utterly indispose and disable thee, that thou canst no more ascend in divine meditation, than a bird can fly when its wings are clipped. Sin cuts the very sinews of this heavenly life.

O, man! What a life dost thou lose? What daily delights dost thou sell for a vile lust! If heaven and hell can meet together, and God become a lover of sin, then mayst thou live in thy sin, and in the tastes of glory; and have a conversation in heaven, though thou cherish thy corruption. And take heed, lest it banish thee from heaven, as it does thy heart. And though thou be not guilty, and knowest no reigning

207

sin in thy soul, think what a sad thing it would be, if ever this should prove thy case. Watch, therefore, especially resolve to keep from the occasions of sin, and out of the way of temptations. What need have we daily to pray, "Lead us not into temptation, but deliver us from evil"!

2. AN EARTHLY MIND is another hindrance carefully to be avoided. God and Mammon, earth and heaven, cannot both have the delight of thy heart. Remember, thou hast to do with the Searcher of hearts. Certainly, so much as thou delightest, and takest up thy rest on earth, so much of thy delight in God is abated. Thine earthly mind may consist with thy outward profession and common duties, but it cannot consist with this heavenly duty. Thou thyself knowest how seldom and cold, how cursory and reserved, thy thoughts have been of the joys above, ever since thou didst trade so eagerly for the world. O, the cursed madness of many that seem to be religious! They thrust themselves into a multitude of employments, till they are so loaded with labours, and clogged with cares, that their souls are as unfit to converse with God, as a man to walk with a mountain on his back; and as unapt to soar in meditation, as their bodies to leap above the sun! And when they have lost that heaven upon earth, which they might have had, they take up with a few rotten arguments to prove it lawful; though, indeed, they cannot.

I advise thee, Christian, who hast tasted the pleasures of a heavenly life, as ever thou wouldst taste of them any more, avoid this devouring gulf of an earthly mind. If once thou come to this, that thou "wilt be rich," thou "fallest into temptation and a snare, and into many foolish and hurtful lusts." Keep these things loose about thee, like thy upper garments, that thou mayst lay them by whenever there is need; but let God and glory be next thy heart. Ever remember, "that the friendship of the world is enmity with God." "Love not the world, neither the things that are in the world. If any man love the world, the love of the Father is not in him." This is plain dealing, and happy he that faithfully receives it!

3. BEWARE OF THE COMPANY OF THE UNGODLY. Not that I would dissuade thee from necessary converse, or from doing them any office of love; especially not from endeavouring the good of their souls, as long as thou hast any opportunity or hope; nor would I have thee to conclude them to be dogs and swine, in order to evade the duty of reproof; nor even to judge them such at all, as long as there is any hope for the better: much less can I approve their practice, who conclude men dogs or swine, before ever they faithfully and lovingly admonished them, or perhaps before they have known them, or spoke with them. But it is the unnecessary society of ungodly men, and too much familiarity with unprofitable companions, that I dissuade you from.

Not only the open profane, the swearer, the drunkard, and the enemies of godliness, will prove hurtful companions to us, though these indeed are chiefly to be avoided; but too frequent society with persons merely civil and moral, whose conversation is empty and unedifying, may much divert our thoughts from heaven. Our backwardness is such that we need the most constant and powerful helps. A stone, or a clod, is as fit to rise and fly in the air as our hearts are naturally to move toward heaven. You need not hinder the rocks from flying up to the sky; it is sufficient that you do not help them: and surely, if our spirits have not great assistance, they may easily be kept from soaring upward, though they should never meet with the least impediment. O, think of this in the choice of your company!

When your spirits are so disposed for heaven, that you need no help to lift them up, but, as flames, you are always mounting, and carrying with you all that is in your way, then, indeed, you may be less careful of your company; but till then, as you love the delights of a heavenly life, be careful herein. What will it advantage thee in a divine life to hear how the market goes, or what the weather is, or is like to be, or what news is stirring! This is the discourse of earthly men. What will it conduce to the raising thy heart God-ward, to hear that this is an able minister, or that an eminent Christian, or this an excellent sermon, or that an excellent book, or to hear some difficult, but unimportant, controversy? Yet this, for the most part, is the sweetest discourse thou are like to have from a formal, speculative, deadhearted professor. Nay, if thou hadst newly been warming thy heart in the contemplation of the blessed joys above, would not this discourse benumb thy affections, and quickly freeze thy heart again?

I appeal to the judgment of any man that hath tried it, and maketh observations on the frame of his spirit. Men cannot well talk of one thing, and mind another, especially things of such different natures. You, young men, who are most liable to this temptation, think seriously of what I say; can you have your hearts in heaven among your roaring companions, in an ale-house or tavern? Or when you work in your shops with those whose common language is oaths, "filthiness, or foolish talking or jesting"? Nay, let me tell you, if you choose such company when you might have better, and find most delight in such, you are so far from a heavenly conversation, that, as yet, you have no title to heaven at all, and in that state shall never come there. If your treasure was there, your heart could not be on things so distant. In a word, our company will be a part of our happiness in heaven, and it is a singular part of our furtherance to it, or hindrance from it.

4. AVOID FREQUENT DISPUTES ABOUT LESSER TRUTHS, AND A RELIGION THAT LIES ONLY IN OPINIONS. They are usually least acquainted with a heavenly life, who are violent disputers about the circumstantials of religion. He whose religion is all in his opinions, will be most fre-

quently and zealously speaking his opinions; and he whose religion lies in the knowledge and love of God and Christ, will be most delight-fully speaking of that happy time when he shall enjoy them. He is a rare and precious Christian, who is skilful to improve well-known truths. Therefore, let me advise you who aspire after a heavenly life, not to spend too much of your thoughts, your time, your zeal, or your speech, upon disputes, that less concern your souls; but when hypo-crites are feeding on husks or shells, do you feed on the joys above.

5. TAKE HEED OF A PROUD AND LOFTY SPIRIT. There is such an antip-athy between this sin and God, that thou wilt never get thy heart near Him, nor get Him near thy heart, as long as this prevaileth in it. If it cast the angels out of heaven, it must needs keep thy heart from heaven. If it cast our first parents out of Paradise, and separated between the Lord and us, and brought His curse on all the creatures here below, it will certainly keep our hearts from Paradise, and in-crease the cursed separation from our God. Intercourse with God will keep men low, and that lowliness will promote their intercourse. When a man is used to be much with God, and taken up in the study of His glorious attributes, he "abhors himself in dust and ashes," and that self-abhorrence is his best preparative to obtain admittance to God again. Therefore, after a soul-humbling day, or in times of trouble, when the soul is lowest, it useth to have freest access to God, and savour most of the life above. The delight of God is in "him that is poor, and of a contrite spirit, and trembleth at His word"; and the delight of such a soul is in God; and then where there is mutual de-light, there will be freest admittance, heartiest welcome, and most frequent converse.

But God is so far from dwelling in the soul that is proud, that He will not admit it to any near access. "The proud He knoweth afar off"; "God resisteth the proud, and giveth grace to the humble." A proud mind is high in conceit, self-esteem, and carnal aspiring; a humble mind is high, indeed, in God's esteem, and in holy aspiring. These two sorts of high-mindedness are most of all opposite to each other, as we see most wars are between princes and princes, and not between a prince and a ploughman. Well, then, art thou a man of worth in thy own eyes? Art thou delighted when thou hearest of thy esteem with men, and much dejected when thou hearest that they slight thee? Dost thou love those best that honour thee, and think meanly of them that do not, though they be otherwise men of godli-ness and honesty? Must thou have thy humours fulfilled, and thy judg-ment be a rule, and thy word a law to all about thee? Art thy passions kindled, if thy word or will be crossed?

Art thou ready to judge humility to be sordid baseness, and knowest not how to submit to humble confession, when thou hast sinned against

God, or injured thy brother? Art thou one that lookest strange at the godly poor, and art almost ashamed to be their companion? Canst thou not serve God in a low place as well as a high? Are thy boastings restrained more by prudence or artifice than humility? Dost thou desire to have all men's eyes upon thee, and to hear them say, "This is he"? Art thou unacquainted with the deceitfulness and wickedness of thy heart? Art thou more ready to defend thy innocence, then accuse thyself, or confess thy fault? Canst thou hardly bear a close reproof, or digest plain dealing? If these symptoms be undeniably in thy heart, thou art a proud person. There is too much of hell abiding in thee, to have any acquaintance with heaven; thy soul is too like the devil, to have any familiarity with God. A proud man makes himself his god, and sets up himself as his idol; how, then, can his affections be set on God? How can he possibly have his heart in heaven? Invention and memory may possibly furnish his tongue with humble and heavenly expressions, but in his spirit there is no more heaven than there is humility.

I speak the more of it, because it is the most common and dangerous sin in morality, and most promotes the great sin of infidelity. O, Christian! If thou wouldst live continually in the presence of thy Lord, lie in the dust, and He will thence take thee up. "Learn of Him to be meek and lowly, and thou shalt find rest unto thy soul." Otherwise thy soul will be "like the troubled sea, when it cannot rest, whose waters cast up mire and dirt"; and instead of these sweet delights in God, thy pride will fill thee with perpetual disquiet. As he that humbleth himself as a little child shall hereafter be greatest in the kingdom of heaven, so shall he now be greatest in the foretastes of that kingdom. God "dwells with a contrite and humble spirit, to revive the spirit of the humble, and to revive the heart of the contrite ones." Therefore, "humble yourselves in the sight of the Lord, and He shall lift you up." And when "others are cast down, then thou shalt say, there is lifting up; and He shall save the humble person."

6. A SLOTHFUL SPIRIT IS ANOTHER IMPEDIMENT TO THIS HEAVENLY LIFE. And I verily think, there nothing hinders it more than this in men of a good understanding. If it were only the exercise of the body, the moving of the lips, the bending of the knee, men would as commonly step to heaven as they go to visit a friend. But to separate our thoughts and affections from the world, to draw forth all our graces, and increase each in its proper object, and hold them to it till the work prospers in our hands; this, this is the difficulty. Reader, heaven is above thee, and dost thou think to travel this steep ascent without labour and resolution? Canst thou get that earthly heart to heaven, and bring that backward mind to God, while thou liest still, and takest thine ease? If lying down at the foot of the hill, and looking toward the top, and

wishing we were there, would serve the turn, then we should have daily travellers to heaven. But "the kingdom of heaven suffereth violence, and the violent take it by force." There must be violence used to get these first-fruits, as well as to get the full possession.

Dost thou not feel it so, though I should not tell thee? Will thy heart get upwards, except thou drive it? Thou knowest that heaven is all thy hope; that nothing below can yield thee rest; that a heart, seldom thinking of heaven, can fetch but little comfort thence; and yet dost thou not lose thy opportunities, and lie below, when thou shouldst walk above, and live with God? Dost thou not commend the sweetness of a heavenly life, and judge those the best Christians that use it, and yet never try it thyself? As the sluggard that stretches himself on his bed, and cries, O that this were working! so dost thou talk, and trifle, and live at thy ease, and say, O that I could get my heart to heaven! How many read books, and hear sermons, expecting to hear of some easier way, or to meet with a shorter course to comfort, than they are ever like to find in Scripture. Or they ask for directions for a heavenly life, and if the hearing them will serve, they will be heavenly Christians; but if we show them their work, and tell them they cannot have these delights on easier terms, then they leave us, as the young man left Christ, sorrowful.

If thou art convinced, reader, that this work is necessary to thy comfort, set upon it resolutely; if thy heart draw back, force it on with the command of reason; if thy reason begin to dispute, produce the command of God, and urge thy own necessity, with the other considerations suggested in the former chapter. Let not such an incomparable treasure lie before thee, with thy hand in thy bosom; nor thy life be a continual vexation, when it might be a continual feast, only because thou will not exert thyself. Sit not still with a disconsolate spirit, while comforts grow before thine eyes, like a man in the midst of a garden of flowers, that will not rise to get them, and partake of their sweetness. This I know, Christ is the fountain; but the well is deep, and thou must get forth this water before thou canst be refreshed with it. I know, so far as you are spiritual, you need not all this striving and violence; but in part you are carnal, and as long as it is so, there is need of labour.

It was a custom of the Parthians not to give their children any meat in the morning, before they saw the sweat on their faces with some labour. And you shall find this to be God's usual course, not to give His children the tastes of His delights till they begin to sweat in seeking after them. Judge, therefore, whether a heavenly life, or thy carnal ease, be better; and, as a wise man, make thy choice accordingly. Yea, let me add for thy encouragement, thou needst not employ thy thoughts more than thou now dost; it is only to fix them upon better and more pleasant objects. Employ but as many serious thoughts every day upon the excellent glory of the life to come, as thou now dost upon worldly affairs, yea, on vanities and impertinences, and thy heart will soon be at heaven. On the whole, it is "the field of the slothful, that is all grown over with thorns and nettles; and the desire of the slothful killeth his joy, for his hands refuse to labour; and it is the slothful man that saith, There is a lion in the way, a lion is in the streets. As the door turneth on its hinges, so doth the slothful upon his bed. The slothful hideth his hand in his bosom; it grieveth him to bring it again to his mouth," though it be to feed himself with the food of life. What is this but throwing away our consolations, and consequently the precious blood that bought them? For "he that is slothful in his work is brother to him that is a great waster." Apply this to thy spiritual work, and study well the meaning of it.

7. CONTENTMENT WITH THE MERE PREPARATIVES TO THIS HEAVENLY LIFE, WHILE WE ARE UTTER STRANGERS TO THE LIFE ITSELF, is also a dangerous and secret hindrance: when we take up the mere study of heavenly things, and the notions of them, or the talking with one another about them; as if this were enough to make us heavenly. None are in more danger of this snare, than those that are employed in leading the devotions of others, especially preachers of the gospel. O how easily may such be deceived! While they do nothing so much as read and study of heaven; preach, and pray and talk of heaven; is not this the heavenly life? Alas! all this is but mere preparation: this is but collecting the materials, not erecting the building itself: it is but gathering the manna for others, and not eating and digesting it ourselves. As he that sits at home may draw exact maps of countries, and yet never see them, nor travel toward them; so may you describe to others the joys of heaven, and yet never come near it in your own hearts.

A blind man, by learning, may dispute of light and colours; so may you set forth to others that heavenly light, which never enlightened your own souls, and bring that fire from the hearts of your people, which never warmed your own hearts. What heavenly passages had Balaam in his prophecies, yet how little of it in his spirit! Nay, we are under a more subtle temptation than any other man to draw us from this heavenly life. Studying and preaching of heaven more resembles a heavenly life, than thinking and talking of the world does; and the resemblance is apt to deceive us. This is to die the most miserable death, even to famish ourselves, because we have bread on our tables; and to die for thirst, while we draw water for others, thinking it enough that we have daily to do with it, though we never drink for the refreshment of our own souls.

SECONDLY:—Having thus showed what hindrances will resist the work, I expect that thou resolve against them, consider them seriously, and avoid them faithfully, or else thy labour will be in vain. I must also tell thee, that I here expect thy promise, as thou valuest the delights of these foretastes of heaven, to make conscience of performing the following duties, particularly:—

1. BE CONVINCED THAT HEAVEN IS THE ONLY TREASURE AND HAPPINESS, and labour to know what a treasure and happiness it is. If thou do not believe it to be the chief good, thou wilt never set thy heart upon it; and this conviction must sink into thy affections; for if it be only a notion, it will have little efficacy. If Eve once supposes she sees more worth in the forbidden fruit, than in the love and enjoyment of God, no wonder if it have more of her heart than God. If your judgment once prefer the delights of the flesh before the delights of the presence of God, it is impossible your heart should be in heaven. As it is ignorance of the emptiness of things below, that makes men so overvalue them, so it is ignorance of the high delights above which is the cause that men so little mind them.

If you see a purse of gold, and believe it to be but counters [counterfeit], it will not entice your affections to it. It is not the real excellence of a thing itself, but its known excellence that excites desire. If an ignorant man see a book containing the secrets of arts or sciences, he values it no more than a common piece, because he knows not what is in it; but he that knows it, highly values it, and can even forbear his meat, drink and sleep to read it. As the Jews killed the Messiah, while they waited for Him, because they did not know Him; so the world cries out for rest, and busily seeks for delight and happiness, because they know it not; for did they thoroughly know what it is, they could not so slight the everlasting treasure.

2. LABOUR ALSO TO KNOW THAT HEAVEN IS THY OWN HAPPINESS. We may confess heaven to be the best condition, though we despair of enjoying it; and we may desire and seek it, if we see the attainment but probable; but we can never delightfully rejoice in it till we are in some measure persuaded of our title to it. What comfort is it to a man that is naked to see the rich attire of others? What delight is it for a man that hath not a house to put his head in to see the sumptuous buildings of others? Would not all this rather increase his anguish and make him more sensible of his own misery? So, for a man to know the excellencies of heaven, and not know whether ever he shall enjoy them, may raise desire and urge pursuit, but he will have little joy.

Who will set his heart on another man's possessions? If your houses, your goods, your cattle, your children were not your own, you would less mind them and less delight in them. O, Christian! rest not, therefore, till you can call this rest your own: bring thy heart to the bar of trial: set the qualifications of the saints on one side, and of thy soul on the other, and then judge how near they resemble. Thou hast the same word to judge thyself by now, as thou must be judged by at the great day. Mistake not the Scripture's description of a saint, that thou neither acquit nor condemn thyself upon mistakes. For as groundless hopes tend to confusion, and are the greatest cause of most men's damnation; so groundless doubts tend to, and are the great cause of, the saints' perplexity and distress. Therefore, lay thy foundation for trial safely, and proceed in the work deliberately and resolutely, nor give over till thou canst say, either thou hast or hast not yet a title to this rest.

O! if men did truly know that God is their own Father, and Christ their own Redeemer and Head, and that those are their own everlasting habitations, and that there they must abide and be happy forever; how could they choose but be transported with the forethoughts thereof! If a Christian could but look upon sun, moon and stars, and reckon all his own in Christ and say, "These are the blessings that my Lord hath procured me and things incomparably greater than these"; what holy raptures would his spirit feel!

The more do they sin against their own comforts, as well as against the grace of the gospel, who plead for their unbelief, and cherish distrustful thoughts of God, and injurious thoughts of their Redeemer; who represent the covenant as if it were of works, and not of grace; and Christ as an enemy, rather than a Saviour; as if He were willing they should die in their unbelief when He hath invited them so often and so affectionately and suffered the agonies that they should suffer. Wretches that we are! to be keeping up jealousies of our Lord, when we should be rejoicing in His love. As if any man could choose Christ, before Christ hath chosen him, or any man were more willing to be happy, than Christ is to make him happy.

Away with these injurious, if not blasphemous thoughts! If ever thou has harboured such thoughts in thy breast, cast them from thee, and take heed how thou ever entertainest them more. God hath written the names of His people in heaven, as you use to write your names or marks on your goods; and shall we be attempting to raze them out and to write our names on the doors of hell? But, blessed be "God, whose foundation standeth sure"; and who "keepeth us by His power through faith unto salvation."

3. LABOUR TO APPREHEND HOW NEAR THY REST IS. What we think near at hand, we are more sensible of than that which we behold at a distance. When judgments or mercies are afar off, we talk of them with little concern; but when they draw close to us, we tremble at, or rejoice in, them. This makes men think on heaven so insensibly, because they conceive it at too great a distance; they look on it as twenty, thirty or forty years off. How much better were it to receive "the sentence of death in ourselves," and to look on eternity as near at hand! While I am thinking, and writing of it, it hasteth near, and I am even entering

into it before I am aware. While thou art reading this, whoever thou art, time posteth on, and thy life will be gone "as a tale that is told." If you verily believed you should die tomorrow, how seriously would you think of heaven tonight! When Samuel had told Saul, "Tomorrow shalt thou be with me"; this struck him to the heart. And if Christ should say to a believing soul, "Tomorrow shalt thou be with me," this would bring him in spirit to heaven beforehand. Do but suppose that you are still entering into heaven, and it will greatly help you more seriously to mind it.

4. LET THY ETERNAL REST BE THE SUBJECT OF THY FREQUENT SERIOUS DISCOURSE; especially with those that can speak from their hearts, and are seasoned themselves with a heavenly nature. It is great pity Christians should ever meet together, without some talk of their meeting in heaven, or of the way to it, before they part. It is pity so much time is spent in vain conversation, and useless disputes, and not a serious word of heaven among them. Methinks we should meet together on purpose to warm our spirits with discoursing of our rest. To hear a Christian set forth that blessed, glorious state, with life and power, from the promises of the Gospel, methinks, should make us say, "Did not our hearts burn within us, while He opened to us the Scriptures?" If a Felix will tremble, when he hears his judgment powerfully represented, why should not the believer be revived, when he hears his eternal rest described? Wicked men can be delighted in talking together of their wickedness; and should not Christians then be delighted in talking of Christ; and should not the heirs of heaven in talking of their inheritance?

This may make our hearts revive, as it did Jacob's to hear the message that called him to Goshen, and to see the chariots that should bring him to Joseph. O that we were furnished with skill and resolution to turn the stream of men's common discourse to these more sublime and precious things! and, when men begin to talk of things unprofitable, that we could tell how to put in a word for heaven, and say, as Peter of his bodily food, "Not so, for I have never eaten any thing that is common or unclean!" O the good that we might both do and receive by this course! Had it not been to deter us from unprofitable conversation, Christ would not have talked of our "giving an account of every idle word in the day of judgment." Say then, as the Psalmist, when you are in company, "Let my tongue cleave to the roof of my mouth, if I prefer not Jerusalem above my chief joy." Then you shall find it true, that a "wholesome tongue is a tree of life."

5. ENDEAVOUR, IN EVERY DUTY, TO RAISE THY AFFECTIONS NEARER TO HEAVEN. God's end in the institution of His ordinances was that they should be as so many steps to advance us to our rest, and by which, in subordination to Christ, we might daily ascend in our affections. Let

this be thy end in using them, and doubtless they will not be unsuccessful. How have you been rejoiced by a few lines from a friend, when you could not see him face to face! And may we not have intercourse with God in His ordinances, though our persons be yet so far remote? May not our spirits rejoice in reading those lines, which contain our legacy and charter for heaven? With what gladness and triumph may we read the expressions of divine love, and hear of our celestial country, though we have not yet the happiness to behold it! Men that are separated by sea and land can by letters carry on great and gainful trades; and may not a Christian, in the wise improvement of duties, drive on this happy trade for rest?

Come, then, renounce formality, custom and applause and kneel down in secret or public prayer with hope to get thy heart nearer to God before thou risest up. When thou openest thy Bible, or other book, hope to meet with some passage of divine truth and such blessing of the Spirit with it, as will give thee a fuller taste of heaven. When thou art going to the house of God, say, "I hope to meet with somewhat from God to raise my affections before I return; I hope the Spirit will give me the meeting, and sweeten my heart with those celestial delights; I hope Christ will 'appear to me in that way, and shine about me with light from heaven'; let me hear His instructing and reviving voice, and cause the scales to fall from my eyes, that I may see more of that glory than I ever yet saw. I hope, before I return, my Lord will bring my heart within the view of rest, and set it before His Father's presence, that I may return as 'the shepherds' from the heavenly vision, 'glorifying and praising God, for all the things I have heard and seen.' "

When the Indians first saw that the English could converse together by letters, they thought there was some spirit enclosed in them. So would by-standers admire, when Christians have communion with God in duties, what there is in those Scriptures, in that sermon, in this prayer, that fills their hearts so full of joy and so transports them above themselves. Certainly God would not fail us in our duties, if we did not fail ourselves. Remember, therefore, always to pray for your minister, that God would put some divine message into his mouth, which may leave a heavenly relish upon your spirit.

6. IMPROVE EVERY OBJECT AND EVERY EVENT, to mind thy soul of its approaching rest. As all providences and creatures are means to our rest, so they point us to that as their end. God's sweetest dealings with us at the present would not be half so sweet as they are if they did not intimate some further sweetness. Thou takest but the bare earnest and overlookest the main sum when thou receivest thy mercies and forgettest thy crown. O that Christians were skilful in this art! You can open your Bibles; learn to open the volumes of creation and providence,

to read there also of God and glory. Thus we might have a fuller taste of Christ and heaven in every common meal, than most men have in a sacrament. If thou prosper in the world, let it make thee more sensible of thy perpetual prosperity. If thou art weary with labour, let it make the thought of thy eternal rest more sweet. If things go cross, let thy desires be more earnest to have sorrows and sufferings for ever cease.

Is thy body refreshed with food or sleep? Remember the inconceivable refreshment with Christ. Dost thou hear any good news? Remember what glad tidings it will be to hear the trump of God, and the applauding sentence of Christ. Art thou delighted with the society of the saints? Remember what the perfect society in heaven will be. Is God communicating Himself to thy spirit? Remember the time of thy highest advancement, when both thy communion and joy shall be full. Dost thou hear the raging noise of the wicked and the confusions of the world? Think of the blessed harmony in heaven. Dost thou hear the tempest of war? Remember the day when thou shalt be in perfect peace, under the wings of the Prince of peace forever. Thus, every condition and creature affords us advantages for a heavenly life, if we had but hearts to improve them.

7. BE MUCH IN THE ANGELICAL WORK OF PRAISE. The more heavenly the employment, the more it will make the spirit heavenly. Praising God is the work of angels and saints in heaven and will be our own everlasting work; and if we were more in it now, we should be liker to what we shall be then. As desire, faith and hope are of shorter continuance than love and joy, so also preaching, prayer and sacraments and all means for expressing and confirming our faith and hope shall cease when our triumphant expressions of love and joy shall abide forever. The liveliest emblem of heaven that I know upon earth is when the people of God, in deep sense of His excellency and bounty, from hearts abounding with love and joy, join together both in heart and voice in the cheerful and melodious singing of His praises. These delights, like the testimony of the Spirit, witness themselves to be of God and bring the evidences of their heavenly parentage along with them.

Little do we know how we wrong ourselves by shutting out of our prayers the praises of God, or allowing them so narrow a room as we usually do, while we are copious enough in our confessions and petitions. Reader, I entreat thee, remember this: let praises have a larger room in thy duties; keep matter ready at hand to feed thy praise, as well as matter for confession and petition. To this end, study the excellencies and goodness of the Lord, as frequently as thy own wants and unworthiness; the mercies thou hast received, and those which are promised as often as the sins thou hast committed. "Praise is comely for the upright. Whoso offereth praise, glorifieth God. Praise ye the Lord, for the Lord is good: sing praises unto His name, for it is pleasant. Let us offer the sacrifice of praise to God continually, that is, the fruit of our lips, giving thanks to His name." Had not David a most heavenly spirit, who was so much in this heavenly work? Doth it not sometimes raise our hearts, when we only read the song of Moses, and the Psalms of David? How much more would it raise and refresh us to be skilful and frequent in the work ourselves!

O the madness of youth, that lay out their vigour of body and mind upon vain delights and fleshly lusts, [vigor] which is so fit for the noblest work of man! And O the sinful folly of many of the saints, who drench their spirits in continual sadness and waste their days in complaints and groans and so make themselves, both in body and mind, unfit for this sweet and heavenly work! Instead of joining with the people of God in His praises, they are questioning their worthiness and studying their miseries, and so rob God of His glory and themselves of their consolation. But the greatest destroyer of our comfort in this duty is our taking up with the tune and melody, and suffering the heart to be idle, which ought to perform the principal part of the work, and use the melody to revive and exhilarate itself.

8. EVER KEEP THY SOUL POSSESSED WITH BELIEVING THOUGHTS OF THE INFINITE LOVE OF GOD. Love is the attractive of love. Few so vile but will love those that love them. No doubt it is the death of our heavenly life to have hard thoughts of God, to conceive of Him as One that would rather damn than save us. This is to put the blessed God into the similitude of Satan. When our ignorance and unbelief have drawn the most deformed picture of God in our imaginations, then we complain that we cannot love Him, nor delight in Him. This is the case of many thousand Christians. Alas, that we should thus blaspheme God, and blast our own joys! Scripture assures us that "God is love; that fury is not in Him; that He hath no pleasure in the death of the wicked, but that the wicked turn from his way, and live." Much more hath He testified His love to His chosen, and His full resolution to save them.

O that we could always think of God as we do of a friend; as of one that unfeignedly loves us, even more than we do ourselves; whose very heart is set upon us to do us good, and hath therefore provided for us an everlasting dwelling with Himself! It would not then be so hard to have our hearts ever with Him! Where we love most heartily, we shall think most sweetly and most freely. I fear most Christians think higher of the love of a hearty friend than of the love of God; and what wonder, then, if they love their friends better than God, and trust them more confidently than God, and had rather live with them than with God?

9. CAREFULLY OBSERVE AND CHERISH THE MOTIONS OF THE SPIRIT OF GOD. If ever thy soul get above this earth, and get acquainted with this heavenly life, the Spirit of God must be to thee as the chariot to Elijah; yea, the very living principle by which thou must move and ascend. O, then, grieve not thy guide, quench not thy life, knock not off thy chariot wheels! You little think how much the life of all your graces and the happiness of your souls depend upon your ready and cordial obedience to the Spirit. When the Spirit urges you to secret prayer, or forbids thee thy transgressions, or points out to thee the way in which thou shouldst go, and thou wilt not regard, no wonder if heaven and thy soul be strange. If thou wilt not follow the Spirit, while it would draw thee to Christ and thy duty, how should it lead thee to heaven, and bring thy heart into the presence of God?

What supernatural help, what bold access, shall the soul find in its approaches to the Almighty, that constantly obeys the Spirit? And how backward, how dull, how ashamed will he be in these addresses, who hath often broke away from the Spirit that would have guided him! Christian reader, dost thou not feel sometimes a strong impression to retire from the world and draw near to God? Do not disobey, but take the offer and hoist up thy sails while this blessed gale may be had. The more of the Spirit we resist, the deeper will be the wound; and the more we obey, the speedier will be our pace.

10. I ADVISE THEE, AS A FURTHER HELP TO THIS HEAVENLY LIFE, NEGLECT NOT THE DUE CARE OF THY BODILY HEALTH. Thy body is a useful servant, if thou give it its due, and no more than its due; but it is a most devouring tyrant, if thou suffer it to have what it unreasonably desires; and it is as a blunted knife if thou unjustly deny it what is necessary to its support. When we consider how frequently men offend on both extremes and how few use their bodies aright, we cannot wonder if they be much hindered in their converse with heaven. Most men are slaves to their appetite, and can scarce deny anything to the flesh, and are therefore willingly carried by it to their sports or profits or vain companions, when they should raise their minds to God and heaven.

As you love your souls, "make not provision for the flesh, to fulfil the lusts thereof"; but remember, "to be carnally-minded is death; because the carnal mind is enmity against God, for it is not subject to the law of God, neither indeed can be. So, then, they that are in the flesh cannot please God. Therefore, brethren, we are debtors, not to the flesh, to live after the flesh. For if ye live after the flesh, ye shall die; but if ye through the Spirit do mortify the deeds of the body, ye shall live." There are a few who much hinder their heavenly joy by denying the body its necessaries, and so making it unable to serve them; if such wronged their flesh only, it would be no great matter; but they wrong their souls also; as he that spoils the house injures the inhabitants. When the body is sick and the spirits languish, how heavily do we move in the thoughts and joys of heaven!

JOHN BUNYAN 1628-1688

The "Shakespeare among divines" singularly resembled any one of a half dozen characters from Shakespeare's own plays. Long wavy hair, parted down the center, fell shoulder-length over white collar and black cavalier robe. S-shaped eyebrows serpentined above thick lids and bulging eyes that veiled penetrating humor and perceptiveness. A spreading mustache separated his mouth from a great bulb of a nose, and a shadowy island of fuzz lodged just under his lower lip. One might easily imagine him clowning his way through A Midsummer Night's Dream, and loving it.

Actually, of course, the Tinker of Bedford filled a far more serious role. His journey from the City of Destruction to Zion via the Slough of Despond, the Wicket Gate, the Empty Tomb and the Cross, the Palace Beautiful, Vanity Fair, the Delectable Mountains, and other way stations, added up to a tortuous and hazardous pilgrimage.

Bunyan was born, he tells us, of a "low, inconsiderable generation." His father labored as a tinker, or mender and vendor of pots and pans. In his day in England, gypsies did this type of work almost exclusively, which has led some to conclude that John had gypsy blood in him. Early in life he decided to follow his father's trade.

After his awakening, so vividly pictured in Grace Abounding, he performed service as a deacon in the Bedford Church. Before long he assayed to preach. Immediately, God bore witness mightily to the word of His grace through Bunyan. With no formal education, his amazing grasp of the doctrines of sin and redemption, his homespun method of stating lessons, his wit, his pungent illustrations took hold of listeners and wooed multitudes to Jesus Christ.

One would expect him to be a Nonconformist, and he was. Because he insisted on conducting services not recognized by the Church of England, the authorities sentenced him to a twelve-year term of imprisonment. With only the Bible, a copy of Fox's Book of Martyrs, and a rich and lively imagination, Bunyan commenced putting together his immortal works.

His Pilgrim's Progress was a phenomenal success, selling one hundred thousand copies in no time. Meanwhile, it has continued its popularity and has enjoyed more of a circulation, the Bible excepted, than any book ever written. Translations have been made in every important language on earth. Lord Macauley once declared it to be the only successful allegory ever created.

Pilgrim's Progress *is a body of divinity spelled out in symbolic language, and stamps Bunyan as a theologian of distinction. Yet he was more than a theologian. His* The Life and Death of Mr. Badman *is an enormously incisive study of the psychology of evil, and ranks with* The Brothers Karamazov *in depth of movement and analysis. Take a single illustration. Bunyan has Badman boast: "I can be religious and irreligious. I can be anything or nothing. I can swear and speak against swearing. I can lie and speak against lying. I can drink, wench, be unclean, and defraud, and not be troubled for it. I can enjoy myself and am master of my own ways, not they of me. This I have attained with much study, care, and pains."*

Bunyan's The Holy War *stands out as an equally exciting drama bringing to light, also in figurative form, the eternal tensions churning in the universe of Mansoul. Says Froude: "The Holy War would have entitled Bunyan to a place among the masters of English literature."*

It would appear that there was no end to the man's versatility. He was, in his own right, a poet with a rustic "beat." Goethe explains that the test of true poetry is the substance which remains when the poetry is reduced to prose. It is interesting to apply the text to Bunyan:

> *The egg's no chick by falling from a hen,*
> *Nor man's a Christian till he's born again . . .*
>
> *Here is a lesson from the swallow:*
> *This pretty bird! Oh, how she flies and sings;*
> *But could she do so if she had no wings?*
> *Her wings bespeak my faith, her songs my peace;*
> *When I believe and sing, my doubtings cease.*

The secret of his fantastic success was probably above everything else his use of the English language. It is sheer wizardry. He stuck to the principle of economy, never inserting a word unless he had to. There are no purple patches of rhetoric. Each word has its proper place, like a gem in a coronet. He shunned the abstract, always chose the concrete. Like his divine Master, he taught in parables. And his diction has the pure strain of the King James Version, in which he was steeped. This is the key to his universality. Little children can understand him, and learned adults too. "A diamond," says Bacon, "is best plain set."

He lived sixteen years after his release from prison. He preached in many churches, ministering for the most part to Baptist communions, where his convictions lay.

His suffering refined him as it refined Job. It was natural for him to rejoice with those who rejoiced and weep with those who wept. He sealed his labor of love with a generous act. Learning of an im-

pending family rupture among acquaintances in a neighboring city, he undertook the trip on horseback for the purpose of effecting a reconciliation. He accomplished his mission, but it proved to be a supreme sacrifice. En route to Bedford, he was overtaken by a severe storm and contracted a serious illness. Ten days later Pilgrim crossed the Jordan River and entered the Celestial City.

Possibly one sentence from his classic book best marks his philosophy of life:

"If you will go with us you must go against wind and tide; you must own religion in his rags, as well as in his silver slippers; and stand by him, too, when bound in irons, as well as when he walketh the streets with applause."

Grace Abounding to the Chief of Sinners:

or A Brief Relation of the Exceeding Mercy of God in Christ, to His Poor Servant, John Bunyan

IN THIS my relation of the merciful working of God upon my soul, it will not be amiss, if, in the first place, I do, in a few words, give you a hint of my pedigree, and manner of bringing up; that thereby the goodness and bounty of God towards me, may be the more advanced and magnified before the sons of men.

In these days, the thoughts of religion were very grievous to me; I could neither endure it myself, nor that any other should; so that, when I have seen some read in those books that concerned Christian piety, it would be as it were a prison to me. Then I said unto God, "Depart from me, for I desire not the knowledge of Thy ways." (Job 21:14) I was now void of all good consideration, heaven and hell were both out of sight and mind; and as for saving and damning, they were least in my thoughts. O Lord, Thou knowest my life, and my ways were not hid from Thee.

Yet this I well remember, that though I could myself sin with the greatest delight and ease, and also take pleasure in the vileness of my companions; yet, even then, if I have at any time seen wicked things, by those who professed goodness, it would make my spirit tremble. As once, above all the rest, when I was in my height of vanity, yet hearing one to swear that was reckoned for a religious man, it had so great a stroke upon my spirit, that it made my heart to ache.

But all this while, I was not sensible of the danger and evil of sin; I was kept from considering that sin would damn me, what religion soever I followed, unless I was found in Christ. Nay, I never thought of Him, nor whether there was one, or no. Thus man, while blind, doth wander, but wearieth himself with vanity, for he knoweth not the way to the city of God. (Eccles. 10:15)

Now therefore I went on in sin with great greediness of mind, still grudging that I could not be so satisfied with it as I would. This did continue with me about a month, or more; but one day, as I was standing at a neighbour's shop-window, and there cursing and swearing, and playing the madman, after my wonted manner, there sat within the woman of the house, and heard me, who, though she was a very loose and ungodly wretch, yet protested that I swore and cursed at that most fearful rate, that she was made to tremble to hear me; and told me further, that I was the ungodliest fellow for swearing that ever she heard in all her life; and that I, by thus doing, was able to spoil all the youth in a whole town, if they came but in my company.

At this reproof I was silenced, and put to secret shame, and that too, as I thought, before the God of heaven; wherefore, while I stood there, and hanging down my head, I wished with all my heart that I might be a little child again, that my father might learn me to speak without this wicked way of swearing; for, thought I, I am so accustomed to it that it is in vain for me to think of a reformation, for I thought it could never be.

But how it came to pass, I know not; I did from this time forward so leave my swearing, that it was a great wonder to myself to observe it; and whereas before I knew not how to speak unless I put an oath before, and another behind, to make my words have authority; now I could, without it, speak better, and with more pleasantness, than ever I could before. All this while I knew not Jesus Christ, neither did I leave my sports and plays.

But quickly after this, I fell in company with one poor man that made profession of religion; who, as I then thought, did talk pleasantly of the Scriptures, and of the matters of religion; wherefore, falling into some love and liking to what he said, I betook me to my Bible, and began to take great pleasure in reading, but especially with the historical part thereof; for, as for Paul's epistles, and Scriptures of that nature, I could not away with them, being as yet but ignorant, either of the corruptions of my nature, or of the want and worth of Jesus Christ to save me.

Thus I continued about a year; all which time our neighbours did take me to be a very godly man, a new and religious man, and did marvel much to see such a great and famous alteration in my life and manners; and, indeed, so it was, though yet I knew not Christ, nor grace, or faith, or hope; and, truly, as I have well seen since, had I then died, my state had been most fearful; well, this, I say, continued about a twelvemonth or more.

But, I say, my neighbours were amazed at this my great conversion, from prodigious profaneness, to something like a moral life; and, truly, so they well might; for this my conversion was as great, as for Tom of Bedlam to become a sober man. Now, therefore, they began to praise, to commend, and to speak well of me, both to my face, and behind my back. Now, I was, as they said, become godly; now, I was become a right honest man. But, oh! when I understood that these were their words and opinions of me, it pleased me mighty well. For though, as yet, I was nothing but a poor painted hypocrite, yet I loved to be talked of as one that was truly godly. I was proud of my godliness, and, indeed, I did all I did, either to be seen of, or to be well spoken of, by man. And thus I continued for about a twelvemonth or more.

Upon a day, the good providence of God did cast me to Bedford, to work on my calling; and in one of the streets of that town, I came where there were three or four poor women sitting at a door in the sun, and talking about the things of God; and being now willing to hear them discourse, I drew near to hear what they said, for I was now a brisk talker also myself in the matters of religion, but now I may say, I heard, but I understood not; for they were far above, out of my reach; for their talk was about a new birth, the work of God in their hearts, also how they were convinced of their miserable state by nature; they talked of how God had visited their souls with His love in the Lord Jesus; and with what words and promises they had been refreshed, comforted, and supported against the temptations of the devil. Moreover, they reasoned of the suggestions and temptations of Satan in particular; and told to each other by which they had been afflicted, and how they were borne up under his assaults. They also discoursed of their own wretchedness of heart, of their unbelief; and did contemn, slight, and abhor their own righteousness, as filthy and insufficient to do them any good.

And methought they spake as if joy did make them speak; and they spake with such pleasantness of Scripture language, and with such appearance of grace in all they said, that they were to me as if they had found a new world, as if they were people that dwelt alone, and were not to be reckoned among their neighbours. (Num. 23:9)

At this I felt my own heart began to shake, as mistrusting my condition to be naught; for I saw that in all my thoughts about religion and salvation, the new birth did never enter into my mind, neither knew I the comfort of the Word and promise, nor the deceitfulness and treachery of my own wicked heart. As for secret thoughts, I took no notice of them; neither did I understand what Satan's temptations were, nor how they were to be withstood and resisted, etc.

One thing I may not omit: There was a young man in our town, to whom my heart before was knit more than to any other, but he being a most wicked creature for cursing, and swearing, and whoring, I now shook him off, and forsook his company; but about a quarter of a year after I had left him, I met him in a certain lane, and asked him how he did; he, after his old swearing and mad way, answered, He was well. But, Harry, said I, why do you swear and curse thus? What will become of you, if you die in this condition? He answered me in a great chafe, What would the devil do for company, if it were not for such as I am?

I cannot now express with what longings and breakings in my soul I cried to Christ to call me. Thus I continued for a time, all on a flame to be converted to Jesus Christ; and did also see that day, such glory in a converted state, that I could not be contented without a share therein. Gold! could it have been gotten for gold, what could I have given for it! had I had a whole world it had all gone ten thousand times over for this, that my soul might have been in a converted state.

How lovely now was everyone in my eyes that I thought to be converted men and women! they shone, they walked like a people that carried the broad seal of heaven about them. Oh! I saw the lot was fallen to them in pleasant places, and they had a goodly heritage. (Ps. 16:6) But that which made me sick was that of Christ, in Mark, He went up into a mountain and called to Him whom He would, and they came unto Him. (Mark 3:13)

This Scripture made me faint and fear, yet it kindled fire in my soul. That which made me fear was this, lest Christ should have no liking to me, for He called "whom He would." But oh! the glory that I saw in that condition did still so engage my heart that I could seldom read of any that Christ did call but I presently wished, Would I had been in their clothes; would I had been born Peter; would I had been born John; or would I had been by and had heard Him when He called them, how would I have cried, O Lord, call me also. But oh! I feared He would not call me.

Sometimes I would tell my condition to the people of God, which, when they heard, they would pity me, and would tell me of the promises; but they had as good have told me that I must reach the sun with my finger as have bidden me receive or rely upon the promise; and as soon as I should have done it, all my sense and feeling was against me; and I saw I had a heart that would sin, and that lay under a law that would condemn.

These things have often made me think of that child which the father brought to Christ, who, while he was yet acoming to Him, was thrown down by the devil, and also so rent and torn by him that he lay and wallowed, foaming. (Luke 9:42; Mark 9:20)

The tempter would also much assault me with this, How can you tell but that the Turks had as good Scriptures to prove their Mahomet the Saviour, as we have to prove our Jesus is? And, could I think, that so many ten thousands, in so many countries and kingdoms, should be without the knowledge of the right way to heaven; if there were indeed a heaven, and that we only, who live in a corner of the earth, should alone be blessed therewith? Everyone doth think his own religion rightest, both Jews and Moors, and Pagans! and how if all our faith, and Christ and Scriptures, should be but a think-so too?

I remember that one day, as I was travelling into the country, and musing on the wickedness and blasphemy of my heart, and considering of the enmity that was in me to God, that Scripture came in my mind, He hath "made peace through the blood of His cross." (Col. 1:20) By which I was made to see, both again and again, and again, that day, that God and my soul were friends by this blood; yea, I saw that the justice of God and my sinful soul could embrace and kiss each other through this blood. This was a good day to me; I hope I shall not forget it.

At another time, as I sat by the fire in my house, and musing on my wretchedness, the Lord made that also a precious word unto me, "Forasmuch, then, as the children are partakers of flesh and blood, He also Himself likewise took part of the same, that through death He might destroy him that had the power of death, that is, the devil, and deliver them who, through fear of death, were all their lifetime subject to bondage." (Heb. 2:14,15) I thought that the glory of these words was then so weighty on me that I was, both once and twice, ready to swoon as I sat; yet not with grief and trouble, but with solid joy and peace.

Oh! now, how was my soul led from truth to truth by God! Even from the birth and cradle of the Son of God to His ascension and second coming from heaven to judge the world.

Truly, I then found, upon this account, the great God was very good unto me; for, to my remembrance, there was not anything that I then cried unto God to make known and reveal unto me but He was pleased to do it for me; I mean not one part of the gospel of the Lord Jesus, but I was orderly led into it. Methought I saw with great evidence, from the relation of the four evangelists, the wonderful work of God, in giving Jesus Christ to save us, from His conception and birth even to His second coming to judgment. Methought I was as if I had seen Him born, as if I had seen Him grow up, as if I had seen Him walk through this world, from the cradle to His cross; to which, also, when He came, I saw how gently He gave Himself to be hanged and nailed on it for my sins and wicked doings. Also, as I was musing on this, His progress, that dropped on my spirit, He was ordained for the slaughter. (I Pet. 1:19,20)

When I have considered also the truth of His resurrection, and have remembered that word, "Touch me not, Mary," etc., I have seen as if He leaped at the grave's mouth for joy that He was risen again and had got the conquest over our dreadful foes. (John 20:17)

I have also, in the spirit, seen Him a man on the right hand of God the Father for me, and have seen the manner of His coming from heaven to judge the world with glory, and have been confirmed in these things by these Scriptures following, Acts 1:9; 7:56; 10:42; Hebrews 7:24; 8:3; Revelation 1:18; I Thessalonians 4:17,18.

Once I was much troubled to know whether the Lord Jesus was both man as well as God, and God as well as man; and truly, in those days, let men say what they would, unless I had it with evidence from heaven, all was as nothing to me, I counted not myself set down in any truth of God. Well, I was much troubled about this point, and could not tell how to be resolved; at last, that in the fifth [chapter of] of Revelations came into my mind, "And I beheld, and lo, in the midst of the throne and of the four beasts, and in the midst of the elders, stood a Lamb." (V. 6) In the midst of the throne, thought I, there is His Godhead; in the midst of the elders, there is His manhood; but oh! methought this did glister! it was a goodly touch, and gave me sweet satisfaction. That other Scripture also did help me much in this, "Unto us a child is born, unto us a son is given; and the government shall be upon His shoulder; and His name shall be called Wonderful, Counsellor, The Mighty God, The Everlasting Father, the Prince of Peace," etc. (Isa. 9:6)

Also, besides these teachings of God in His Word, the Lord made use of two things to confirm me in these things; the one was the errors of the Quakers, and the other was the guilt of sin; for as the Quakers did oppose His truth, so God did the more confirm me in it, by leading me into the Scriptures that did wonderfully maintain it.

The errors that this people then maintained were: (1) That the holy Scriptures were not the Word of God. (2) That every man in the world had the spirit of Christ, grace, faith, etc. (3) That Christ Jesus, as crucified, and dying 1600 years ago, did not satisfy divine justice for the sins of the people. (4) That Christ's flesh and blood was within the saints. (5) That the bodies of the good and bad that are buried in the churchyard shall not arise again. (6) That the resurrection is past with good men already. (7) That that man Jesus, that was crucified between two thieves on Mount Calvary, in the land of Canaan, by Jerusalem, was not ascended up above the starry heavens. (8) That He should not, even the same Jesus that died by the hands of the Jews, come again at the last day, and as man judge all nations, etc.

Many more vile and abominable things were in those days fomented by them, by which I was driven to a more narrow search of the Scriptures, and was, through their light and testimony, not only enlightened, but greatly confirmed and comforted in the truth; and, as I said, the guilt of sin did help me much, for still as that would come upon me, the blood of Christ did take it off again, and again, and again, and that too, sweetly, according to the Scriptures. O friends! cry to God to reveal Jesus Christ unto you; there is none teacheth like Him.

But before I had got thus far out of these my temptations, I did greatly long to see some ancient godly man's experience, who had writ some hundreds of years before I was born; for those who had writ in our days, I thought, but I desire them now to pardon me, that they had writ only that which others felt, or else had, through the strength of their wits and parts, studied to answer such objections as they perceived others were perplexed with, without going down themselves into the deep. Well, after many such longings in my mind, the God in whose hands are all our days and ways, did cast into my hand, one day, a book of Martin Luther; it was his comment on the Galatians —it also was so old that it was ready to fall piece from piece if I did but turn it over. Now I was pleased much that such an old book had fallen into my hands; the which, when I had but a little way perused, I found my condition, in his experience, so largely and profoundly handled, as if his book had been written out of my heart. This made me marvel; for thus thought I, This man could not know anything of the state of Christians now, but must needs write and speak the experience of former days.

Besides, he doth most gravely, also, in that book, debate of the rise of these temptations, namely, blasphemy, desperation, and the like; showing that the law of Moses as well as the devil, death, and hell hath a very great hand therein, the which, at first, was very strange to me; but considering and watching, I found it so indeed. But of particulars here I intend nothing; only this, methinks, I must let fall before all men, I do prefer this book of Martin Luther upon the Galatians, excepting the Holy Bible, before all the books that ever I have seen, as most fit for a wounded conscience.

And now I found, as I thought, that I loved Christ dearly; oh! methought my soul cleaved unto Him, my affections cleaved unto Him; I felt love to Him as hot as fire; and now, as Job said, I thought I should die in my nest; but I did quickly find that my great love was but little, and that I, who had, as I thought, such burning love to Jesus Christ, could let Him go again for a very trifle; God can tell how to abase us, and can hide pride from man.

Quickly after this my love was tried to purpose. For after the Lord had, in this manner, thus graciously delivered me from this great and sore temptation, and had set me down so sweetly in the faith of His holy gospel, and had given me such strong consolation, and blessed evidence from heaven touching my interest in His love through Christ; the tempter came upon me again, and that with a more grievous and dreadful temptation than before.

And that was, To sell and part with this most blessed Christ, to exchange Him for the things of this life, for anything. The temptation lay upon me for the space of a year, and did follow me so continually that I was not rid of it one day in a month, no, not sometimes one hour in many days together, unless when I was asleep.

Now was the battle won, and down fell I, as a bird that is shot from the top of a tree, into great guilt, and fearful despair. Thus getting out of my bed, I went moping into the field; but God knows, with as heavy a heart as mortal man, I think, could bear; where, for the space of two hours, I was like a man bereft of life, and as now past all recovery, and bound over to eternal punishment.

And withal, that Scripture did seize upon my soul, "Or profane person, as Esau, who for one morsel of meat, sold his birthright. For ye know how that afterward, when he would have inherited the blessing, he was rejected; for he found no place of repentance, though he sought it carefully with tears." (Heb. 12:16,17)

These words were to my soul like fetters of brass to my legs, in the continual sound of which I went for several months together. But about ten or eleven o'clock one day, as I was walking under a hedge, full of sorrow and guilt, God knows, and bemoaning myself for this hard hap, that such a thought should arise within me; suddenly this sentence bolted in upon me, The blood of Christ remits all guilt. At this I made a stand in my spirit; with that, this word took hold upon me, "The blood of Jesus Christ, His Son, cleanseth us from all sin." (I John 1:7)

About this time I took an opportunity to break my mind to an ancient Christian, and told him all my case; I told him, also, that I was afraid that I had sinned the sin against the Holy Ghost; and he told me he thought so too. Here, therefore, I had but cold comfort; but, talking a little more with him, I found him, though a good man, a stranger to much combat with the devil. Therefore, I went to God again, as well as I could, for mercy still.

Now, also, the tempter began afresh to mock my soul another way, saying that Christ, indeed, did pity my case, and was sorry for my loss; but forasmuch as I had sinned and transgressed, as I had done, He could by no means help me, nor save me from what I feared; for my sin was not of the nature of theirs for whom He bled and died, neither was it counted with those that were laid to His charge when He hanged on the tree. Therefore, unless He should come down from heaven and die anew for this sin, though, indeed, He did greatly pity me, yet I could have no benefit of Him.

These things may seem ridiculous to others, even as ridiculous as they were in themselves, but to me they were most tormenting cogitations; every one of them augmented my misery, that Jesus Christ should have so much love as to pity me when He could not help me; nor did I think that the reason why He could not help me was because His merits were weak, or His grace and salvation spent on them already, but because His faithfulness to His threatening would not let Him extend His mercy to me. Besides, I thought, as I have already hinted, that my sin was not within the bounds of that pardon that was wrapped up in a promise; and if not, then I knew assuredly, that it was more easy for heaven and earth to pass away than for me to have eternal life. So that the ground of all these fears of mine did arise from a steadfast belief that I had of the stability of the holy Word of God, and, also, from my being misinformed of the nature of my sin.

But the next day, at evening, being under many fears, I went to seek the Lord; and as I prayed, I cried, and my soul cried to Him in these words, with strong cries: O Lord, I beseech Thee, show me that Thou hast loved me with everlasting love. (Jer. 31:3) I had no sooner said it but, with sweetness, this returned upon me, as an echo or sounding again, "I have loved thee with an everlasting love." Now I went to bed at quiet; also, when I awaked the next morning, it was fresh upon my soul—and I believed it.

But yet the tempter left me not; for it could not be so little as an hundred times that he that day did labour to break my peace. Oh! the combats and conflicts that I did then meet with as I strove to hold by this word; that of Esau would fly in my face like to lightning. I should be sometimes up and down twenty times in an hour, yet God did bear me up and keep my heart upon this word, from which I had also, for several days together, very much sweetness and comfortable hopes of pardon; for thus it was made out to me, I loved thee whilst thou was committing this sin, I loved thee before, I love thee still, and I will love thee for ever.

One day, as I was passing in the field, and that too with some dashes on my conscience, fearing lest yet all was not right, suddenly this sentence fell upon my soul, "Thy righteousness is in heaven"; and methought withal, I saw, with the eyes of my soul, Jesus Christ at God's right hand; there, I say, is my righteousness; so that wherever I was, or whatever I was a-doing, God could not say of me, He wants my righteousness, for that was just before Him. I also saw, moreover, that it was not my good frame of heart that made my righteousness better, nor yet my bad frame that made my righteousness worse; for my righteousness was Jesus Christ Himself, the same yesterday, and today, and forever. (Heb. 13:8)

Now did my chains fall off my legs indeed, I was loosed from my affliction and irons, my temptations also fled away; so that, from that time, those dreadful Scriptures of God left off to trouble me; now went I also home rejoicing for the grace and love of God. So when I came home, I looked to see if I could find that sentence, Thy righteousness is in heaven; but could not find such a saying, wherefore my heart began to sink again, only that was brought to my remembrance, he "of God is made unto us wisdom, and righteousness, and sanctification, and redemption"; by this word I saw the other sentence true. (I Cor. 1:30)

Now I saw Christ Jesus was looked on of God and should also be looked upon by us, as that common or public person, in whom all the whole body of His elect are always to be considered and reckoned; that we fulfilled the law by Him, rose from the dead by Him, got the victory over sin, death, the devil, and hell, by Him; when He died, we died; and so of His resurrection. "Thy dead men shall live, together with My dead body shall they arise," said He. (Isa. 26:19) And again, "After two days will He revive us; in the third day He will raise us up, and we shall live in His sight" (Hos. 6:2); which is now fulfilled by the sitting down of the Son of man on the right hand of the Majesty in the heavens, according to that to the Ephesians, He "hath raised us up together, and made us sit together in heavenly places in Christ Jesus." (Eph. 2:6)

When I went first to preach the Word abroad, the doctors and priests of the country did open wide against me. But I was persuaded of this, not to render railing for railing, but to see how many of their carnal professors I could convince of their miserable state by the law, and of the want and worth of Christ; for, thought I, This shall answer for me in time to come, when they shall be for my hire before their faces. (Gen. 30:33)

I never cared to meddle with things that were controverted, and in dispute amongst the saints, especially things of the lowest nature; yet it pleased me much to contend with great earnestness for the word of faith and the remission of sins by the death and sufferings of Jesus; but I say, as to other things, I should let them alone, because I saw they engendered strife, and because that they neither, in doing nor in leaving undone, did commend us to God to be His. Besides, I saw my work before me did run in another channel even to carry an awakening word; to that therefore did I stick and adhere.

In my preaching I have really been in pain, and have, as it were, travailed to bring forth children to God; neither could I be satisfied unless some fruits did appear in my work. If I were fruitless it mattered not who commended me; but if I were fruitful, I cared not who did condemn. I have thought of that, "He that winneth souls is wise" (Prov. 11:30); and again, "Lo, children are an heritage of the Lord; and the fruit of the womb is his reward. As arrows in the hand of a mighty man, so are children of the youth. Happy is the man that hath filled his quiver full of them; they shall not be ashamed, but they shall speak with the enemies in the gate." (Ps. 127:3-5)

It pleased me nothing to see people drink in opinions if they seemed ignorant of Jesus Christ, and the worth of their own salvation; sound conviction for sin, especially for unbelief, and an heart set on fire to be saved by Christ, with strong breathing after a truly sanctified soul; that it was that delighted me; those were the souls I counted blessed.

But in this work, as in all other, I had my temptations attending me, and that of diverse kinds, as sometimes I should be assaulted with great discouragement therein, fearing that I should not be able to speak the Word at all to edification; nay, that I should not be able to speak sense unto the people; at which times I should have such a strange faintness and strengthlessness seize upon my body that my legs have scarce been able to carry me to the place of exercise.

But when Satan perceived that his thus tempting and assaulting of me would not answer his design, to wit, to overthrow my ministry, and make it ineffectual, as to the ends thereof; then he tried another way, which was to stir up the minds of the ignorant and malicious, to load me with slanders and reproaches; now therefore I may say, that what the devil could devise, and his instruments invent, was whirled up and down the country against me, thinking, as I said, that by that means they should make my ministry to be abandoned.

It began therefore to be rumoured up and down among the people, that I was a witch, a jesuit, a highwayman, and the like.

To all which, I shall only say, God knows that I am innocent. But as for mine accusers, let them provide themselves to meet me before the tribunal of the Son of God, there to answer for all these things, with all the rest of their iniquities, unless God shall give them repentance for them, for the which I pray with all my heart.

But that which was reported with the boldest confidence, was, that I had my misses, my whores, my bastards, yea, two wives at once, and the like. Now these slanders, with the other, I glory in, because but slanders, foolish, or knavish lies, and falsehoods cast upon me by the devil and his seed; and should I not be dealt with thus wickedly by the world, I should want one sign of a saint, and a child of God. "Blessed are ye (said the Lord Jesus) when men shall revile you, and persecute you, and shall say all manner of evil against you falsely for My sake; rejoice, and be exceeding glad, for great is your reward in

heaven; for so persecuted they the prophets which were before you."
(Matt. 5:11,12)

These things, therefore, upon mine own account, trouble me not;
no, though they were twenty times more than they are. I have a good
conscience, and whereas they speak evil of me, as an evil doer, they
shall be ashamed that falsely accuse my good conversation in Christ.

So then, what shall I say to those that have thus bespattered me?
Shall I threaten them? Shall I chide them? Shall I flatter them? Shall
I intreat them to hold their tongues? No, not I, were it not for that
these things make them ripe for damnation, that are the authors and
abettors, I would say unto them, Report it, because it will increase
my glory.

Therefore I bind these lies and slanders to me as an ornament, it
belongs to my Christian profession to be vilified, slandered, reproached
and reviled; and since all this is nothing else, as my God and my
conscience do bear me witness, I rejoice in reproaches for Christ's sake.

Now as Satan laboured by reproaches and slanders, to make me
vile among my countrymen, that, if possible, my preaching might be
made of none effect, so there was added hereto a long and tedious imprisonment, that thereby I might be frightened from my service for
Christ, and the world terrified, and made afraid to hear me preach, of
which I shall in the next place give you a brief account.

A Brief Account of the Author's Imprisonment

Having made profession of the glorious gospel of Christ a long
time, and preached the same about five years, I was apprehended at
a meeting of good people in the country, among whom, had they let
me alone, I should have preached that day, but they took me away from
amongst them, and had me before a justice; who, after I had offered
security for my appearing at the next sessions, yet committed me, because my sureties would not consent to be bound that I should preach
no more to the people.

I never had in all my life so great an inlet into the Word of God
as now; those Scriptures that I saw nothing in before, are made in this
place and state to shine upon me; Jesus Christ also was never more
real and apparent than now; here I have seen Him and felt Him indeed; O that word, We have not preached unto you cunningly devised
fables (II Pet. 1:16); and that, God raised Christ from the dead, and
gave Him glory, that your faith and hope might be in God (I Pet.
1:21), were blessed words unto me in this my imprisoned condition.

Before I came to prison, I saw what was a-coming, and had especially
two considerations warm upon my heart; the first was how to be able
to endure, should my imprisonment be long and tedious; the second
was how to be able to encounter death, should that be here my por-

tion; for the first of these, that Scripture, Colossians 1:11, was great information to me, namely, to pray to God to be "strengthened with all might, according to His glorious power, unto all patience and long-suffering with joyfulness." I could seldom go to prayer before I was imprisoned, but not for so little as a year together, this sentence, or sweet petition, would, as it were, thrust itself into my mind, and persuade me, that if ever I would go through long-suffering, I must have all patience, especially if I would endure it joyfully.

As to the second consideration, that saying, II Corinthians 1:9, was of great use to me, "But we had the sentence of death in ourselves, that we should not trust in ourselves, but in God which raiseth the dead." By this Scripture I was made to see, that if ever I would suffer rightly, I must first pass a sentence of death upon everything that can properly be called a thing of this life, even to reckon myself, my wife, my children, my health, my enjoyments, and all, as dead to me, and myself as dead to them. "He that loveth father or mother, son or daughter, more than Me, is not worthy of Me." (Matt. 10:37)

But notwithstanding these helps, I found myself a man, and compassed with infirmities; the parting with my wife and poor children hath oft been to me in this place as the pulling the flesh from my bones, and that not only because I am somewhat too fond of those great mercies, but also because I should have often brought to mind the many hardships, miseries and wants that my poor family was like to meet with, should I be taken from them, especially my poor blind child, who lay nearer my heart than all I had besides; O the thoughts of the hardship I thought my blind one might go under, would break my heart to pieces.

I will tell you a pretty business; I was once above all the rest in a very sad and low condition for many weeks; at which time also I being but a young prisoner, and not acquainted with the laws, had this lay much upon my spirit, That my imprisonment might end at the gallows for aught that I could tell. Now, therefore, Satan laid hard at me to beat me out of heart, by suggesting thus unto me, But how if when you come indeed to die, you should be in this condition; that is, as not to savour the things of God, nor to have any evidence upon your soul for a better state hereafter? For indeed at that time all the things of God were hid from my soul.

Wherefore, when I at first began to think of this, it was a great trouble to me; for I thought with myself, that in the condition I now was in, I was not fit to die, neither indeed did think I could, if I should be called to it: besides, I thought with myself, if I should make a scrabbling shift to clamber up the ladder, yet I should either with quaking, or other symptoms of faintings, give occasion to the enemy to reproach the way of God and His people, for their timorousness.

This therefore lay with great trouble upon me, for methought I was ashamed to die with a pale face, and tottering knees, for such a cause as this.

Wherefore, I prayed to God that He would comfort me, and give me strength to do and suffer what He should call me to; yet no comfort appeared, but all continued hid; I was also at this time so really possessed with the thought of death, that oft I was as if I was on the ladder with a rope about my neck; only this was some encouragement to me, I thought I might now have an opportunity to speak my last words to a multitude, which I thought would come to see me die; and, thought I, if it must be so, if God will but convert one soul by my very last words, I shall not count my life thrown away, nor lost.

But yet all the things of God were kept out of my sight, and still the tempter followed me with, But whither must you go when you die? What will become of you? Where will you be found in another world? What evidence have you for heaven and glory, and an inheritance among them that are sanctified? Thus was I tossed for many weeks, and knew not what to do; at last this consideration fell with weight upon me, That it was for the Word and the way of God that I was in this condition, wherefore I was engaged not to flinch a hair's breadth from it.

I thought also, that God might choose whether He would give me comfort now or at the hour of death, but I might not therefore choose whether I would hold my profession or no: I was bound, but He was free; yea, it was my duty to stand to His word, whether He would ever look upon me or no, or save me at the last: wherefore, thought I, the point being thus, I am for going on, and venturing my eternal state with Christ, whether I have comfort here or no; if God doth not come in, thought I, I will leap off the ladder even blindfold into eternity, sink or swim, come heaven, come hell, Lord Jesus, if Thou wilt catch me, do; if not, I will venture for Thy name.

I find to this day seven abominations in my heart: (1) Inclinings to unbelief. (2) Suddenly to forget the love and mercy that Christ manifesteth. (3) A leaning to the works of the law. (4) Wanderings and coldness in prayer. (5) To forget to watch for that I pray for. (6) Apt to murmur because I have no more, and yet ready to abuse what I have. (7) I can do none of those things which God commands me, but my corruptions will thrust in themselves, "When I would do good, evil is present with me."

These things I continually see and feel, and am afflicted and oppressed with; yet the wisdom of God doth order them for my good. (1) They make me abhor myself. (2) They keep me from trusting my heart. (3) They convince me of the insufficiency of all inherent righteousness. (4) They show me the necessity of flying to Jesus. (5) They press me to pray unto God. (6) They show me the need I have to watch and be sober. (7) And provoke me to look to God, through Christ, to help me, and carry me through this world. *Amen.*

JONATHAN EDWARDS 1703—1758

It would be an interesting experiment to assume the role of Inquiring Reporter, stop ten people on the street at random, and ask, "Do you know anything about Jonathan Edwards?" If there were any answer, it might be something like this: "Jonathan Edwards? Wasn't he that man who preached a sermon on 'Sinners in the Hands of an Angry God'?"

He was indeed. But actually that famed sermon is only the tiniest fragment of Jonathan Edwards' contribution to the world of religion and culture. In his book, American Literature and Christian Doctrine, *Randall Stewart makes the unqualified assertion that Edwards is not only the greatest of all American theologians and philosophers, but the greatest of our pre-nineteenth century writers as well. Those who know the corpus of his writing will be inclined to agree.*

"Childhood shows the man as morning shows the day," said Milton. Jonathan Edwards, the only son in a family of eleven children, gave evidence of precocity early in life. At six he studied Latin. Before he matriculated at Yale (at thirteen) he was acquainted with Latin, Greek, and Hebrew. He was graduated with the equivalent of magna cum laude *before that badge of distinction came into use.*

After graduation he tutored at Yale, then served a Scots-Presbyterian church in New York City. In 1727, he received a call to assist his grandfather, Solomon Stoddard, in Northampton, Massachusetts. Jonathan married the daughter of a New Haven clergyman, the fascinating Sarah Pierrepont.

When Mr. Stoddard died, the church called the young assistant to succeed him. Edwards worked hard, spending as much as thirteen hours a day in his study. He espoused Calvinist teachings with enthusiasm. Northampton was then a small city of wealth and culture. At the same time a good deal of vulgarity and looseness of life were undermining morals.

In 1734 a revival broke out. Three hundred people confessed their faith in Christ. Edwards overflowed with joy.

Six years later, George Whitefield journeyed through New England, including Northampton, preaching evangelistic messages. History knows the movement as the Great Awakening. Over fifty thousand people professed conversion. One hundred and fifty new churches were organized. It was during the Awakening that Edwards delivered his sermon, "Sinners in the Hands of an Angry God." While he was preaching men, women, and young people rose to their feet, wept, and begged God for mercy.

Excesses followed in the wake of the revival. Edwards felt that he must discourage hysterical exhibitionism and shallow emotionalism, and for it he was criticized by numbers of New England ministers as well as by laymen.

Coincidentally, he added to his local unpopularity by exposing what he thought was a breach of morals. Some people were reported to be reading clandestinely a book on the subject of midwifery. Edwards attacked their conduct from the pulpit.

A third development helped produce what turned out to be an eruption. Mr. Stoddard had established a precedent of admitting worshipers to the Communion table without inquiring into their spiritual state. Edwards developed a conscience on the matter. He decided that he could not serve the Lord's Supper to anyone not able or willing to make a public profession of faith in Christ. When the smoke cleared and the ashes settled, Jonathan Edwards was out of a pastorate, out of an income, and out of public favor.

The church at Stockbridge, Massachusetts, issued him a call. He accepted, and for the next ten years he preached to a small congregation and to a tribe of Indians living near the town. In this period he turned out his best writings. He became famous throughout the world (Northampton excepted) as a brilliant and resourceful scholar.

In 1757, Princeton University (then called the College of New Jersey) invited him to be president. He accepted. Less than six weeks after he took the president's chair in 1758, Death sat down with him.

His sermons, tracts, and books reflect a subtle beauty, a knowledge that is encyclopedic, and also a total consecration to the will of God. But, as Mr. Stewart has indicated, he was more than a theologian. "He was one of America's five or six major artists who happened to work with ideas instead of with poems or novels. He was much more of a psychologist and a poet than a logician, and though he devoted his genius to topics derived from the body of divinity—the will, virtue, sin—he traced them in the manner of the very finest spectators, in the manner of Augustine, Aquinas, and Pascal, as problems not of dogma but of life." So writes Perry Miller.

A brooding pathos hovered over this descendant of the great New England Puritans. A mysterious film, like the envelope of vapor surrounding the planet Venus, shut him off from his fellows. He was a lonely soul. "I have a constitution," he confesses, "with a disagreeable dullness and stiffness, much unfitting me for conversation." Lonely, wistful, poignantly sensitive—he was a solitary Ozymandias standing on the floor of the desert while "boundless and bare, the lone and level sands stretch away." He felt his hurts ever so deeply. Further-

more the shadow of John Locke crossed him continuously. He was always the empiricist: experience was his watchword. Even the forensic doctrine of justification he could not detach from sensation, from feeling.

The pendulum is swinging back; at last Jonathan Edwards is coming into his own. The Ivy League is astir. Scholars from Harvard, Princeton, and Yale have been busy bringing out new editions of his works. Does this preview a new day for his theology, and for his empiricism? Perhaps so. Perhaps, in his own words, "If the great things of religion are rightly understood, they will affect the heart."

An Unpublished Essay on the Trinity

JONATHAN EDWARDS

'TIS COMMON when speaking of the Divine happiness to say that God is infinitely happy in the enjoyment of Himself, in perfectly beholding and infinitely loving, and rejoicing in, His own essence and perfections, and accordingly it must be supposed that God perpetually and eternally has a most perfect idea of Himself, as it were an exact image and representation of Himself ever before Him and in actual view, and from hence arises a most pure and perfect act or energy in the Godhead, which is the Divine love, complacence and joy.

The knowledge or view which God has of Himself must necessarily be conceived to be something distinct from His mere direct existence. There must be something that answers to our reflection. The reflection as we reflect on our own minds carries something of imperfection in it. However, if God beholds Himself so as thence to have delight and joy in Himself He must become his own object. There must be a duplicity. There is God and the idea of God, if it be proper to call a conception of that that is purely spiritual an idea.

If a man could have an absolutely perfect idea of all that passed in his mind, all the series of ideas and exercises in every respect perfect as to order, degree, circumstance and for any particular space of time past, suppose the last hour, he would really to all intents and purpose be over again what he was that last hour. And if it were possible for a man by reflection perfectly to contemplate all that is in his own mind in an hour, as it is and at the same time that it is there in its first and direct existence; if a man, that is, had a perfect reflex or contemplative idea of every thought at the same moment or moments that that thought was and of every exercise at and during the same time that that exercise was, and so through a whole hour, a man would really be two during that time, he would be indeed double, he would be twice at once. The idea he has of himself would be himself again.

Note, by having a reflex or contemplative idea of what passes in our own minds I don't mean consciousness only. There is a great difference between a man's having a view of himself, reflex or contemplative idea of himself so as to delight in his own beauty or excellency, and a mere direct consciousness. Or if we mean by consciousness of what is in our own minds anything besides the mere simple existence in our minds of what is there, it is nothing but a power by reflection to view or contemplate what passes.

Therefore as God with perfect clearness, fullness and strength, understands Himself, views His own essence (in which there is no distinction of substance and act but which is wholly substance and wholly act), that idea which God hath of Himself is absolutely Himself. This representation of the Divine nature and essence is the Divine nature and essence again: so that by God's thinking of the Deity must certainly be generated. Hereby there is another person begotten, there is another Infinite Eternal Almighty and most holy and the same God, the very same Divine nature.

And this Person is the second person in the Trinity, the Only Begotten and dearly Beloved Son of God; He is the eternal, necessary, perfect, substantial and personal idea which God hath of Himself; and that it is so seems to me to be abundantly confirmed by the Word of God.

Nothing can more agree with the account the Scripture gives us of the Son of God, His being in the form of God and His express and perfect image and representation: (II Cor. 4:4) "Lest the light of the glorious Gospel of Christ Who is the image of God should shine unto them." (Phil. 2:6) "Who being in the form of God." (Col. 1:15) "Who is the image of the invisible God." (Heb. 1:3) "Who being the brightness of His glory and the express image of His person."

Christ is called the face of God (Exod. 33:14): the word [A.V. presence] in the original signifies face, looks, form or appearance. Now what can be so properly and fitly called so with respect to God as God's own perfect idea of Himself whereby He has every moment a view of His own essence: this idea is that "face of God" which God sees as a man sees his own face in a looking glass. 'Tis of such form or appearance whereby God eternally appears to Himself. The root that the original word comes from signifies to look upon or behold: now what is that which God looks upon or beholds in so eminent a manner as He doth on His own idea or that perfect image of Himself which He has in view. This is what is eminently in God's presence and is therefore called the angel of God's presence or face. (Isa. 63:9)

But that the Son of God is God's own eternal and perfect idea is a thing we have yet much more expressly revealed in God's Word. First, in that Christ is called "the wisdom of God." If we are taught in the Scripture that Christ is the same with God's wisdom or knowledge, then it teaches us that He is the same with God's perfect and eternal idea. They are the same as we have already observed and I suppose none will deny. But Christ is said to be the wisdom of God (I Cor. 1:24, Luke 11:49, compare with Matt. 23:34); and how much doth Christ speak in Proverbs under the name of Wisdom especially in the 8th chapter.

The Godhead being thus begotten by God's loving an idea of Himself and shewing forth in a distinct subsistence or person in that idea, there proceeds a most pure act, and an infinitely holy and sacred energy arises between the Father and Son in mutually loving and delighting in each other, for their love and joy is mutual, (Prov. 8:30) "I was daily His delight rejoicing always before Him." This is the eternal and most perfect and essential act of the Divine nature, wherein the Godhead acts to an infinite degree and in the most perfect manner possible. The Deity becomes all act, the Divine essence itself flows out and is as it were breathed forth in love and joy. So that the Godhead therein stands forth in yet another manner of subsistence, and there proceeds the third Person in the Trinity, the Holy Spirit, viz., the Deity in act, for there is no other act but the act of the will.

We may learn by the Word of God that the Godhead or the Divine nature and essence does subsist in love. (I John 4:8) "He that loveth not knoweth not God; for God is love." In the context of which place I think it is plainly intimated to us that the Holy Spirit is that Love, as in the 12th and 13th verses. "If we love one another, God dwelleth in us, and His love is perfected in us; hereby know we that we dwell in Him . . . because He hath given us of His Spirit." 'Tis the same argument in both verses. In the 12th verse the apostle argues that if we have love dwelling in us we have God dwelling in us, and in the 13th verse He clears the force of the argument by this that love is God's Spirit. Seeing we have God's Spirit dwelling in us, we have God dwelling in [in us], supposing it as a thing granted and allowed that God's Spirit is God. 'Tis evident also by this that God's dwelling in us and His love or the love that He hath exerciseth, being in us, are the same thing. The same is intimated in the same manner in the last verse of the foregoing chapter. The apostle was, in the foregoing verses, speaking of love as a sure sign of sincerity and our acceptance with God, beginning with the 18th verse, and He sums up the argument thus in the last verse, and hereby do we know that He abideth in us by the Spirit that He hath given us.

The Scripture seems in many places to speak of love in Christians as if it were the same with the Spirit of God in them, or at least as the prime and most natural breathing and acting of the Spirit in the soul. (Phil. 2:1) "If there be therefore any consolation in Christ, any comfort of love, any fellowship of the Spirit, if any bowels and mercies, fulfil ye my joy that ye be likeminded, having the same love, being of one accord, of one mind." (II Cor. 6:6) "By kindness, by the Holy Ghost, by love unfeigned." (Romans 15:30) "Now I beseech you, brethren, for the Lord Jesus Christ's sake, and for the love of the Spirit." (Col. 1:8) "Who declared unto us your love in the Spirit." (Rom. 5:5) "Having the love of God shed abroad in our hearts by the Holy Ghost which is given to us." (See notes on this text.) (Gal. 5:13-16) "Use not liberty for an occasion to the flesh, but by love serve one another. For all the law is fulfilled in one word, even in this: Thou shalt love thy neighbour as thyself. But if ye bite and devour one another, take heed that ye be not consumed one of another. This I say then, "Walk in the Spirit, and ye shall not fulfill the lusts of the flesh." The Apostle argues that Christian liberty does not make way for fulfilling the lusts of the flesh in biting and devouring one another and the like, because a principle of love which was the fulfilling of the law would prevent it, and in the 16th verse he asserts the same thing in other words: "This I say then walk in the Spirit and ye shall not fulfill the lusts of the flesh."

The third and last office of the Holy Spirit is to comfort and delight the souls of God's people, and thus one of His names is the Comforter, and thus we have the phrase of "Joy in the Holy Ghost." (I Thess. 1:6) "Having received the Word in much affliction with joy of the Holy Ghost." (Rom. 14:17) "The kingdom of God is ... righteousness, and peace, and joy in the Holy Ghost." (Acts 9:31) "Walking in the fear of the Lord and in the comfort of the Holy Ghost." But how well doth this agree with the Holy Ghost being God's joy and delight, (Acts 13:52) "And the disciples were filled with joy and with the Holy Ghost"—meaning as I suppose that they were filled with spiritual joy.

This is confirmed by the symbol of the Holy Ghost, viz., a dove, which is the emblem of love or a lover, and is so used in Scripture, and especially often so in Solomon's Song, (1:5) "Behold thou art fair; my love, behold thou art fair; thou hast dove's eyes": i.e. "Eyes of love," and again 4:1, the same words; and 5:12, "His eyes are as the eyes of doves," and 5:2, "My love, my dove," and 2:14 and 6:9; and this I believe to be the reason that the dove alone of all birds (except the sparrow in the single case of the leprosy) was appointed to be offered in sacrifice because of its innocency and because it is the emblem of love, love being the most acceptable sacrifice to God. It was under this similitude that the Holy Ghost descended from the Father on Christ at

His baptism, signifying the infinite love of the Father to the Son, Who is the true David, or beloved, as we said before.

The same was signified by what was exhibited to the eye in the appearance there was of the Holy Ghost descending from the Father to the Son in the shape of a dove, as was signified by what was exhibited to the eye in the voice there was at the same time, viz., "This is My well Beloved Son in Whom I am well pleased."

(That God's love or His loving kindness is the same with the Holy Ghost seems to be plain by Psalm 36:7-9, "How excellent (or how precious as 'tis in the Hebrew) is Thy loving kindness O God, therefore the children of men put their trust under the shadow of Thy wings, they shall be abundantly satisfied (in the Hebrew "watered") with the fatness of Thy house and Thou shalt make them to drink of the river of Thy pleasures; for with Thee is the fountain of life and in Thy light shall we see light."

Doubtless that precious loving kindness and that fatness of God's house and river of His pleasures and the water of the fountain of life and God's light here spoken [of] are the same thing; by which we learn that the Holy anointing oil that was kept in the House of God, which was a type of the Holy Ghost, represented God's love, and that the "River of water of life" spoken of in the 22nd [chapter] of Revelation, which proceeds out of the throne of God and of the Lamb, which is the same with Ezekiel's vision of Living and life-giving water, which is here [in Ps. 36] called the "Fountain of life and river of God's pleasures," is God's loving-kindness.

But Christ Himself expressly teaches us that by spiritual fountains and rivers of water of life is meant the Holy Ghost. (John 4:14; 7:38, 39). That by the river of God's pleasures here is meant the same thing with the pure river of water of life spoken of in Revelation 22:1, will be much confirmed if we compare those verses with Revelation 21:23, 24; 22:1,5. (See the note on chapter 21, 23, 24.) I think if we compare these places and weigh them we cannot doubt but that it is the same happiness that is meant in this Psalm which is spoken of there.)

So this well agrees with the similitudes and metaphors that are used about the Holy Ghost in Scripture, such as water, fire, breath, wind, oil, wine, a spring, a river, a being poured out and shed forth, and a being breathed forth. Can there any spiritual thing be thought, or anything belonging to any spiritual being to which such kind of metaphors so naturally agree, as to the affection of a Spirit. The affection, love or joy, may be said to flow out as water or to be breathed forth as breath or wind. But it would [not] sound so well to say that an idea or judgment flows out or is breathed forth.

It is no way different to say of the affection that it is warm, or to compare love to fire, but it would not seem natural to say the same of perception or reason. It seems natural enough to say that the soul is poured out in affection or that love or delight are shed abroad: (Rom. 5:5) "The love of God is shed abroad in our hearts," but it suits with nothing else belonging to a spiritual being.

This is that "river of water of life" spoken of in the 22nd [chapter] of Revelation, which proceeds from the throne of the Father and the Son, for the rivers of living water or water of life are the Holy Ghost, by the same apostle's own interpretation (John 7:38, 39); and the Holy Ghost being the infinite delight and pleasure of God, the river is called the river of God's pleasures (Ps. 36:8), not God's river of pleasures, which I suppose signifies the same as the fatness of God's House, which they that trust in God shall be watered with, by which fatness of God's House I suppose is signified the same thing which oil typifies.

It is a confirmation that the Holy Ghost is God's love and delight, because the saints communion with God consists in their partaking of the Holy Ghost. The communion of saints is twofold: 'tis their communion with God and communion with one another, (I John 1:3) "That ye also may have fellowship with us, and truly our fellowship is with the Father and with His Son, Jesus Christ." Communion is a common partaking of good, either of excellency or happiness, so that when it is said the saints have communion or fellowship with the Father and with the Son, the meaning of it is that they partake with the Father and the Son of their good, which is either their excellency and glory (II Peter 1:4, "Ye are made partakers of the Divine nature"; Heb. 12:10, "That we might be partakers of His holiness;" John 17:22, 23, "And the glory which Thou hast given Me I have given them, that they may be one, even as we are one, I in them and Thou in Me"); or of their joy and happiness: (John 17:13) "That they might have My joy fulfilled in themselves."

But the Holy Ghost being the love and joy of God is His beauty and happiness, and it is in our partaking of the same Holy Spirit that our communion with God consists: (II Cor. 13:14) "The grace of the Lord Jesus Christ, and the love of God, and the communion of the Holy Ghost, be with you all, *Amen.*" They are not different benefits but the same that the Apostle here wisheth, viz., the Holy Ghost: in partaking of the Holy Ghost, we possess and enjoy the love and grace of the Father and the Son, for the Holy Ghost is that love and grace, and therefore I suppose it is that in that forementioned place, (I John 1:3) we are said to have fellowship with the Son and not with the Holy Ghost, because therein consists our fellowship with the Father and the Son, even in partaking with them of the Holy Ghost.

In this also eminently consists our communion with the Son that we drink into the same Spirit. This is the common excellency and joy and happiness in which they all are united; 'tis the bond of perfectness by which they are one in the Father and the Son as the Father is in the Son.

I can think of no other good account that can be given of the apostle Paul's wishing grace and peace from God the Father and the Lord Jesus Christ in the beginning of his Epistles, without ever mentioning the Holy Ghost,—as we find it thirteen times in his salutations in the beginnings of his Epistles,—but [i.e., except] that the Holy Ghost is Himself love and grace of God the Father and the Lord Jesus Christ; and in his blessing at the end of his second Epistle to the Corinthians where all three Persons are mentioned he wishes grace and love from the Son and the Father [except that] in the communion or the partaking of the Holy Ghost, the blessing is from the Father and the Son in the Holy Ghost. But the blessing from the Holy Ghost is Himself, the communication of Himself. Christ promises that He and the Father will love believers (John 14:21,23), but no mention is made of the Holy Ghost, and the love of Christ and the love of the Father are often distinctly mentioned, but never any mention of the Holy Ghost's love.

(This I suppose to be the reason why we have never any account of the Holy Ghost's loving either the Father or the Son, or of the Son's or the Father's loving the Holy Ghost, or of the Holy Ghost's loving the saints, tho these things are so often predicated of both the other Persons.)

And this I suppose to be that blessed Trinity that we read of in the Holy Scriptures. The Father is the Deity subsisting in the prime, unoriginated and most absolute manner, or the Deity in its direct existence. The Son is the Deity generated by God's understanding, or having an idea of Himself and subsisting in that idea. The Holy Ghost is the Deity subsisting in act, or the Divine essence flowing out and breathed forth in God's Infinite love to and delight in Himself. And I believe the whole Divine essence does truly and distinctly subsist both in the Divine idea and Divine love, and that each of them are properly distinct Persons.

It is a maxim amongst divines that everything that is in God is God which must be understood of real attributes and not of mere modalities. If a man should tell me that the immutability of God is God, or that the omnipresence of God and authority of God is God, I should not be able to think of any rational meaning of what he said. It hardly sounds to me proper to say that God's being without change is God, or that God's being everywhere is God, or that God's having a right of government over creatures is God.

But if it be meant that the real attributes of God, viz., His understanding and love are God, then what we have said may in some measure explain how it is so, for Deity subsists in them distinctly; so they are distinct Divine Persons.

One of the principal objections that I can think of against what has been supposed is concerning the Personality of the Holy Ghost—that this scheme of things does not seem well to consist with [the fact] that a person is that which hath understanding and will. If the three in the Godhead are Persons they doubtless each of them have understanding, but this makes the understanding one distinct person and love another. How therefore can this love be said to have understanding? (Here I would observe that divines have not been wont to suppose that these three had three distinct understandings, but all one and the same understanding.)

In order to clear up this matter let it be considered that the whole Divine office is supposed truly and properly to subsist in each of these three, viz., God and His understanding and love, and that there is such a wonderful union between them that they are, after an ineffable and inconceivable manner, One in Another, so that One hath Another and they have communion in One Another and are as it were predicable One of Another; as Christ said of Himself and the Father "I am in the Father and the Father in Me," so may it be said concerning all the Persons in the Trinity, the Father is in the Son and the Son in the Father, the Holy Ghost is in the Father, and the Father in the Holy Ghost, the Holy Ghost is in the Son, and the Son in the Holy Ghost, and the Father understands because the Son Who is the Divine understanding is in Him, the Father loves because the Holy Ghost is in Him, so the Son loves because the Holy Ghost is in Him and proceeds from Him, so the Holy Ghost or the Divine essence subsisting is Divine, but understands because the Son the Divine Idea is in Him.

Understanding may be predicated of this love because it is the love of the understanding both objectively and subjectively. God loves the understanding and that understanding also flows out in love so that the Divine understanding is in the Deity subsisting in love. It is not a blind love. Even in creatures there is consciousness included in the very nature of the will or act of the soul, and tho perhaps not so that it can so properly be said that it is a seeing or understanding will, yet it may truly and properly be said so in God by reason of God's infinitely more perfect manner of acting so that the whole Divine essence flows out and subsists in this act, and the Son is in the Holy Spirit tho it does not proceed from Him by reason (of the fact) that the understanding must be considered as prior in the order of nature to the will or love or act, both in creatures and in the Creator. The understanding is so in the Spirit that the Spirit may be said to know, as the Spirit of God is truly and perfectly said to know and to search all things, even the deep things of God.

(All the Three are Persons for they all have understanding and will. There is understanding and will in the Father, as the Son and the Holy Ghost are in Him and proceed from Him. There is understanding and will in the Son, as He is understanding and as the Holy Ghost is in Him and proceeds from Him. There is understanding and will in the Holy Ghost as He is the Divine will and as the Son is in Him.

Nor is it to be looked upon as a strange and unreasonable figment that the Persons should be said to have an understanding or love by another person's being in them, for we have Scripture ground to conclude so concerning the Father's having wisdom and understanding or reason that it is by the Son's being in Him; because we are there informed that He is the wisdom and reason and truth of God, and hereby God is wise by His own wisdom being in Him. Understanding and wisdom is in the Father as the Son is in Him and proceeds from Him. Understanding is in the Holy Ghost because the Son is in Him, not as proceeding from Him but as flowing out in Him.)

But I don't pretend fully to explain how these things are and I am sensible a hundred other objections may be made and puzzling doubts and questions raised that I can't solve. I am far from pretending to explaining the Trinity so as to render it no longer a mystery. I think it to be the highest and deepest of all Divine mysteries still, notwithstanding anything that I have said or conceived about it. I don't intend to explain the Trinity. But Scripture with reason may lead to say something further of it than has been wont to be said, tho there are still left many things pertaining to it incomprehensible.

It seems to me that what I have here supposed concerning the Trinity is exceeding analogous to the Gospel scheme and agreeable to the tenor of the whole New Testament and abundantly illustrative of Gospel doctrines, as might be particularly shewn, would it not exceedingly lengthen out this discourse.

I shall only now briefly observe that many things that have been wont to be said by orthodox divines about the Trinity are hereby illustrated. Hereby we see how the Father is the fountain of the Godhead, and why when He is spoken of in Scripture He is so often, without any addition or distinction, called God, which has led some to think that He only was truly and properly God. Hereby we may see why in the economy of the Persons of the Trinity the Father should sustain the dignity of the Deity, that the Father should have it as His office to uphold and maintain the rights of the Godhead and should be God not only by essence, but as it were, by His economical office.

Hereby is illustrated the doctrine of the Holy Ghost. Proceeding [from] both the Father and the Son. Hereby we see how that it is possible for the Son to be begotten by the Father and the Holy Ghost to proceed from the Father and Son, and yet that all the Persons should be Co-eternal. Hereby we may more clearly understand the equality of the Persons among themselves, and that they are every way equal in the society or family of the three.

They are equal in honour: besides the honour which is common to them all, viz., that they are all God, each has His peculiar honour in the society or family. They are equal not only in essence, but the Father's honour is that He is, as it were, the Author of perfect and Infinite wisdom. The Son's honour is that He is that perfect and Divine wisdom itself the excellency of which is that from whence arises the honour of being the author or Generator of it. The honour of the Father and the Son is that they are infinitely excellent, or that from them infinite excellency proceeds; but the honour of the Holy Ghost is equal for He is that Divine excellency and beauty itself.

Tis the honour of the Father and the Son that they are infinitely holy and are the fountain of holiness, but the honour of the Holy Ghost is that holiness itself. The honour of the Father and the Son is [that] they are infinitely happy and are the original and fountain of happiness and the honour of the Holy Ghost is equal for He is infinite happiness and joy itself.

The honour of the Father is that He is the fountain of the Deity as He from Whom proceed both the Divine wisdom and also excellency and happiness. The honour of the Son is equal for He is Himself the Divine wisdom and is He from Whom proceeds the Divine excellency and happiness, and the honour of the Holy Ghost is equal for He is the beauty and happiness of both the other Persons.

By this also we may fully understand the equality of each Person's concern in the work of redemption, and the equality of the Redeemed's concern with them and dependence upon them, and the equality and honour and praise due to each of them. Glory belongs to the Father and the Son that they so greatly loved the world: to the Father that He so loved that He gave His Only Begotten Son: to the Son that He so loved the world as to give up Himself.

But there is equal glory due to the Holy Ghost for He is that love of the Father and the Son to the world. Just so much as the two first Persons glorify themselves by showing the astonishing greatness of their love and grace, just so much is that wonderful love and grace glorified Who is the Holy Ghost. It shows the Infinite dignity and excellency of the Father that the Son so delighted and prized His honour and glory that He stooped infinitely low rather than [that] men's salvation should be to the injury of that honour and glory.

It showed the infinite excellency and worth of the Son that the Father so delighted in Him that for His sake He was ready to quit His anger and receive into favour those that had [deserved?] infinitely ill at His Hands, and what was done shews how great the excellency and worth of the Holy Ghost Who is that delight which the Father and the Son have in each other: it shows it to be Infinite. So great as the worth of a thing delighted in is to any one, so great is the worth of that delight and joy itself which he has in it.

Our dependence is equally upon each in this office. The Father appoints and provides the Redeemer, and Himself accepts the price and grants the thing purchased; the Son is the Redeemer by offering Himself and is the price; and the Holy Ghost immediately communicates to us the thing purchased by communicating Himself, and He is the thing purchased. The sum of all that Christ purchased for men was the Holy Ghost: (Gal. 3:13,14) "He was made a curse for us . . . that we might receive the promise of the Spirit through faith."

What Christ purchased for us was that we have communion with God [which] is His good, which consists in partaking of the Holy Ghost: as we have shown, all the blessedness of the Redeemed consists in their partaking of Christ's fullness, which consists in partaking of that Spirit which is given not by measure unto him: the oil that is poured on the head of the Church runs down to the members of His body and to the skirts of His garment (Ps. 133:2). Christ purchased for us that we should have the favour of God and might enjoy His love, but this love is the Holy Ghost.

Christ purchased for us true spiritual excellency, grace and holiness, the sum of which is love to God, which is [nothing] but the indwelling of the Holy Ghost in the heart. Christ purchased for us spiritual joy and comfort, which is in a participation of God's joy and happiness, which joy and happiness is the Holy Ghost as we have shewn. The Holy Ghost is the sum of all good things. Good things and the Holy Spirit are synonymous expressions in Scripture: (Matt. 7:11) "How much more shall your Heavenly Father give *the Holy Spirit* to them that ask Him." The sum of all spiritual good which the finite have in this world is that spring of living water within them which we read of (John 4:10), and those rivers of living water flowing out of them which we read of (John 7:38,39), which we are there told means the Holy Ghost; and the sum of all happiness in the other world is that river of water of life which proceeds out of the throne of God and the Lamb, which we read of (Rev. 22:1), which is the River of God's pleasures and is the Holy Ghost and therefore the sum of the Gospel invitation to come and take the water of life (verse 17).

The Holy Ghost is the purchased possession and inheritance of the saints, as appears because that little of it which the saints have in this world is said to be the earnest of that purchased inheritance. (Eph. 1:14) Tis an earnest of that which we are to have a fulness of hereafter. (II Cor. 1:22; 5:5) The Holy Ghost is the great subject of all

Gospel promises and therefore is called the Spirit of promise. (Eph. 1:13) This is called the promise of the Father (Luke 24:49), and the like in other places. (If the Holy Ghost be a comprehension of all good things promised in the Gospel, we may easily see the force of the Apostle's arguing (Gal. 3:2), "This only would I know, Received ye the Spirit by the works of the law or by the hearing of faith?") So that it is God of Whom our good is purchased and it is God that purchases it and it is God also that is the thing purchased.

Thus all our good things are of God and through God and in God, as we read in Romans 11:36: "For of Him and through Him and to Him (or in Him as *eis* is rendered, I Cor. 8:6) are all things." "To Whom be glory forever." All our good is of God the Father, it is all through God the Son, and all is in the Holy Ghost as He is Himself all our good. God is Himself the portion and purchased inheritance of His people. Thus God is the Alpha and the Omega in this affair of redemption.

If we suppose no more than used to be supposed about the Holy Ghost, the concern of the Holy Ghost in the work of redemption is not equal with the Father's and the Son's, nor is there an equal part of the glory of this work belonging to Him: merely to apply to us or immediately to give or hand to us the blessing purchased, after it was purchased, as subservient to the other two Persons, is but a little thing [compared] to the purchasing of it by the paying an Infinite price, by Christ offering up Himself in sacrifice to procure it, and it is but a little thing to God the Father's giving His infinitely dear Son to be a sacrifice for us and upon His purchase to afford to us all the blessings of His purchased.

But according to this there is an equality. To be the love of God to the world is as much as for the Father and the Son to do so much from love to the world, and to be the thing purchased was as much as to be the price. The price and the thing bought with that price are equal. And it is as much as to afford the thing purchased, for the glory that belongs to Him that affords the thing purchased arises from the worth of that thing that He affords and therefore it is the same glory and an equal glory; the glory of the thing itself is its worth and that is also the glory of him that affords it.

There are two more eminent and remarkable images of the Trinity among the creatures. The one is in the spiritual creation, the soul of man. There is the mind, and the understanding or idea, and the spirit of the mind as it is called in Scripture, i.e., the disposition, the will or affection. The other is in the visible creation, viz., the Sun. The father is as the substance of the Sun. (By substance I don't mean in a philosophical sense, but the Sun as to its internal constitution.) The Son is as the brightness and glory of the disk of the Sun or that bright and glorious form under which it appears to our eyes. The Holy Ghost is the action of the Sun which is within the Sun in its intestine heat, and, being diffusive, enlightens, warms, enlivens and comforts the world. The Spirit as it is God's Infinite love to Himself and happiness in Himself, is as the internal heat of the Sun, but as it is that by which God communicates Himself, it is as the emanation of the sun's action, or the emitted beams of the sun.

The various sorts of rays of the sun and their beautiful colours do well represent the Spirit. They well represent the love and grace of God and were made use of for this purpose in the rainbow after the flood, and I suppose also in that rainbow that was seen round about the throne by Ezekiel (Ezek. 1:28; Rev. 4:3) and round the head of Christ by John (Rev. 10:1), or the amiable excellency of God and the various beautiful graces and virtues of the Spirit. These beautiful colours of the sunbeams we find made use of in Scripture for this purpose, viz., to represent the graces of the Spirit, as (Ps. 68:13) "Though ye have lien among the pots, yet shall be as the wings of a dove covered with silver, and her feathers with yellow gold," i.e., like the light reflected in various beautiful colours from the feathers of a dove, which colours represent the graces of the Heavenly Dove.

The same I suppose is signified by the various beautiful colours reflected from the precious stones of the breastplate, and that these spiritual ornaments of the Church are what are represented by the various colours of the foundation and gates of the new Jerusalem (Rev. 21; Isaiah 54:11, etc.) and the stones of the Temple (I Chron. 29:2); and I believe the variety there is in the rays of the Sun and their beautiful colours was designed by the Creator for this very purpose, and indeed that the whole visible creation which is but the shadow of being is so made and ordered by God as to typify and represent spiritual things, for which I could give many reasons. (I don't propose this merely as an hypothesis but as a part of Divine truth sufficiently and fully ascertained by the revelation God has made in the Holy Scriptures.

I am sensible what kind of objections many will be ready to make against what has been said, what difficulties will be immediately found, How can this be? And how can that be?

I am far from affording this as any explication of this mystery, that unfolds and renews the mysteriousness and incomprehensibleness of it, for I am sensible that however by what has been said some difficulties are lessened, others that are new appear, and the number of those things that appear mysterious, wonderful and incomprehensible, is increased by it. I offer it only as a farther manifestation of what of Divine truth the Word of God exhibits to the view of our minds concerning this great mystery.

I think the Word of God teaches us more things concerning it to be believed by us than have been generally believed, and that it exhibits many things concerning it exceeding [i.e., more] glorious and wonderful than have been taken notice of; yea, that it reveals or exhibits many more wonderful mysteries than those which have been taken notice of; which mysteries that have been overvalued are incomprehensible things and yet have been exhibited in the Word of God tho they are an addition to the number of mysteries that are in it. No wonder that the more things we are told concerning that which is so infinitely above our reach, the number of visible mysteries increases.

When we tell a child a little concerning God he has not an hundredth part so many mysteries in view on the nature and attributes of God and His works of creation and Providence as one that is told much concerning God in a Divinity School; and yet he knows much more about God and has a much clearer understanding of things of Divinity and is able more clearly to explicate some things that were dark and very unintelligible to him. I humbly apprehend that the things that have been observed increase the number of visible mysteries in the Godhead in no other manner than as by them we perceive that God has told us much more about it than was before generally observed.

Under the Old Testament the Church of God was not told near so much about the Trinity as they are now. But what the New Testament has revealed, tho it has more opened to our view the nature of God, yet it has increased the number of visible mysteries and they thus appear to us exceeding wonderful and incomprehensible. And so also it has come to pass in the Church being told [i.e., that the churches are told] more about the incarnation and the satisfaction of Christ and other Gospel doctrines.

It is so not only in Divine things but natural things. He that looks on a plant, or the parts of the bodies of animals, or any other works of nature, at a great distance where he has but an obscure sight of it, may see something in it wonderful and beyond his comprehension, but he that is near to it and views them narrowly indeed understands more about them, has a clearer and distinct sight of them, and yet the number of things that are wonderful and mysterious in them that appear to him are much more than before, and, if he views them with a microscope, the number of the wonders that he sees will be increased still but yet the microscope gives him more a true knowledge concerning them.)

God is never said to love the Holy Ghost nor are any epithets that betoken love anywhere given to Him, tho so many are ascribed to the Son, as God's Elect, The Beloved, He in Whom God's soul delighteth, He in Whom He is well pleased, etc. Yea such epithets seem to be ascribed to the Son as tho He were the object of love exclusive of all other persons, as tho there were no person whatsoever to share the love of the Father with the Son. To this purpose evidently He is called God's Only Begotten Son, at the time that it is added, "In Whom He is well pleased." There is nothing in Scripture that speaks of any acceptance of the Holy Ghost or any reward or any mutual friendship between the Holy Ghost and either of the other Persons, or any command to love the Holy Ghost or to delight in or have any complacence in [the Holy Ghost], tho such commands are so frequent with respect to the other Persons.

That knowledge or understanding in God which we must conceive of as first is His knowledge of every thing possible. That love which must be this knowledge is what we must conceive of as belonging to the essence of the Godhead in it's first subsistence. Then comes a reflex act of knowledge and His viewing Himself and knowing Himself and so knowing His own knowledge and so the Son is begotten. There is such a thing in God as knowledge of knowledge, an idea of an idea. Which can be nothing else than the idea or knowledge repeated.

The world was made for the Son of God especially. For God made the world for Himself from love to Himself; but God loves Himself only in a reflex act. He views Himself and so loves Himself, so He makes the world for Himself viewed and reflected on, and that is the same with Himself repeated or begotten in His own idea, and that is His Son. When God considers of making any thing for Himself He presents Himself before Himself and views Himself as His End, and that viewing Himself is the same as reflecting on Himself or having an idea of Himself, and to make the world for the Godhead thus viewed and understood is to make the world for the Godhead begotten and that is to make the world for the Son of God.

The love of God as it flows forth ad extra is wholly determined and directed by Divine wisdom, so that those only are the objects of it that Divine wisdom chooses, so that the creation of the world is to gratify Divine love as that is exercised by Divine wisdom. But Christ is Divine wisdom so that the world is made to gratify Divine love as exercised by Christ or to gratify the love that is in Christ's heart, or to provide a spouse for Christ. Those creatures which wisdom chooses for the object of Divine love as Christ's elect spouse and especially those elect creatures that wisdom chiefly pitches upon and makes the end of the rest of creatures.

GILBERT TENNENT 1703–1764

Gilbert Tennent and his three brothers absorbed their knowledge of the classics, Hebrew, theology, plus a rich Irish brogue, from their father. All four followed him into the ministry. The Tennents immigrated to America when Gilbert was fourteen. The sons helped Mr. Tennent found the "Log College," near Philadelphia.

Even though he had not attended theological seminary, Gilbert was able to pass the tests for licensure required of him by the Presbytery of Philadelphia.

In 1725 he took up his initial pastoral labors in the Presbyterian Church of New Castle, Delaware. For some unknown reason he left the church abruptly soon after he was installed. Both his church and presbytery complained of the action; the synod rebuked him. It was the first of a cycle of explosive events in an explosive life.

The young licentiate received a call to a church in New Brunswick, New Jersey. The Presbytery of Philadelphia laid hands on his head and ordained him. The congregation he ministered to was composed for the most part of English-speaking Dutch. With another pastor named Freylinghuysen, who preached in the Dutch language to a group of recent immigrants from Holland, he carried on his work. Both congregations used the same building for worship.

Tennent thought that his preaching was ineffectual, that too few were being converted under him. A rather serious ailment put him aside for some months. During the period of his illness, he engaged in much heart-examining and prayer. When he recuperated, two new features were noticeable in his preaching: one, a ring of power; and two, a somewhat harsh condemnation of others.

In 1739 George Whitefield arrived in America, and the Great Awakening flamed up. Gilbert Tennent was one of the sparks. On hearing him sermonize, Whitefield wrote a friend, "He went to the Bottom indeed, and did not daub with untempered Mortar. . . . Hypocrites must soon be converted or enraged at his Preaching."

Tennent accompanied Whitefield to New York, watched him conduct evangelistic services, and studied his methods with boyish enthusiasm. Applying what he learned, he emulated the English minister's approach on a trip through South Jersey and Maryland, and with extraordinary success.

Whitefield went back to England. In 1740, several New England revivalists, having learned of Tennent's zeal and wishing to have some-

*one follow up Whitefield's tour, invited him to water the seed White-
field had sown. He accepted with pleasure.*

*In Boston, he addressed greater crowds than Whitefield had drawn.
He also brought down the wrath of certain Church leaders by his
pointed preachment. Perry Miller has referred to him as a "burly, salty,
downright man." Others, like Thomas Prince, charged that he was
totally without polish, but admit that he had arrived at deep and terrible
convictions. One impatient Bostonian stated in a communication that
he "preached like a Boatswain of a Ship, calling the Sailors to come to
Prayers and be damned." Timothy Cutler described him as "a minister
impudent and saucy; and told them all they were damned, damned,
damned." Cutler went on to say, "This charmed them; and in the
dreadfullest winter I ever saw, people wallowed in the snow night and
day for the benefit of his beastly braying."*

*No one, not his most articulate opponent, denied that Gilbert's
preaching was powerful, or said that it was without effect. In numerical
results, more responded to his invitations than ever had at the Whitefield meetings. His visits to over twenty New England communities always bore fruit.*

*Next, he became embroiled in a disputation in the Synod of Phila-
delphia. He and others enthusiastic for "conscious conversion" and for
Whitefield's revivalistic methods charged their brethren with being
interested in orthodoxy but not in experimental religion. At Notting-
ham, Pennsylvania, he preached his fiery sermon, "The Danger of an
Unconverted Ministry," which served to widen the breach between
the two parties. The Synod of Philadelphia arraigned Tennent for
disregarding its authority and for disturbing the peace of the Church.
The upshot was that he and a group of friends and sympathizers withdrew from their presbytery, and the seventeen-year schism was initiated.*

*A churchman named Hancock took the occasion to ridicule him in
the* Braintree Examiner *under the title of an article: "Gilbert against
Tennent." He retaliated by publishing his reply: "The Examiner Examined; or Gilbert Tennent, Harmonious."*

*In 1743, he left New Brunswick to shepherd a flock in Philadelphia.
From then on his career grew less spectacular. He mellowed with age,
as most men do. He even wrote articles and made public pronouncements expressing his regret that he had once been so vituperative.*

*A complete individualist, he was buried, by request, under the middle
aisle of the Second Presbyterian Church of Philadelphia. Later his body
was exhumed and moved to suburban Abington.*

The Solemn Scene of the Last Judgment

GILBERT TENNENT, A.M.

> Seeing it is a righteous thing with God to recompense Tribulation to them that trouble you; And to you who are troubled rest with us, when the Lord Jesus shall be revealed from heaven, with His mighty Angels, In flaming Fire, taking Vengeance on them that know not God, and that obey not the Gospel of our Lord Jesus Christ: Who shall be punished with everlasting Destruction from the Presence of the Lord, and from the Glory of His Power
>
> —II Thessalonians 1:6-9

IT IS a most dreadful and afflictive Sight! to behold vast Multitudes of unhappy Sinners, who are inconsiderately hastening upon the swift *Torrent of Time* to that Great *Ocean of Eternity*, whence there is no returning; without considering what will be the Consequence of their present Impieties, the severe Examination they shall undergo before the great Judge of Heaven and Earth, the everlasting State of Misery and Woe which they shall be finally and irrevocably fixed in, except they repent; after a few fleeting Moments they are expired! It's a strange, to Amazement, to behold intelligent Creatures endow'd with rational and noble Powers, so far degenerated from their own Order, so far sunk into brutish Stupidity; so far forgetting the Dignity of their Nature and Design of their Being, as to be chiefly intent upon, and prospective about, the securing and amassing temporary and perishing Vanities; while in the meantime they indulge the supinest Negligence about the Concerns of their everlasting State!

As to that determinate *Time* of the last Judgment, that is known only to God, and reserv'd as a secret in the divine Bosom from all Mortals; and that for very wise Reasons; viz., to awaken our Fears, excite our Diligence, and support our Patience: That not knowing the exact Time of our Lord's coming, we may be every Day expecting of it, and preparing for it. In the meantime it may be asserted, that the coming of the Son of Man will be very *sudden* and *unexpected: The Day of the Lord*, says the Apostle Peter, *will come as a Thief in the Night*, i.e., when it is not looked for; *the Heavens shall pass away with a great Noise, and the Elements shall melt with fervent heat.* (2 Pet. 3:10) *At Midnight*, i.e., in the secure State of the Church, there will be a great Cry, *Behold the Bridegroom cometh! Go ye out to meet*

Him. As it was in the Days of Noah and Lot, so will it be in the Days of the Son of Man: They eat, they drank, married and were given in Marriage. They shall indulge themselves in the securest Sensuality, and little dream of so terrible an Event. For *as a Snare will it come on all that dwell on the Face of the Earth.* While Sinners cry, *Peace, Peace, sudden Destruction shall come upon them as a Travail on a Woman with Child.*

The *Place* of Judgment, it is probable, will be the Region of the Air; so near to the Earth as to render the great Judge and His judicial Process visible to all its Inhabitants. Hence is that of the Apostle to the *Thessalonians,* that the Righteous *will be caught up in the Clouds, to meet their Lord in the Air.* (I Thes. 4:17)

For as the Father hath Life in Himself, so hath He given to the Son to have Life in Himself, and hath given Him Authority to execute Judgment also, because He is the Son of Man: And indeed it is highly reasonable that the Person who is to transact this grand Affair, should be God and Man in one Person, in order to pass a righteous Sentence upon all the Thought, Words, and Actions of reasonable Creatures; and to execute it, nothing less than infinite Knowledge and infinite Power are necessary.

Now these are Properties peculiar to the supreme Being. The secret Springs of Action, from which their Guilt or Goodness is principally derived, devoid of all Disguise, are only open to the all-penetrating Eye of God. Not to say that as the divine Nature is only capable to execute so difficult a Task, so it is only worthy of the Honours of it. To pass a determinative sentence upon the everlasting State of Men and Angels, is a Dignity too sacred and venerable for any mere Creature to sustain. The holy Lamb of God is only worthy to open the Seals of the Book of God's invariable Purposes, and to assign to Men and Angels, those endless Rewards and Punishments, that are suited to their different Works (Rev. 5:9, 12).

The *Sinfulness of Sin* will be doubtless hereby expos'd, and made to appear in its crimson Aggravations, and flagrant Malignancy; in that it turns the softest Compassion, into the sternest Severity; obliging the merciful Saviour, who came from the Bosom of His blessed Father (that Throne of the brightest Glory, that Seat of the sweetest Felicity, that Center of the sternest Majesty) into a miserable World, and thereby the most astonishing Stoop of Condescending Excellency, having assum'd the human Nature with His Deity, endured inconceivable Pain and extreme Misery, in order to save Souls from everlasting and deserved Ruin, and purchase for them an endless and a glorious Life: That He, I say, after such vast Expense of Labour and of Blood, should be obliged by Sin, to banish Impenitents into eternal Death; *This, This,* affords the most detestable Idea of Sin that can possibly enter into a human Mind.

It might be further observed concerning the Wisdom of this Constitution of Christ to be the Judge of the Universe, that thereby the undisturbed Harmony of the divine Attributes will be eminently apparent; which here we have but very imperfect Notions of. For at the same time will be executed upon different Objects, the mildest Clemency and most awful Severity, the richest Mercy and everest Justice, the heaviest Vengeance and the noblest Love!

And it must needs inspire the Hearts of all good Men with great Magnanimity, and peculiar Pleasure; to think that that Saviour, whom they love and serve from the Heart, is to be their supreme and final Judge. So on the contrary, it can't but discourage and distress the Hearts of the Ungodly, to think that that Jesus whose Doctrine they have discredited, and whose Laws they have disobeyed, will determine their everlasting State. Hence in that solemn and Soul-affecting Passage of the Apostle *John* in the *Revelations*, the 1st Chapter and the 7th Verse, *Behold, He cometh in the Clouds, and every Eye shall see Him.* To this I may add one Consideration more, namely, That it is more than probable that the Power of the last Judgment is an illustrious Branch of the *Kingly Office* of the Lord Jesus, confer'd upon Him by God the Father, as a Reward of His deep Humiliation and astonishing Abasure. See Phil. 2:8,9: *And being found in Fashion as a Man, He humbled Himself, and became obedient unto Death, even the Death of the Cross. Wherefore also God hath highly exalted Him, and given Him a Name which is above every Name.*

This leads me to consider the 2nd Particular included in our Text, namely, the *Appearance* of this Judge whom the Father hath constituted, in that terrible Day of God, when the grand and solemn Scene of eternal Judgment shall be open'd; and no doubt will be full of inexpressible Pomp, and tremendous Majesty; as our Text informs us: *Then the Lord Jesus shall be revealed from Heaven, with His mighty Angels in flaming Fire.* Now the Heavens conceal Him, but then they shall disclose their Lord and Ornament, to the Admiration of the whole Universe; *for every Eye shall see Him!*

The eternal Son of God shall descend visibly from the heavenly Paradise, that Throne of majestic Beauty and refulgent Glory, attended with all possible Ensigns of Power, and inconceivable Grandeur. He will come guarded with a Train of innumerable and mighty Angels: He will come environed with a vast and glorious Retinue of perfected Spirits; these will attend the great Judge of Heaven and Earth, the descending God, through the airy Regions, to the Seat of Judgment; in order to grace that magnificient Solemnity, with the august State!

These holy and mighty Angels will doubtless be employed as Ministers of Justice and Mercy at that great Day, in summoning Criminals to the Bar, and executing their woeful Sentence upon them; as well as gathering in the Elect, and accompanying them to their blissful Mansions. No doubt these Nobles of the Court of Heaven will appear in their brightest Robes. And we are told, that our great Lord Himself will be reveal'd *in flaming Fire*. When the Law was given by *Moses* upon *Sinai*, the Mount trembled for Fear, and was wrapt in Fire and Smoke; and the Voice in the midst of the Flames; which struck the whole Hosts of Israel, with the utmost Consternation.

Now if the Lord appear'd with so much Majesty and Terror when the Law was given, how much more when He comes to avenge the Breaches of it. This Mass of Fire, which the Text mentions, being added to the Splendor of His Glorified Body, "will," as one well expresses it, "cause Him to outshine the *Sun* in His Meridian Bloom and Beauty, and drown all the Lights of Heaven with the conquering Brightness of His Appearance. So that when He comes from His ethereal Palace, and appears upon the eastern Heaven, the immense Sphere of visible Glory that shall surround Him, will in the Twinkling of an Eye spread and diffuse itself over all Creation, and cause both the Heavens and Earth to glitter like flaming Fire."

It is with the utmost Magnificence, that the holy Scriptures describe the second Coming of the SON OF MAN! When He came as a *Saviour*, His divine Glory was veil'd with the Mantle of His Humanity: He who was God over all blessed forever, appeared in the Form of a Servant, was willingly exposed to Poverty and Contempt, with all the painful Maladies to which the human Nature is subject! But when He comes as a *Judge*, He will assume a Splendor and Greatness suitable to the Glory of His Deity; suitable to the Dignity of His Character! The Face of the Heavens will be convuls'd into a flaming Scroll, and the deep Foundations of the Earth shall shake, while its Surface, being torn by Earthquakes, shall send forth Rivers of Fire!

In the meantime while the Heavens and Earth are covered with a general Ruin! the dreadful Clangor (or Blast) of the Archangel's Trumpet, which shall awake the dead out of their secure Recesses; the awful Roarings of the great Ocean, with terrible Peals of Thunder from the Heavens above, and hideous Murmurs from the Earth beneath; and the dreadful Shrieks of damned Creatures, now expecting to hear their final Doom pronounc'd; shall so mingle and confound their Groans, that the whole Face of things shall present a doleful Scene of the most hideous, horrible and confus'd Ruin!

How dreadful will it be at this *Juncto*, for the Wicked, to behold the Son of Man coming in the Clouds of Heaven, in the most triumphant Manner, with Myriads of the heavenly Hosts attending on Him; encompass'd with Power and great Glory! Descending from Heaven with a Shout, with the Voice of the Archangel and with the Trump of God! When our Lord appeared on the Mount of Transfiguration, His Face did shine as the Sun, and His Raiment was white as the Light: How splendid then must His Venture be at this glorious Solemnity?

We may be help'd to some Idea of the Lustre of Christ's Appearance, by considering that memorable Passage of the Apostle John (Rev. 1:13-17). *"And in the midst of the Seven golden Candlesticks, one like unto the Son of Man, clothed with a Garment down to the Foot, and girt with a golden Girdle. His Head and His Hairs were white as Snow, and His Eyes were as a Flame of Fire; and His Feet like unto fine Brass, as if they burned in a furnace; and His Voice as the Sound of many Waters. And He had in His right Hand seven Stars; and out of His Mouth went a sharp two-edged Sword; and His Countenance was as the Sun shineth in his Strength."* We are also inform'd, that *He will come in His own and in His Father's Glory;* the Light and Beauty, the Splendor and Majesty of which, is to us, in our present State, inconceivable and inexpressible!

"When He comes to Judgment, saith one, it will be with His own glorify'd Body of pure and immaculate Splendor, with His Hair shining like Threads of Light, His Eyes sparkling with Beams of Majesty; displaying a soft beautiful Lustre and dazzling Glory round about it." His Throne is said to be great and white, i.e., pure and immaculate, stately and magnificent; and from it are said to proceed Lightnings, and Thunderings and Voices. Yea, so terrible and insupportable will be the Majesty of the Judge seated on His Throne, that the Heavens and Earth are said to flee from His Face! If in the Time of His humble Abasure, there appeared such Majesty in His Aspect, and those who came to apprehend Him went backwards and fell to the Ground, how will His Enemies be able then to abide the Day of His Wrath; when He will appear in His most exalted Glory and Magnificence!

The Thunder of the Archangel's Trumpet, being accompanied with the almighty Power of Christ, shall resound to the utmost Limits of the Globe, strike the Concave of the Heavens, and pierce the darkest Caverns, the most remote and silent Recesses of the Earth and Sea, and rouse their Inhabitants from the Sleep of Death: That the whole rational Creation who have ever lived in all the past Ages, since the Foundation of the world: and shall hereafter come into Existence, to the utmost Period and extreme Verge of the Line of Time, may appear at once, in a universal Rendezvous, before the dread Tribunal of the Lord Jesus Christ, to receive their final Doom.

Then the haughtiest Monarchs, the subtilest Politicians, the boldest Heroes, being disrob'd of the trifling Ensigns of their present State and Greatness, will forget their former Power, Courage, and Grandeur, and cry to the Mountains to hide them from the Face of the Lamb that sits upon the Throne. They shall be forced to bow to that Saviour, whom they here contemned, and implore His Favour, but in vain, He will be inexorable to their unseasonable and rueful Crys. Their Lamentations over Sin, and Supplications for Mercy and Pardon, might here in the Time of Life and Health be serviceable to them; but then it will be *too late! too late!* The Master of the House will rise up,' and shut too the Door of Mercy and Salvation against such wilfull Impenitents!

We may reasonably imagine, That when the Souls and Bodies of the Wicked are united, their Hearts will be torn with the most terrible Convulsions of Guilt, Fear and Shame! O! With what Confusion, Horror and Reluctance, will impenitent *Caitiffs* be drag'd to the Bar of Judgment, to hear their most secret Impieties openly expos'd, and their awful Doom pronounc'd, before the Whole Creation! While crowds of innumerable Devils are at their Hells, ready to Witness against them, and hale them to the infernal Furnace! While before them is that Lord Jesus who once offered Himself to be their Saviour, but now is their angry Judge! When they behold His Eyes as Flames of Fire, and hear His Voice as the sound of many Waters, how will their hearts be rack'd with the acutest Pain! Especially when they behold the Elements above their Heads melting with fervent Heat, and the massy Earth trembling and burning under their Feet; and everywhere around them the wildest Confusion and most deplorable Ruin blended together in a promiscuous Chaos, void of Beauty and of Order!

And in the meantime, none in Heaven or in Earth to pity, or help them in their Extremity! But on the contrary, the great God and the Lord Jesus Christ who here offered His Love, and entreated them to accept it, in the most importunate and moving Strains, now frowning on them, and laughing at their Calamity! Yea and all the Hosts of Angels, and Armies of glorify'd Saints, rejoicing in their deserved Destruction! In which God's Justice will have a glorious but terrible Triumph.

The vast Assembly of the Quick and Dead being thus brought before the burning Tribunal! There will be a Separation made, the *Goats* will be put on the *Left Hand* of Christ, and the *Sheep* at His *Right!* (Matt. 25:33) Here it is impossible fully to discern between the Righteous and the Wicked, presumptuous Hypocrites will crowd amongst pious Souls, with their specious Pretences; and sometimes deceive the most judicious; But there their Fraud and Subtilty will be fully detected, and their Persons separated from the Congregation of the Righteous, not one abhorred Hypocrite will be suffered to intrude into that venerable and innumerable Army of the Saints.

And then not only *great Crimes* will be examined, but those *lesser Evils* which many little consider, and think there is no Harm in now.

264   *The Solemn Scene of the Last Judgment*

Our Lord Himself informs us, *that every idle Word that Men shall speak, they shall give an Account thereof, in the Day of Judgment.* And Alas! What a dreadful account this will be to many? (Matt. 12) And as the Wickedness of the Wicked will thus be dissected, and laid open: So on the contrary, the Duties of Piety and Charity, which good Men have done shall be proclaim'd with Honour: Their secret Sighs, Prayers, Tears, Sufferings for Righteousness Sake; those silent Virtues, which they here labour'd to conceal, as much as they could from others Observance with avail of Modesty, shall then come into Remembrance, be mentioned honourably, and rewarded openly. *I was hungry and ye gave me food, sick and in Prison and ye visited me, naked and ye clothed me.* The least charitable Action of a gracious Person, even to the *Cup of cold Water*, shall neither be forgotten, or pass unrewarded: for it is a righteous Thing with God, to recompence Tribulation to them that trouble You, and to such as are troubled, rest.

Then shall the King, the Judge from His Throne of Glory, *say to them on His Right Hand, Come ye blessed of my Father, inherit the Kingdom prepared for you from the Foundation of the World.* (Matt. 25:34) O precious Sentence! O Good Lord Jesus! how sweet are thy Words! and how happy are thy People! What can be conceiv'd more full of divine Consolation? Whoever accuses, asperses or condemns you, you are blessed by my Father, justify'd and approv'd of by Him, *Come;* on earth you were slighted and deserted by my Enemies, and your false friends, but I will never forsake you; *Come*, from a sinful and miserable World under the Shadow of my Wings, into the Embraces of my Bosom, and enjoy the Delights of my Love; *Come*, inherit that glorious Kingdom, that princely Portion, which was prepared for you from everlasting, in the Purposes of my Father, and in the Fulness of Time purchased for you by my Blood, and continued to you by my Intercession; *Come*, and possess that unspeakable Honour, and unmerited Happiness, for which you were prepared by the sanctifying Operations of the Holy Spirit; *Come*, and dwell with God and holy Angels; *Come*, and drink the Delights of Heaven, the crystal streams of Life which flow from the Throne of God; *Come*, ye troubled and weary Souls who have been troubled by Sinners, and weary of Sin, and *inherit the Rest prepared for you!* O! It is not possible to express with Words, the Rivers of Joy and Gladness, which will run into the Hearts of the Glorify'd! and make them triumph on this Occasion with Joy unspeakable and full of Glory!

Now after their joyful Sentence is pass'd, they will be honourably conducted by Hosts of Angels to the City of the great God.

After this will succeed the Sentence of the Wicked: These impure and unholy souls, being sufficiently detected, and convict'd of their ungrateful Rebellion against God, in breaking His Law and slighting His Gospel, must then hear these dreadful Words from the Mouth of Christ, *Go ye accursed into everlasting Fire, prepared for the Devil and His Angels.* What can be conceiv'd more full of Terror than His Sentence? Ye bless'd yourselves in your prosperity and false Hope, and were flattered by others; but now you are accursed by God, cursed to all Eternity: You wanted God to depart from you in this World, you lik'd not the Knowledge of His Ways, and slighted the Company of His Servants, and now you must depart from them for ever: *Go* ye accursed into never-ending Torments, prepar'd for the vilest and most malignant Spirits: Ye would obey their Suggestions, while ye contemned my Authority, quench'd my repeated Calls, and abus'd my Mercy! And now ye must dwell with these infernal Ghosts forever, and inherit the Burnings prepar'd for them! I shall never offer you abused Mercy any more; but ye shall be punished with everlasting Destruction from my gracious Presence by my glorious Power!

After the Sentence is pronounc'd by the great Judge, immediately it shall be executed. Then will these unhappy wretches be drag'd from the Judgment-Seat, to that terrible *Tophet,* whose Flames are kindled by the Breath of God! Forever banished from the ravishing Sweets of God's Presence, from the amiable Society of Saints and Angels! From the blissful Regions of Light and Love! From all the Joys and Glories of the heavenly Paradise! And the least Hope of ever attaining them! To be tormented in the burning Lake, that gloomy Vault of thick Darkness, frightful Horror, and extreme Despair! With the Strings of their accusing Consciences! The Upbraidings and Severities of Devils! The continual Roarings, and awful Lamentations of damned Companions; and the fearful and inconceivably terrible Vengeance of the most high God, pour'd forth upon them in full and never-ending Vials. The Shame, Confusion and Anguish of such miserable Souls, cannot be fully conceiv'd or express'd.

And all you who slight the precepts, Promises, and Offers of the glorious Gospel of the Grace of God, remember as you are condemned already (John 3:36), that then, except ye repent, that Sentence will be executed against you; A terrible Damnation expects you if ye continue in your Sins, it will be more tolerable for *Sodom* and *Gomorrha* in the Day of the Lord, than for you. Hell from beneath is moved to meet you at your coming. If pious *Moses* was so affected with the Sight of God, upon Mount *Sinai,* that he did exceedingly Fear and Quake (Heb. 12:21): If zealous *Isaiah* was so much affected with Fear, by beholding of a small glimpse of God's Glory, when the Seraphs cry'd, *Holy, holy, holy, is the Lord of Hosts,* that he complain'd, *Wo is me! for I am undone!* (Isa. 6:5)

If faithful *Daniel* was so surprised with a Vision, that he swoon'd

away with the dread thereof! (Dan. 10:8,11) Then how will you
who are condemn'd by complicated Guilt, and covered with the basest
Deformity; be able to bear up under the Appearance of the Judge of
Heaven and of Earth; whose Loins will be girded as with the finest
Gold of *Uphaz;* His Body like the Beryl, and His Face as the Appearance of Lightning, and His Eyes as Lamps of Fire, His Arms and His
Feet like polish'd Brass, and the Voice of His Words like the Voice
of a Multitude. If the Joints of *Belshazzar's* Knee were loosn'd by
trembling, in the midst of his Grandeur and Jollitry! by the Appearance of but a Handwriting upon the Wall, what Fear and Trembling
shall possess you! Guilty Dust! Strip'd of all your present Comforts
and Ornaments; when you behold the Lord of Jesus appearing in the
greatest Majesty and highest Glory!

If the Appearance of a temporal Judge in scarlet Robes, strikes such
a Damp in a guilty Prisoner at the Bar, what Horror shall tear your
Bosoms, if ye repent now, when ye behold the Son of God coming
in the Clouds of Heaven, or seated on His blazing Throne of judgment!
If this Minute we heard the Heavens groan and roar with piercing
Claps of Thunder and were encompass'd with terrible and sudden
Flashes of Lightning, from the murmuring Clouds, and in the meantime
felt the labouring Earth tremble under our Feet, ready to open it's
Mouth and devour us, and beheld the Lord Jesus descending to the
Seat of Judgment, from the opening Heavens, on a Body of Light
brighter than the Sun, with all His holy Angels about Him; what pale
frighted Countenances and trembling Hearts would there be amongst
us, what crying to God for Mercy and Pardon.

But because Christ defers His coming, stupid Sinners will not believe it, and consider it, so as to prepare for it! But be assured, my
Brethren, that Christ will as certainly come to judge you as tho' you
now saw Him coming from Heaven. All ye miserable Souls, who are
guilty of any of those Evils I before express'd, and to continue in
them, believe it, the Time hastens when the Lord Jesus shall be
reveal'd from Heaven with His mighty Angels, in flaming Fire, to
take Vengeance on you; to inflict Punishments with Jealousy and in-
censed Indignation, suited to the Number and Heinousness of your
Crimes. Then shall ye be punished with everlasting Destruction, from
the Presence of the Lord, and from the Glory of His Power. Ye
shall be forever deprived of the gracious Presence of God, and expos'd
to an intense, continual and eternal Destruction! God's stern Justice
and almighty Power, will be glorified, in your utter and eternal Ruin!
Dear Brethren! If these Things will not affect you, I know not what
will; even a Pagan *Felix* trembled when he heard this Subject discoursed
of; but alas some of our Gospel Sinners are more hardened than the
Pagans!

In the last Place, I exhort you, my Brethren, in the Name and

Bowels of Christ, and by all that should be clear to you, that you would quickly endeavour to *prepare* for Christ's Coming to Judgment, which may be very speedily for you, even before tomorrow Morning. In the Parable of the Virgins we read, that *at Midnight there was a great Cry, behold the Bridegroom cometh!* The Means I would prescribe to you for that End, are, a frequent Meditation upon Death and Judgment, Examination, Prayer, and a speedy Reformation. *Let the wicked Man forsake his way.*

O! methinks, the Consideration of the last Judgment shou'd deter us from secret sins, and excite us to a conscientious Performance of the secret Duties of Religion! feeling that then that which is now done in Corners will be published on the House Tops; i.e., in the most open and conspicuous Manner possible. But my dear brethren! That which I wou'd especially and passionately recommend to you, as a principal and absolutely necessary Preparative, for the Judgment of the great God, is that you would speedily and vehemently labour to be acquainted with experimental and vital Religion: Namely, Justification from the Guilt of Sin, by the Grace of Christ; and Sanctification from the Power of Sin by the Spirit of Christ.

O Sinner! *Agree with thine Adversary quickly, whiles thou art in the Way with him; lest at any Time the Adversary deliver thee to the Judge, and the Judge deliver thee to the Officer, and thou be cast into Prison. Verily I say unto thee, Thou shalt by no Means come out thence, till thou hast paid the uttermost Farthing.* (Matt. 5:25,26)

O Brethren! Wash your Hearts from Wickedness; How long shall vain Thoughts lodge within you. Cleanse your Hands, ye sinners, and purify your Hearts, ye double-minded, be afflicted and mourn and weep:—Life is short, Eternity is long, Death is near, and the Judge at the Door; in a little Time ye will be past all Remedy, if ye repent not; if there be any Convictions of Sin and Danger, in any of you, encourage and preserve them by Consideration and Supplication to God, as the most invaluable Jewels. Such unnecessary Conversation with ungodly People. *Forsake the Foolish and live.*—Be humbly resolute in God's service, whatever it cost you, for true Religion is its own reward here, and how much so will it be hereafter. *The Sufferings of this present World are not worthy to be compar'd with that Weight of Glory which shall be revealed.* If it seem Evil to others to serve God in a profligate and perverse Age, let it not do so to you. O Sinners! I beseech you by the tender Mercies of God, that you would not always halt between two Opinions, *God* and *Baal.* If ye will faithfully observe these Things, the Day of *Christ* will be a Day of refreshing to you; and you will long for it, with the poor Church; and say, *Come,* Lord Jesus, *come quickly,* even so come thou blessed Son of God! *Amen, Amen.*

JOHN WESLEY 1703-1791

In the year 1735, two young Oxford graduates, John and Charles Wesley, sailed for America intending to carry on missionary work among the Indians. A sudden violent storm at sea threw the passengers into a state of consternation. People cried out in terror, wept, whimpered, cursed, or asked God for mercy. The Wesleys themselves were stricken with fear. On board were a number of Moravian Christians whose conduct contrasted vividly with that of the other passengers, exhibiting a poise and serenity which so impressed the brothers that for the first time in their lives they doubted their own conversion.

Arrived in Georgia, the Wesleys set about seeking to persuade the natives to live better lives. The response was disheartening. Frustrated, Charles soon returned to England and later John gave up and followed him. On shipboard he wrote, "I went to America to convert the Indians; but oh! who shall convert me?"

John Wesley was then an ordained minister in the Church of England. His great-grandfather, grandfather, and father had been clergymen before him. Back in England, he continued to preach, but still without results. Remembering the Moravians and immersing themselves in the writings of Luther, Charles first, then John, came to realize that justification was secured by faith and not by the works of the law. Resting now on Christ alone, peace and consolation came to their troubled hearts.

At once, they began to preach the doctrine of "instantaneous conversion." The doors of the Church of England were closed to them, so they joined Whitefield in open-air campaigns. In 1738 Methodism came to birth. Its leaders never dreamed that eventually the Methodist movement would break with the Church of England and develop into a separate church.

John Wesley owned rare administrative gifts. He organized societies and dispatched bands of workers all over England who emphasized the necessity of the experience of conversion. A rigid disciplinarian, he held his followers to simplicity in dress, abstinence from amusements, and "holy living." Wherever his workers went, multitudes of conversions occurred, often punctuated by weeping, groaning, and screaming.

The Methodists met bitter persecution. Wesley, himself an itinerant evangelist, walked the valley of the shadow of death for half a century. His Journal reads like Paul's missionary saga. At Bristol, "the streets filled with people shouting, cursing, and swearing, and ready to swallow the ground with fierceness of rage." At London, "I had no sooner stepped out of the coach than the mob, who were gathered in great numbers about the door, quite closed in on me." At Long-Lane he was stoned. At Pelton, a company of drunkards all but mobbed him to death. Again, at Falmouth, he barely escaped with his life. A friend testified that at Bowling Green he witnessed Wesley shamefully treated by a desperate crowd. "I stood at the table upon which Mr. Wesley was standing; and while I heard the shouting of the crowd, and saw dead animals and cabbage stalks flying around his hoary head, I was filled with pity and horror." Through all the testings Wesley displayed incredible fortitude, a calm and sweet spirit, and frequently prayed for those who did him wrong.

He wrote several books and many hymns, though as a hymn-writer he never attained the stature of his brother Charles. John's famous motto was, "The world is my parish." He traveled some 225,000 miles during his years of service. He seldom preached less than 500 sermons a year.

John Wesley sincerely believed Methodism to be a return to primitive Christianity. He taught, over against Calvin, that repentance and faith preceded regeneration in temporal sequence. He also was persuaded that sanctification could reach a point of perfection in this life. His most severe opponents, however, were forced to admit that he led an unimpeachably godly life. Spurgeon, who disagreed heartily with his Arminianism, wrote in his autobiography that he honestly believed were the Saviour to add two more disciples to the Twelve, He would choose Wesley and Whitefield.

His dying words: "Best of all, God is with us."

The Natural Condition of the Natural Man

JOHN WESLEY

And God saw that the wickedness of man was great in the earth, and that every imagination of the thoughts of his heart was only evil continually. —Genesis 6:5

HOW widely different is this from the fair pictures of human nature which men have drawn in all ages! The writings of many of the ancients abound with gay descriptions of the dignity of man; whom some of them paint as having all virtue and happiness in his composition, or, at least, entirely in his power, without being beholden to any other being; yea, as self-sufficient, able to live on his own stock, and little inferior to God Himself.

Nor have Heathens alone, men who are guided in their researches by little more than the dim light of reason, but many likewise of them that bear the Name of Christ, and to whom are entrusted the oracles of God, spoken as magnificently concerning the nature of man, as if it were all innocence and perfection. Accounts of this kind have particularly abounded in the present century; and perhaps in no part of the world more than in our own country. Here not a few persons of strong understanding, as well as extensive learning, have employed their utmost abilities to show, what they termed, "the fair side of human nature." And it must be acknowledged, that, if their accounts of him be just, man is still but "a little lower than the angels"; or, as the words may be more literally rendered, "a little less than God."

Is it any wonder, that these accounts are very readily received by the generality of men? For who is not easily persuaded to think favourably of himself? Accordingly, writers of this kind are most universally read, admired, applauded. And innumerable are the converts they have made, not only in the gay but the learned world. So that it is now quite unfashionable to talk otherwise, to say any thing to the disparagement of human nature; which is generally allowed, notwithstanding a few infirmities, to be very innocent, and wise, and virtuous!

But, in the mean time, what must we do with our Bibles?—for they will never agree with this. These accounts, however pleasing to flesh and blood, are utterly irreconcilable with the Scriptural. The Scripture avers, that "by one man's disobedience all men were constituted sinners"; that "in Adam all died," spiritually died, lost the life and the image of God; that fallen, sinful Adam then "begat a son in his own likeness";—nor was it possible he should beget him in any other; for "who can bring a clean thing out of an unclean?"—that consequently we, as well as other men, were by nature "dead in trespasses and sins," "without hope, without God in the world," and, therefore "children of wrath;" that every man may say, "I was shapen in wickedness, and in sin did my mother conceive me"; that "there is no difference," in that "all have sinned and come short of the glory of God," of that glorious image of God wherein man was originally created.

And hence, when "the Lord looked down from heaven upon the children of men, he saw they were all gone out of the way; they were altogether become abominable, there was none righteous, no, not one," none that truly sought after God: just agreeable to this, to what is declared by the Holy Ghost in the words above recited, "God saw," when He looked down from heaven before, "that the wickedness of man was great in the earth"; so great, that "every imagination of the thoughts of his heart was only evil continually."

This is God's account of man: from which I shall take occasion, first, to show what men were before the flood: secondly, to inquire, whether they are not the same now: and, thirdly, to add some inferences.

I am, first, by opening the words of the text, to show what men were before the flood. And we may fully depend on the account here given: for God saw it, and He cannot be deceived. He "saw that the wickedness of man was great":—not of this or that man; not of a few men only; not barely of the greater part, but of man in general; of men universally. The word includes the whole human race, every partaker of human nature. And it is not easy for us to compute their numbers, to tell how many thousands and millions they were.

The earth then retained much of its primeval beauty and original fruitfulness. The face of the globe was not rent and torn as it is now; and spring and summer went hand in hand. It is therefore probable, it afforded sustenance for far more inhabitants than it is now capable of sustaining; and these must be immensely multiplied, while men begat sons and daughters for seven or eight hundred years together. Yet, among all this inconceivable number, only "Noah found favour with God." He alone (perhaps including part of his household) was an exception from the universal wickedness, which, by the just judgment of God, in a short time after brought on universal destruction. All the rest were partakers in the same guilt as they were in the same punishment.

"God saw all the imaginations of the thoughts of his heart";—of his soul, his inward man, the spirit within him, the principle of all his inward and outward motions. He "saw all the imaginations":—it is not possible to find a word of a more extensive signification. It includes whatever is formed, made, fabricated within; all that is or passes in the soul; every inclination, affection, passion, appetite; every temper, design, thought. It must of consequence include every word and action, as naturally flowing from these fountains, and being either good or evil according to the fountain from which they severally flow.

Now God saw that all this, the whole thereof, was evil;—contrary to moral rectitude; contrary to the nature of God, which necessarily includes all good; contrary to the divine will, the eternal standard of good and evil; contrary to the pure, holy image of God, wherein man was originally created, and wherein he stood when God, surveying the works of His hands, saw them all to be very good; contrary to justice, mercy, and truth, and to the essential relations which each man bore to his Creator and his fellow-creatures.

But was there not good mingled with the evil? Was there not light intermixed with the darkness? No, none at all: "God saw that the whole imagination of the heart of man was only evil." It cannot indeed be denied, but many of them, perhaps all, had good motions put into their heart; for the Spirit of God did then also "strive with man," if haply he might repent, more especially during that gracious reprieve, the hundred and twenty years, while the ark was preparing. But still "in his flesh dwelt no good things"; all his nature was purely evil: it was wholly consistent with itself, and unmixed with any thing of an opposite nature.

However, it may still be matter of inquiry, "Was there no intermission of this evil? Were there no lucid intervals, wherein something good might be found in the heart of man?" We are not here to consider, what the grace of God might occasionally work in his soul; and, abstracted from this, we have no reason to believe, there was any intermission of that evil. For God, who "saw the whole imagination of the thoughts of his heart to be only evil," saw likewise, that it was always the same, that it "was only evil continually"; every year, every day, every hour, every moment. He never deviated into good.

Such is the authentic account of the whole race of mankind which he who knoweth what is in man, Who searcheth the heart and trieth the reins, hath left upon record for our instruction. Such were all men before God brought the flood upon the earth. We are, secondly, to inquire, whether they are the same now.

And this is certain, the Scripture gives us no reason to think any otherwise of them. On the contrary, all the above-cited passages of Scripture refer to those who lived after the flood. It was above a thousand years after, that God declared by David concerning the children of men, "They are all gone out of the way" of truth and holiness; "there is none righteous, no, not one." And to this bear all the

Prophets witness, in their several generations. So Isaiah, concerning God's peculiar people (and certainly the Heathens were in no better condition), "The whole head is sick, and the whole heart faint. From the sole of the foot even unto the head there is no soundness . . . but wounds, and bruises, and putrefying sores." The same account is given by all the Apostles, yea, by the whole tenor of the oracles of God. From all these we learn, concerning man in his natural state, un-assisted by the grace of God, that "every imagination of the thoughts of his heart is" still "evil, only evil," and that "continually."

And this account of the present state of man is confirmed by daily experience. It is true, the natural man discerns it not: and this is not to be wondered at. So long as a man born blind continues so, he is scarce sensible of his want: much less, could we suppose a place where all were born without sight, would they be sensible of the want of it. In like manner, so long as men remain in their natural blindness of understanding, they see the state they were in before; they are then deeply convinced, that "every man living," themselves especially, are, by nature, "Altogether vanity"; that is, folly and ignorance, sin and wickedness.

We see, when God opens our eyes, that we were before without God, or rather, Atheists in the world. We had, by nature, no knowledge of God, no acquaintance with Him. It is true, as soon as we came to the use of reason, we learned "the invisible things of God, even His eternal power and Godhead, from the things that are made." From the things that are seen we inferred the existence of an eternal, powerful Being, that is not seen. But still, although we acknowledged His being, we had no acquaintance with Him. As we know there is an Emperor of China, whom yet we do not know; so we knew there was a King of all the earth, yet we knew Him not. Indeed we could not by any of our natural faculties. By none of these could we attain the knowledge of God. We could no more perceive Him by our natural understanding, than we could see Him with our eyes. For "no one knoweth the Father but the Son, and he to whom the Son willeth to reveal Him. And no one knoweth the Son but the Father, and he to whom the Father revealeth Him."

We read of an ancient King who, being desirous to know what was the natural language of men, in order to bring the matter to a certain issue, made the following experiment:—he ordered two infants, as soon as they were born, to be conveyed to a place prepared for them, where they were brought up without any instruction at all, and without even hearing a human voice. And what was the event? What, that when they were at length brought out of their confinement, they spake no language at all; they uttered only inarticulate sounds, like those of other animals.

Were two infants in like manner to be brought up from the womb without being instructed in any religion, there is little room to doubt but (unless the grace of God interposed) the event would be just the same. They would have no religion at all: they would have no more knowledge of God than the beasts of the field, than the wild ass's colt. Such is natural religion, abstracted from traditional, and from the influences of God's Spirit!

And having no knowledge, we can have no love of God: we cannot love Him we know not. Most men talk indeed of loving God, and perhaps imagine they do; at least, few will acknowledge they do not love Him: but the fact is too plain to be denied. No man loves God by nature, any more than he does a stone, or the earth he treads upon. What we love we delight in; but no man has naturally any delight in God. In our natural state we cannot conceive how any one should delight in Him. We take no pleasure in Him at all; He is utterly tasteless to us. To love God! it is far above, out of our sight. We cannot, naturally, attain unto it.

We have by nature, not only no love, but no fear of God. It is allowed, indeed, that most men have, sooner or later, a kind of senseless, irrational fear, properly called "superstition"; though the blundering Epicureans gave it the name of "religion." Yet even this is not natural, but acquired; chiefly by conversation or from example. By nature "God is not in all our thoughts": we leave Him to manage His own affairs, to sit quietly, as we imagine, in heaven, and leave us on earth to manage ours; so that we have no more of the fear of God before our eyes, than of the love of God in our hearts.

Thus are all men "Atheists in the world." But Atheism itself does not screen us from idolatry. In his natural state, every man born into the world is a rank idolater. Perhaps, indeed, we may not be such in the vulgar sense of the word. We do not, like the idolatrous Heathens, worship molten or graven images. We do not bow down to the stock of a tree, to the work of our own hands. We do not pray to the angels or saints in heaven, any more than to the saints that are upon the earth. But what then? We have set up our idols in our hearts; and to these we bow down, and worship them: we worship ourselves, when we pay that honour to ourselves which is due to God only. Therefore, all pride is idolatry; it is ascribing to ourselves what is due to God alone. And although pride was not made for man, yet where is the man that is born without it? But hereby we rob God of His unalienable right, and idolatrously usurp His glory.

But pride is not the only sort of idolatry which we are all by nature guilty of. Satan has stamped his own image in our heart in self-will also. "I will," said he before he was cast out of heaven, "I will sit upon the sides of the north": I will do my own will and pleasure, inde-

pendently of that of my Creator. The same does every man born into
the world say, and that in a thousand instances; nay, and avow it too,
without ever blushing upon the account, without either fear or shame.
Ask the man, "Why did you do this?" He answers, "Because I had a
mind to it." What is this but, "Because it was my will"; that is, in
effect, because the devil and I are agreed; because Satan and I govern
our actions by one and the same principle. The will of God, mean time,
is not in his thoughts, is not considered in the least degree; although it
be the supreme rule of every intelligent creature, whether in heaven or
earth, resulting from the essential, unalterable relation which all creatures bear to their Creator.

So far we bear the image of the devil, and tread in his steps. But at
the next step we leave Satan behind; we run into an idolatry whereof
he is not guilty: I mean, love of the world; which is now as natural to
every man, as to love his own will. What is more natural to us than
to seek happiness in the creature, instead of the Creator?—to seek that
satisfaction in the works of his hands, which can be found in God
only? What more natural than "the desire of the flesh"? that is, of the
pleasure of sense in every kind?

Men indeed talk magnificently of despising these low pleasures, particularly men of learning and education. They affect to sit loose to
the gratification of those appetites wherein they stand on a level with
the beasts that perish. But it is mere affectation! for every man is
conscious to himself, that in this respect he is, by nature, a very beast.
Sensual appetites, even those of the lowest kind, have, more or less, the
dominion over him. They lead him captive; they drag him to and fro,
in spite of his boasted reason. The man, with all his good breeding,
and other accomplishments, has no pre-eminence over the goat: nay, it
is much to be doubted, whether the beast has not the pre-eminence
over him.

A considerable difference indeed, it must be allowed, there is between
man and man, arising (beside that wrought by preventing grace) from
difference of constitution and of education. But, notwithstanding this,
who, that is not utterly ignorant of himself, can here cast the first stone
at another? Who can abide the test of our blessed Lord's comment on
the Seventh Commandment?—"He that looketh on a woman to lust
after her hath committed adultery with her already in his heart." So
that one knows not which to wonder at most, the ignorance or the insolence of those men who speak with such disdain of them that are
overcome by desires which every man has felt in his own breast; the
desire of every pleasure of sense, innocent or not, being natural to
every child of man.

And so is "the desire of the eye": the desire of the pleasures of the
imagination. These arise either from great, or beautiful, or uncommon

objects;—if the two former do not coincide with the latter; for perhaps it would appear, upon a diligent inquiry, that neither grand nor beautiful objects please any longer than they are new; that when the novelty of them is over, the greatest part, at least, of the pleasure they give is over; and in the same proportion as they become familiar, they become flat and insipid. But let us experience this ever so often, the same desire will remain still. The inbred thirst continues fixed in the soul; nay, the more it is indulged, the more it increases, and incites us to follow after another, and yet another object; although we leave every one with an abortive hope, and a deluded expectation."

A third symptom of this fatal disease,—the love of the world, which is so deeply rooted in our nature, is "the pride of life"; the desire of praise, of the honour that cometh of men. This the greatest admirers of human nature allow to be strictly natural; as natural as the sight, or hearing, or any other of the external senses. And are they ashamed of it, even men of letters, men of refined and improved understanding? So far from it, that they glory therein! They applaud themselves for their love of applause! Yea, eminent Christians, so called, make no difficulty of adopting the saying of the old, vain Heathen, "Not to regard what men think of us is the work of a wicked and abandoned mind." So that to go calm and unmoved through honour and dishonour, through evil report and good report, is with them a sign of one that is, indeed, not fit to live: "away with such a fellow from the earth!"

But would one imagine that these men had ever heard of Jesus Christ or His Apostles; or that they knew Who it was that said, "How can ye believe who receive honour one of another, and seek not the honour which cometh of God only?" But if this be really so, if it be impossible to believe, and consequently to please God, so long as we receive or seek honour one of another, and seek not the honour which cometh of God only; then in what a condition are all mankind! the Christians as well as Heathens! since they all seek honour one of another! since it is as natural for them so to do, themselves being the judges, as it is to see the light which strikes upon their eye, or to hear the sound which enters their ear; yea, since they account it a sign of a virtuous mind, to seek the praise of men, and of a vicious one, to be content with the honour that cometh of God only!

I proceed to draw a few inferences from what has been said. And, first, from hence we may learn one grand fundamental difference between Christianity, considered as a system of doctrines, and the most refined Heathenism. Many of the ancient Heathens have largely described the vices of particular men. They have spoken much against their covetousness, or cruelty; their luxury, or prodigality. Some have dared to say that "no man is born without vices of one kind or another."

But still as none of them were apprized of the fall of man, so none of them knew of his total corruption. They knew not that all men were empty of all good, and filled with all manner of evil. They were wholly ignorant of the entire depravation of the whole human nature, of every man born into the world, in every faculty of his soul, not so much by those particular vices which reign in particular persons, as by the general flood of Atheism and idolatry, of pride, self-will, and love of the world.

This, therefore, is the first grand distinguishing point between Heathenism and Christianity. The one acknowledges that many men are infected with many vices, and even born with a proneness to them; but supposes withal, that in some the natural good much over-balances the evil: the other declares that all men are "conceived in sin," and "shapen in wickedness";—that hence there is in every man a "carnal mind, which is enmity against God; which is not, cannot be, subject to" His "law"; and which so infects the whole soul, that "there dwelleth in" him, "in his flesh," in his natural state, "no good thing"; but "every imagination of the thoughts of his heart is evil," only evil, and that "continually."

Hence we may, secondly, learn, that all who deny this, call it "original sin," or by any other title, are but Heathens still, in the fundamental point which differences Heathenism from Christianity. They may, indeed, allow, that men have many vices; that some are born with us; and that, consequently, we are not born altogether so wise or so virtuous as we should be; there being few that will roundly affirm, "We are born with as much propensity to good as to evil," and that "Every man is, by nature, as virtuous and wise as Adam was at his creation." But here is the shibboleth: Is man by nature filled with all manner of evil? Is he void of all good? Is he wholly fallen? Is his soul totally corrupted? Or, to come back to the text, is "every imagination of the thoughts of his heart only evil continually?" Allow this, and you are so far a Christian. Deny it, and you are but an Heathen still.

We may learn from hence, in the third place, what is the proper nature of religion, of the religion of Jesus Christ. It is God's method of healing a soul which is thus diseased. Hereby the great Physician of souls applies medicines to heal this sickness; to restore human nature, totally corrupted in all its faculties. God heals all our Atheism by the knowledge of Himself, and of Jesus Christ whom he hath sent; by giving us faith, a divine evidence and conviction of God, and of the things of God,—in particular, of this important truth, "Christ loved me, and gave Himself for me." By repentance and lowliness of heart, the deadly disease of pride is healed; that of self-will by resignation, a meek and thankful submission to the will of God; and for the love of the world in all its branches, the love of God is the sovereign remedy. Now, this is properly religion, "faith" thus "working by love": working the genuine meek humility, entire deadness to the world, with a loving, thankful acquiescence in, and conformity to, the whole will and word of God.

Indeed, if man were not thus fallen, there would be no need of all this. There would be no occasion for this work in the heart, this renewal in the spirit of our mind. The superfluity of godliness would then be a more proper expression than the "superfluity of naughtiness." For an outside religion, without any godliness at all, would suffice to all rational intents and purposes. It does, accordingly, suffice, in the judgment of those who deny this corruption of our nature. They make very little more of religion than the famous Mr. Hobbes did of reason. According to him, reason is only "a well-ordered train of words": according to them, religion is only a well-ordered train of words and actions. And they speak consistently with themselves; for if the inside be not full of wickedness, if this be clean already, what remains, but "cleanse the outside of the cup"? Outward reformation, if their supposition be just, is indeed the one thing needful.

But ye have not so learned the oracles of God. Ye know, that He who seeth what is in man gives a far different account both of nature and grace, of our fall and our recovery. Ye know that the great end of religion is, to renew our hearts in the image of God, to repair that total loss of righteousness and true holiness which we sustained by the sin of our first parent. Ye know that all religion which does not answer this end, all that stops short of this, the renewal of our soul in the image of God, after the likeness of Him that created it, is no other than a poor farce, and a mere mockery of God, to the destruction of our own soul.

O beware of all those teachers of lies, who would palm this upon you for Christianity! Regard them not, although they should come unto you with all the deceivableness of unrighteousness; with all smoothness of language, all decency, yea, beauty and elegance of expression, all professions of earnest good-will to you, and reverence for the Holy Scriptures. Keep to the plain, old faith, "once delivered to the saints," and delivered by the Spirit of God to our hearts. Know your disease! Know your cure! Ye were born in sin: therefore, "ye must be born again," born of God. By nature ye are wholly corrupted: by grace ye shall be wholly renewed. In Adam ye all died: in the second Adam, in Christ, ye all are made alive. "You that were dead in sins hath He quickened": He hath already given you a principle of life, even faith in Him Who loved you and gave Himself for you! Now, "go on from faith to faith," until your whole sickness be healed, and all that "mind be in you which was also in Christ Jesus!"

The Repentance of Believers

Repent ye, and believe the Gospel. —MARK 1:15

IT IS generally supposed, that repentance and faith are only the gate of religion; that they are necessary only at the beginning of our Christian course, when we are setting out in the way to the kingdom. And this may seem to be confirmed by the great apostle, where, exhorting the Hebrew Christians to "go on to perfection," he teaches them to *leave* these "first principles of the doctrine of Christ"; "not laying again the foundation of repentance from dead works, and of faith towards God"; which must at least mean, that they should comparatively leave these, that at first took up all their thoughts, in order to "press forward towards the prize of the high calling of God in Christ Jesus."

And this is undoubtedly true, that there is a repentance and a faith, which are, more especially, necessary at the beginning: a repentance, which is a conviction of our utter sinfulness, and guiltiness, and helplessness; and which precedes our receiving that kingdom of God, which our Lord observes, is "within us"; and a faith, whereby we receive that kingdom, even "righteousness, and peace, and joy in the Holy Ghost."

But, notwithstanding this, there is also a repentance and a faith, (taking the words in another sense, a sense not quite the same, nor yet entirely different), which are requisite after we have "believed the gospel"; yea, and in every subsequent stage of our Christian course, or we cannot "run the race which is set before us." And this repentance and faith are full as necessary, in order to our *continuance* and *growth* in grace, as the former faith, and repentance were, in order to our *entering* into the kingdom of God.

But in what sense are we to repent and believe, after we are justified? This is an important question, and worthy of being considered with the utmost attention.

And first, in what sense are we to repent?

Repentance, frequently means an inward change, a change of mind from sin to holiness. But we now speak of it in quite a different sense, as it is one kind of self-knowledge, the knowing ourselves sinners, yea, guilty, helpless sinners, even though we know we are children of God.

Indeed when we first know this; when we first find redemption in the blood of Jesus; when the love of God is first shed abroad in our hearts, and his kingdom set up therein; it is natural to suppose that we are no longer sinners, that all our sins are not only covered but destroyed. As we do not then feel any evil in our hearts, we readily imagine none is there. Nay, some well-meaning men have imagined this not only at that time, but ever after; having persuaded themselves, that when they were justified, they were entirely sanctified: yea, they have laid it down as a general rule, in spite of Scripture, reason, and experience. These sincerely believe, and earnestly maintain, that all sin is destroyed when we are justified; and that there is no sin in the heart of a believer; but that it is altogether clean from that moment. But though we readily acknowledge, "he that believeth is born of God," and "he that is born of God doth not commit sin": yet we cannot allow that he does not *feel* it within: it does not *reign,* but it does remain. And a conviction of the sin which *remains* in our heart, is one great branch of the repentance we are now speaking of.

For it is seldom long before he who imagined all sin was gone, feels there is still *pride* in his heart. He is convinced both that in many respects he has thought of himself more highly than he ought to think, and that he has taken to himself the praise of something he had received, and gloried in it as though he had not received it; and yet he knows he is in the favour of God. He cannot, and ought not, "to cast away his confidence." "The Spirit" still "witnesses with" his "spirit, that he is a child of God."

Nor is it long before he feels *self will* in his heart; even a will contrary to the will of God. A will every man must inevitably have as long as he has an understanding. This is an essential part of human nature, indeed of the nature of every intelligent being. Our blessed Lord Himself had a will as a man; otherwise He had not been a man. But His human will was invariably subject to the will of His Father. At all times, and on all occasions, even in the deepest affliction, He could say, "Not as I will, but as thou wilt." But this is not the case at all times, even with a true believer in Christ. He frequently finds his will more or less exalting itself against the will of God. He wills something, because it is pleasing to nature, which is not pleasing to God; and he wills (is averse from) something, because it is painful to nature, which is the will of God concerning him. Indeed, suppose he continues in the faith, he fights against it with all his might: but this very thing implies that it really exists, and that he is conscious of it.

Now self will, as well as pride, is a species of *idolatry;* and both are directly contrary to the love of God. The same observation may be made concerning the *"love of the world."* But this likewise even true believers are liable to feel in themselves; and every one of them does feel it, more or less, sooner or later, in one branch or another. It is true, when he first "passes from death unto life," he desires nothing more but God. He can truly say, "All my desire is unto thee, and unto the remembrance of thy name": "Whom have I in heaven but thee, and there is none upon earth that I desire beside thee!" But it is not so always. In process of time he will feel again, though perhaps only for a few moments, either "the desire of the flesh," or "the desire of the eye," or "the pride of life." Nay, if he does not continually watch and pray, he may find *lust* reviving; yea, and thrusting sore at him that he may fall, till he has scarce any strength left in him. He may feel the assaults of *inordinate affection;* yea, a strong propensity to "love the creature more than the Creator"; whether it be a child, a parent, a husband or wife, or "the friend that is as his own soul." He may feel, in a thousand various ways, a desire of earthly things or pleasures. In the same proportion he will forget God, not seeking his happiness in Him, and consequently being a "lover of pleasure more than a lover of God."

If he does not keep himself every moment, he will again feel *the desire of the eye;* the desire of gratifying his imagination with something great, or beautiful, or uncommon. In how many ways does this desire assault the soul? Perhaps with regard to the poorest trifles, such as dress, or furniture; things never designed to satisfy the appetite of an immortal spirit. Yet, how natural it is for us, even after we have "tasted of the powers of the world to come," to sink again into these foolish, low desires of things that perish in the using! How hard is it, even for those who know in whom they have believed, to conquer but one branch of the desire of the eye, curiosity; constantly to trample it under their feet; to desire nothing, merely because it is new!

And how hard it is even for the children of God wholly to conquer the *pride of life!* St. John seems to mean by this nearly the same with what the world terms the sense of honour. This is no other than a desire of, and delight in, "the honour that cometh of men"; a desire and love of praise; and, which is always joined with it, a proportionable *fear of dispraise.* Nearly allied to this is *evil shame;* the being ashamed of that wherein we ought to glory. And this is seldom divided from the *fear of man,* which brings a thousand snares upon the soul. Now where is he, even among those that seem strong in faith, who does not find in himself a degree of all these evil tempers? So that even these are but in part "crucified to the world"; for the evil root still remains in their heart.

And do we not feel other tempers, which are as contrary to the love of our neighbour as these are to the love of God? The love of our neighbour "thinketh no evil." Do not we find anything of the kind? Do we never find any *jealousies,* any *evil surmisings,* any groundless or unreasonable suspicions? He that is clear in these respects, let him cast the first stone at his neighbour. Who does not sometimes feel other tempers or inward motions, which he knows are contrary to brotherly love? If nothing of *malice, hatred,* or *bitterness,* is there no touch of *envy?* Particularly towards those who enjoy some real or supposed good which we desire but cannot attain? Do we never find any degree of *resentment,* when we are injured or affronted; especially by those whom we peculiarly loved, and whom we had most laboured to help or oblige? And does injustice or ingratitude never excite in us any desire of *revenge?* Any desire of returning evil for evil, instead of "overcoming evil with good"? This also shows how much is still in our heart which is contrary to the love of our neighbour.

Covetousness, in every kind and degree, is certainly as contrary to this as to the love of God; whether *the love of money,* which is too frequently "the root of all evil"; or a desire of *having more,* or increasing in substance. And how few, even of the real children of God, are entirely free from both! Indeed, one great man, Martin Luther, used to say, He "never had any covetousness in him (not only in his converted state, but) ever since he was born." But, if so, I would not scruple to say, he was the only man born of a woman (except him that was God as well as man?) who had not, who was born without it. Nay, I believe, never was any one born of God, that lived any considerable time after, who did not feel more or less of it many times, especially in the latter sense. We may therefore set it down as an undoubted truth, that covetousness, together with pride, and self will, and anger, remain in the hearts even of them that are justified.

It is their experiencing this, which has inclined so many serious persons to understand the latter part of the seventh chapter to the Romans, not of them that are "under the law," that are convinced of sin, which is undoubtedly the meaning of the apostle, but of them that are "under grace"; that are "justified freely through the redemption that is in Christ." And it is most certain, they are thus far right:—there does still *remain,* even in them that are justified, a *mind* which is in some measure *carnal* (so the apostle tells even the believers at Corinth, "Ye are carnal"); *a heart bent to backsliding,* still ever ready to "depart from the living God"; a propensity to pride, self will, anger, revenge, love of the world, yea, and all evil; a root of bitterness, which, if the restraint were taken off for a moment, would instantly spring up; yea, such a depth of corruption, as, without clear light from God, we cannot possibly conceive. And a conviction of all this sin *remaining* in *their hearts,* is the repentance which belongs to them that are justified.

But we should likewise be convinced, that as sin remains in our hearts, so it *cleaves* to all our words and actions. Indeed it is to be feared, that many of our words are more than mixed with sin; that they are sinful altogether; for such undoubtedly is all *uncharitable conversation;* all which does not spring from brotherly love; all which does not agree with that golden rule, "What ye would that others should

do to you, even so do unto them." Of this kind is all backbiting, all
tale-bearing, all whispering, all evil-speaking, that is, repeating the faults
of absent persons; for none would have others repeat his faults when
he is absent. Now how few are there, even among believers, who are
in no degree guilty of this; who steadily observe the good old rule, "Of
the dead and the absent—nothing but good!" And suppose they do,
do they likewise abstain from *unprofitable conversation?* Yet all this
is unquestionably sinful, and "grieves the Holy Spirit of God": yea,
and "for every idle word that men shall speak, they shall give an account
in the day of judgment."

But let it be supposed that they continually "watch and pray," and
so do "not enter into this temptation"; that they constantly set a watch
before their mouth, and keep the door of their lips; suppose they exercise themselves herein, that *all* their "conversation may be in grace,
seasoned with salt, and meet to minister grace to the hearers"; yet do
they not daily slide into useless discourse, notwithstanding all their
caution? And even when they endeavour to speak for God, are their
words pure, free from unholy mixtures? Do they find nothing wrong
in their very *intention?* Do they speak merely to please God, and not
partly to please themselves? Is it wholly to do the will of God, and not
their own will also? Or, if they begin with a single eye, do they go on
"looking unto Jesus," and talking with Him all the time they are talking with their neighbour? When they are reproving sin, do they feel
no anger or unkind temper to the sinner? When they are instructing the
ignorant, do they not find any pride, any self-preference? When they
are comforting the afflicted, or provoking one another to love and to
good works, do they never perceive any inward self-commendation;
"Now you have spoke well?" Or any vanity, a desire that others should
think so, and esteem them on the account? In some or all of these respects, how much sin cleaves to the best *conversation* even of believers? The conviction of which is another branch of the repentance,
which belongs to them that are justified.

And how much sin, if their conscience is thoroughly awake, may
they find cleaving to *their actions also?* Nay, are there not many of
these, which, though they are such as the world would not condemn,
yet cannot be commended, no, nor excused, if we judge by the word
of God? Are there not many of their actions, which, they themselves
know, are not to the glory of God? Many, wherein they did not even
aim at this; which were not undertaken with an eye to God? And of
those that were, are there not many, wherein their eye is not singly
fixed on God? Wherein they are doing their own will, at least as much
as His; and seeking to please themselves as much, if not more, than to
please God?—And while they are endeavouring to do good to their
neighbour, do they not feel wrong tempers of various kinds?

Hence their good actions, so called, are far from being strictly such; being polluted with such a mixture of evil? Such are their works of *mercy*. And is not the same mixture in their works of *piety*? While they are hearing the word, which is able to save their souls, do they not frequently find such thoughts as make them afraid lest it should turn to their condemnation, rather than their salvation? Is it not often the same case, while they are endeavouring to offer up their prayers to God, whether in public or private? Nay, while they are engaged in the most solemn service, even while they are at the table of the Lord, what manner of thoughts arise in them? Are not their hearts sometimes wandering to the ends of the earth?—sometimes filled with such imaginations, as make them fear lest all their sacrifice should be an abomination to the Lord? So that they are now more ashamed of their best duties, than they were once of their worst sins.

Again: How many *sins of omission* are they chargeable with? We know the words of the apostle, "To him that knoweth to do good, and doeth it not, to him it is sin." But do they not know a thousand instances wherein they might have done good, to enemies, to strangers, to their brethren, either with regard to their bodies or their souls, and they did it not? How many omissions have they been guilty of, in their duty towards God? How many opportunities of communicating, of hearing His word, of public or private prayer, have they neglected! So great reason had even that holy man, Archbishop Ussher, after all his labours for God to cry out almost with his dying breath, "Lord, forgive me my sins of omission!"

But, besides these outward omissions, may they not find in themselves *inward defects* without number? Defects of every kind: they have not the love, the fear, the confidence, they ought to have, towards God. They have not the love which is due to their neighbour, to every child of man; no, nor even that which is due to their brethren, to every child of God, whether those that are at a distance from them, or those with whom they are immediately connected. They have no holy temper in the degree they ought; they are defective in everything;—in a deep consciousness of which they are ready to cry out with M. DeRenty, "I am a ground all overrun with thorns"; or with Job, "I am vile: I abhor myself, and repent as in dust and ashes."

A conviction of their *guiltiness* is another branch of that repentance which belongs to the children of God. But this is cautiously to be understood, and in a peculiar sense. For it is certain, "there is no condemnation to them that are in Christ Jesus," that believe in Him, and, in the power of that faith, "walk not after the flesh, but after the Spirit." Yet can they no more bear the *strict justice* of God, now than before they believed. This pronounces them to be still *worthy of death*, on all the preceding accounts. And it would absolutely condemn them thereto, were it not for the atoning blood. Therefore they are thoroughly convinced, that they still *deserve* punishment, although it is hereby turned aside from them. But here there are extremes on one hand and on the other, and few steer clear of them. Most men strike on one or the other, either thinking themselves condemned when they are not, or thinking they *deserve* to be acquitted. Nay, the truth lies between: they still *deserve*, strictly speaking, only the damnation of hell. But what they deserve does not come upon them, because they "have an advocate with the Father." His life, and death, and intercession, still interpose between them and condemnation.

A conviction of their *utter helplessness*, is yet another branch of this repentance. I mean hereby two things: First, that they are no more able now *of themselves* to think one good thought, to form one good desire, to speak one good word, or do one good work, than before they were justified; that they have still no kind or degree of strength *of their own;* no power either to do good, or resist evil; no ability to conquer or even withstand the world, the devil, or their own evil nature. They can, it is certain, do all these things; but it is not by their own strength. They have power to overcome all these enemies; for "sin hath no more dominion over them": but it is not from nature, either in whole or in part; it is the *mere* gift of God: nor is it given all at once, as if they had a stock laid up for many years; but from moment to moment.

By this helplessness I mean, secondly, an absolute inability to deliver ourselves from that guiltiness or desert of punishment whereof we are still conscious; yea, and an inability to remove, by all the grace we have (to say nothing of our natural powers), either the pride, self-will, love of the world, anger, and general proneness to depart from God, which we experimentally know to *remain* in the heart, even of them that are regenerate; or the evil which, in spite of all our endeavours, cleaves to all our words and actions. Add to this, an utter inability wholly to avoid uncharitable, and much more unprofitable, conversation; and an inability to avoid sins of omission, or to supply the numberless defects we are convinced of; especially the want of love, and other right tempers, both to God and man.

If any man is not satisfied of this, if any believes that whoever is justified is able to remove these sins out of his heart and life, let him make the experiment. Let him try whether, by the grace he has already received, he can expel pride, self-will, or inbred sin in general. Let him try whether he can cleanse his words and actions from all mixture of evil; whether he can avoid all uncharitable and unprofitable conversation, with all the sins of omission; and, lastly, whether he can supply the numberless defects which he still finds in himself. Let him not be discouraged by one or two experiments, but repeat the trial again and again; and the longer he tries, the more deeply will he be convinced of his utter helplessness in all these respects.

Indeed this is so evident a truth, that well nigh all the children of God, scattered abroad, however they differ in other points, yet generally agree in this; that although we may, "by the Spirit, mortify the deeds of the body"; resist and conquer both outward and inward sin; although we may *weaken* our enemies day by day;—yet we cannot *drive them out*. By all the grace which is given at justification, we cannot extirpate them. Though we watch and pray ever so much, we cannot wholly cleanse either our hearts or hands. Most sure we cannot till it shall please our Lord to speak to our hearts again, to speak the second time, Be clean: and then only the leprosy is cleansed. Then only, the evil root, the carnal mind, is destroyed; and inbred sin subsists no more. But if there be no such second change, if there be no instantaneous deliverance after justification, if there be *none but* a gradual work of God (that there is a gradual work none denies), then we must be content, as well as we can, to remain full of sin till death; and, if so, we must remain guilty till death, continually *deserving* punishment. For it is impossible the guilt, or desert of punishment, should be removed from us, as long as all this sin remains in our heart, and cleaves to our words and actions. Nay, in rigorous justice, all we think, and speak, and act, continually increases it.

In this sense we are to *repent*, after we are justified. And till we do so, we can go no farther. For, till we are sensible of our disease it admits of no cure. But, supposing we do thus repent, then are we called to "believe the gospel."

And this also is to be understood in a peculiar sense, different from that wherein we believed in order to justification. Believe the glad tidings of great salvation, which God hath prepared for all people. Believe that He who is "the brightness of His Father's glory, the express image of His person," is "able to save unto the uttermost all that come unto God through Him." He is able to save you from all the sin that still remains in your heart. He is able to save you from all the sin that still cleaves to all your words and actions. He is able to save you from sins of omission and to supply whatever is wanting in you.

It is true, this is impossible with man; but with God all things are possible. For what can be too hard for Him, who hath "all power in heaven and in earth"? Indeed his bare power to do this is not a sufficient foundation for our faith that He will do it, that He will thus exert His power, unless He hath promised it. But this He has done; He has promised it over and over, in the strongest terms. He has given us these "exceeding great and precious promises," both in the Old and the New Testament.

You have therefore good reason to believe, He is not only able but *willing* to do this; to cleanse you from all your filthiness of flesh and spirit; to "save you from all your uncleannesses." This is the thing which you now long for; this is the faith which you now particularly need, namely, that the Great Physician, the Lover of my soul, is willing to make me clean. But is He willing to do this tomorrow or today? Let Him answer for Himself. "Today, if ye will hear" my "voice, harden not your hearts." If you put it off till tomorrow, you harden your hearts; you refuse to hear His voice. Believe therefore that He is willing to save you *today*. He is willing to save you *now*. "Behold, now is the accepted time." He now saith, "Be thou clean!" Only believe; and you also will immediately find, "All things are possible to him that believeth."

Continue to believe in Him that loved thee, and gave Himself for thee; that bore all thy sins in His own body on the tree; and He saveth thee from all condemnation, by His blood continually applied. Thus it is that we continue in a justified state. And when we go on "from faith to faith," when we have faith to be cleansed from indwelling sin, to be saved from all our uncleannesses, we are likewise saved from all that *guilt*, that *desert* of punishment, which we felt before. So that then we must say, not only,

> Every moment, Lord, I *want*
> The merit of thy death;

but, likewise, in the full assurance of faith,

> Every moment, Lord, I *have*
> The merit of thy death!

For, by that faith in His life, death, and intercession for us, renewed from moment to moment, we are every whit clean, and there is not only now no condemnation for us, but no such desert of punishment as was before, the Lord cleansing both our hearts and lives.

By the same faith we feel the power of Christ every moment resting upon us, whereby alone we are what we are; whereby we are enabled to continue in spiritual life, and without which, notwithstanding all our present holiness, we should be devils the next moment. But as long as we retain our faith in Him, we "draw water out of the wells of salvation." Leaning on our beloved, even Christ in us the hope of glory, who dwelleth in our hearts by faith, who likewise is ever interceding for us at the right hand of God, we receive help from Him to think, and speak, and act what is acceptable in His sight. Thus does He "prevent" them that believe, in all their "doings, and further them with his continual help," so that all their designs, conversations, and actions are "begun, continued, and ended in Him." Thus doth He "cleanse the thoughts of their hearts, by the inspiration of His Holy Spirit, that they may perfectly love Him, and worthily magnify His holy name."

Thus it is, that in the children of God, repentance and faith exactly answer each other. By repentance, we feel the sin remaining in our hearts, and cleaving to our words and actions: by faith we receive the power of God in Christ, purifying our hearts, and cleansing our hands. By repentance we are still sensible that we deserve punishment for all our tempers, and words, and actions: by faith we are conscious that our Advocate with the Father is continually pleading for us, and thereby continually turning aside all condemnation and punishment from us.

By repentance we have an abiding conviction, that there is no help in us: by faith we receive not only mercy, "but grace to help in" *every* "time of need." Repentance disclaims the very possibility of any other help: faith accepts all the help we stand in need of, from Him that hath all power in heaven and earth. Repentance says, "Without Him I can do nothing": Faith says, "I can do all things through Christ strengthening me." Through Him I can not only overcome, but expel, all the enemies of my soul. Through Him I can "love the Lord my God with all my heart, mind, soul, and strength"; yea, and "walk in holiness and righteousness before Him all the days of my life."

From what has been said, we may easily learn the mischievousness of that opinion, that we are *wholly* sanctified when we are justified; that our hearts are then cleansed from all sin. It is true, we are then delivered, as was observed before, from the dominion of outward sin; and, at the same time, the power of inward sin is so broken, that we need no longer follow, or be led by it: but it is by no means true, that inward sin is then totally destroyed; that the root of pride, self will, anger, love of the world, is then taken out of the heart; or that the carnal mind, and heart bent to backsliding, are entirely extirpated. And to suppose the contrary, is not, as some may think, an innocent, harmless mistake. No, it does immense harm: it entirely blocks up the way to any farther change—for it is manifest, "They that are whole do not need a physician, but they that are sick." If, therefore, we think we are quite made whole already, there is no room to seek any farther healing. On this supposition it is absurd to expect a farther deliverance from sin, whether gradual or instantaneous.

On the contrary, a deep conviction that we are not yet whole; that our hearts are not fully purified; that there is yet in us a "carnal mind," which is still in its nature "enmity against God"; that a whole body of sin remains in our heart, weakened indeed, but not destroyed; shows, beyond all possibility of doubt, the absolute necessity of a farther change. We allow, that at the very moment of justification, we are *born again:* in that instant we experience that inward change, from "darkness into marvellous light"; from the image of the brute and the devil, into the image of God; from the earthly, sensual, devilish mind, to the mind which was in Christ Jesus. But are we then *entirely* changed? Are we *wholly* transformed into the image of Him that created us? Far from it: we still retain a depth of sin: and it is the consciousness of this, which constrains us to groan for a full deliverance, to Him that is mighty to save.

Hence it is, that those believers who are not convinced of the deep corruption of their hearts, or but slightly, and as it were notionally convinced, have little concern about *entire sanctification.* They may possibly hold the opinion, that such a thing is to be, either at death, or some time, they know not when, before it. But they have no great uneasiness for the want of it, and no great hunger or thirst after it. They cannot, until they know themselves better, until they repent in the sense above described, until God unveils the inbred monster's face, and shows them the real state of their souls. Then only, when they feel the burden, will they groan for deliverance from it. Then, and not till then, will they cry out, in the agony of their soul,

> Break off the yoke of inbred sin,
> And fully set my spirit free!
> I cannot rest, till pure within;
> Till I am wholly lost in thee.

We may learn from hence, secondly, that a deep conviction of our *demerit,* after we are accepted (which, in one sense, may be termed *guilt*) is absolutely necessary, in order to our seeing the true value of the atoning blood; in order to our feeling that we need this as much, after we are justified, as ever we did before. Without this conviction we cannot but account the blood of the covenant *as a common thing,* something of which we have not now any great need, seeing all our past sins are blotted out. Yea, but if both our hearts and lives are thus unclean, there is a kind of guilt which we are contracting every moment, and which, of consequence, would every moment expose us to fresh condemnation, but that—

> He ever lives above,
> For us to intercede,
> His all-atoning love,
> His precious blood to plead.

It is this repentance, and the faith intimately connected with it, which are expressed in those strong lines—

> I sin in every breath I draw,
> Nor do thy will, nor keep thy law,
> On earth, as angels do above:
> But still the fountain open stands,
> Washes my feet, my heart, my hands,
> Till I am perfected in love.

We may observe, thirdly, a deep conviction of our utter *helpless-ness*, of our total inability to retain anything we have received, much more to deliver ourselves from the world of iniquity remaining both in our hearts and lives, teaches us truly to live upon Christ by faith, not only as our Priest, but as our King. Hereby we are brought to "magnify Him," indeed; to "give Him all the glory of His grace"; to make Him a whole Christ, an entire Saviour; and truly "to set the crown upon His head." These excellent words, as they have frequently been used, have little or no meaning; but they are fulfilled in a strong and deep sense, when we thus, as it were, go out of ourselves, in order to be swallowed up in Him; when we sink into nothing, that He may be all in all. Then His almighty grace having abolished "every high thing which exalted itself against Him," every temper, and thought, and word, and work, "is brought to the obedience of Christ."

Londonderry, April 24, 1767.

GEORGE WHITEFIELD 1714–1770

Two hundred miners standing in the field near the colliery at Bedworth, Warwickshire, listened with astonishment while a young Oxford graduate explained how they might have their sins forgiven. In the town of Bedworth colliers were rated heathen, animals, brutes who had no use in life other than to wrest coal from the earth. To be treated with respect and interest was a new experience. The unlicensed preacher could see "white gutters made by their tears, which plentifully fell down their black cheeks."

It was a new experience for George Whitefield as well. In truth, his act was a novelty in England. Hitherto the churches, sedate and respectable, had served as the only sounding boards for the Gospel. Now the vast cathedral of nature was about to be utilized.

Three days later a bishop in the Church of England said to Whitefield, "If you preach or expound anywhere in this diocese till you have a license, I will first suspend and then excommunicate you."

Whitefield disregarded the warning. In very little time the rebel was drawing open-air congregations of thousands. Opposition to his methods mounted. Both Church and State tried to block him. A campaign of vilification only increased his popularity with the public. As with his divine Lord, who also preached by lakes and streams, so it was with George Whitefield: "The common people heard him gladly."

His father, a tavernkeeper, died when George was two, and his mother supported her family by operating the tavern. It provided an unsavory background for children. George learned to sell liquor over the counter and pocket the money. He also learned just about every other vice in the spectrum of evil: "It would be endless to recount the sins and offenses of my younger days."

At eighteen he entered Oxford, where he came in contact with the ideas that were to form Methodism, the Wesley brothers, and the "Holy Club." Oddly, he came to an understanding of the saving truths of the Gospel before John and Charles Wesley.

"With what joy, joy unspeakable, even joy that was full of, and big with, glory, was my soul filled when the weight of sin fell off!"

It is paradoxical that he had made up his mind to preach even before his conversion. Under the dominion of the Spirit of God his natural gifts came into their full flow. He possessed unusual dramatic powers. At one service, addressing a group of sailors, he described a ship about to founder at sea. In the midst of the description, he paused and said,

"*What next?*" *A sailor sprang to his feet and shouted, "Take the long-boat!" The actor David Garrick said that Whitefield could make an audience weep simply by enunciating the word Mesopotamia. His clear resonant voice could be heard with no difficulty whatever by as many as a hundred thousand people.*

As Whitefield's fame spread, he was given more and more of a hearing by men and women from all strata of social life. Seven times he crossed the Atlantic. He evangelized from Georgia to New England, where he led in the Great Awakening. In thirty years he delivered an aggregate of 18,000 sermons, Stuart Henry estimates. He preached in and out of pulpits; on barrels, on city walls, on ships, on horseback; in parks, in halls and in theaters; at race courses, and once on a gallows. It is impossible to compute the numbers who professed faith under his preaching.

Inevitably, he became a controversial figure. A confirmed Calvinist, he found himself in articulate disagreement with his good friend John Wesley. Their correspondence on predestination has its amusing features.

"Dear George," wrote Wesley, "I have read what you have written on the subject of predestination, and God has taught me to see that you are wrong and that I am right."

"Dear John," Whitefield replied, "I have read what you have written on the subject of predestination, and God has taught me that I am right and you are wrong."

He branded certain leaders of the Church of England as blind, unregenerate, carnal, lukewarm and unskillful guides. A prominent archbishop, he said, knew no more about Christianity than Mohammed. The clergy counterattacked by questioning his sanity. In New England, he labeled the universities "centers of darkness." Since these were church-endowed institutions, his criticism called down the indignation of ministers and educators alike. Jonathan Edwards, who admired him tremendously, nevertheless deplored his censorious attitude toward his brethren.

He also stirred up all manner of discussion among intellectuals. Horace Walpole condemned him as an arch rogue, Alexander Pope as a braying ass. Samuel Foote descended to the lowest form of assault, calling him Dr. Squintum, because of his crossed eyes. On the other hand, Benjamin Franklin applauded his work, and publicly defended him against the charge of commercialism. Cowper wrote of him:

> *Paul's love of Christ, and*
> *steadiness unbribed,*
> *Were copied close in him, and*
> *well transcribed . . .*

The day before his marvelous voice was stilled forever he was on his way to Boston. Throngs of New Englanders crowded the highway and begged him to preach. Although seriously ill, he interrupted his journey, climbed up on a hogshead and spoke for two hours. "His voice," says Abel Stevens, "flowed on until the candle which he held in his hand burned away and went out in its socket."

From the Autobiography of George Whitefield

I CAN truly say, I was froward from my mother's womb. I was so brutish as to hate instruction, and used purposely to shun all opportunities of receiving it. I soon gave pregnant proofs of an impudent temper. Lying, filthy talking and foolish jesting, I was much addicted to, even when very young. Sometimes I used to curse, if not swear. Stealing from my mother I thought no theft at all, and used to make no scruple of taking money out of her pocket before she was up. I have frequently betrayed my trust, and have more than once spent money I took in the house in buying fruits, tarts, etc., to satisfy my sensual appetite. Numbers of Sabbaths have I broken, and generally used to behave myself very irreverently in God's sanctuary. Much money have I spent in plays, and in common entertainments of the age. Cards and reading romances were my heart's delight. Often have I joined with others in playing roguish tricks, but was generally, if not always, happily detected. For this I have often since, and do now, bless and praise God.

I had some early convictions of sin, and once I remember when some persons (as they frequently did) made it their business to tease me, I immediately retired to my room, and, kneeling down, with many tears prayed over that Psalm wherein David so often repeats these words: "But in the name of the Lord will I destroy them." I was always fond of being a clergyman, used frequently to imitate the minister's reading prayers, etc. Part of the money I used to steal from my parent I gave to the poor, and some books I privately took from others (for which I have since restored fourfold) I remember were books of devotion.

One morning, as I was reading a play to my sister, said I, "Sister, God intends something for me which we know not of. As I have been diligent in business, I believe many would gladly have me for an apprentice; but every way seems to be barred up, so that I think

God will provide for me some way or other that we cannot apprehend."

How I came to say these words I knew not. God afterwards showed me that they came from Him. Having thus lived with my mother for some considerable time, a young student, who was once my school-fellow, and then a servitor of Pembroke College, Oxford, came to pay my mother a visit. Amongst other conversation, he told her how he had discharged all college expenses that quarter, and received a penny. Upon that my mother immediately cried out, "This will do for my son." Then, turning to me, she said, "Will you go to Oxford, George?" I replied, "With all my heart." Whereupon, having the same friends that this young student had, my mother, without delay, waited on them. They promised their interest to get me a servitor's place in the same college. She then applied to my old master, who much approved of my coming to school again.

Being now near the seventeenth year of my age, I was resolved to prepare myself for the holy sacrament, which I received on Christmas-day. I began now to be more and more watchful over my thoughts, words and actions. I kept following Lent, fasting Wednesday and Friday, thirty-six hours together. My evenings, when I had done waiting upon my mother, were generally spent in acts of devotion, reading Drelincourt upon Death and other practical books; and I constantly went to public worship twice a day. Being now upper boy, by God's help I made some reformation amongst my school-fellows. I was very diligent in reading and learning the classics, and in studying my Greek Testament, but was not yet convinced of the absolute unlawfulness of playing at cards, and of reading and seeing plays, though I had some scruples about it.

I had not been long at the university before I found the benefit of the foundation I had laid in the country for a holy life. I was quickly solicited to join in their excess of riot with several who lay in the same room. God, in answer to prayers before put up, gave me grace to withstand them: and once, in particular, it being cold, my limbs were so benumbed by sitting alone in my study, because I would not go out amongst them, that I could scarcely sleep all night. But I soon found the benefit of not yielding; for, when they perceived they could not prevail, they let me alone as a singular odd fellow.

All this while I was not fully satisfied of the sin of playing at cards and reading plays, till God, upon a fast-day, was pleased to convince me: for, taking a play to read a passage out of it to a friend, God struck my heart with such power, that I was obliged to lay it down again; and, blessed be His name, I have never read any such book again.

God enabled me to do much good to many, as well as to receive much from the despised Methodists, and made me instrumental in converting one who is lately come out into the church, and I trust will prove a burning and shining light.

Several short fits of illness was God pleased to visit and to try me with, after my first acquaintance with Mr. Wesley. My new convert was a help-meet for me in those and in all other circumstances; and, in company with him and several other Christian friends, did I spend many sweet and delightful hours. Never did persons, I believe, strive more earnestly to enter in at the strait gate. They kept their bodies under even to an extreme. They were dead to the world, and willing to be accounted as the dung and off-scouring of all things, so that they might win Christ. Their hearts glowed with the love of God, and they never prospered so much in the inward man, as when they had all manner of evil spoken against them falsely without.

The first thing I was called to give up for God was what the world calls my fair reputation. I had no sooner received the sacrament publicly on a week-day at St. Mary's but I was set up as a mark for all the polite students that knew me to shoot at. By this they knew that I was commenced Methodist. For though there is a sacrament at the beginning of every term, at which all, especially the seniors, are, by statute, obliged to be present, yet so dreadfully has that once faithful city played the harlot, that very few masters, and no undergraduates (but the Methodists), attend upon it.

Mr. Charles Wesley (whom I must always mention with the greatest deference and respect), walked with me from the church even to the college. I confess to my shame I would gladly have excused him; and the next day going to his room, one of our fellows passing by, I was ashamed to be seen to knock at his door. But, blessed be God, this fear of man gradually wore off. As I had imitated Nicodemus in his cowardice, so, by the divine assistance, I followed him in his courage. I confessed the Methodists more and more publicly every day. I walked openly with them, and chose rather to bear contempt with those people of God, than to enjoy the applause of almost-Christians for a season.

God only knows how many nights I have lain upon my bed groaning under the weight I felt, and bidding Satan depart from me in the name of Jesus. Whole days and weeks have I spent in lying prostrate on the ground, and begging freedom from those proud, hellish thoughts that used to crowd in upon and distract my soul. But God made Satan drive out Satan. For these thoughts and suggestions created such a self-abhorrence within me, that I never ceased wrestling with God, till He blessed me with a victory over them. Self-love, self-will, pride and envy, buffeted me in their turns, that I was resolved either to die or conquer. I wanted to see sin as it was, but feared, at the same time, lest the sight of it should terrify me to death.

Whilst my inward man was thus exercised, my outward man was not unemployed. I soon found what a slave I had been to my sensual appetite, and now resolved to get the mastery over it by the help of Jesus Christ. Accordingly, by degrees, I began to leave off eating fruits, and such like, and gave the money I usually spent in that way to the poor. Afterwards I always chose the worst sort of food, though my place furnished me with variety. I fasted twice a week. My apparel was mean. I thought it unbecoming a penitent to have his hair powdered. I wore woollen gloves, a patched gown, and dirty shoes; and though I was then convinced that the kingdom of God did not consist in meats and drinks, yet I resolutely persisted in these voluntary acts of self-denial, because I found them great promoters of the spiritual life.

As I daily got strength, by continued, though almost silent prayer, in my study, my temptations grew stronger also, particularly for two or three days before deliverance came. Near five or six weeks I had now spent in my study, except when I was obliged to go out. During this time I was fighting with my corruptions, and did little else besides kneeling down by my bedside, feeling, as it were, a heavy pressure upon my body, as well as an unspeakable oppression of mind, yet offering up my soul to God, to do with me as it pleased Him. It was now suggested to me that Jesus Christ was among the wild beasts when He was tempted, and that I ought to follow His example; and being willing, as I thought, to imitate Jesus Christ, after supper I went into Christ's Church Walk, near our college, and continued in silent prayer under one of the trees for near two hours, sometimes kneeling upon my knees, all the while filled with fear and concern lest some of my brethren should be overwhelmed with pride. The night being stormy, it gave me awful thoughts of the day of judgment. I continued, I think, till the great bell rung for retirement to the college, not without finding some reluctance in the natural man against staying so long in the cold.

The next night I repeated the same exercise at the same place. But the hour of extremity being now come, God was pleased to make an open show of those diabolical devices by which I had been deceived.

By this time I had left off keeping my diary, using my forms, or scarce my voice in prayer, visiting the prisoners, etc. Nothing remained for me to leave, unless I forsook public worship, but my religious friends. Now it was suggested that I must leave them also for Christ's sake. This was a sore trial; but rather than not be, as I fancied, Christ's disciple, I resolved to renounce them, though as dear to me as my own soul. Accordingly, the next day being Wednesday, whereon we kept one of our weekly fasts, instead of meeting with my brethren as usual, I went out into the fields and prayed silently by myself. Our evening meeting I neglected also; and went not to breakfast, according to appointment, with Mr. Charles Wesley, the day following. This, with many other concurring circumstances, made my honoured friend, Mr. Charles Wesley, suspect something more than ordinary was the matter. He came to my room, soon found out my case, apprized me of my danger if I would not take advice; and recommended me to his brother John, Fellow of Lincoln College, as more experienced in the spiritual life. God gave me (blessed be His holy name!) a teachable temper; I waited upon his brother, with whom from that time I had the honour of growing intimate. He advised me to resume all my externals, though not to depend upon them in the least. From time to time he gave me directions as my various and pitiable state required; and at length, by his excellent advice and management of me, under God, I was delivered from those wiles of Satan. "Praise the Lord, O my soul, and all that is within me praise His holy name."

About this time God was pleased to enlighten my soul and bring me into the knowledge of His free grace and the necessity of being justified in His sight by faith only. This was more extraordinary, because my friends at Oxford had rather inclined to the mystic divinity. And one of them (a dear servant of the Lord) lately confessed he did not like me so well when at Oxford as the rest of his brethren, because I held justification by faith only; and yet, he observed, I had most success. But, blessed be God, most of us have now been taught this doctrine of Christ, and I hope shall be willing to die in the defence of it. It is the good old doctrine of the Church of England, it is what the holy martyrs in Queen Mary's time sealed with their blood, and which I pray God, if need be, that I and my brethren may seal with ours.

My dear reader, whosoever thou art, I pray to God that what I have now written may not prove a savour of death unto death, but a savour of life unto life unto thy soul! Many, I fear, through ignorance, prejudice, and unbelief, when they read this, will contradict and blaspheme. Be not thou of this number; but, if thou art yet unaffected with the contagion of the world, I pray God to keep thee so; for, believe me, innocence is better than repentance; and though sin may afford thee some brutish present pleasure, yet the remembrance of it afterwards is exceeding bitter. If thou art immersed in sin as I was, take no encouragement from me to continue in it on the one hand, nor despair of mercy on the other. Let God's goodness to me lead thee also to repentance. The same Lord is rich unto all that call upon Him through faith in Christ Jesus.

If, through divine grace, I have done anything praise-worthy, not unto me, but unto God give all the glory! If thou art awakened to a sense of the divine life, and art hungering and thirsting after that righteousness which is by faith only in Christ Jesus, and the indwelling of the Spirit in thy heart, think it not absolutely necessary to pass through all the temptations that have beset me round about on every side. It is in the spiritual as in the natural life—some feel more, others less—but all experience some pangs and travails of soul, before the Man

Christ Jesus is formed within them, and brought forth and arrived unto the measure of His fulness who filleth all in all! If God deals with thee in a most gentle way, yet so as that a thorough work of conversion is effected in thy heart, thou oughtest to be exceeding thankful; or if He should lead thee through a longer wilderness than I have passed through, thou needest not complain. The more thou art humbled now, the more thou shalt be exalted thereafter. One taste of Christ's love in thy heart will make amends for all. And if thou hast felt the powers of the world to come, and been made partaker of the Holy Ghost, know thou wilt rejoice, and give thanks for what God hath done for my soul.

To conclude: May all that peruse these few sheets be as much affected alternately with grief and joy in reading as I have been in writing them! They will then have the desired effect, and cause many thanksgivings to be offered in my behalf to that God who has called me out of darkness into His marvellous light! And that thou, Oh reader, whoever thou art, mayst experience the like and greater blessings, is the hearty prayer of

Thy soul's friend and servant,

GEO. WHITEFIELD

DAVID BRAINERD 1718–1747

The Yale junior was to be dismissed from school. He had been guilty of two misdemeanors: he had attended a service of worship when forbidden to do so by the college rector, and he had inadvertently dropped a remark about one of his teachers in the presence of a freshman. The freshman dutifully reported the remark to an acquaintance. Eventually it reached the office of the rector, who sent for the offender and gave him the choice of apologizing publicly for his sins or leaving the college. The young man, David Brainerd, decided not to apologize, and so bade farewell to the hallowed halls of Yale.

David was the third son of a family of eleven, of fine old New England stock. His father, Jonathan Edwards recounts in his Life and Diary of David Brainerd, *was "The Worshipful Hezekiah Brainerd, Esq., one of his majesty's council for that colony." His great-grandfather was the first of the Puritan preachers to migrate to America.*

The Brainerd children were reared in an atmosphere of piety. When David was fourteen the parents died.

He early experienced the prophetic constraint and looked forward almost impatiently to the day when he would be able to declare the glories of his God and King. At twenty-six he was licensed by his presbytery to preach. He turned down the offers of two pastorates in order to bear the Good News to the American Indians. As Jonathan Edwards wrote, "And having put his hand to the plow, he looked not back, but gave himself, heart, and soul, and mind, and strength, to his chosen mission, with unfaltering purpose, with apostolic zeal, with a heroic faith that feared no danger and surmounted every obstacle, and with an earnestness of mind that wrought wonders on savage lives and whole communities."

He made western Massachusetts the theater of his labors, later preached to tribes living along the Susquehanna and Delaware rivers. Not satisfied to teach through an interpreter, he studied and learned the language of the Indians.

His work necessitated taking long rides on horseback. Wilderness hardships, lack of proper food, overwork, and a consuming passion to win as many to Christ as possible in his lifetime drained his meager physical resources. He was never a well man, even as a youth. His diary is full of pathetic jottings on the subject: "I felt my bodily strength fail." "Distressed with an extreme pain in my head, attended with sickness in my stomach." "Shattered with the violence of the fever." "*My body was inexpressibly weak, followed continually with agues and fevers.*" *Along with his physical weakness, he suffered from a proneness to periodic melancholy and dejection.*

Brainerd fell in love with Jonathan Edwards' daughter, Jerusha. They became engaged but never married. Brainerd's last painful months were passed in Northampton at the Edwards' manse. Mr. Edwards notes that Jerusha was of much the same spirit with Mr. Brainerd. "She had constantly taken care of him and attended him in his sickness for nineteen weeks before his death, devoting herself to it with great delight because she looked on him as an eminent servant of Jesus Christ." One of his last statements was, "We shall spend a happy eternity together."

She survived him by five months.

Brainerd's devotional life has moved multitudes to yearn for a closer walk with God. His absolute surrender of every area of his being to the Lord's service puts to shame the indolence of hosts of Christ's followers. His vision of dying men lighted a flame in the heart of Henry Martyn and impelled him to go to India. His love for the American Indian so impressed Jonathan Edwards that while serving the Stockbridge congregation Edwards gave part of his time to preaching to a local tribe.

The Diary of David Brainerd, *though not written for the purpose of publication, has proved to be a fountain of gardens, a well of living water, and flowing streams from Lebanon. Its line has gone out through all the earth and its words to the end of the world. In that momentous hour when the books will be opened and a greater book than the diary will be opened, many unquestionably will rise up and call the Wilderness Missionary blessed.*

Extracts from the Diary of David Brainerd

T HE many disappointments, great distresses and perplexity which I experienced, put me into a most horrible frame of contesting with the Almighty; with an inward vehemence and virulence, finding fault with His ways of dealing with mankind. I found great fault with the imputation of Adam's sin to his posterity; and my wicked heart often wished for some other way of salvation than by Jesus Christ. Being like the troubled sea, my thoughts confused, I used to contrive to escape the wrath of God by some other means. I had strange projects, full of atheism, contriving to disappoint God's designs and decrees concerning me, or to escape His notice, and hide myself from Him. But when, upon reflection, I saw these projects were vain, and would not serve me, and that I could contrive nothing for my own relief; this would throw my mind into the most horrid frame, to wish there was no God, or to wish there were some other God that could control him. These thoughts and desires were the secret inclinations of my heart, frequently acting before I was aware; but, alas! they were mine, although I was frightened when I came to reflect on them.

When I considered, it distressed me to think, that my heart was so full of enmity against God; and it made me tremble, lest his vengeance should suddenly fall upon me. I used before to imagine, that my heart was not so bad as the scriptures and some other books represented it. Sometimes I used to take much pains to work it up into a good frame, a humble submissive disposition; and hoped there was then some goodness in me. But, on a sudden, the thoughts of the strictness of the law, or the sovereignty of God, would so irritate the corruption of my heart, that I had so watched over, and hoped I had brought to a good frame, that it would break over all bounds, and burst forth on all sides, like floods of waters when they break down their dams.

"The sovereignty of God. I could not bear, that it should be wholly at God's pleasure, to save or damn me, just as he would. That passage (Rom. 9:11-23) was a constant vexation to me, especially verse 21. Reading or meditating on this, always destroyed my seeming good frames: for when I thought I was almost humbled, and almost resigned, this passage would make my enmity against the sovereignty of God appear. When I came to reflect on the inward enmity and blasphemy, which arose on this occasion, I was the more afraid of God, and driven further from any hopes of reconciliation with him. It gave me a dreadful view of myself; I dreaded more than ever to see myself in God's hands, at his sovereign disposal; and it made me more opposite than ever to submit to his sovereignty; for I thought God designed my damnation.

It was the sight of truth concerning myself, truth respecting my state, as a creature fallen and alienated from God, and that consequently could make no demands on God for mercy, but must subscribe to the absolute sovereignty of the divine Being; the sight of the truth, I say, my soul shrank away from, and trembled to think of beholding. Thus, he that doth evil, as all unregenerate men continually do, hates the light of truth, neither cares to come to it, because it will reprove his deeds, and show him his just deserts. (John 3:26) Some time before, I had taken much pains, as I thought, to submit to the sovereignty of God; yet I mistook the thing,—and did not once imagine, that seeing and being made experimentally sensible of this truth, which my soul now so much dreaded and trembled at, was the frame of soul which I had so earnestly desired.

I had ever hoped, that when I had attained to that humiliation, which

I supposed necessary to precede faith, then it would not be fair for God to cast me off; but now I saw it was so far from any goodness in me, to own myself spiritually dead, and destitute of all goodness, that, on the contrary, my mouth would be forever stopped by it; and it looked as dreadful to me, to see myself, and the relation I stood in to God—I a sinner and criminal, and He a great Judge and Sovereign— as it would be to a poor trembling creature, to venture off some high precipice. Hence I put it off for a minute or two, and tried for better circumstances to do it in; either I must read a passage or two, or pray first, or something of the like nature or else put off my submission to God's sovereignty with an objection, that I did not know how to sub- mit. But the truth was I could see no safety in owing myself in the hands of a sovereign God, and could lay no claim to anything better than damnation.

I continued, in this state of mind till the Sabbath evening following, when I was walking again in the same solitary place, where I was brought to see myself lost and helpless, as before mentioned. Here, in a mournful melancholy state, I was attempting to pray; but found no heart to engage in that or any other duty; my former concern, exercise, and religious affections were now gone. I thought that the Spirit of God had quite left me; but still was not distressed; yet disconsolate, as if there was nothing in heaven or earth could make me happy. Having been thus endeavoring to pray—though, as I thought, very stupid and senseless—for near half an hour; then, as I was walking in a dark thick grove, unspeakable glory seemed to open to the view and apprehension of my soul. I do not mean any external brightness, for I saw no such thing; nor do I intend any imagination of a body of light, somewhere in the third heavens, or anything of that nature; but it was a new inward apprehension or view that I had of God, such as I never had before, nor anything which had the least resemblance of it.

I stood still; wondered; and admired! I knew that I never had seen before anything comparable to it for excellency and beauty; it was widely different from all the conceptions that ever I had of God, or things divine. I had no particular apprehension of any one person in the Trinity, either the Father, the Son, or the Holy Ghost; but it appeared to be Divine glory. My soul rejoiced with joy unspeakable, to see such a God, such a glorious divine Being; and I was inwardly pleased and satisfied that he should be God over all forever and ever. My soul was so captivated and delighted with the excellency, loveliness, great- ness, and other perfections of God, that I was even swallowed up in him; at least to that degree, that I had no thought (as I remember) at first, about my own salvation, and scarce reflected that there was such a creature as myself.

LORD'S DAY, APRIL 18. I retired early this morning into the woods for prayer; had the assistance of God's Spirit, and faith in exercise; and was enabled to plead with fervency for the advancement of Christ's kingdom in the world, and to intercede for dear, absent friends. At noon, God enabled me to wrestle with him, and to feel, as I trust, the power of divine love, in prayer. At night I saw myself infinitely indebted to God, and had a view of my failures in duty. It seemed to me, that I had done, as it were, nothing for God, and that I never had lived to him but a few hours of my life.

APRIL 20. This day, I am twenty-four years of age. O how much mercy have I received the year past! How often has God caused his goodness to pass before me! And how poorly have I answered the vows I made this time twelvemonth, to be wholly the Lord's, to be forever devoted to his service! The Lord help me to live more to his glory for the time to come. This has been a sweet, a happy day to me; blessed be God. I think my soul was never so drawn out in intercession for others, as it has been this night. Had a most fervent wrestle with the Lord tonight for my enemies; and I hardly ever so longed to live to God and to be altogether devoted to him; I wanted to wear out my life in his service, and for his glory.

LORD'S DAY, MAY 9. I think I never felt so much of the cursed pride of my heart, as well as the stubbornness of my will before. O dreadful! what a vile wretch I am! I could submit to be nothing, and to lie down in the dust. O that God would humble me in the dust! I felt myself such a sinner, all day, that I had scarce any comfort. O, when shall I be delivered from the body of this death! I greatly feared, lest through stupidity and carelessness I should lose the benefit of these trials. O that they might be sanctified to my soul! Nothing seemed to touch me but only this, that I was a sinner. Had fervency and refreshment in social prayer in the evening.

LORD'S DAY, AUG. 14. I had much more freedom in public, than in private. God enabled me to speak with some feeling sense of divine things; but perceived no considerable effect. . . . Spent most of the day in labor, to procure something to keep my horse on in the winter. Enjoyed not much sweetness in the morning; was very weak in body through the day; and thought that this frail body would soon drop into the dust; and had some very realizing apprehensions of a speedy entrance into another world. In this weak state of body, I was not a little distressed for want of suitable food. I had no bread, nor could I get any. I am forced to go or send ten or fifteen miles for all the bread I eat; and sometimes it is mouldy and sour before I eat it, if I get any considerable quantity. And then again I have none for some days together, for want of an opportunity to send for it, and cannot find my horse in the woods to go myself; and this was my case now; but through divine goodness I had some Indian meal, of which I made little cakes, and fried them. Yet I felt contented with my circumstances, and sweetly resigned to God. In prayer I enjoyed great freedom; and blessed God as much for my present circumstances, as if I had been a king; and thought that I found a disposition to be contented in any circumstances. Blessed be God.

[This day he wrote to his brother John, at Yale college, the following letter:]

Kaunaumeek, Dec. 27, 1743.

DEAR BROTHER:

I long to see you, and to know how you fare in your journey through a world of inexpressible sorrow: where we are compassed about with "vanity, confusion, and vexation of spirit." I am more weary of life, I think, than ever I was. The whole world appears to me like a huge vacuum, a vast empty space, whence nothing desirable, or at least satisfactory, can possibly be derived; and I long daily to die more and more to it; even though I obtain not that comfort from spiritual things which I earnestly desire. Worldly pleasures, such as flow from greatness riches, honors, and sensual gratifications, are infinitely worse than none. May the Lord deliver us more and more from these vanities.

I have spent most of the fall and winter hitherto in a very weak state of body; and sometimes under pressing inward trials and spiritual conflicts; but "having obtained help from God, I continue to this day"; and am now somewhat better in health, than I was some time ago. I find nothing more conducive to a life of Christianity, than a diligent, industrious, and faithful improvement of precious time. Let us then faithfully perform that business, which is allotted to us by divine Providence, to the utmost of our bodily strength, and mental vigor. Why should we sink, and grow discouraged with any particular trials and perplexities, which we are called to encounter in the world? Death and Eternity are just before us; a few tossing billows more will waft us into the world of spirits, and we hope, through infinite grace, into endless pleasures, and uninterrupted rest and peace. Let us then "run, with patience, the race set before us." (Heb. 12:1,2) And, O, that we could depend more upon the living God, and less upon our own wisdom and strength! Dear brother, may the God of all grace comfort your heart, and succeed your studies, and make you an instrument of good to his people in your day. This is the constant prayer of

Your affectionate brother,
DAVID BRAINERD.

JUNE 26. In the morning, my desires seemed to rise, and ascend up freely to God. Was busy most of the day in translating prayers into the language of the Delaware Indians; met with great difficulty, because my interpreter was altogether unacquainted with the business. But though I was much discouraged with the extreme difficulty of that work, yet God supported me; and especially in the evening, gave me sweet refreshment. In prayer, my soul was enlarged, and my faith drawn into sensible exercise; was enabled to cry to God for my poor Indians; and though the work of their conversion appeared impossible with man, yet with God I saw all things were possible. My faith was much strengthened, by observing the wonderful assistance God afforded his servants Nehemiah and Ezra, in reforming his people, and re-establishing his ancient church. I was much assisted in prayer for my dear Christian friends, and for others whom I apprehended to be Christless; but was more especially concerned for the poor Heathen, and those of my own charge; was enabled to be instant in prayer for them; and hopeful that God would bow the heavens and come down for their salvation.

It seemed to me, that there could be no impediment sufficient to obstruct that glorious work, seeing the living God, as I strongly hoped, was engaged for it. I continued in a solemn frame, lifting up my heart to God for assistance and grace, that I might be more mortified to this present world, that my whole soul might be taken up continually in concern for the advancement of Christ's kingdom. Earnestly desired that God would purge me more, more, that I might be as a chosen vessel to bear his name among the heathens. Continued in this frame till I fell asleep.

LORD'S DAY, JULY 1. In the morning, was perplexed with wandering vain thoughts; was much grieved, judged and condemned myself before God. O how miserable did I feel, because I could not live to God! At ten, rode away with a heavy heart, to preach to my Indians. Upon the road I attempted to lift up my heart to God; but was infested with an unsettled wandering frame of mind; and was exceeding restless and perplexed, and filled with shame and confusion before God. I seemed to myself to be "more brutish than any man"; and thought, none deserved to be "cast out of God's presence" so much as I. If I attempted to lift up my heart to God, as I frequently did by the way, on a sudden, before I was aware, my thoughts were wandering "to the ends of the earth"; and my soul was filled with surprise and anxiety, to find it thus. Thus also, after I came to the Indians, my mind was confused; and I felt nothing sensibly of that sweet reliance on God, with which my soul has been comforted in days past. Spent the forenoon in this posture of mind, and preached to the Indians without any heart.

In the afternoon I felt still barren, when I began to preach; and for about half an hour, I seemed to myself to know nothing, and to have nothing to say to the Indians; but soon after, I found in myself a spirit of love, and warmth, and power, to address the poor Indians; and God helped me to plead with them, to "turn from all the vanities of the Heathen, to the living God." I am persuaded that the Lord touched their consciences; for I never saw such attention raised in them. When I came away from them, I spent the whole time while I was riding to my lodgings, three miles distant, in prayer and praise to God. After I had rode more than two miles, it came into my mind to dedicate myself to God again; which I did with great solemnity, and unspeakable satisfaction; especially gave up myself to him renewedly in the work of the ministry. This I did by divine grace, I hope, without any exception or reserve; not in the least shrinking back from any difficulties that might attend this great and blessed work. I seemed to be most free, cheerful, and full in this dedication of myself. My whole soul cried "Lord, to thee I dedicate myself! O accept of me, and let me be thine forever, Lord, I desire nothing else; I desire nothing more. O come, come Lord, accept a poor worm. Whom have I in heaven but thee? And there is none upon earth that I desire beside thee."

After this, was enabled to praise God with my whole soul, that he had enabled me to devote and consecrate all my powers to him in this solemn manner. My heart rejoiced in my particular work as a missionary; rejoiced in my necessity of self-denial in many respects; and still continued to give up myself to God and implore mercy of him, praying incessantly, every moment with sweet fervency. My nature being very weak of late, and much spent, was now considerably overcome: my fingers grew very feeble, and somewhat numb, so that I could scarcely stretch them out straight: and when I lighted from my horse, could hardly walk; my joints seemed all to be loosed. But I felt abundant strength in the inner man. Preached to the white people; God helped me much, especially in prayer. Sundry of my poor Indians, were so moved as to come to meeting also; and one appeared much concerned.

OCT. 3 We went on our way into the wilderness, and found the most difficult and dangerous travelling, by far, that ever any of us had seen. We had scarce anything else but lofty mountains, deep valleys, and hideous rocks, to make our way through. However, I felt some sweetness in divine things, part of the day, and had my mind intensely engaged in meditation on a divine subject. Near night my beast on which I rode, hung one of her legs in the rocks, and fell down under me; but through divine goodness, I was not hurt. However, she broke her leg; and being in such a hideous place, and near thirty miles from any house, I saw nothing that could be done to preserve her life, and so was obliged to kill her, and to prosecute my journey on foot. This accident made me admire the divine goodness to me, that my bones were not broken, and the multitude of them filled with strong pain. Just at dark, we kindled a fire, cut up a few bushes, and made a shelter over our heads, to save us from the frost, which was very hard that night; and committing ourselves to God by prayer, we lay down on the ground, and slept quietly.

NOV. 22. Came on my way from Rockciticus to the Delaware. Was very much disordered with a cold and pain in my head. About six at night, I lost my way in the wilderness, and wandered over rocks and mountains, down hideous steeps, through swamps, and most dreadful and dangerous places; and, the night being dark, so that few stars could be seen, I was greatly exposed. I was much pinched with cold, and distressed with an extreme pain in my head, attended with sickness at my stomach; so that every step I took was distressing to me. I had little hope for several hours together, but that I must lie out in the woods all night, in this distressed case. But about nine o'clock, I found a house through the abundant goodness of God, and was kindly entertained.

Thus I have frequently been exposed, and sometimes lain out the whole night: but God has hitherto preserved me; and blessed be his name. Such fatigues and hardships as these serve to wean me from the earth; and, I trust, will make heaven the sweeter. Formerly, when I was thus exposed to rain, cold, etc., I was ready to please myself with the thoughts of enjoying a comfortable house, a warm fire, and other outward comforts; but now these have less place in my heart (through the grace of God), and my eye is more to God for comfort. In this world I expect tribulation; and it does not now, as formerly, appear strange to me. I do not in such seasons of difficulty flatter myself that it will be better hereafter: but rather think how much worse it might be; how much greater trials others of God's children have endured; and how much greater are yet perhaps reserved for me. Blessed be God, that he makes the thoughts of my journey's end, and of my dissolution, a great comfort to me, under my sharpest trials; and scarce ever lets these thoughts be attended with terror or melancholy; but they are attended frequently with great joy.

JUNE 22. About noon rode to the Indians again, and next night preached to them. Found my body much strengthened, and was enabled to speak with abundant plainness and warmth. The number, which at first consisted of seven or eight persons, was now increased to nearly thirty. There was not only a solemn attention among them, but some considerable impression, it was apparent, was made upon their minds by divine truth. Some began to feel their misery, and perishing state, and appeared concerned for a deliverance from it. The power of God evidently attended the word; so that several persons were brought under great concern for their souls, and made to shed many tears, and to wish for Christ to save them.

My soul was much refreshed and quickened in my work; and I could not but spend much time with them in order to open both their misery and their remedy. This was indeed a sweet afternoon to me. While riding, before I came to the Indians, my spirits were refreshed, and my soul enabled to cry to God almost incessantly, for many miles together. In the evening also, I found that the consolations of God were not small. I was then willing to live, and in some respects desirous of it, that I might do something for the dear kingdom of Christ; and yet death appeared pleasant; so that I was in some measure in a strait between two; having a desire to depart. I am often weary of this world, and want to leave it on that account; but it is desirable to be drawn, rather than driven out of it.

LORD'S DAY, JUNE 23. Preached to the Indians, and spent the day with them. Their number still increased; and all with one consent seemed to rejoice in my coming among them. Not a word of opposition was heard from any of them against Christianity, although in times past they had been as much opposed to anything of that nature, as any Indians whatsoever. Some of them not many months before, were enraged with my interpreter, because he attempted to teach them something of Christianity.

JUNE 28. The Indians being now gathered, a considerable number of them, from their several and distant habitations, requested me to preach twice a day to them; being desirous to hear as much as they possibly could while I was with them. I cheerfully complied with their request, and could not but admire the goodness of God, who I was persuaded, had inclined them thus to inquire after the way of salvation. In the evening my soul was revived, and my heart lifted up to God in prayer for any poor Indians, myself, and friends, and the dear church of God. O how refreshing, how sweet was this! Bless the Lord, O my soul, and forget not his goodness and tender mercy!

AUG. 8. A young Indian woman, who, I believe, never knew before that she had a soul, nor ever thought of such a thing, hearing that there was something strange among the Indians, came to see what was the matter. In her way to the Indians she called at my lodgings; and when I told her that I designed presently to preach to the Indians, laughed, and seemed to mock, but went however to them. I had not proceeded far in my discourse before she felt effectually that she had a soul; and, before I had concluded my discourse, was so convinced of her sin and misery, and so distressed with concern for her soul's salvation, that she seemed like one pierced through with a dart, and cried out incessantly. She could neither go nor stand, nor sit on her seat without being held up. After public service was over, she lay flat on the ground, praying earnestly, and would take no notice of, nor give any answer to any who spoke to her. I hearkened to hear what she said, and perceived the burden of her prayer to be, "Guttummaukalummeh wechaumeh kmelch Nolah," i.e. "Have mercy on me, and help me to give you my heart." Thus she continued praying incessantly for many hours together. This was indeed a surprising day of God's power, and seemed enough to convince an Atheist of the truth, importance, and power of God's word.

SEPT. 5. Discoursed to the Indians from the parable of the sower. Afterwards I conversed particularly with sundry persons; which occasioned them to weep, and even to cry out in an affecting manner, and seized others with surprise and concern. I doubt not but that a divine power accompanied what was then spoken. Several of these persons had been with me to Crossweeksung; and there had seen, and some of them, I trust, felt, the power of God's word, in an affecting and saving manner. I asked one of them, who had obtained comfort and given hopeful evidences of being truly religious, "Why he now cried?" He replied, "When the thought how Christ was slain like a lamb, and spilt his blood for sinners, he could not help crying, when he was alone"; and thereupon burst into tears, and cried again. I then asked his wife who had likewise been abundantly comforted, why she cried? She answered, "that she was grieved that the Indians here would not come to Christ, as well as those at Crossweeksung." I asked her if she found a heart to pray for them; and whether Christ had seemed to be near her of late in prayer, as in times past; which is my usual method of expressing a sense of the divine presence. She replied, "yes, He had been near to her, and at times when she had been praying alone, her heart loved to pray so, that she could not bear to leave the place, but wanted to stay and pray longer."

SEPT. 20. In the evening the Indians met together, nearly a hundred of them, and danced around a large fire, having prepared ten fat deer for the sacrifice. The fat of the inwards they burnt in the fire while they were dancing, and sometimes raised the flame to a prodigious height; at the same time yelling and shouting in such a manner, that they might easily have been heard two miles or more. They continued their sacred dance nearly all night, after which they ate the flesh of the sacrifice, and so retired each one to his own lodging. I enjoyed little satisfaction; being entirely alone on the island as to any Christian company, and in the midst of this idolatrous revel; and having walked to and fro till body and mind were pained and much oppressed, I at length crept into a little crib made for corn, and there slept on the poles.

LORD'S DAY, SEPT. 21. Spent the day with the Indians on the island. As soon as they were well up in the morning, I attempted to instruct them, and labored for that purpose to get them together; but soon found they had something else to do, for near noon they gathered together all their powows, or conjurers, and set about half a dozen of them playing their juggling tricks, and acting their frantic distracted postures, in order to find out why they were then so sickly upon the island, numbers of them being at that time disordered with a fever and bloody flux. In this exercise they were engaged for several hours, making all the wild, ridiculous and distracted motions imaginable; sometimes singing, sometimes howling, sometimes extending their hands to the utmost stretch, and spreading all their fingers,—they seemed to push with them as if they designed to push something away, or at least keep it off at arm's-end; sometimes stroking their faces with their hands, then spirting water as fine as mist; sometimes sitting flat on the earth, then bowing down their faces to the ground; then wringing their sides as if in pain and anguish, twisting their faces, turning up their eyes, grunting, puffing, etc.

"When I was in this region in May last, I had an opportunity of learning many of the notions and customs of the Indians, as well as observing many of their practices. I then traveled more than a hundred and thirty miles upon the river, above the English settlements: and in that journey, met with individuals of seven or eight distinct tribes, speaking as many different languages. But of all the sights I ever saw among them, or indeed anywhere else, none appeared so frightful, or so near akin to what is usually imagined of infernal powers, none ever excited such images of terror in my mind, as the appearance of one who was a devout and zealous reformer, or rather, restorer of what he supposed was the ancient religion of the Indians.

He made his appearance in his pontifical garb, which was a coat of boar skins, dressed with the hair on, and hanging down to his toes; a pair of bear-skin stockings; and a great wooden face painted, the one half black, the other half tawny, about the color of an Indian's skin, with an extravagant mouth, cut very much awry; the face fastened to a bearskin cap, which was drawn over his head. He advanced towards me with the instrument in his hand, which he used for music in his idolatrous worship; which was a dry tortoise-shell with some corn in it, and the neck of it drawn on to a piece of wood, which made a very convenient handle. As he came forward, he beat his tune with the rattle, and danced with all his might, but did not suffer any part of his body, not so much as his fingers to be seen. No one would have imagined from his appearance or actions, that he could have been a human creature, if they had not had some intimation of it otherwise. When he came near me, I could not but shrink away from him although it was then noonday, and I knew who it was; his appearance and gestures were so prodigiously frightful. He had a house consecrated to religious uses, with divers images cut upon the several parts of it. I went in, and found the ground beat almost as hard as a rock, with their frequent dancing upon it.

I discoursed with him about Christianity. Some of my discourse he seemed to like, but some of it he disliked extremely. He told me that God had taught him his religion, and that he never would turn from it; but wanted to find some who would join heartily with him in it; for the Indians, he said, were grown very degenerate and corrupt. He had thoughts, he said, of leaving all his friends, and traveling abroad, in order to find some who would join with him; for he believed that God had some good people somewhere, who felt as he did. He had not always, he said, felt as he now did; but had formerly been like the rest of the Indians, until about four or five years before that time. Then, he said, his heart was very much distressed, so that he could not live among the Indians, but got away into the woods, and lived alone for some months. At length, he says, God comforted his heart, and showed him what he should do; and since that time he had known God, and tried to serve him; and loved all men, be they who they would, so as he never did before.

He treated me with uncommon courtesy, and seemed to be hearty in it. I was told by the Indians, that he opposed their drinking strong liquor with all his power; and that, if at any time he could not dissuade them from it by all he could say, he would leave them, and go crying into the woods. It was manifest that he had a set of religious notions which he had examined for himself, and not taken for granted, upon bare tradition; and he relished or disrelished what ever was spoken of a religious nature, as it either agreed or disagreed with his standard. While I was discoursing, he would sometimes say "Now that I like; so God has taught me"; etc., and some of his sentiments seemed very just. Yet he utterly denied the existence of a devil, and declared there was no such creature known among the Indians of old times, whose religion he supposed he was attempting to revive.

He likewise told me, that departed souls all went southward; and that the difference between the good and the bad, was this; that the former were admitted into a beautiful town with spiritual walls; and that the latter would forever hover around these walls, in vain attempts to get in. He seemed to be sincere, honest, and conscientious in his own way, and according to his own religious notions; which was more than I ever saw in any other pagan. I perceived that he was looked upon and derided among most of the Indians, as a precise zealot, who made a needless noise about religious matters; but I must say that there was something in his temper and disposition, which looked more like true religion, than anything I ever observed amongst other heathens.

But alas! how deplorable is the state of the Indians upon this river! The brief representation which I have here given of their notions and manners, is sufficient to show that they are "led captive by Satan at his will," in the most eminent manner; and methinks might likewise be sufficient to excite the compassion, and engage the prayers, of pious souls for these their fellow men, who sit "in the region of the shadow of death."

It is remarkable, that God began this work among the Indians at a time when I had the least hope, and, to my apprehension, the least rational prospect of seeing a work of grace propagated among them; my bodily strength being then much wasted by a late tedious journey to the Susquehannah, where I was necessarily exposed to hardships and fatigues among the Indians; my mind being, also, exceedingly depressed with a view of the unsuccessfulness of my labors. I had little reason so much as to hope, that God had made instrumental in the saving conversion of any of the Indians, except my interpreter and his wife. Hence I was ready to look upon myself as a burden to the honorable society which employed and supported me in this business, and began to entertain serious thoughts of giving up my mission; and almost resolved, I would do so at the conclusion of the present year, if I had then no better prospect of special success in my work than I had hitherto had.

I cannot say that I entertained these thoughts because I was weary of the labors and fatigues which necessarily attended my present business, or because I had light and freedom in my own mind to turn any other way; but purely through dejection of spirit, pressing discouragement, and an apprehension of its being unjust to spend money consecrated to religious uses, only to civilize the Indians, and bring them to an external profession of Christianity. This was all which I could see any prospect of effecting, while God seemed, as I thought, evidently to frown upon the design of their saving conversion, by withholding the convincing and renewing influences of His blessed Spirit from attending the means which I had hitherto used with them for that end.

It is remarkable how God providentially, and in a manner almost unaccountable, called these Indians together, to be instructed in the great things that concerned their souls; and how He seized their minds with the most solemn and weighty concern for their eternal salvation, as fast as they came to the place where His word was preached. When I first came into these parts in June, I found not one man at the place I visited, but only four women and a few children; but before I had been here many days they gathered from all quarters, some from more than twenty miles distant; and when I made them a second visit in the beginning of August, some came more than forty miles to hear me. Many came without any intelligence of what was going on here, and consequently without any design of theirs, so much as to gratify their curiosity. Thus it seemed as if God had summoned them together from all quarters for nothing else but to deliver His message to them; and that He did this, with regard to some of them, without making use of any human means; although there was pains taken by some of them to give notice to others at remote places.

The effects of this work have likewise been very remarkable. I doubt not but that many of these people have gained more doctrinal knowledge of divine truths, since I first visited them in June last, than could have been instilled into their minds by the most diligent use of proper and instructive means for whole years together, without such a divine influence. Their pagan notions and idolatrous practices, seem to be entirely abandoned in these parts. They are regulated, and appear regularly disposed in the affairs of marriage; an instance whereof I have given in my journal of August 14. They seem generally divorced from drunkenness, their darling vice, the "sin that easily besets them"; so that I do not know of more than two or three who have been steady hearers, that have drunk to excess since I first visited them; although before it was common for some or other of them to be drunk almost every day; and some of them seem now to fear this sin in particular, more than death itself. A principle of honesty and justice appears in many of them; and they seem concerned to discharge their old debts, which they have neglected, and perhaps scarcely thought of for years past.

Their manner of living, is much more decent and comfortable than formerly, having now the benefit of that money which they used to consume upon strong drink. Love seems to reign among them, especially those who have given evidence of having passed a saving change; and I never saw any appearance of bitterness or censoriousness in these, nor any disposition to "esteem themselves better than others," who had not received the like mercy.

LORD'S DAY, DEC. 29. Preached from John 3:1-5. A number of white people were present, as is usual upon the Sabbath. The discourse was accompanied with power, and seemed to have a silent, but deep and piercing influence upon the audience. Many wept and sobbed affectionately. There were some tears among the white people, as well as the Indians. Some could not refrain from crying out; though there were not so many so exercised. But the impressions made upon their hearts appeared chiefly by the extraordinary earnestness of their attention, and their heavy sighs and tears.

After public worship was over, I went to my house, proposing to preach again after a short season of intermission. But they soon came in, one after another, with tears in their eyes, to know "what they should do to be saved." The divine Spirit in such a manner set home upon their hearts what I spake to them, that the house was soon filled with cries and groans. They all flocked together upon this occasion; and those whom I had reason to think in a Christless state, were almost universally seized with concern for their souls. It was an amazing season of power among them; and seemed as if God had bowed the heavens and come down. So astonishingly prevalent was the operation upon old as well as young, that it seemed as if none would be left in a secure and natural state, but that God was now about to convert all the world. I was ready to think then, that I should never again despair of the conversion of any man or woman living, be they who or what they would.

MARCH 9. Methinks it would have refreshed the heart of any who truly love Zion's interests, to have been in the midst of this divine influence, and seen the effects of it upon saints and sinners. The place of worship appeared both solemn and sweet, and was so endeared by a display of the divine presence and grace, that those who had any relish for divine things could not but cry, "How amiable are thy tabernacles, O Lord of hosts!" After public worship was over, numbers came to my house, where we sang and discoursed of divine things; and the presence of God seemed here also to be in the midst of us.

While we were singing the woman mentioned in my journal of February 9, who I may venture to say, if I may be allowed to say so much of any person I ever saw, was "filled with joy unspeakable and full of glory"; and could not but burst forth in prayer and praises to God before us all with many tears; crying sometimes in English, and sometimes in Indian, "O blessed Lord! do come, do come! O do take me away; do let me die and go to Jesus Christ! I am afraid if I live I shall sin again. O do let me die now! O dear Jesus, do come! I cannot stay, I cannot stay! O how can I live in this world? do take my soul away from this sinful place! O let me never sin any more! O what shall I do, what shall I do, dear Jesus! O dear Jesus!"

In this ecstasy she continued some time, uttering these and similar expressions incessantly. The grand argument she used with God to take her away immediately was, that "if she lived she should sin against him." When she had a little recovered herself, I asked her, if Christ was now sweet to her soul? Whereupon, turning to me with tears in her eyes, and with all the tokens of deep humility I ever saw in any person, she said, "I have many times heard you speak of the goodness and the sweetness of Christ, that he was better than all the world. But oh! I knew nothing what you meant. I never believed you, I never believed you! But now I know it is true;" or words to that effect. I answered, "And do you see enough in Christ for the greatest of sinners?" She replied, "O enough, enough for all the sinners in the world, if they would but come." When I asked her, "if she could not tell them of the goodness of Christ":—Turning herself about to some Christless souls who stood by and were much affected, she said, "O there is enough in Christ for you if you would but come. O strive, strive to give up your hearts to him," etc. On hearing something of the glory of heaven mentioned, that there was no sin in that world, she again fell into the same ecstasy of joy and desire of Christ's coming, repeating her former expressions, "O dear Lord, do let me go! O what shall I do; what shall I do. I want to go to Christ. I cannot live. O do let me die."

SEPT. 27. Spent this day as well as the whole week past, under a great degree of bodily weakness, exercised with a violent cough, and a considerable fever. I had no appetite for any kind of food; and frequently brought up what I ate, as soon as it was down; oftentimes had little rest in my bed, owing to pains in my breast and back. I was able, however, to ride over to my people, about two miles, every day, and take some care of those who were then at work upon a small house for me to reside in among the Indians. I was sometimes scarce able to walk, and never able to sit up the whole day, through the week. Was calm and composed, and but little exercised with melancholy, as in former seasons of weakness.

Whether I should ever recover or no, seemed very doubtful; but this was many times a comfort to me, that life and death did not depend upon my choice. I was pleased to think, that he who is infinitely wise, had the determination of this matter: and that I had no trouble to consider and weigh things upon all sides, in order to make the choice, whether I should live or die. Thus my time was consumed; I had little strength to pray, none to write or read, and scarce any to meditate; but through divine goodness, I could with great composure look death in the face, and frequently with sensible joy. O how blessed it is, to be habitually prepared for death! The Lord grant, that I may be actually ready also!

MARCH 28. Was taken this morning with violent griping pains. These pains were extreme, and constant for several hours; so that it seemed impossible for me, without a miracle, to live twenty-four hours in such distress. I lay confined to my bed the whole day, and in distressing pains, all the former part of it; but it pleased God to bless means for the abatement of my distress. Was exceedingly weakened by this pain, and continued so for several days following; being exercised with a fever, cough, and nocturnal sweats. In this distressed case, so long as my head was free of vapory confusions, death appeared agreeable to me. I looked on it as the end of toils, and an entrance into a place "where the weary are at rest"; and think I had some relish for the entertainments of the heavenly state; so that by these I was allured and drawn, as well as driven by the fatigues of life. O, how happy it is, to be drawn by desires of a state of perfect holiness!

JUNE 18. I was taken exceedingly ill, and brought to the gates of death by the breaking of small ulcers in my lungs, as my physician supposed. In this extremely weak state, I continued for several weeks, and was frequently reduced so low, as to be utterly speechless, and not able so much as to whisper a word. Even after I had so far revived, as to walk about the house, and to step out of doors, I was exercised every day with a faint turn, which continued usually four or five hours; at which times, though I was not so utterly speechless, but that I could say Yes, or No, yet I could not converse at all, nor speak one sentence, without making stops for breath; and divers times this season my friends gathered round my bed to see me breathe my last, which they expected every moment, as I myself also did.

How I was, the first day or two of my illness with regard to the exercise of reason, I scarcely know. I believe I was somewhat shattered with the violence of the fever at times; but the third day of my illness, and constantly afterwards, for four or five weeks together, I enjoyed as much serenity of mind, and clearness of thought, as perhaps I ever did in my life. I think that my mind never penetrated with so much ease and freedom into divine things, as at this time; and I never felt so capable of demonstrating the truth of many important doctrines of the gospel, as now. As I saw clearly the truth of those great doctrines which are justly styled the doctrines of grace, so I saw with no less clearness, that the essence of religion consisted in the soul's conformity to God, and acting above all selfish views, for His glory, longing to be for Him, to live to Him, and please and honor Him in all things; and this from a clear view of His infinite excellency and worthiness in Himself, to be loved, adored, worshipped and served by all intelligent creatures.

Thus I saw, that when a soul loves God with a supreme love, he therein acts like the blessed God Himself who most justly loves Himself in that manner. So when God's interest and his are become one, and he longs that God should be glorified, and rejoices to think that he is unchangeably possessed of the highest glory and blessedness herein, also, he acts in conformity to God. In like manner when the soul is fully resigned to, and rests satisfied and content with the divine will, here it is also conformed to God.

SEPT. 19. Near night, while I attempted to walk a little, my thoughts turned thus: "How infinitely sweet it is, to love God, and be all for him!" Upon which it was suggested to me, "You are not an angel, not lively and active." To which my whole soul immediately replied, "I as sincerely desire to love and glorify God, as any angel in heaven." Upon which it was suggested again, "But you are filthy, not fit for heaven."

Hereupon instantly appeared the blessed robes of Christ's righteousness, in which I could not but exult and triumph; and I viewed the infinite excellency of God, and my soul even broke with longings, that God should be glorified. I thought of dignity in heaven; but instantly the thought returned, "I do not go to heaven to get honor, but to give all possible glory and praise." O how I longed that God should be glorified on earth also!

O, I was made—for eternity—if God might be glorified! Bodily pains I cared not for; though I was then in extremity, I never felt easier. I felt willing to glorify God in that state of bodily distress, as long as He pleased I should continue in it. The grave appeared really sweet, and I longed to lodge my weary bones in it: but Oh, that God might be glorified! this was the burden of all my cry. Oh, I knew that I should be active as an angel, in heaven; and that I should be stripped of my filthy garments! so that there was no objection. But, O to love and praise God more, to please Him forever! this my soul panted after, and even now pants for while I write. O that God might be glorified in the whole earth! "Lord let thy kingdom come." I longed for a spirit of preaching to descend and rest on ministers, that they might address the consciences of men with closeness and power. I saw that God "had the residue of the Spirit"; and my soul longed that it should be "poured from on high." I could not but plead with God for my dear congregation, that He would preserve it, and not suffer His great name to lose its glory in that work; my soul still longing that God might be glorified.

SEPT. 24. My strength began to fail exceedingly; which looked further as if I had done all my work; however, I had strength to fold and superscribe my letter. About two I went to bed, being weak and much disordered, and lay in a burning fever till night, without any proper rest. In the evening, I got up, having lain down in some of my clothes; but was in the greatest distress, that ever I endured, having an uncommon kind of hiccough; which either strangled me, or threw me into a straining to vomit; and at the same time was distressed with griping pains. O the distress of this evening! I had little expectation of my living the night through, nor indeed had any about me; and I longed for the finishing moment!—I was obliged to repair to bed by six o'clock; and through mercy enjoyed some rest; but was grievously distressed at turns with the hiccough.—My soul breathed after God,— "When shall I come to God, even to God, my exceeding joy?" Oh for His blessed likeness!

SEPT. 25. This day, I was unspeakably weak, and little better than speechless all the day; however, I was able to write a little, and felt comfortably in some part of the day. O it refreshed my soul, to think of former things, of desires to glorify God, of the pleasures of living to Him! O, blessed God, I am speedily coming to Thee, I hope. Hasten the day, O Lord, if it be Thy blessed will, O come, Lord Jesus, come quickly. *Amen.*

SEPT. 26. I felt the sweetness of divine things, this forenoon; and had the consolation of a consciousness that I was doing something for God.

LORD'S DAY, SEPT. 27. This was a very comfortable day to my soul; I think I awoke with God. I was enabled to lift up my soul to God, early this morning; and while I had little bodily strength, I found freedom to lift up my heart to God for myself and others. Afterwards, was pleased with the thought of speedily entering into the unseen world.

FRANCIS ASBURY 1745–1816

It was inevitable that Methodism, rising in England, should spread to England's American colonies. In 1771, John Wesley sent the first two missionaries across the Atlantic to shepherd the 316 members who had already emigrated and to extend the frontiers of the movement. Francis Asbury was one of the two pioneers.

The next year Wesley appointed Asbury "assistant." Wesley's plan for America was to duplicate that which he was using in England. The circuit riders were to be known as "helpers," the superintendents of circuits, "assistants."

Asbury had been converted at thirteen. Not long after his awakening he began to lead meetings. Wesley licensed him at age eighteen as a local preacher. As he grew into maturity he became burdened for the colonists in expanding America and told Wesley so. He was therefore a natural choice for missionary activity.

Asbury, now twenty-five, established his headquarters in Baltimore. For a while the colonists hesitated to open their homes for services, as Methodism lay under the veil of suspicion because of the evangelistic methods of its adherents, who were nominally still within the Church. Gradually the mistrust evaporated, since Asbury appeared to be a churchman of good sense and unusual intelligence. His orbit of operation took in six counties surrounding Baltimore. He made the circuit once every three weeks. His efforts to convert people to Christ prospered, and quickly Wesleyan societies sprang up along the Atlantic seaboard.

In the new world men were more tolerant than in the old, and persecution did not pose the major problem. Asbury contended with other difficulties. He suffered from physical infirmities, and constantly sustained some form of bodily affliction, especially from a chronic throat infection. Also, Methodism was having its growing pains. J. M. Buckley remarks pointedly, "Those who suppose that in early Methodism human nature was extinguished by divine grace, to be undeceived need only read Asbury's Journal, *which records that in this conference there were debates 'relative to the conduct of some who had manifested a desire to abide in the cities and live like gentlemen, and that when three years out of four had been already spent in that city. Money had been wasted, improper leaders appointed, many of our rules broken.' "*

The American Revolution checked the progress of Methodism for a season. The close connection between John Wesley and British co-

lonial governors, especially in the South, cast the movement in a bad light with the colonial patriots, and all of the preachers in the first American Conference of Methodists were recent arrivals from the homeland. All returned to England save Asbury, at the outbreak of war. Poor Asbury had to hide out in the home of a friend in Delaware during the years 1778–79 until his devotion to the colonies became accepted.

Peace restored, the Methodists moved forward with renewed vigor. Wesley appointed one of his assistants, Thomas Coke, as joint superintendent with Asbury over the American constituency. Moreover, he conferred upon the two the right to administer the sacraments. Until this point, the Methodists had depended upon the clergy of the Church of England for the Lord's Supper and baptism. The action was a step toward the formation of a new denomination.

That step was consummated in 1784. At a conference held in Baltimore, Asbury, Coke, and other leaders, with Wesley's approval, formally constituted themselves into a body to be called the Methodist Episcopal Church, "in which liturgy [as presented by the Reverend John Wesley] should be read and the sacraments be administered by a superintendent, elders, and deacons, who shall be ordained by a presbytery, using the Episcopal form, as prescribed in the Rev. Mr. Wesley's prayer-book."

Francis Asbury was ordained a deacon, then an elder, then a superintendent, and later a bishop. Together with Coke and William Black of Nova Scotia he is to be recognized as the founding father of American Methodism.

There is a striking parallel between Asbury and Wesley. Both were individuals of tremendous vitality and executive ability. Both were tireless workers. Both were molders of men, and entirely devoted to Christ. Asbury outrode Wesley in his circuit tours, totaling 270,000 miles, perhaps the greatest mileage ever compiled by a horseman.

The last entry in his journal reads: "My consolations are great. I live in God from moment to moment."

Selections from *The Character and Career of Francis Asbury*

Asbury's Early Years

MY FATHER'S NAME was Joseph, and my mother's Elizabeth Asbury. They were people in common life, were remarkable for honesty and industry, and had all things needful to enjoy. Had my father been as saving as laborious he might have been wealthy. As it was, it was his province to be employed as a farmer and gardener by the two richest families in the parish. My parents had but two children—a daughter, called Sarah, and myself.

My lovely sister died in infancy. She was a favorite, and my dear mother, being very affectionate, sunk into deep distress at the loss of a darling child, from which she was not relieved for many years. It was under this dispensation that God was pleased to open the eyes of her mind, she living in a very dark, dark, dark day and place. She now began to read almost constantly when leisure presented the opportunity. When a child, I thought it strange my mother should stand by a large window poring over a book for hours together. From my childhood, I may say, I have neither dared an oath, nor hazarded a lie.

The love of truth is not natural, but the habit of telling it I acquired very early; and so well was I taught, that my conscience would never permit me to swear profanely. I learned from my parents a certain form of words for prayer, and I well remember my mother strongly urged my father to family reading and prayer. The singing of psalms was much practiced by them both. My foible was the ordinary foible of children;—fondness for play; but I abhorred mischief and wickedness, although my mates were among the vilest of the vile for lying, swearing, fighting, and whatever else boys of their age and evil habits were likely to be guilty of.

From such society I very often returned home uneasy and melancholy; and, although driven away by my better principles, still I would return, hoping to find happiness where I never found it. Sometimes I was much ridiculed, and called Methodist Parson, because my mother invited any people who had the appearance of religion to her house.

I was sent to school early, and began to read the Bible between six and seven years of age, and greatly delighted in the historical part of it. My schoolmaster was a great churl, and used to beat me cruelly. This drove me to prayer, and it appeared to me that God was near to me. My father having but the one son, greatly desired to keep me at school, he cared not how long; but in this design he was disappointed, for my master, by his severity, had filled me with such horrible dread, that with me any thing was preferable to going to school. I lived some time in one of the wealthiest and most ungodly families we had in the parish.

Here I became vain, but not openly wicked. Some months after this I returned home and made my choice, when about thirteen years and a half old, to learn a branch of business at which I wrought about six years and a half. During this time I enjoyed great liberty, and in the family was treated more like a son or an equal than an apprentice.

Soon after I entered on that business God sent a pious man, not a Methodist, into our neighborhood, and my mother invited him to our house. By his conversation and prayers I was awakened before I was fourteen years of age. It was now easy and pleasing to leave my companions, and I began to pray morning and evening, being drawn by the cords of love as with the bands of a man. I soon left our blind priest and went to West Bromwich church.

Here I heard Ryland, Stillingfleet, Talbot, Bagnall, Mansfield, Hawes, and Venn—great names, and esteemed Gospel ministers. I became very serious, reading a great deal—Whitefield and Cennick's Sermons, and every good book I could meet with. It was not long before I began to inquire of my mother who, where, what were the Methodists. She gave me a favorable account, and directed me to a person that could take me to Wednesbury to hear them. I soon found this was not the Church —but it was better. The people were so devout: men and women kneeling down, saying *Amen*. Now, behold! they were singing hymns. Sweet sound! Why, strange to tell! the preacher had no prayer-book, and yet he prayed wonderfully! What was yet more extraordinary, the man took his text, and had no sermon-book. Thought I, "This is wonderful indeed! It is certainly a strange way, but the best way." He talked about confidence, assurance, etc., of which all my flights and hopes fell short. I had no deep convictions, nor had I committed any deep known sins.

At one sermon, some time after, my companion was powerfully wrought on. I was exceedingly grieved that I could not weep like him, yet I knew myself to be in a state of unbelief. On a certain time, when we were praying in my father's barn, I believe the Lord pardoned my sins and justified my soul; but my companions reasoned me out of this belief, saying, "Mr. Mather said a believer was as happy as if he was in heaven." I thought I was not as happy as I would be there, and gave up my confidence, and that for months; yet I was happy, free from guilt and fear, and had power over sin, and felt great inward joy.

After this, we met for reading and prayer, and had large and good meetings, and were much persecuted, until the persons at whose houses we held them were afraid, and they were discontinued. I then held meetings frequently at my father's house, exhorting the people there, as also at Sutton Colefield, and several souls professed to find peace through my labors. I met class awhile at Bromwich Heath, and met in band at Wednesbury. I had preached some months before I publicly appeared in the Methodist meetinghouses, but when my labors became more public and extensive some were amazed, not knowing how I had exercised elsewhere.

Behold me now a local preacher! The humble and willing servant of any and of every preacher that called on me by night or by day—being ready, with hasty steps, to go far and wide to do good—visiting Derbyshire, Staffordshire, Warwickshire, Worcestershire, and indeed almost every place within my reach, for the sake of precious souls, preaching, generally, three, four, and five times a week, and at the same time pursuing my calling. I think when I was between twenty-one and twenty-two years of age I gave myself up to God and His work, after acting as a local preacher near the space of five years. It is now the 19th of July, 1792. I have been laboring for God and souls about thirty years or upward.

Some time after I had obtained a clear witness of my acceptance with God, the Lord showed me, in the heat of youth and youthful blood, the evil of my heart. For a short time I enjoyed, as I thought, the pure and perfect love of God, but this happy frame did not long continue, although at seasons I was greatly blessed. While I was a traveling preacher in England I was much tempted, finding myself exceedingly ignorant of almost every thing a minister of the Gospel ought to know. How I came to America, and the events which have happened since my journal will show.

Asbury's Reflections on Shipboard

THURSDAY, 12. I will set down a few things that lie on my mind. Whither am I going? To the New World. What to do? To gain honor? No, if I know my own heart. To get money? No; I am going to live to God, and to bring others so to do. In America there has been a work of God; Some moving first among the Friends, but in time it declined; likewise by the Presbyterians, but among them also it declined. The people God owns in England are the Methodists. The doctrines they preach, and the discipline they enforce, are, I believe, the purest of any people now in the world. The Lord has greatly blessed these doctrines and this discipline in three kingdoms: they must, therefore, be pleasing to Him. If God does not acknowledge me in America, I will soon return to England. I know my views are upright; may they never be otherwise!

An Assault from Satan

FRIDAY, 13. I packed up my clothes and books to be ready for my departure, and had an agreeable conversation with Mr. O. The next day some of my friends were so unguarded and imprudent as to commend me to my face. Satan, ready for every advantage, seized the opportunity, and assaulted me with self-pleasing, self-exalting ideas. But the Lord enabled me to discover the danger, and the snare was broken. May He ever keep me humble, and little, and mean in my own eyes!

Ballast Necessary—Puffs of Applause

FRIDAY, JUNE 2. The Lord is pleased to show me the danger which a preacher is in of being lifted up by pride, and falling into the condemnation of the devil. How great is the danger of this! A considerable degree of ballast is highly necessary to bear frequent and sudden puffs of applause. Lord, fill me with genuine humility, that the strongest gusts from Satan or the world may never move me!

Marines in Norfolk—Reflection

TUESDAY, 3. My heart is fixed, trusting the Lord. I sincerely desire to be entirely His—to spend the remnant of my days and strength altogether for God. A company of marines have been ashore at Norfolk, ransacked the printing-office, and taken the printers and press with them. The inhabitants soon after embodied and got under arms. The people are also repairing the fort, which, if put in order, may sink all the ships that shall attempt to come into the harbor. But if it is thought expedient to watch and fight in defense of our bodies and property, how much more expedient it is to watch and fight against sin and Satan in defense of our souls, which are in danger of eternal damnation! But small dangers at hand have a greater effect on fallen man than the greatest dangers which are thought to be at a distance. But, alas! the one may be as near as the other!

"Ended Where We Began"

LORD'S DAY, 18. I preached twice at Petersburg. The last subject was the rich man and Lazarus, which struck the people with great solemnity, and many seemed to feel the power of God. On Monday there were two Baptist preachers among the congregation. After the sermon was ended they desired to speak with me. So we conversed about three hours on experimental, practical, and controversial divinity, but ended where we began. I thank the Lord, my mind was kept in peace and coolness. No doubt Satan is very active in promoting religious controversies. Many take a controversial spirit for the spirit of religion, while others dispute away what little religion they have. "Only by pride cometh contention. The wisdom that cometh from above is pure and peaceable."

Reflection

THURSDAY, 7. Alas for fallen man! He fears his fellow-creatures, whose breath is in their nostrils, but fears not Him who is able to destroy body and soul in hell. If fire and sword at a small distance can so alarm us, how will poor impenitent sinners be alarmed when they find, by woeful experience, that they must drink the wine of the wrath of God, poured out without mixture?

Heaven and Earth Contrasted

LORD'S DAY, 10. The congregations were but small, so great has the consternation been. But I know the Lord governeth the world; therefore these things shall not trouble me. I will endeavor to be ready for life or death; so that, if death should come, my soul may joyfully quit this land of sorrow, and go to rest in the embraces of the blessed Jesus. O delightful felicity! There is no din of war; no unfriendly persecutors of piety; no enchanting world with concealed destruction; no malevolent spirit to disturb our peace; but all is purity, peace, and joy.

Preaching for Souls, Not for Silver

WEDNESDAY, 23. Preached at a new place in a meadow to about one hundred people, who were wild enough; after preaching, had to ride twelve miles for my dinner. In this our labor we have to encounter hunger, heat, and many restless nights with mosquitoes, unwholesome provisions, and bad water. But all this is for souls; were it for silver, I should require a great sum. But the Lord is not unrighteous to forget our labor of love, and our reward is with Him.

Chatham County

MONDAY, 24. Cool, like the fall. I am kept in peace. Rose with a sense of God's presence; have only time to pray and write my journal. Always upon the wing, as the rides are so long, and bad roads; it takes me many hours, as in general I walk my horse. I crossed Rocky River about ten miles from Haw River. It was rocky, sure enough; it is in Chatham county, North Carolina. I can see little else but cabins in these parts, built with poles: and such a country as no man ever saw for a carriage. I narrowly escaped being overset; was much affrighted, but Providence keeps me, and I trust will. I crossed Deep River in a flatboat, and the poor ferry-man sinner swore because I had not a silver shilling to give him. I rode to friend Hinton's, borrowed a saddle, and rode near six miles to get three, as we were lost.

Asbury's Trust in Providence Confirmed

SATURDAY, FEBRUARY 3. Visited my old friend, Fullford. He is feeble in body, and not much at ease in his worldly possessions, yet happy in God.

Brother Poythress frightened me with the idea of the Great Swamp, the east end of the Dismal; but I could not consent to ride sixty miles round, so we ventured through, and neither we nor our horses received any injury. Praise the Lord! Our passing unharmed through such dangers and unhealthy weather feelingly assures me that I am kept by the immediate interposition of His providence. I preached in the new chapel, I hope not in vain. I am now surrounded with waters and hideous swamps, near the head of Pasquotank River.

Conference at Charleston—Riotous Demonstrations

FRIDAY, MARCH 14. Our conference began, and we had a very free, open time. Saturday night I preached on "I have set watchmen upon thy walls," etc. On the Sabbath, on "The Lord turned and looked on Peter," etc. It was a gracious season, both in the congregation and in the love-feast. While another was speaking in the morning to a very crowded house, and many outside, a man made a riot at the door. An alarm at once took place, the ladies leaped out at the windows of the church, and a dreadful confusion ensued. Again, while I was speaking at night, a stone was thrown against the north side of the church, then another on the south, and a third came through the pulpit window and struck near me inside the pulpit. I, however, continued to speak on my subject, "How beautiful upon the mountains," etc.

A Journey Through the Wilderness—Graves of the Slain

TUESDAY, 11. Crossed Kentucky River. I was strangely outdone for want of sleep, having been greatly deprived of it in my journey through the wilderness; which is like being at sea, in some respects, and in others worse. Our way is over mountains, steep hills, deep rivers, and through muddy creeks; a thick growth of reeds for miles together, and no inhabitants but wild beasts and savage men. Sometimes, before I am aware, my ideas would be leading me to be looking out ahead for a fence, and I would, without reflection, try to recollect the houses we should have lodged at in the wilderness. I slept about an hour the first night, and about two the last. We ate no regular meal; our bread grew short, and I was much spent.

I saw the graves of the slain—twenty-four in one camp. I learn that they had set no guard, and that they were up late, playing at cards.

A poor woman of the company had dreamed three times that the Indians had surprised and killed them all; she urged her husband to entreat the people to set a guard, but they only abused him, and cursed him for his pains. As the poor woman was relating her last dream, the Indians came upon the camp; she and her husband sprung away, one east, the other west, and escaped. She afterward came back, and witnessed the carnage. These are some of the melancholy accidents to which the country is subject for the present. As to the land, it is the richest body of fertile soil I have ever beheld.

Reception at Stratford

TUESDAY, 7. We came to Stratford. Good news—they have voted that the town-house shall be shut. Well, where shall we preach? Some of the selectmen—one at least—granted access. I felt unwilling to go, as it is always my way not to push myself into any public house. We had close work on Isaiah 55:67; some smiled; some laughed, some swore, some talked, some prayed, some wept. Had it been a house of our own, I should not have been surprised had the windows been broken. I refused to preach there any more, and it was well I did, for two of the esquires were quite displeased at our admittance. We met the class, and found some gracious souls. The Methodists have a society consisting of twenty members, some of them converted, but they have no house of worship. They may now make a benefit of a calamity—being denied the use of other houses, they will the more earnestly labor to get one of their own. The Presbyterians and the Episcopalians have each one, and both are elegant buildings.

"Hail, Happy Death!"

FRIDAY, 26. We rode twenty-six miles to the Little Levels. O what a solitary country is this! We have now one hundred and twenty miles before us, fifty of which is a wilderness. There is a guard at two houses on our route, but I do not fear. Nature is spent with labor. I would not live always. Hail, happy death! Nothing but holiness, perfect love, and then glory for me!

Another Journey Through Wilderness

TUESDAY, 7. We rode down to the Crab Orchard, where we found company enough, some of whom were very wild. We had a company of our own, and refused to go with them. Some of them gave us very abusive language, and one man went up on a hill above us and fired a pistol toward our company. We resolved to travel in our order, and bound ourselves by honor and conscience to support and defend each other, and to see every man through the wilderness.

But we could not depend upon wicked and unprincipled men, who would leave and neglect us, and even curse us to our faces. Nor were we at liberty to mix with swearers, liars, drunkards, and, for aught we know, this may not be the worst with some. We were about fourteen or fifteen in company, and had twelve guns and pistols. We rode on near the defeated camp, and rested till three o'clock under great suspicion of the Indians. We pushed forward, and by riding forty-five miles on Wednesday, and about the same distance on Thursday, we came safe to Robinson's station about eight o'clock.

Asbury in Philadelphia in the Midst of Contagion

FRIDAY, 6. We rode to the city. Ah! how the ways mourn! how low-spirited are the people while making their escape! I judge the people die from fifty to one hundred in a day. Some of our friends are dying, others flying.

SUNDAY, 8. I preached on Isa. 58:1: "Cry aloud, spare not, lift up thy voice like a trumpet, and show my people their transgression, and the house of Jacob their sins." The people of this city are alarmed, and well they may be. I went down to Ebenezer [a church in the lower part of the city], but my strength was gone; however, I endeavored to open and apply Micah 6:9. The streets are now depopulated, and the city wears a gloomy aspect. All night long my ears and heart were wounded with the cry of fire! And what made it still more serious, two young men were killed by the fall of a wall, one of whom was a valuable member of our society. Poor Philadelphia! the lofty city, He layeth it low! We appointed Tuesday, 9th, to be observed as a day of humiliation. I preached on I Kings 8:37-40, and had a large and very serious weeping congregation. The preachers left the city on Monday; I continued in order to have the minutes of conference printed.

Ecclesiastical Chains—A Prophecy

SUNDAY, 10. Brother R., though sick, went to Coventry, and I was left alone at Tolland, where I preached in the forenoon, on Acts 2:37,38, with some freedom, and in the afternoon on Colossians 2:6, and found it heavy work. After meeting I was taken with a dysentery, (attended with great sinking of bodily powers), which held me most of the night. Monday I was better, and preached in a school-house at Ellington. I felt great dejection of spirit, but no guilt or condemnation. Ah! here are the iron walls of prejudice; but God can break them down. Out of fifteen United States thirteen are free, but two are fettered with ecclesiastical chains—taxed to support ministers who are chosen by a small committee and settled for life.

My simple prophecy is, that this must come to an end with the present century. The Rhode Islanders began in time, and now are free. Hail, sons of liberty! Who first began the war? Was it not Connecticut and

Massachusetts? and priests are now saddled upon them. I heard——
read a most severe letter from a citizen of Vermont, to the clergy and
Christians of Connecticut, striking at the foundation and principle of
the hierarchy, and the policy of Yale College and the independent
order. It was expressive of the determination of the Vermonters to continue free from ecclesiastical fetters, to follow the Bible, and give
liberty, equal liberty, to all denominations of professing Christians. If
so, why may not the Methodists (who have been repeatedly solicited)
visit these people also?

Indian Barbarities—A Thrilling Narrative

MONDAY, 9. I hobbled over the ridge, through the capital part of
Russell county, sixteen miles to B.'s. These people have lived in peace
ever since the death of Ben, the half-blooded Indian warrior, who was
shot through the head while carrying off two women. He was a dreadful wicked wretch, who, by report, may have been the agent of death
to nearly one hundred people in the wilderness and in Russell. Here I
preached to a few insensible people, and had time to read, write, and
sleep in quiet. Yesterday our prayers were requested on behalf of
F.D. This day in the evening Brother K. was called upon to perform
her funeral solemnities. Perhaps she has been as great a female sufferer
as I have heard of. The following account, in substance, was taken
from her own mouth, some time ago, by J. Kobler, who performed
her funeral rites.

Her maiden name was Dickenson. She was married to a Mr. Scott,
and lived in Powell's Valley, at which time the Indians were very
troublesome, often killing and plundering the inhabitants. On a certain
evening, her husband and children being in bed, eight or nine Indians
rushed into the house. Her husband being alarmed started up, when
all that had guns fired at him. Although he was badly wounded he broke
through them all and got out of the house. Several of them closely
pursued him, and put an end to his life. They then murdered and
scalped all her children before her eyes, plundered her house, and took
her prisoner. The remainder of the night they spent around a fire in
the woods, drinking, shouting and dancing. The next day they divided
the plunder with great equality. Among the rest of the goods was one of
Mr. Wesley's hymn-books. She asked them for it, and they gave it to
her; but when they saw her often reading therein they were displeased,
called her a conjurer, and took it from her. After this they traveled
several days' journey toward the Indian towns; but, said she, my grief
was so great I could hardly believe my situation was a reality, but
thought I dreamed.

To aggrevate my grief one of the Indians hung my husband's and
my children's scalps to his back, and would walk the next before me.

In walking up and down the hills and mountains I was worn out with fatigue and sorrow. They would often laugh when they saw me almost spent, and mimic my panting for breath. There was one Indian who was more humane than the rest. He would get me water, and make the others stop when I wanted to rest. Thus they carried me on eleven days' journey, until they were all greatly distressed with hunger. They then committed me to the care of an old Indian at the camp, while they went off hunting.

While the old man was busily employed in dressing a deer-skin, I walked backward and forward through the woods, until I observed he took no notice of me. I then slipped off, and ran a considerable distance and came to a cane-brake, where I hid myself very securely. Through most of the night I heard the Indians searching for me, and answering each other with a voice like that of an owl. Thus was I left alone in the savage wilderness, far away from any inhabitants, without a morsel of food, or any kind of help but the common Saviour and friend of all.

To Him I poured out my complaint in fervent prayer that He would not forsake me in this distressing circumstance. I then set out in the course that I thought Kentucky lay, though with very little expectation of seeing a human face again, except that of the savages, whom I looked upon as so many fiends from the bottomless pit, and my greatest dread was that of meeting some of them while wandering in the wilderness.

One day as I was traveling I heard a loud human voice and a prodigious noise, like horses running. I ran into a safe place and hid myself, and saw a company of Indians pass by, furiously driving a gang of horses which they had stolen from the white people. I had nothing to subsist upon but roots, young grapevines, and sweet-cane, and such like produce of the woods. I accidently came where a bear was eating a deer, and drew near in hopes of getting some; but he growled and looked angry, so I left him, and quickly passed on.

At night when I lay down to rest I never slept, but I dreamed of eating. In my lonesome travels I came to a very large shelving rock, under which was a fine bed of leaves. I crept in among them, and determined there to end my days of sorrow. I lay there several hours, until my bones ached in so distressing a manner that I was obliged to stir out again. I then thought of and wished for home, and traveled on several days, till I came where Cumberland River breaks through the mountain.

I went down the cliffs a considerable distance until I was affrighted, and made an attempt to go back, but found the place down which I had gone was so steep that I could not return. I then saw but one way that I could go, which was a considerable perpendicular distance down to the bank of the river. I took hold of the top of a little bush, and for

half an hour prayed fervently to God for assistance. I then let myself
down by the little bush until it then broke, and I went down with great
violence to the bottom. This was early in the morning, and I lay there
a considerable time, with a determination to go no further.

About ten o'clock I grew so thirsty that I concluded to crawl to the
water and drink, after which I found I could walk. The place I came
through, as I have been since informed, is only two miles, and I was
four days in getting through it. I traveled on until I came to a little
path, one end of which led to the inhabitants, and the other to the
wilderness. I knew not which end of the path to take. After standing
and praying to the Lord for direction, I turned to take the end that
led to the wilderness. Immediately there came a little bird of a dove-
color near to my feet, and fluttered along the path that led to the
inhabitants. I did not observe this much at first, until it did it a second
or third time. I then understood this as a direction of Providence, and
took the path which led me to the inhabitants. Immediately after her
safe arrival she embraced religion, and lived and died an humble fol-
lower of Christ.

Generosity of a Poor Black

TUESDAY, 21. My mind has been greatly afflicted, so that my sleep
has been much interrupted, yet there was a balm for this: a poor black,
sixty years of age, who supports herself by picking oakum and the
charity of her friends, brought me a French crown, and said she had
been distressed on my account, and I must have her money. But no!
although I have not three dollars to travel two thousand miles, I will
not take money from the poor. I am very unwell, my soul and body
is distressed; ah! that such trifles should affect me. I have read four
books of Moses critically.

"A Worthless Lump of Misery and Sin"

SUNDAY, JUNE 18. I was only able to speak about fifteen minutes. I
recover but slowly. The constant resort of the wealthy and poor
visiting me made me much ashamed that they should look after such
a worthless lump of misery and sin.

Asbury's Burden

SATURDAY, 26. I stayed at the house to read, write and plan a little.
I tremble and faint under my burden—having to ride about six thousand miles annually, to preach from three to five hundred sermons a
year, to write and read so many letters, and read many more—all this
and more, besides the stationing of three hundred preachers, reading
many hundred pages, and spending many hours in conversation by day

and by night with preachers and people of various characters, among whom are many distressing cases.

Death of Washington—Matchless Man

SATURDAY, 4. Slow moved the northern post on the eve of New Year's day, and brought the heart-distressing information of the death of Washington, who departed this life December 14, 1799.

Washington, the calm, intrepid chief, the disinterested friend, first father, and temporal savior of his country under Divine protection and direction. A universal cloud sat upon the faces of the citizens of Charleston; the pulpits clothed in black—the bells muffled—the paraded soldiery—a public oration decreed to be delivered on Friday, 14th of this month—a marble statue to be placed in some proper situation— these were the expressions of sorrow, and these the marks of respect paid by his feeling fellow-citizens to the memory of this great man. I am disposed to lose sight of all but Washington—matchless man! At all times he acknowledged the providence of God, and never was he ashamed of his Redeemer. We believe he died not fearing death. In his will he ordered the manumission of his slaves—a true son of liberty in all points.

Death of Asbury's Mother—Tribute to Her Memory

John Pawson's letter, and fifty copies of a volume of sermons, came safely to hand. His and other letters concerning the work of God I read to my brethren. While in Baltimore, I received an account of the death of my mother, which I fear is true. And here I may speak safely concerning my very dear mother. Her character to me is well known. Her paternal descent was Welsh; from a family ancient and respectable, of the name of Rogers. She lived a woman of the world until the death of her first and only daughter, Sarah Asbury. This afflictive providence graciously terminated in the mother's conversion. When she saw herself a lost and wretched sinner she sought religious people, but "in the times of this ignorance" few were "sound in the faith" or "faithful to the grace given."

Many were the days she spent chiefly in reading and prayer; at length she found justifying grace and pardoning mercy. So dim was the light of truth around her, from the assurance she found, she was at times inclined to believe in the final perseverance of the saints. For fifty years her hands, her house, her heart were open to receive the people of God and ministers of Christ, and thus a lamp was lighted up in a dark place called Great Barre, in Great Britain. She was an afflicted yet most active woman, of quick bodily powers and masculine understanding. Nevertheless, "so kindly all the elements were mixed in her," her strong mind quickly felt the subduing influences of that Christian sympathy which "weeps with those who weep," and "rejoices with those who do rejoice."

As a woman and a wife she was chaste, modest, blameless; as a mother (above all the women in the world would I claim her for my own) ardently affectionate. As a "mother in Israel" few of her sex have done more by a holy walk to live, and by personal labor to support the Gospel and to wash the saints' feet. As a friend she was generous, true, and constant. Elizabeth Asbury died January 6th, 1802, aged eighty-seven or eighty-eight years. There is now, after fifty years, a chapel within two or three hundred yards of her dwelling. I am now often drawn out in thankfulness to God, who hath saved a mother of mine, and, I trust, a father also, who are already in glory, where I hope to meet them both.

Absury's Reasons for a Life of Celibacy

FRIDAY, 27. We reached Georgetown. I have suffered in my flesh, and have had "deep waters" of a temporal and spiritual nature to wade through. If I should die in celibacy, which I think quite probable, I give the following reasons for what can scarcely be called by choice: I was called in my fourteenth year; I began my public exercises between sixteen and seventeen; at twenty-one I traveled; at twenty-six I came to America—thus far I had reasons enough for a single life. It had been my intention of returning to Europe at thirty years of age; but the war continued, and it was ten years before we had a settled, lasting peace —this was no time to marry or be given in marriage. At forty-nine I was ordained superintendent bishop in America.

Among the duties imposed upon me by my office was that of traveling extensively, and I could hardly expect to find a woman with grace enough to enable her to live but one week out of the fifty-two with her husband; besides, what right has any man to take advantage of the affections of a woman, make her his wife, and by a voluntary absence subvert the whole order and economy of the marriage state, by separating those whom neither God, nature, nor the requirements of civil society permit long to be put asunder?—it is neither just nor generous.

I may add to this that I had little money, and with this little administered to the necessities of a beloved mother until I was fifty-seven. If I have done wrong, I hope God and the sex will forgive me. It is my duty now to bestow the pittance I may have to spare upon the widows and fatherless girls, and poor married men.

WILLIAM CAREY 1761–1834

The challenge struck like a thunderclap, during a ministers' meeting at Northamptom, England, in 1786. One of the clergy present had invited the others to offer suggestions for a general discussion. For some moments nothing was said. At last William Carey, the preacher-cobbler from Moulton, rose and asked, "Do the brethren not think that the command given by our Lord to the Apostles to teach all nations is obligatory on all succeeding ministers to the end of the world, seeing that the accompanying promise is of equal extent?"

The question was like the hurling of a stone into a nest of bees. Furiously the bees swarmed out to attack. The chairman of the meeting glared at Carey sourly and shouted, "You are a miserable enthusiast for asking such a question! Certainly nothing can be done before another Pentecost, when an effusion of miraculous gifts, including the gift of tongues, will give effect to the commission of Christ as at first."

Fortunately for England—and India—William Carey did not believe the proposition. To him it was a neat bit of rationalizing.

Out of the incident came his Enquiry into the Obligations of Christians to Use Means for the Conversion of the Heathens. *Copies swept over the Island Kingdom.*

Carey continued to preach every Sabbath and to mend shoes through the week. Over his bench hung a map of the great unevangelized world. As he worked, he would cast a compassionate eye at the dark areas of the globe which were habitations of cruelty, regions where millions sat in darkness and in the shadow of death, knowing nothing of the mercy of God or the sweetness of the love of Jesus. Out of the cobbler's heart a prayer would wing its course to the heavenly throne-room: "Lord, here am I; send me!"

Nine years after the publication of the Enquiry, *a Baptist Missionary Society was organized, largely through Carey's effort. The society appointed him and another applicant named Thomas to do service in the East Indies.*

It was a dangerous undertaking. Parliament had passed a law declaring that any subject of the king traveling to or from the East Indies without a license from the East India Company would be fined and imprisoned. And like Abraham, the two men were going out not knowing where they would settle.

They never reached their destination. The company officials made them leave the ship at India. There, for forty years Carey studied, taught, suffered, preached, wrote, and worked for reforms in what is possibly the most amazing and heroic chapter in the history of missions.

He translated the New Testament into Kashmiri—the first book ever published in that language. His translations of Christian literature into six other dialects were important works. He mastered and taught Sanskrit, produced Oriental grammars and dictionaries, and brought the study of the languages of India to life, both among natives and civil servants. He agitated against the hideously cruel customs of widow-burning and child-drowning until the British Government finally outlawed the practices. All this was in addition to his evangelistic preaching, which he carried on endlessly. He laid the foundation for the Church in India.

How one man was able to perform the deeds he did in both scholarship and evangelism, and at the same time endure all the hardships thrust upon him, remains a mystery. At first the natives mistrusted and ridiculed him; the foreigners in India held him in contempt. For twelve years he lived with a wife who was deranged. His co-worker turned out to be a personality most eccentric, almost impossible to get along with. His salary was absurdly low, and like the Apostle, he often had to engage in secular work for his support. Incidentally, he became one of the outstanding amateur horticulturalists of his time.

Honors came to him in his last years. Brown University conferred on him the degree of Doctor of Divinity. He was elected as a corresponding member of the Horticultural Society of London, and of the Geological Society, and made a Fellow of the Linnaean Society. The renowned preacher, Robert Hall, spoke of him as, "The first of missionaries, and the instrument of diffusing more religious knowledge among his contemporaries than has fallen to the lot of any individual since the Reformation."

His life-long motto was:

> *"Expect great things from a great God;*
> *Attempt great things for a great God."*

Selections from

An Enquiry into the Obligations of Christians to Use Means for the Conversion of the Heathens

in Which the Religious State of the Different Nations of the World, the Success of Former Undertakings, and the Practicability of Further Undertakings, Are Considered By William Carey

> For there is no difference between the Jew and the Greek; for the same Lord over all, is rich unto all that call upon Him. For whosoever shall call upon the name of the Lord shall be saved. How then shall they call on Him, in Whom they have not believed? And how shall they believe in Him of Whom they have not heard? and how shall they hear without a Preacher? and how shall they preach except they be sent? —PAUL (Romans 10:12-15)

Introduction

AS OUR BLESSED Lord has required us to pray that His kingdom may come, and His will be done on earth as it is in heaven, it becomes us not only to express our desires of that event by words, but to use every lawful method to spread the knowledge of His name. In order to do this, it is necessary that we should become, in some measure, acquainted with the religious state of the world; and as this is an object we should be prompted to pursue, not only the Gospel of our Redeemer, but even by the feelings of humanity, so an inclination to conscientious activity therein would form one of the strongest proofs that we are the subjects of grace, and partakers of that spirit of universal benevolence and genuine philanthropy, which appear so eminent in the character of God Himself.

Sin was introduced amongst the children of men by the fall of Adam, and has ever since been spreading its baneful influence. By changing its appearances to suit the circumstances of the times, it has grown up in ten thousand forms, and constantly counteracted the will and designs of God. One would have supposed that the remembrance of the deluge would have been transmitted from father to son, and have perpetually deterred mankind from transgressing the will of their Maker; but so blinded were they, that in the time of Abraham, gross wickedness prevailed wherever colonies were planted, and the iniquity of the Amorites was great, though not yet full.

After this, idolatry spread more and more, till the seven devoted nations were cut off with the most signal marks of divine displeasure. Still, however, the progress of evil was not stopped, but the Israelites themselves too often joined with the rest of mankind against the God of Israel. In one period the grossest ignorance and barbarism prevailed in the world; and afterwards, in a more enlightened age, the most daring infidelity, and contempt of God; so that the world which was once overrun with ignorance, now by wisdom knew not God, but changed the glory of the incorruptible God as much as in the most barbarous ages, into an image made like to corruptible man, and to birds, and four-footed beasts, and creeping things. Nay, as they increased in science and politeness, they ran into more abundant and extravagant idolatries.

Yet God repeatedly made known his intention to prevail finally over all the power of the Devil, and to destroy all his works, and set up His own kingdom and interest among men, and extend it as universally as Satan had extended his. It was for this purpose that the Messiah came and died, that God might be just, and the justifier of all that should believe in Him. When he had laid down His life, and taken it up again, He sent for His disciples to preach the good tidings to every creature, and to endeavor by all possible methods to bring over a lost world to God. They went forth according to their divine commission, and wonderful success attended their labors; the civilized Greeks, and uncivilized barbarians, each yielded to the cross of Christ, and embraced it as the only way of salvation.

Since the apostolic age many other attempts to spread the Gospel have been made, which have been considerably successful, notwithstanding which a very considerable part of mankind are still involved in all the darkness of heathenism. Some attempts are still making, but they are inconsiderable in comparison of what might be done if the whole body of Christians entered heartily into the spirit of the divine command on this subject. Some think little about it, others are unacquainted with the state of the world, and others love their wealth better than the souls of their fellow creatures.

In order that the subject may be taken into more serious consideration, I shall enquire, whether the commission given by our Lord to His disciples be not still binding on us,—take a short view of former undertakings,—give some accounts of the present state of the world,—consider the practicability of doing something more than is done,—and the duty of Christians in general in this matter.

An Enquiry Whether the Commission Given by Our Lord to His Disciples Be not Still Binding on Us

Our Lord Jesus Christ, a little before His departure, commissioned His apostles to "Go, into all the world, and preach the Gospel to every creature." This commission was as extensive as possible, and laid them under obligation to disperse themselves into every country of the habitable globe, and preach to all the inhabitants, without exception of limitation. They accordingly went forth in obedience to the command, and the power of God evidently wrought with them.

Many attempts of the same kind have been attended with various success; but the work has not been taken up, or prosecuted of late years (except by a few individuals) with that zeal and perseverance with which the primitive Christians went about it. It seems as if many thought the commission was sufficiently put in execution by what the apostles and others have done; that we have enough to do to attend to the salvation of our own countrymen; and that, if God intends the salvation of the heathen, He will some way or other bring them to the Gospel, or the Gospel to them.

It is thus that multitudes sit at ease, and give themselves no concern about the far greater part of their fellow sinners, who to this day are lost in ignorance and idolatry. There also seems to be an opinion existing in the minds of some, that because the apostles were extraordinary officers and have no proper successors, and because many things which were right for them to do would be utterly unwarrantable for us, therefore it may not be immediately binding on us to execute the commission, though it was so upon them. To the consideration of such persons I would offer the following observations.

First, If the command of Christ to teach all nations be restricted to the apostles, or those under the immediate inspiration of the Holy Ghost, then that of baptizing should be so too; and every denomination of Christians, except the Quakers do wrong in baptizing with water at all.

Secondly, If the command of Christ to teach all nations be confined to the apostles, then all such ordinary ministers who have endeavored to carry the Gospel to the heathens, have acted without warrant, and run before they were sent. Yea, and though God has promised the most glorious things to the heathen world by sending His Gospel to them, yet whoever goes first, or indeed at all, with the message, unless he have a new and special commission from heaven, must go without any authority for so doing.

Thirdly, If the command of Christ to teach all nations extend only to the apostles, then, doubtless, the promise of the divine preference in this work must be so limited; but this is worded in such a manner as expressly precludes such an idea. Lo, I am with you always, to the end of the world.

It was not the duty of Paul to preach Christ to the inhabitants of Otaheite, because no such place was then discovered, nor had he any means of coming at them. But none of these things can be alleged by us in behalf of the neglect of the commission given by Christ. We cannot say that it is repealed, like the commands of the ceremonial law; nor can we plead that there are no objects for the command to be exercised upon. Alas! the far greater part of the world, as we shall see presently, are still covered with heathen darkness! Nor can we produce a counter-revelation, concerning any particular nation, like that to Paul and Silas, concerning Bithynia; and, if we could, it would not warrant our sitting still and neglecting all the other parts of the world; for Paul and Silas, when forbidden to preach to those heathens, went elsewhere, and preached to others. Neither can we allege a natural impossibility in the case.

It has been said that we ought not to force our way, but to wait for the openings, and leadings of Providence; but it might with equal propriety be answered in this case, neither ought we to neglect embracing those openings of Providence which daily present themselves to us. What openings of Providence do we wait for? We can neither expect to be transported into the heathen world without ordinary means, nor to be endowed with the gift of tongues, etc., when we arrive there. These would not be providential interpositions, but miraculous ones. Where a command exists nothing can be necessary to render it binding but a removal of those obstacles which render obedience impossible, and these are removed already. Natural impossibility can never be pleaded so long as facts exist to prove the contrary.

Have not the popish missionaries surmounted all those difficulties which we have generally thought to be insuperable? Have not the missionaries of the Unitas Fratrum, or Moravian Brethren, encountered the scorching heat of Abyssinia, and the frozen climes of Greenland, and Labrador, their difficult languages, and savage manners? Or have not English traders, for the sake of gain, surmounted all those things which have generally been counted insurmountable obstacles in the way of preaching the Gospel?

Witness the trade to Persia, the East Indies, China, and Greenland, yea even the accursed slave trade on the coasts of Africa. Men can insinuate themselves into the savor of the most barbarous clans, and uncultivated tribes, for the sake of gain; and how different soever the circumstances of trading and preaching are, yet this will prove the possibility of ministers being introduced there; and if this is but thought a sufficient reason to make the experiment, my point is gained.

It has been said that some learned divines have proved from Scripture that the time is not yet come that the heathen should be converted; and that first the witnesses must be slain, and many other prophecies fulfilled. But admitting this to be the case (which I must doubt) yet if any objection is made from this against preaching to them immediately, it must be founded on one of these things; either that the secret purpose of God is the rule of our duty, and then it must be as bad to pray for them as to preach to them; or else that none shall be converted in the heathen world till the universal downpouring of the Spirit in the last days. But this objection comes too late, for the success of the Gospel has been very considerable in many places already.

It has been objected that there are multitudes in our own nation, and within our immediate spheres of action, who are as ignorant as the South Sea savages, and that therefore we have work enough at home, without going into other countries. That there are thousands in our own land as far from God as possible, I readily grant, and that this ought to excite us to tenfold diligence in our work, and in attempts to spread divine knowledge amongst them is a certain fact; but that it ought to supersede all attempts to spread the Gospel in foreign parts seems to want proof. Our own countrymen have the means of grace, and may attend on the Word preached if they choose it. They have the means of knowing the truth, and faithful ministers are placed in almost every part of the land, whose spheres of action might be much extended if their congregations were but more hearty and active in the cause; but with them the case is widely different, who have no Bible, no written language (which many of them have not), no ministers, no good civil government, nor any of those advantages which we have. Pity therefore, humanity, and much more Christianity, call loudly for every possible exertion to introduce the Gospel amongst them.

Section II. Containing a Short Review of Former Undertakings for the Conversion of the Heathen

[The story of missions in the book of Acts is omitted.]

Thus far the history of the Acts of the Apostles informs us of the success of the Word in the primitive times; and history informs us of its being preached about this time in many other places. Peter speaks of a church in Babylon; Paul proposed a journey to Spain, and it is generally believed he went there, and likewise came to France and Britain. Andrew preached to the Scythians, north of the Black Sea. John is said to have preached in India, and we know that he was at the Isle of Patmos, in the Achipelago. Philip is reported to have preached in upper Asia, Scythia, and Phrygia; Bartholomew in India, on this side the Ganges, Phrygia, and Armenia; Matthew in Arabia, or Asiatic Ethiopia, and Parthia; Thomas in India, as far as the coast of Coromandel, and some say in the island of Ceylon; Simon, the Canaanite, in

Egypt, Cyrene, Mauritania, Libya, and other parts of Africa, and from thence to have come to Britain; and Jude is said to have been principally engaged in the lesser Asia, and Greece.

Their labors were evidently very extensive, and very successful; so that Pliny the Younger, who lived soon after the death of the apostles, in a letter to the emperor Trajan, observed that Christianity had spread, not only through towns and cities, but also through whole countries. Indeed before this, in the time of Nero it was so prevalent that it was thought necessary to oppose it by an Imperial Edict, and accordingly the proconsuls, and other governors, were commissioned to destroy it.

After this they had great encouragement under several emperors, particularly Constantine and Theodosius, and a very great work of God was carried on; but the ease and affluence which in these times attended the church, served to introduce a flood of corruption, which by degrees brought on the whole system of popery, by means of which all appeared to be lost again; and Satan set up his kingdom of darkness, deceit, and human authority over conscience, through all the Christian world.

In the time of Constantine, one Frumentius was sent to preach to the Indians, and met with great success. A young woman who was a Christian, being taken captive by the Iberians, or Georgians, near the Caspian Sea, informed them of the truths of Christianity, and was so much regarded that they sent to Constantine for ministers to come and preach the Word to them. About the same time some barbarous nations having made irruptions into Thrace, carried away several Christians captive, who preached the Gospel; by which means the inhabitants upon the Rhine, and the Danube, the Celtae, and some other parts of Gaul, were brought to embrace Christianity. About this time also James of Nisbia, went into Persia to strengthen the Christians, and preach to the heathens; and his success was so great that Adiabene was almost entirely Christian. About the year 372, one Moses, a monk, went to preach to the Saracens, who then lived in Arabia, where he had great success; and at this time the Goths, and other northern nations, had the kingdom of Christ further extended amongst them, but which was very soon corrupted with Arianism.

About the year 500, the Scythians overran Bulgaria, and Christianity was extirpated; but about 870 they were reconverted. Poland began to be brought over about the same time, and afterwards, about 960 or 990, the work was further extended amongst the Poles and Prussians. The work was begun in Norway in 960, and in Muscovy in 989; the Swedes propagated Christianity in Finland, in 1168; Luthuania became Christian in 1386, and Samogitia in 1439.

The Spaniards forced popery upon the inhabitants of South America, and the Portuguese in Asia. The Jesuits were sent into China in 1552. Xavier, whom they call the apostle of the Indians, labored in the East Indies and Japan, from 1541 to 1552, and several missions of Capuchins were sent to Africa in the seventeenth century. But blind zeal, gross superstition, and infamous cruelties, so marked the appearances of religion all this time, the professors of Christianity needed conversion, as much as the heathen world.

A few people had fled from the general corruption, and lived obscurely in the valleys of Piedmont and Savoy, who were like the seed of the church. Some of them were now and then necessitated to travel into other parts, where they faithfully testified against the corruptions of the times. About 1369 Wickliffe began to preach the faith in England, and his preaching and writings were the means of the conversion of great numbers, many of whom became excellent preachers; and a work was begun which afterwards spread in England, Hungary, Bohemia, Germany, Switzerland, and many other places.

John Huss and Jerome of Prague, preached boldly and successfully in Bohemia and the adjacent parts. In the following century Luther, Calvin, Melanchthon, Bucer, Martyn, and many others, stood up against all the rest of the world; they preached, and prayed, and wrote; and nations agreed one after another to cast off the yoke of popery, and to embrace the doctrine of the Gospel.

In England, episcopal tyranny succeeded to popish cruelty, which, in the year 1620, obliged many pious people to leave their native land and settle in America; these were followed by others in 1629, who laid the foundations of several Gospel churches, which have increased amazingly since that time, and the Redeemer has fixed His throne in that country, where but a little time ago, Satan had universal dominion.

Section IV. The Practicability of Something Being Done, More Than What Is Done, for the Conversion of the Heathen

The impediments in the way of carrying the Gospel among the heathen must arise, I think, from one or other of the following things; —either their distance from us, their barbarous and savage manner of living, the danger of being killed by them, the difficulty of procuring the necessaries of life, or the unintelligibleness of their languages.

First, As to their distance from us, whatever objections might have been made on that account before the invention of the mariner's compass, nothing can be alleged for it, with any color of plausibility in the present age. Men can now sail with as much certainty through the Great South Sea, as they can through the Mediterranean, or any lesser Sea. Yea, and providence seems in a manner to invite us to the trial, as there are to our knowledge trading companies, whose commerce lies in many of the places where these barbarians dwell.

Secondly, As to their uncivilized, and barbarous way of living, this can be no objection to any, except those whose love of ease renders them unwilling to expose themselves to inconveniences for the good of others.

It was no objection to apostles and their successors, who went among the barbarous Germans and Gauls, and still more barbarous Britons! They did not wait for the ancient inhabitants of these countries to be civilized before they could be Christianized, but went simply with the doctrine of the Cross; and Tertullian could boast that "those parts of Britain which were proof against the Roman armies, were conquered by the Gospel of Christ."

It was no objection to an Eliot, or a Brainerd, in later times. They went forth, and encountered every difficulty of the kind, and found that cordial reception of the Gospel produced those happy effects which the longest intercourse with Europeans, without it, could never accomplish. It is no objection to commercial men. It only requires that we should have as much love to the souls of our fellow creatures, and fellow sinners, as they have for the profits arising from a few otter-skins, and all these difficulties would be easily surmounted.

After all, the uncivilized state of the heathen, instead of affording an objection against preaching the Gospel to them, ought to furnish an argument for it. Can we as men, or as Christians, hear that a great part of our fellow creatures, whose souls are as immortal as ours, and who are as capable as ourselves, of adoring the Gospel, and contributing by their preaching, writings, or practices to the glory of our Redeemer's name, and the good of his church, are enveloped in ignorance and barbarism? Can we hear that they are without the Gospel, without government, without laws, and without arts and sciences, and not exert ourselves to introduce amongst them the sentiments of men, and of Christians? Would not the spread of the Gospel be the most effectual means of their civilization? Would not that make them useful members of society?

Thirdly, In respect to the danger of being killed by them, it is true that whoever does go must put his life in his hand, and not consult with flesh and blood; but do not the goodness of the cause, the duties incumbent on us as the creatures of God, and Christians, and the perishing state of our fellow men, loudly call upon us to venture all and use every warrantable exertion for their benefit?

Paul and Barnabas, who hazarded their lives for the name of our Lord Jesus Christ, were not blamed as being rash, but commended for so doing, while John Mark who through timidity of mind deserted them in their perilous undertaking, was branded with censure. After all, as has been already observed, I greatly question whether most of the barbarities practiced by the savages upon those who have visited them, have not originated in some real or supposed affront, and were therefore, more properly, acts of self-defense, than proofs of ferocious dispositions. No wonder if the imprudence of sailors should prompt them to offend the simple savage, and the offense be resented; but Eliot, Brainerd, and the Moravian missionaries, have been very seldom molested. Nay, in general the heathen have shewed a willingness to hear the word; and have principally expressed their hatred of Christianity on account of the vices of nominal Christians.

Fourthly, As to the difficulty of procuring the necessaries of life, this would not be so great as may appear at first sight; for though we could not procure European food, yet we might procure such as the natives of those countries which we visit, subsist upon themselves. And this would only be passing through what we have virtually engaged in by entering on the ministerial office.

A Christian minister is a person who in a peculiar sense is not his own; he is the servant of God, and therefore ought to be wholly devoted to Him. By entering on that sacred office he solemnly undertakes to be always engaged, as much as possible, in the Lord's work, and not to choose his own pleasure, or employment, or pursue the ministry as something that is to subserve his own ends, or interests, or as a kind of by-work. He engages to go where God pleases, and to do, or endure what He sees fit to command, or call him to, in the exercise of his function. He virtually bids farewell to friends, pleasures, and comforts, and stands in readiness to endure the greatest sufferings in the work of his Lord and Master.

It is inconsistent for ministers to please themselves with thoughts of a numerous auditory, cordial friends, a civilized country, legal protection, affluence, splendor, or even a competency. The slights, and hatred of men, and even pretended friends, gloomy prisons, and tortures, the society of barbarians of uncouth speech, miserable accommodations in wretched wildernesses, hunger and thirst, nakedness, weariness, and painfulness, hard work, but little worldly encouragement, should rather be the objects of their expectation.

Thus the apostles acted, in the primitive times, and endured hardness, as good soldiers of Jesus Christ; and though we, living in a civilized country where Christianity is protected by law, are not called to suffer these things in staying while we continue here, yet I question whether all are justified in staying here, while so many are perishing without means of grace in other lands.

Sure I am that it is entirely contrary to the spirit of the Gospel for its ministers to enter upon it from interested motives, or with great worldly expectations. On the contrary the commission is a sufficient call to them to venture all, and, like the primitive Christians, go everywhere preaching the Gospel.

It might be necessary, however, for two, at least, to go together, and in general I should think it best that they should be married men, and to prevent their time from being employed in procuring necessaries, two, or more, other persons, with their wives and families, might also accompany them, who should be wholly employed in providing for them.

In most countries it would be necessary for them to cultivate a little spot of ground just for their support, which would be a resource to them, whenever their supplies failed. Not to mention the advantages they would reap from each other's company, it would take off the enormous expense which has always attended undertakings of this kind, the first expense being the whole; for though a large colony needs support for a considerable time, yet so small a number would, upon receiving the first crop, maintain themselves. They would have the advantage of choosing their situation, their wants would be few; the women, and even the children, would be necessary for domestic purposes; and a few articles of stock, as a cow or two, and a bull, and a few other cattle of both sexes, a very few utensils of husbandry, and some corn to sov their land, would be sufficient.

Fifthly, As to learning their languages, the same means would be found necessary here as in trade between different nations. In some cases interpreters might be obtained, who might be employed for a time; and where these were not to be found, the missionaries must have patience, and mingle with the people, till they have learned so much of their language as to be able to communicate their ideas to them in it. It is well known to require no very extraordinary talents to learn, in the space of a year, or two at most, the language of any people upon earth, so much of it at least, as to be able to convey any sentiments we wish to their understandings.

The missionaries must be men of great piety, prudence, courage, and forbearance; of undoubted orthodoxy in their sentiments, and must enter with all their hearts into the spirit of their mission; they must be willing to leave all the comforts of the life behind them, and to encounter all the hardships of a torrid, or a frigid climate, an uncomfortable manner of living, and every other inconvenience that can attend this undertaking. Clothing, a few knives, powder and shot, fishing-tackle, and the articles of husbandry above-mentioned, must be provided for them; and when arrived at the place of their destination, their first business must be to gain some acquaintance with the language of the natives (for which purpose two would be better than one), and by all lawful means to endeavor to cultivate a friendship with them, and as soon as possible let them know the errand for which they were sent.

They must endeavor to convince them that it was their good alone which induced them to forsake their friends and all the comforts of their native country. They must be very careful not to resent injuries which may be offered to them, not to think highly of themselves, so as to despise the poor heathens, and by those means lay a foundation for their resentment, or rejection of the Gospel. They must take every opportunity of doing them good, and laboring, and traveling, night and day, they must instruct, exhort, and rebuke, with all long suffering, and anxious desire for them, and, above all, must be instant in prayer for the effusion of the Holy Spirit upon the people of their charge. Let but missionaries of the above description engage in the work, and we shall see that it is not impracticable.

It might likewise be of importance, if God should bless their labors, for them to encourage any appearances of gifts amongst the people of their charge; if such should be raised up, many advantages would be derived from their knowledge of the language and customs of their countrymen; and their change of conduct would give great weight to their ministrations.

Section V. An Enquiry into the Duty of Christians in General, and What Means Ought to be Used, in Order to Promote This Work

If the prophecies concerning the increase of Christ's kingdom be true, and if what has been advanced, concerning the commission given by Him to His disciples being obligatory on us, be just, it must be inferred that all Christians ought heartily to concur with God in promoting His glorious designs, for he that is joined to the Lord is one Spirit.

One of the first, and most important of those duties which are incumbent upon us, is fervent and united prayer. However, the influence of the Holy Spirit may be set at nought, and run down by many, it will be found upon trial, that all means which we can use, without it, will be ineffectual. If a temple is raised for God in the heathen world, it will not be by might, nor by power, nor by the authority of the magistrate, or the eloquence of the orator; but by my Spirit, saith the Lord of Hosts. We must therefore be in real earnest in supplicating His blessings upon our labors.

The most glorious works of grace that have ever taken place have been in answer to prayer which should encourage us to persist, and increase in that important duty. I trust our monthly prayer-meetings for the success of the Gospel have not been in vain. It is true a want of importunity too generally attends our prayers; yet unimportunate, and feeble as they have been, it is to be believed that God has heard, and in a measure answered them. The churches that have engaged in the practice have in general since that time been evidently on the increase; some controversies which have long perplexed and divided the church, are more clearly stated than ever; there are calls to preach the Gospel in many places where it has not been usually published.

A glorious door is opened, and is likely to be opened wider and wider, by the spread of civil and religious liberty, accompanied also by a diminution of the spirit of popery; a noble effort has been made to abolish the inhuman slave trade, and though at present it has not been so successful as might be wished, yet it is to be hoped it will be persevered in, till it is accomplished. In the meantime it is a satisfaction to consider that the late defeat of the abolition of the slave trade has proved the occasion of a praiseworthy effort to introduce a free settlement, at Sierra Leone, on the coast of Africa; an effort which, if succeeded with a divine blessing, not only promises to open a way for honorable commerce with that extensive country, and for the civilization of its inhabitants, but may prove the happy means of introducing amongst them the Gospel of our Lord Jesus Christ.

These are events that ought not to be overlooked; they are not to be reckoned small things; and yet perhaps they are small compared with what might have been expected, if all had cordially entered into the spirit of the proposal, so as to have made the cause of Christ their own, or in other words to have been so solicitous about it, as if their own advantage depended upon its success. If a holy solicitude had prevailed in all the assemblies of Christians in behalf of their Redeemer's kingdom, we might probably have seen before now, not only an open door for the Gospel, but many running to and fro, and knowledge increased; of a diligent use of those means which providence has put in our power, accompanied with a greater blessing than ordinary from heaven.

Many can do nothing but pray, and prayer is perhaps the only thing in which Christians of all denominations can cordially and unreservedly unite; but in this we may all be one, and in this the strictest unanimity ought to prevail. Were the whole body thus animated by one soul, with what pleasure would Christians attend on all the duties of religion, and with what delight would their ministers attend on all the business of their calling.

We must not be contented however with praying, without exerting ourselves in the use of means for the obtaining of those things we pray for. Were the children of light, but as wise in their generation as the children of this world, they would stretch every nerve to gain so glorious a prize, nor ever imagine that it was to be obtained in any other way.

When a trading company have obtained their charter they usually go to its utmost limits; and their stocks, their ships, their officers, and men are so chosen, and regulated, as to be likely to answer their purpose; but they do not stop here, for encouraged by the prospect of success, they use every effort, cast their bread upon the waters, cultivate friendship with every one from whose information they expect the least advantage. They cross the widest and most tempestuous seas, and encounter the most unfavorable climates; they introduce themselves into the most barbarous nations, and sometimes undergo the most affecting hardships; their minds continue in a state of anxiety and suspense, and a longer delay than usual in the arrival of their vessels agitates them with a thousand changeful thoughts, and foreboding apprehensions, which continue till the rich returns are safe arrived in port.

But why these fears? Whence all these disquietudes, and this labor? Is it not because their souls enter into the spirit of the project and their happiness in a manner depends on its success? Christians are a body whose truest interest lies in the exaltation of the Messiah's kingdom. Their charter is very extensive, their encouragements exceeding great, and the returns promised infinitely superior to all the gains of the most lucrative fellowship. Let then every one in his station consider himself as bound to act with all his might, and in every possible way for God.

Suppose a company of serious Christians, ministers and private persons, were to form themselves into a society, and make a number of rules respecting the regulation of the plan, and the persons who are to be employed as missionaries, the means of defraying the expense, etc. This society must consist of persons whose hearts are in the work, men of serious religion, and possessing a spirit of perseverance; there must be a determination not to admit any person who is not of this description, or to retain him longer than he answers to it.

From such a society a committee might be appointed whose business it should be to procure all the information they could upon the subject, to receive contributions, to enquire into the characters, tempers, abilities and religious views of the missionaries, and also to provide them with necessaries for their undertakings.

They must also pay a great attention to the views of those who undertake this work; for want of this the missions to the Spice Islands, sent by the Dutch East India Company, were soon corrupted, many going more for the sake of settling in a place where temporal gain invited them, than of preaching to the poor Indians. This soon introduced a number of indolent, or profligate persons, whose lives were a scandal to the doctrines which they preached; and by means of whom the Gospel was ejected from Ternate, in 1694, and Christianity fell into great disrepute in other places.

If there is any reason for me to hope that I shall have any influence upon any of my brethren, and fellow Christians, probably it may be more especially amongst them of my own denomination. I would therefore propose that such a society and committee should be formed amongst the particular Baptist denomination.

I do not mean by this, in any wise to confine it to one denomination of Christians. I wish with all my heart, that every one who loves our Lord Jesus Christ in sincerity, would in some way or other engage in it. But in the present divided state of Christendom, it would be more likely for good to be done by each denomination engaging separately in the work, than if they were to embark in it conjointly. There is room enough for us all, without interfering with each other; and if no unfriendly interference took place, each denomination would bear good will to the other, and wish, and pray for its success, considering it as upon the whole friendly to the great cause of true religion; but if all were intermingled, it is likely their private discords might throw a damp upon their spirits, and much retard their public usefulness.

In respect to contributions for defraying the expenses, money will doubtless be wanting; and suppose the rich were to embark a portion of that wealth over which God has made them stewards, in this important undertaking, perhaps there are few ways that would turn to a better account at last.

Nor ought it to be confined to the rich; if persons in more moderate circumstances were to devote a portion, suppose a tenth, of their annual increase to the Lord, it would not only correspond with the practice of the Israelites, who lived under the Mosaic economy, but of the patriarchs Abraham, Isaac, and Jacob, before that dispensation commenced. Many of our most eminent forefathers amongst the Puritans followed that practice; and if that were but attended to now there would not only be enough to support the ministry of the Gospel at home, and to encourage village preaching in our respective neighborhoods, but to defray the expenses of carrying the Gospel into the heathen world.

If congregations were to open subscriptions of one penny, or more per week, according to their circumstances, and deposit it as a fund for the propagation of the Gospel, much might be raised in this way. By such simple means they might soon have it in their power to introduce the preaching of the Gospel into most of the villages in England; where, though men are placed whose business it should be to give light to those who sit in darkness, it is well known that they have it not. Where there was no person to open his house for the reception of the Gospel, some other building might be procured for a small sum, and even then something considerable might be spared for the Baptist, or other committees, for propagating the Gospel amongst the heathen.

Many persons have of late left off the use of West India sugar on account of the iniquitous manner in which it is obtained. Those families who have done so, and have not substituted anything else in its place, have not only cleansed their hands of blood, but have made a saving to their families, some of sixpence, and some of a shilling a week. If this, or a part of this were appropriated to the uses before-mentioned, it would abundantly suffice. We have only to keep the end in view, and have our hearts thoroughly engaged in the pursuit of it, and means will not be very difficult.

We are exhorted to lay up treasure in heaven, where neither moth nor rust doth corrupt, nor thieves break through and steal. It is also declared that whatsoever a man soweth, that shall he also reap. These Scriptures teach us that the enjoyments of the life to come, bear a near relation to that which now is; a relation similar to that of the harvest, and the seed. It is true all the reward is of mere grace, but it is nevertheless encouraging; what a treasure, what a harvest must await such characters as Paul, and Eliot, and Brainerd, and others, who have given themselves wholly to the work of the Lord. What a heaven will it be to see the many myriads of poor heathens, of Britons amongst the rest, who by their labors have been brought to the knowledge of God. Surely a crown of rejoicing like this is worth aspiring to. Surely it is worthwhile to lay ourselves out with all our might, in promoting the cause, and the kingdom of Christ.

ROBERT MURRAY McCHEYNE 1813–1843

One day a boy who had run away from home and gotten in trouble received a letter from his pastor, Robert Murray McCheyne.

Following the salutation, Mr. McCheyne plunged into the heart of the matter: "Would the forgiveness of sins make you less happy than you are: Perhaps you will tell me that you are very happy as you are. I quite believe you. I know that I was very happy when I was unforgiven. . . . I fancy few boys were ever happier than I was. No sorrows clouded my brow—no tears filled my eyes, unless over some nice story-book; so that I know that you say quite true, when you say that you are happy as you are. But ah! is not this just the saddest thing of all, that you should be happy whilst you are a child of wrath,—that you should smile, and eat, and drink, and be merry and sleep sound, when this very night you may be in hell? Happy while unforgiven!— a terrible happiness. . . . Now, do you think it would not give you more happiness to be forgiven,—to be able to put on Jesus, and say, 'God's anger is turned away'? Would you not be happier at work, and happier in the house, and happier in your bed? I can assure you the pleasures of being forgiven are as superior to the pleasures of an unforgiven man, as heaven is higher than hell. The peace of being forgiven reminds me of the calm, blue sky, which no earthly clamors can disturb. It lightens all labor, sweetens every morsel of bread, and makes a sick-bed all soft and downy; yea, it takes away the sorrow of death."

The letter illustrates the depth of yearning that McCheyne exercised over mortal souls. It is not to be wondered that, when he preached, rocky hearts were cracked and tears washed many a cheek. It is not to be wondered that all Scotland was moved by his deadly earnestness. It is not to be wondered that, on the day of his funeral, business was suspended in his parish, and every street, every window was crowded with those who knew that a prince had fallen in Israel. Not a few hardened characters felt a secret awe creep over them as they followed the funeral procession to the cemetery.

McCheyne attended Edinburgh University and after graduation continued his studies at the Divinity Hall, where he sat at the feet of the scholarly Dr. Thomas Chalmers. He had decided to go into the ministry chiefly to please his brother. It was in seminary that he entered into conscious fellowship with Jesus Christ and was given a clear view of what it meant to be justified by faith. He knew then that he must preach the unsearchable riches of Christ.

He had only one charge in his ministerial career, St. Peter's Presbyterian Church in Dundee. But his flaming holiness and his zeal for the expansion of Zion's walls made a wide impact. Had his health permitted, he would undoubtedly have carried the Gospel around the world. He did make one trip to Palestine, and preached to Arabs and Jews. And his diary is studded with notes showing what a prominent part the Great Commission played in his reflections. "Why is a missionary life so often an object of my thought?" "I am now willing, if God shall open the way, to go to India." "To go, or to stay,—to be here till death, or to visit foreign shores, whatsoever, wheresoever, whensoever Thou pleasest."

When the youthful minister passed along the streets of Dundee, people said of him what the Shunammite woman said of Elisha, "This is an holy man of God." McCheyne did not think so. The banner over him was humility. "What a mass of corruption I have been!" "How great a portion of my life have I spent wholly without God in the world, given up to sense and to the perishing things around me!" "I know I am proud; and yet I do not know the half of that pride." "What change is there in the heart! Wild, earthy affections there are here; strong, coarse passions; bands both of iron and silk."

He deplored controversy for the sake of controversy, yet was not afraid to stand up and be numbered with the minority when an issue was raised touching the honor of Christ the King. There were giants in those days, men of intellectual stature, moral girth, and spiritual power—leaders like Thomas Chalmers and the Bonar brothers with whom McCheyne stood shoulder-to-shoulder in the fight against unbelief in the high councils of the Church and against state control of the body of Christ. Those hardy sons of Scotland were not only fair as the moon and clear as the sun, they were also terrible as an army with banners.

He departed to be with Christ at thirty, the age when his Redeemer began His public ministry. Excerpts from his diary are like exhalations from an eastern garden out of which flows the scent of camphor and spikenard, calamus and cinnamon, myrrh and aloes, with all the chief spices. Andrew Bonar's Memoirs and Remains of Robert Murray McCheyne has inspired tens of thousands of readers. With superior artlessness it tells the story of one of God's noblemen who, "during the last years of his short life, walked calmly in almost unbroken fellowship with the Father and the Son."

Christ, the Son of God—Our Only Message!

IT WAS Jesus Christ and Him crucified that John preached. "That which we have seen and heard, declare we unto you." This was the preaching of John the Baptist: "Behold the Lamb of God, which taketh away the sins of the world." He pointed to Jesus. This was the preaching of Philip (Acts 8:5): "Philip went down to Samaria, and preached Christ unto them." And when he came to the Ethiopian eunuch, "he preached unto him Jesus." This was the preaching of Paul: "I determined to know nothing among you, but Jesus Christ and Him crucified." This was the beginning, and middle, and end of the preaching of Paul.

This was the preaching of John: To declare all that he had seen with his eyes, heard with his ears, handled with his hands, of Immanuel—this was the object of his life, this was the Alpha and Omega of his preaching. He knew that Jesus was like the alabaster box, full of spikenard, very costly; and his whole labor was to break the box and pour forth the good ointment before the eyes of fainting sinners, that they might be attracted by the sweet savor. He knew that Jesus was a bundle of myrrh, and His whole life was spent in opening it out to sinners, that they might be overcome by the refreshing odors. He carried about the savor of Christ with him wherever he went. He knew that Jesus was the Balm of Gilead, and his labor was to open out this bruised balm before the eyes of sick souls, that they might be healed.

I. The things John preached concerning Christ.

1. His eternity.—"That which was from the beginning." John had often heard Jesus speak of His eternity. "In the beginning was the Word." "Before Abraham was, I am," He remembered how Jesus said in prayer in the garden, "Glorify me with the glory which I had with Thee before the world was." "Thou lovedst Me before the foundation of the world." John thus knew that He was the Eternal One, that He was before all visible things, for He made them all. By Him God made the world. Even at the time John was leaning on His bosom, he felt that it was the bosom of the Uncreated One. John always declared this; he loved to make Him known. O beloved! if you have come to lean on the bosom of Jesus, you have come to the Uncreated One—the Eternal One.

2. His eternal pre-existence with the Father,—John knew, from Proverbs 8:30, that Jesus had been with the Father: "Then I was by Him, as one brought up with Him, and I was daily His delight, re-

joicing always before Him." He had heard Jesus tell many of the secrets of His Father's bosom, from which he knew that He had been with the Father: "All things that I have heard of My Father I have made known unto you." He had heard Jesus plainly say, "I came forth from the Father, and am come into the world." "Again I leave the world, and go to the Father." John felt, even when Jesus was washing his feet, that this was the man that was God's fellow. Even when he saw Jesus on the cross, with His pale lips and bleeding hands and feet, like a tortured worm, and "no man," he knew that this was the Man that was God's Fellow. He lived to declare this. Do you thus look to Jesus? Have you beheld the glory, as of the only begotten of the Father, full of grace and truth? O tempest-tossed soul, this is He that comes to save thee!

3. His eternal life.—John knew that Jesus was the Author of all natural life, that not a man breathes, no beast of the forest roars, no bird stoops on the wing, but they all receive the stream of life from the hand of Immanuel. He had seen Jesus raise the ruler's daughter from the dead, and call Lazarus from the tomb. He knew that Jesus was the Author of all life in the soul. He had heard Jesus say, "As the Father raiseth up the dead, and quickeneth whom He will, even so the Son quickeneth whom He will." "My sheep know My voice, and I give unto them eternal life."

Above all, he had felt in his own soul that Christ was the Eternal Life. In that morning, when he sat with his father Zebedee in the boat, mending their nets, Jesus said, "Follow me!" and the life entered into his soul, and he found it a never-failing spring of life. Christ was his life; therefore did he make Him known as the Eternal Life. Even when he saw Him give up the ghost; when he saw His pale, lifeless body, the stiff hands and feet, the glazed eye, the body cold as the rocky tomb where they laid Him; still he felt that this was the Eternal Life. O beloved! do you believe that He is the life of the world? Some of you feel your soul to be dead—lifeless in prayer—lifeless in praise. Oh look on Him whom John declares to you! All is death without Him. Bring your dead soul into union with Him, and He will give you eternal life.

4. His Being Manifested.—O beloved, if Jesus had not been manifested, you had never been saved! It would have been quite righteous in God to have kept His Son in His own bosom, to have kept that jewel in His own place upon the throne of heaven. God would have been the same lovely God; but we would have lain down in a burning hell. If that Eternal Life which was with the Father had remained in His glory as the Living One, then you and I would have borne our own curse. But He was manifested: "God was manifest in the flesh, justified in the Spirit, seen of angels, believed on in the world, received up into glory."

John saw Him: he saw His lovely countenance; he beheld His glory, as the glory of the only begotten of the Father, full of grace and truth. He saw that better Sun veiled with flesh that could not keep the beams of His Godhead from shining through. He saw Him on the Mount, when His face shone like the sun. He saw Him in the garden, when He lay upon the ground. He saw Him on the cross, when He hung between earth and heaven. He looked upon Him—many a time he looked upon His heavenly countenance—his eye met His eye.

He heard Him, heard the voice that said, "Let there be light!" He heard the voice like the sound of many waters. He heard all His gracious words—His words concerning God and the way of peace. He heard Him say to a sinner, "Be of good cheer, thy sins are forgiven thee."

He handled Him, he put his hands in His hands, his arms around His arms, and his head upon His bosom. Perhaps he handled His body when it was taken from the cross, touched the cold clay of Immanuel. O beloved, it is a manifested Christ we declare unto you. It is not the Son in the bosom of the Father; that would never have saved you. It is Jesus manifested in flesh. The Son of God living and dying as man in the stead of sinners; Him we declare unto you.

Learn the true way of coming to peace.—It is by looking to a manifested Jesus. Some of you think you will come to peace by looking in to your own heart. Your eye is riveted there. You watch every change there. If you could only see a glimpse of light there, oh, what joy it would give you! If you could only see a melting of your stony heart, if you could only see your heart turning to God, if you could only see a glimpse of the image of Jesus in your heart, you would be at peace; but you cannot, all is dark within. Oh, dear souls, it is not there you will find peace! You must avert the eye from your bosom altogether. You must look to a declared Christ. Spread out the record of God concerning His Son. The Gospels are the narrative of the heart of Jesus, of the work of Jesus, of the grace of Jesus. Spread them out before the eye of your mind, till they fill your eye. Cry for the Spirit to breathe over the page, to make a manifested Christ stand out plainly before you; and the moment that you are willing to believe all that is there spoken concerning Jesus, that moment you will wipe away your tears, and change your sighs for a new song of praise.

II. The object John had in view by preaching Christ.

1. That ye may have fellowship with us.—To have fellowship with another is to have things in common with him. Thus, in Acts. 4:32, the first Christians were "of one heart and of one soul; neither said any that aught of the things which he possessed was his own, but they had all things in common." They had all their goods in common; they shared what they had with one another. That is what John desired in

spiritual things—that we should share with him in his spiritual things, share and share alike.

In Forgiveness.—Some people think it impossible to have the same forgiveness that the apostles had, that it would be very bold to think of tasting the same. But is it not far bolder to say that John is a liar, and that the Holy Spirit is a liar? For he here says plainly, that all his preaching, and all his desire was, that you should have fellowship with Him. Yes, sinner, forgiveness is as open to you as it was to John. The blood that washed him is ready to wash you as white as snow. John had the same need of Christ that the vilest of you have. Only look to a declared Immanuel; clear your eye from unbelief, and look at a freely-revealed Jesus, and you will find the same forgiveness is as free to you as it was to John.

In the same love of Jesus.—John was the disciple whom Jesus loved. Just as Daniel was the prophet whom He greatly loved," a man greatly beloved," so John was the disciple whom Jesus loved. At the Last Supper which Jesus had in this world, John leaned upon His bosom. He had the nearest place to the heart of Christ of any in all this world. Perhaps you think it is impossible you can ever come to that. Some of you are trembling afar off; but you, too, if you will only look where John points you, if you will only believe the full record of God about Jesus, will share the love of Jesus with John, you will be one of His peculiarly beloved ones. Those that believe most, get most love; they come nearest to Jesus—they do, as it were, lay their head on His breast; and no doubt you will one day really share that bosom with John. If you believe little, you will keep far off from Jesus.

In the same fatherly dealings as John.—John experienced many wonderful dealings of God. He experienced many of the prunings of the Father. He was a fruitful branch, and the Father pruned him that he might bring forth more fruit. When he was very old, he was banished to Patmos, an island in the Aegean Sea, and, it is supposed, made a slave in the mines there. He was a companion in tribulation; but he had many sweet shinings of the Father's love to his soul. He had sweet revelations of Christ in the time of his affliction; and he was joyfully delivered out of all his troubles. He experienced peculiarly the fatherly dealings of God. And so may you do, believer. Look where John looked, believe as John believed; and, like him, you will find that you have a Father in heaven, who will care for you, who will correct you in measure, who will stay His rough wind in the day of His east wind, who will preserve you unto His heavenly kingdom.

2. That ye may have fellowship with the Father.—O beloved, this is so wonderful, that I could not have believed it, if I had not seen it! Shall a hell-deserving worm come to share with the holy God? Oh the depth and the length of the love of God, it passeth knowledge!

In His holiness.—A natural man has not a spark of God's holiness in him. There is a kind of goodness about you. You may be kind, pleasant, agreeable, good-natured, amiable people; there may be a kind of integrity about you, so that you are above stealing or lying; but as long as you are in a natural state, there is not a grain of God's holiness in you. You have not a grain of that absolute hatred against all sin which God has; you have none of that flaming love for what is lovely, pure, holy, which dwells in the heart of God. But the moment you believe on a manifested Christ, that moment you receive the Spirit, the same Spirit which dwells in the infinite bosom of the Father dwelleth in you; so you become partakers of God's holiness, you become partakers of the Divine nature. You will not be as holy as God; but the same stream that flows through the heart of God will be given you. Ah! does not your heart break to be holier? Look then to Jesus, and abide in Him, and you will share the same spirit with God Himself.

In His joy.—No joy is like the Divine joy. It is infinite, full, eternal, pure unmingled joy. It is light, without any cloud to darken it; it is calm, without any breath to ruffle it. Clouds and darkness are round about Him, storms and fire go before Him; but within all is peace ineffable, unchangeable. Believers in some measure share in this joy. First, All things happen according to the good pleasure of His will. He has foreordained whatsoever comes to pass. Nothing comes unprepared upon God. Many things are hateful in His sight, yet, looking on the whole, He can delight in all. If you have come to Christ, you will have some drops of His joy. You can look upon all events with a calm, holy joy, knowing that your Father's will and purposes alone shall stand. Second, The conversion of souls. There is joy in the presence of the angels of God over one sinner repenting, more than over ninety-nine who need no repentance. I have no doubt that this is one of the great elements of His joy—seeing souls brought into His favour. He loves to save; He delighteth in mercy; He delights when He can be a just God and a Saviour. If you are come to Christ, you will have the same joy.

3. That ye may have fellowship with the Son.

We share with the Son in His justification.—Once Jesus was unjustified; once there were sins laid to His charge—the sins of many. It was this that occasioned His agony in the garden, on the cross. His only comfort was, "He is near that justifieth me." He knew the time would be short. But now the wrath of God has all fallen upon Him. The thunderclouds of God's anger have spent all their lightnings on His head. The vials of God's wrath have poured out their last drops upon Him. He is now justified from all the sins that were laid upon Him. He has left them with the graveclothes. His fellow men and devils laid all sins to His charge; He was silent. Do you believe this record concerning the Son? Do you cleave to Jesus as yours? Then you have fellowship with Him in His justification. You are as much justified as Christ is. There is as little guilt lying upon you as there is upon Christ. The vials of wrath have not another drop for you. You are justified from all things.

In His adoption.—When Jesus went up to heaven, He said, "I go to My Father." When He entered heaven, the word of God was "Thou art My Son; sit Thou on My right hand until I make Thine enemies Thy footstool." Oh, it was a blessed exchange, when He left the frowns and curses of this world for the embrace of His Father's arms; when He left the thorny crown for a crown of glory; when He came from under the wrath of God into the fatherly love of God! Such is your change, you that believe in Jesus. You have fellowship with the Son, you share in His adoption. He says, "I ascend to My Father and your Father." God is as much your Father as He is Christ's Father, your God as Christ's God. Oh, what a change! for an heir of hell to become an heir of God, and joint-heir with Christ; to inherit God; to have a son's interest in God! Eternity alone will teach you what is in that word, "heir of God."

4. That your joy may be full.—Other joys are not filling.

Creature joys only fill a small part of the soul. Money, houses, lands, music, entertainments, friends, these are not filling joys; they are just drops of joys. But Christ revealed makes the cup run over. "Thou anointest my head with oil, my cup runneth over."

Believing in a manifested Christ fills the heart full of joy. "In Thy presence is fullness of joy." Christ brings the soul into God's presence. One smile of God fills the heart more than ten thousand smiles of the world.

You that have nothing but creature joy, hunting after butterflies, feeding upon carrion, why do you spend money for that which is not bread? You that are afflicted, tempest-tossed, and not comforted, look to a manifested Jesus. According to your faith so be it unto you. Believe none, and you will have no joy. Believe little, and you will have little joy. Believe much, and you will have much joy. Believe all, and you will have all joy, and your joy will be full. It will be like a bowl running over, good measure, pressed down, and running over. *Amen.*

JOHN CHARLES RYLE 1816–1900

John Charles Ryle drifted into an Oxford church one Sunday morning after the service had begun. He was then the embodiment of youthful success, as men of the world count success. His father, a member of the House of Commons, had fallen heir to a large fortune, owned property, held banking interests, enjoyed an annual income of over fifteen thousand pounds. As for John, whatever he turned his hand to also prospered. Handsome of feature and striking of figure, he had captained the cricket teams at Eton and at Oxford, rowed with the Oxford crew, besides winning a name as an intellectual. Yet all these honors left him strangely dissatisfied. A recent illness had plunged him into the Slough of Despond and sent him to the Bible for comfort. It was a new experience, as he was later to admit: "I never read a word of my Bible from the time I was seven to the time I was twenty-one."

The stranger in the lectern was reading the Scripture lesson as young Ryle took his pew. The passage happened to be the second chapter of Ephesians. Slowly, and with telling solemnity, the words of the eighth verse distilled on the collegian's parched spirit like dew on grass: "For by grace—are ye saved—through faith—and that—not of yourselves:—it is the gift of God." From that moment to the last recorded syllable of this life no doubt ever lingered in John's mind that the Word of God was living and powerful, sharper than any two-edged sword. There and then he jettisoned his own imperfect works, donned the beautiful garments of Christ's righteousness, rested in the crucified and risen Son of God as set forth in the terms of the Gospel. He left the church that morning in joyous communication with the God of all grace.

After graduation and a stint in the army, he started to study law, intending to follow his father in the House of Commons. But then with blinding suddenness financial disaster struck, and the Ryle fortune was wiped out in a few hours. The son, poor in property but rich toward God, interpreted the event as the divine means of thrusting him into the ministry. Nor was he disobedient to the heavenly vision. Presently he became curate of the church at Exbury, near the Isle of Wight.

It was a far cry from the fabulous estate at Henbury to the humble parish in southern England. Still he accepted the assignment as God's will and entered his duties happily. Tempted at first to emulate the flowing pulpit delivery of the great Henry Melville, he quickly checked the temptation, and rather, as Marcus Loane has expressed it, "crucified his style." He preached not with the wisdom of words lest the cross of Christ be made of none effect. The people of Exbury responded with genuine appreciation, and the church went forward in a marvelous manner.

In 1843 he was appointed Rector of St. Thomas Church in Winchester. Soon after he made the change, a horrible accident occurred near his parish. At Great Yarmouth a suspension bridge crowded with men and women broke down, plunging the multitude into the waters below. About one hundred of the victims drowned. Ryle capitalized on the opportunity to warn readers of the uncertainties of life by publishing a Gospel tract. In reality it was the setting off of a movement, for out of it emerged the idea of a series known as the Ipswich Tracts. Before his death, Bishop Ryle was to write three hundred messages in pamphlet form. Their printings would pass the twelve-million mark and be read in a dozen different languages. People all over the world otherwise unreached were thus to know the tidings of redemption and release.

Ryle next moved to Suffolk in East Anglia, where he was successively Rector of Helminghaus and Vicar of Stradbroke. In 1880, when he was Dean Designate of Salisbury Cathedral, Queen Victoria made him the first bishop of the Diocese of Liverpool. There he rounded out his fruitful career, held in high regard by friend and adversary.

Bishop Ryle was militantly evangelical in his views, holding fast to Reformation doctrine to the end. "I believe in the plenary inspiration of every word of the original text of Holy Scripture." The cross winds of destructive Biblical criticism and the Back-to-Rome movement led by John Henry Newman caught him squarely in the center. Both thrusts he resisted with all the force of his aroused soul. "Our honored fathers in the last century . . . stood firm, and held their ground; let us do likewise," he said.

He turned out over twenty volumes in all. His Expository Thoughts on the Gospels *provides a storehouse of devotional material for lovers of the Bible. His language is vigorous and full of pith and point. He loved to use the epigram: "What we weave in time, we wear in eternity." "Meddle with no man's person, but spare no man's sin." "Here is rock," he said of the Word of God. "All else is sand."*

"His virile personality dominated two generations of Evangelicals, and set an ineradicable mark upon a third," said one of his contemporaries. When he was called to a higher field than the See of Liverpool, a fellow churchman referred to him as "that man of granite, with the heart of a child."

Only One Way of Salvation

IS THERE MORE than one road to heaven? Is there more than one way in which the soul of man can be saved? This is the question which I propose to consider in this paper, and I shall begin the consideration by quoting a text of Scripture: "Neither is there salvation in any other: for there is none other name under heaven given among men, whereby we must be saved." (Acts 4:12)

These words are striking in themselves; but they are much more striking if we observe when and by whom they were spoken.

They were spoken by a poor and friendless Christian, in the midst of a persecuting Jewish Council. It was a grand confession of Christ.

They were spoken by the lips of the Apostle Peter. This is the man who, a few weeks before, forsook Jesus and fled: this is the very man who three times over denied his Lord. There is another spirit in him now! He stands up boldly before priests and Sadducees, and tells them the truth to their face:—"This is the stone that was set at nought of you builders, which is become the head of the corner. Neither is there salvation in any other: for there is none other name under heaven given among men, whereby we must be saved."

I. First, let me explain the doctrine laid down by St. Peter.

Let us make sure that we rightly understand what the Apostle means. He says of Christ, "Neither is there salvation in any other." Now what does this mean? On our clearly seeing this very much depends.

He means that no one can be saved from sin,—its guilt, its power, and its consequences,—excepting by Jesus Christ.

He means that no one can have peace with God the Father,—obtain pardon in this world, and escape wrath to come in the next,—excepting through the atonement and mediation of Jesus Christ.

In Christ alone God's rich provision of salvation for sinners is treasured up: by Christ alone God's abundant mercies come down from heaven to earth. Christ's blood alone can cleanse us; Christ's righteousness alone can clothe us; Christ's merit alone can give us a title to heaven. Jews and Gentiles, learned and unlearned, kings and poor men,—all alike must either be saved by the Lord Jesus, or lost for ever.

And the Apostle adds emphatically, "There is none other name under heaven given among men, whereby we must be saved." There is no other person commissioned, sealed, and appointed by God the Father to be the Saviour of sinners, excepting Christ. The keys of life and death are committed to His hand, and all who would be saved must go to Him.

There was but one place of safety in the day when the flood came upon the earth: that place was Noah's ark. All other places and devices, —mountains, towers, trees, rafts, boats,—all were alike useless. So also there is but one hiding-place for the sinner who would escape the storm of God's anger; he must venture his soul on Christ.

There was but one man to whom the Egyptians could go in time of famine, when they wanted food.—They must go to Joseph: it was a waste of time to go to any one else. So also there is but One to whom hungering souls must go, if they would not perish for ever: they must go to Christ.

There was but one word that could save the lives of the Ephraimites in the day when the Gileadites contended with them, and took the fords of Jordan (Judges 12): they must say "Shibboleth," or die. Just so there is but one Name that will avail us when we stand at the gate of heaven: we must name the Name of Jesus as our only hope, or be cast away everlastingly.

Such is the doctrine of the text. "No salvation but by Jesus Christ;— in Him plenty of salvation,—salvation to the uttermost, salvation for the very chief of sinners;—out of Him no salvation at all." It is in perfect harmony with our Lord's own words in St. John's Gospel,—"I am the way, the truth, and the life: no man cometh unto the Father, but by Me." (John 14:6) It is the same thing that Paul tells the Corinthians: —"Other foundation can no man lay than that is laid which is Jesus Christ." (1 Cor. 3:11) And it is the same that St. John tells us in his first Epistle:—"God hath given to us eternal life, and this life is in His Son. He that hath the Son hath life, and he that hath not the Son of God hath not life." (1 John 5:12) All these texts come to one and the same point,—no salvation but by Jesus Christ.

Let us make sure that we understand this before we pass on. Men are apt to think, "This is all old news;—these are ancient things: who knoweth not such truths as these? Of course, we believe there is no salvation but by Christ." But I ask my readers to mark well what I say. Make sure that you understand this doctrine, or else by and by you will stumble, and be offended at the statements I have yet to make in this paper.

We are to venture the whole salvation of our souls on Christ, and on Christ only. We are to cast loose completely and entirely from all other hopes and trusts. We are not to rest partly on Christ,—partly on doing all we can,—partly on keeping our church,—partly on receiving the sacrament. In the matter of our justification Christ is to be *all*. This is the doctrine of the text.

Heaven is before us, and Christ the only door into it; hell beneath us, and Christ alone able to deliver us from it; the devil behind us, and Christ the only refuge from his wrath and accusations; the law against us, and Christ alone able to redeem us; sin weighing us down, and Christ alone able to put it away. This is the doctrine of the text.

Now do we see it? I hope we do. But I fear many think so who may find, before laying down this paper that they do not.

II. Let me, in the second place, supply some reasons why the doctrine of the text must be true.

I might cut short this part of the subject by one simple argument: "God says so." "One plain text," said an old divine, "is as good as a thousand reasons."

But I will not do this. I wish to meet the objections that are ready to rise in many hearts against this doctrine, by pointing out the strong foundations on which it stands.

1. Let me then say, for one thing, the doctrine of the text must be true *because man is what man is.*

Now what is man? There is one broad, sweeping answer, which takes up the whole human race: man is a sinful being. All children of Adam born into the world, whatever be their name or nation, are corrupt, wicked, and defiled in the sight of God. Their thoughts, words, ways, and actions are all, more or less, defective and imperfect.

Is there no country on the face of the globe where sin does not reign? Is there no happy valley, no secluded island, where innocence is to be found? Is there no tribe on earth, where, far away from civilization, and commerce, and money, and gunpowder, and luxury, and books, morality and purity flourish? No! there is none. Look over all the voyages and travels you can lay your hand on, from Columbus down to Cook, and from Cook to Livingstone, and you will see the truth of what I am asserting. The most solitary islands of the Pacific Ocean,—islands cut off from all the rest of the world,—islands where people were alike ignorant of Rome and Paris, London, and Jerusalem,—these islands, when first discovered, have been found full of impurity, cruelty, and idolatry. The footprints of the devil have been traced on every shore. The veracity of the third chapter of Genesis has everywhere been established. Whatever else savages have been found ignorant of, they have never been found ignorant of sin.

But are there no men and women in the world who are free from this corruption of nature? Have there not been high-minded and exalted beings who have every now and then lived faultless lives? Have there not been some, if it be only a few, who have done all that God requires, and thus proved that sinless perfection is a possibility?

No! there have been none. Look over all the biographies and lives of the holiest Christians; mark how the brightest and best of Christ's people have always had the deepest sense of their own defectiveness and corruption. They groan, they mourn, they sigh, they weep over their own shortcomings: it is one of the common grounds on which they meet. Patriarchs and Apostles, Fathers and Reformers, Episcopalians and Presbyterians, Luther and Calvin, Knox and Bradford, Rutherford and Bishop Hall, Wesley and Whitefield, Martyn and McCheyne,—all are alike agreed in feeling their own sinfulness. The more light they have, the more humble and self-abased they seem to be; the more holy they are, the more they seem to feel their own unworthiness.

Now what does all this seem to prove? To my eyes it seems to prove that human nature is so tainted and corrupt that, left to himself, no man could be saved. Man's case appears to be a hopeless one without a Saviour,—and that a mighty Saviour too. There must be a Mediator, an Atonement, an Advocate, to make such poor sinful beings acceptable with God; and I find this nowhere, excepting in Jesus Christ. Heaven for man without a divine Intercessor, eternal life for man without an eternal Saviour,—in one word, salvation without Christ,—all alike, in the face of the plain facts about human nature, appear utter impossibilities.

I lay these things before thinking men, and I ask them to consider them. I know it is one of the hardest things in the world to realize the sinfulness of sin. To say we are all sinners is one thing; to have an idea what sin must be in the sight of God is quite another. Sin is too much part of ourselves to allow us to see it as it is; we do not feel our own moral deformity. We are like those animals in creation which are vile and loathsome to our senses, but are not so to themselves, nor yet to one another: their loathsomeness is their nature, and they do not perceive it. Just in the same way our corruption is part and parcel of ourselves, and at our best we have but a feeble comprehension of its intensity.

But this we may be sure of,—if we could see our own lives with the eyes of the angels who never fell, we should never doubt this point for a moment. In a word, no one can really know what man is, and not see that the doctrine of our text must be true. We are shut up to the Apostle Peter's conclusion. There can be no salvation except by Christ.

2. Let me say another thing. The doctrine of our text must be true, *because God is what God is.*

Now what is God? That is a deep question indeed. We know something of His attributes: He has not left Himself without witness in creation; He has mercifully revealed to us many things about Himself in His Word. We know that God is a Spirit,—eternal, invisible, almighty,—the Maker of all things, the Preserver of all things,—holy, just, all-seeing, all-knowing, all-remembering,—infinite in mercy, in wisdom, in purity.

But alas, after all, how low and grovelling are our highest ideas, when we come to put down on paper what we believe God to be! How many words and expressions we use whose full meaning we cannot fathom! How many things our tongues say of Him which our minds are utterly unable to conceive!

How small a part of Him do we see! How little of Him can we possibly know! How mean and paltry are any words of ours to convey any idea of Him who made this mighty world out of nothing, and with whom one day is as a thousand years, and a thousand years as one day! How weak and inadequate are our poor feeble intellects to form any conception of Him who is perfect in all His works,—perfect in the greatest as well as perfect in the smallest,—perfect in appointing the days and hours and minutes and seconds in which Jupiter, with all his satellites, shall travel round the sun,—perfect in forming the smallest insect that creeps over a few feet of our little globe! How little can our busy helplessness comprehend a Being who is ever ordering all things, in heaven and earth, by universal providence: ordering the rise and fall of nations and dynasties, like Nineveh and Carthage; ordering the exact length to which men like Alexander and Tamerlane and Napoleon shall extend their conquests; ordering the least step in the life of the humblest believer among His people: all at the same time, all unceasingly, all perfectly,—all for His own glory.

The blind man is no judge of the paintings of Rubens or Titian; the deaf man is insensible to the beauty of Handel's music; the Greenlander can have but a faint notion of the climate of the tropics; the South Sea islander can form but a remote conception of a locomotive engine, however well you may describe it. There is no faculty in their minds which can take in these things; they have no set of thoughts which can comprehend them; they have no mental fingers to grasp them. And just in the same way, the best and brightest ideas that man can form of God, compared to the reality which we shall one day see, are weak and faint indeed.

But one thing, I think, is very clear: and that is this. The more any man considers calmly what God really is, the more he must feel the immeasurable distance between God and himself: the more he meditates, the more he must see that there is a great gulf between him and God. His conscience, I think, will tell him, if he will let it speak, that God is perfect, and he imperfect; that God is very high, and he very low; that God is glorious majesty, and he a poor worm; and that if ever he is to stand before Him in judgment with comfort, he must have some mighty Helper, or he will not be saved.

And what is all this but the very doctrine of the text with which I began this paper? What is all this but coming round to the conclusion I am urging upon my readers? With such an One as God to give account to, we must have a mighty Saviour. To give us peace with such a glorious Being as God, we must have an Almighty Mediator, a Friend and Advocate on our side,—an Advocate who can answer every charge that can be laid against us, and plead our cause with God, on equal terms. We want this, and nothing less than this. Vague notions of mercy will never give true peace. And such a Saviour, such a Friend, such an Advocate is nowhere to be found excepting in the Person of Jesus Christ.

I lay this reason also before thinking men. I know well that people may have false notions of God as well as everything else, and shut their eyes against truth. But I say boldly and confidently, no man can have really high and honourable views of what God is, and escape the conclusion that the doctrine of our text must be true. We are shut up to the truth of St. Peter's declaration. There can be no possible salvation but by Jesus Christ.

3. Let me say, in the third place, this doctrine must be true, *because the Bible is what the Bible is.* If we do not believe the doctrine, we must give up the Bible as the only rule of faith.

All through the Bible, from Genesis down to Revelation, there is only one simple account of the way in which man must be saved. It is always the same: only for the sake of our Lord Jesus Christ,—through faith; not for our own works and deservings.

We see it dimly revealed at first: it looms through the mist of a few promises; but there it is.

We have it more plainly afterwards: it is taught by the pictures and emblems of the law of Moses, the schoolmaster dispensation.

We have it still more clearly by and by: the Prophets saw in visions many particulars about the Redeemer yet to come.

We have it fully at last, in the sunshine of New Testament history: Christ incarnate,—Christ crucified,—Christ rising again,—Christ preached to the world.

But one golden chain runs through the whole volume: no salvation excepting by Jesus Christ. The bruising of the serpent's head foretold in the day of the fall; the clothing of our first parents with skins; the sacrifices of Noah, Abraham, Isaac, and Jacob; the passover, and all the particulars of the Jewish law,—the high priest, the altar, the daily offering of the lamb, the holy of holies entered only by blood, the scape goat, the cities of refuge;—all are so many witnesses to the truth set forth in the text. All preach with one voice, salvation only by Jesus Christ.

In fact, this truth appears to be the grand object of the Bible, and all the different parts and portions of the Book are meant to pour light upon it. I can gather from it no ideas of pardon and peace with God excepting in connection with this truth. If I could read of one soul in it who was saved without faith in a Saviour, I might perhaps not speak so confidently. But when I see that faith in Christ,—whether a coming Christ or a crucified Christ,—was the prominent feature in the religion of all who went to heaven;—when I see Abel owning Christ in his "better sacrifice" at one end of the Bible, and the saints in glory in John's vision rejoicing in Christ at the other end of the Bible;—when I see a man like Cornelius, who was devout, and feared God, and gave alms and prayed, not told that he had done all, and would of course be saved, but ordered to send for Peter, and hear of Christ;—when I see all these things, I say, I feel bound to believe that the doctrine of the text is the doctrine of the whole Bible. The Word of God, fairly examined and interpreted, shuts me up to the truth laid down by St. Peter. No salvation, no way to heaven, excepting by Jesus Christ.

Such are the reasons which seem to me to confirm the truth which forms the subject of this paper. What man is,—what God is,—what the Bible is,—all appear to me to lead on to the same great conclusion: no possible salvation without Christ. I leave them here, and pass on.

III. And now, in the third and last place, let me shout some consequences which flow naturally out of the doctrine declared by St. Peter.

There are few parts of the subject which seem to me more important than this. The truth I have been trying to set before my readers bears so strongly on the condition of a great proportion of mankind, that I consider it would be mere affectation on my part not to say something about it. If Christ is the only way of salvation, what are we to feel about many people in the world? This is the point I am now going to take up.

I believe that many persons would go with me so far as I have gone, and would go no further. They will allow my premises: they will have nothing to say to my conclusions. They think it uncharitable to say anything which appears to condemn others. For my part I cannot understand such charity. It seems to me the kind of charity which would see a neighbour drinking slow poison, but never interfere to stop him;—which would allow emigrants to embark in a leaky, ill-found vessel, and not interfere to prevent them,—which would see a blind man walking near a precipice, and think it wrong to cry out, and tell him there was danger.

The greatest charity is to tell the greatest quantity of truth. It is no charity to hide the legitimate consequences of such a saying of St. Peter as we are now considering, or to shut our eyes against them. And I solemnly call on every one who really believes there is no salvation in any but Christ,—and none other name given under heaven whereby we must be saved,—I solemnly call on that person to give me his attention, while I set before him some of the tremendous consequences which the doctrine we are considering involves.

I am not going to speak of the heathen who have never heard the Gospel. Their final state is a great depth, which the mightiest minds have been unable to fathom: I am not ashamed of leaving it alone. One thing only I will say. If any of the heathen, who die heathen, are saved, I believe they will owe their salvation, however little they may know it on this side of the grave, to the work and atonement of Christ. Just as infants and idiots among ourselves will find at the last day they owed all to Christ, though they never knew Him, so I believe it will be with the heathen, if any of them are saved, whether many or few. This at any rate I am sure of—there is no such thing as creature merit. My own private opinion is that the highest Archangel (though, of course in a very different way and degree from us) will be found in some way to owe his standing to Christ; and that things in heaven, as well as things on earth, will be found ultimately all indebted to the Name of Jesus. But I leave the case of the heathen to others, and will speak of matters nearer home.

a. One mighty consequence then which seems to be learned from the text which forms the keynote of this paper, is the utter uselessness of any religion without Christ.

There are many to be found in Christendom at this day who have a religion of this kind. They would not like to be called Deists, but Deists they are. That there is a God, that there is what they are pleased to call Providence, that God is merciful, that there will be a state after death,—this is about the sum and substance of their creed; and as to the distinguishing tenets of Christianity, they do not seem to recognize them at all. Now I denounce such a system as a baseless fabric,—its seeming foundation man's fancy,—its hopes an utter delusion. The god of such people is an idol of their own invention, and not the glorious God of the Scriptures,—a miserably imperfect being, even on their own showing,—without holiness, without justice, without any attribute but that of vague, indiscriminate mercy. Such a religion may possibly do as a toy to live with: it is far too unreal to die with. It utterly fails to meet the wants of man's conscience: it offers no remedy; it affords no rest for the soles of our feet; it cannot comfort, for it cannot save. Let us beware of it, if we love life. Let us beware of a religion without Christ.

b. Another consequence to be learned from the text is, the folly of any religion in which Christ has not the first place.

I need not remind my readers how many hold a system of this kind. The Socinian tells us that Christ was a mere man; that His blood had no more efficacy than that of another; that His death on the cross was not a real atonement and propitiation of man's sins; and that, after all, doing is the way to heaven, and not believing. I solemnly declare that I believe such a system is ruinous to men's souls. It seems to me to strike at the root of the whole plan of salvation which God has revealed in the Bible, and practically to nullify the greater part of the Scriptures.

It overthrows the priesthood of the Lord Jesus, and strips Him of His office. It converts the whole system of the law of Moses, touching sacrifices and ordinances, into a meaningless form. It seems to say that the sacrifice of Cain was just as good as the sacrifice of Abel. It turns man adrift on a sea of uncertainty, by plucking from under him the finished work of a divine Mediator. Let us beware of it, no less than of Deism, if we love life. Let us beware of the least attempt to depreciate and undervalue Christ's Person, offices, or work. The name whereby alone we can be saved, is a name above every name, and the slightest contempt poured upon it is an insult to the King of kings. The salvation of our souls has been laid by God the Father on Christ, and no other. If He were not very God of very God, He never could accomplish it, and there could be no salvation at all.

c. Another consequence to be learned from our text is, the great error committed by those who add anything to Christ as necessary to salvation.

It is an easy thing to profess belief in the Trinity, and reverence for our Lord Jesus Christ, and yet to make some addition to Christ as the ground of hope, and so to overthrow the doctrine of the text as really and completely as by denying it altogether.

The Church of Rome does this systematically. She adds things to Christianity over and above the requirements of the Gospel, of her own invention. She speaks as if Christ's finished work was not a sufficient foundation for a sinner's soul, and as if it were not enough to say, "Believe on the Lord Jesus Christ, and thou shalt be saved." She sends men to priests and confessors, to penances and absolution, to masses and extreme unction, to fasting and bodily mortification, to the Virgin Mary and the saints,—as if these things could add to the safety there is in Christ Jesus. And in doing this she sins against the doctrine of God's Word with a high hand. Let us beware of any Romish hankering after additions to the simple way of the Gospel, from whatever quarter it may come.

But I fear the Church of Rome does not stand alone in this matter. I fear there are thousands of professing Protestants who are often erring in the same direction, although, of course, in a very different degree. They get into a way of adding, perhaps insensibly, other things to the Name of Christ, or attaching an importance to them which they never ought to receive. The ultra Churchman in England, who thinks God's covenanted mercies are tied to episcopacy,—the ultra Presbyterian in Scotland, who cannot reconcile prelacy with an intelligent knowledge of the Gospel,—the ultra Free-kirk man by his side, who seems to think lay patronage and vital Christianity almost incompatible, —the ultra Dissenter, who traces every evil in the Church to its connection with the State, and can talk of nothing but the voluntary system,—the ultra Baptist, who shuts out from the Lord's table every one who has not received his peculiar views of adult baptism,—the ultra Plymouth Brother, who believes all knowledge to reside with his own body, and condemns every one outside as a poor weak babe;—all these, I say, however unwittingly, exhibit a most uncomfortable tendency to add to the doctrine of our text. All seem to me to be practically declaring that salvation is not to be found simply and solely in Christ. All seem to me to be practically adding another name to the Name of Jesus, whereby men must be saved,—even the name of their own party and sect. All seem to me to be practically replying to the question, "What shall I do to be saved?" not merely, "Believe on· the Lord Jesus Christ," but also "Come and join us."

Now I call upon every true Christian to beware of such ultraism, in whatever form he may be inclined to it. In saying this I would not be misunderstood. I like every one to be decided in his views of ecclesiastical matters, and to be fully persuaded of their correctness. All I ask is, that men will not put these things in the place of Christ, or place them anywhere near Him, or speak of them as if they thought them needful to salvation. However dear to us our own peculiar views may be, let us beware of thrusting them in between the sinner and the Saviour. In the things of God's Word, be it remembered, addition, as well as subtraction, is a great sin.

d. The last consequence which seems to me to be learned from our text is, the utter absurdity of supposing that we ought to be satisfied with a man's state of soul, if he is only earnest and sincere.

This is a very common heresy indeed, and one against which we all need to be on our guard. There are thousands who say in the present day, "We have nothing to do with the opinions of others. They may perhaps be mistaken, though it is possible they are right and we wrong: but, if they are sincere and earnest, we hope they will be saved, even as we." And all this sounds liberal and charitable, and people like to fancy their own views are so! To such an extreme length has this erroneous idea run, that many are content to describe a Christian as "an earnest man," and seem to think this vague definition is quite sufficient!

Now I believe such notions are entirely contradictory to the Bible, whatever else they may be. I cannot find in Scripture that any one ever got to heaven merely by sincerity, or was accepted with God if he was only earnest in maintaining his own views. The priests of Baal were earnest and sincere when they cut themselves with knives and lancets till the blood gushed out; but that did not prevent Elijah from commanding them to be treated as wicked idolaters.—Manasseh, King of Judah, was doubtless earnest and sincere when he burned his children in the fire to Moloch; but who does not know that he brought on himself great guilt by so doing?—The Apostle Paul, when a Pharisee, was earnest and sincere while he made havoc of the Church, but when his eyes were opened he mourned over this special wickedness. Let us beware of allowing for a moment that sincerity is everything, and that we have no right to speak ill of a man's spiritual state because of the opinions he holds, if he is only earnest in holding them. On such principles, the Druidicial sacrifices, the car of Juggernaut, the Indian suttees, the systematic murders of the Thugs, the fires of Smithfield might each and all be defended. It will not stand: it will not bear the test of Scripture. Once allow such notions to be true, and we may as well throw our Bibles aside altogether. Sincerity is not Christ, and therefore sincerity cannot put away sin.

I dare be sure these consequences sound very unpleasant to the minds of some who may read them. But I say, calmly and advisedly, that a religion without Christ, a religion that takes away from Christ, a religion that adds anything to Christ, a religion that puts sincerity in the place of Christ,—all are dangerous: all are to be avoided, because all are alike contrary to the doctrine of Scripture.

Some readers may not like this. I am sorry for it. They think me uncharitable, illiberal, narrow-minded, bigoted, and so forth. Be it so. But they will not tell me my doctrine is not that of the Word of God and of the Church of England, whose minister I am. That doctrine is, salvation in Christ to the very uttermost,—but out of Christ no salvation at all.

I feel it a duty to bear my solemn testimony against the spirit of the day we live in, to warn men against its infection. It is not Atheism I fear so much, in the present times, as Pantheism. It is not the system which says nothing is true, so much as the system which says everything is true. It is not the system which says there is no Saviour, so much as the system which says there are many saviours, and many ways to peace!—It is the system which is so liberal, that it dares not say anything is false. It is the system which is so charitable, that it will allow everything to be true. It is the system which seems ready to honour others as well as our Lord Jesus Christ, to class them all together, and to think well of all. Confucius and Zoroaster, Socrates and Mahomet, the Indian Brahmins and the African devil-worshippers, Arius and Pelagius, Ignatius Loyola and Socinus,—all are to be treated respectfully: none are to be condemned. It is the system which bids us smile complacently on all creeds and systems of religion. The Bible and the Koran, the Hindu Vedas and the Persian Zendavesta, the old wives' fables of Rabbinical writers and the rubbish of Patristic traditions, the Racovian catechism and the Thirty-nine Articles, the revelations of Emanuel Swedenborg and the book of Mormon of Joseph Smith,—all, all are to be listened to: none are to be denounced as lies. It is the system which is so scrupulous about the feelings of others, that we are never to say they are wrong. It is the system which is so liberal that it calls a man a bigot, if he dares to say, "I know my views are right." This is the system, this is the tone of feeling which I fear in this day, and this is the system which I desire emphatically to testify against and denounce.

What is it all but a bowing down before a great idol, speciously called liberality? What is it all but a sacrificing of truth upon the altar of a caricature of charity? What is it all but the worship of a shadow, a phantom, and an unreality? What can be more absurd than to profess ourselves content with "earnestness," when we do not know what we are earnest about? Let us take heed lest we are carried away by the delusion. Has the Lord God spoken to us in the Bible, or has He not? Has He shown us the way of salvation plainly and distinctly in that Bible, or has He not? Has He declared to us the dangerous state of all out of that way, or has He not? Let us gird up the loins of our minds, and look these questions fairly in the face, and give them an honest answer. Tell us that there is some other inspired book beside the Bible, and then we shall know what you mean. Tell us that the whole Bible is not inspired, and then we shall know where to meet you. But grant for a moment that the Bible, the whole Bible, and nothing but the Bible is God's truth, and then I know not in what way we can escape the doctrine of the text. From the liberality which says everybody is right, from the charity which forbids us to say anybody is wrong, from the peace which is bought at the expense of truth,—may the good Lord deliver us!

For my own part, I frankly confess, I find no resting-place between downright distinct Evangelical Christianity and downright infidelity, whatever others may find. I see no half-way house between them; or else I see the houses that are roofless and cannot shelter my weary soul. I can see consistency in an infidel, however much I may pity him. I can see consistency in the full maintenance of Evangelical truth. But as to a middle course between the two,—I cannot see it; and I say so plainly. Let it be called illiberal and uncharitable. I can hear God's voice nowhere except in the Bible, and I can see no salvation for sinners in the Bible excepting through Jesus Christ. In Him I see abundance: out of Him I see none. And as for those who hold religions in which Christ is not all, whoever they may be, I have a most uncomfortable feeling about their safety. I do not for a moment say that none of them will be saved; but I say that those who are saved will be saved by their disagreement with their own principles, and in spite of their own systems. The man who wrote the famous line, "He can't be wrong whose life is in the right," was a great poet undoubtedly, but he was a wretched divine.

Let me conclude this paper with a few words by way of application.

1. First of all, if there is no salvation excepting in Christ, let us make sure that we have an interest in that salvation ourselves. Let us not be content with hearing, and approving, and assenting to the truth, and going no further. Let us seek to have a personal interest in this salvation. Let us not rest till we know and feel that we have got actual possession of that peace with God which Jesus offers, and that Christ is ours, and we are Christ's. If there were two, or three, or more ways of getting to heaven, there would be no necessity for pressing this matter. But if there is only one way, who can wonder that I say, "Make sure that you are in it."

2. Secondly, if there is no salvation excepting in Christ, let us try to do good to the souls of all who do not know Him as a Saviour. There are millions in this miserable condition,—millions in foreign lands, millions in our own country, millions who are not trusting in Christ. We ought to feel for them if we are true Christians; we ought to pray for them; we ought to work for them, while there is yet time. Do we really believe that Christ is the only way to heaven? Then let us live as if we believed it.

Let us look round the circle of our own relatives and friends, count them up one by one, and think how many of them are not yet in Christ. Let us try to do good to them in some way or other, and act as a man should act who believes his friends to be in danger. Let us not be content with their being kind and amiable, gentle and good-tempered, moral and courteous. Let us rather be miserable about them till they come to Christ, and trust in Him. I know all this may sound like enthusiasm and fanaticism. I wish there was more of it in the world. Anything, I am sure, is better than a quiet indifference about the souls of others, as if everybody was in the way to heaven. Nothing, to my mind, so proves our little faith, as our little feeling about the spiritual condition of those around us.

3. Thirdly, if there is no salvation excepting in Christ, let us love all who love the Lord Jesus in sincerity, and exalt Him as their Saviour, whoever they may be. Let us not draw back and look shy on others, because they do not see eye to eye with ourselves in everything. Whether a man be a Free-kirk man or an Independent, a Wesleyan or a Baptist, let us love him if he loves Christ, and gives Christ His rightful place. We are all fast travelling toward a place where names and forms and Church-government will be nothing, and Christ will be all. Let us get ready for that place betimes, by loving all who are in the way that leads to it.

This is the true charity, to believe all things and hope all things, so long as we see Bible doctrines maintained and Christ exalted. Christ must be the single standard by which all opinions must be measured. Let us honour all who honour Him: but let us never forget that the same apostle Paul who wrote about charity, says also, "If any man love not the Lord Jesus Christ, let him be Anathema." If our charity and liberality are wider than what of the Bible, they are worth nothing at all. Indiscriminate love is no love at all, and indiscriminate approbation of all religious opinions, is only a new name for infidelity. Let us hold out the right hand to all who love the Lord Jesus, but let us beware how we go beyond this.

4. Lastly, if there is no salvation excepting by Christ, we must not be surprised if ministers of the Gospel preach much about Him. They cannot tell us too much about the Name which is above every name. We cannot hear of Him too often. We may hear too much about controversy in sermons,—we may hear too much of works and duties, of forms, of ceremonies, of sacraments and ordinances,—but there is one subject which we never hear too much of: we can never hear too much of Christ.

When ministers are wearied of preaching Him, they are false ministers: when people are wearied of hearing of Him, their souls are in an unhealthy state. When ministers have preached Him in all their lives, the half of His excellence will remain untold. When hearers see Him face to face in the day of His appearing, they will find there was more in Him than their hearts ever conceived.

Let me conclude this paper with the words of an old writer, to which I desire humbly to subscribe. "I know no true religion but Christianity; no true Christianity but the doctrine of Christ: the doctrine of His divine Person, of His divine office, of His divine righteousness, and of His divine Spirit, which all that are His receive. I know no true ministers of Christ but such as make it their business, in their calling, to commend Jesus Christ in His saving fulness of grace and glory, to the faith and love of men; no true Christian but one united to Christ by faith and love, unto the glorifying of the Name of Jesus Christ, in the beauty of Gospel holiness. Ministers and Christians of this spirit have been for many years my brethren and companions, and I hope shall ever be, whithersoever the hand of God shall lead me".—(Robert Traill)

ROSWELL D. HITCHCOCK 1817–1887

Roswell Dwight Hitchcock was the sixth in descent from Luke Hitch-cock, a freeman of New Haven, hence of good hardy stock. Wash-ington Academy, Amherst College, and Andover Theological Seminary claim him as a graduate of note. He was from the beginning an ex-cellent student, gripped always by an unquenchable intellectual thirst.

While Hitchcock was studying at Andover, he helped support him-self by teaching at Phillips Academy. Later, he was chosen to be principal of an academy at Jaffrey, New Hampshire. He tutored at Amherst from 1839 to 1842.

The Congregational Church licensed him to preach. He spent eight years alternately serving the First Congregational Church of Exeter, New Hampshire, and doing post-graduate work in Germany.

In 1852, Bowdoin College appointed him Professor of Natural and Revealed Religion. He taught theology for three years.

Union Theological Seminary of New York made him Washburn Professor of Church History. He remained there until his retirement, officiating as president of the faculty the last seven years of his academic life.

Like many American scholars who expose their minds to brilliant destructive Biblical criticism, Hitchcock was deeply affected by Ger-man rationalism. He reacted from it, however, and eventually returned to the conservative position, as his message on the atonement makes clear.

Dr. Hitchcock is best known for his writings. His earliest product was a biography of Edward Robinson. There followed his monumental New and Complete Analysis of the Holy Bible, *applauded by theo-logians, ministers, educators, and leaders in all walks of life. Talmage, Cuyler, Mark Hopkins, C. S. Brown, and James McCosh, with others, were lavish in their praise of it. Philip Schaff wrote: "As may be expected from the ability and culture of Professor Hitchcock, and the great amount of labor he bestowed upon it and to the injury of his health, his* Analysis of the Bible *is not only an improvement upon its predecessors, but in many respects a new work. It enables students to see the Bible's wonderful unity, variety, and the completeness of its teachings, which form one of the strongest evidences of its divine origin."*

Hitchcock edited the American Theological Review *for seven years. In 1871 he was elected president of the Palestine Exploration Society.*

His book Socialism, *completed in 1879, is a sweeping broadside against everything Lasalle and Marx espoused, so piercing and timely that one might judge it to have been written in the mid–twentieth century.* "His [Karl Marx's] voluminous work 'On Capital' shows us what he is, and what he does," *Hitchcock says indignantly.* "He cares no more for Germany than he cares for Greece or Egypt. He loudly proclaims his allegiance only to labor, though living himself, as Lasalle did, in luxury."

The final paragraph of his second chapter is startlingly contemporary, uncannily anticipating George Orwell's Animal Farm:

"We had better be calling things by their right name. This is no Paradise of men, but of animals: of dull oxen first, each under his own end of the yoke by day, and each at night in his own stall, yokes and stalls all alike; presently, it will be of dogs, each growling and gnawing his well-picked bone; by and by it will be of wolves, howling and chasing down the belated teams; but at last it will be of tigers, tearing one another to pieces in the jungle. So the chapter and so the volume, ends, this tragic volume of human history: at the bottom of the final page, after a fashion of the old printers, Memento mori, *with skull and cross-bones, though not of man, but of beast. The evolution ends. Beast thou art and unto beast thou shalt return. Whether Law or Gospel, science said it; and so it is."*

Roswell Dwight Hitchcock's last official act was to preside at the dedication of new Union Theological Seminary buildings. The institution had moved from its old quarters on University Place to a new home on Lenox Hill. Dr. Hitchcock congratulated the trustees, members of the faculty, and students on securing what would surely be the school's permanent home. The "permanent home" enjoyed a duration of twenty-three years.

Dr. Hitchcock, with Job, believed that the fear of the Lord was the beginning of wisdom, and to depart from evil, understanding. Upon this principle his mind could continuously reach out and up, while his faith kept pace with the expansion of his intellectual horizons. For Hitchcock, Jesus Christ was the hinge on which the portals of history turned. In Him were stored up all the treasures of wisdom and knowledge.

"Amid the fluctuations of modern opinion he was tranquil and composed, because he had found one Divine life running through the ages, and knew that He Who had always been with His Church would abide with it until the end of the world."

Eternal Atonement

ROSWELL D. HITCHCOCK, D.D., LL.D.

And all that dwell upon the earth shall worship Him, whose names are not written in the book of life of the Lamb slain from the foundation of the world. —Revelation 13:8

MY SUBJECT is the Lamb slain from the foundation of the world. My text is Revelation 13:8, the precise import of which is disputed; and I will therefore give you the rival renderings. As we have been used to it in the Authorized Version, it reads, "Written in the book of life of the Lamb slain from the foundation of the world." The Anglican Revisers, following the lead of Alford, make no essential change; "Written in the book of life of the Lamb that hath been slain from the foundation of the world." The American Revisers following the lead of Bengel, DeWette, and many others, would have it; "Written from the foundation of the world in the book of life of the Lamb that hath been slain." The American rendering makes the *election* eternal. The Anglican rendering makes the *atonement* eternal.

The prevalent opinion no doubt has been that the atonement is simply an historic fact, dating back now some nineteen hundred years; and that only the *purpose* of it is eternal. But Johann Wessel, the great German theologian who died only six years after Martin Luther was born, got hold of the idea that not election only, but atonement also, is an eternal act. And this, it seems to me, is both rational and Scriptural. Eternal election, profoundly considered, requires eternal atonement for its support. Both are eternal, as all Divine realities are eternal.

If the passage in Revelation were given up, we should still have to deal with I Peter 1:19,20, where the Lamb is spoken of as foreknown before the foundation of the world, but manifested at the end of the times; eternal reality becoming temporal fact. We should still have to deal with John 17:24, which also carries back into eternity the redeeming relationship between the Father and the Son. Even on Calvary, as temporal actuality, the Lamb slain is only a figure of speech, and, of course, it can be no more than a figure of speech as eternal reality in the bosom of God. But whether in time, or in eternity— whether on Calvary or in the bosom of God, the figure must stand for something. For us the meaning is, and must be, that not election only, but atonement also is eternal.

And so the relationship of God to moral evil stands forth as an eternal relationship. Not that evil is itself eternal; but God always knew it and always felt it. It may help our thinking in this direction to re-member that there is a sense in which creation itself is eternal; not independently eternal, but of God's Will, dependently eternal.

There must nothing be said, or thought, in mitigation of the ethical verdict against moral evil. The hatefulness of it, no matter what its chronology may be, is simply unspeakable. Violated law is monstrous. Unmindfulness of God, Who has always been so mindful of us, is mean. Never to pray, either in one's closet or in one's family, is against all the proprieties. Idolatry is childish and contemptible. Profaneness of speech is scandalous. Neglect of holy time is robbery. Disobedience to parents is shameful. Murder is hideous. Unchastity murders the soul, is indeed both murder and suicide.

And so of all the rest. Theft, falsehood, and even inordinate desire are abominable. Imagine a community, larger or smaller—a family, a township, a state, or a nation, where the Ten Commandments are per-sistently trampled under foot, and you will have imagined a community intolerable even to itself. And—if this be our human judgment, what must the Divine judgment be? The more pure and righteous a moral being is, the more squarely he must antagonize, the more intensely he must hate, the more surely he must punish impurity and unrighteous-ness. Volcanic fire inside the globe, forked lightning outside of it, are faint emblems of holy wrath. Wrong doing is the one thing nowhere, and never, to be either condoned or endured.

Physical accident, bodily sickness, financial disaster, social bereave-ment may all be pitied. But when a thoroughly bad man stands revealed, only lightning is logical. He that sows the wind ought to reap the whirlwind.

It was a great philosopher who stood amazed at the starry sky, and at the moral sense in man. Well he might. There is no softness in the midnight sky; only cold blue marble, and a steady blaze that never relents and is never tired. You cannot endure that blaze, you dare not risk yourself out alone among those gleaming orbs with a guilty secret in your bosom. The universe is instinct with law that never abdicates. Remorse is not repentance; and even repentance washes out no stain. Self-forgiveness is impossible. The trumpet is always sounding; every day is a judgment-day; and every one of us goes to the left. Gehenna is only the logical goal of sin.

Nor should any attempt be made to get at the genesis of moral evil. The beginning of it is simply inconceivable. The whole thing is a mystery, and must be let alone. Moral evil is not eternal; or there would be two infinities. Nor is it a creature of God; or God would be divided against Himself. And yet it had the Divine permission, whatever that may be imagined to have been.

With every attribute roused and alert—infinity of power, infinity of wisdom, infinity of holiness, God stood by and let evil enter. Angels revolted first, somewhere among the stars. Mankind revolted. Was evil really unavoidable in a proper moral system? If so, immorality is not immoral. Evil that is really essential to good should not be considered evil. It would be only the bitter bud of the fragrant blossom and the luscious fruit.

Or, putting it in another form, will you say that God could not have prevented evil? He certainly could have prevented it. In Heaven today, what is the security of saints and angels, of your own dear sainted mother, of Gabriel himself, but God's own grace, constraining the will of every saint, contraining the will of every seraph? What is human sin but the abuse of human appetites, of human passions, of human faculties, in themselves all innocent? Study the lesson of our Lord's temptation in the desert. Certainly, He was not tempted as we are, by inflamed appetites and passions, by impaired and disordered faculties. But He possessed all these natural appetites, passions and faculties, and they were put to a real and tremendous strain.

That "great duel" as Milton calls it, was no sham fight; one or the other had to go down. Christ was gnawed by hunger, but refused to eat. He saw what might be done by a brilliant miracle towards inaugurating His Jewish ministry, but refused to work it. He saw the short, Satanic path to Messianic dominion, but chose Gethsemane and Calvary. Now the first Adam was just as cool and just as innocent as the second Adam. And, with more of grace to strengthen him, he too might have stood.

There was no real necessity for that first human disobedience. It was sheer, wanton, gratuitous, inexplicable apostasy. Somewhat more of Divine constraint, and the catastrophe would certainly have been averted. Call it non-prevention, call it permission, call it anything you please, somehow sin entered in spite of God's hating it. It came knocking for admission, and God's shoulder was not against the gate. For some reason, or reasons, not revealed, perhaps not revealable, God thought it best not to put His shoulder against the gate. The hateful and hated thing pushed through. Ormuzd let in Ahriman. I thank the Persian for these two words. They embody and emphasize the historic dualism of good and evil.

The *historic* dualism, you will observe I say; there is no other dualism. God is One; and Master of all. The Divine permission of hateful and hated evil, when we fairly apprehend it, is a tremendous statement, which might well be challenged, were not the thing itself so undeniably a fact. This is as far as we can go. Here we halt, with our bruised and throbbing foreheads hard up against the granite cliff.

Practically, historic sin finds relief in historic redemption. Apparently, there was little, if any, interval between the two. Sin came, perhaps, with the noon tide rest. "In the cool of the day"—that same day, most likely, the offended Lord came walking in the garden. The colloquy had a sharp beginning, but a mellow ending. The bitten heel would finally crush the biting head. And the struggle at once began. The Lord came down very close to His erring, guilty, frightened children. And they clung very closely to Him. We are in great danger of underrating that primitive economy of grace. The record is very brief, and the oriental genius of it seems strange to us. But we see an altar there; and it can have had but one meaning.

Ages after, in all the nobler ethnic religions—Egyptian, Indian, Persian, and Pelasgic—we encounter echoes and survivals of that first vouchsafement of revelation. In all the great religions, we find one God; in all of them, personal immortality, with retribution; in most of them Divine Triads; in two of them at least, the resurrection of the body. If it be true, as we may well believe, that Socrates is now in Heaven, singing the new song, it is because he sacrificed; and he sacrificed, whether he fully understood it or not, because of that colloquy in the garden. And if that sufficed for him, the Providence of God is justified. Historic sin is fairly matched, and overmatched by historic redemption.

But the Lamb slain from the foundation of the world, suggests a far sublimer theodicy. We are taken back behind the human ages, behind all time, into awful infinite depths, into the very bosom of the Triune God. Theological science recognizes two Trinities which it calls economic and essential. The former began with historic redemption and kept pace with it. Father, Son and Spirit stood for law, redemption and regeneration. It was economic Trinity that suggested essential Trinity. But for the historic process, the question might not have seemed worth asking, whether God is One only, or Three also, and Three in One.

The Hebrew mind, as represented by Philo, was only just beginning to be Trinitarian, when Christ's life in the flesh compelled the Hebrew mind, as represented by Peter, Paul, and John, to a new theology. After Pentecost, bald Unitarianism was anachronous. Christian experience logically required three Divine Persons, of one and the same Divine Essence. Economic Trinity required essential Trinity.

Essential Trinity is anything but an arbitrary conception of God. Wiclif taught it at Oxford as a necessary doctrine of reason. Trinity is another name for the self-consciousness, and self-communion, of God. Father, Son and Spirit are vastly more than the revelation of God to man; they are the revelation of God to Himself, and the intercourse of God with Himself. They suggest infinite fulness and richness of being.

Our scientific definitions of God do not amount to much. At best, they formulate only very inadequate conceptions of Him. It is assumed that these scientific definitions of God take us farther than the Biblical descriptions of God. We had better not feel too sure of that. Attributes in action may impart a better knowledge than attributes abstractly defined. Pictures for children may be better than creeds and catechisms. What we need is to see God in the life both of nature, and of man. This the Hebrew Prophets enable us to do by their anthropomorphic and anthropopathic pictures of God. If you say the pictures are childish, then I must say that we *are* children, all of us, and had better be children.

It is no real scandal to science to be told that "the *eyes* of the Lord are in every place, beholding the evil and the good," that "the *eyes* of the Lord are upon the righteous and His *ears* are open unto their cry"; that the Lord "*smelled* a sweet savor" from Noah's altar; while wicked men are consumed by "the *breath* of His nostrils" that "the *voice* of the Lord breaketh the cedars of Lebanon"; and He "*walketh* upon the wings of the wind"; and that at last, in the Messianic time, the Lord will make "bare His holy arm in the eyes of all the nations."

God is not a mere aggregate of attributes. He has a Personality as distinct and positive as yours and mine. But the Personality is infinite in all its outgoings. God's Being is a vast abyss which no plummet has ever sounded. Imagine all you can of boundless power, constantly at work; of boundless intelligence, constantly at work; of boundless passion, constantly at work; God is all that, and immeasurably more than that.

What right has any one to say that God is passionless? God Himself has never said it. He is NOT passionless. Like the sun, He is all aflame; He rejoices in the truth; He hates a lie. He is pleased with what is right, and displeased with what is wrong. Good men are the apple of His eye; bad men His abomination and His scorn. Rendered literally, "God is a righteous Judge, and a God Who is angry every day." (Ps. 7:11)

But God is love. So says John in that famous passage, over which theologians are still disputing, whether the meaning be that love is only one of the Divine attributes, or is that very essence of God, into which every other attribute may be resolved. Some of the profoundest thinkers of our day accept these three words of John, "God is love," as the final definition of God. Sunshine striking a tear-drop, may give us the seven colors of the rainbow; but the seven colors are all one blessed light.

God creates, governs, judges, punishes, pities, redeems, and saves; but love is the root of all. It was love that created this wondrous universe, to which science can set no bounds. It was love that created angels, some of whom rebelled, and were "delivered into chains of darkness." (II Pet. 2:4) It was love that created this human brotherhood, all of whom have rebelled and gone astray. This rebellion was permitted; but was rebellion all the same. God feels it; and has always felt it. Absalom has broken his father's heart; and we are Absalom. The grand old King goes up over Olivet weeping, with his head covered, and his feet bare; and that King is God. Only He is the King Eternal, and His agony over sin is also eternal. This agony of God over human sin is the Lamb slain from the foundation of the world. God Himself atones, to Himself atones; and so atonement is both eternal and divine.

In that matchless epitome of the Gospel—the parable of the Prodigal Son, reported only by Luke, not a word is said, not a glimpse is given, of the father of the Prodigal during all that interval between the departure and the return. A veil is drawn over all those bitter, weary years. So has God yearned and suffered in the silent depths of His own eternity, waiting and watching for the repentant Prodigal. This yearning, grieved, and suffering God is the God and Father of our Lord and Saviour Jesus Christ; Son of God, Son of Mary. This sinless child should have had no griefs of His own. His sorrows could have been only those old eternal shadows of permitted sin. The Cross on which He died, flinging out its arms as if to embrace the world, lifted up its head toward the Lamb slain from the foundation of the world. Our hearts now go back to Calvary; and from Calvary they go up to God.

ALEXANDER MACLAREN 1826–1910

"I cannot recall ever having had any hesitation as to being a minister; it seems to me it must have been simply taken for granted by my father and my mother and myself; it just had to be."

So wrote young Alexander Maclaren to a friend from the Baptist College at Stepney, London. Some Christian ministers can point to the day and even the hour when they received their call to service. With others it amounted to a growing conviction. A third group had the predilection from childhood. Maclaren was obviously in this third category.

In 1845, having finished college, he received an invitation to fill the pulpit of the Portland Chapel in Southampton one Sunday. He accepted, delivering two sermons. The church at the time was pastorless. The members enjoyed his preaching so much that they asked him to continue as stated supply for three months. Again he agreed, but with some trepidation. The church was in barren condition spiritually. Maclaren confided to his family, "If the worst comes to the worst I shall at all events not have to reflect that I killed a flourishing plant but only assisted at the funeral of a withered one."

At the end of the three months, the people of the congregation were sure he was the Lord's choice to preach the Word to them. They voted to call him, and he said Yes a third time.

He married his cousin, Marian Maclaren, a lovely girl with deep brown eyes and delicately beautiful features. For thirty years they lived together as heirs of the grace of life. Upon Marian's exodus, her bereaved husband said, "There was never a cloud between us and she never did a thing or spoke a word that was not full of love and unselfishness." Two daughters were born to them.

Alexander Maclaren was a shy person. Consequently, he did not enjoy visitation and shunned social contacts. He was criticized for not being a good pastor, and readily admitted it. If he was to be a physician of value, he wrote, he must give himself unceasingly to prayer and the study and ministry of the Word.

The Portland Chapel grew in numbers and in the faith under Mr. Maclaren's teaching.

In 1858, thirteen years after he had accepted his first call, a second came to him. The Union Chapel in Manchester invited him to preach after the regular minister had resigned. He did, and twenty-four hours later a committee waited on him to ask him if he would be willing to take over the vineyard, now vacant. He would.

It was his second and last charge, and he was to be with it for the next fifty fruitful years.

If Spurgeon is the prince of preachers, Alexander Maclaren is the prince of expositors. In his first years in the pulpit he may have yielded to the temptation to use high-flown language. It did not last long. "I have abjured forever all the rubbish of intellectual preaching," he said. "The sole purpose lies in the true, simple, sincere setting forth of the living Christ." In season and out of season, he expounded God's whole counsel. In consequence, there was in his preaching a fountain freshness, a perennial power, a wholesome and healthy balance which, under God, converted and edified and enriched his hearers in all wisdom and knowledge. His sermons, hundreds of which exist in printed form, still delight, stimulate, and challenge the hearts and minds of avid readers.

What was the secret of his success in teaching Scripture? His answer: "I sometimes think that a verse in the Psalms carries the whole path of homiletics: 'While I was musing the fire burned; then spake I with my tongue.' Patient meditation, resulting in kindled emotions and the flashing-up of truth with warmth and light—and not till then—the rush of speech 'moved by the Holy Ghost'—there are the processes which will make sermons live things with hands and feet, as Luther's words were said to be. 'Then spake I,' not 'Then sat I down at my desk and wrote it out all down to be majestically read out of a manuscript in a leather bag.' "

Once in 1893, he was invited to address the Assembly of the Free Church of Scotland. He aroused some ire among the Presbyterian brethren when he advised them, "Burn your manuscripts."

Maclaren used sermon notes, but sparingly. His fertile mind was so filled with sacred writings that he needed no script. Always before a sermon or lecture in public, he would be overcome with nervous agitation. It vanished as soon as he launched into his message. And frequently after the service, waves of depression would engulf him, and he wanted to be alone.

A Baptist by conviction, Maclaren had a truly catholic spirit and attitude. Many times he addressed other communions and bodies, and he interested himself deeply in Manchester's moral and philanthropic enterprises. All of his gifts—his trained intellect, his vivid imagination, his flawless taste in literary expression—were dedicated to the cause of truth and righteousness, and were generously blessed of his Lord.

At the evening of his life there was sunlight. He ripened gracefully, enjoyed his friendships to the end, and retained his intellectual vigor until his final hours on earth.

Over his burial place a plaque carries the simple words: "In Christo, in Pace, in Spe" ("In Christ, in Peace, in Hope"). Only his name is added.

Who Can Forgive Sins but God Only?

ALEXANDER MACLAREN, D.D.

Mark 2:1-12

MARK alone gives Capernaum as the scene of this miracle. The excitement which had induced our Lord to leave that place had been allowed "some days" to quiet down, "after" which He ventures to return, but does not seem to have sought publicity, but to have remained in "the house"—probably Peter's. There would be at least one woman's heart there, which would love to lavish grateful service on Him. But "He could not be hid," and, however little genuine or deep the eagerness might be, He will not refuse to meet it. Mark paints vividly the crowd flocking to the humble home, overflowing its modest capacity, blocking the doorway, and clustering round it outside as far as they could hear Christ's voice. "He was speaking the Word to them," proclaiming His mission, as He had done in their synagogue, when He was interrupted by the events which follow, no doubt to the gratification of some of His hearers, who wanted something more exciting than "teaching."

Peter's house was, probably, one of no great pretensions or size, but like hundreds of poor men's houses in Palestine still—a one-storied building, with a low, flat roof, mostly earth, and easily reached from the ground by some outside stair. It would be somewhat difficult to get a sick man and his bed up there, however low, and somewhat free-and-easy dealing with another man's house to burrow through the roof a hole big enough for the purpose; but there is no impossibility, and the difficulty is part of the lesser of the incident, and is recognised expressly in the narrative by Christ's notice of their "faith."

We can fancy the blank looks of the four bearers, and the disappointment on the sick man's thin face and weary eyes, as they got to the edge of the crowd, and saw that there was no hope of forcing a passage. Had they been less certain of a cure, and less eager, they would have shouldered their burden and carried him home again. They could well have pleaded sufficient reason for giving up the attempt. But "we cannot" is the coward's word. "We must" is the earnest man's. If we have any real consciousness of our need to get to Christ, and any real wish to do so, it is not a crowd round the door that will keep us back. Difficulties test, and therefore increase, faith. They develop a sanctified

385

ingenuity in getting over them, and bring a rich harvest of satisfaction when at last conquered.

These four eager faces looked down through the broken roof, when they had succeeded in dropping the bed right at Christ's feet, with a far keener pleasure than if they had just carried him in by the door. No doubt their act was inconvenient; for, however light the roofing, some rubbish must have come down on the heads of some of the notabilities below. And, no doubt, it was interfering with property as well as with propriety. But here was a sick man, and there was his Healer; and it was their business to get the two together somehow. It was worth risking a good deal to accomplish. The rabbis sitting there might frown at rude intrusiveness; Peter might object to the damage to his roof; some of the listeners might dislike the interruption to His teaching; but Jesus read the action of the bearers and the consent of the motionless figure on the couch as the indication of "their faith," and His love and power responded to its call.

Note the unexpected gift with which Christ answers this faith. None of them speak a word throughout the whole incident. The act of the bearers and the condition of the sick man spoke loudly enough. Obviously, all five must have had, at all events, so much "faith" as went to the conviction that He could and would heal; and this faith is the occasion of Christ's gift. The bearers had it, as is shown by their work. It was a visible faith, manifest by conduct. He can see the hidden heart; but here He looks upon conduct, and thence infers disposition.

Faith, if worth anything, comes to the surface in act. Was it faith of the bearers, or of the sick man, which Christ rewarded? Both. As Abraham's intercession delivered Lot, as Paul in the shipwreck was the occasion of safety to all the crew, so one man's faith may bring blessings on another. But if the sick man had not had faith too, he would not have let himself be brought at all, and would certainly not have consented to reach Christ's presence by so strange and, to him, dangerous a way—painfully hoisted up some narrow stair, and then perilously let down, at the risk of cords snapping, or hands letting go, or quilts tearing.

His faith, apparently, was deeper than theirs; for Christ's answer, though it went far beyond his or their expectations, must have been moulded to meet his deepest sense of need. We mark it in the tender greeting "son," or, as the margin has it, "child"—possibly pointing to the man's youth, but more probably an appellation revealing the mingled love and dignity of Jesus, and taking this man into the arms of His tenderness. The palsy may have been the consequence of "fast" living; but, whether it were so or no, Christ saw that in the dreary hours of solitary inaction to which it had condemned the sufferer, remorse had been busy gnawing at his heart, and that pain had done its best work by leading to penitence. Therefore He spoke to the conscience before He touched the bodily ailment, and met the sufferer's deepest and most deeply felt disease first. He goes to the bottom of the malady with His cure.

These great words are not only closely adapted to the one case before Him, but contain a general truth, worthy to be pondered by all philanthropists. It is of little use to cure symptoms unless you cure diseases. The tap-root of all misery is sin; and, until it is grubbed up, hacking at the branches is sad waste of time. Cure sin, and you make the heart a temple and the world a paradise. We Christians should hail all efforts of every sort for making men nobler, happier, better physically, morally, intellectually; but let us not forget that there is but one effectual cure for the world's misery, and that is wrought by Him who has borne the world's sins.

Note the snarl of the scribes. "Certain of the scribes," says Mark—not being much impressed by their dignity, which, as Luke tells us, was considerable. He says that they were "Pharisees and doctors of the law . . . out of every village of Galilee and Judea and Jerusalem" itself, who had come on a formal errand of investigation. Their tempers would not be improved by the tearing up of the roof, nor sweetened by seeing the "popularity" of this doubtful young Teacher, who showed that He had the secret, which they had not, of winning men's hearts. Nobody came crowding to them, nor hung on their lips.

Professional jealousy has often a great deal to do in helping zeal for truth to sniff out heresy. The whispered cavillings are graphically represented. The scribes would not speak out, like men, and call on Jesus to defend His words. If they had been sure of their ground, they should have boldly charged Him with blasphemy; but perhaps they were half suspicious that He could show good cause for His speech. Perhaps they were afraid to oppose the tide of enthusiasm for Him. So they content themselves with comparing notes among themselves and wait for Him to entangle Himself a little more in their nets. They affect to despise Him. "This man" is meant for contempt. If He were so poor a creature, why were they there, all the way from Jerusalem, some of them? They overdo their part. The short, snarling sentences of their muttered objections, as given in the Revised Version [1881], may be taken as shared among three speakers, each bringing his quota of bitterness.

One says, "Why doth" He "thus speak"? Another curtly answers, "He blasphemeth"; while a third formally states the great truth on which they rest their indictment. Their principle is impregnable. Forgiveness is a Divine prerogative, to be shared by none, to be grasped by none, without, in the act, diminishing God's glory. But it is not enough to have one premise of your syllogism right. Only God forgives sins; and if this man says that He does, He, no doubt, claims to be, in some sense, God. But whether He "blasphemeth" or no depends on what the scribes do not stay to ask; namely, whether He has the right so to claim: and, if He has, it is they, not He, who are the blasphemers.

We need not wonder that they recoiled from the right conclusion, which is the Deity of Jesus. Their fault was not their jealousy for the Divine honour, but their inattention to Christ's evidence in support of His claims, which inattention had its roots in their moral condition, their self-sufficiency, and absorption in trivialities of externalism. But we have to thank them for clearly discerning and bluntly stating what was involved in our Lord's claims, and for thus bringing up the sharp issue—blasphemer, or God manifest in the flesh.

Note our Lord's answer to the cavils. Mark would have us see something supernatural in the swiftness of Christ's knowledge of the muttered criticisms. He perceived it "straightway" and "his spirit," which is tantamount to saying, by Divine discernment, and not by the medium of sense, as we do. His spirit was a mirror, in which looking He saw externals. In the most literal and deepest sense, He does "not judge after the sight of His eyes, neither reprove after the hearing of His ears."

The absence from our Lord's answer of any explanation that He was only declaring the Divine forgiveness and not Himself exercising a Divine prerogative, shuts us up to the conclusion that He desired to be understood as exercising it. Unless His pardon is something quite different from the ministerial announcement of forgiveness, which His servants are empowered to make to penitents, He wilfully led the cavillers into error.

His answer starts with a counter-question—another "why" to meet their "why." It then puts into words what they were thinking; namely, that it was easy to assume a power the reality of which could not be tested. To say "Thy sins be forgiven," and to say "Take up thy bed," are equally easy. To effect either is equally beyond man's power; but the one can be verified and the other cannot, and, no doubt, some of the scribes were maliciously saying, "It is all very well to pretend to do what cannot be tested. Let Him come out into daylight, and do a miracle which we can see." He is quite willing to accept the challenge to test His power in the invisible realm of conscience by His power in the visible region.

The remarkable construction of the long sentence in verses 10 and 11, which is almost verbally identical in the three Gospels, parenthesis and all, sets the suddenness of the turn from the scribes to the patient before us with dramatic force. Mark that our Lord claims "authority" to forgive, the same word which has been twice in the people's mouths in reference to His teaching and to His sway over demons. It implies not only power, but rightful power, and that authority He wields as "Son of man" and "on earth."

This is the first use of that title in Mark. It is Christ's own designation of Himself, never found on other lips except the dying Stephen's. It implies His Messianic office, and points back to Daniel's great prophecy; but it also asserts His true manhood and His unique relation to humanity, as being Himself its sum and perfection,—not *a*, but *the*, Son of man. Now the wonder which He would confirm by His miracle is that such a manhood, walking on earth, has lodged in it the Divine prerogative. He who is the Son of man must be something *more* than man, even the Son of God. His power to forgive is both derived and inherent, but, in either aspect, is entirely different from the human office of announcing God's forgiveness.

For once, Christ seems to work a miracle in response to unbelief, rather than to faith. But the real occasion of it was not the cavils of the scribes, but the faith and need of the man and His friends; while the silencing of unbelief, and the enlightenment of honest doubt, was but a collateral benefit.

Note the cure and its effect. This is another of the miracles in which no vehicle of the healing power is employed. The word is enough; but here the word is spoken, not as to the disease, but to the sufferer; and in his obedience, he receives strength to obey. Tell a palsied man to rise and walk! His disease is such that he cannot. But if he believes that Christ has power to heal, he will try to do as he is bid; and, as he tries, the paralysis steals out of the long-unused limbs.

Jesus makes us able to do what He bids us do. The condition of healing is faith, and the test of faith is obedience. We do not get strength till we put ourselves into the attitude of obedience. The cure was immediate; and the cured man, who was "borne of four" into the healing presence, walked away, with his bed under his arm, "before them all." They were ready enough to make way for him then. And what said the wise doctors to it all? We do not hear that any of them were convinced. And what said the people? They were "amazed," and they "glorified God," and recognised that they had seen something quite new. That was all. Their glorifying God cannot have been very deep-seated, or they would have better learned the lesson of the miracle. Amazement was but a poor result.

No emotion is more transient or less fruitful than gaping astonishment; and that, with a little varnish of acknowledgment of God's power, which led to nothing, was all the fruit of Christ's mighty work. Let us hope that the healed man carried his unseen blessing in a faithful and grateful heart, and consecrated his restored strength to the Lord who healed him!

T. DE WITT TALMAGE 1832–1902

A threefold cord, said Solomon, is not easily broken. A triple cord of three offices—clergyman, lecturer, editor—bound Thomas De Witt Talmage to an exciting and colorful life. He became one of the most controversial figures in America in the latter half of the nineteenth century.

Originally he planned to practice law. Halfway through college, he changed his mind and decided to enter the ministry. He attended New Brunswick Theological Seminary, and upon graduation was ordained in the Dutch Reformed Church and assumed charge of a congregation in Belleville, New Jersey. Three years later he was called to a church in Syracuse, New York.

From Syracuse he went to the Second Dutch Reformed Church of Philadelphia. Following a successful seven-year pastorate, he transferred to the Brick Church in Brooklyn. He was a man of fine appearance, with distinguished bearing, strong features, magnetic personality, and remarkable fluency. He attracted large crowds whenever he preached. In no time the facilities in the Brick Church became inadequate, and a large tabernacle was built for him.

Meanwhile, a storm was in the making. His flair for the dramatic, his unusual gestures, his graphic illustrations were drawing fire from the public. Newspapermen called him a pulpit clown and a mountebank. In 1879 his presbytery preferred charges against him, accusing him of "falsehood and deceit . . . using improper methods of preaching which tend to bring religion into contempt." He was acquitted by a narrow margin.

Much publicity accompanied the indictment, which he was quick to capitalize on. Soon after the incident, he happened to be traveling in the Holy Land. With no little fanfare, he baptized a man in the Jordan River. Again he was plunged into the vortex of controversy. The action proved that he was a sensationalist, a headline-hunter, his enemies said.

Unabashed, he continued to preach.

During his career as a minister he married three times, death taking his first two wives. Three times his churches were demolished by fire. Around the world, over three thousand newspapers carried his sermons. He lectured on an average of fifty times a year.

In 1889, he left the pulpit to turn his attention and gifts to journalism. He first edited Christians at Work, *and later* The Christian Herald.

Adverse criticism notwithstanding, Talmage unquestionably had a love for the Gospel of the Son of God, and proclaimed it fearlessly. He was a wizard of the illustration and selected from an astonishingly wide range of knowledge to drive home his points. In one sermon, "The Hornet's Mission," object lessons are borrowed from the Hittites and the Canaanites, from Judea, Persia, Bithynia, Holland, England, Africa, Germany, and America.

His diction was pure and refreshing, singularly free from clichés and hackneyed phrases. In a message to young people, he closes with an appeal that must have stirred many a youthful pulse: "O Christian workers, my heart is high with hope. The dark horizon is blooming into the morning of which the prophets spoke, and of which poets have dreamed, and of which painters have sketched. The mountains will kiss the morning radiant and effulgent, and all the waves of the sea will become the crystal keys of a great organ, on which the fingers of everlasting joy shall play the grand march of a world redeemed."

Jealousy

A Diabolical Sin That Sets One-half the World Against the Other

T. DE WITT TALMAGE

THERE IS an old sin, haggard, furious, monstrous and diabolical, that has for ages walked and crawled the earth. It combines all that is obnoxious in the races, human, quadrupedal, ornithological, reptilian and insectile, horned, tusked, hoofed, fanged, stinged; the eye of a basilisk, the tooth of an adder, the jaws of a crocodile, the crushing folds of an anaconda, the slyness of a scorpion, the tongue of a cobra, and the coil of the worm that never dies. It is in every community, in every church, in every legislative hall, in every monetary institution, in every drawing-room levee, in every literary and professional circle. It whispers, it hisses, it lies, it debauches, it blasphemes, it damns.

It is grief at the superiority of others; their superiority in talent, or wealth, or beauty, or elegance, or virtue, or social, or professional, or political recognition. It is the shadow of other people's success. It is the shiver in our pocket-book because it is not so fat as some one else's pocket-book. It is the twinge in our tongue because it is not so eloquent as some one else's tongue. It is the flutter in our robes because they are not so lustrous as some one else's robes. It is the earthquake under our house because it is not so many feet front deep as our neighbor's house.

It is the thunder of other people's popularity souring the milk of our kindness. It is the father and mother of one-half of the discontent and outrages, and detractions, and bankruptcies, and crimes, and woes of the human race.

The First Case of Jealousy

It was antediluvian as much as it is postdiluvian. It put a rough stick in the hands of the first boy that was ever born, and said to him: "Now, Cain, when Abel is looking the other way, crush in his skull; for his sacrifice has been accepted and yours rejected." And Cain picked up the stick as though just to walk with it, and while Abel was watching some birds in the tree-top, or gazing at some water-fall, down came the blow of the first assassination, which has had its echo in all the fratricides, matricides, homicides, infanticides and regicides of all ages and all nations.

This passion of jealousy so disturbed Caligula at the prominence of some of the men of his time, that he cut a much-admired curl from the brow of Cincinnatus, and took the embroidered collar from the neck Torquatus, and had Ptolemaeus killed because of his purple robe, which attracted too much attention. After Columbus had placed America as a gem in the Spanish crown, jealousy set on the Spanish courtiers to depreciate his achievement, and aroused animosities till the great discoverer had his heart broken. Urged on by this bad passion, Dionysius flayed Plato because he was wiser than himself, and Philixenus because his music was too popular. Jealousy made Korah lie about Moses and Succoth depreciate Gideon.

Jealousy made the trouble between Jacob and Esau. That hurled Joseph into the pit. That struck the twenty-three fatal wounds into Julius Caesar. That banished Aristides. That fired Antony against Cicero. Tiberius exiled an architect because of the fame he got for a beautiful porch, and slew a poet for his fine tragedy. That set Saul in a rage against David. How graphically the Bible puts it when it says: "Saul eyed David." It seems to take possession of both eyes and makes them flash and burn like two port-holes of hell. "Saul eyed David." That is, he looked at him as much as to say: "You little upstart, how dare you attempt anything great. I will grind you under my heel. I will exterminate you, I will, you miserable homunculus. Crouch, crawl, slink into that rat-hole. I will teach those women to sing some other song, instead of "Saul has slain his thousands, but David his tens of thousands." When Voltaire heard that Frederick the Great was forgetting him and putting his literary admiration on Bacaulard d'Arnaud, the old infidel leaped out of his bed and danced the floor in a maniacal rage, and ordered his swiftest horses hooked up to carry him to the Prussian palace.

That despicable passion of jealousy led Napoleon I to leave in his will a bequest of 5000 francs to the ruffian who shot at Wellington when the victor of Waterloo was passing through Paris. That stationed the grouty elder brother at the back door of the homestead when the prodigal son returned, and threw a chill on the family reunion while that elder brother complained, saying: "Who ever heard of giving roast veal to such a profligate?" Ay, that passion rose up and under the darkest cloud that ever shadowed the earth, and amid the loudest thunder that ever shook the mountains, and amid the wildest flash of lightning that ever blinded or stunned the nations, hung up on two pieces of rough lumber back of Jerusalem the kindest, purest, lovingest nature that Heaven could delegate, and stopped not until there was no power left in hammer, or bramble, or javelin to hurt the dead Son of God.

That passion of jealousy, livid, hungry, unbalked, rages on, and it now pierces the earth like a fiery diameter and encircles it like a fiery circumference. It wants both hemispheres. It wants the heavens. It would, if it could, capture the palace of God, and dethrone Jehovah, and chain the Almighty in eternal exile, and after the demolition of the universe would cry: "Satisfied at last, here I am, alone, the undisputed and everlasting I, me, mine, myself!" That passion keeps all Europe perturbed. Nations jealous of Germany, of England, of Russia, and those jealous of each other, and all of them jealous of America.

Go into all occupations and professions, and if you want to know how much jealousy is yet to be extirpated, ask master builders what they think of each other's houses, and merchants what their opinion is of merchants in the same line of business in the same street, and ask doctors what they think of doctors, and lawyers what they think of lawyers, and ministers what they think of ministers, and artists what they think of artists. As long as men and women in any department keep down and have a hard struggle they will be faintly praised and the remark will be: "Oh, yes, he is a good, clever sort of a fellow." "She is rather, yes, somewhat, quite—well, I may say, tolerable nice kind of a woman." But let him or her get a little too high and off goes the aspiring head by social or commercial decapitation.

Remember that envy dwells more on small defects of character than on great forces; makes more of the fact that Domitian amused himself by transfixing flies with his penknife than of his great conquests; more of the fact that Handel was a glutton than that he created imperishable oratorios; more of Coleridge's opium habit than of his writing "Christabel" and "The Ancient Mariner"; more of the fact that Addison drank too much than of the fact that he was the editor of the "Spectator"; jealousy that derided and abused Copernicus even to his death-bed;

more of man's peccadilloes than of his mighty energies; more of his defeats than of his victories.

Jealousy Among Doctors

Look at the sacred and heaven-descended science of healing, and then see Dr. Mackenzie, the English surgeon, who prolonged the life of the Crown Prince of Germany until he became Emperor. Yet so great were the medical jealousies that for a time Dr. Mackenzie dared not walk the streets of Berlin. He was under military guard. The medical students of Germany could hardly keep their hands from him. The old doctors of Germany were writhing with indignation. The fact is that in prolonging Frederick's life for several months Dr. Mackenzie saved the peace of Europe. There was not an intelligent man on either side of the ocean that did not fear for the result if the throne passed immediately from wise and good old Emperor William to his inexperienced grandson. But when, under the medical treatment of Dr. Mackenzie, the Crown Prince Frederick took the throne, a wave of satisfaction and confidence rolled over Christendom. But what shall the world do with the doctor who prolonged his life? "Oh," cried out the medical jealousies of Europe, "destroy him; of course, destroy him."

What a brutal scene of jealousy we had in this country when President Garfield lay dying. There were faithful physicians that sacrificed their other practice and sacrificed their health for all time in fidelity to that death-bed. Doctors Bliss and Hamilton and Agnew went through anxieties and toils and fatigues such as none but God could appreciate. Nothing pleased many of the medical profession. The doctors in charge did nothing right. We who did not see the case knew better than those who agonized over it in the sick-room for many weeks. I, who never had anything worse than a run-round on my thumb, which seemed to me at the time was worthy all the attention of the entire medical fraternity, had my own ideas as to how the President ought to be treated. And in proportion as physicians and laymen were ignorant of the case, they were sure the treatment practiced was a mistake. And when in post-mortem the bullet dropped out of a different part of the body from that in which it was supposed to have been lodged, about 200,000 people shouted: "I told you so!" "There! I knew it all the time." There are some doctors who would rather have the patient die under the treatment of their own schools than have them get well under some other pathy.

Yea, look at the clerical profession. I am sorry to say that in matters of jealousy it is no better than other professions. There are now in all denominations a great many young clergymen who have a faculty for superior usefulness. But they are kept down and kept back and crippled by older ministers who look askance at these rising evangelists. They are snubbed. They are jostled. They are patronizingly advised. It is suggested to them that they had better know their place. If here and there one with more nerve and brain, and consecration, and divine force go past the seniors who want to keep the chief places, the young are advised in the words of Scripture: "Tarry at Jericho till their beards are grown."

They are charged with sensationalism. They are compared to rockets that go up in a blaze and come down sticks, and the brevity of their career is jubilantly prophesied. If it be a denomination with bishops, a bishop is implored to sit down heavily on the man who will not be moulded; or if a denomination without bishops, some of the older men with nothing more than their own natural heaviness and theological avoirdupois are advised to flatten out the innovator. In conferences and presbyteries, and associations and conventions there is often seen the most damnable jealousy. Such ecclesiastical tyrants would not admit that jealousy had any possession of them, and they take on a heavenly air, and talk sweet oil and sugar plums, and balm of a thousand flowers, and roll up their eyes with an air of unctuous sanctity when they simply mean the destruction of those over whom they pray and sniffle. There are cases where ministers of religion are derelict and criminal, and they must be put out.

Like Cutting a Roasted Ox

But in the majority of cases that I have witnessed in ecclesiastical trials, there is a jealous attempt to keep men from surpassing their theological fellows, and as at the presidential elections in country places the people have a barbecue, which is a roasted ox round which the people dance with knives, cutting off a slice here, and pulling out a rib there, and sawing off a beefsteak yonder, and having a high time; so most of the denominations of Christians keep on hand a barbecue in which some minister is roasted while the Church courts dance around with their sharp knives of attack, and one takes an ear, another a hand, another a foot, and it is hard to tell whether the ecclesiastical plaintiffs of this world or the demons of the nether world most enjoy it. Albert Barnes, than whom no man has accomplished more good in the last thousand years, was decreed to sit silent for a year in the pew of his own church while some one else occupied his pulpit, the pretended offence being that he did not believe in a limited atonement, but the real offence the fact that all the men who tried him put together would not equal one Albert Barnes.

Yes; amid all professions and business, and occupations, and trades, and amid all circles needs to be heard what God says in regard to envy and jealousy, which, though not exactly the same, are twins: "Envy is the rottenness of the bone"; "Where envy and strife is, there is confusion and every evil work"; "Jealousy is the rage of man." That which has downed kings and emperors, and apostles, and reformers, and ministers of religion, and thousands of good men and women, is too mighty for you to contend against unaided. The evil has so many roots of such infinite convolution that nothing but the energy of omnipotence can pull it out.

Away with the accursed, stenchful, blackening, damning crime of jealousy. Allow it to stay and it will eat up and carry off all the religion you can pack into your soul for the next half-century. It will do you more harm than it does any one it leads you to assail. It will delude you with the idea that you can build yourself up by pulling somebody else down. You will make more out of the success of others than out of their misfortunes. Speak well of everybody. Stab no man in the back. Be a honey-bee rather than a spider; be a dove rather than a buzzard.

Surely this world is large enough for you and all your rivals. God has given you a work to do. Go ahead and do it. Mind your own business. In all circles, in all businesses, in all professions there is room for straightforward successes. Jealousy entertained will not only bedwarf your soul, but it will flatten your skull, bemean your eye, put pinchedness of look about your nostril, give a bad curl to the lip, and expel from your face the divine image in which you were created. When you hear a man or woman abused, drive in on the defendant's side. Watch for excellences in others rather than for defects, morning-glories instead of night-shade. If some one is more beautiful than you, thank God that you have not so many perils of vanity to contend with. If some one has more wealth than you, thank God that you have not so great stewardship to answer for. If some one is higher up in social position, thank God that those who are down need not fear a fall. If some one gets higher office in Church or State than you, thank God there are not so many to wish for the hastening on of your obsequies.

The Duke of Dantzig, in luxurious apartments, was visited by a plain friend, and to keep his friend from jealousy the Duke said: "You can have all I have if you will stand twenty paces off and let me shoot at you one hundred times."

"No, no," said his friend.

"Well," said the Duke, "to gain all my honors I faced on the battle-field more than a thousand gunshots fired not more than ten paces off."

A minister of small congregation complained to a minister of large congregation about the sparseness of his attendants. "Ah," said one of large audience, "my son, you will find in the day of judgment that you had quite enough people for whom to be held accountable."

A Substitute

Substitute for jealousy an elevating emulation. Seeing others good, let us try to be better. Seeing others industrious, let us work more hours. Seeing others benevolent, let us resolve on giving larger percentage of our means for charity. May God put congratulations for others into our right hand and cheers on our lips for those who do brave and useful things. Life is short at the longest; let it all be filled up with helpfulness for others, work and sympathy for each other's misfortunes, and our arms be full of white mantles to cover up the mistakes and failures of others. If an evil report about some one come to us, let us put on the most favorable construction, as the Rhone enters Lake Leman foul and comes out crystalline. Do not build so much on the transitory differences of this world, for soon it will make no difference to us whether we had ten million dollars or ten cents, and the ashes into which the tongue of Demosthenes dissolved are just like the ashes into which the tongue of the veriest stammerer went.

If you are assailed by jealousy, make no answer. Take it as a compliment, for people are never jealous of a failure. Until your work is done, you are invulnerable. Remember how our Lord behaved under such exasperations. Did they not try to catch Him in His word? Did they not call Him the victim of intoxicants? Did they not misinterpret Him from the winter of the year 1 to the spring of the year 33—that is, from His first infantile cry to the last groan of His assassination? Yet He answered not a word. But so far from demolishing either His mission or His good name, after near nineteen centuries He outranks everything under the skies, and is second to none above them, and the archangel makes salaam at His footstool. Christ's bloody antagonists thought that they had finished Him when they wrote over the cross His accusation in three languages—Hebrew, Greek and Latin—not realizing that they were by that act introducing Him to all nations, since Hebrew is the holiest language, and Greek the wisest of tongues, and Latin the widest spoken.

You are not the first man who had his faults looked at through a microscope and his virtues through the wrong end of a telescope. Pharaoh had the chief butler and baker endungeoned, and tradition says that all the butler had done was to allow a fly in the king's cup, and all the baker had done was to leave a gravel in the king's bread. The world has the habit of making a great ado about what you do wrong and forgetting to say anything about what you do right, but the same God will take care of you who provided for Merlin, the Christian martyr, when hidden from his pursuers in a hay-mow in Paris, a hen came and laid an egg close by him every morning, thus keeping him from starvation. Blessed are they that are persecuted, although persecution is a severe cataplasm. Ointment may smart the wound before healing it. What a soft pillow to die on if when we leave the world we can feel that, though a thousand people may have wronged us, we have wronged no one; or having made envious and jealous attack on others, we have repented of the sin and as far as possible made reparation.

CHARLES HADDON SPURGEON 1834–1892

The Surrey Gardens Music Hall, with a seating capacity of twelve thousand, overflowed with Londoners from every section of the city. They had come to hear the rising young Baptist minister, Charles Haddon Spurgeon. He had just started to pray when, without warning, from several areas of the auditorium the cry went up, "Fire!" Instantly, the congregation panicked. Shouting and screaming, people rushed toward the exits, trampling others underfoot. In vain Spurgeon pleaded for order. There was no fire, he said. The whole thing was a terrible trick planned by thieves and pickpockets. No one listened to him, and when the uproar at last died down, seven had been crushed to death and nearly thirty seriously injured.

The calamity plunged Spurgeon into a state of shock. He came out of it eventually, but not without scar tissue. Throughout his lifetime, periodically, the nightmarish spectacle, like Banquo's ghost, came back to haunt, sometimes to prostrate him. In those dark moments, one sublime truth would flow like healing ointment into his tortured mind and bring him peace: "Amidst much tumult, and divers rushings to and fro of troublous thoughts, our souls have returned to the dearest object of our desires, and we have found it no small consolation, after all to say, 'It matters not what shall become of us; God hath highly exalted Him, *and given* Him *a name which is above every name; that at the name of* Jesus *every knee should bow.'"*

From his youth until the hour God kissed away his spirit, the person of Jesus Christ filled the horizon of Charles Haddon Spurgeon.

One Sabbath morning in Colchester he, at sixteen, wandered into a Primitive Methodist Chapel, oppressed with a sense of guilt and wretchedly unhappy. The regular minister did not appear. A layman stood in his place and took as his text, "Look unto me and be ye saved, all the ends of the earth." That man, I thought, was really stupid, Spurgeon *said later. He was obliged to stick to his text because he had little else to say.*

He spoke for a few minutes, then riveted his eyes on the squirming boy seated among fifteen other listeners and said, "Young man, you look very miserable." He lifted his hands and cried out, "Young man, look to Jesus Christ! Look! Look! Look! You have nothin' to do but look and live."

Spurgeon obeyed. "I would have almost looked my eyes away. . . . I could have risen that instant and sung with the most enthusiastic of them, of the precious blood of Jesus, and the simple faith that looks to this alone. . . . I thought I could have danced my way home."

Soon thereafter he began to preach, first at informal gatherings in homes, then in churches. He became known as "The Boy Preacher of the Fens." He moved upward to the church at Waterbeach, thence to the New Park Street Chapel in Southwark, and finally to the Metropolitan Tabernacle in London. Uneducated in formal channels, he was, nevertheless, one of the most learned men of his generation. His fifteen-hundred-page autobiography, compiled from his diary by Mrs. Spurgeon, is a literary mine interstratified with rich veins of classical English, fresh and original thoughts, flashing epigrams: "Once I, like Mazeppa, lashed to the wild horse of my lust, bound hand and foot, incapable of resistance, was galloping on with hell's wolves behind me, howling for my body and soul as their just and lawful prey. Then came a mighty hand which stopped that wild horse, cut my bands, set me down, and brought me into liberty."

He never received ordination, never practiced it. "We do not believe in laying empty hands on empty heads."

"The Prince of Preachers" planted himself firmly in the current of historic Calvinism: "The old truth that Calvin preached, that Augustine preached, that Paul preached, is the truth that I must preach today, or else be false to my conscience and my God. I cannot shape the truth; I know of no such thing as paring off the rough edges of a doctrine. John Knox's gospel is my gospel. That which thundered through Scotland must thunder through England again."

Not content with the ministry of the Word as the sole facet of service, he established a college for training ministers, an orphanage, and a mission. He wrote extensively. Many of his books and sermons have been translated into other languages.

No minister enjoyed the lighter side of life more than Spurgeon. He used to say there was as much holiness in a laugh as in a cry. At a certain meeting when contributions for the new tabernacle were brought in, it was announced that a Mr. Pig had given the church a guinea. "Hm," said Charles Haddon drily, "a guinea pig." At Dunnington, he was introduced to a deacon named Alway. Spurgeon held out his hand and said, "Rejoice in the Lord, Alway." Again, John Campbell was once showing him a book, Thorn on Infant Baptism. Campbell remarked, "There is a thorn in the flesh for you," and the great Baptist preacher quipped, "Finish the quotation, my brother—'the messenger of Satan to buffet me.'"

During what he called the "Downgrade Controversy," when an assault was leveled against the basic doctrines of the faith, Spurgeon rose up in holy wrath and led the counterattack. "We can allow a thousand opinions in the world, but that which infringes upon the doctrine of covenant salvation through the imputed righteousness of our Lord Jesus

*Christ—against that we must and will, enter our hearty, all-solemn pro-
test as long as God spares us. As good stewards, we must maintain the
cause of truth against all comers."*

*Of all the people on earth, he scored as most contemptible the miser-
able men who sat listlessly in the galleries while in the arena the soldiers of Jesus Christ engaged the enemies of truth in a struggle to the
death. "We shall soon have to handle truth, not with kid gloves, but
with gauntlets, the gauntlets of holy courage and integrity. Go on, ye
warriors of the cross, for the King is at the head of you. . . . The old
faith must be triumphant."*

*It is just possible that Wordsworth, patient poet that he was, might
forgive a paraphrase on his tribute to Milton in his London, 1802:*

> *Spurgeon! thou should'st be living at this hour:*
> *England hath need of thee!*

Three Crucifixions!

CHARLES HADDON SPURGEON

But God forbid that I should glory, save in the cross of our Lord
Jesus Christ, by whom the world is crucified unto me, and I unto the
world.   —Galatians 6:14

WHENEVER we rebuke other people we should be prepared to
clear ourselves of their offence. The apostle had been rebuking
those who wished to glory in the flesh. In denouncing false teachers
and upbraiding their weak-minded followers he used sharp language,
while he appealed to plain facts and maintained his ground with strong
arguments; and this he did without fear of being met by a flank movement, and being charged with doing the same things himself.

Very fitly, therefore, does he contrast his own determined purpose
with their plausible falseness. They were for making a fair show in the
flesh, but he shrunk not from the deepest shame of the Christian profession; nay, so far from shrinking, he even counted it honour to be
scorned for Christ's sake, exclaiming, "God forbid that I should glory,
save in the Cross of our Lord Jesus Christ." The Galatians, and all others
to whom his name was familiar, well knew how truly he spoke; for the
manner of his life as well as the matter of his teaching had supplied evidence of this assertion, which none of his foemen could gainsay.

There had not been in all his ministry any doctrine that he extolled more highly than this of "Christ crucified"; nor any experience that he touched on more tenderly than this "Fellowship with Christ in His sufferings"; nor any rule of conduct that he counted more safe than this following in the footsteps of Him who "endured the Cross, despising the shame, and is set down at the right hand of the throne of God." His example accorded with his precept. God grant, of His grace, that there may always be with us the like transparent consistency. Sometimes when we notice an evil, and protest as boldly and conscientiously as we can against it, we feel that our protest is too obscure to have much influence; it will then be our very best resource resolutely to abstain from the evil ourselves, and so, at least in one person, to overthrow its power.

If you cannot convert a man from his error by an argument, you can at least prove the sincerity of your reasoning by your own behaviour; and thus, if no fortress is captured, you will at least "hold the fort," and you may do more: your faithfulness may win more than your zeal. Vow faithfully within your own heart, and say frankly to your neighbour, "You may do what you will; but as for me, God forbid that I should remove the old landmarks, or seek out new paths, however inviting, or turn aside from that which I know to be the good old way." A determined resolution of that sort, fully adhered to, will often carry more weight and exert more influence on the mind of an individual, especially of a waverer, than a host of arguments. Your actions will speak more loudly than your words.

The apostle in the present case warms with emotion at the thought of anybody presuming to set a carnal ordinance in front of the Cross, by wishing to glory in circumcision or any other outward institution. The idea of a ceremony claiming to be made more of than faith in Jesus provoked him, till his heart presently grew hot with indignation, and he thundered forth the words, "God forbid!" He never used the sacred Name with lightness; but when the fire was hot within him he called God to witness that he did not, and could not, glory in anything but the Cross. Indeed, there is to every true-hearted believer something shocking and revolting in the putting of anything before Jesus Christ, be it what it may, whether it be an idol of superstition or a toy of scepticism, whether it be the fruit of tradition or the flower of philosophy.

Do you want new Scriptures to supplement the true sayings of God? Do you want a new Saviour who can surpass Him whom the Father hath sealed? Do you want a new sacrifice that can save you from sins which His atoning blood could not expiate? Do you want a modern song to supersede the new song of "Worthy is the Lamb that was slain"? "O foolish Galatians!" said Paul. O silly Protestants! I am inclined to say. We might go on in these times to speak warmly to many of the parties around us—the doting Ritualists, the puffed-up Rationalists, and the self-exalting school of modern thought. I marvel not at Paul's warmth. I only wish that some who think so little of doctrinal discrepancies, as they call them, could but sympathise a little with his holy indignation when he saw the first symptoms of departure from godly simplicity and sincerity.

Do you not notice that a little dissembling of a dear brother made him withstand him to his face? When a whole company turned the cold shoulder to the Cross of Christ it made him burn with indignation. He could not brook it. The Cross was the centre of his hopes; around it his affections twined; there he had found peace to his troubled conscience. God forbid that he should allow it to be trampled on. Besides, it was the theme of his ministry. "Christ crucified" had already proved the power of God to salvation to every soul who had believed the life-giving message as he proclaimed it in every city. Would any of you, he asks, cast a slur on the Cross—you who have been converted—you before whose eyes Jesus Christ hath been evidently set forth crucified among you?

How his eyes flash; how his lips quiver; how his heart grows hot within him; with what vehemence he protests: "God forbid that I should glory, save in the Cross of our Lord Jesus Christ." He spreads his eagle wing, and rises into eloquence at once, while still his keen eye looks fiercely upon every enemy of the Cross whom he leaves far beneath. Oftentimes in his epistles you observe this. He burns, he glows, he mounts, he soars, he is carried clean away as soon as his thoughts are in fellowship with his Lord Jesus, that meek and patient Sufferer, who offered Himself a sacrifice for our sins. When his tongue begins to speak of the glorious work which the Christ of God has done for the sons of men it finds a sudden liberty, and he becomes as "A hind let loose; he giveth goodly words." May we have something of that glow within our breasts tonight, and whenever we think of our Lord. God forbid that we should be cold-hearted when we come near to Jesus; God forbid that we should ever view with heartless eye and lethargic soul the sweet wonders of that Cross on which our Saviour loved and died. The main part of our subject lies in Christ crucified, in whom Paul gloried. I call your attention to the language; "God forbid that I should glory, save in the Cross." Some popular authors and public speakers, when they have to state a truth, count it necessary to clothe it in very delicate language. They, perhaps, do not quite intend to conceal its point and edge; but, at any rate, they do not want the projecting angles and bare surfaces of the truth to be too observable, and therefore they cast a cloak around it; they are careful to scabbard the sword of the Spirit. The apostle Paul might have done so here if he had chosen, but he disdains the artifice. He presents the truth "in the worst possible form," as his opponents say—"in all its naked hideousness," as the Jew would have it; for he does not say, "God forbid that I should glory, save in the death of Christ"; but in the Cross.

You do not realize, I think—we cannot do so in these days—how the use of that word "Cross" would grate on ears refined in Galatia and elsewhere. In those days it meant the felon's tree, the hangman's gibbet; and the apostle, therefore, does not hesitate to put it just so: "Save in that gibbet on which my Master died." We have become so accustomed to associate the name of "the Cross" with other sentiments that it does not convey to us that sense of disgrace which it would inflict upon those who heard Paul speak. A family sensitively shrinks if one of its members has been hanged; and much the same would be the natural feeling of one who was told that his leader was crucified. Paul puts it thus boldly he lets it jar thus harshly though it may prove to some a stumbling-block, and to others foolishness; but he will not cloak it, he glories in "the Cross!"

On the other hand, I earnestly entreat you to observe how he seems to contrast the glory of the person with the shame of the suffering; for it is not simply the death of Christ, nor of Jesus, nor of Jesus Christ, nor of the Lord Jesus Christ, but of "our Lord Jesus Christ." Every word tends to set forth the excellence of His person, the majesty of His character, and the interest which all the saints have in Him. It was a Cross, but it was the Cross of our Lord: let us worship Him! It was the Cross of our Lord Jesus the Saviour: let us love Him! It was the Cross of our Jesus Christ the anointed Messiah: let us reverence Him! Let us sit at His feet and learn of Him! Each one may say, "It was the Cross of my Lord Jesus Christ": but it sweetens the whole matter, and gives a largeness to it when we say, "It was the Cross of our Lord Jesus Christ." Oh yes, we delight to think of the contrast between the precious Christ and the painful Cross, the Son of God and the shameful gibbet. He was Immanuel, God with us; yet did He die the felon's death upon the accursed tree.

Paul brings out the shame with great sharpness, and the glory with great plainness. He does not hesitate in either case, whether he would declare the sufferings of Christ or the glory that should follow. What did he mean, however, by the Cross? Of course he cared nothing for the particular piece of wood to which those blessed hands and feet were nailed, for that was mere materialism, and has perished out of mind. He means the glorious doctrine of justification—free justification—through the atoning sacrifice of Jesus Christ. This is what he means by the Cross—the expiation for sin which our Lord Jesus Christ made by His death, and the gift of eternal life freely bestowed on all those who by grace are led to trust in Him. To Paul the Cross meant just what the brazen serpent meant to Moses. As the brazen serpent in the wilderness was the hope of the sin-bitten, and all that Moses had to do was to bid them look and live, so to-day the Cross of Christ—the atonement of Jesus Christ—is the hope of mankind, and our mission is continually to cry, "Look and live! Look and live!"

It is this doctrine, this Gospel of Christ crucified, at which the present age, with all its vaunted culture and all its vain philosophies, sneers so broadly, it is this doctrine wherein we glory. We are not ashamed to put it very definitely: we glory in substitution, in the vicarious sacrifice of Jesus in our stead. He was "made sin for us Who knew no sin, that we might be made the righteousness of God in Him." "All we like sheep have gone astray: we have turned every one to his own way; and the Lord hath laid on Him the iniquity of us all." "Christ hath redeemed us from the curse of the law, being made a curse for us: for it is written, Cursed is everyone that hangeth on a tree." We believe in the imputation of sin to the innocent Person of our covenant Head and Representative, in the bearing of the penalty by that substituted One, and the clearing by faith of those for whom He bore the punishment of sin.

Now we glory in this. We glory in it, not as men sometimes boast in a creed, which they have received by tradition from their forefathers, for we have learned this truth, each one for himself by the inward teaching of the Holy Ghost, and therefore it is very dear to us. We glory in it with no empty boast, but to the inward satisfaction of our own hearts; we prove that satisfaction by the devout consecration of our lives to make it known. We have trusted our souls to its truth. If it be a fable our hopes are for ever shipwrecked, our all is embarked in that venture. We are quite prepared to run that risk, content to perish if this salvation should fail us. We live upon this faith. It is our meat and our drink. Take this away there is nothing left us in the Bible worth the having. It has become to us the head and front of our confidence, our hope, our rest, our joy. Instead of being ashamed to preach it, we wish that we could stand somewhere where all the inhabitants of the earth should hear us, and we would thunder it out day and night. So far from being ashamed of acknowledging it, we count it to be our highest honour and our greatest delight to tell it abroad, as we have opportunity, among the sons of men.

But why do we rejoice in it? Why do we glory in it? The answer is so large that I cannot do more than glance at its manifold claims on our gratitude. We glory in it for a thousand reasons. We fail to see anything in the doctrine of atonement that we should not glory in. We have heard a great many dogs bark against it, but dogs will bay the moon in her brightness, and therefore we mind not their howlings. Their noise has sometimes disturbed though never yet has it frightened us. We have not yet heard a cavil against our Lord or an argument against His atoning Blood which has affected our faith the turn of a hair. The Scriptures affirm it, the Holy Ghost bears witness to it, and its effect upon our inner life assures us of it. The analogy between Jewish fasts and festivals and our Christian faith endorses it; there is a chasm that no man yet has been able to bridge without it; it lightens our conscience, gladdens our hearts, inspires our devotion, and elevates our aspirations; we are wedded to it, and daily glory in it.

In the Cross of Christ we glory, because we regard it as a matchless exhibition of the attributes of God. We see there the love of God desiring a way by which He might save mankind, aided by His wisdom, so that a plan is perfected by which the deed can be done without violation of truth and justice. In the Cross we see a strange conjunction of what once appeared to be two opposite qualities—justice and mercy. We see how God is supremely just; as just as if He had no mercy, and yet infinitely merciful in the gift of His Son. Mercy and justice in fact become counsel upon the same side, and irresistibly plead for the acquittal of the believing sinner. We can never tell which of the attributes of God shines most glorious in the sacrifice of Christ; they each one find a glorious high throne in the Person and Work of the Lamb of God that taketh away the sin of the world. Since it has become, as it were, the disc which reflects the character and perfections of God it is meet that we should glory in the Cross of Christ; and none shall stay us of our boasting.

We glory in it next, as the manifestation of the love of Jesus. He was loving inasmuch as He came to earth at all; loving in feeding the hungry, in healing the sick, in raising the dead. He was loving in His whole life; He was embodied charity, the Prince of philanthropists, the King of kindly souls. But, oh, His death!—His cruel and shameful death —bearing as we believe He did, the wrath due to sin, subjecting Himself to the curse, though in Him was no sin—this shows the love of Christ at its highest altitude, and therefore do we glory in it, and will never be ashamed to do so. We glory in the Cross, moreover, because it is the putting away of sin. There was no other way of making an end of sin, and making reconciliation for inquity. To forgive the transgressions without exacting the penalty would have been contrary to all threatenings of God. It would not have appeased the claims of justice, nor satisfied the conscience of the sinner. No peace of mind can be enjoyed without pardon, and conscience declares that no pardon can be obtained without an atonement. We should have distracted ourselves with the fear that it was only a reprieve, and not a remission, even if the most comforting promises had been given unsealed with the atoning Blood.

The instincts of nature have convinced men of this truth, for all the world over religion has been associated with sacrifice. Almost every kind of worship that has ever sprung up among the sons of men has had sacrifice for its most prominent feature; crime must be avenged, evil and sin cry from the ground, and a victim is sought to avert the vengeance. The heart craves for something that can calm the conscience: that craving is a relic of the ancient truth learned by man in primeval ages.

Now, Christ did make His soul an offering for sin, when His own self He bare our sins in His own body on the tree. With His expiring breath He said, "It is finished!" Oh, wondrous grace! Pardon is now freely published among the sons of men, pardon of which we see the justice and validity. As far as the east is from the west, so far hath God removed our transgressions from us by the death of Christ. This and this alone will put away sin, therefore in this Cross of Christ we glory; yea, and in it alone will we glory evermore. It has put away our sins, blessed be God, so that this load and burden no more weigh us down! We do not speak at random now. It has breathed hope and peace and joy into our spirits. I am sure that no one knows how to glory in the Cross unless he has had an experimental acquaintance with its peace-breathing power. I speak what I do know, and testify what I have felt. The burden of my sin laid so heavy upon me that I would sooner have died than have lived. Many a day, and many a night, I felt the flames of hell in the anguish of my heart, because I knew my guilt, but saw no way of righteous forgiveness. Yet in a moment the load went from me, and I felt overflowing love to the Saviour. I fell at His feet awe-stricken that ever He should have taken away my sin and made an end of it. That matchless deed of love won my heart to Jesus. He changed my nature and renewed my soul in that same hour, But, oh, the joy I had.

Those who have sunk to the very depths of despair, and risen in a moment to the heights of peace and joy unspeakable, can tell you that they must glory in the Cross and its power to save. Why, sirs, we must believe according to our own conscience. We cannot believe that inward witness. We only wish that others had been as deeply convinced of sin, and as truly led to the Cross to feel their burden roll from off their shoulder as we have been, and then they, too, would glory in the Cross of Christ. Since then we have gone with this remedy in our hands to souls that have been near despair, and we have never found the medicine to fail. Many and many a time have I spoken to people so depressed in spirit that they seemed not far from the madhouse, so heavy was their sense of sin; yet have I never known the matchless music of Jesus' Name, in any case, fail to charm the soul out of its despondency.

"They looked unto Him, and were lightened: and their faces were not ashamed." Men who, because they thought there was no hope for them, would have desperately continued in sin, have read that word "hope" written in crimson lines upon the Saviour's dying body, and they have sprung up into confidence, have entered into peace, and henceforth have begun to lead a new life. We glory in the Cross because of the peace it brings to every troubled conscience which receives it by faith: our own case has proved to our own souls its efficacy, and what we have seen in others has confirmed our confidence. Yet we should not glory so much in the Cross, were we not convinced that it is the greatest moral power in all the world. We glory in the Cross because it gets at men's hearts when nothing else can reach them. The story of the dying Saviour's love has often impressed those whom all the moral lectures in the world could never have moved. Judged and condemned by the unanswerable reasonings of their own consciences, they have not had control enough over their passions to shake off the captivity in which they were held by the temptations that assailed them at every turn, till they have drawn near to the Cross of Jesus, and from pardon have gathered hope, and from hope have gained strength to master sin.

When they have seen their sin laid on Jesus, they have loved Him, and hated the sin that made Him to suffer so grievously as their Substitute. Then the Holy Ghost has come upon them, and they have resolved, with Divine strength, to drive out the sin for which the Saviour died; they have begun a new life, aye, and they have continued in it, sustained by that same sacred power which first constrained them, and now they look forward to be perfected by it through the power of God.

Where are the triumphs of infidelity in rescuing men from sin? Where are the trophies of philosophy in conquering human pride? Will you bring us harlots that have been made chaste; thieves that have been reclaimed; angry men, of bear-like temper, who have become harmless as lambs, through scientific lectures? Let our amateur philanthropists, who suggest so much and do so little, produce some instances of the moral transformations that have been wrought by their sophistries. Nay; they curl their lips, and leave the lower orders to the City Missionary and the Bible Woman. It is the Cross that humbles the haughty, lifts up the fallen, refines the polluted, and gives a fresh start to those who are forlorn and desperate. Nothing else can do it. The world sinks lower and lower into the bog of its own selfishness and sin. Only this wondrous lever of the atonement, symbolized by the Cross of Christ, can lift our abject race to the place of virtue and honour which it ought to occupy. We glory in the Cross for so many reasons that I cannot hope to enumerate them all. While it ennobles our life, it invigorates us with hope in our death. Death is now deprived of its terrors to us, for Christ has died. We like Him, can say, "Father, into Thy hands we commend our spirit." His burial has perfumed the grave; His resurrection has paved the road to immortality. He rose and left a lamp behind which shows an outlet from the gloom of the sepulchre. The paradise He immediately predicted for Himself and for the penitent who hung, from mortal pains to immortal joys. "Absent from the body, present with the Lord," is the cheering prospect. Glory be to Christ for ever and for ever that we have this doctrine of "Christ crucified" to preach.

The second crucifixion exhibits the WORLD CRUCIFIED. The apostle says that the world was crucified to him. What does he mean by this? He regarded the world as nailed up like a felon, and hanged upon a cross to die. Well, I suppose he means that its character was condemned. He looked out upon the world which thought so much of itself, and said, "I do not think much of thee poor world! Thou art like a doomed malefactor." He knew that the world had crucified its Saviour—crucified its God. It had gone to such length of sin that it had hounded perfect innocence through the streets. Infinite benevolence it had scoffed at and maligned. Eternal truth it had rejected, and preferred a lie; and the Son of God, who was love incarnate, it had put to the death of the Cross. "Now," says Paul, "I know thy character, O world! I know thee! and I hold thee in no more esteem than the wretch abhorred for his crimes, who is condemned to hang upon the gibbet and so end his detested life."

This led Paul, since he condemned its character, utterly to despise its judgment. The world said, "This Paul is a fool. His Gospel is foolishness and he himself is a mere babbler." "Yes," thought Paul, "a deal you know of it!" In this we unite with him. What is your judgment worth? You did not know the Son of God, poor blind world! We are sure that He was perfect, and yet you hunted Him to death. Your judgment is a poor thing, O world! You are crucified to us.

Now, there are a great many people who could hardly endure to live if they should happen to be misjudged by the world or what is called "society." Oh yes, we must be respectable. We must have every man's good word, or we are ready to faint. Paul was of another mind. What cared he for aught the world might say? How could he wish to please a world so abominable that it had put his Lord to death! He would sooner have its bad opinion than its good. It were better to be frowned at than to be smiled upon by a world that crucified Christ. Certainly, its condemnation is more worth having than its approbation if it can put Christ to death: so Paul utterly despised its judgment, and it was crucified to him.

Now, we are told to think a great deal about "public opinion," "popular belief," "the growing feeling of the age," "the sentiment of the period," and "the spirit of the age." I should like Paul to read some of our religious newspapers; and yet I could not wish the good man so distasteful a task, for I dare say he would sooner pine in the Mammertine prison than do so; but, still, I should like to see how he would look after he had read some of those expressions about the necessity of keeping ourselves abreast with the sentiment of the period. "What," would he say, "the sentiment of the world! It is crucified to me! What can it matter what its opinion is? We are of God, little children and the whole world lieth in the wicked one; would ye heed what the world that is lying in the wicked one thinks of you or of the truth of your Lord? Are you going to smooth your tongue, and soften your speech, to please the world that lieth in the wicked one!" Paul would be indignant with such a proposition. He said, "the world is crucified to me." Hence he looked upon all the world's pleasures as so much rottenness, a carcase nailed to a cross.

Can you fancy Paul being taken to the Colosseum at Rome? I try to imagine him made to sit on one of those benches to watch a combat of gladiators. There is the emperor: there are all the great peers of Rome and the senators; and there are those cruel eyes all gazing down upon men who shed each other's blood. Can you picture how Paul would have felt if he had been forced to occupy a seat at that spectacle? It would have been martyrdom to him. He would have closed his eyes and ears against the sight of what Rome thought to be the choicest pleasure of the day. They thronged the imperial city; they poured in mighty streams into the theatre each day to see poor beasts tortured, or men murdering one another; that was the world of Paul's day; and he rightly judged it to be a crucified felon. If he was compelled to see the popular pleasures of today upon which I will say but little, would he not be well-nigh as sick of them as he would have been of the amusements of the amphitheatre at Rome?

To Paul, too, all the honours of the age must have been crucified in like manner. Suppose that Paul settled his mind to think of the wretches who were reigning as emperors in his day! I use the word advisedly, for I would not speak evil of dignities; but really I speak too well of them when I call them wretches. They seem to have been inhuman monsters—"tyrants whose capricious folly violated every law of nature and decency," to whom every kind of lust was a daily habit, and who even sought out new inventions of sensuality, calling them new pleasures. As Paul thought of the iniquities of Napoli, and all the great towns to which the Romans went in their holidays—Pompeii and the like—oh, how he loathed them! And I doubt not that if the apostle were to come here now, if he knew how often rank and title are wont to sink all true dignity in shameful dissipation, and what flagrant profligacy is to be found in high quarters, he might as justly consider all the pomps and dignities and honours of the world that now is to be as little worth as a putrid carcase hanging on a tree and rotting in the sun. He says, "The world is crucified to me: it is hanging on the gallows to me, I think so little of its pleasures and of its pomps."

Alike contemptuously did Paul judge of all the treasures of the world. Paul never spent as much time as it would take to wink his eye in thinking of how much money he was worth. Having food and raiment he was therewith content. Sometimes he had scarcely that. He casually thanks the Philippians for ministering to his necessities, but he never sought to store anything, nor did he live with even half a thought of aggrandizing himself with gold and silver. "No," he said, "this will all perish with the using," and so he treated the world as a thing crucified to him.

Now, Christian men can you say as much as this—that the world in its mercantile aspect, as well as in its money vices and its manifold frivolities, is a crucified thing to you? Now, look what the world says. "Make money, young man, make money! Honestly if you can, but by all means make money. Look about you, for if you are not sharp you will not succeed. Keep your own counsel, and rather play the double than be the dupe. Your character will rise with the credit you get on "Change." Now, suppose that you get the money, what is the result? The net result, as I often find it, is a paragraph in one of the newspapers to say that So-and-so Esquire's will was proved in the Probate Court under so many thousands. Then follows a grand squabble among all his relatives which shall eat him up. That is the consummation of a life of toil and care and scheming. He has lived for lucre, and he has to leave it behind. There is the end of that folly.

I have sometimes thought of the contrast between the poor man's funeral and the rich man's funeral. When the poor man dies there are his sons and daughters weeping with real distress, for the death of the father brings sadness and sympathy into that house. The poor man is to be buried, but it can only be managed by the united self-denials of all his sons and daughters. There is Mary out at service; she, perhaps, contributes more than the others towards the funeral, for she has no family of her own. The elder son and the younger brothers all pinch themselves to pay a little; and the tears that are shed that evening when they come home from the grave are very genuine: they do suffer, and they prove their sorrow by rivalling one another in the respect they pay to their parent.

Now you shall see the rich man die. Of course everybody laments the sad loss: it is the proper thing. Empty carriages swell the procession to the grave by way of empty compliment. The mourners return, and there is the reading of that blessed document the will; when that is read the time for tears is over in almost every case. Few are pleased; the one whom fortune favours is the envy of all the rest. Sad thoughts and sullen looks float on the surface, not in respect of the man's departure, but concerning the means he has left and the mode in which he has disposed of them. Oh, it is a poor thing to live for, the making of money and the hoarding of it. But still the genius of rightly getting money can be consecrated to the glory of God. You can use the wealth of this world in the service of the Master. To gain is not wrong.

It is only wrong when grasping becomes the main object of life, and grudging grows into covetousness which is idolatry. To every Christian that, and every other form of worldliness ought to be crucified, so that we can say, "For me to live is not myself, but it is Christ; I live that I may honour and glorify Him."

When the apostle said that the world was crucified to him he meant just this. "I am not enslaved by any of its pursuits. I care nothing for its maxims. I am not governed by its spirit. I do not court its smiles. I do not fear its threatenings. It is not my master, nor am I its slave. The whole world cannot force Paul to lie, or to sin, but Paul will tell the world the truth, come what may." You recollect the words of Palissy, the potter, when the king of France said to him that if he did not change his religion, and cease to be a Huguenot, he was afraid that he should have to deliver him up to his enemies. "Sire," said the potter, "I am sorry to hear you say, 'I am afraid,' for all the men in the world could not make Palissy talk like that. I am afraid of nobody, and I must do nothing but what is right."

Oh, yes; the man that fears God and loves the Cross has a moral backbone which enables him to stand, and he snaps his fingers at the world. "Dead felon!" says he, "dead felon! Crucifier of Christ! Cosmos thou callest thyself. By comely names thou wouldst fain be greeted. Paul is nothing in thine esteem; but Paul is a match for thee, for he thinks as much of thee as thou dost of him, and no more." Hear him as he cries, "The world is crucified unto me, and I unto the world." To live to serve men is one thing, to live to bless them is another: and this we will do, God helping us, making sacrifices for their good. But to fear men, to ask their leave to think, to ask their instructions as to what we shall speak, and how we shall say it—that is a baseness we cannot brook. By the grace of God, we have not so degraded ourselves and never shall. "The world is crucified to me," says the apostle, "by the Cross of Christ."

Then he finishes up with the third crucifixion, which is, I AM CRUCIFIED TO THE WORLD. We shall soon see the evidence of this crucifixion if we notice how they poured contempt upon him. Once Saul was a great rabbi, a man profoundly versed in Hebrew lore, a Pharisee of the Pharisees, and much admired. He was also a classic scholar and a philosophic thinker, a man of great mental powers, and fit to take the lead in learned circles. But when Paul began to preach Christ crucified —"Bah," they said, "he is an utter fool! Heed him not!" Or else they said, "Down with him! He is an apostate!" They cursed him. His name brought wrath into the face of all Jews that mentioned it, and all intelligent Greeks likewise. "Paul? He is nobody!" He was everybody when he thought their way: he is nobody now that he thinks in God's way.

And then they put him to open shame by suspecting all his motives, and by misrepresenting all his actions. It did not matter what Paul did; they were quite certain that he was self-seeking; that he was endeavoring to make a fine thing of it for himself. When he acted so that they were forced to own that he was right, they put it in such a light that they made it out to be wrong. There were some who denied his apostleship, and said that he was never sent of God; and others questioned his ability to preach the Gospel. So they crucified poor Paul one way and another to the full.

They went further still. They despised, they shunned him. His old friends forsook him. Some got out of the way, others pointed at him the finger of scorn in the streets. His persecutors showed their rancour against him, now stoning him with lynch-law, and anon with a semblance of legality dragging him before the magistrates. Paul was crucified to them. As for his teaching, they decried him as a babbler—a setter-forth of strange gods. I dare say they often sneered at the Cross of Christ which he preached as a nine days' wonder, an almost exploded doctrine, and said, "If you do but shut the mouths of such men as Paul, it will soon be forgotten." I have heard them say in modern times to lesser men, "Your old-fashioned Puritanism is nearly dead, ere long it will be utterly extinct!" But we preach Christ crucified; the same old doctrine as the apostle preached, and for this by the contempt of the worldly wise we are crucified.

Now, dear Christian friends, if you keep to the Cross of Christ you must expect to have this for your portion. The world will be crucified to you, and you will be crucified to the world. You will get the cold shoulder. Old friends will become open foes. They will begin to hate you more than they loved you before. At home your foes will be the men of your own household. You will hardly be able to do anything right. When you joined in their revels you were a fine fellow; when you could drink, and sing a lascivious song, you were a jolly good fellow; but now they rate you as a fool; they scout you as a hypocrite; and slanderously blacken your character. Let their dislike be a badge of your discipleship, and say, "Now also the world is crucified to me, and I unto the world. Whatever the world says against me for Christ's sake is the maundering of a doomed malefactor, and what do I care for that? And, on the other hand, if I be rejected and despised, I am only taking what I always expected—my crucifixion—in my poor humble way, after the manner of Christ Himself, Who was despised and rejected of men."

The moral and the lesson of it all is this. Whatever comes of it, still glory in Christ. Go in for this, dear friends, that whether ye be in honour or in dishonour, in good report or in evil report, whether God multiply your substance and make you rich, or diminish it and make you poor, you still glory in the Cross of Christ. If you have health, and strength, and vigour to work for Him, or if you have to lie upon a bed of languishing and bear in patience all your heavenly Father's will, resolve that you will still glory in the Cross. Let this be the point of your glorifying throughout your lives. Go down the steeps of Jordan, and go through Jordan itself, still glorying in the Cross, for in the heaven of glory you will find that the blood-bought hosts celebrate the Cross as the trophy of their redemption.

Are you trusting in the Cross? Are you resting in Jesus? If not, may the Lord teach you this blessed privilege. There is no joy like it. There is no strength like it. There is no life like it. There is no peace like it. At the Cross we find our heaven. While upon the Cross we gaze all heavenly, holy things abound within our hearts. If you have never been there, the Lord lead you there at this very hour; so shall you be pardoned, accepted, and blest for aye. The Lord grant that you all may be partakers of this grace for Christ's sake. Amen.

DWIGHT L. MOODY 1837–1899

A man named Edward Kimball paused before the shoestore in downtown Boston, wondering whether or not he should go in and speak to the seventeen-year-old clerk who worked inside. The youngster, Dwight L. Moody, was a member of his Sunday school class. Not too well grounded in the Scriptures, of course. Only recently, while Kimball was telling the story of Moses leading the Israelites out of Egypt, Moody had burst out, "That Moses must have been smart!" *Still, Kimball reflected, he has a soul that needs to be quickened and I've got to speak to him about his relation to Christ some time. So it might as well be now.*

He marched into the store and found young Moody in the rear, wrapping a pair of shoes. With some hesitation but with no lack of love, Mr. Kimball stated his mission. A few minutes later D. L. Moody was no longer an inquirer but a firm believer in the Son of God.

Saul Kane of Masefield's The Everlasting Mercy, *when touched by the hand of God, looked out on a totally new and different world of nature. Even*

> *The station brook to my new eyes*
> *Was babbling out of Paradise . . .*

It was the same with Moody. "I thought the old sun shone brighter than it ever had before. I thought it was just smiling upon me. Do you know I fell in love with the birds? I had never cared for them before. It seemed to me I was in love with all creation."

He moved to Chicago, where he worked as a commercial traveler. He attended the Plymouth Congregational Church, and promptly became a doer of the Word as well as a hearer. Within a few Sundays he had brought enough young people to church to fill four pews.

Gradually Moody branched off into mission Sunday school work. He seemed to be blessed with a King Midas propensity for golden results: everything he touched prospered. He founded two Sunday schools and finally a church. Still, he was anything but a fluent speaker. After a mid-week service at which he had tried to say a few words, someone advised him that he would serve God most effectively by keeping still.

The Civil War convulsed America. Dwight gave himself to evangelistic activity under the auspices of the Christian Commission. During the second year of the war he married.

When the armistice was signed he returned to Chicago and to his Sunday school efforts. To these and to Young Men's Christian Association service he now gave all his time. His missionary activity among Chicago's youth so flourished that he began to be known throughout the Midwest, and was in demand as a speaker at various conventions.

Attending a convention in Indianapolis in 1870, he met and heard Ira Sankey sing for the first time. He was delighted with Sankey's singing and personality, and invited him to take charge of the music at an open-air service he was about to hold. Sankey agreed. All went so well that the singer, as had Mr. Moody, gave up his secular work in order to enter the field of evangelism. The pattern was set for the next twenty-nine years: they were to labor as the Moody-Sankey team until Moody died.

A prophet is not without honor save in his own country. It was in England that Moody was first catapulted to great fame as an evangelistic speaker. He led services in York, then Sunderland, then Newcastle. From there he went to Scotland. Everywhere immense crowds converged on him. Staid Scotland was stirred as it had never been before. "The meetings," said Dr. John Cairns, "were unparalleled in the history of Scottish, perhaps of British Christianity." This trip across the Atlantic was the first of many he and Sankey were destined to make in their years of campaigning.

Back in America, they led gigantic rallies in the leading cities of the nation. At the World's Fair in Chicago in 1893, services were conducted in the largest halls in the city. Thousands took their initial stand for Jesus Christ.

Mr. Moody established the Bible Institute in Chicago, which since his day has grown to be one of the largest in the world. He also founded educational institutions at Mt. Hermon and Northfield, Massachusetts. He is buried at Round Top, on the Northfield campus.

D. L. Moody impressed his generation with his intense love for God and for the souls of men. In addition, he was a shrewd observer of human nature, a practically minded leader. He was preaching in a church one evening when he noticed several of his listeners dozing. He stopped preaching, and said, "Now some of you good people think you need a baptism of the Holy Spirit when what you need most is some good fresh air. Let us all stand and sing a hymn while the ushers open the windows and let fresh air circulate in here."

His sermons are essentially Christ-centered. They were never geared to impress, but to convict and to turn hearers from darkness to light. They are plain, down-to-earth messages, as full of homely illustrations as Lincoln's discourses. In all honesty, D. L. Moody could have said, "My speech and my preaching were not in persuasive words of man's wisdom, but in demonstration of the Spirit, and of power, that your faith should not stand in the wisdom of men, but in the power of God."

The Work of the Holy Ghost

DWIGHT L. MOODY

I REMEMBER once when I was first converted, I spoke in a Sabbath-school, and there seemed to be a great deal of interest, and quite a number rose for prayer, and I remember I went out quite rejoiced; but an old man followed me out—I have never seen him since. I never had seen him before, and don't even know his name—but he caught hold of my hand and gave me a little bit of advice. I didn't know what he meant at the time, but he said, "Young man, when you speak again, honor the Holy Ghost." I was hastening off to another church to speak, and all the way over it kept ringing in my ears—"Honor the Holy Ghost," and I said to myself, "I wonder what the old man means."

I have found out since what he meant, and I think that all that have been to work in the vineyard of the Lord have learned that lesson, that if we honor Him in our efforts to do good, He will honor us and work through us; but if we don't honor Him, we will surely break down. The only work that is going to stand to eternity is the work done by the Holy Ghost, and not by any one of us. We may be used as His instruments, but the work that will stand to eternity is that done by the Holy Ghost; and every conversion in these meetings, that is not by the power of the Holy Ghost, will not stand. They may be impressions that may last for a few weeks or months, but then they will pass away like the morning cloud; and I firmly believe that if a man or woman be not converted by the Holy Ghost, we will not see them in heaven.

But I want now to call your attention to the Holy Ghost as a Person. He has been in the world ever since man has been in it. We are told here in the second Epistle of Peter, 1st chapter and 21st verse: "For the prophecy came not in old time by the will of man, but holy men of God spake as they were moved by the Holy Ghost." Every holy man that has ever spoken in this world has been inspired and prompted by the Holy Ghost, and has been moved by the Holy Ghost to speak, and if he has not been so moved, the words are just like the clouds, they will soon be gone and be of no permanent effect. They won't last; but the words that abide and live forever are the words prompted by the Holy Ghost, or accompanied by the Holy Ghost.

Now I want to call your attention to an important truth, because I really believe I was a Christian ten years before I believed it. I went into a church once and heard an old minister say that the Holy Ghost was a Person. I thought the old man was wrong, and could not believe that the Holy Ghost was a Person. I did not know my Bible then as well as I do now, but I went home and got my Bible, and went to work to study it out, and have been thoroughly convinced ever since that the Holy Ghost is a Person as much as God the Father is, and as much as Jesus Christ the Son is. Some may say that it is a mystery, and there are a good many things that are mysterious on their face. Now turn to the 14th chapter of John, 16th and 17th verses: "And I will pray the Father, and He shall give you another Comforter, that He may abide with you forever. Even the Spirit of Truth, whom the world cannot receive because it seeth Him not, neither knoweth Him; but ye know Him, for He dwelleth with you and shall be in you."

Now, if the Holy Ghost were not a person, Christ would not have said, "Who." To be sure He is a Spirit, but at the same time He is a Person, the same as God the Father is. God is a Spirit, and yet He is a Person. Three times in this last verse it says "Him," and once "Who." Then in the 26th verse of the same chapter: "But The Comforter which is the Holy Ghost, whom the Father will send in My Name, He shall teach you all things, and bring all things to your remembrance whatsoever I have said unto you," He shall do it. Then there are a good many other verses, and I want to call your attention to one or two more, just to show this fact, that He is a Person. Whenever Christ spoke of the Holy Ghost, He always spoke of Him as "He," or "Him," and we won't honor the Holy Ghost unless we make Him a Person, and one of the Persons of the Trinity—the Father, son and Holy Ghost.

When Christ got ready to go away He taught His disciples to baptize the people in the Name of the Father, Son and Holy Ghost. Now, not only that, but we get life through Him. It is through the Holy Ghost that we get life. We would in reality not know Christ but for the Holy Ghost. It is the Holy Ghost that imparts life. We must be born of the Spirit—that is love. Not only that, but if we turn over to Peter, First Epistle, 3d chapter and 18th verse, we will find that Christ was raised by the power of the Holy Ghost: "For Christ also hath once suffered for sins, the just for the unjust, that He might bring us to God, being put to death in the flesh, but quickened by the Spirit"; and every dead soul that has been brought to life has been brought to life by the power of the Holy Ghost. They are dead in sin until the Holy Ghost brings them to life, until the Spirit of God moves upon the waters. There is no life or power for a man to serve God until he is first born of the Spirit, until he has been quickened by the Holy Ghost, until he has been raised as Christ's dead body was raised. So dead souls must be raised, and when they have been raised by that power then they can serve God.

Now the work of the Holy Ghost is also to impart love. Just turn to Romans 5:5: "And hope maketh not ashamed; because the love of God is shed abroad in our hearts by the Holy Ghost, which is given unto us." The real fruit that we look for in a young convert is love; and I think it is one of the strongest proofs that this religion of Jesus Christ is divine, that it is the same all the world over. Even in the heart of China you will find if a man is converted he will love his enemies. The love of God is in that man's heart. What do we as Christians feel and want to-day? What is the great lack of the church? Why are so many complaining about the coldness of the church? It is because we have not got this love.

If the Holy Ghost is a power in the church, shedding abroad love in our hearts, there won't be any complaint. Go into a society of young converts. If you could have been in our meeting last night you would have seen love and joy in every face, except a few inquiring ones. They all tell the same story. They were of different nationalities, perhaps, but they had only one story to relate. They loved every one, and told how much love and pity they felt for all. And if a man gets up and talks bitterly against any one, and professes to be a young convert, you may believe it is a spurious conversion. It is counterfeit. It has not got the ring of heaven in it, because a man when he is converted will love every one. Not only that, but I have noticed this, that when a man is full of the Holy Ghost he is the very last man to be complaining of other people. He loves everybody too tenderly. He loves even a cold church, and is anxious to lift them up and bring them to a kinder feeling and sympathy.

And I want to say here that I think a good many people have gotten into this habit of coldness. A man told me the other day that he felt it to be his duty to go up to a certain church and open on them when he got a chance for their lukewarmness, and I thought if he could just get a look at these young converts here he would feel differently. For when a man is himself cold he looks upon everybody else as cold too. When a man is himself warm he will talk about everybody else in the same view as of himself; he will talk about the love of God that is in our hearts, and that is what we want. If we only just felt filled with love, how easy it would be to reach man! All these barriers between us would be broken down. If you can only convince the greatest blasphemer and infidel in New York that you really love him you can reach him. What we want, therefore, is this love, and that is the work of the Holy Ghost to impart; and let us pray to-day that the love of God may be shed abroad in all our hearts.

The Holy Ghost not only imparts love, too, but hope. That is another thing the church wants—more hope. When a church is hopeful, then the work advances; when it is discouraged and disheartened, the work does not advance; and I have learned this, that the hopeful Christians that are all the time looking on the bright side are the very ones that God delights to honor by using as His instruments, while He never employs for His best work those who are always looking on the dark side. Let the Holy Ghost come into a church and convert a few, imparting the hope that it does impart, and see how the work of the church will suddenly go on.

If you will only let Jesus Christ come into the church He will do the work well. The trouble is we want our own way. We want the Holy Ghost to work in *our* way, and if He doesn't come in that way we think sometimes it is not the work of God because it has not come in the usual way. My grandfather told me in his day there was a great revival and every one came to the anxious bench, "but now they don't do so," said he, "and I don't believe it is the work of God." That is the way a great many talk. God never repeats Himself. Because God did a certain thing through one instrument at one time, it is no sign that He will do it the same way all the time. What we want to do is to let the Holy Ghost work *in His own way* and He will impart hope, and the Holy Ghost is very hopeful the moment He gets in.

Another thing we want in the church is liberty. If you had been to that young converts' meeting last night, you would have seen perfect liberty—three or four trying to get the floor at once. There was no trouble in speaking there. But go into some of our churches, and where is that essential liberty? A great many Christians are like Lazarus when he came forth—he was bound hand and foot; but Christ said, "Loose him and let him go." And so Christians want to feel that liberty they *should* feel when Christ calls them to be His disciples. Where the Spirit of the Lord is there is liberty. Many think to themselves before they get up to speak: "Now, what will Mrs. B., say when I get up, if I don't talk as well as the minister? and "Oh, if I could speak as well as Brother A., wouldn't I give my testimony quickly! but I haven't got any eloquence, and cannot speak like an orator." Don't you know, my friend, it is not the most fluent man that has the greatest effect with a jury? It is the man who tells the truth. And in speaking of your experience, God will help you if you trust in Him, and you will find after a simple trial that you have perfect liberty.

The trouble is we have a great many Christians who have only got as far as the 3d chapter of John, and so far as liberty to come out and speak up for God is concerned, they don't know anything about it. We want this spirit of liberty so as to be qualified for God's work. A friend of mine told me once, that when he went to a boarding-house, he could always tell who the boarders were, for they never alluded to family matters, but sat down to the table and talked of outside matters; but when the son came in he would go into the sitting-room to see if there were any letters, and inquire after the family, and show in many ways his interest in the household. It doesn't take five minutes to tell that he is not a boarder and that the others are. And so it is with the church of God. You see these boarders in church every Sunday morning, but they don't take any interest. They come to criticise, and that is about all that constitutes a Christian nowadays. They are boarders in the house of God, and we have got too many boarders. What we want is liberty.

A friend of mine said he was down in Natchez before the war, and he and a friend of his went out riding one Saturday—they were teaching school through the week—and they drove out back from Natchez. It was a beautiful day, and they saw an old slave coming up, and they thought they would have a little fun. They had just come to a place where there was a fork in the roads, and there was a sign-post which read, "Forty miles to Liberty." One of the young men said to the old darkey driver, "Sambo, how old are you?" "I don't know, massa. I guess I'se about eighty." "Can you read?" "No, sah; we don't read in this country. It's agin the law." "Can you tell what is on that sign-post?" "Yes, sah, it says 'Forty miles to Liberty.' " "Now, why don't you take that road and go there?" The old man's countenance changed, and he said, "Oh, young massa, that is all a sham. If that post pointed out the road to the liberty that God gives, we might try it. There could be no sham in that."

My friend said he had never heard anything more eloquent from the lips of any preacher. God wants all His sons to have liberty. He does not want us bound, as so many of us are bound, by a sort of fear. The Holy Ghost casts out fear. It is the spirit of love and liberty. There ought to be perfect liberty in all our religious meetings, in all our social meetings. If there were, how long would it be before there would be a wonderful reformation in this country if they all had this spirit of liberty? A friend of mine asked a judge in his church to go out to a school-house in the country with him one day, where he was going to preach. He said to the judge that he would like to have him go, and the judge said he would like to go along. He told the judge he would like to have him speak to the people. The judge said, "Oh, I could not do that." "Why can't you? You can speak in your court well enough, without any trouble. Why cannot you speak here? Suppose you just try it?" When they got out there the judge refused to do it, but the minister said, "I want to put the judge into the witness box and question him." And the judge got his lips open at last, and told how he was converted, and how the Spirit of God came down upon him. And there was mighty power in what he said, and the result was that many were converted, and the judge has been a working Christian ever since.

I think there are hundreds bound, as he was, by station. A man who had been a professing Christian for three years I met at a meeting, and I knew he had been a professing Christian, and I supposed of course he had prayed in public. I noticed that he hesitated when I asked him, but he rose, and as soon as he had opened his lips the words came easily. I heard him tell a friend afterward that that night he felt as if he had been converted a second time. How many there are in the church that are bound to silence by long habit and that have not yet got their liberty! And one reason is because you do not ask God for it. Oh, open your lips and the Spirit of God will come upon you, and you will have liberty.

There are so many people who are just between the two beliefs, or between belief and unbelief. I pity that class of people. What God wants is for us to have perfect liberty. Where the Spirit of the Lord is you will have this liberty. I want to call your attention to this fact. What is the work of the Holy Ghost? Why is it that when the Holy Ghost wakes up some men they get so angry? Because the Holy Ghost testifies against the world. That is what He has come to do—to convince men of their sins. It is a good sign sometimes to see a man get mad and storm out of the house. A man went out of this building so a few days ago, but he did not rest in it; he found Christ soon after. When the Spirit of God wakes some men up they wake up in anger. I want to read the 7th and 8th verses of the 16th chapter of John: "Nevertheless, I tell you the truth. It is expedient for you that I go away, for if I go not away, the Comforter will not come unto you; but if I depart I will send Him unto you. And when He is come He will reprove the world of sin, and of righteousness, and of judgment." I do not believe a man was ever convicted of sin by any preacher in the world. It is the work of the Holy Ghost. If He does not do it they won't be converted.

It would be very easy for the Holy Ghost to convict every man here of sin. Then shall we not ask Him to do it? All that He has to do is to open a man's eyes and he will see at once that he is a sinner. When the Holy Ghost opens a man's eyes he will soon find out what a miserable sinner he is. The work of the Holy Ghost is to testify of Christ; He comes for that purpose. I believe the world would have forgotten Christ's death as soon as they forgot His birth, if it had not been for the Holy Ghost. It had only been thirty years since His birth, and all those wonderful scenes had happened in Bethlehem, and it was well known in Jerusalem; yet it seems to have been forgotten until Christ came. And they would have forgotten His death if it had not been for the Holy Ghost. He came to testify for Jesus Christ that He had risen.

He saw Him in heaven, and he came to tell us He was there at the right hand of God. He convinced men on the day of Pentecost, three thousand of them. He does not talk of Himself, but of Christ.

In the 15th chapter of John, the 26th verse, it says, "But when the Comforter is come, whom I will send unto you from the Father, even the Spirit of Truth, which proceedeth from the Father, He shall testify of me." If a man preaches Christ faithfully the Holy Ghost will bless his preaching, because he will testify and carry home the truth. He knows that Christ has risen and is sitting at the right hand of God, and has been raised for our justification. Do you believe, my friends, that He who died outside of the walls of Jerusalem the death of a common prisoner, the cruel death of the cross, do you believe that the preaching of that man after it had taken place would have had any power over this audience, except for the Holy Ghost?

Some people do not believe in the supernatural working of the Holy Ghost, and the supernatural power of His influence. Every Christian man and every Christian woman has felt the power of the Holy Ghost. When the Holy Ghost first opened my eyes, I thought how blind I had been! That is the way with the world now; it is blind, but does not know it. He came into the world that the blind might see and recover. And the world is deaf, but does not know it. And so the world turns around and says people go mad on the subject of religion. When people are mad they think every one else is. I think it would take but a few minues to prove that the world had gone clean crazy. The Holy Ghost is our teacher. He will teach us and show us things to come. He comes to speak of Christ, not of Himself.

A man came to me the other day and said he was going down to Florida, where my wife and family are, and wanted to know if I had any message to send. Well, I sent them a message; but suppose when the man went down there he should go and see my wife and should begin and talk about himself, and not say a word about me. That would not cheer their hearts; they would want to hear about me. That would make their hearts warm. The Holy Ghost teaches us this lesson of self-forgetfulness. Every one of us Christians wants more of the Holy Ghost. Let us all give ourselves up to the influence of His Spirit, who will lead us on to liberty and life and peace and joy.

People are running off after books and they are running after this and that minister to ask them if they have not committed the unpardonable sin. Just let me read this verse: "Because"—now Christ gives a reason—"because, they said, he hath an unclean spirit." I don't know but there are men living who have committed the unpardonable sin, but I have never met one. I never heard of a man who thought the Lord Jesus Christ cast out devils by the power of the devil. I never met a man who thought the Holy Ghost was a devil, and it is a question in my mind if there is any man in this city who has committed an unpardonable sin against the Holy Ghost. If you say you have resisted the Holy Ghost, well, we have all of us done that, I think. Ah, *how* we resisted until we hadn't any more strength and could not resist any longer; and then just simply accepted Christ. A man may die in his sins resisting the Holy Ghost. I don't remember of ever hearing any man swear in my life by the Holy Ghost, except once, and then I looked upon him expecting him to fall dead, and my blood ran cold when I heard him. I have heard a great many profane men, and have travelled considerably, but I have met only this one man who swore by the Holy Ghost.

Now, if any here have said that Christ was possessed of the devil, and that He cast out demons by the power of the devil, and have blasphemed the power of the Holy Ghost in that way, then it may be you have committed that sin; but I never met any one. But I can hear some of you saying, "I have blasphemous thoughts; they come flitting into my mind." Well, many of the best Christian people in the world have them. I have met men very eminent in the service of God who have these thoughts come upon them, but they don't harbor or entertain them; they drive them off. That is Satan. No doubt but that we all have these thoughts in our mind, but if we don't entertain them, but drive them off, we don't sin. The sin is in harboring and entertaining them.

Let me call your attention to another thought—that we are sealed by the Holy Ghost. We are washed and cleansed by the blood, and when a soul is washed and cleansed by the precious blood of Christ, then he becomes a temple for the Holy Ghost to dwell in. The Holy Ghost dwells with only those that have been cleansed by the blood. The 30th verse of the fourth chapter of Ephesians says that we are sealed by the Holy Ghost unto the day of redemption. That is the work of the Holy Spirit. After we have been cleansed and purified, then the Holy Ghost can seal us for the day of redemption; and who is to going to break God's seal? Can Satan do it? Can all the infernal powers break that seal? Can man do it? Can all the world itself do it? Can God break His *own* seal? If we are sealed for the day of redemption, that seal will not be broken. And I want to call your attention to another very precious truth, and that is that the Holy Ghost dwells with every one that is sealed for the day of redemption.

Now, I have got a great many letters against that hymn, "Come, Holy Spirit, Heavenly Dove," and I hear a great many people complain about our singing that hymn and praying for the Holy Ghost to come. They say He came on the day of Pentecost, and has been here ever since. But when we pray for Him to come, it is that He may anoint us afresh, that He may endow us with fresh power. There is such a thing as a man just having life, but not having the power, and so when we pray that the Holy Ghost may come upon us with power that we may be anointed, that is a different thing. Then in First Corinthians, 3rd chapter, 16th verse, it says: "Know ye not that ye are the temple of God and that the Spirit of God dwelleth in you?" The Holy Ghost dwells in you. He dwells with us. He doesn't just come to visit us and then leave us. I don't believe there is a Christian here but what would fall into some grievous sin inside of forty-eight hours if it was not for the Holy Ghost dwelling in us. It is He that gives us power over the world and over Satan.

Now I want this thing clearly understood. We believe firmly that any man that has been cleansed by the blood, redeemed by the blood, and been sealed by the Holy Ghost, the Holy Ghost dwells in him. And a thought I want to call your attention to is this, that God has a good many children who have just barely got life, but no power for service. You might say safely, I think, without exaggeration, that nineteen out of every twenty of professed Christians are of no earthly account so far as building up Christ's kingdom; but on the contrary they are standing right in the way, and the reason is because they have just got life and have settled down, and have not sought for power. The Holy Ghost coming upon them with power is distinct and separate from conversion. If the Scripture doesn't teach it I am ready to correct it.

Let us look and see what God says, and if you will look in the third and fourth chapters of Luke you will see that all these thirty years that Christ had been in Nazareth He had been a son, but now the Holy Ghost comes upon Him for service, and He goes back to Nazareth and finds a place where it is written: "The Spirit of the Lord God is upon me, because He hath anointed me to preach the gospel to the poor. He has sent me to heal the broken-hearted, to proclaim liberty to the captive, to recover sight to the blind, to set at liberty them that are bruised." And for three years we find Him preaching the kingdom of God, casting out devils, and raising the dead, while for thirty years that He was at Nazareth, we hear nothing of Him. He was a son all the while, but now He is anointed for service; and if the Son of God has got to be anointed, do not His disciples need it, and shall we not seek for it, and shall we barely rest with conversion?

In the 7th chapter of John, 38th and 39th verses, Jesus says, "He that believeth on me, as the Scripture hath said, out of his belly shall flow rivers of living water. But this spake He of the Spirit, which they that believe on Him should receive, for the Holy Ghost was not yet given, because that Jesus was not yet glorified." Now, do you tell me that Peter and John and James and the rest of those men had not been converted at that time? Had they been three years with the Son of God and had not been born of the Spirit? Had not Nicodemus been born of the Spirit, and had not men been converted before them? Yes, but they were saints without power and must tarry in Jerusalem until imbued with power from on high. I believe we should accomplish more in one week than we should in years if we had only this fresh baptism. Then turn to the 20th chapter of John, 22d verse, "And when he had said this He breathed on them and said unto them, Receive ye the Holy Ghost." Now that is the second time. They must have received the Holy Ghost when they were converted; they must have been sealed by the Holy Ghost for the day of redemption; and now Christ breathes upon them and says, "Receive ye the Holy Ghost." Do you think they did not receive it? Of course they did; and yet they were instructed to go to Jerusalem and tarry there until they got power.

It seems to me we have got about three classes of Christians. The first class, in the 3d chapter of John, were those who had got to Calvary and there got life. They believed on the Son and were saved, and there they rested satisfied. They did not seek anything higher. Then, in the 4th chapter of John, we come to a better class of Christians. There it was a well of living water bubbling up. There are a few of these, but they are not a hundredth part of the first class. But the best class is in the 7th chapter of John, "Out of his belly shall flow rivers of living water." That is the kind of Christian we ought to be.

When I was a boy I used to have to pump water for the cattle. Ah, how many times I have pumped with that old right hand until it ached! and many times I used to pump when I could not get any water, and I was taught that when the pump was dry I must pour a pail of water down the pump and then I could get the water up. And that is what Christians want—a well of living water. We will have plenty of grace to spare; all we need ourselves and plenty for others. We have got into the way now of digging artesian wells better. They don't pump now to get the water, but when they dig the well they cut down through the gravel and through the clay perhaps one thousand or two thousand feet, not stopping when they can pump the water up, but they cut to a lower strata, and the water flows up abundantly of itself.

And so we ought, every one of us, to be like artesian wells. God has got grace enough for every one of us, and if we were only full of the Holy Ghost what power we would have! The influence of these meetings would be felt not only through New York, but through the whole country. A learned doctor said once, speaking of Christ's holiness, "You fill a tumbler of water to the brim and then just touch it and the water flows out; and so Christ was so full of truth that when the woman touched Him virtue flowed out and healed her." Every one of us should be as full of the Holy Ghost as this, and then men will see that we have an unseen power. We must not be satisfied with just having life, but we want this power. How many times we have preached and taught and it has been like the wind! And why? Because our hearts were not full, and we did not have that anointing.

Peter's heart was full and he had the anointing of the Holy Spirit when he accused the Jews of having crucified the Lord. This same man Peter, who only a few days before denied the Lord, stood up and preached with unction. It was not the same Peter. Suppose that little girl who had heard him deny his Master, and swear that he did not know Christ, had heard him preaching His Name afterward? I can imagine how she would wonder. She would look at him and say, "Isn't that the man that said he did not know Him, and swore to me and said he did not know Christ?" She might have said, "Well, he looks like the same man, but it cannot be." Instead of being afraid of one little crowd of people, he charged it home to the whole nation, saying, "You have crucified our Lord."

When a man is full of the Holy Ghost, he has boldness. He is not afraid to declare the Gospel truth in all its simplicity and drive it right home, even if he drives a man out of doors. We need boldness. In the 33d verse of that same chapter (acts 2) it says, "Therefore being by the right hand of God exalted, and having received of the Father the promise of the Holy Ghost . . ." Now, I believe the gift of the Holy Ghost that is spoken of there is a gift for certain, but one that we have mislaid, overlooked, and forgotten to seek for. If a man is only converted, and we get him into the church, we think the work is done, and we let him go right off to sleep. Instead of urging him to seek the gift of the Holy Ghost, that he may be anointed for the work, we let him sleep and slumber. This world would soon be converted, if all such were baptized with the Holy Ghost.

We find Philip, a deacon, going down to Samaria to preach. We find that Stephen, the first martyr, was a layman. The Spirit of the Word of God came down upon him and he could not help preaching. When a man is full of the Holy Ghost, he cannot help working for the Lord. We would indeed have a stir in the church if we were baptized with the Holy Ghost. The cry would be, "Here am I, Lord; use me, send me!" We would all be anxious to be used in God's service. Some people say if you are once sealed by the Holy Ghost you need never to seek for it again, that He is with you from that time, and if you are once full of the Holy Ghost you remain so. I heard of a man in the last half-hour who said that it is the teaching of Scripture and of our experience. Do you not all know of some men who were full of the Holy Ghost a year ago, and were anointed, and there was a mighty power upon them, and that have already lost their strength, as Sampson lost his?

But Sampson regained his strength, and those who have so lost it may regain theirs a second time, and many times.

Let us not be trying to live on the old story. We cannot work now on grace that we had years ago. What we want is further baptism. The 4th chapter of Acts, 31st verse, says: "And when they had prayed, the place was shaken where they were assembled together; and they were filled with the Holy Ghost, and they spake the word of God with boldness." There were Peter and James and John and the rest of them there, those very men that were filled with the Holy Ghost at Pentecost. There the Holy Ghost came a second time to them. They must have been converted by the power of the Holy Ghost away back there where it is said "the Holy Ghost breathed upon them." They must have been brought under its influence a second time then, and a third time in the 2d chapter of Acts, and in the 4th chapter of Acts a fourth time.

Some one asked a minister if he had ever received a second blessing since he was converted. "What do you mean?" was the reply. "I have received ten thousand since the first." A great many think because they have been filled once, they are going to be full for all time after; but O, my friends, we are leaky vessels, and have to be kept right under the fountain all the time in order to keep full. If we are going to be used by God we have to be very humble. A man that lives close to God will be the humblest of men. I heard a man say that God always chooses the vessel that is close at hand. Let us keep near Him. But we will have to keep down in the dust; lift up our head and think that we are something and somebody, He lays us aside. If we want this power, we have to give God all the glory. I believe the reason we do not get this power more than we do is because we do not know how to use it. We would be taking all the credit to ourselves and saying, "Don't I do a great work?" and begin and boast about it. There are hundreds of thousands I believe that God would take up and use and give us a great baptism if we would only give Him the glory. We have not learned the lesson of humility yet, that we are nothing and God is everything.

The true idea of preaching is to cry down yourself and the devil and to preach up on no one but God. That is the kind of preaching that He wants. If a man only wants to preach Christ and keep himself behind the cross, the Holy Ghost will use him, and he will be anointed for service. In the 19th chapter of Acts, they went down there at Ephesus, and they found twelve men, and said to them, "Have you received the Holy Ghost since you believed?" The early Christians looked for that; but what would our converts do now if that question were put to them? They would rub their eyes and say they never heard of such a thing, and, what do you mean by receiving the Holy

Ghost for service? That is the reason men dare not speak to their neighbors about Christ, and the reason why every night so many go away from here that are anxious about their souls, and yet the man, the Christian who sits next them, has not the moral courage to speak to them about Christ and salvation.

I. M. HALDEMAN 1845–1933

The venerable I. M. Haldeman began his Sunday morning sermon in his typical staccato, machine-gun style of speaking. He had no sooner gotten into the message when the congregation noticed him hesitate as though groping for words. Finally, there was a long pause. Then in a subdued voice he said, "Dear friends, for the first time in sixty years I have forgotten everything I was going to say." A few minutes later, he pronounced the benediction and dismissed the worshipers.

That evening he made his confession in deep humility. He had of late been guilty, he said, of the sin of pride. It was his conviction that the Lord had purposely blurred his memory that morning to teach him that his sufficiency, even in the matter of memorizing as well as delivering the Word, must be of God. Those who heard him preach that night said that he spoke for one and a half hours, and that he rose to planes of greatness never reached before.

Isaac Massey Haldeman was born in Concordville, Delaware County, Pennsylvania. When he was seven, the Haldeman family moved to West Chester. At nineteen, he went into business with his father, who would have been satisfied to have him continue in secular work. Mrs. Haldeman entertained other ideas. She had dedicated Isaac, as a child, to God and set him apart for the prophetic ministry. When, in 1886, he was brought under the dominion of Christ she could, like Samson's mother in Samson's youth, begin to trace the movements of the Spirit in her boy.

James Trickett, pastor of the West Chester Church, baptized and received him into membership. Soon afterward, he invited young Haldeman to preach for him. He consented, and to the amazement of the community it was the starting of a revival in West Chester that lasted a month, with Isaac evangelizing every night for thirty consecutive nights. His mother's chalice of joy overflowed.

His first pastorate was the Brandywine Baptist Church in Delaware County, the church in which he had received ordination. It is estimated that in four years, two hundred people were brought into the church, most of them on confession of faith.

In '875, the Delaware Avenue Baptist Church of Wilmington, Delaware, sent for him. He went there in the summer of that year. During the fall and winter months, approximately four hundred were added to the church. So strong was his emphasis on salvation by faith that the citizens of Wilmington came to refer to him as "Only Believe" Haldeman.

His third and final field, to extend across four decades, was the First Baptist Church of New York City. As a seasoned veteran of the pulpit he attracted wide attention in the metropolitan area with his magnificent powers of speech and faithfulness to the Gospel. One who listened to him with great profit has thus described him: "As a preacher he is exceedingly rich in imagery, clothing his ideas as they flow from a fountain of clear and logical thought with choice words and fitting metaphors. He also speaks extempore."

One of the special features of Dr. Haldeman's work was his interest in young men giving consideration to or preparing for the ministry. His personal counseling and encouragements to a goodly number of warriors of the cross now on the firing line made a permanent impact on mind and character alike.

Legion are the anecdotes surrounding him, marking him out as an individualist. After attending a certain meeting of the old Baptist Association of New York, he is reported to have said, "It opened with prayer and closed with devils."

His views on future prophecy are well known. In his latter years he preached practically every Sunday evening on some aspect of the Saviour's return. Once at a congregational business meeting his parishioners decided that it would be necessary to spend about fifteen thousand dollars for repairs on the church building; unfortunately there was no money in the treasury. Dr. Haldeman said, "Well, let's go ahead and repair because the Lord is going to come before we shall have to pay for it."

In the first World War his only son gave up his life. The funeral service was held in the church. As the pallbearers bearing the casket moved away from the chancel, the courageous father, tears streaming down his face, walked down the aisle before the procession repeating Jesus' words, "I am the resurrection and the life. . . ."

Aging Caleb had fought a good fight and had reached the period of retirement. Joshua asked him what property he would like to have for his pension. He said, "Give me Hebron." Hebron was a mountain city built on the edge of a frowning precipice, and was known to be a stronghold of giants. Caleb requested it. I. M. Haldeman, long after he might have laid down his sword and trowel, continued to wield them with the zest of an adolescent. Almost to the point of his death he held forth the Word of God, hating compromise, despising the opinions of men, loving the glorious Gospel of the blessed God with burning and undivided heart. Like Eleazar, "his hand clave unto the sword."

The Judgment Seat of Christ

I. M. HALDEMAN

M Y THEME tonight is "*The Judgment Seat of Christ.*" "*For we shall all stand before the judgment seat of Christ. . . . So then every one of us shall give an account of himself to God.*" (Romans 14:10,12) The Bible is a book of judgments. These judgments are manifold and recorded in fullest detail. Some are immediate and brief. There are others extending in their course over a thousand years.

There are *four* great and distinctive judgments.

THE JUDGMENT OF THE CROSS. The cross was neither the place nor the act of a suicide. It was not a martydom. It was something more than a brutal murder (though murder and brutal it was). It was a judgment. *It was the judgment of God against man.* It was God's judgment against man's nature as well as deeds. It was God's judgment against the world considered as a *system.* On that Cross God was judging Christ His Son as the representative of the natural man and his system called the world.

From the beginning God had been pursuing sin. At the Cross He came up with it and overtook it in the personal representation of it by His Son. He dealt with Him there as very sin, as *the Great Criminal of the Universe.* All the essential as well as governmental antagonism of God to sin swept forth and broke like a descending deluge upon that perfect and sinless Son. Speaking anticipatively of this hour, the Lord Himself by the Spirit through David cries out: "*All thy waves and thy billows are gone over me.*"

And again through David He cries: "Mine iniquities (the iniquities of those whom He represented and whose iniquities He made His own) have taken hold on me, so that I am not able to look up; they are more than the hairs of mine head."

By the mouth of the prophet Jeremiah, looking forward and entering into the ordained anguish of the Cross, He pours forth the soul-stirring and pathetic lamentation of His heart: "Is it nothing to you, all ye that pass by? Behold, and see if there be any sorrow like unto my sorrow which is done unto me, wherewith the Lord (the Father) hath afflicted me in the day of *his fierce anger.*"

Out from the midst of that black tempest of wrath, indignation and judgment where He suffers in the name of and as the representative of sinful men, suddenly there comes the amazing cry: "*My God, my God,*

432

why hast Thou forsaken Me?" That uttered agony expresses a fact and foretells a condition. The fact is, the sinless, holy, perfect Son of God and God the Son, the Son who from all eternity was in the bosom of the Father, the Son who in the flesh He assumed for the Father's glory, told Him out, and ceaselessly magnified Him, that Son in that hour upon the Cross was forsaken of the Father, the Father turned His back upon Him, hid His face from Him and left Him in the sunless, starless midnight of a complete and infinite repudiation; withdrew from Him every manifestation of His Fatherly love, left Him to sink under and be swallowed up by the endless, measureless billows of wrath in which every surge of every wave was a deeper and ever deeper drowning agony of helpless and hopeless despair.

The condition foretold by that cry which rent the earth, echoed to the farthest reach of the universe and pierced with pain the heart of listening angels is the condition of every soul forsaken at last of God. A fact and a condition! *The fact*—that all who have not received the salvation bought at this fearful price of the cross will be forsaken. *The condition*—agony, agony uttered and expressed in one eternally repeated and eternally unanswered question, "My God, my God, why hast thou forsaken me?"

The aspect of the judgment of the Cross is twofold. *Because* the death of Christ met the law, the government and the being of God, it has obtained a stay in proceedings against the individual sinner. *Because* that Cross is the demonstration of the unimpeachable righteousness of God, it has enabled Him to bring the world upon mercy ground where He can deal with it in grace, justify the ungodly and still be just. The Cross has set Christ before the world as the sacrifice for sin provided of God, and as the substitute the sinner is invited of God to claim.

The moment any sinner, be he ever so stained, so sunken and hopeless in sin, offer up Christ on the Cross by faith as his sacrifice for sin and claims Him as his personal substitute, as having taken his place and suffered for him, that moment the Father accepts the death of the Cross for the believing sinner, counts him to have died in the Person of His Son, counts the wrath which fell upon the Son as having fallen on the believer, reckons the believer's sins as fully transferred to the Son (so that He is *made sin* for the believer), reckons that the righteousness of Christ's obedience unto death is freely transferred to the believer, sees the believer as having passed through the judgment with Christ on the Cross, justifies him before the demands of the law and accepts him as *His own very righteousness* in His now risen, ascended, glorified and priestly Son.

On the basis of this Divine and exact justification the Son of God in His office and function as the Second Adam, the *New Head* of the race, communicates of His own life and nature to the justified and accepted believer. That believer has passed out of death into life. He is one with God in Christ. He is eternally saved. He has been delivered and saved by the judgment of the Cross.

So complete, so ample and so immediately available is this provided salvation that tonight, at this present moment, any individual sinner here, though he be as black as hell's deepest darkness and no man on earth be willing to lend him a hand, if he will in child-like simplicity take God at His Word, claim the crucified Christ as his sacrificial substitute, say believingly in his inmost soul, as though he talked face to face with God, "Almighty and Holy Lord, I ought to be eternally ruined, swept out of Thy presence and denied every joy, death, endless, hopeless is my due; but I claim Thy Son hanging on that Cross for such as I, accept all the judgments that fell on Him as having fallen on me and as having satisfied for every claim against me. Count His agony and damnation as mine and as completely and finally suffered there." Let any sinner here say that, mean that in honest, claiming faith and God will accept you, accept you quicker than the flash of a second. He will brush away every cloud of condemnation that hangs above you. You shall never stand at the judgment bar of doom. You shall be saved now and safe forever more.

This is the judgment of the Cross and the salvation it brings.

THE JUDGMENT SEAT OF CHRIST. This is the judgment next in order. (The others we shall deal with at a later time.) *At the Judgment Seat of Christ, the Christian will not be judged in respect to life and salvation, but exclusively for work and service as a Christian.* And this is in the nature of the case. Primarily because the death of Christ has met the judgment originally due the believer. When the believer claimed the death of Christ as his sacrifice for sin and claimed Him as a personal substitute, the believer was at once delivered from his standing and place as a sinner under doom of forfeited life, accepted as not guilty, justified and reckoned as righteous in the righteousness of Christ and in Christ as his actual righteousness; that is to say, he received not only an *imputed*, but, *imparted* righteousness.

So clear and clean is this transaction between the believer and a once-crucified Christ that were I with other believers at this moment summoned to that Judgment Seat, did Justice appear before me with a naked sword and in stern and merciless tones say unto me that my life was a sinful failure, or infraction of Divine law, and that I must pay what I owed with my life, that rightly and fittingly I deserved to be banished from God and the glory of His presence forever I would turn and point to that great crimson blot uplifted on a Cross between two thieves and I should say:

"O Justice, as much as you know of all the sin in my nature, all the sin I am and all the sin I have done, I know it too; but, Justice, yonder on the Cross I was judged, punished, executed and done to death in the Person of my Substitute, the Substitute whom the Infinite and Almighty God Himself provided. I have paid all the debt I owe to the law, the government and the Being of God. I have not fallen short in one jot or tittle of the law's demand. I have paid to the last element of my being every thing the *conscience* of God could require. God has not winked at any debt I owe or have partially paid. He has required it all. He has got it all, and He got it all in my Substitute, in every drop of blood His Son, my Substitute, shed for me. The *conscience of God* is satisfied concerning me and *my conscience is at rest in the satisfied conscience of God.*" I would say that. When I said that, Justice would sheathe the double-edged and gleaming sword and turn away.

No matter who you are, *worst* or *best* of men, the moment you turn and claim the crucified Son of God as your sacrificial substitute, you are safe. Safe because Justice cannot demand payment twice, once from *your surety* and *then* from you.

While it is true that we as Christians have done no work, nor could do any that would save us, we have been saved that we might do good works; as it is written:—"Created in Christ Jesus unto good works which God hath before ordained that we should walk in them." "What wilt Thou have me *to do?*" was Paul's first question. It is typical, suggestive and all-revealing.

We are here, as Christians, for service; we are here to take the place of witnesses. There are many Christians who imagine if they just live what they call the Christian life and never say a word about Christ, they are efficiently and satisfactorily witnessing for Him. It is a great and grievous mistake. *Before all else*, we must *speak* of Him. Our *lips* must give clear and vibrant testimony concerning Him. We must tell about the death of the Cross. We must talk of the empty grave, of a risen, ascended and Coming Lord; we must assure those about us that there is a present salvation in His Name and we must be clear and strong to say there is "none other name under heaven given among men whereby we must be saved!" This is what the early disciples did. This is what Paul did.

Surely in all history nothing is more dramatic nor more appealing than the scene in Herod's judgment hall at Caesarea where with manacled hands and guarded by Roman soldiers he stands before the dissolute king and his beautiful paramour, speaking with unfaltering lips and Divine passion to the astounded and brilliant throng of that Christ of God whom blinded Jews had hung upon a tree; whom God had raised from the dead and set Him at His own right hand in the heaven far above all principalities and powers, higher than the heavens as the Redeemer and Saviour, not only of Jew but Gentile also, even the very Romans before him; and speaking in such fashion, with such deep-set convictions and consciousness of truth that he wrenched from the lips of Agrippa himself the involuntary cry, "Almost thou persuadest *me* to be a Christian."

Not only Paul, not only the called apostles spoke, but Christians in the quiet of private life. Wherever they went and in whatsoever occupation engaged, mind and heart were full of the wondrous truth that God had so loved the world He gave His only begotten Son to die for men. The light from an open grave so flashed upon them that they could not hide it in the dark of silence. Their hearts were so full of the wonder, the glory and the benediction of a Risen Lord that out of the abundance thereof their lips spoke with gladness the joyful tidings.

Testifying of Christ with the tongue, that is the function of the Christian. *This dispensation began with tongues.* Pentecost was the risen Lord's declaration that He would have His disciples go forth and tell the story of His death and resurrection. This is the function of every Christian, to talk of Christ, not the Christ who lived and walked among men and blessed them merely, but Christ crucified, Christ the Sacrifice for sin, Christ the Substitute for the sinner, Christ risen, glorified, the present Saviour of every believing sinner. You need not wait for the preacher to tell it. You can tell it. This is your obligation as a witness. But a witness must have a character. A witness whose character is not good is of no avail. He may tell the truth, but his testimony does not count. Yonder is a man on the witness stand. He has told the truth, the exact truth in the case, nothing less and nothing more than the absolute truth; but if the attorney who is against him is keen enough he will summon those who will declare this witness is not to be believed upon his oath; that his reputation for dishonesty is widely known, he can be bought and sold. Let him do this and the testimony of that witness will be ruined, the jury will pay no heed to it.

A Christian who lives an inconsistent life, whose speech is full of unbelief, of doubt or worldliness, carelessness and open sin; a Christian who continually does things no Christian ought to do and who goes where a faithful and devoted Christian ought never to go, becomes sooner or later, in so far as the world outside goes, a worthless witness. No matter how much truth he may tell, nor how well and earnestly he may tell it, the world will not believe him; they look upon him as a faker, a hypocrite, an unworthy betrayer of the Lord whose Name he wears.

In order to be an efficient witness for Christ so that our testimony shall have a hearing and the work of the Spirit be unhindered, we are under bonds as Christians to build up individual character, a character that shall verify what we profess and preach. And do you think this is an easy matter? An easy thing in this world, here in this city where ten thousand forces are seeking to drag you from the path of Christian consistency and faith, and when the coordinate and resisting power of evil and unbelief come from within yourself? You never know what depths of sin and wickedness of hell are in your nature till you turn and start to walk the path that leads to God and Christ, the path that is paved with righteousness and truth, but bordered with grinning fiends or smiling serpents who stretch out hands to help the traitor in your soul; a path in which sometimes the devil meets you arrayed as an angel of light and in the name of righteousness seeks to guids your feet into the way of enticing sin. I have had earnest genuine Christians come to me filled with heartaches and lamentation. I have had them say to me, "We never knew what sinful and perverse natures we had till we tried to serve the Lord."

You cannot escape from that nature. Like Saint Anthony, you may flee from the city and hide in the cave, but sin and shame and devil and beautiful wantonness will be there in vision of a thousand-fold quickened imagination with whispered word and pictured form to tempt, to fool and lead you all unwillingly astray.

I say to you it is a fight, a battle fierce in which all the powers of darkness will rise up within you and about you to pull you down and away. Neither by tongue of orator nor pen of logician could the *super-naturalness*, the absolute divinity and Heaven birth of Christianity be more overwhelmingly and unanswerably demonstrated than by this upheaval of evil and wicked antagonism and this *internal revolt* of human nature in the regenerated Child of God. To live the Christ life, the life of spirituality and heavenward aspiration, to say "No" to material appetite, to rebuke passion, offer love for hate, purity for impurity and unselfishness for selfishness; in short, the dethronement of the flesh and the enthronement of the Spirit, surely this is not natural, it is not of man nor of earth, but of Heaven and God alone.

If you are a Christian, this is the conflict into which you are called and this is your work, to meet assault and resist, to go forward, fight the good fight of faith and to win. The supernatural life must be upper-most in you; as it is written:

> For though we walk in the flesh, we do not war after the flesh: (For the weapons of our warfare are not carnal, but mighty through God to the pulling down of strongholds.) Casting down imaginations, and every high thing that exalteth itself against the knowledge of God, and bringing into captivity every thought to the obedience of Christ.

This a part of our function, if we would be faithful and truthful witnesses for Christ, to so live that we win for Christ and Christ wins for Himself in us in the life that we live.

As Christians, we are each one of us called to be good "ministers" of Christ. But ministering in its true sense means serving others in the

Name of Christ. We are to minister to the saints, to look after the "household of faith," to visit the sick and the fatherless in their affliction, to take care of the needy, comfort the troubled, build up and strengthen the faith of others. We are to give of our substance. Do you imagine that God prospers any of us in this world that we may wholly spend our substance on ourselves? The only time I recall the Son of God applied the epithet "fool" to any one was when he spoke of the man who laid up treasure for himself and *"was not rich toward God";* so He said was every one like him who made his own life the deposit of his wealth and had nothing for God—*a very fool,* a fool of fools.

The matter of giving is at bottom a moral and spiritual test. Many Christians count it no sacrifice to give largely for that which gives them the return of satisfaction, of personal comfort and joy. They spend it on themselves, considering self always first, giving self the benefit of lavish expenditure and economizing on God. The Christian who refuses to give to the Lord, who holds back on the plea of economy bears witness that his heart is not right with God and that his appreciation of the salvation which for a while robbed heaven of its glory goes no greater length than the lip which professes what the heart does not feel. We are here as the stewards of God. We are here to give liberally and that liberality is measured not alone by the amount but by the impulse of the heart, the quickness of the hand and the spirit in which the gift is made.

We are here to win souls for Christ, to bring them to Him that He may save them. As of old wherever He came they sought out the sick, the lame, the blind, the leper and the halt that they might but touch the hem of His garment and be healed, we likewise are to seek the sin sick, the spiritually blind, the morally paralyzed, the social leper, those who are undone and lost and bring them with the hands of faith and prayer and lay them at His feet. We are to speak the simple word and tell them to touch Him with the touch of faith, to believe and "only believe" and they shall be saved.

We are to speak this word of hope and invitation on the street corner, in the seat of cars, in the office, in the store, wherever and whenever the door of opportunity is opened by the Lord. "A word spoken in due season, how good it is. It is like apples of gold in pictures of silver." We are here as Christians to do whatever our hand finds to do. We are to do it with all our might, for "the night cometh when no man can work." We are here to mean business for God, and we shall be examined at the Judgment Seat of Christ for the way in which we have endeavored to fill our missions as Christians.

It is for this we shall appear at the Judgment Seat of Christ. *At this Judgment Seat our Lord will reveal Himself as very God and each*

*Christian will have to give a faithful and intimate account of himself
or herself to Him as such.*

From all eternity He was God, God the Son and God the Word.
From all eternity He was in the "form" of God, and therefore the visi-
bility, the outgoing and forth-putting of God.

In the hour when His Judgment Seat is set, each Christian will be
summoned to meet Him, not only as the crucified and risen Man, the
Saviour of all who own Him, but as living God and Eternal Judge.
Each Christian must give an account to Him. You cannot give an
account for me. I cannot give an account for you. You must give an
account for yourself. I give an account for myself. That word "account" means "speech," "narrative," "reason." We will have to make
our speech to Him, give a narrative of our lives as Christians. We shall
have to give a reason for what we did and what we did not do. We
shall have to tell him why we neglected His Holy Word, the exercise
of prayer, the house of God; and why again and again we refused
to meet the responsibility of the profession we made or the service
into which He called us. Everything will come out in that all-searching
light.

There is a way in which the sins and failures, the short-comings and
the mistakes of your life as a Christian may be removed from your
soul. One way in which these things may not be known, may not con-
front you at the Judgment Seat of Christ, and that way—*Confession*;
as it is written:

"If we (Christians) confess our sins, He is faithful and just to forgive
us our sins, and to cleanse us from all unrighteousness."

Confessed sins will not appear at the Judgment Seat of Christ. Un-
confessed sins will be revealed and will weigh the scales of judgment
in relation to our work and service. O that I could impress you as
Christians with the necessity of confession. The Romanist goes to
confession. He bares all things. He pours all out in the ears of the listening priest. The priest gives him what he claims to be full and complete absolution.

You need to go to confession. You need to pour your heart out into
the ears of the listening priest, *not* in the ears of any priest on earth;
no such confession is warranted of God. The doctrine is the invention
of man. The claim to give absolution is treason to God and wicked
blasphemy. You have a Priest. That Priest is in heaven. He is your
risen Lord and Saviour. He is in heaven within the veil, seated upon
the throne, a high priest after the order of Melchizedek. He is there
to act on your behalf. This is His great and ever *unfinished* work.
The work of redemption was finished, but His work as priest, as intercessor and advocate for His Church, for individual Christians is un-

ceasing. His ears are ever open to hear. He is waiting always to take up our slightest petition and present it before His Father's throne. He is anxious to hear our confession. He is ready to make that confession turn to our welfare and peace. The mode and way of this action is very simple. Come to Him. Confess all that is upon your heart and soul. Keep nothing back. Make no attempt to exculpate or justify yourself. Give up the idea of seeking scapegoats for your own responsible failure. Tell the truth at any cost to your pride. Take sides with the Lord against yourself. Put your confession free and full into His hands and leave it there. There is immense moral and spiritual value in this act of confession. As you confess, as you bring to light the evil in you and judge it with the judgment of God, you will learn more and more to hate it and turn away from it. At this Judgment Seat all things will be adjusted by the Lord. All things will be righted and regulated.

If any one owes you a debt, it will have to be acknowledged and paid. If a Christian has wronged you in any fashion, hurt you by an idle word or the spreading of a false and irresponsible report, such an one will have to apologize to you before high heaven and the assembled host; and all this is in the nature of the case, for the Son of God Himself has said here in relation to this world:

If thou bring thy gift to the altar, and there rememberest that thy brother hath aught against thee; Leave there thy gift before the altar, and go thy way; first be reconciled to thy brother, and then come and offer thy gift.

If reconciliation and adjustment must be made here, *how much more in that hour* when everything is to be settled and the crooked made straight. At that Judgment Seat no good thing you have ever done in the Name of Christ and for His sake will be forgotten; as it is written:

"Judge nothing before the time, until the Lord come, who both will bring to light the hidden things of darkness, and will make manifest the counsels of the hearts: *and then shall every man have praise of God.*"

The kindly smile, the cup of cold water in His Name, the cheery word spoken in the fitting season, the clasp of hand by which you lifted another to firmer footing in the way of faith; all this will be remembered.

The Christian who at the Judgment Seat of Christ is judged and determined as faithful will receive a reward. He will be permitted to enter in and share the joy of the Lord. The "joy of the Lord" is twofold. There is the joy which enabled Him to endure the Cross, despising the shame; as it is written:

Who, for the joy that was set before Him, endured the Cross, despising the shame.

What think you was it which made Him press forward to Jerusalem in that last and awful passover time when He knew He was Himself to be the chosen and eternal victim: What held Him in the heart-break of that last supper when all the shadows were deepening round Him? What made Him bend His will in Gethsemane and yield it wholly to the Father's claim, drinking the cup the Father gave Him to the very dregs even while the blood sweat dripped from His brow? What sealed His lips in the hour of trial and made Him withhold the power by which He had raised the dead and stilled the storm? Why did He not use that power in His own defense and scatter His foes as by the blast of a whirlwind? What led Him to restrain the prayer for the sixty thousand tall, strong-limbed angels the Father was ready to give Him, had He but asked it? Why did He hang in such amazingly apparent helplessness upon the Cross when with but a word He gave salvation to the repentant thief dying by His side and opened paradise to the fresh believing soul? Why did He endure the agony, the horror, all the untranslatable woe but partially expressed in the universe-splitting cry as of one forsaken? What gave Him impulse and furnished Him strength whereby He not only endured the Cross, but rising in moral grandeur and balanced conscience above its shame, endured it, despised it, and counted it as naught?

There is but one answer. And this is the answer—"*The joy that was set before Him.*" The joy through that agony, that anguish and shame of becoming your Redeemer, your Saviour and mine.

One of the joys in that joyful sharing of the joy of Christ will be the privilege, not only of rulership, but sitting at the feet of the King Himself, and from time to time, listening as He shall unfold the written Word which long ago, He Himself as the living Word, inspired; for in letters of light I read this rare and wondrous affirmation:

And it shall come to pass in the last days, that the mountain of the Lord's house shall be established in the top of the mountains, and shall be exalted above the hills; and all nations shall flow into it. And many people shall go and say, Come ye, and let us go up to the mountain of the Lord, to the house of the God of Jacob; and He *will teach us of His ways*, and we will walk in His paths: for out of Zion shall go forth the law, *and the word of the Lord from Jerusalem.*

Who can measure the joy of listening to His Divine and human voice as He shall unfold the first chapter of Genesis and tell the story of that wide sweep of ages between the first and second verses; that hour when with His own spoken Word, and as Himself the Word, He set the heavens and the earth in their course; that mysterious moment when the cataclysmic crash came which flung the earth from its original orbit out of the original sunlight into the dark and formless void of chaos, the resurrection of the earth out of the woeful night and watery waste, the six days remaking of it as the dwelling place of man and the long ordained arena of redemption, the revelation of the love of God.

O the joy of walking with Him through the sacred ways of Palestine, sitting with Him as did the disciples of old, and with those very disciples again upon the brow of Olivet, listening while He unbares the deeper secrets of the Cross, the countless eternity, the mysteries and the endless wonders of redeeming grace.

The Christian who shall not be found faithful will suffer loss. He cannot enter into the joy of the Lord. Those who have preached and by their preaching have built nothing better than wood, hay and stubble on the foundation of Christ will be judged as unfaithful stewards of the Word of God. At that Judgment Seat the preachers who have been willing to make the Church a rubbish heap will be fully revealed. Men who have mixed law and grace, the righteousness of God with the righteousness of man; who have preached prohibition, socialism and state legislation; like Lot, have endeavored to clean up Sodom, and like Lot in Sodom, have vexed their righteous but unspiritual souls with their daily and manifested inability to keep it clean. O what rubbish heaps some churches are! Everything under heaven preached but the Gospel of the Grace of God. The life of Christ proclaimed, but not His death, evolution from below instead of regeneration from above, the first birth and not the second, appeals made to the inhering, self-redemptive powers in man instead of exhortation to claim redeeming blood. Everywhere the watchword, "Toleration." The right to think and go as you please in matters of religion; modern thought and not first century thought, the word of man and not the Word of God, goodness taught and not Godness; the present life the only life worth while, one religion as good as another.

Romanism which teaches an earthly priesthood and a continually sacrificed Christ as good as Protestantism which teaches one sacrifice once for all and one Priest alone and in heaven; Judaism which denies the Deity of Christ and looks upon Him as a cool deceiver or a weakling failure, and Christian Science which denies the Trinity, the personality of God, the fact of sin and death and owns Jesus simply as an idea and no longer a fact, just as good as any other system that makes use of the Name of God; Christ Himself owned as a moralist, at best a reformer and never a personal and only Saviour of men, the Bible not the exclusive Word of God and by no means the only revelation of God to man.

O what rubbish heaps some churches are! All sorts of means used to draw the people, street cleaners with their band, baseball experts to talk on the benefit of physical sobriety, regular habits and cleanliness, lectures, moving show pictures, ice cream suppers, dramatic entertainments, social clubs, military companies, minstrel shows, burlesques and dancing. All this is wood, hay and stubble. Like wood, hay and stubble, it is big, bulks greatly, gives the idea of being busy, occupied, doing things; but like wood, hay and stubble, the bigger the bulk the bigger the bonfire it will make; for all such religious rubbish will be burned away on the day of the Lord. Not only so, multitudes of those who are brought into the churches, who become its members give no sign of a change of life, give no evidence of spiritual income and spiritual outgo, who are in reality as lifeless as wood, hay and stubble; who have swelled the list of "conversions" and have made a good numerical showing in annual reports, these will be shown on the day of the Lord as elements of churchly rubbish, and witness of the worthlessness of the work of those who "added" them to the church.

The preachers who in spite of all the blindness and blundering of their wood, hay and stubble work have been really regenerated, have had some element of Divine life, the foolish and deceived workers who have mistaken quantity for quality, will in that hour when they stand at the Judgment Seat of Christ be accused of unfaithfulness to their trust and shall suffer loss. None of these shall enter into and share the joy of the Lord. They cannot take part in the kingdom on the earth.

Christians who have refused to give of their substance; who have been willing to spend it on themselves, but not on God; that class of Christians who are always revolting against "expense" in the Church and Judas-like are continually talking of "this waste," these shall miss the joy of the Lord. Christians who live notoriously and intentionally inconsistent lives; who openly dishonor the Name of Christ; who are impervious to spiritual appeal; who claim the assurance of salvation; who no doubt really believe, but refuse to bring forth the things which accompany salvation; these shall suffer loss. Amiable Christians, decent Christians, Christians who always go to church, but never do anything for Christ; who sit still on the cushioned seats of easy security and repeat to themselves as complacent justification, "not of works lest any man should boast."

Think of it! Redeemed by blood, made partakers of the Divine nature, indwelt by the Holy Ghost, linked up to a risen Christ, claiming all the guarantees of salvation; and *yet* never doing anything for Him who has done all things for them. O the pitiableness of it. *Redeemed and doing nothing for Christ.* And these all shall suffer loss, the loss of what they might have had.

Christ as Judge is already imminently before the door of the Church. This is the Divine and Holy Ghost way of saying that the coming of Christ *for* His Church is *imminent.* So imminent is it that the Holy Ghost says He is before the door. If the door should be opened the

Church would find herself face to face with Him, not only as her Saviour but as her righteous Judge.

And this is the announced order; as it is written:

The time is come that *judgment must begin at the house of God.*

While many predicted events are between us and the appearing of Christ in glory, many things which form the burden of prophetic warning and find their amplified accent in our Lord's discourse and are uttered and illuminated for us in the parenthetic chapters of Revelation, those terrible chapters which extend from the sixth to the nineteenth, between us and the coming of the Lord *for* the Church, there is not a single fore-announced event. It may be at any hour and, therefore, *at any moment.* He has only to speak, the door will be opened.

According to the Word of God, the testimony of the Son of God and the corroborative and unbroken testimony of the Apostles, *there is not the thickness of tissue paper between us who are Christians and the Judgment Seat of Christ.* In the light of this tremendous judicial imminency, the corollary of the present opportunity is immensely self-evident. As Christians, we ought to arouse. We ought to make our calling and election sure.

What an unspeakable experience it would be if before morning we should be summoned to the Judgment Seat of Christ and learn sooner or later that we could not pass the examination with honor to ourselves nor glory to the Lord! The Apostle John speaks of being put to shame in that hour, as it is written in I John 2:28:

And now, little children, abide in Him; that, when He shall appear, we may have confidence, and not be ashamed before Him at His coming.

O what disaster, what shame if for the sake of a dance, a game of cards, a glass of wine, a night in the theatre; what a disaster if for the sake of self-pleasure, self-gratification of any sort, an unwillingness to be strong and steadfast and to stand for truth, a compromise and failure by the way; what disaster, what indescribable shame if we should find we were shut out from that golden hour, that splendid sweep of a thousand heaven-illuminated years.

It is time to awake and let go the grip upon the things of earth; time to let the vision of heaven and heavenly things enter in and possess the soul; time to let go the handfuls of dust we call our plans, plans already slipping through our loosening fingers and falling into the ever-opening trench men call a grave; time to realize God in our daily experience, be as conscious of God as we are of the winds that blow or the heat that burns, or the circumstance that disturbs, hinders or makes us turn; time to arouse because should the voice call and the hand of power lift us to the judgment seat, we should be ready without hesitation and wholly unafraid to answer and say:

"Here, Lord, am I."

To you who are unsaved, listen to the word of warning: If Christ should come tonight, or tomorrow, you would be left behind to certain woe and sorrow which even the symbols given of God fail fully to reveal. At the last you would die. For a thousand years you would be held in the prison house of the underworld. Then would come the second resurrection, the second death. As a forever disembodied soul you would pass out into eternity where the cry of anguish would ring through the endless and hopeless darkness, "My God, my God, why hast Thou forsaken me?"

Hear me, I pray! Get into Christ, let Christ get into you. Take God at His word, believe the record, stand on the promise, offer Christ as your sacrifice, claim Him as your substitute; say, "O God, death is my doom and death is my due; but, Thou hast given Thy Son for such as I. Accept the judgment which fell on Him as though it had fallen on me. By His bloody pains, His anguish and His woe, let me go free. Accept me in His name, make me Thy child and Thine forever more." Say that and mean it, and quickly as you say it God will accept you and save you.

God forbid you should trifle! God forbid any one of you here in spite of the love of God, the blood of Christ, the call of the Gospel, the conviction of the Spirit and the prayers of those who love you, God forbid you should be among those in eternity who shall take up the cry, not the cry of adoration and praise from the lips of the blood-washed and enraptured hosts, but the cry wrenched from the sunless souls of the unredeemed, that unspeakably awful cry which shall make a universe to quiver—"Lost! Lost! We are forever lost." God forbid it.

J. GRESHAM MACHEN 1881–1937

Speaking at a Westminster Seminary alumni dinner in Cleveland in 1934, Dr. Gordon A. MacLennan, a minister in the (then) United Presbyterian Church, said, "What is it in Dr. Machen that stands out above everything else? I have given much thought to my own question. To me the answer does not lie in his scholarship, or in his teaching ability, or in his literary skill, great as all these are. In my opinion the one feature about him that overshadows everything else is this: his burning passion to see the Lordship of Christ exercised in His church."

Unless one understands this, he will never understand John Gresham Machen, his moves or his moods. But for that one overruling passion he would have been content to lodge in the quiet eye of the hurricane undisturbed by the fury of the storm that howled about him. How good and how pleasant it would have been to stay out of theological controversy, quietly confine all his energies to classroom instruction and scholarly writing! But historic Christianity was in conflict, the honor of the Son of God was involved, and Machen was of sterner stuff than to sit at rest and disregard the frontal attack against his Lord.

Nurtured in a godly home, finely instructed at Johns Hopkins University and Princeton Theological Seminary, he went to Germany for his graduate work and exposed his mind to brilliant if essentially destructive Biblical criticism. It was the proving ground of his faith, and though there were times when the test rocked his soul, he came out of the struggle strong in his confidence in the complete trustworthiness of the Word of God.

His "one increasing purpose," a progressive love for the pre-eminence of Christ, explains the quality of writings that flowed from his pen. The Origin of Paul's Religion, Christianity and Liberalism, What Is Faith? *and later,* The Virgin Birth of Christ, *represent the ultimate in Christian scholarship and at the same time reveal the depths of tremendous moral earnestness in the writer.*

In 1929, when Princeton Seminary was reorganized in a way that virtually insured the locking out of the pure Calvinism that school had stood for, Machen and three other professors withdrew and formed Westminster Theological Seminary to perpetuate a consistent witness to the Reformed Faith.

Machen contended that Galatians 1:8, "Though we, or an angel from heaven, preach any other gospel unto you than that which we have preached unto you, let him be accursed," summarized all that Scripture

446

has to say about the exclusive character of the Christian message, and that it enjoined total non-compliance with Christ-dishonoring error. Having taken his stand on the principle, there was no turning back. Logic and conviction compelled him to carry the fight against unbelief into the courts of the Church.

Like Luther, Machen learned that the role of reformer is thorny and dangerous. For the purity of doctrine and for the carrying out of his ordination vows he put his ecclesiastical life on the line—and lost it. He was ejected from the Church and was instrumental in launching the Orthodox Presbyterian Church. Soon afterward he passed away.

One of the surprising tributes to his character comes from Pearl Buck. She said: "I admired Dr. Machen very much while I disagreed with him at every point. And we had much the same fate. I was kicked out of the back door of the Church and he was kicked out the front door. . . . The man was admirable. He never gave in one inch to anyone."

There was a side to Dr. Machen the public never knew. Frequently, on a Saturday evening he would dispatch a crier through the seminary buildings with the message: "All right, boys, don't be tightwads!" This was the signal to congregate in "Das's headquarters." There the room overflowed with oranges, grapes, dates, apples, nuts, and ginger ale. Das would be seated at the checkerboard like the Autocrat of the Breakfast Table, ready to take on all challengers. No one can recall his ever losing.

While teaching at Princeton, Machen roomed unobtrusively in Alexander Hall. Every day a maid would make up his bed. One morning a student burst into his room and found Das pulling the bedding from the Beautyrest. He looked as guilty as the small boy caught with his hand in the forbidden cooky jar. He mumbled an apology.

"You see," he explained, "I like it fixed a certain way."

"Sir, why don't you show the maid how you want it fixed?" the student said. "I'm sure she'd be glad to oblige."

"Oh, I couldn't do that," said the eminent professor. "She'd lose face."

Some day perhaps people will understand why he was greatly loved by servants and by children.

The Good Fight of Faith

DR. J. GRESHAM MACHEN*

And the peace of God, which passeth all understanding, shall keep
your hearts and minds through Christ Jesus.   —Philippians 4:7

"Fight the good fight of faith"   —I Timothy 6:12

T HE APOSTLE PAUL was a great fighter. His fighting was partly
against external enemies—against hardships of all kinds. Five times
he was scourged by the Jews, three times by the Romans; he suffered
shipwreck four times; and was in perils of waters, in perils of robbers,
in perils by his own countrymen, in perils by the heathen, in perils in
the city, in perils in the wilderness, in perils in the sea, in perils among
false brethren. And finally he came to the logical end of such a life,
by the headsman's axe. It was hardly a peaceful life, but was rather a
life of wild adventure. Lindbergh, I suppose, got a thrill when he
hopped off to Paris, and people are in search of thrills today; but if
you wanted a really unbroken succession of thrills, I think you could
hardly do better than try knocking around the Roman Empire of the
first century with the Apostle Paul, engaged in the unpopular business
of turning the world upside down.

But these physical hardships were not the chief battle in which Paul
was engaged. Far more trying was the battle that he fought against the
enemies in his own camp. Everywhere his rear was threatened by an
all-engulfing paganism or by a perverted Judaism that had missed the
real purpose of the Old Testament law. Read the Epistles with care, and
you see Paul always in conflict. At one time he fights paganism in life,
the notion that all kinds of conduct are lawful to the Christian man,
a philosophy that makes Christian liberty a mere aid to pagan license.
At another time, he fights paganism in thought, the sublimation of the
Christian doctrine of the resurrection of the body into the pagan doctrine of the immortality of the soul.

At still another time, he fights the effort of human pride to substitute
man's merit as the means of salvation for Divine grace; he fights the
subtle propaganda of the Judaizers with with its misleading appeal to
the Word of God. Everywhere we see the great apostle in conflict for
the preservation of the church. It is as though a mighty flood were

* The last sermon preached by Dr. J. Gresham Machen at Princeton

448

seeking to engulf the church's life; dam the break at one point in the levee, and another break appears somewhere else. Everywhere paganism was seeping through; not for one moment did Paul have peace; always he was called upon to fight.

Fortunately, he was a true fighter; and by God's grace he not only fought, but he won. At first sight indeed he might have seemed to have lost. The lofty doctrine of Divine grace, the center and core of the Gospel that Paul preached, did not always dominate the mind and heart of the subsequent church. The Christianity of the Apostolic Fathers, of the Apologists, of Irenaeus, is very different from the Christianity of Paul. The church meant to be faithful to the apostle; but the pure doctrine of the Cross runs counter to the natural man, and not always, even in the church, was it fully understood. Read the Epistle to the Romans first, and then read Irenaeus, and you are conscious of a mighty decline. No longer does the Gospel stand out sharp and clear; there is a large admixture of human error; and it might seem as though Christian freedom, after all, were to be entangled in the meshes of a new law.

The human instruments which God uses in great triumphs of faith are no pacifists, but great fighters like Paul himself. Little affinity for the great apostle has the whole tribe of considerers of consequences, the whole tribe of the compromisers ancient and modern. The real companions of Paul are the great heroes of the faith. But who are those heroes? Are they not true fighters, one and all? Tertullian fought a mighty battle against Marcion; Athanasius fought against the Arians; Augustine fought against Pelagius; and as for Luther, he fought a brave battle against kings and princes and popes for the liberty of the people of God. Luther was a great fighter; and we love him for it. So was Calvin; so were John Knox and all the rest. It is impossible to be a true soldier of Jesus Christ and not fight.

God grant that you—students in this seminary—may be fighters, too! Probably you have your battles even now; you have to contend against sins gross or sins refined; you have to contend against the sin of slothfulness and inertia; you have, many of you, I know very well, a mighty battle on your hands against doubt and despair. Do not think it strange if you fall thus into divers temptations. The Christian life is a warfare after all. John Bunyan rightly set it forth under the allegory of a Holy War; and when he set it forth, in his greater book, under the figure of a pilgrimage, the pilgrimage too, was full of battles.

There are indeed, places of refreshment on the Christian way; the House Beautiful was provided by the King at the top of the Hill Difficulty, for the entertainment of pilgrims, and from the Delectable Mountains could sometimes be discerned the shining towers of the City of God. But just after the descent from the House Beautiful, there was the battle with Apollyon and the Valley of Humiliation, and later came the Valley of the Shadow of Death. Yes, the Christian faces a mighty conflict in this world. Pray God that in that conflict you may be true men; good soldiers of Jesus Christ, not willing to compromise with your great enemy, not easily cast down, and seeking ever the renewing of your strength in the Word and ordinances and prayer!

If you decide to stand for Christ, you will not have an easy life in the ministry. Of course, you may try to evade the conflict. All men will speak well of you if, after preaching no matter how unpopular a Gospel on Sunday, you will only vote against that Gospel in the councils of the church the next day; you will graciously be permitted to believe in supernatural Christianity all you please if you will only *act* as though you did *not* believe in it, if you will only make common cause with its opponents. Such is the program that will win the favor of the church. A man may believe what he pleases, provided he does not believe anything strongly enough to risk his life on it and fight for it. "Tolerance" is the great word. Men even ask for tolerance when they look to God in prayer. But how can any Christian possibly pray such a prayer as that? What a terrible prayer it is, how full of disloyalty to the Lord Jesus Christ!

There is a sense, of course, in which tolerance is a virtue. If by it you mean tolerance on the part of the state, the forbearance of majorities toward minorities, the resolute rejection of any measures of physical compulsion in propagating either what is true or what is false, then of course, the Christian ought to favor tolerance with all his might and main, and ought to lament the widespread growth of intolerance in America today. Or if you mean by tolerance forbearance toward personal attacks upon yourself, or courtesy and patience and fairness in dealing with all errors of whatever kind, then again tolerance is a virtue. But to pray for tolerance apart from such qualifications, in particular to pray for tolerance without careful definition of that of which you are to be tolerant, is just to pray for the breakdown of the Christian religion; for the Christian religion is intolerant to the core.

There lies the whole offense of the Cross—and also the whole power of it. Always the Gospel would have been received with favor by the world IF it had been presented merely as *one way* of salvation; the offense came because it was presented as the *only way*, and because it made relentless war upon all other ways. God save us, then, from this "tolerance" of which we hear so much. God deliver us from the sin of making common cause with those who deny or ignore the blessed Gospel of Jesus Christ! God save us from the deadly guilt of consenting to the presence as our representatives in the church of those who lead Christ's little ones astray; God make us, whatever else we are, just faithful messengers, who present, without fear or favor, not our word, but the Word of God.

But if you are such messengers, you will have the opposition, not only of the world, but increasingly, I fear, of the Church. I cannot tell you that your sacrifice will be light. No doubt it would be noble to care nothing whatever about the judgment of our fellow men. But to such nobility I confess that I for my part have not quite attained, and I cannot expect you to have attained to it. I confess that academic preferments, easy access to great libraries, the society of cultured people, and in general the thousand advantages that come from being regarded as respectable people in a respectable world—I confess that these things seem to me to be in themselves good and desirable things. Yet the servant of Jesus Christ, to an increasing extent, is being obliged to give them up. Certainly, in making that sacrifice we do not compain; for we have something with which all that we have lost is not worthy to be compared. Still, it can hardly be said that any unworthy motives of self-interest can lead us to adopt a course which brings us nothing but reproach.

Where, then, shall we find a sufficient motive for such a course as that; where shall we find courage to stand against the whole current of the age; where shall we find courage for this fight of faith? I do not think that we shall obtain courage by any mere lust of conflict. In some battles that means may perhaps suffice. Soldiers in bayonet practice were sometimes, and for all I know still are, taught to give a shout when they thrust their bayonets at imaginary enemies; I heard them doing it even long after the armistice in France. That serves, I suppose, to overcome the natural inhibition of civilized man against sticking a knife into human bodies. It is thought to develop the proper spirit of conflict. Perhaps it may be necessary in some kinds of war. But it will hardly serve in this Christian conflict. In this conflict I do not think we can be good fighters simply by being resolved to fight. For this battle is a battle of love; and nothing ruins a man's service in it so much as a spirit of hate.

No, if we want to learn the secret of this warfare, we shall have to look deeper; and we can hardly do better than turn again to that great fighter, the Apostle Paul. What was the secret of his power in the mighty conflict; how did he learn to fight?

The answer is paradoxical; but it is very simple. Paul was a great fighter because he was at peace. He who said, "Fight the good fight of faith," spoke also of "the peace of God which passeth all understanding"; and in that peace the sinews of his war were found. He fought against the enemies that were without because he was at peace within; there was an inner sanctuary in his life that no enemy could disturb. There, my friends, is the great central truth. You cannot fight

successfully with beasts, as Paul did at Ephesus; you cannot fight successfully against evil men, or against the devil and his spiritual powers
of wickedness in high places, unless when you fight against those
enemies there is One with Whom you are at peace.

But if you are at peace with that One, then you can care little what
men may do. You can say with the apostles, "We must obey God rather
than men"; you can say with Luther, "Here I stand, I cannot do otherwise, God help me. *Amen*"; you can say with Elisha, "They that be
with us are more than they that be with them"; you can say with Paul,
"It is God that justifieth, who is he that condemneth?" Without that
peace of God in your hearts, you will strike little terror into the
enemies of the Gospel of Christ. You may amass mighty resources for
the conflict; you may be great masters of ecclesiastical strategy; you
may be very clever, and very zealous too; but I fear that it will be of
little avail. There may be a tremendous din; but when the din is over,
the Lord's enemies will be in possession of the field. No, there is no
other way to be a really good fighter. You cannot fight God's battle
against God's enemies unless you are at peace with Him.

But how shall you be at peace with Him? Many ways have been
tried. How pathetic is the age-long effort of sinful man to become
right with God; sacrifice, lacerations, almsgiving, morality, penance,
confession! But alas, it is all of no avail. Still there is that same awful
gulf. It may be temporarily concealed; spiritual exercises may conceal
it for a time; penance or the confession of sin unto men may give a
temporary and apparent relief. But the real trouble remains; the burden is still on the back; Mount Sinai is still ready to shoot forth flames;
the soul is still not at peace with God. How then shall peace be obtained?

My friends, it cannot be attained by anything in us. Oh, that that
truth could be written in the hearts of every one of you! Oh, that it
could be written in letters of flame for all the world to read! Peace with
God cannot be attained by any act or any mere experience of man; it
cannot be attained by good works, neither can it be attained by confession of sin, neither can it be attained by any psychological results
of an act of faith. We can never be at peace with God unless God first
be at peace with us. But how can God be at peace with us? Can He
be at peace with us by ignoring the guilt of sin? by descending from
His throne? by throwing the universe into chaos? by making wrong
to be the same as right? by making a dead letter of His holy law?
"The soul that sinneth it shall die," by treating His eternal laws as
though they were the changeable laws of man?

Oh, what an abyss were the universe if that were done, what a mad
anarchy, what a wild demon-riot! Where could there be peace if God
were thus at war with Himself; where could there be a foundation if

God's laws were not sure? Oh, no, my friends, peace cannot be attained for man by the great modern method of dragging God down to man's level; peace cannot be attained by denying that right is right and wrong is wrong; peace can nowhere be attained if the awful justice of God stand not forever sure.

How then can we sinners stand before that Throne? How can there be peace for us in the presence of the justice of God? How can He be just and yet justify the ungodly? There is one answer to these questions. It is not our answer. Our wisdom could never have discovered it. It is God's Answer. It is found in the story of the Cross. We deserved eternal death because of sin; the eternal Son of God, because He loved us, and because He was sent by the Father Who loved us too, died in our stead, for our sins, upon the Cross. That message is despised today; upon it the visible church as well as the world pours out the vials of its scorn, or else does it even less honor by paying it lip-service and then passing it by. Men dismiss it as a "theory of the atonement," and fall back upon the customary commonplaces about a principle of self-sacrifice, or the culmination of a universal law, or a revelation of the love of God, or the hallowing of suffering, or the similarity between Christ's death and the death of soldiers who perished in the great war.

In the presence of such blindness, our words often seem vain. We may tell men something of what we think about the Cross of Christ, but it is harder to tell them what we *feel*. We pour forth our tears of gratitude and love; we open to the multitude the depths of our souls; we celebrate a mystery so tender, so holy, that we might think it would soften even a heart of stone. But all to no purpose. The Cross remains foolishness to the world, men turn coldly away, and our preaching seems but vain. And then comes the wonder of wonders! The hour comes for some poor soul, even through the simplest and poorest preaching; the message is honored, not the messenger; there comes a flash of light into the soul, and all is as clear as day. "He loved me and gave Himself for me," says the sinner at last, as he contemplates the Saviour upon the Cross. The burden of sin falls from the back, and a soul enters into the peace of God.

Have you yourselves that peace, my friends? If you have, you will not be deceived by the propaganda of any disloyal church. If you have the peace of God in your hearts, you will never shrink from controversy; you will never be afraid to contend earnestly for the Faith. Talk of peace in the present deadly peril of the Church, and you show, unless you be strangely ignorant of the conditions that exist, that you have little inkling of the true peace of God. Those who have been at the foot of the Cross will not be afraid to go forth under the banner of the Cross to a holy war of love.

Where are you going to stand in the great battle which now rages

in the church? Are you going to curry favor with the world by standing aloof; are you going to be "conservative liberals" or "liberal
conservatives" or "Christians who do not believe in controversy," or
anything else so self-contradictory and absurd? Are you going to be
Christians, but not Christians overmuch? Are you going to stand
coldly aloof when God's people fight against ecclesiastical tyranny
at home and abroad? Are you going to excuse yourselves by pointing
out personal defects in those who contend for the Faith today? Are
you going to be disloyal to Christ in external testimony until you
can make all well within your own soul? Be assured, you will never
accomplish your purpose if you adopt such a program as that. Witness bravely to the Truth that you already understand, and more will
be given you; but make common cause with those who deny or ignore
the Gospel of Christ, and the enemy will forever run riot in your life.

There are many hopes that I cherish for you men, with whom I am
united by such ties of affection. I hope that you may be gifted preachers;
I hope that you may have happy lives; I hope that you may have adequate support for yourselves and for your families; I hope that you
may have good churches. But I hope something for you far more
than all that. I hope above all that, wherever you are and however
your preaching may be received, you may be true witnesses for the
Lord Jesus Christ; I hope that there may never be any doubt where
you stand, but that always you may stand squarely for Jesus Christ, as
He is offered to us, not in the experiences of men, but in the blessed
written Word of God.

Many have been swept from their moorings by the current of the
age; a church grown worldly often tyrannizes over those who look for
guidance to God's Word alone. But this is not the first discouraging
time in the history of the church; other times were just as dark, and
yet always God has watched over His people, and the darkest hour
has sometimes preceded the dawn. So even now God has not left Himself without a witness. In many lands there are those who have faced
the great issue of the day and have decided it aright, who have preserved true independence of mind in the presence of the world; in
many lands there are groups of Christian people who in the face of
ecclesiastical tyranny have not been afraid to stand for Jesus Christ.
God grant that you may give comfort to them as you go forth from
this seminary; God grant that you may rejoice their hearts by giving
them your hand and your voice. To do so you will need courage.
Far easier is it to curry favor with the world by abusing those whom
the world abuses, by speaking against controversy, by taking a balcony
view of the struggle in which God's servants are engaged.

But God save you from such a neutrality as that! It has a certain
worldly appearance of urbanity and charity. But how cruel it is to

burdened souls; how heartless it is to those little ones who are looking to the Church for some clear message from God! God save you from being so heartless and so unloving and so cold! God grant, instead, that in all humility but also in all boldness, in reliance upon God, you may fight the good fight of faith. Peace is indeed yours, the peace of God which passeth all understanding. But that peace is given you, not that you may be onlookers or neutrals in love's battle, but that you may be good soldiers of Jesus Christ.

Index of Scripture Passages